Management Accounting Manual 2001/2002

Management Accounting Manual 2001/2002

Al Bhimani, BSc, MBA, PhD, CMA

*Senior Lecturer in Accounting and Finance,
London School of Economics and Political Science*

ABG Professional Information
40 Bernard Street
London
WC1N 1LD
Tel: +44(0)20 7920 8991
Fax: +44(0)20 7920 8992
E-mail: info@abgpublications.co.uk
Website: www.abgweb.com

© 2001 The Institute of Chartered Accountants in England and Wales

ISBN 1 85388 051 5

All rights reserved. No part of this publication may be reproduced or transmitted in any form or by any means, or stored in any retrieval system of any nature without prior permission, except for permitted fair dealing under the Copyright, Designs and Patents Act 1988, or in accordance with the terms of a licence issued by the Copyright Licensing Agency in respect of photocopying and/or reprographic reproduction. Application for permission for other use of copyright material, including to reproduce extracts in other published works shall be made to the publisher. Full acknowledgement to author, publisher and source must be given.

No responsibility for loss occasioned to any person acting or refraining from action as a result of any material in this publication can be accepted by the author or publisher.

British Library Cataloguing-in-Publication Data

A catalogue record for this book is available from the British Library.

Typeset by Servis Filmsetting Ltd, Manchester.
Printed by Bell & Bain, Glasgow

Preface

In a world of accelerated corporate change, management and accounting are becoming increasingly integrated. Sound business judgement today signifies a recognition that globalisation impacts the managerial task; emerging communication technologies and web-based tools alter the organisational potential; and leveraging knowledge-focused and intangible assets influence the basis of value creation. *Management Accounting Manual* is intended to capture the multifaceted issues which the finance function in modern enterprises has to address in order to effectively mobilise economic transformations. The message which runs through the Manual is that whilst the business context may change, one business priority remains: practising cutting-edge management accounting.

Management Accounting Manual seeks to provide help so organisations realise this priority. It provides front-seat detailed expositions of how vanguard management accounting tools are applied in a diversity of enterprises. It discusses and explains in a straightforward but focused way, a full diversity of conventional and emerging management accounting methodologies. Ultimately, *Management Accounting Manual* is a comprehensive enabler, useful to any enterprise which considers revenue maximisation and cost minimisation as its starting point as well as its ultimate goal.

Whilst *Management Accounting Manual* deals with the managerial potential of emerging accounting techniques, it also seeks to report on the latest cost management methodologies written about in the applied accounting press. It illustrates their viability, strengths, shortcomings and repercussions in real life organisations rather than simply documenting their conceptual underpinnings.

The Manual includes more than twenty-five detailed case studies centering around the application and implications of various management accounting methods. These case studies do not simply provide an outline of technical details or financial consequences but delve also into the organisational and implementational implications stemming from the adoption of innovative managerial accounting tools.

The pages which follow comprehensively encompass emerging and established management accounting techniques, concepts and philosophies, and

Preface

discuss their applicability and operation in real-world organisations. Extensive cross-referencing allows for swift reference but the writing style and text interlinkages also permit chapters to be read in their entirety to afford a thorough exposé of specific management accounting issues in terms of methodology, implementations and practice.

Al Bhimani,
September 2001.

Contents

	page
Preface	v
List of figures and tables	xv

Chapter 1 Management accounting and the finance function	**1**
1.1 Introduction	1
1.2 Achieving 'world-class' financial management	3
Orientation	3
Processes	4
Organisation of people	5
Control	11
1.3 Change management in the finance function	12
1.4 The future of management accounting	13

Chapter 2 Established cost management approaches	**17**
2.1 Introduction and background	17
Pre-1900 to the present: job costing	17
Early 1900s to the present: standard costing	18
1980s onwards: activity-based costing	18
2.2 Cost behaviour	19
2.3 Cost estimation	19
Account classification	19
Engineering method	20
Scattergraphs	20
Regression analysis	22
2.4 Break-even analysis	24
The break-even point	24
Examples of break-even calculations in action	24
2.5 Contribution margin analysis	28
An example	28
A case study: determining a price bid	29
A case study: Kim Basinger's replacement cost	38
2.6 Standard costing and variance analysis	48
An example	48
2.7 Costing using standard costs	52

Contents

	An example	52
	Why are standard costing systems widely used?	54

Chapter 3 Financial analysis and working capital management — **57**

3.1	Introduction	57
3.2	Profitability ratios	57
3.3	Solvency ratios	63
	Typical ratios	68
3.4	Working capital management	69
	Working capital management checklist	70
	An example	72
3.5	Economic value added (EVA®)	78
3.6	EVA® versus residual income	81
3.7	Accounting ratios and e-businesses	82
	A case study: EVA® and financial improvement	86

Chapter 4 Investment appraisal in modern enterprises — **114**

4.1	Introduction	114
4.2	The case for discounting cash flows	114
4.3	From counting to discounting	116
	Return on investment and the accounting rate of return	116
	Payback	118
	Net present value	119
	Internal rate of return	121
	Real options-based capital budgeting	125
4.4	Strategic investment appraisal	127
	Phase one: positioning	127
	Phase two: appraisal	127
	Phase three: selection	128
	Phase four: benefits tracking	128
	A case study: capital budgeting in action	134

Chapter 5 Changing technologies and cost management — **141**

5.1	Technology, processes and accounting	141
5.2	Just-in-time systems	142
	An example	145
	A case study: work reorganisation and cost effects	147
5.3	Enterprise resource planning	176
	A case study: integration through ERP	181
5.4	Numerical control machines	185
5.5	Computer-aided design and computer-aided manufacturing (CAD/CAM)	187

5.6	Flexible manufacturing systems	190
	Material handling systems	191
	A case study: rethinking plant layout	193
	A case study: investing in AMT	200

Chapter 6   Activity accounting — 247

6.1	Introduction and background	247
6.2	What drives costs?	248
6.3	The logic of activity accounting	249
6.4	Scope versus scale	251
6.5	Long-term versus short-term cost behaviour	251
6.6	What is an activity?	252
6.7	When to replace your costing system	253
6.8	Determining cost drivers	256
	A case study: cost-based decisions	258
6.9	Activity accounting design issues	271
	ABC and lean enterprises	273
	Top management support	274
	ABC training	276
	ABC and consultants	276
	Clarity of objectives	277
6.10	Achieving the right fit	277
6.11	Why ABC can fail	278
	Increasing revenue	279
	Reducing cost	280
	Product redesign	282
6.12	Economics versus organisational reality	282
	The legacy of bygone rationalities	283
6.13	Change strategies	283
	A case sudy: ABC implementation success	284
	A case study: ABC in a service context	288
	More lessons	289
6.14	ABC and the 'death spiral'	289
	The outcome – year one	291
	The start of the death spiral – year two	292
	The progress of the death spiral – year three	292
	The effects on profits	294
	The long run	294
6.15	Gap between theory and practice	295
	Strategy versus finance	296
	Clarifying business objectives	296
	Heading ABM: don't choose an accountant	296
	The usefulness of a pilot system	297

Contents

	How much complexity?	297
	A case study: achieving balance	299
6.16	Resistance to change	316
	A case study: the effective design of an ABM system	317
6.17	Tangible costs versus intangible benefits	321
	Cost-centre control	323
	Activity-level control	325
	Lot-level control	326
	Lot-level tracking	326
	Design trade-offs	328
	Activity-based management with actuals only	328
6.18	Outdated habits	330
	A case study: cost analysis versus business analysis	332
6.19	The choice of software	358
6.20	Activity-based budgetary control	358
	What activity-based budgeting can bring	359
	A case study: activity-based budgeting in action	360

Chapter 7 Time and cost management — 365

7.1	Product life-cycle costing	365
7.2	Time and product life-cycles	369
	Trade-offs between cost and time	369
7.3	Life-cycle costs in selected industries	370
7.4	Role of ABM in new product development	371
	Cost and time drivers	372
7.5	The role of TQM	374
7.6	The role of strategy	375
7.7	Activities and continuous improvement	376
	Steps to continuous improvement	378
7.8	The theory of constraints	380
	Managing constraints	380
	Controversies about TOC	381
	The goal is to make money – not reduce cost	381
7.9	Throughput	381
	Inventory (I)	383
	Operating expense (OE)	383
	Bottlenecks and constraints	385
	Ways to prevent wasting constraint time	386
7.10	Throughput accounting	387
	An example	388
	A case study: redirecting managerial attention	388
	Calculating throughput time	394
7.11	Integrating ABC, TOC and financial reporting	398

	Constrained and non-constrained activities	401
	Interdependencies among activities	402
	Effects on financial reporting	404
7.12	Activity mapping	405
	Dependency grids	407
	Using activity analyses to find bottlenecks	407
	An example	408
7.13	Activity mapping and the theory of constraints	409
	Three steps to using activity maps	410
	A case study: dealing with bottlenecks	412
7.14	Non-financial performance measures	431

Chapter 8 Quality and cost management — **437**

8.1	Quality: how much is enough?	437
8.2	What is quality?	438
	Conformance and non-conformance	439
	Hidden costs and customers	443
8.3	The cost of not minding quality costs	444
	A case study: developing COQ information	444
8.4	Making COQ work	453
	Successful use of COQ	454
	Returns on quality	455
	A case study: assessing quality and product line performance	458
	A case study: achieving quality improvements	465
	A case study: using cost of quality in environmental management	507

Chapter 9 Strategy and cost management — **519**

9.1	Business planning	519
9.2	Linking plans to strategy	519
	Competitive differentiation	521
	Core competencies	524
9.3	SWOT analysis	525
	Environmental analysis	527
	Structured strategy generation	527
9.4	The mission	528
	Building a sense of mission	530
	Mission statements	533
9.5	Why do strategies fail?	536
	1. The strategy is not worth implementing	537
	2. People are not clear how the strategy will be implemented	538
	3. Customers and staff do not fully understand the strategy	538

Contents

	4. Individual responsibilities for implementing the change are not clear	538
	5. Chief executives and senior managers step out of the picture once implementation begins	538
	6. The 'brick walls' are not recognised	539
	7. Forgetting to 'mind the shop'	539
9.6	Strategic management accounting	539
	SMA criteria	540
	Implementing SMA	547
9.7	Who needs SMA?	549
9.8	Linking customer value to product costs	553
	A case study: achieving strategic cost analysis	561
	A case study: strategy and financial reporting	577
9.9	Customer profitability analysis	593
	A case study: developing customer profitability information	593
9.10	Key features of analyses of customer profitability	597
	Implementing customer profitability analysis	599
	Strategy and customer profitability analysis	599
	New directions in analysing customer profitability	602

Chapter 10 Target cost management — 605

10.1	Target versus kaizen costing	605
10.2	The basis for target costing	606
	Corporate planning	606
	Developing the new project	606
	Determining the basic plan for a specific new product	606
	Product design	608
	Production transfer plan	608
10.3	Target costing principles	610
	A case study: implementing target costing	610
10.4	Target costing as an integrative management process	614
	Phase 1	616
	Phase 2	617
	Phase 3	619
	Management planning systems	619
	Procedural aspects of target costing	620
	Consumer perspective	622
	Critical activities	623
	Reducing cost at the detail design stage	624
	Reducing cost at the mass production stage	625
10.5	Implementation issues	627
	A case study: market strategy and target costing	628

A case study: redesigning the product	646
A case study: dealing with market pricing pressures	656

Chapter 11 Performance measurement and cost management — 685

11.1 The goals of performance measures	685
Problems with traditional evaluation systems	685
Improvements to traditional evaluation systems	686
11.2 Which new performance measures?	687
11.3 Performance measures for stakeholders	688
The vital link	689
Monitoring employee safety	690
Key variables	690
A case study: measuring workers' performance	693
The need for measures that perform	714
Strategic business information and performance measurement	719
Developing non-financial metrics	727
11.4 Corporate board information and budgetary control	731
11.5 Metrics and customer satisfaction	739
Steps to improve customer satisfaction	740
Metrics versus measures	740
Making metrics useful	742
The balanced scorecard at ADI	743
11.6 The balanced scorecard	744
11.7 Four dimensions that matter	744
The financial perspective	745
The customer perspective	745
The internal-business-process perspective	746
The learning-and-growth perspective	746
11.8 The balanced scorecard and strategy	747
A case study: organisational processes and the balanced scorecard	749
11.9 Balanced scorecards can fail!	760
11.10 Commandments of balanced scorecards	762
A case study: strategy and budgetary control	763

List of tables and figures

		page
Chapter 1	**Management accounting and the finance function**	
Figure 1.1	Developments in the processing of financial transactions since 1950	8
Table 1.1	Different approaches to control	11
Table 1.2	Managing barriers to change	12
Chapter 2	**Established cost management approaches**	
Figure 2.1	A scattergraph	21
Figure 2.2	Cost/volume/profit chart	25
Table 2.1	CVP Company income statement for year ended 31 December 2001	27
Table 2.2	Quality Dairy, 2000 mix product information	31
Table 2.3	Quality Dairy cost sheets – Regular milkshake and 10% ice cream mix – April 2001	32
Table 2.4	Quality Dairy – Cost Centre Number Three 2000 overhead costs – Mix department and receiving, pasteurisation and separation department	34
Table 2.5	Incremental costs of the McDonald's order	36
Table 2.6	Quality Dairy cost sheets – Overhead allocated on a per gallon basis – Regular milkshake mix and 10% ice cream	38
Table 2.7	Minimum damages, according to Main Line's plaintiff expert ($US)	42
Table 2.8	Maximum damages, according to Main Line's plaintiff expert ($US)	43
Table 2.9	Revenue needed for profit differentials, defence expert ($US)	44
Table 2.10	Main line minimum profit with contractual payments deducted ($US)	46
Table 2.11	Revised maximum lost profits ($US million)	48
Table 2.12	Redd Co. income statement for the month ended 31.10.01	49
Table 2.13	Redd Co. income statement for the month ended 31.10.01	49

List of tables and figures

Table 2.14	Redd Co. performance report for the month ended 30.11.01	51
Table 2.15	Redd Co. calculations to obtain variance values	51
Chapter 3	**Financial analysis and working capital management**	
Table 3.1	Key profitability ratios	58
Table 3.2	Ratio Co. comparative balance sheet at 31.12.01 and 2000	59
Table 3.3	Ratio Co. comparative income statement for the years ended 31.12.01 and 2000	59
Table 3.4	Ratio Co. calculation of the asset turnover ratio	60
Table 3.5	Ratio Co. calculation of the rate earned on total assets	60
Table 3.6	Ratio Co. calculation of the rate earned on shareholders' equity	61
Table 3.7	Ratio Co. calculation of the rate earned on ordinary shareholders' equity	62
Table 3.8	Ratio Co. calculation of earnings per share on ordinary shares	63
Table 3.9	Ratio Co. calculation of price/earnings ratio on ordinary shares	63
Table 3.10	Ratio Co. calculation of dividend yield on ordinary shares	63
Table 3.11	Examples of solvency ratios	64
Table 3.12	Ratio Co. calculation of working capital and current ratio	65
Table 3.13	Ratio Co. calculation of acid-test ratio	65
Table 3.14	Ratio Co. calculation of debtor's turnover	66
Table 3.15	Ratio Co. calculation of number of days' sale to collection	66
Table 3.16	Ratio Co. calculation of inventory turnover	66
Table 3.17	Ratio Co. calculation of number of days' sales in inventory	67
Table 3.18	Ratio Co. calculation of the ratio of plant assets to long-term liabilities	68
Table 3.19	Ratio Co. calculation of ratio of shareholders' equity to liabilities	68
Table 3.20	Typical ratios by industry sector	69
Table 3.21	Company A's current working capital performance	73
Figure 3.1	Actual terms taken vs terms agreed (days)	73
Figure 3.2	Aged debtor days	74
Figure 3.3	Stock days for four divisions	75
Table 3.22	Improving working capital management	76
Table 3.23	European average payment periods (days)	77

List of tables and figures

Table 3.24	Weighted-average cost of capital (example of calculation)	79
Figure 3.4	OutSource Inc's balance sheet	91
Figure 3.5	OutSource Inc's statement of income	92
Figure 3.6	Balance sheet	99
Figure 3.7	Financial data input and calculation of interest rates/expense	101
Figure 3.8	OutSource Inc. pertinent information extracted from the footnotes to the annual report	103
Figure 3.9	Balance sheet	104
Figure 3.10	OutSource Inc. summary of NOPAT and capital	106
Chapter 4	**Investment appraisal in modern enterprises**	
Table 4.1	Anticipated cash flow	120
Table 4.2	The present value of a stream of cash flows	121
Table 4.3	The present value of net cash flows	122
Table 4.4	Analysis	124
Table 4.5	Financial analysis	125
Figure 4.1	Principal option definition form	129
Table 4.6	Main objectives and outputs of the appraisal phase	131
Table 4.7	Types of financial cost and benefit	132
Table 4.8	Main objectives and outputs of the selection phase	133
Table 4.9	Main objectives and outputs of the benefits tracking phase	134
Table 4.10	Net cash flows and present value analysis of alternatives in the absence of competing products	137
Table 4.11	Net cash flows and net present value analysis of alternatives assuming entry by competition	138
Table 4.12	Net cash flows and net present value analysis of entering the market from the competitor's perspective	140
Chapter 5	**Changing technologies and cost management**	
Table 5.1	Classification of costs in traditional and just-in-time environments	144
Table 5.2	JIT Co. entries made under a backflush accounting system	145
Table 5.3	JIT Co. entries made under a traditional costing system	145
Table 5.4	Contrasting performance measures under traditional and just-in-time environments	147
Figure 5.1	Previous production process layout	149
Figure 5.2	New conversion processing layout	153
Figure 5.3	Kenco's product cost flows	154
Figure 5.4	Backflush and product costing system	154

List of tables and figures

Figure 5.5	Bidding sheet – Front End Loader Edges (FEL)	160
Figure 5.6	Weekly production and cost report	161
Figure 5.7	Weekly performance measures	164
Table 5.5	Product miscosting alternatives and effects	169
Figure 5.8	The three levels of the SAP project	182
Figure 5.9	SAP decision model	184
Table 5.6	NC machines: problems and solutions	186
Table 5.7	CAD/CAM: problems and solutions	188
Table 5.8	FMS: problems and solutions	191
Table 5.9	AS/RS: problems and solutions	192
Figure 5.10	Original plan layout	194
Figure 5.11	Rantoul redesigned plant layout	196
Figure 5.12	Rantoul redesigned plant layout	197
Figure 5.13	East River Plant (A) – Tube Shop Manual Line	205
Figure 5.14	East River Plant (A) – Proposal-to-shipment process	206
Figure 5.15	Project/contract cost monitoring	209
Figure 5.16	CIM Line Savings Summary ($US)	215
Figure 5.17	Tube Shop CIM Line – Process flow/machine count/headcount	216
Figure 5.18	Existing overhead cost allocation system	220
Figure 5.19	East River Plant (B) – Bay 7 Manufacturing – Major activities and cost drivers	231
Figure 5.20	East River Plant (B) – Tube Shop expense profile	232
Figure 5.21	East River Plant (B) – Bay 7 Automated line – Conversion cost estimate comparison on selected contracts	234
Chapter 6	**Activity accounting**	
Figure 6.1	Optimal cost system	255
Table 6.1	Cost drivers appropriate to activity categories	258
Table 6.2	TAP Co. balance sheet as of 31 December 2001	259
Table 6.3	TAP Co. schedule of sales revenues by model for the year ended 31 December 2001	259
Table 6.4	TAP Co. schedule of profitability by model: conventional cost management system for the year ended 31 Dec 2001	260
Table 6.5	TAP Co. schedule of profitability by vehicle: conventional cost management system for the year ended 31 Dec 2001	260
Table 6.6	Comparisons of accounting systems on gross margin for the year ended 31 Dec 2001	261
Table 6.7	Activities and costs for purchasing for the year ended 31 Dec 2001	262

List of tables and figures

Table 6.8	Activities and costs for production planning and control for the year ended 31 Dec 2001	262
Table 6.9	Activities and costs for inventory control for the year ended 31 Dec 2001	263
Table 6.10	Activities and costs for quality control and inspection for the year ended 31 Dec 2001	264
Table 6.11	Revised schedule of profitability by model: activity-based cost management system for the year ended 31 Dec 2001	265
Table 6.12	Revised schedule of direct labour utilisation: conventional cost management	265
Table 6.13	Revised schedule of profitability by model: conventional cost management system for the next model year	266
Table 6.14	Comparison of direct labour utilisation for the next model year	267
Table 6.15	Revised schedule of profitability by model: activity-based cost management system for the next model year	267
Table 6.16	Saving by product line	269
Table 6.17	Activities and costs for quality control and inspection for the year ended 31 Dec 2001	269
Figure 6.2	Initial response to ABC data	279
Figure 6.3	Choose initial change approach	280
Figure 6.4	Analyse fidget price	281
Figure 6.5	Change fidget price	281
Table 6.18	Cost pools, activities and cost drivers	290
Table 6.19	Product, cost and market characteristics	291
Table 6.20	Year 3 operating results	293
Table 6.21	Profits over three years	294
Figure 6.6	Original Standard Soap Works Co. – Process flow diagram	300
Figure 6.7	Standard Soap change in sales mix	303
Figure 6.8	ACMS System timeline	305
Figure 6.9	Proposed customer profitability analysis datafile	306
Figure 6.10	Restatement of income statement G/L accounts	307
Figure 6.11	Standard Soap works – Bid price estimator sheet	309
Figure 6.12	Job cost comparisons	310
Figure 6.13	Case data tables	311
Table 6.22	Standard activity frequencies for planned volumes	323
Figure 6.14	Cost Centre Control using standard activity rates	324
Figure 6.15	Activity control using standard activity rates	325
Figure 6.16	Lot Control using standard activity rates	327
Figure 6.17	Activity cost per sort device	329

List of tables and figures

Figure 6.18	From focus on functions toward focus on processes	323
Figure 6.19	California winery shipments (thousands of case)	336
Figure 6.20	Wine production in case equivalents	337
Figure 6.21	Consolidated balance sheets, The Chalice Wine Group, Ltd (thousands)	338
Figure 6.22	1991 Meritage Wine product costs	339
Figure 6.23	Costs per acre to establish and operate a vineyard	341
Figure 6.24	Assets required to establish and operate a 30 acre vineyard	341
Figure 6.25	History of California grape prices per ton	342
Figure 6.26	Stellar Wines financial statements (in thousands)	343
Figure 6.27	Riverside Wine Company, 1992	344
Figure 6.28	Winemaking cost – ABC approach	345
Figure 6.29	Bottling costs – per case	346
Figure 6.30	Barrel depreciation	347
Figure 6.31	1991 Lyford Meriage White	348
Figure 6.32	Condensed comparative income statements, The Chalice Wine Group	350
Figure 6.33	Value chain profitability analysis	351
Figure 6.34	The value chain – 1991 Cimarron Meritage White (per case)	352
Figure 6.35	Product cost (1991 Meritage White), several versions	356
Figure 6.36	Lyford Wines: a different approach	357
Figure 6.37	The evolution of 'Buyer Power' in California.	357
Figure 6.38	Understanding the business for profit improvement	358
Chapter 7	**Time and cost management**	
Figure 7.1	Product life-cycle	365
Figure 7.2	Life-cycle cost: the producer's perspective	366
Figure 7.3	Cost impact versus decision	367
Figure 7.4	LCC decision relationships	369
Figure 7.5	Cost-saving window of opportunity	370
Figure 7.6	Advantages of Pioneers	371
Figure 7.7	Trade-offs among objectives	373
Figure 7.8	Development cycle length	374
Table 7.1	Production of products X and Y	388
Table 7.2	Example of bottleneck improvements	390
Figure 7.9	Inventory calculations for material number 614	396
Figure 7.10	Throughput days per weighted average material $	396
Figure 7.11	Calculation of material cost and throughput time for a batch of product	397
Figure 7.12	Throughput time for all products shipped on a given date	398

List of tables and figures

Figure 7.13	Activity Y: operating expenses and activity levels	400
Figure 7.14	Throughput time for all products shipped on a given date	401
Figure 7.15	Southern Pulp Company – Flowchart of pulp and chemical processes	428
Figure 7.16	Southern Pulp Company – Summary of results – simulation run of PULP2 model	430
Figure 7.17	Southern Pulp Company – Summary of results – simulation run of PULP3 model	432
Chapter 8	**Quality and cost management**	
Figure 8.1	Estimated annual failure costs	450
Figure 8.2	The Xerox ROA calculation (the impact of cost quality)	457
Figure 8.3	Production line profitability – Scenario A: prior to losing the Virginia contract	463
Figure 8.4	Production line profitability – Scenario B: without to losing the Virginia contract	464
Figure 8.5	Production line profitability – Scenario C: with double volume of commercial paint	465
Figure 8.6	Latex cost per gallon of paint	466
Figure 8.7	Assignment of overhead	466
Figure 8.8	Engine build-up	471
Figure 8.9	Engine build-up – shop bar chart	472
Figure 8.10	Engine build-up	473
Figure 8.11	Engine build-up – cost analysis	475
Figure 8.12	Engine build-up – Activity: install exhaust plug and sleeve – value analysis worksheet	476
Figure 8.13	Engine build-up – install exhaust plug and sleeve	477
Figure 8.14	Engine build-up – install exhaust plug and sleeve	478
Figure 8.15	Engine build-up – pareto of activities	479
Figure 8.16	Engine build-up – pareto of activities	480
Figure 8.17	737 engine build-up – shop bar chart	481
Figure 8.18	737 engine build-up – operations and inspection record: wire and bundle installation	482
Figure 8.19	Section of division's performance goals	487
Figure 8.20	Division organisation transformation	488
Figure 8.21	Total division process and activity analysis	490
Figure 8.22	Division organisation cost	491
Figure 8.23	Product definition change activities	493
Figure 8.24	Engineering operations – non-value added activities	494
Figure 8.25	Committed change process	496
Figure 8.26	Committed change process – value added timeline (calendar days)	498

List of tables and figures

Figure 8.27	Product revision record (PRR)	499
Figure 8.28	Causes for revisions to product revision records (PRR)	500
Figure 8.29	Primary Federal Environmental Acts	508
Figure 8.30	1993 Financial highlights (in thousands)	508
Figure 8.31	Union Pacific Railroad Environmental Policy	509
Figure 8.32	Excerpts from Quality System Procedure 1002, Cost of Quality Control Processes	511

Chapter 9	**Strategy and cost management**	
Figure 9.1	Eras of management theory and practice	522
Figure 9.2	Porter's generic strategies	522
Figure 9.3	Making SWOT analysis work	526
Figure 9.4	Mission and strategy	532
Figure 9.5	UK brewery's mission analysis	533
Figure 9.6	Mission statements	534
Figure 9.7	Organisation's value chain	541
Figure 9.8	Relative cost graphs for firms A and B	542
Table 9.1	Product cost structure comparisons	546
Figure 9.9	Conventional versus strategic management accounting	550
Figure 9.10	Management accountants' involvement in strategic planning activities	552
Figure 9.11	Desired involvement in SMA	553
Figure 9.12	Factors in strategic formulation	554
Figure 9.13	Strategic decision making	555
Figure 9.14	SMA definitions by those who practice SMA	556
Figure 9.15	Strategic cost analysis: example for a fast-food supplier	558
Figure 9.16	Memorandum., Reichard Maschinen GmbH, Grinding Machines Division	562
Figure 9.17	Relevant costs per 100 rings	567
Figure 9.18	Comparison of incremental profitability per 100 rings	569
Figure 9.19	Annual contribution of plastic and steel rings	574
Figure 9.20	Exit the replacement rings business	576
Figure 9.21	Possible exit strategy	577
Figure 9.22	Competitive strategy considerations	579
Figure 9.23	Projected income statements under two competitive strategies for the month ended 31 Dec 2001	581
Figure 9.24	Balance sheet as at October 31 2000	581
Figure 9.25	Pro forma balance sheet as at 31 Dec 2001	584
Figure 9.26	Startup, breakdown of fees charged for the twelve months ended 31 Dec 2001	585
Figure 9.27	Breakdown of fees charged for the 12 months ended 31 Dec 2001	591

List of tables and figures

Figure 9.28	Calculation of opportunity cost associated with growth Option 3	592
Figure 9.29	Profile of customer groupings of Blue Ridge	594
Figure 9.30	Customer profitability analysis of large customers of Blue Ridge	596
Figure 9.31	Cumulative customer profitability analysis	600
Figure 9.32	Decision grid analysis	600
Figure 9.33	Customer production contribution analysis	601

Chapter 10 Target cost management

Figure 10.1	Form for classification of target costs (motor car)	607
Figure 10.2	Cost tables: the key to cost estimation	614
Figure 10.3	Closing the gap with design-to-cost and value engineering	615
Figure 10.4	Flow of chart costing activities through Daihatsu Motors	621
Figure 10.5	Summary of sales by distribution channel	629
Figure 10.6	B&B's product line price list based on the 'rule of thumb' pricing mode	633
Figure 10.7	Current Batdorf & Bronson income statement	635
Figure 10.8	Sales by product and distribution channel	637
Figure 10.9	Cost of beans sold	639
Figure 10.10	Cost of packaging/shipping supplies	640
Figure 10.11	Analysis of competitors	644
Figure 10.12	Engineering and customer-related product function areas	649
Figure 10.13	Production processes for Maeva-2	651
Figure 10.14	A process-function relationship map	652
Figure 10.15	Tracking cost reductions via a process-function relationship map	654
Figure 10.16	MosCo Inc. income statement	657
Figure 10.17	MosCo Inc. FY94 product cost worksheet	658
Figure 10.18	FY94 used capacity and process costs worksheet	662
Figure 10.19	FY94 spending summary by organisation	663
Figure 10.20	MosCo Inc. – FY94 Activity-based spending summary by organisation	664
Figure 10.21	MosCo Inc. – FY94 Direct activity-based spending summary	667
Figure 10.22	MosCo Inc. – FY94 Support group activity-based spending summary	668
Figure 10.23	FY94 revised product cost worksheet	669
Figure 10.24	FY94 used capacity and process costs worksheet	669
Figure 10.25	MosCo Inc. – FY95	671
Figure 10.26	MosCo Inc. – FY95	672

List of tables and figures

Figure 10.27	MosCo Inc. – FY96	673
Figure 10.28	MosCo Inc. – FY96	673
Figure 10.29	'Offitol' pro forma income statement	675
Figure 10.30	FY95 'Offitol' pro forma income statement worksheet	676
Figure 10.31	MosCo Inc. – FY96 'Offitol' pro forma income statement worksheet	677
Figure 10.32	MosCo Inc. – FY95&FY96 capacity available	682

Chapter 11 Performance measurement and cost management

Figure 11.1	Performance evaluation system model	687
Table 11.1	Use of financial performance measure in the division	687
Figure 11.2	Financial performance measures recently introduced or being considered for introduction	688
Figure 11.3	Hierarchial development of meaningful performance measures	689
Table 11.2	Examples of variables monitored by performance measures and indicators	689
Figure 11.4	Examples of worker-safety process performance measures and indicators	691
Figure 11.5	Current warehouse layout	695
Figure 11.6	Velky Potraveniny warehouse date	696
Figure 11.7	Task flow and responsibilities by job titles	699
Figure 11.8	Current process flow	701
Figure 11.9	Velky Potraveniny's current bonus program for warehouse employees	702
Figure 11.10	Current measures of performance by job/function	704
Table 11.3	Financial and non-financial measures commonly used in assessing performance	716
Figure 11.11	Application of the SBI process: supply chain management	724
Figure 11.12	Application of the SBI process: further breakdown of the first objectives in its critical factors	725
Figure 11.13	Application of the SBI process	727
Figure 11.14	From design to sales	728
Figure 11.15	Sherwin-Williams' managerial process	733
Figure 11.16	Sherwin-Williams: Summary of required budget documents	735
Figure 11.17	Sherwin-Williams: annual income and expense summary	736
Figure 11.18	Sherwin-Williams five-year sales, profit, net assets employed and cash flow summary	737
Figure 11.19	Sherwin-Williams: profit before tax change analysis	738
Figure 11.20	Balancing four-dimensions of strategic concern	748
Figure 11.21	Repertory Theatre of St. Louis vision statement	765

List of tables and figures

Figure 11.22 Organisation chart 767
Figure 11.23 History of subscriptions 1979–1994 estimate 769
Figure 11.24 Financial data 1986–87 through 1993–94 770
Figure 11.25 Glossary 771
Figure 11.26 Attendance and revenue data 1986–87 through 1993–94 773
Figure 11.27 Expense breakdown 1992–93 774
Figure 11.28 Expense detail 1992–93 775
Figure 11.29 Production expense report 778
Figure 11.30 Five-year projections 1994–95 through 1998–99 782

Chapter 1
Management accounting and the finance function

1.1 Introduction

1.1.1 The business environment is experiencing a period of unprecedented change, and such ongoing change is now accepted as an integral part of organisational life. The key issue currently facing organisations is that of how to adapt or respond to the increasing velocity of change. New markets are emerging and maturing at previously unimagined speed, whilst old markets vanish or are revitalised by new approaches. Recent years have seen a dramatic growth in scientific knowledge both social and pure. Innovative approaches to management within changing market structures are providing the established order with fierce competition.

1.1.2 One key element in sustaining a viable level of competitive advantage in the changing environment relates to the role of finance and accounting (the finance function) within the organisation. Finance may be viewed as adding value through participation in the management and business processes, in addition to providing proactive support to operational and senior managers and the board. The function of finance and accounting is now deemed more crucial than ever in ensuring that the quality of management information and decision support makes an even greater contribution to a company's success, whilst maintaining the integrity of business systems and controls. In many companies, particularly those competing in international markets, organisational subunits set themselves targets of achieving, for example, 'world-class operations'. This challenge applies equally to the finance function, which in many leading companies is seeking to identify world-class financial performance through a variety of techniques and to bring those parts of their activities most crucial to the success of their business up to speed.

1.1.3 One traditional objective of management accounting has been to help organisations plan their future and then monitor performance to ensure that the planned objectives are achieved. Much of management accounting, therefore continues to be concerned with analysing, investigating and forecasting information which is not financial in nature, but an understanding of which is essential to ensuring that financial forecasts are soundly based and that differences in performance are properly explained. However, within modern organisations, management accounting's roles are fast changing, becoming wider and more far reaching.

1.1.4 Across Europe there are different approaches to management accounting (Bhimani, 1996) and in some countries the term 'controllership' is more widely used, with 'accounting' referring principally to historical bookkeeping. Finance-related terms must be used within the organisational context to which they relate. This is especially so in that increasingly, management accountants engage in providing control support for both operational tasks and strategic management activities.

1.1.5 The UK-based Chartered Institute of Management Accountants (CIMA) defines management accounting as:

> 'The application of the principles of accounting and financial management to create, protect, preserve and increase value so as to deliver that value to the stakeholders of profit and not-for-profit enterprises, both public and private. Management accounting is an integral part of management, requiring the identification, generation, presentation, interpretation and use of information relevant to:
> - formulating business strategy;
> - planning and controlling activities;
> - decision-making;
> - efficient resource usage;
> - performance improvement and value enhancement;
> - safeguarding tangible and intangible assets;
> - corporate governance and internal control.' (CIMA, 2000)

1.1.6 Most of the research into management accounting techniques is carried out by academics or the professional institutes dedicated to management accounting such as CIMA and others:

- Canada – CMA Canada
- USA – Institute of Management Accountants.

1.1.7 These bodies come together internationally in a subcommittee of the International Federation of Accountants (IFAC) known as the Financial and Management Accounting Committee (FMAC), which has published fundamental principles for the preparation of management accounting information (referred to as International Management Accounting Practice Statements).

1.2 Achieving 'world-class' financial management

1.2.1 The role of finance and accounting, and particularly of the finance director and senior members of his team, is increasingly moving away from traditional responsibilities into many different areas. Finance directors are finding that they are expected to be involved in actively formulating business objectives and strategies, and in enhancing competitive advantage through, for example, helping to re-engineer business processes, whilst continuing to ensure that the business is properly controlled.

1.2.2 In order to make this contribution, certain closely related elements need to be in place. These are: orientation, processes and systems, organisation of people, and the control framework. Finance activities should seek to meet the needs of an organisation. How organisations achieve this will vary significantly depending on the organisational context, the business itself and the nature of the industry. However, the manner in which different organisations aspire to world-class finance is dependent on having an appropriate balance of a number of elements. These include orientation, processes, organisation of people and control.

Orientation

1.2.3 Orientation is the 'glue' that binds together other dimensions of the finance framework and it relates to the manner in which finance interacts with the rest of the business. There is, in many companies, an increasingly shared responsibility across the business for financial work and controls. Finance teams are participating more in the management of the business and, conversely, other line managers are becoming more aware of financial issues. Greater emphasis is also being placed on the use of emerging technologies and systems as 'enablers' to free up time and to drive down the cost of administrative processing activities.

1.2.4 Finance teams in many organisations are responsible for corporate oversight and stewardship and are sometimes oriented internally to the corporate hierarchy. Finance at times operates as an independent assessor of business plans and actions.

1.2.5 In some organisations the finance function is organised as a bureaucracy with fixed routines for processing financial data. Finance work relates to external accountability and technical compliance with rules and regulations. Where finance takes a competitive team orientation, it is focused on the external markets and works hand-in-hand with business managers. A

Management accounting and the finance function

positive contribution is sought from the finance team, not because this is required by corporate rules, but because they have demonstrated that they understand the business and can add to the quality of business management and decision-making. The success of finance within such environments is judged by the perceived value added by the finance team.

1.2.6 One example that supports the importance of adopting the 'competitive team' orientation relates to two companies in the automotive industry. An American corporation, USCO, was concerned about the service from, and cost of, its finance function and initiated a comparative study with a Far East partner, FECO. The study identified a number of factors which yielded a competitive advantage to FECO, including:

- less complex reporting and profit centre structures;
- highly integrated systems;
- financial accountability devolved to the business units;
- a significant degree of cross-over from accounting to analysis.

1.2.7 More significantly, the study identified that these factors were supported by a highly team-oriented operating philosophy characterised by trust, and the disposal of many so-called accounting activities to non-finance staff. In cost terms, FECO needed a smaller finance function as cost and productivity control was lodged with responsible individuals within the business units, i.e., engineers/plant controllers, etc.

1.2.8 There are many factors that affect how finance relates to, and works with, the rest of the business. These include the culture and history of the organisation, the way in which the business is organised, the influence and personal style of both the finance director and the chief executive, and the measurement practices adopted. In addition, an important consideration for the finance director revolves around achieving a fine balance between the 'competitive team' orientation and the maintenance of integrity in financial activities. Of essence here is how far finance is able to integrate with other business activities and units without endangering professional integrity.

Processes

1.2.9 Many businesses recognise that to create and sustain competitive advantage it is necessary to ensure the effective execution of core business processes – in other words, those key processes which generate an outcome valued by customers. In addition to supporting the effective operation of the core business processes, finance needs to consider how to re-engineer its supporting processes to improve service, quality and cost. An example of process improvement may be taken from an information services company which identified substantial opportunities to reduce costs and improve customer service in one of its processes. The results from the re-engineering exercise were dramatic.

1.2.10 One financial management process that needs special mention is that of performance measurement. Finance is uniquely positioned to ensure that measures are established to help the business convert strategy into performance. Information will come from many sources to provide a potentially balanced view of business performance, which will incorporate a range of measures including customer perspectives, non-financial measures, organisational learning and business environment indicators. In addition, the measures should seek to be consistent throughout the organisation and track performance across the core business processes as well as the separate functions.

Organisation of people

1.2.11 Although there is great diversity in the ways in which organisations structure themselves and their finance function, a growing trend across some enterprises has been to attempt to achieve the advantages of both the centralised and the decentralised approaches via a small team of specialists at the centre (e.g., tax and treasury), strong analytical and advisory support at business unit or process level, and the establishment of service centres for efficient volume transaction processing on behalf of a number of business units.

1.2.12 The US-based Institute of Management Accountants carried out a '1999 Practice Analysis of Management Accounting', in which it noted that the role of management accountants was very different in 1999 to what it had been in the past. Growing numbers of management accountants spend the bulk of their time as internal consultants or business analysts within their companies. Technological advances have liberated them from the mechanical aspects of accounting. They spend less time preparing standardised reports and more time analysing and interpreting information. Many have moved from the isolation of accounting departments to be physically positioned in the operating departments with which they work. Management accountants work on cross-functional teams, they have extensive face-to-face communications with people throughout their organisations, and they are more actively involved in decision-making.

1.2.13 In many organisations, management accountants take on leadership roles in their teams and are sought out for 'value added' information. They may be seen as trusted advisors.

Management accounting and the finance function

1.2.14 In some organisations, the role of management accountant has changed from serving internal customers to being a business partner. A business partner is seen as an equal member of the decision-making team. As a business partner, a management accountant has the authority and responsibility to tell an operating executive why particular types of information may or may not be relevant to the business decision at hand, and he is expected to suggest ways to improve the quality of the decision.

1.2.15 Many companies are reviewing the feasibility of outsourcing transaction processing – an important activity but not one which is likely to yield competitive advantage for most companies. This is especially so in the emerging digitised economy where it makes sense to devolve operational accounting and information processing to an off-base application service provider (ASP). The ASP may provide services that constitute its core strength more cheaply and effectively. The enterprise is then free to focus on its own core functions and expertise. But such possibilities are recent phenomena. Since the Second World War there has been a massive change in the way in which financial transactions are processed, with a huge consequential reduction in the number of staff required. The technical developments that have taken place may be summarised as:

1950s

- card-posting ledger machines with no calculating capability or card sorting/printing machines;
- calculation by comptometer operator;
- labour was cheap and plentiful, detailed standard costing systems were built, requiring large numbers of staff to drive them.

1960s

- punched card-driven computers and magnetic stripe ledger posting machines;
- electronic calculators;
- standard costing systems reached their peak.

1970s

- mainframe computers became widely used;
- beginnings of financial modelling;
- financial application packages became available for all ledger systems.

Achieving 'world-class' financial management

1980s

- computer performance/price capability escalated dramatically;
- personal computers/spreadsheets became universal with major increases in productivity of management accounting staff;
- standard costing systems became too expensive to maintain and started to decline;
- activity-based costing generated interest but was not widely applied;
- functionality of financial application packages became almost universally accepted.

1990s

- move from mainframe to distributed computer systems;
- trend towards financial transaction processing centres within distributed environment serving many subsidiaries/countries;
- functional transaction processing becoming more and more integrated and embedded in operational (e.g., manufacturing, sales and marketing) systems;
- escalating demand from management for better performance measurement systems and improvements to budgeting and forecasting, met in part by development of activity-based management, strategic cost analysis and the pursuit of more balanced scorecard measures.

1.2.16 The opening decade of the twenty-first century is set to usher in further changes on a mass scale. The advent of Internet-based commercial transactions is driven in part by technological changes in hardware structures, software possibilities and the emergence of novel possibilities for information retrieval, processing and presentation. But, perhaps more importantly, it is the confluence of both technological advance and the shifting business challenges within the emerging digitised economy which will force through transformational business change at its most fundamental. The Internet is currently in its infancy, but it has already altered what were seen as well-grounded principles underpinning the functioning of the modern enterprise. The role of finance within this context is set to undergo important new changes.

1.2.17 The impact of some of these developments and trends is represented in Figure 1.1, based on information from, and observation of, selected large companies in the commercial and industrial sectors. During this period of steep decline in the number of people employed in finance, the amount of qualified accountants employed in industry and commerce outside auditing has escalated. The quality mix within finance has therefore increased and this aligns with the whole trend towards greater demand in some sectors for enhanced participation by finance in management.

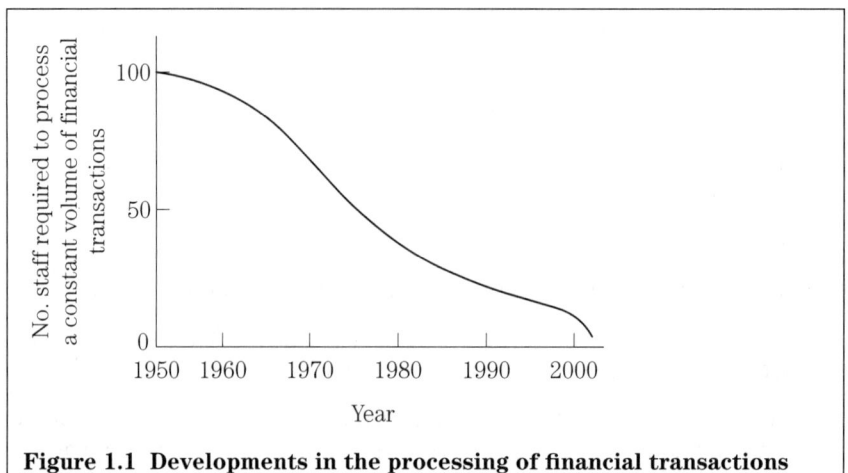

Figure 1.1 Developments in the processing of financial transactions since 1950

1.2.18 Many professional finance and accountancy bodies across the globe presuppose that these trends will move towards a structure with small numbers of:

- highly skilled cost management professionals working as part of management teams to develop strategy, plan the business and manage performance;
- specialists in tax, internal audit, etc.;
- specialist technicians responsible for ensuring that integrity of financial transactions and management information is maintained throughout distributed and integrated systems, most of which are run by non-financial personnel.

1.2.19 In their Management Accounting Guideline entitled *A Strategic Role for Treasury* (1999), CMA Canada note that moving corporate treasury from its traditional role of financial efficiency to a strategic role of organisational effectiveness presents a challenge for the management accountant. Today's strategic treasury initiatives are both technically complex and organisationally sensitive, thus offering the management accountant the opportunity to facilitate organisational understanding and communication concerning their

Achieving 'world-class' financial management

intent and purpose. The role of the management accountant as business partner will seek to be strengthened.

1.2.20 The impetus to broaden the scope of corporate treasury to include organisational effectiveness will possibly come from the company's senior management teams. However, as a business partner or as a member of the senior management team, it is expected that the management accountant will make a valuable contribution to such initiatives by creating an awareness of the strategic possibilities and by providing a framework for possible implementation.

1.2.21 As part of corporate treasury, as a member of another area of finance organisation, or as an outside consultant, the management accountant will perhaps have the opportunity to:

- develop an understanding of the strategic goals of the organisation and the ways in which chosen change initiatives contribute to those goals;
- identify current strategic treasury practices that are most complementary to the company's desired change initiatives;
- secure hard and on-line sources of information in order to keep up to date on strategic treasury initiatives, best practices and competitive performance metrics;
- develop a discussion framework for strategic treasury initiatives, including, where relevant, the most important accounting and tax questions and concerns applicable to each;
- identify reliable in-house and external professional sources that can best resolve those questions and/or concerns;
- establish a due diligence corporate policy and an approval framework for corporate treasury strategic initiatives; and
- communicate all of the above to senior management and the entire business organisation.

1.2.22 In the future, management accountants will also seek to help corporate treasuries develop a plan to move them away from the practice of financial efficiency to that of financial effectiveness. This may involve:

- conducting an assessment (or diagnostic) of where the company is on its journey to organisational change and effectiveness;
- conducting a similar assessment (or diagnostic) of where corporate treasury stands in relation to the corporation's overall commitment to organisational change;

Management accounting and the finance function

- identifying, with assistance from human resource experts, the skill sets and competencies required for a world-class treasury operation;
- developing a strategy for closing the identified gaps that might include elements of both financial efficiency and financial effectiveness; and
- suggesting ways in which treasury can build an organisation that continuously learns and contributes to the economic value of the firm.

1.2.23 In their Management Accounting Guideline entitled *Financial Risk Management* (1999), the Canadian body also states that as an active participant in the financial risk management process, the role of the management accountant is to include:

- sensitising top management to its risk management exposures and responsibilities;
- setting objectives (ultimately based on, yet contributing to, corporate strategy and policy choices);
- providing financial planning in relation to corporate strategy and asset/liability management;
- identifying underlying business risks and financial exposures;
- measuring the nature and extent of these exposures and risks and how they might offset each other or create diversification effects – quantitative analysis and interpretation are essential here;
- formulating and managing hedging strategies for financial and operating risks, using various capital and debt structure alternatives and incorporating tax aspects of derivatives applications;
- collaborating with the treasury function, particularly with regard to transfer pricing and multi-currency accounting (including constantly updating currency gains and losses);
- controlling policy implementation;
- monitoring hedge performance;
- providing internal accounting for reporting and control of derivatives;
- reporting results; and
- integrating performance measurement and financial risk management.

1.2.24 Today's management accountant is deemed not only to require skills in accounting, but also to have a sound understanding of the practice of management in other functions of the business. Traditionally, this has meant understanding the role of marketing, sales, production, distribution, research and development plus other support functions such as human resources and IT. However, as an increasing number of companies move to a more 'process'-oriented and digitised view of their operations, the management accountant will be required to understand and support such a novel frame of organisational reference.

Control

1.2.25 The final element is one that is viewed as being of increasing significance. Finance has always had a great deal of responsibility for establishing and maintaining appropriate controls. It is increasingly being recognised that it is no longer acceptable for control to be regarded solely as the responsibility of finance. It is a shared responsibility and, whilst finance will inevitably be expected to take a lead, managers throughout the business are being expected to take responsibility for control. The contrast between the traditional approach to control and the broader view now being developed is set out in Table 1.1.

Table 1.1 Different approaches to control

Traditional approach	Best demonstrated practice
Control is the responsibility of finance	Control is the responsibility of every manager and employee. Finance's role is to highlight risk areas and monitor the application of controls
Control is focused on financial controls and procedures	Control is exercised through raising employees' understanding of how they fit in to the organisation, encouraging staff to take greater responsibility for activities in their area, focusing on quality levels by monitoring failure rates, and emphasising self-checking
Control checks are applied at the end of discrete business activities (i.e., post-event)	Controls are built into business processes rather than 'added on'. This is assisted by reorganising activities into business processes rather than discrete functions, so that staff have a better understanding of the significance of their role
Responsibilities are segregated so that few people understand a complete process	Segregation of duties is an outmoded concept in some industries, e.g., the IT industry. As manpower levels are reduced, businesses focus more on system checks (where processes are heavily automated) and control checks embedded in the business processes

Management accounting and the finance function

Control problems are addressed by adding more people and by exercising greater control centrally	The sources of risk are identified and performance measures put in place to monitor activity in the areas of greatest risk, e.g., focusing on cash flows, margins, stock levels, asset movements. Managers are responsible for complete business processes; this responsibility increases their insight and awareness of control issues

1.3 Change management in the finance function

1.3.1 The management of financial functions is today seen as facing the same necessity to implement change as with other functions, in addition to the need to meet a variety of challenges to pursued change. Typically, resistance to change exhibited by effective managers is underpinned by sound reasons. Table 1.2 identifies certain established views as to how barriers to change can be overcome. These approaches are required by financial management professionals seeking to effect 'good practice' change management within their departments.

Table 1.2   Managing barriers to change

Barrier	Explanation	Action to resolve
Loss of control	A feeling of powerlessness arises when change is done *to* us rather than *by* us	Active involvement in the process
Excess uncertainty	Simply not knowing enough about the next step makes comfort impossible	Complete information
The 'difference' effect	Asking people to renounce the past completely can cause too much stress	Minimise the number of differences. Make changes manageable
Loss of face	Accepting change can often mean that people admit that things in the past were wrong. Many people are certain to resist this	Put actions in a positive light
Concerns about future competence	People with these concerns rarely express them openly – they are expressed in the many reasons why the change should be avoided	Supply adequate training
Ripple effect	Change disrupts plans, projects, personal and family activities Inadvertent ripples sent out by the change will generate resistance	Flexibility of response

More work	Change almost always means more work and extra effort	Recognise, support and reward effort
Past resentments	Past unresolved grievances will resurface during the change process	Bring them into the open and deal with them
The threat is real	The threat represented in change is real to many people	Avoid creating 'losers' where at all possible

1.4 The future of management accounting

1.4.1 Many management accountingcommentators have pondered over the role of the field in the future. Some prognostications are less urging than others and, just as change pundits vociferously exhort rethinking and reorganisation, so calls for change in management accounting continue to espouse alteration in practice if not in essence. McNair (1997), for instance, holds that the primary objectives for any reshaping of the finance function must be to:

- provide information utility with accurate, timely and relevant information available to all levels of the organisation, on demand, with no errors;
- become a highly effective and efficient provider of quality services to all internal and external customers;
- act in the capacity of an internal financial consultant, providing financial and business expertise to the organisation;
- educate managers throughout the organisation on the meaning, use, and structure of the financial reporting process and the estimates that underlie it;
- participate actively on teams focused on product and process design and improvement.

1.4.2 In other words, the finance function of the new millennium is, in McNair's view, to embrace analysis and a value added orientation. It will seek to be a consultative business partner and advisor, a participant and leader in decision-making. It will also seek to be strategically oriented and focused on performance enhancement.

1.4.3 According to McNair, to achieve these objectives companies are deploying novel business designs in the finance area. Three basic components – namely business consultants, business analysts, and technical specialists –

Management accounting and the finance function

comprise redesigned finance processes to facilitate the use of resources freed from transaction processing so that they can be re-engaged with the organisation.

1.4.4 Sheridan (1998) is more specific about the transformation currently being witnessed by the finance function in terms of the substance of new information requirements. In his view, the finance organisation is already changing under the pressure of various forces. For instance, he perceives that the need to manage outsourced activities and service centres (quite often far from the company's main operating centre), and to cope with new business alliances and partnerships, causes finance staff to introduce specific structures to deal with such novel management issues. Environmental matters and the demands of governance where the social pressures are often far ahead of the strictly legal ones also necessitate new types of information and facilities for its exchange.

1.4.5 Increased demand for information transparency will bring with it additional costs, and expectations that savings must be sought to finance these will continue to emerge.

1.4.6 Sheridan notes that many organisations are already facing the prospect of having to answer for their general corporate demeanour and to make evident for instance the basis of trading in foreign countries, political payments at home and abroad, labour policies in the Third World, policies on safety, health and green issues, equal opportunities, the employment of disabled people, pension scheme safeguards, etc. Sheridan rightly questions whether the provision of such general non-financial information will remain the province of finance. If so, it will bring into question issues concerning the size of the finance department and the nature of expertise best suited to deal with novel information construction and reporting requirements.

1.4.7 Whilst many management accounting approaches continue to emerge, the problem seems not always to be one of too few management accounting solutions, but rather of inadequately prepared management accountants. King (1997) believes that many management accountants are excluded from management decision-making because of their training which emphasises precision and accuracy at the expense of relevance. King suggests that recognising that there is more judgement – and less precision – in accounting is a first step in what may have to be an extensive programme to add to the role accountants could play in the twenty-first century. Without repositioning, the future of the management accountant as a key organisational player will be under question.

The future of management accounting

1.4.8 Foster (1996) likewise believes that change is required in the way in which management accountants operate. Management accounting is in a continual state of adaptation as the knowledge base in the field increases and business environments change. In Foster's view, management accounting has often been portrayed as focusing too much on internal reporting and on providing information for statutory financial reporting. This portrayal is now seen as inadequate. Beyond 2000, it will be even more inadequate. In future, decisions about which activities to outsource and how to structure joint ventures with other organisations will be critical management responsibilities. Management will seek financial information to help plan and monitor ongoing relationships with external partners.

1.4.9 According to Flegm (1996), skill with numbers is not enough. Accountants of the future must seek to become experts in the basic disciplines of business, whilst also becoming generalists who can manage different disciplines, communicate with clients, and motivate employees. Such calls have often been made of management accountants, but in a complex and fast-changing digitised economy where the medium is as important as the reported message, the accounting professional will be called upon to be increasingly integrative and holistic.

1.4.10 Whilst some quarters seek a more encompassing role for management accounting, the call for more strategic management accountants likewise rings loud. Kaplan (1995) considers that advances in the past 10 years have made it possible for management accountants to become part of their organisation's value added team. Kaplan believes that management accountants should participate in the formulation and implementation of strategy, and help translate strategic intent and capabilities into operational and managerial measures.

1.4.11 Management accountants must move away from being scorekeepers of the past and instead become the designers of the organisation's critical management information systems. Whilst existing performance measurement systems, even systems based on activity accounting (see Chapter **6** focus on improving existing processes, there is a need to become more 'balanced'. In Kaplan's opinion, the balanced scorecard focuses on what new processes are needed to achieve breakthrough performance objectives for customers and shareholders (see Chapter **11**).

1.4.12 This call has been echoed in other ways which seek greater balance and changes in management accountants' patterns of behaviour (Johnson, 1995). In the past, management accountants focused on how to disclose and report financial accounting numbers, especially cost numbers,

Management accounting and the finance function

so that managers could draw on them for more useful information. According to Johnson (1995), instead of focusing on achieving targets, companies intent on achieving positive long-term results should focus on mastering disciplined and standardised patterns of behaviour. Management accountants should work to create channels through which people enquire openly about purpose and method. In this light, Borthick and Roth (1997) note that the management accounting system of the future will be a large, real-time database whose data managers anywhere will be able to retrieve, manipulate and analyse new problems as they arise. The choice faced by companies is whether to be startled by what the future has in store or to embrace the future by implementing organisation-wide database systems to reap the benefits of improved data access.

1.4.13 What seems evident is that each decade brings with it pressures for changing management accounting as well as different perceptions of the implications of such pressures. The late 1990s heralded in the 'New Economy' where past conceptions of proper organisational management were viewed as being in need of change. A renaissance of liberalisation from the past is deemed essential by many old industrial firms facing competition from new giants that only five years earlier were non-existent. The Internet economy has made many 'modern' management information processing techniques ancestral. Bricks and mortar cardinal principles have been questioned and sometimes replaced by evolving clicks and mortar truths. Life-cycle costing (see Chapter **7** takes on a new tone *within* an Internet time pace. Balanced scorecard adopters must tackle new forms of imbalance. Activity accounting systems must now appeal to cyber-based cost drivers. Target cost management (see Chapter **10**) must today capture the nuances of ephemeral web markets. Whilst little can be said of where the future will take management accounting – if anywhere – pundits will continue to dwell on what is essential for its wellbeing.

Chapter 2
Established cost management approaches

2.1 Introduction and background

2.1.1 The first and last two decades of the twentieth century saw more thinking and development in the field of costing than the years in between. Moreover, the field of management accounting has seen more calls for change in the past decade than it has in the whole of its prior history. Altering management philosophies, different work organisation approaches, emerging flexible production technologies and a fast-changing global business climate are factors that have underlined calls for reform (Bhimani, 2000). Management accountants agree that established cost management approaches continue to be appropriate for use in many organisational situations, but that novel management accounting techniques are required for a diversity of contexts. This section reviews conventional cost management techniques and principles which continue to show usefulness and widespread application in modern-day organisations.

2.1.2 An understanding of costs is fundamental to many aspects of management because unless they are controlled an organisation may risk becoming unprofitable and imperilling its existence. In addition, cost information is needed for a number of accounting processes, such as the development of product cost data for the valuation of finished goods stock. Whilst the management of cost is seen as important, the concept is hard to define. There is no such thing as an 'absolute' or 'true' cost – costs can only be expressed within a set of rules or conventions.

2.1.3 Cost management has evolved over the course of the twentieth century under the principal concepts of job costing, standard costing and, ultimately, activity-based costing.

Pre-1900 to the present: job costing

2.1.4 Material and labour costs are recorded for each unit of production and overheads may be recovered, usually on the basis of direct labour hours. Job costing is commonly used where the units of production are large, as, for example, in building chemical plants or specialised heavy machinery.

Early 1900s to the present: standard costing

2.1.5 Standard costs reflect notions of optimum cost of materials and labour directly used for production. Overhead costs are often included, usually by recovery on the basis of direct labour or machine hours. Actual costs are then measured and compared with the standards and variances investigated. Standard costing is most commonly used in industries where there are many identical units of production – for example, automotive components or white goods. It can also be applied to service industries such as banking and insurance. The vast majority of companies today use standard or job costing for the valuation of stock.

1980s onwards: activity-based costing

2.1.6 Although the principles of activity analysis (see Chapter **6**) had been used for many years, an extension of this approach to areas formerly regarded as 'overheads' was proposed in the early 1980s. This was notably couched as a challenge to conventional methods of overhead apportionment. Many companies have carried out activity-based cost analyses which have proved valuable in providing a new perspective on product costing and as a basis for efficiency gains. Fewer companies have implemented ongoing activity-based costing systems for day-to-day cost monitoring or stock valuation. Research into and interest in activity techniques continues at a high level.

2.1.7 Cheatham and Cheatham (1996) suggest that of US manufacturers, 'only about 36 per cent of companies are using ABC as their main system while the vast majority use a standard cost system'. Innes, Mitchell and Sinclair (2000) report that a growing number of large UK firms are rejecting activity accounting approaches following implementations. Nevertheless, over 17 per cent of large firms have adopted the technique and another 20 per cent are actively considering it.

2.1.8 An increased knowledge of a variety of other cost management techniques has also emerged since the early 1980s. Examples are backflush accounting (Chapter **5**), target cost management (Chapter **10**), quality costing (Chapter **8**), throughput accounting and life-cycle costing (Chapter **7**). Presently, the concern is to consider established cost management approaches including cost-volume-profit relationships and standard costing systems. The starting point is to gain an understanding of cost behaviour.

2.2 Cost behaviour

2.2.1 Knowledge of cost behaviour is fundamental to many internal accounting activities including cost estimation, product costing and cost-based decision-making. Conceptually, operating costs can readily be subdivided into two categories: fixed and variable.

2.2.2 Variable costs are costs that change in total as the volume of activity changes. For example, assume that product A requires £5 of direct materials per unit. The total direct materials cost of manufacturing 10,000 units is £50,000; 20,000 units require direct materials of £100,000, and so on. The unit cost of the direct materials (£5) remains constant with changes in volume, but total variable costs increase with increased activity. Direct labour and direct materials are variable costs. Items such as supplies, electricity, indirect materials and sales commissions are ordinarily also examples of variable costs.

2.2.3 Fixed costs, on the other hand, remain constant in total as the volume of activity changes over a defined relevant range. For example, straight-line depreciation of £200,000 on factory buildings and equipment will not change, regardless of whether 10,000 units or 20,000 units of product are manufactured. Outside the relevant range of activities, further fixed costs may have to be incurred. Although fixed costs do not vary in total with changes in volume of activity, the unit cost will change with changes in activity. If volume increases, the unit cost will decrease, and if volume decreases, the unit cost will increase. For example, the unit cost of straight-line depreciation of £200,000 for 10,000 units is £20, and for 20,000 units of product, the unit cost is £10. Examples of other fixed costs include property insurance and taxes, rent and office salaries. Although such costs do not vary in total with changes in volume of activity, they may change due to other factors. For example, changes in property insurance rates will change the total property insurance cost. Some costs will also jump in discrete amounts showing an element of step variability.

2.3 Cost estimation

2.3.1 The behaviour of costs may be estimated using a variety of approaches. Some commonly used methods are considered below.

Account classification

2.3.2 A basic method of cost estimation is account classification. This procedure requires a limited amount of data and relies heavily on the accountant's

Established cost management approaches

professional judgement. When this method is used, the accountant obtains actual production and cost data for a single period. Each production cost account is analysed to determine its status as fixed, variable or semi-variable (i.e., a cost which has both a fixed and a variable component). All costs are classified as fixed or variable and are totalled in these two categories. In order to do this, a subjective estimate must be made of the variable and fixed portion of semi-variable costs. Variable unit production costs are estimated by dividing total variable costs by the number of units produced and the following cost estimating equation is derived:

$$\hat{y} = ax + b$$

where $\hat{y}$ is the estimated total cost, a the estimated variable unit cost, b the estimated fixed costs (if the range of observed activity points covers zero), and x the number of units produced (or the activity in question which is thought to relate to cost incursions). The 'cap' is inserted over the dependent variable y to indicate that the equation is used to estimate total costs. An actual value of y may not equal the estimated $\hat{y}$.

Engineering method

2.3.3 The engineering approach requires various physical inputs to be estimated. For example, material input can be estimated by analysing product blueprints and specifications. If the variables of the estimating equation are the volumes of each product produced, then the rate of increase in the cost per unit of the product is determined by pricing the derived inputs using current cost rates.

2.3.4 For example, a specific operation may be deemed to be achievable using 0.8 direct labour hours, and this would represent a standard based on natural working conditions, using perhaps a specific machine and assuming the deployment of a trained worker who can comfortably maintain the required pace of work as part of his ordinary functions.

2.3.5 The engineering method is expensive to adopt but does not rely on the availability of past data on operations or productivity.

Scattergraphs

2.3.6 If it is assumed that there is only one relevant independent variable (x above), then a scattergraph analysis might be used to separate a mixed cost into its fixed and variable components. To perform such an analysis, the actual observations that have been collected are graphed and cost behaviour

Cost estimation

is visually estimated. Suppose, for instance, that the following data are available for total costs versus units produced:

Costs	Units
£500	48
£600	62
£650	66
£700	68
£770	79

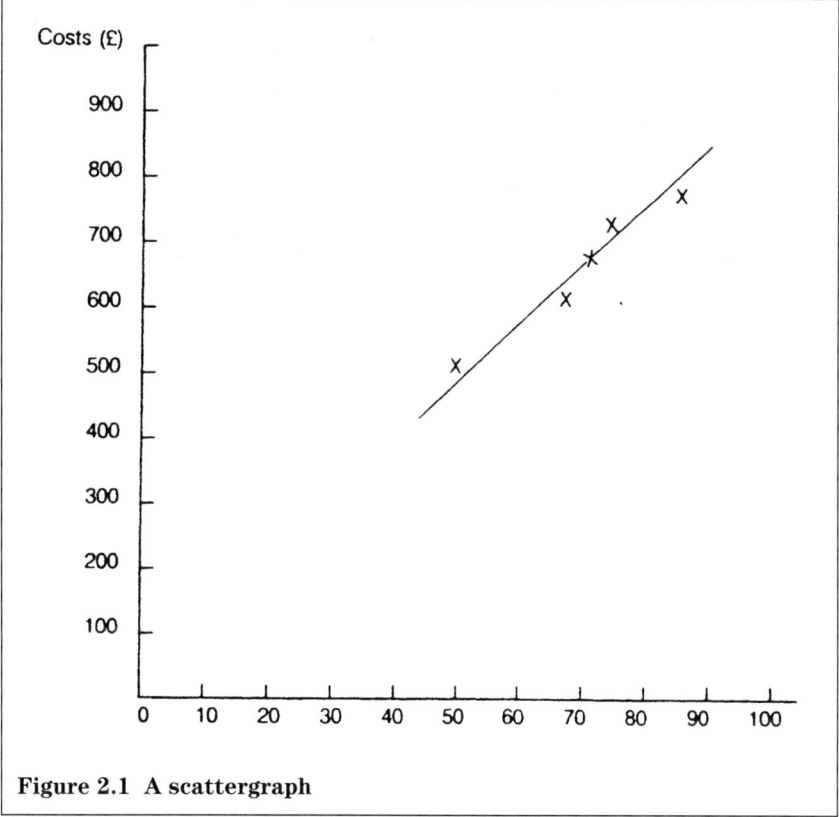

Figure 2.1 A scattergraph

2.3.7 Figure 2.1 provides a rough representation of the situation because it would be drawn manually and would rely on the interpretation and judgement of the individual doing the estimations. A slight variation of the method is the high-low approach, which makes use of just two observations (the highest and the lowest activities points) in constructing the estimating line.

Established cost management approaches

Clearly, no judgement is required here but the method is likely to yield improbable results if the two points happen to be outliers.

Regression analysis

2.3.8 Simple linear regression (also termed 'least squares analysis') takes the estimating line as represented by the above form of the equation. It assumes that there is a single independent variable (x) and that the relationship between it and the dependent variable (y) is linear. The objective is to construct a good fitting line through all the data points that are available. Regression is based on mathematical principles that ensure a best-fitting line. To understand the method further, it is necessary to consider how 'best' is operationally defined. Many statistical computer packages and hand-held calculators will process the sample data to provide values for a and b in the equation above.

2.3.9 Suppose the following data were available:

Production volume (units)	Labour costs (£)
105	990
44	460
61	600
42	440
77	740
78	760
87	850
31	330
103	1,000
84	810
53	540
40	430
56	560
37	390
69	670
93	930

2.3.10 For the particular set of data for x and y values, the regression equation would be:

$$y = 60.48 + 0.8955x$$

2.3.11 Although regression identifies the best-fitting line using a given variable and a given data set, it does not ensure that the equation is useful. There is a burden on the user to select appropriate variables for the analysis. The mere fact that a least squares best-fitting line can be derived from

Cost estimation

two sets of data should not be taken to suggest causality or even some logical association between the two.

2.3.12 The coefficient of determination (r^2) is one indicator of the potential usefulness of a regression equation. This value will range between 0 and 1 and is a measure of the accuracy of the fit of the line to the sample data (for the above example, $r^2 = 0.99$). The higher the r^2 the better, but correlation does not imply causality. Two variables can be highly correlated but need not be causally related. Thus, professional judgement needs to be exercised in selecting independent variables.

2.3.13 The r^2 statistic can be useful in deciding which of several possible regression equations should be selected. For example, suppose overhead costs have been regressed with; (1) direct labour hours, and (2) machine hours. The equation with the highest r^2 value would be a favoured candidate assuming that the r^2 is significant, i.e., exceeds 0.3 (and that other statistics for the regression model are not in conflict with this conclusion).

2.3.14 Where there is a choice between using different independent variables that are deemed equally useful, the organisation may opt for one over the others on the basis of ease of collection.

2.3.15 Another relevant statistic to consider is the standard error of the estimate (s_e) which is a measure of the 'average' difference between the actual observations of the dependent variable in the sample and the values predicted by the regression equation. It essentially signals the extent of 'scatter' – the calculated regression line. A lower value is thus preferable to a high value (the value for the above example is 8.47, which is relatively small). Another useful statistic is the standard error of the estimate for the parameter a (s_a). This statistic is a measure of the sampling error that results from estimating the true coefficient that exists in the population. It is reflective of the uncertainty of the slope of the calculated regression line. Again, the lower the value, the better.

2.3.16 Regression analysis can be a useful tool for estimating costs and can be used as a forecasting technique for certain management decisions. It is important to recognise that it relies on assumptions. One limitation is the range of values for which the equation should be used. The results can be misleading when used to estimate costs for values of the independent variable that are outside the range observed in the sample. Attempting to extrapolate outside this range has its problems in that the real relationship may be very different from that within the range. This is why the intercept term (b) cannot be taken to infer a plausible fixed cost level if the original observation points did not include a reading at zero activity level. Simple regression assumes there is a linear relationship between the two variables

Established cost management approaches

in the population. The model will fit a straight line to the data even if the actual relationship is not linear.

2.4 Break-even analysis

2.4.1 Many management accounting practices have been in use for decades and continue to serve important roles in the management of modern enterprises. These include and break-even analysis, contribution margin analysis, standard costing and variance analysis. Their use relies on an understanding of cost behaviour.

The break-even point

2.4.2 Once costs have been classified into their fixed and variable components, their effects on profit, along with revenues and volume, can be understood via cost/volume/profit analysis. Cost/volume/profit analysis can be used to indicate the revenues necessary to achieve the break-even point in operations or to indicate the revenues or sales unit level necessary to achieve a desired or target profit.

2.4.3 The point in the operations of an enterprise at which revenues and expired costs are exactly equal is called the break-even point. At this level of operations, an enterprise will neither realise an operating income nor incur an operating loss. Break-even analysis can be applied to past periods but is most useful when visualising future performance scenarios as a guide to business planning. When concerned with future prospects and future operations, the approach will rely upon estimates. The reliability of the analysis is thus greatly influenced by the accuracy of the estimates.

2.4.4 The break-even point can be computed by means of a mathematical formula which indicates the relationship between revenue, costs and capacity. The data required are:

- total estimated fixed costs for a future period, such as a year;
- total estimated variable costs for the same period, stated as a percentage of net sales.

Examples of break-even calculations

2.4.5 Assume that an organisation's fixed costs are estimated at $90,000 and that the expected variable costs are 60 per cent of sales. The maximum sales at 100 per cent capacity are $400,000. The break-even point is $225,000 of sales, computed as follows:

Break-even analysis

Break-even sales	(£)	=	Fixed costs (£) + Variable costs (as % of break-even sales)	
	S		£900,000 + 60%s	
	40%S		£90,000	
	S	=	£225,000	
Sales			£225,000	
Expenses				
Variable costs (225,000 × 60%)			£135,000	
Fixed costs			£90,000	£225,000
Operating profit				0

2.4.6 This is also shown in the graph in Figure 2.2.

2.4.7 The break-even point can be expressed either in terms of total sales or in terms of units of sales. For example, if the unit selling price is £25, the break-even point can be expressed as either £225,000 of sales or 9,000 units (£225,000/£25). The break-even point can be affected by changes in the fixed costs, unit variable costs and unit selling price.

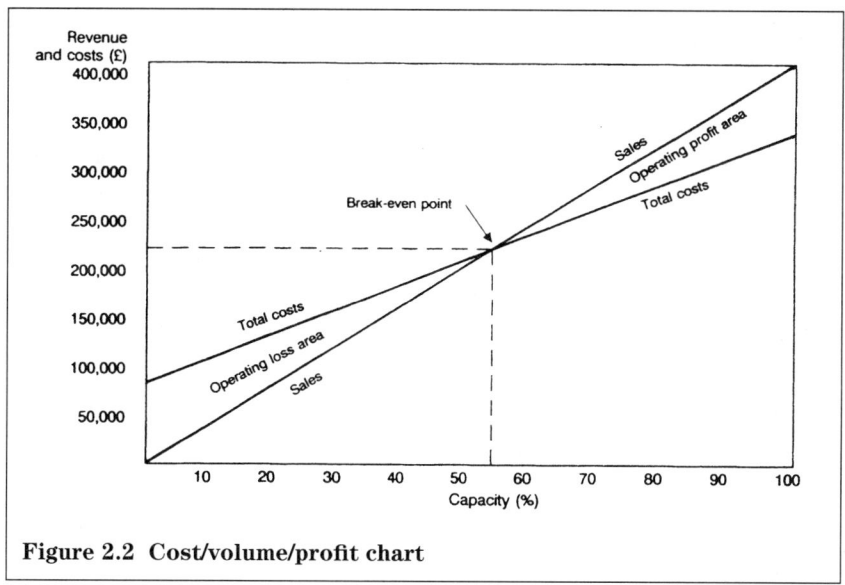

Figure 2.2 Cost/volume/profit chart

Established cost management approaches

2.4.8 At the break-even point, sales and costs are exactly equal. By modifying the break-even equation, the sales volume required to earn a desired amount of profit may be estimated. For this purpose, a factor for desired profit is added to the standard break-even formula.

2.4.9 Consider a situation in which fixed costs are estimated at £200,000, variable costs are estimated at 60 per cent of sales, and the desired profit is £100,000. The sales volume is £750,000, computed as follows:

Sales	(£)	=	Fixed costs (£) + Variable costs (as % of sales) + Desired profit
	S	=	£200,000 + 60%S + £100,000
	40%S	=	£300,000
	S	=	£750,000

2.4.10 The validity of the computation is shown as follows:

Sales		750,000		
Expenses:				
Variable costs (750,000 × 60%)		£450,000		
Fixed costs			£200,000	£650,000
Operating profit				£100,000

2.4.11 The break-even point for an enterprise selling two or more products can be calculated on the basis of a specified sales mix. If the sales mix is assumed to be constant, the break-even point and the sales necessary to achieve desired levels of operating profit can be readily calculated.

2.4.12 Consider the following data for the CVP company.

Product	Selling price per unit	Variable cost per unit	Sales mix
A	£90	£70	80%
B	£140	£95	20%
	Fixed costs = £200,000		

2.4.13 To compute the break-even point when several products are sold, it is useful to think of the individual products as contributing to a weighted average product. These computations are as follows:

Unit selling price of W: ($90×0.8) + ($140×0.2) = $100

Unit variable cost of W: ($70×0.8) + ($95×0.2) = $75

2.4.14 The variable costs for enterprise product W are therefore expected to be 75 per cent of sales ($75/$100). The break-even point can be determined in the normal manner using the equation as follows:

Break-even sales ($) = Fixed costs ($) + Variable costs (as % of break-even sales)

Break-even sales S = $200,000 + 75% S

Break-even sales 25% S = $200,000

Break-even sales S = $800,000

2.4.15 The break-even point of $800,000 of sales of enterprise product W is equivalent to 8,000 total sales units ($800,000/$100). Since the sales mix for products A and B is 80 per cent and 20 per cent respectively, the break-even quantity of A is 6,400 units (8,000×80%) and for B it is 1,600 units (8,000×20%) units. A verification of the analysis is given in Table 2.1.

Table 2.1 CVP Company income statement for year ended 31 December 2001

	Product A	Product B	Total
Sales			
6,400 units × $90	$576,000		$576,000
1,600 units × $140		$224,000	$224,000
Total sales	$576,000	$224,000	$800,000
Variable costs			
6,400 units × $70	$448,000		$448,000
1,600 units × $95		$152,000	$152,000
Total variable costs	$448,000	$152,000	$600,000
Fixed costs			$200,000
Total costs			$800,000
Operating profit			0

Established cost management approaches

2.4.16 The reliability of cost/volume/profit analysis depends upon the validity of several assumptions. One major assumption is that there is no change in stock quantities during the year – that is, the quantity of units in the beginning stock equals the quantity of units in the ending stock. When changes in stock quantities occur, the computations for cost/volume/profit analysis become more complex.

2.4.17 For cost/volume/profit analysis, a relevant range of activity is assumed within which all costs can be classified as either fixed or variable. Within the relevant range, which is usually a range of activity over which the company is likely to operate, the unit variable costs and the total fixed costs will not change. Moreover, the sales mix remains constant for a multi-product environment.

2.5 Contribution margin analysis

2.5.1 The classification of costs according to the way in which they behave enables particular types of short run decision to be made (i.e., one year or less). Contribution margin analysis relies on an appreciation of fixed versus variable cost components. Contribution margin represents sales net of variable costs. In other words, the contribution margin represents the amount available to cover fixed costs for a period and ultimately to produce a profit. Morse (1981) provides a useful example of the application of contribution margin computation for a special order decision.

An example

2.5.2 The Taylor Radio Co. has developed the following predetermined unit cost estimates at a production and sales volume of 25,000 units:

Direct materials	£20
Direct labour	£15
Variable factory overhead	£5
Fixed factory overhead	£10
Variable selling and admininstrative	£5
Fixed selling and admininstrative	£2
Total	£57

2.5.3 A special order has been received from a foreign distributor to purchase 2,000 radios at £47 each. The company has sufficient excess capacity and does not currently compete in any foreign market. Accepting the special

Contribution margin analysis

order will result in special selling and administrative expenses of £500. There will be no additional variable selling and administrative expenses. Should the order be accepted?

2.5.4 The relevant unit costs are direct materials, direct labour and variable factory overhead. They total £40 per unit. Hence, the unit contribution margin if the order is accepted is £7. The total contribution margin of £14,000 (£7×2,000) far exceeds the contract's fixed costs of £500. Accordingly, the contract contributes £13,500 to common fixed costs and profits. The relevant costs to include in the analysis are the incremental costs of the contract, and not the allocated fixed costs.

2.5.5 Suppose now that Taylor can reduce the direct materials cost by £2 per unit and direct labour costs by £3 per unit if it purchases component XR72 from a domestic supplier at a cost of £5.50 per unit. Accepting the order will permit Taylor to rent one of its buildings to a local firm for £20,000 per year. Should Taylor make or buy component XR72?

2.5.6 The incremental unit cost of buying is £0.50 per unit. However, buying will result in incremental revenues of £20,000 per year. At a volume of 25,000 units, the incremental profit from buying is £20,000 − £0.50(25,000) = £7,500. It appears desirable to buy. Given the focus on incremental costs, this approach to short run decision-making is sometimes referred to as incremental cost analysis. What is important to ask regarding incremental costs is whether the costs differ between alternative courses of action being considered and whether they relate to the future. Only such costs are deemed 'relevant' in incremental cost analysis.

A case study: determining a price bid

2.5.7 The following case examines a company's pricing decision for a large order from a customer. It encompasses a variety of cost management issues.

2.5.8 Quality Dairy is a large milk-processing company located in Birmingham. Founded in 1890, Quality was a small, privately held company until 1960 when it was purchased by the regional milk co-operative, owned and operated by and for dairy farmers. Quality's primary role in the co-operative is to provide an outlet for all surplus milk produced by member farmers. The government supports the price of milk by guaranteeing to purchase unlimited amounts of butter, powdered milk and cheese at set prices. Thus, Quality provides the means by which co-operative members ensure that they receive full price for all milk produced.

Established cost management approaches

2.5.9 Any skim milk or cream that Quality is unable to use in products sold to commercial customers is either converted into non-fat dry milk and sold to the government or sold to a creamery. Although sales of surplus milk products to the government and the creamery are not profitable, Quality is able to remain moderately profitable due to its commercial business. Net income averages £1,000,000 per year and return on equity is about 10 per cent. The majority of Quality's profits come from its mix business and sales of condensed skim and non-fat powdered milk. The condensed and powdered milk is sold to other dairies and food processors in lorry-load quantities.

2.5.10 The dairy industry is plagued by a constant surplus of butterfat, which is churned into butter and sold to the government at a loss. As a result, Quality sells its surplus butterfat to a creamery for £0.20 per pound of butterfat less than its direct costs (milk cost plus transportation). About 40 years ago Quality, in an effort to find a profitable market for some of its butterfat, began manufacturing ice cream, soft serve and milkshake mixes (referred to collectively as mixes) for wholesale markets. Quality offers all mixes in chocolate and vanilla flavours. The primary customers are ice cream stands and fast food chains, whose orders range in size from five gallons to 800 gallons per delivery. Management views the mix business as the most profitable part of Quality's operations, and wishes to expand the sales volume of this business.

2.5.11 Marketing information: Quality is the acknowledged leader in the market in terms of quality of product, and its prices are also normally among the highest. Mr Smith, the general manager of Quality, attributed this reputation for quality to his firm's specialisation in the production of mixes. Quality's competitors are dairies that produce a full line of products, including bottled milk, cottage cheese, butter, packaged frozen ice cream, and buttermilk. In addition, Quality has the best mix laboratory and quality control departments in the industry. It is also known for its excellent customer service. Although Quality does not hold a large market share in any major geographical market (30 per cent is its largest market share), it is by far the largest manufacturer of mixes in Birmingham. This volume allows Quality to produce relatively large batches of each type of mix almost daily, keeping costs down while ensuring the delivery of fresh products. A listing of Quality's mix products is presented in Table 2.2.

Contribution margin analysis

Table 2.2 Quality Dairy, 2000 mix product information (adapted from Adams, 1997)

	% butterfat content	Price per gallon £	% of sales mix	Total kgs sold	kgs of butterfat sold	Annual batches produced
14% ice cream mix	14	4.08	1	1,000,000	140,000	200
12% ice cream mix	12	3.74	6	5,000,000	600,000	300
10% ice cream mix	10	3.33	26	25,000,000	2,500,000	400
Soft serve mix	6	2.68	43	50,000,000	3,000,000	400
Regular milkshake mix	3.5	2.17	21	30,000,000	1,050,000	400
Low fat milkshake mix	1	1.80	3	5,000,000	50,000	300
Totals			100	116,000,000	7,340,000	2,000

2.5.12 Mr Smith is concerned that Quality's prices are considerably higher than those of most competitors, despite the apparent cost advantages it has relative to other dairies. Quality's prices seem particularly out of line for the 10 per cent and 12 per cent ice cream mixes. In fact, these products with higher butterfat content represent a much smaller percentage of sales than they did 10 years ago. The high-butterfat mixes are also losing market share. Mr Smith, holder of an MSc in Engineering from Glasgow University, suspects that competing dairies are selling at a loss to attract business, since Quality is a more efficient mix producer than any of its competitors.

2.5.13 Most mix customers are on three-day-per-week delivery schedules. Each customer is called the day before delivery and orders are recorded by order clerks. The mix products are packaged in 2.5-gallon plastic bags and sold in five-gallon increments (two bags in a plastic milk crate). Each morning at 4.00am at least 12 lorries leave for either a Monday-Wednesday-Friday route or a Tuesday-Thursday-Saturday route. During the peak demand months of June, July and August, six routes on each cycle are split each day to meet the seasonal volume, resulting in 18 lorries leaving each morning. Each lorry can carry 4,000 gallons of mix, and, except for the June-August surge, operate well below capacity. In the winter months, delivery lorries often leave the plant up to 70 per cent empty. It is not possible to combine the routes in winter however, because combined routes would take more hours than a driver is allowed to work in a day.

Established cost management approaches

2.5.14 Cost accounting system: target mix prices are set based on full manufacturing cost, plus delivery cost, plus direct selling and administrative cost, plus a mark-up. The accountant's staff prepare monthly updates of mix costs, which then become the basis for pricing decisions. The April 2001 cost sheet for both the regular milk shake mix and 10 per cent ice cream mix is presented in Table 2.3. Raw material costs (butterfat, skim, sugar, other ingredients and packaging) are computed using the average actual cost of material for the month and the actual product formula used in making the product. Farmers are paid for milk on the basis of the butterfat and skim content of milk sent to Quality. Therefore, the cost of milk in the mix products is directly traceable to Quality's purchase cost. Overhead is applied to products using a predetermined overhead rate based on last year's costs and volume.

Table 2.3 Quality Dairy cost sheets
Regular milkshake mix and 10% ice cream mix
April 2001

	Regular milkshake mix per gallon		10% ice cream mix per gallon	
Direct costs:				
Butterfat	(0.35# @ $0.91)	$0.319	(1# @ $0.91)	$0.910
Skim	(9.15# @ $0.12)	$1.098	(8.5# @ $0.12)	$1.020
Sugar		$0.140		$0.120
Other ingredients		$0.020		$0.020
Packaging		$0.030		$0.030
Total		$1.607		$2.100
Overhead:				
Factory overhead[a]	(0.35# @ $0.493)	$0.173	(1# @ $0.493)	$0.493
Delivery[a]	(0.35# @ $0.26)	$0.091	(1# @ $0.26)	$0.260
Selling & administrative[a]	(0.35# @ $0.04)	$0.014	(1# @ $0.04)	$0.040
Total mix cost		$1.885		$2.893
Mark-up (15%)		$0.283		$0.434
Target selling price		$2.168		$3.327

[a] Applied on the basis of butterfat content

2.5.15 For pricing purposes, two non-manufacturing costs are assigned to mix products: (1) delivery costs, and (2) selling and administrative costs. Delivery costs of £1,908,000 in 2000 include all lorry driver wages and benefits, maintenance, depreciation and fuel costs associated with the delivery of mix products. The delivery manager estimates that each delivery stop costs Quality about £10 whether five gallons or 500 gallons are delivered. The £10 cost represents the average time it takes to drive from one customer location to the next, as well as the time it takes to park, get the customer to open the cooler, engage in small talk with the customer, and complete the paperwork. At £10 per stop, the total 2000 'fixed' delivery costs total £840,000. Management believes that the rest of 2000's total delivery cost of £1,908,000 varies primarily with the volume of mix delivered.

2.5.16 The selling and administrative costs assigned to mix products include order, billing and sales costs related to the mix products. These costs totalled £293,600 in 2000. Each order takes about the same amount of time to process, bill and service. Quality processed 84,000 orders in 2000. General selling and administrative costs, including management salaries, finance and accounting costs, and laboratory costs, are not attributed directly to mix products. These costs are covered by the 15 per cent mark-up on costs that Quality applies to mix products in setting target prices.

2.5.17 The factory has three cost centres:

- the condensing department;
- the drying department, where powdered milk is created form condensed milk; and
- the rest of the plant's costs, which include the mix department and the pasteurisation and separation department. In the third cost centre, which is the focus of this case, all costs are allocated to the mix products on the basis of pounds of butterfat (cream bears no overhead cost from the pasteurisation and separation department even though it contains butterfat).

2.5.18 Detailed costs for the third cost centre are presented in Table 2.4.

Established cost management approaches

Table 2.4 Quality Dairy Cost centre number three 2000 overhead costs

Mix department and receiving, pasteurisation and separation department

	Cost
Mix department:	
Depreciation	£900,000
Labour	£1,478,070
Utilities and other	£129,000
Department total	£2,507,070
Receiving, pasteurisation and separation:	
Depreciation	£421,000
Labour	£672,550
Utilities and other	£18,000
Department total	£1,111,550
Cost Centre Three total	£3,618,620
2000 butterfat pounds (from Table 2.2)	£7,340,000
2001 predetermined overhead rate per pound of butterfat	£0.493

2.5.19 Whole milk is received from farmers and stored in one of six receiving towers with a capacity of up to 1,000,000lbs each. All milk is then pasteurised and separated. The cream (40 per cent butterfat) is sold by the lorry-load or used in mix products. The skim is sent to the condensing department or used in mix products. The condensed skim milk is sold as is by the lorry-load or dried into powdered non-fat dry milk. Quality received and processed 600,000,000lbs of milk in 2000. Management believes that pasteurisation and separation costs vary with the volume of milk received.

2.5.20 The mix department is composed of several large mixing vats (up to 10,000 gallons in size) in which cream, skim, sugar, flavouring and other ingredients are combined into the final mix products. Each flavour of each mix product is produced in a separate batch. The primary conversion costs in the mix department consist of depreciation and substantial costs related to cleaning the vats and the extensive piping used to transport the various milk product ingredients. Department capacity is constrained by the number of batches that can be produced in the existing vats and associated plumbing. Utility costs are also closely related to the number of mix batches produced, because for each batch the mixing, cleaning and cooling equipment must run for about the same amount of time.

Contribution margin analysis

2.5.21 The finished mix product is then pumped to the bottling area where plastic bags are filled, placed in crates and sent by conveyor to the cooler. Approximately £500,000 of the mix department labour costs, referred to as bottling costs, are related to filling the bags, placing the crates of mix in the cooler and loading them onto the delivery lorries. Handling takes the same amount of time per crate regardless of the product involved. The remaining mix department labour cost is related to setting up, mixing the ingredients and cleaning the equipment.

2.5.22 The McDonald's Order: Quality has an opportunity to bid on a contract to supply regular milkshake mix to all 30 McDonald's restaurants in the Midlands area. Each restaurant will receive three deliveries per week. The contract is desirable because it is high-volume, year-round business, and Mr Smith is eager to win the contract. A representative of McDonald's has approached Mr Smith and informed him that, as a result of its reputation for quality and service, Quality will be awarded the contract if it matches a competing bid of £1.94 per gallon. Mr Smith thus wishes to prepare a cost analysis of the McDonald's offer.

2.5.23 Quality has just completed the installation of new equipment that will double its packaging capacity for mixes, the only existing constraint on the volume of mix produced. The McDonald's contract is expected to increase mix sales to approximately 1,000,000 gallons per year. The increased volume will not increase the number of regular milkshake mix batches produced. The delivery manager estimates that the McDonald's order will require the purchase of three additional refrigerated delivery trucks at a cost of £150,000 each. They have useful lives of 10 years. Additional lorries would only need to be operated during the three peak summer months (there is sufficient surplus space on trucks serving existing delivery routes to handle the McDonald's volume the rest of the year) with an incremental gas and maintenance cost of £2,000 per lorry per summer month. Five additional summer drivers will also be needed at a cost of £3,500 per month per driver. The sales manager, who is pushing hard for the contract, argues that the McDonald's business is particularly good for Quality because it is much less seasonal than most of Quality's mix sales, and each store is a relatively high-volume customer.

2.5.24 Based on cost estimates from the existing system presented in Table 2.3 should the McDonald's order be accepted? If one accepts the cost calculations from the current system, the McDonald's order will not yield the desired target 15 per cent mark-up of £0.28. However, the £1.94 will generate a mark-up of £0.055 per gallon. The sales manager will argue that given the volume and the opportunity to break into the McDonald's business, the

Established cost management approaches

£0.055 per gallon profit is acceptable for initial penetration pricing. This type of subjective pricing based on the cost calculations in Table 2.3 is typical of how Quality has always determined prices for special orders.

2.5.25 What is the minimum price Quality can charge McDonald's and still increase net income by £0.05 per gallon? Incremental costs for regular milkshake mix are presented in Table 2.5. Since Quality must receive only about £1.75 per gallon to earn an incremental income of £0.05, management could be inclined to accept it based on this analysis. Two important assumptions underlie the relevant cost analysis. First, the firm must have excess capacity. Since Quality has just completed installation of new equipment that doubles mix capacity, the only capacity constraint appears to be delivery lorries, which have been accounted for in the relevant cost analysis. Second, management must believe that this is a unique opportunity. For Quality, basing the decision on a relevant cost analysis is dubious, because McDonald's represents a significant and ongoing business relationship.

Table 2.5 Incremental costs of the McDonald's order

Incremental cost item	Incremental cost per gallon (£)
Butterfat[a]	0.319
Skim[a]	1.098
Sugar[a]	0.140
Other ingredients a	0.020
Packaging	0.030
Bottling labour (£500,000/11,600,000 gallons of mix)	0.043
Incremental delivery (£115,500/1,000,000 gallons)[b]	0.116
Butterfat savings[c]	(0.070)
Incremental cost per gallon	1.696
Minimum profit	0.050
Minimal incremental price	1.746

[a] From Table 2.3.
[b] Depreciation costs of £45,000 per year, gas and maintenance costs of £18,000 per year and salaries of £52,500 per year.
[c] Quality loses £0.20 per pound of surplus butterfat sold to the creamery. The 3.5 per cent mix uses 0.35lb of butterfat per gallon, which avoids a loss of £0.07 per gallon.

2.5.26 It is easy to overlook the opportunity cost savings represented by the sale of 350,000lbs (3.5 per cent of the 10,000,000lbs of McDonald's mix) of butterfat per year to McDonald's that would otherwise be sold to the gov-

Contribution margin analysis

ernment at a loss of $0.20 per pound. Although the $0.07 per gallon savings (350,000lbs of butterfat not sent to the creamery multiplied by the $0.20 savings divided by 1,000,000 gallons) is not large, conceptually, this opportunity cost should be an important part of Quality's cost system because the avoidance of this loss is one stated reason why Quality is in the mix business.

2.5.27 What is Quality's basic mix strategy and is the McDonald's order consistent with this strategy? From a strategic perspective, Quality probably should not accept the current order. Quality's strategy is to be the quality and service leader in the mix business, not to be the low-price leader. By selling to McDonald's at a discount, it is likely to damage its premium image and upset current customers. Also, McDonald's may purchase Quality's mix at a higher price anyway because of the superior quality and service. An even more fundamental strategic problem relates to the reason why Quality is in the mix business to begin with: to find an outlet for surplus butterfat. Thus, Quality should be focusing its marketing attention on high-butterfat products rather than the regular milkshake mix. Note that raw milk also averages about 3.5 per cent butterfat. A strategic cost system should include a butterfat opportunity cost saving in the calculation of mix prices. A key point here is that the existing overhead allocation system based on butterfat is in conflict with this fundamental strategy because it encourages the sale of low-butterfat products and discourages the sale of high-butterfat products. Strategy implications are discussed further in Chapter **9**.

2.5.28 The order does have some strategic value. It significantly increases Quality's volume, particularly in the slack winter months. One might argue that by aggressively pricing McDonald's and other volume orders, Quality, because of its size and efficiencies, could drive competitors out of the mix business and eventually impose higher prices. However, since most of Quality's competitors are full-line dairies where mix represents only a small portion of their business, they are likely to remain long run competitors even if their mix business is temporarily discontinued. Costs to re-enter the mix business are low for existing dairies.

2.5.29 What are the consequences of the current allocation procedures? How could Mr Smith improve the product costing system used in determining target prices? The current allocation system systematically overstates the cost of the high-butterfat items and understates the cost of low-butterfat items. This occurs not only with the factory overhead allocation, but also with the delivery and selling and administrative costs. The result of this inadequate costing process over time is a 'death spiral', whereby fewer and fewer of the over-costed, high-butterfat products are sold. As fewer high-butterfat products are produced and sold, the total pounds of the butterfat over which

Established cost management approaches

overhead costs are allocated declines more rapidly than costs. This increases the overhead costs per pound of butterfat, which increases the cost and selling price of the high-butterfat items, and ultimately causes a further decline in sales of these products. At a minimum, Quality should recalculate mix costs using a volume-based cost driver such as gallons or kilograms of product. Since there is considerable product and volume diversity, an activity-based costing (ABC) system might be a useful extension of the volume-based allocation basis (ABC is further discussed in Chapter **6**.

2.5.30 What is the cost of 10 per cent and regular milkshake mix? The most appropriate single cost driver for Quality is gallons of product (kilograms of product will yield the same result). Gallons matches the cost behaviour of the bottling and delivery activities fairly well. Alternative allocation bases, such as number of batches, would more heavily burden the low-volume, high-butterfat products. Except for the overhead costs in the pasteurisation and separation department ($0.019 per gallon), mix production is a batch, not a joint process. The milk costs are not joint costs because the cost of the materials (butterfat and skim) that pass through the joint process remains identifiable after the split-off.

2.5.31 A calculation of Quality's cost for regular milkshake mix and 10 per cent ice cream mix based on a gallons-of-product allocation base is presented in Table 2.6. It is clear from the table that a $1.94 price for the McDonald's order is well below Quality's full cost. The price can only be justified on a penetration pricing basis. It is also obvious that Quality can significantly reduce the price of its 10 per cent and higher ice cream mixes, which will certainly increase market share and increase the sales of surplus butterfat. As a result of reviewing the McDonald's order, Quality may recalculate all mix prices using gallons as the allocation base. The new cost calculations could lead Quality to reduce the target prices for six per cent and higher butterfat products and increase the target prices for milkshake mixes.

Table 2.6
Quality Dairy cost sheets
Overhead allocated on a per gallon basis
Regular milkshake mix and 10 per cent ice cream mix

	Regular milkshake mix per gallon		10% ice cream mix per gallon	
Direct costs:				
Butterfat	(0.35# @ $0.91)	$0.319	(1# @ $0.91)	$0.910
Skim	(9.15# @ $0.12)	$1.098	(8.5# @ $0.12)	$1.020

Contribution margin analysis

Sugar		$0.140		$0.120
Other ingredients		$0.020		$0.020
Packaging		$0.030		$0.030
Overhead:				
Variable factory[a]	($0.185/ gallon)	$0.185	($0.185/ gallon)	$0.185
Fixed factory[b]	($0.127/ gallon)	$0.127	($0.127/ gallon)	$0.127
Delivery[c]	($0.165/ gallon)	$0.165	($0.165/ gallon)	$0.165
Selling & administrative[d]	($0.025/ gallon)	$0.025	($0.025/ gallon)	$0.025
Butterfat savings[e,f]		($0.070)		($0.200)
Total cost		$2.039		$2.402
Mark-up (15%)		$0.306		$0.306
Target selling price		$2.345		$2.762

[a] ($1,478,070 + $672,550)/11,600,000 gallons
[b] ($900,000 + $129,000 + $421,000 + $18,000)/11,600,000 gallons of mix
[c] $0.26 × 7,340,000# of butterfat/11,600,000 gallons
[d] $0.04 × 7,340,000# of butterfat/11,600,000 gallons
[e] 0.35# of butterfat per gallon × $0.20 savings
[f] 1# of butterfat per gallon × $0.20 savings
(Source: adapted with permission from Adams, 1997.)

A case study: Kim Basinger's replacement cost

2.5.32 Another case study relying on an understanding of contribution analysis and relevant costing is that of the widely publicised case of *Main Line Pictures vs Basinger*. Main Line sued actress Kim Basinger in 1991, alleging that she caused the company to lose profits of between US$5 million and US$10 million by withdrawing from a controversial film project in breach of contract. Main Line argued that it would have earned a pre-tax profit on the film in the range of US$3 million to US$8 million if Basinger had remained on set. The profit figures were calculated from pre-sale contract amounts and the film's budgeted cost. Main Line also argued that it now expected to lose US$2 million on the film when it was made, primarily because Basinger's replacement did not have the same box office appeal. Basinger argued that only a handful of very successful films could generate profits to Main Line in the dollar amounts cited due to the many contractual claims against those profits by others. In addition, her presence in the film was no guarantee that the film would be successful. At issue in this case are

Established cost management approaches

the reliability and reasonableness of the numbers used in Main Line's lost profit computation.

2.5.33 In the *Basinger* case, the primary issue for jurists and other legal enthusiasts was whether Basinger breached an actual contractual agreement or simply engaged in the usual caprice of Hollywood deal-making. As Barton, Shenkir and Marinas (1996) suggest, the press was awash at the time with stories declaiming the lack of integrity in Hollywood deals and discussing the possible adverse implications for actors and production companies in general.

2.5.34 The film *Boxing Helena* was no less controversial than the legal issue. It involves a woman who is injured in a car accident. The doctor who 'rescues' her amputates her injured legs and unhurt arms and keeps her hostage in a box, hoping she will eventually fall in love with him. Basinger testified that she withdrew from the starring role, after ongoing negotiations, because of concerns about her character's personality and involvement in graphic scenes of an adult nature.

2.5.35 Main Line, however, had US$3 million in potential domestic and US$7.6 million in foreign pre-sale agreements based on Basinger's participation in the film. After her withdrawal, a lesser-known actress, Sherilyn Fenn (known for her role in the cult television series *Twin Peaks*) was engaged, resulting in only US$2.7 million in foreign pre-sale agreements and no domestic distributor as at the time of trial. Main Line contended that it incurred significant financial damage as a direct result of Basinger's withdrawal from the project.

2.5.36 Of concern here is how to value the actual damage incurred by Main Line if there were a breach of contract. Any value is particularly tenuous given the fact that; (1) a film with Basinger was never made, and (2) a reliable revenue prediction for a specific film is very difficult, and frequently impossible, to obtain before the film is released. Both Main Line and Basinger presented expert witnesses to deal with the problem.

Revenues and costs for a film production
2.5.37 A film project generates revenue to its producer through rentals based on box office receipts and ancillary sources such as home video, cable and network television. Independent producers (i.e., those not affiliated with major studios) typically attempt to raise the capital to produce their films through pre-sale contracts. In a pre-sale contract, a film distributor will agree to distribute a film to theatres in a certain geographic area in return for a fee guarantee. For example, a distributor in Europe contracts to dis-

Contribution margin analysis

tribute a film and agrees to pay the producer US$5 million against an amount calculated as the revenue to the distributor (based on box office receipts or 'gross') less a 40 per cent distribution fee and less the costs of advertising, making the copies of the movie (prints), and other distribution elements such as freight. The producer can then borrow against that contract from a bank to help finance the film's production cost, or the distributor can advance production funds to the producer against its own contract.

2.5.38 If the film generates revenue to the distributor in Europe of, for example, US$15 million (based on total tickets sold), the distributor will calculate the payment to the producer as US$15 million less the 40 per cent distribution fee, less the cost of prints, advertising and other miscellaneous distribution costs. Suppose the cost of prints, advertising and other miscellaneous distribution elements is US$3 million. Then the producer would be paid:

US$15 million − (40% × US$15 million) − US$3 million = US$6 million

2.5.39 But regardless of the film's actual success at the box office, the payment could not be less than the guarantee of US$5 million.

2.5.40 The producer's costs in a film production are the outlays for acquiring the rights to the script, fees to the actors, director and production personnel, film stock and processing, camera rentals, sets, costumes, special effects, and post-production costs of editing, sound and music. The producer will deliver a master copy of the film from which prints can be made, but the actual cost of the prints, advertising and other distribution elements are borne by the distributor until they are recouped from the producer's share of the box office receipts.

2.5.41 Often there will be contractual arrangements that will call for the producer to share net profits, and in some cases revenues, with key actors, the directors and others. While direct costs are charged to the individual film projects as incurred (job order costing), there can be common overhead costs that will require allocation to individual films. Naturally, this allocation will affect the payments made to net profit participants and thus it has been a longstanding source of controversy – and litigation – in the industry. But overhead allocation is more of an issue with major studios who produce 15 to 20 films per year than with independent producers who may produce only one or two films per year.

2.5.42 Testimony by Main Line's expert: Dr Louis L. Wilde (a University Professor of Economics and Consultant) appeared as an expert witness for

Established cost management approaches

the plaintiff. Wilde testified that the minimum profit differential (and therefore financial loss to Main Line) was US$5.1 million. This analysis is presented in Table 2.7.

Table 2.7 Minimum damages, according to Main Line's plaintiff expert (in US$ million)

	With Basinger	Without Basinger	Difference
Foreign pre-sales			
Firm	6.8	2.7	4.1
Probable	0.8	n/a	0.8
Total foreign	7.6	2.7	4.9
Domestic pre-sales	3.0	0.0	3.0
Total revenue	10.6	2.7	7.9
Production budget	(7.6)[a]	(4.8)[b]	(2.8)
Net profit/(loss)	23.0	(2.1)	5.1

[a] Per testimony of producer that film would be made for amount of foreign pre-sales
[b] Actual budget for film as produced

2.5.43 Wilde worked from the definition that damages were 'a measure of the compensation that would be required to put the person [who was breached] in the position [he] would have been in had there not been a breach in terms of the economic losses to [him]. . ..' Wilde simply compared what Main Line expected to make with Basinger to what Main Line was actually able to make on the same package without Basinger – the difference (presumably a loss) was the damage to Main Line.

2.5.44 Wilde emphasised that a focus on 'net profit differential' was especially appropriate because a differential, or incremental value, is independent of the specific values for revenue or expenses. For example, suppose the film without Basinger eventually performed better than the US$2.7 million pre-sale amount, generating ultimate revenues of US$12.7 million. Wilde claimed that his profit differential of US$5.1 million would still hold even at the higher revenue amount. Revenues of US$12.7 million for the film without Basinger equate to a profit of US$7.9 million (US$12.7 in revenue less US$4.8 in costs). Thus, according to Wilde, the Basinger film would have earned a profit of US$13 million (US$7.9 plus US$5.1).

Table 2.8
Maximum damages, according to Main Line's plaintiff expert (in US$ million)

	With Basinger	Without Basinger	Difference
Foreign pre-sales			
Firm	6.8	2.7	4.1
Probable	0.8	n/a	0.8
Total foreign	7.6	2.7	4.9
Domestic pre-sales	7.6[a]	0.0	7.6
Total revenue	15.2	2.7	12.5
Production budget	(7.6)[b]	(4.8)[c]	(2.8)
Net profit/(loss)	7.6	(2.1)	9.7

[a] Domestic pre-sales adjusted for market inefficiency. Put into 1:1 ratio with foreign pre-sales.
[b] Per testimony of producer that film would be made for amount of foreign pre-sales.
[c] Actual budget for film as produced.

2.5.45 Wilde also calculated a maximum profit differential (Table 2.8). He argued that the private negotiations for the price of domestic distribution lacked market efficiency and, therefore, did not fully reflect the eventual market price of the film if it were released. This flaw in the domestic revenue estimate did not apply to the foreign pre-sales, according to Wilde, because:

> 'The foreign pre-sale markets are very well organised. They meet in well-defined places . . . Buyers and sellers come together. The products are there. The transactions take place. Not down in the pit the way the stock market works, but in a relatively short period of time. Information is very good.'

2.5.46 Therefore, the foreign pre-sale markets (e.g., Cannes Film Festival, American Film Market, MIFED-International Film, TV Film and Documentary Market, etc.) possess greater market efficiency.

2.5.47 To adjust the privately negotiated domestic price to what would be expected in the public market (i.e., box office), Wilde studied the average ratios of domestic to foreign sales for movies of the same genre. Wilde concluded that the ratio of domestic to foreign for this type of film was 1:1. Therefore, the potential domestic revenue amount should be revised to equal the foreign pre-sales amount. This means an upward adjustment of US$4.6 million in the domestic revenue to US$7.6 million. With this change, the maximum profit differential is US$9.7 million.

Established cost management approaches

2.5.48 As a 'gut level check' of his analysis and the revenue differentials, Wilde also compared the average revenue of Basinger films (excluding *Batman*) with the average revenue of Fenn films. He found that Basinger films had an average revenue of US$19 million and Fenn films, an average revenue of only US$1.6 million.

2.5.49 Testimony by Basinger's expert: Bruce St J Lilliston, a lawyer and specialist in independent film finance and production contracts, appeared as an expert witness for Basinger. Lilliston took the position that in order for an independently produced film to yield a net profit of US$5.1 million to Main Line (the minimum profit differential of Main Line's expert), it would have to generate worldwide distribution revenues of US$82 million. This would come primarily from theatres, video and television (Table 2.9). The analysis assumes the film without Basinger exactly breaks even. If total revenue of the same size was generated by *Boxing Helena*, it would place it fourth in the list of top performing independent films released between 1985 and 1991, following *Dirty Dancing* and above *Nightmare on Elm Street, Part IV*.

2.5.50 Lilliston also presented evidence that to yield the maximum profit differential of US$9.6 million, *Boxing Helena* would have to generate worldwide distribution revenues of US$144 million, placing it third in the list of top performing independent films, following *Teenage Mutant Ninja Turtles* and above *Dirty Dancing*.

2.5.51 Lilliston then testified that 'big stars in a movie' do not necessarily equate to big revenues. He displayed a chart showing a list of films with well-known stars that had under-performed at the box office. Included in the list was *Homer and Eddie* starring Whoopi Goldberg, which had a box office gross of US$14,000 against a cost of US$14 million. Also appearing in the list was *Hudson Hawk* starring Bruce Willis, which generated a box office gross of US$17 million against a cost of US$54 million.

Table 2.9
Revenue needed for profit differentials, defence expert (in US$)

	Maximum	Minimum
Total revenue	144,207,655	82,288,150
Avg. worldwide distribution fees (40%)	(57,683,062)	(32,915,260)
Prints & advertising	(12,000,000)	(12,000,000)
Amount payable to producer	74,524,593	37,372,890
Production budget (assumed)	(7,600,000)	(7,600,000)
Gross profit	66,924,593	29,772,890
Deferment payable to Main Line	(250,000)	(250,000)
Deferment payable to Caland[a]	(250,000)	(250,000)

Contribution margin analysis

Net profit	66,424,593	29,272,890
Participation payment (20.5%)[b]	(13,617,042)	(6,000,943)
Net profit after participation	52,807,551	23,271,947
Level 1 split:		
50% to Main Line to US$2 million	(2,000,000)	(2,000,000)
50% to Caland to US$2 million	(2,000,000)	(2,000,000)
Net profit for Level 2 split	48,807,551	19,271,947
Level 2 split:		
15% to Main Line	(7,321,132)	(2,890,792)
85% to Caland	(41,486,419)	(16,381,155)
Summary of payments to Main Line:		
Deferment	250,000	250,000
Level 1	2,000,000	2,000,000
Level 2	7,321,132	2,890,792
Total payments to Main Line	9,571,132	5,140,792

[a] Philippe Caland is identified in court documents as a partner with Main Line in the project but is not a plaintiff in the lawsuit.
[b] Profit participation to actors Kim Basinger and Ed Harris, and writer/director Jennifer Lynch.

Note: 'Amount payable to producer' in this table is termed 'Total revenue' in Tables 2.7 and 2.8.

2.5.52 The following additional information also emerged from the case:

- Basinger was to be paid US$600,000 in guaranteed compensation to appear in *Boxing Helena* with another US$400,000 to be paid out of producer revenues 'before the bank' was paid on the production loan to finance the film. Basinger received US$3 million to appear in *Final Analysis* following her withdrawal from *Boxing Helena*.

- As mentioned previously, foreign pre-sales are typically used by independent producers to secure production loans from banks that provide financing for the production costs. This was the case with *Boxing Helena*.

- The domestic distribution deal cited in Wilde's testimony had not been finalised before Basinger withdrew from the project.

- One of the partners in Main Line advanced US$1.7 million against domestic revenues to help cover production costs on the Fenn film. In other words, the advance would be repaid from domestic revenues.

- Main Line president Carl Mazzocone testified on the subject of the US$2.8 million difference between the two production budgets (with and without Basinger):

Established cost management approaches

> 'Well, Miss Fenn and [co-star] Julian Sands both received US$100,000. The difference is Kim Basinger would have received US$1 million. I had to bank US$1 million even though I was paying US$600,000 up front, and Mr Harris [co-star] would have made US$500,000. So there is a difference there. I also would have had increased producer's fees and would have made more money.
>
> And, lastly, the other increase was that I wanted to build a set of this [on a soundstage] instead of using a real house, you have so many limitations and drawbacks [with a real house]. It takes longer. So when you build a set, even though it costs more money to build a set, you will actually save money because it's faster.'

2.5.53 The verdict: Barton, Shenkir and Marinas (1996) report that the jury (in a 9:3 vote) awarded Main Line US$7,421,694 in damages for breach of contract and unanimously added US$1,500,000 for bad faith denial of the contract. A request for punitive damages of between US$1 million and US$2 million was denied. Basinger appealed the decision and later filed for bankruptcy protection.

2.5.54 In 1994, the judgment was reversed on appeal and remanded to the lower court. The Appeals Court concluded that jury instructions failed to draw a sufficient distinction between the liability of Basinger and the liability of her production company, Mighty Wind Productions.

2.5.55 Barton, Shenkir and Marinas (1996) suggest that the primary flaw in the plaintiff's calculation of lost profits is its failure to include a deduction for the various claims on those profits by others including Basinger herself. If Basinger had remained with the project and Main Line had, in fact, shown a profit of US$3 million (minimum), an extrapolation of the defence expert's testimony would have Philippe Caland, Ed Harris, Jennifer Lynch and Basinger share in it as shown in Table 2.10. The term 'gross profit' is used here to be consistent with Table 2.9. There, profit claims lower the minimum profit to US$1,243,750. By a similar analysis, the US$7.6 million maximum profit amount (Table 2.8) would become US$2,496,675 when the contractual profit claims are deducted.

Table 2.10 Main Line minimum profit with contractual payments deducted (in US$)

Gross profit	3,000,000
Deferment payable to Main Line	(250,000)
Deferment payable to Caland	(250,000)
Net profit	2,500,000
Participation payments (20.5%) – Basinger/Harris/Lynch	512,500
Net profit after participation	1,987,500

Contribution margin analysis

Level 1 split:	
50% to Main Line to US$2 million	(993,750)
50% to Caland to US$2 million	(993,750)
Net profit for Level 2 split:	0
Level 2 split:	
15% to Main Line	0
85% to Caland	0
Summary of payments to Main Line	
Deferment	250,000
Level 1	993,750
Level 2	0
Total payments to Main Line	1,243,750

2.5.56 The point of this exercise is to demonstrate that Main Line would not have kept all of the cash shown as 'profit' by the plaintiff. In fact, at the US$3 million profit level, Main Line retains only 41 per cent of it (33 per cent at the US$7.6 million level).

2.5.57 Barton, Shenkir and Marinas (1996) also note that the second major problem in the plaintiff's lost profit calculation is the failure to include an amount for domestic revenues in the 'Without Basinger' FILM. According to trial testimony, one of the partners in main Line advanced US$1.7 million against domestic revenues to permit the production of the film after Basinger withdrew (and the domestic distribution deal collapsed).

2.5.58 Plaintiff's expert merely ignored potential domestic revenues because there were no contracts executed by the trial date. But it would be relatively easy to argue that the Main Line partner would not have advanced the money if he did not feel somewhat confident that he would be repaid after the film was distributed. Also, including the US$1.7 million in minimum revenues would remove the somewhat implausible presumption that Main Line would proceed with the production of a film while expecting to lose US$2 million on it. This latter point is related to the defence attorney's discussion of mitigation of damages ('He has a duty under the law to minimise his loss', quoted early in the case). For the maximum computation, it can be suggested that domestic revenues for the 'Without Basinger' film be set at a 1:1 ratio with foreign revenues or US$2.7 million. It would be illogical to use the plaintiff expert's 1:1 ratio for one film project and not the other.

2.5.59 Without any further adjustment beyond these two items, the Main Line minimum damage amount falls to US$1.6 million and the maximum damage amount falls to US$2.2 million (Table 2.11).

Established cost management approaches

Table 2.11 Revised maximum lost profits (US$ million)

	With Basinger	Without Basinger	Difference
Foreign pre-sales			
Firm	6.8	2.7	4.1
Probable	0.8	n/a	0.8
Total foreign	7.6	2.7	4.9
Domestic pre-sales	7.6	2.7	4.9
Total revenue	15.2	5.4	9.8
Production budget	(7.6)	(4.8)	(2.8)
Gross profit	7.6	0.6	7.0
Contractual profit claims	(5.1)	(0.3)	(4.8)
Net profit	2.5	0.3	2.2

(Source: adapted with permission from Barton, Shenkir and Marinas, 1996.)

2.6 Standard costing and variance analysis

2.6.1 A standard cost may be defined as the budgeted cost for one unit of a particular resource. One objective of using standard costs is to provide a tool for investigating deviations between expectations and outcomes. The actual profit for a year may differ from plan depending on how far sales and costs have deviated from expected values. The variance between volume expectations and actual activity is also an essential component of the investigation. This requires a consideration of 'flexible' rather than 'static' activity volumes. A useful illustration of the use of standard costs to investigate differences between expectations and outcomes follows.

An example

2.6.2 For October 2001, the Redd Co. budgeted sales at 30,000 units at a selling price of £10 each and a variable cost of £6 each. Actual sales were 28,000 units. Table 2.12 shows that net income was £17,000 less than budgeted.

2.6.3 One could conclude that the reduced sales caused net income to be reduced by £20,000. It would appear that variable costs were £5,000 less than expected, helping to offset the reduced sales. However, this is misleading. The £5,000 favourable variance was derived by comparison of the actual costs for 28,000 units with the budgeted costs for 30,000 units. Such a comparison is inappropriate. Costs are expected to be lower if sales are lower. In fact, the firm can reduce variable costs to zero by selling nothing.

Standard costing and variance analysis

Table 2.12 Redd Co. income statement for the month ended 31 October 2001

	Budget (30,000 units)	Actual (28,000 units)	Variance
Sales	£300,000	£280,000	£20,000 U
Variable costs	£180,000	£175,000	£5,000 F
Contribution margin	£120,000	£105,000	£15,000 U
Fixed costs	£50,000	£52,000	£2,000 U
Net income	£70,000	£53,000	£17,000 U

F = favourable
U = unfavourable

2.6.4 It is necessary to prepare a flexible budget that shows total variable costs for 28,000 units rather than 30,000 units, at a variable cost per unit of £6. This is illustrated in Table 2.13, which shows that variable costs are not £5,000 favourable but £7,000 unfavourable. In other words, since the company sold only 28,000 units, variable costs should have been only £168,000 (£6×28,000 units). Instead, they were £175,000.

Table 2.13 Redd Co. income statement for the month ended 31 October 2001

	Budget (28,000 units)	Actual (28,000 units)	Variance
Sales	£280,000	£280,000	–
Variable costs	£168,000	£175,000	£7,000 U
Contribution margin	£112,000	£105,000	£7,000 U
Fixed costs	£50,000	£52,000	£2,000 U
Net income	£62,000	£53,000	£9,000 U

U = unfavourable

2.6.5 Fixed cost variances total £2,000 unfavourable. Notice that the budget for fixed costs is £50,000 in both the 'static' budget (for 30,000 units) and the 'flexible' budget (for 28,000 units). By definition, fixed costs do not change within a relevant range. Assuming a relevant range of 0–50,000 units for Redd Co.'s fixed costs, these costs would be the same for both 28,000 units and 30,000 units of sales. Thus, within the relevant range the flexible budget shows the same amount of fixed costs. However, outside the relevant range, the flexible budget would also show different levels of fixed costs. A detailed analysis of specific items of fixed cost would reveal those costs that resulted in the £2,000 unfavourable variance.

Established cost management approaches

2.6.6 Actual net income was $17,000 less than budgeted net income; $9,000 of that $17,000 was caused by variances in costs. Specifically, variable costs were $7,000 more than they should have been for the achieved level of activity, 28,000 units, and fixed costs were $2,000 more than they should have been. The fact that actual sales in units were less than budgeted also caused net income to be less than expected. This difference is referred to as the sales variance. The sales variance shows how much contribution margin was lost because budgeted sales were not achieved. Thus:

Sales variance	= (Actual unit sales − Budgeted unit sales) × Contribution margin per unit
Sales variance	= (28,000 units − 30,000 units) × $4 per unit
	= −2,000 units × $4 per unit
	= $8,000 U

U = unfavourable

2.6.7 The calculation above shows that because sales were 2,000 units less than expected, net income was $8,000 less than expected, resulting in an unfavourable sales variance. The $17,000 unfavourable variance in net income is as follows:

Sales variance	$8,000 U
Variable cost variances	$7,000 U
Fixed cost variances	$2,000 U
Net income variance	$17,000 U

U = unfavourable

2.6.8 In summary, the company failed to achieve its budgeted net income of $70,000 because lost sales resulted in an $8,000 decrease in expected net income, variable cost variances resulted in a $7,000 decrease in expected net income, and fixed cost variances resulted in a $2,000 decrease in expected net income. The details of these variances can be further analysed to determine more specific reasons why they occurred.

2.6.9 We can view a standard cost system as an accounting system under which all manufacturing costs are charged to production at standard costs. This practice is in contrast to an actual cost system, which charges actual costs to production as they are incurred, or to an actual/normal cost system, which charges actual direct material and direct labour costs to production but charges variable and fixed factory overhead at a predetermined, or standard, rate. Consider the following standards for Redd:

Standard costing and variance analysis

Unit cost	
Direct material (2.5lbs per unit at $70 per lb)	$1.75
Direct labour (0.25 hours per unit at $8 per hour)	$2.00
Factory overhead (0.25 hours per unit at $4 per DLH)	$1.00
Total standard variable cost per unit	$4.75

2.6.10 For November 2001 Redd Co. budgeted production for 12,000 units. However, only 10,000 units were produced. A performance report based on a flexible budget of 10,000 units may be prepared as shown in Table 2.14. The budgeted amounts in the performance report are based on the standard variable costs per unit multiplied by 10,000 units. The performance report shows that the total variable cost variance for November was unfavourable by $2,335.

Table 2.14 Redd Co. performance report for the month ended 30 November 2001

	Budget	Actual	Variance
Direct material	$17,500	$16,900	$600 F
Direct labour	$20,000	$21,735	$1,735 U
Variable factory overhead	$10,000	$11,200	$1,200 U
Totals	$47,500	$49,835	$2,335 U

F = favourable
U = unfavourable

2.6.11 To illustrate how standard costs are used in analysing variances, suppose that Redd Co. is applying variable factory overhead on the basis of direct labour hours rather than the units produced. Table 2.15 indicates the calculations that must be performed in order to obtain variance values for each variable cost category. The actual material and labour costs and quantities used are obtained from the company's records.

Table 2.15 Redd Co. calculations to obtain variance values

Material price variance
(Actual quantity × Actual price) − (Actual quantity × Standard price)
(AQ × AP) − (AQ × SP)
(26,000 lb × $0.25) − (26,000 × $0.70) = $1,300 F
Material usage (or efficiency) variance
(Actual quantity × Standard price) − (Standard quantity allowed for flexible budget × Standard price)

51

Established cost management approaches

> (AQ × SP) − (SQA × SP)
> (26,000 × $0.70) − (25,000 lb × $0.70) = $700 U
>
> Labour rate variance
> (Actual hours × Actual rate) − (Actual hours × Standard rate)
> (AH × AR) − (AH × SR)
> (2,700 hr × $8.05) − (2,700 hr × $8.00) = $135 U
>
> Labour efficiency variance
> (Actual hours × Standard rate) − (Standard hours allowed for flexible budget × Standard rate)
> (AH × SR) × (SAH × SR)
> (2,700 hr × $8.00) − (2,500 hr × $8.00) = $1,600 U
>
> Overhead spending variance
> Actual cost incurred − (Actual hours × Standard rate)
> $11,200 − (2,700 hr × $4.00) = $400 U
>
> Overhead efficiency variance
> (Actual hours × Standard rate) − (Standard hours allowed for flexible budget × Standard rate)
> (AH × SR) − (SHA × SR)
> (2,700 hr × $4.00) − (2,500 hr × $4.00) = $800 U

2.6.12 Individual variances will provide information on the efficiency and effectiveness with which organisational resources are used.

2.7 Costing using standard costs

2.7.1 Standard costs provide a useful means for costing products. For a manufacturing company, labour and material costs can often be predetermined to coincide with actual costs incurred. Overhead costs, however, may pose costing problems in that not all overhead costs per unit will be known at any one stage of the financial period. For costing a contract, it is thus useful to determine a volume-based method of allocating overhead costs. The link between overhead cost incursion and a volume variable such as units produced, or labour cost or machine hours worked, can be statistically tested using a regression analysis package for example.

An example

2.7.2 Consider the Contract Co., which uses a budgeted overhead rate in applying overhead to production orders on a labour cost basis for

Costing using standard costs

Department A and on a machine-hour basis for Department B. At the beginning of 2001, the company made the following estimations:

	Department A	Department B
Direct labour	$128,000	
Machine-hours		20,000
Factory overhead	$144,000	$150,000
Overhead rates	112.5% of direct labour	$7.50 per machine-hour

2.7.3 During January, the cost record for job order no.500 which consisted of 20 units of product shows the following:

	Department A	Department B
Materials requisitioned	$20	$40
Direct labour cost	$32	$21
Machine-hours		13

2.7.4 The total departmental costs are then determined to obtain the unit product costs:

Department A		Department B	
Raw materials	$20.00	Raw materials	$40.00
Direct labour	$32.00	Direct labour	$21.00
Factory department overhead applied (32×112.5%)	$36.00	Factory department overhead applied (13×$7.50)	$97.50
Total	$88.00		$158.50
Total costs	$88 + $158.50 = $246.50		
	$246.50 × 20 − $13.25 per unit		

2.7.5 An adjustment will likely be made for deviations between budgeted overhead rates and the actual costs incurred. Thus, suppose that at the end of 2001 it is found that actual factory overhead cost amounts to $160,000 in Department A and $138,000 in Department B and that the actual direct labour cost is $148,000 in Department A and the actual machine-hours are 18,000 in Department B. Then the over-applied or under-applied overhead amount for each department and for the factory as a whole can be readily calculated:

Established cost management approaches

Department A:	Applied overhead (112.5% of £148,000)		£166,500
	Actual overhead		£160,000
	Over-applied overhead	£6,500	
Department B:	Applied overhead (18,000 × £7.50)		£135,000
	Actual overhead		£138,000
	Under-applied overhead	(£3,000)	
Total over-applied factory overhead		(£3,500)	

2.7.6 It is to be noted that the extent of the variances and therefore cost misallocations is dependent principally on the choice of overhead allocation base and the accuracy of the rate at which it is allocated. If the difference is significant in relation to the year end accounts, an adjustment to the overhead value of inventory at the year end can be calculated. (See Horngren *et al.*, 2002 for a more detailed exposition.)

Why are standard costing systems widely used?

2.7.7 The use of standard costing is appropriate for organisations with activities that consist of a series of repetitive operations. This would include many manufacturing organisations given that their processes are often of a repetitive nature. Standard costing cannot be readily applied to activities of a non-repetitive nature as there is little basis for observing recurring actions and processes with continuity. Thus standards cannot be set.

2.7.8 Standard costing systems are used in many organisations because they provide cost information for a variety of different purposes including the following (see Drury, 1999):

- enabling future costs to be predicted for decision-making purposes;
- providing difficult-to-achieve targets which are motivational;
- assisting budget setting and managerial performance evaluation;
- providing useful and convenient information for understanding the physical and monetary resource requirements of production budgets;
- acting as a control device by highlighting those activities which deviate from plans and enabling management by exception, i.e., highlighting out of control situations requiring corrective action. The use of a standard costing system means that variances can be analysed in great detail. Actions can be readily taken in terms of evolving change;

Costing using standard costs

- simplification of cost tracing to products for profit measurement and stock valuation. Standard costing systems are ordinarily set up to maintain records at standard cost, merely providing efficient information exchange and monitoring. Stock and cost of goods sold are recorded at standard cost and actual costs are derived by writing off variances arising during the period as period costs.

2.7.9 Drury notes that the usefulness of standard costing systems in a modern business enterprise may be questionable in that:

- cost structures are rapidly changing;
- actions that are inimical to a 'just-in-time' philosophy may be encouraged;
- continuous improvements may be discouraged;
- direct labour as a category may be over-emphasised;
- feedback reporting can be delayed.

2.7.10 Many critics of standard costing argue that the focus on price and efficiency, factors to the exclusion of a proper consideration of quality variables is detrimental. In addition, the use of the volume variance to measure utilisation of capacity while ignoring over-production can lead to unnecessary build-ups of stock levels.

2.7.11 The price variance is the traditional price variance computed on materials purchased. It has been criticised on the grounds that over-emphasis on price leads purchasing managers to ignore quality. However, Cheatham and Cheatham (1996) note that price is a legitimate concern that should not be overlooked. Moreover, if low quality materials are purchased in order to gain a low price, an unfavourable 'Quality Variance' can be calculated.

2.7.12 The 'Efficiency Variance' is based on the difference between the actual amount of material used and the standard amount for total production. The traditional Efficiency (or Quantity) Variance is the difference between the actual amount of material used and the standard amount for good production. The traditional variance is in fact a combination of quality and efficiency factors and it may be argued that quality is best treated as a separate variance.

2.7.13 The Quality Variance may be viewed as the standard cost of units produced that did not meet specifications (the difference between total

55

Established cost management approaches

units produced and good units produced). Traditionally, this variance is buried in the efficiency variances of the various inputs.

2.7.14 Suppose for instance that a company used 2lbs of material per finished unit at a standard cost of £1.00 per lb. Assume further that 4,900lbs were used in the production of 2,500 total units, of which 100 were defective. Traditional variance analysis would show an unfavourable Efficiency Variance of £100 computed from the difference between the standard cost of the 4,800lbs that should have been used to produce the 2,400 good units and the 4,900lbs actually used.

2.7.15 According to Cheatham and Cheatham (1996), a better breakdown of the traditional variance would show a favourable Efficiency Variance of £100 and an unfavourable Quality Variance of £200. The Production Department did use only 4,800lbs to produce 2,500 units, which should have required 5,000lbs. The fact that some of these units were defective should appear as a Quality Variance. The Quality Variance is £200 unfavourable representing £2.00 per unit invested in 100 defective units.

2.7.16 The analysis also yields a Production Variance reflecting the difference between the standard cost of good units produced and the scheduled amount of production. The goal in a flexible production environment might be to produce exactly what is needed for sales orders. A variance from scheduled production is unfavourable since excess production results in unnecessary build-up of stock, while too little results in sales orders not being fulfilled. One critical factor is the cost of the capital invested in excess stock. It is desirable to highlight this cost in responsibility reports by applying a cost of capital figure to the excess.

2.7.17 Although the above analysis pertains to materials, labour and volume-related variable overhead can be analysed in a similar manner. Given that there is no difference between labour purchased and labour used in production, the labour input variances would include the traditional Rate Variance as well as the updated Efficiency Variance.

2.7.18 In terms of a Volume Variance, aside from showing a budget variance for the various elements of fixed overhead, there is a need for further analysis. The updated Production Variance serves the same purpose.

Chapter 3
Financial analysis and working capital management

3.1 Introduction

3.1.1 The efficiency and effectiveness of planning and controlling operations can be quantitatively assessed through a series of ratios and calculations. The information that is usually contained in an enterprise's financial statements is historical but offers a starting point for such analysis, which can be used to guide future operations. Although financial statements as part of corporate annual reports are ordinarily in the public domain for listed companies, it is essential for finance managers to understand the perception of the enterprise from an external viewpoint. Moreover, the financial implications of operational activities also have an impact on financial statements.

3.1.2 Most organisations will be concerned about their ability to pay debts, manage their debtors, plan their cash flows, minimise inventory costs and earn income. Such concerns can be categorised into a number of key dimensions, which in turn are supported by different ratio computations. When analysing accounts, the following sequence of steps may be followed:

- glance at key results to gain an introductory overview;

- read the reports of the directors and the auditors;

- calculate ratios in terms of profitability and solvency;

- interpret and summarise the analysis.

3.1.3 Two principal dimensions identified in the third step (profitability and solvency) are considered below.

3.2 Profitability ratios

3.2.1 Profitability refers to the ability of an enterprise to earn income. Table 3.1 lists the key profitability ratios (as suggested by Fess and Warren, 1985).

Financial analysis and working capital management

Table 3.1 Key profitability ratios

Ratio	Calculation	Use
Ratio of net sales to assets	Net sales / Average total assets (excluding long-term investments)	To assess the effectiveness in the use of assets
Rate earned on total assets	(Net income + Interest expense) / Average total assets	To assess the profitability of the assets
Rate earned on shareholders' equity	Net income / Average shareholders' equity	To assess the profitability of the investment by shareholders
Rate earned on shareholders' equity	(Net income − Preferred dividends) / Average ordinary shareholders' equity	To assess the profitability of the investment by holders of ordinary shares
Earnings per share on ordinary shares	(Net income − Preferred dividends) / Shares of ordinary shareholders outstanding	
Dividends per share of ordinary shares	Dividends / Ordinary shares outstanding	To indicate the extent to which earnings are being distributed to holders of ordinary shares
Price/earnings ratio	Market price per share of ordinary shares / Earnings per share on ordinary shares	To indicate the relationship between market value of ordinary shares and earnings
Dividend yield	Dividends per ordinary share / Market price per ordinary share	To indicate the rate of return to ordinary shares in terms of dividends
Number of times interest charges earned	(Income before income tax + Interest expense) / Interest expense	To assess the risk to bondholders in terms of number of times interest charges were earned

Profitability ratios

3.2.2 Consider the data given in Tables 3.2 and 3.3 for the Ratio Co.

Table 3.2 Ratio Co. comparative balance sheet at 31 December 2001 and 2000

	2001	2000
Assets		
Current assets	550,000	533,000
Long-term investments	95,000	177,500
Plant assets (net)	444,500	470,000
Intangible assets	50,000	50,000
Total assets	£1,139,500	£1,230,550
Liabilities		
Current liabilities	210,000	243,000
Long-term liabilities	100,000	200,000
Total liabilities	£310,000	£443,000
Shareholders' equity		
Preferred 6% shares, £100 par	150,000	150,000
Ordinary shares, £10 par	500,000	500,000
Related earnings	179,000	137,500
Total shareholders' equity	829,500	787,500
Total liabilities and shareholders' equity	£1,139,500	£1,230,500

(Source: adapted from Fess and Warren, *Managerial Accounting*, 1st edition, 1985).

Table 3.3 Ratio Co. comparative income statement for the years ended 31 December 2001 and 2000

	2001	2000
Sales	1,530,000	1,234,000
Sales returns and allowances	32,500	34,000
Net sales	1,498,000	1,200,000
Cost of goods sold	1,043,000	820,000
Gross profit	455,000	380,000
Selling expenses	191,000	147,000
General expenses	104,000	97,400
Total operating expenses	295,000	244,400
Operating income	160,000	135,600
Other income	8,500	11,000
	168,500	146,600
Other expense	6,000	12,000
Income before income tax	162,500	134,600
Income tax	71,500	58,100
Net income	£91,000	£76,500

3.2.3 The asset turnover ratio is a profitability measure that shows how effectively a firm utilises its assets. In computing the ratio, any long-term

Financial analysis and working capital management

investments should be excluded from total assets because they are wholly unrelated to sales of goods or services. Assets used in determining the ratio may be the total at the end of the year, the average at the beginning and end of the year, or the average of the monthly totals. The basic data and the ratio of net sales to assets for Ratio Co. are given in Table 3.4.

Table 3.4 Ratio Co. calculation of the asset turnover ratio

	2001	2000
Net sales	£1,498,000	£1,200,000
Total assets (excluding long-term investments):		
Beginning of year	1,053,000	1,010,000
End of year	1,044,500	1,053,000
Total	£2,097,500	£2,063,000
Average	£1,048,750	£1,031,500
Ratio of net sales to assets	1.4:1	1.2:1

3.2.4 The ratio improved to a minor degree in 2001, largely due to the increase in sales volume. A comparison of the ratio with those of other enterprises in the same industry would be helpful in assessing Ratio Co.'s effectiveness in the utilisation of assets.

3.2.5 The rate earned on total assets is a measure of the profitability of the assets, without regard to the equity of creditors and shareholders in the assets. The rate is therefore not affected by differences in methods of financing an enterprise.

3.2.6 The rate earned on total assets is derived by adding interest expense to net income and dividing this sum by total assets. By adding interest expense to net income, the profitability of the assets is determined without considering the means of financing the acquisition of the assets. The calculation of the rate earned by Ratio Co. on total assets is shown in Table 3.5.

Table 3.5 Ratio Co. calculation of the rate earned on total assets

	2001	2000
Net income	91,000	76,500
Plus interest expense	6,000	12,000
Total	£97,000	£88,500
Total assets:		
Beginning of year	1,230,500	1,187,500
End of year	1,139,500	1,230,500
Total	£2,370,000	£2,418,000
Average	£1,185,000	£1,209,000
Rate earned on total assets	8.2%	7.3%

Profitability ratios

3.2.7 The rate earned on total assets for 2001 indicates an improvement over that for 2000. A comparison with other companies and with industry averages would also be useful in evaluating the effectiveness of Ratio Co.'s management performance.

3.2.8 Another relative measure of profitability is obtained by dividing net income by total shareholders' equity. In contrast to the rate earned on total assets, the rate earned on shareholders' equity emphasises income in relation to the amount invested by the shareholders. The amount of the total shareholders' equity throughout the year varies for several reasons – the issue of additional shares, the payment of dividends and the gradual accrual of net income. If monthly figures are not available, the average of the shareholders' equity at the beginning and the end of the year is used. The calculation is shown in Table 3.6.

Table 3.6 Ratio Co. calculation of the rate earned on shareholders' equity

	2001	2000
Net income	$91,000	$76,500
Shareholders' equity:		
Beginning of year	787,000	750,000
End of year	829,500	787,500
Total	$1,617,000	$1,537,500
Average	$808,500	$768,750
Rate earned on shareholders' equity	11.3%	10.0%

3.2.9 The rate earned by a thriving enterprise on the equity of its shareholders is usually higher than the rate earned on total assets. The reason for the difference is that the amount earned on assets acquired through the use of funds provided by creditors is more than the interest charges paid to creditors. This tendency of the rate on shareholders' equity to vary disproportionately from the rate on total assets is sometimes termed 'leverage'. Ratio Co.'s rate on shareholders' equity for 2001 of 11.3 per cent compares favourably with the rate of 8.2 per cent earned on total assets. The leverage factor of 3.1 per cent (11.3 – 8.2) for 2001 also compares favourably with the 2.7 per cent (10.0 – 7.3) differential for the preceding year.

3.2.10 When a corporation has both preferred and ordinary shares outstanding, the rate earned on ordinary shareholders' equity is the net income less preferred dividend requirements for the period, stated as a percentage of the average equity of the ordinary shareholders.

3.2.11 Ratio Co. has $150,000 of preferred 6 per cent non-participating shares outstanding at both balance sheet dates, hence annual preferred

Financial analysis and working capital management

dividends amount to £9,000. The ordinary shareholders' equity is the total shareholders' equity reduced by the nominal value of the preferred shares (£150,000). The basic data and the rate earned on ordinary shareholders' equity are set out in Table 3.7.

Table 3.7 Ratio Co. calculation of the rate earned on ordinary shareholders' equity

	2001	2000
Net income	91,000	76,500
Preferred dividends	9,000	9,000
Remainder – identified with ordinary shares	£82,000	£67,500
Ordinary shareholders' equity:		
Beginning of year	637,500	600,000
End of year	679,500	637,500
Total	£1,317,000	£1,237,500
Average	£658,500	£618,750
Ratio earned on ordinary shareholders' equity	12.5%	10.9%

3.2.12 The rate earned on ordinary shareholders' equity differs from the rates earned by Ratio Co. on total assets and total shareholders' equity. Such a situation occurs where there are borrowed funds and also preferred shares outstanding, which rank ahead of the ordinary shares in their claim on earnings. The concept of leverage can be applied to the use of funds from the sale of preferred shares as well as from borrowing. Funds from both sources can be used in an attempt to increase the return on ordinary shareholders' equity.

3.2.13 One profitability measure included in the income statement in corporate annual reports is earnings per share on ordinary shares. If a company has issued only one class of share, the earnings per share are determined by dividing net income by the number of shares outstanding. If there are both preferred and ordinary shares outstanding, the net income must be reduced first by the amount necessary to meet the preferred dividend requirements.

3.2.14 Any changes in the number of shares outstanding during the year, such as would result from stock dividends or stock splits, should be disclosed in quoting earnings per share on ordinary shares. Also, if there are any non-recurring (extraordinary, etc.) items in the income statement, the income per share before such items should be reported along with net income per share. In addition, if there are convertible bonds or preferred shares outstanding, the amount reported as net income per share should be stated without considering the conversion privilege, followed by net income per share, assuming that conversion had occurred. The data on the earnings per share of common stock for Ratio Co. are as set out in Table 3.8.

Solvency ratios

Table 3.8 Ratio Co. calculation of earnings per share on ordinary shares

	2001	2000
Net income	91,000	76,500
Preferred dividends	9,000	9,000
Remainder – identified with ordinary shares	₤82,000	₤67,500
Shares of ordinary shares outstanding	50,000	50,000
Earnings per share on ordinary shares	₤1.64	₤1.35

3.2.15 Earnings per share can be presented in conjunction with dividends per share data to indicate the relationship between earnings and dividends and the extent to which the corporation is retaining its earnings for use in the business. The price/earnings (P/E) ratio on ordinary shares is computed by dividing the market price per share of ordinary shares at a specific date by the annual earnings per share. Table 3.9 sets out the P/E ratio calculation for Ratio Co., assuming market prices per ordinary share of 20 1/2 at the end of 2001 and 13 1/2 at the end of 2000.

Table 3.9 Ratio Co. calculation of price/earnings ratio on ordinary shares

	2001	2000
Market price per share of ordinary shares	₤20.50	₤13.50
Earnings per share of ordinary shares	₤1.64	₤1.35
Price/earnings ratio on ordinary shares	12.5	10.0

3.2.16 The dividend yield on ordinary shares is a profitability measure that shows the rate of return to ordinary shareholders in terms of cash dividend distributions. The dividend yield is computed by dividing the annual dividends paid per ordinary share by the market price per share at a specific date. Table 3.10 sets out Ratio Co.'s dividend yield calculation assuming dividends of ₤0.80 and ₤0.60 per ordinary share and market prices per ordinary share of ₤20.50 and ₤13.50 at the end of 2001 and 2000 respectively.

Table 3.10 Ratio Co. calculation of dividend yield on ordinary shares

	2001	2000
Dividends per share of ordinary shares	₤0.80	₤0.60
Market price per share of ordinary shares	₤20.50	₤13.50
Dividends yield on ordinary shares	3.9%	4.4%

3.3 Solvency ratios

3.3.1 Solvency refers to the ability of a business to meet its financial obligations as they fall due. The focus is usually on the possibility of liquidating liabilities. Table 3.11 lists examples.

Financial analysis and working capital management

Table 3.11 Examples of solvency ratios

Ratio	Calculation	Use
Working capital	Current assets − Current liabilities	To indicate the ability to meet currently maturing obligations
Current ratio	Current assets / Current liabilities	
Acid-test ratio	Quick assets / Current liabilities	To indicate instant debt-paying ability
Debtors' turnover	Net sales on account / Average debtors	To assess the efficiency in collecting receivables and in the management of credit
Number of days' sales in debtors	Debtors, end of year / Average daily sales on account	
Inventory turnover	Cost of goods sold / Average inventory	To assess the efficiency in the management of inventory
Number of days' sales in inventory	Inventory, end of year / Average daily cost of goods sold	
Ratio of plant assets to long-term liabilities	Plant assets (net) / Long-term liabilities	To indicate the margin of safety to long-term creditors
Ratio of shareholders' equity to liabilities	Total stockholders' equity / Total liabilities	To indicate the margin of safety to creditors

(Source: adapted from Fess and Warren, 1985.)

3.3.2 The current assets of an enterprise net of its current liabilities at a certain moment in time is working capital. The absolute amount of working capital and the flow of working capital during a period of time can be used to evaluate a company's ability to meet maturing obligations. Although useful for making intra-period comparisons within a company, these absolute amounts are difficult to use in comparing companies of different sizes or in comparing such amounts with industry figures.

3.3.3 The relationship between current assets and current liabilities can also be expressed through the current ratio, or the working capital ratio. The

Solvency ratios

ratio is computed by dividing the total of current assets by the total of current liabilities. The working capital and the current ratio for Ratio Co. are shown in Table 3.12.

Table 3.12 Ratio Co. calculation of working capital and current ratio

	2001	2000
Current assets	550,000	533,000
Current liabilities	210,000	243,000
Working capital	$340,000	$290,000
Current ratio	2.6:1	2.2:1

3.3.4 The current ratio is a more dependable indication of solvency than is working capital. A ratio that measures the 'instant' debt-paying ability of a company is the 'acid-test ratio' or 'quick ratio'. It is the ratio of the sum of cash, receivables and marketable securities, which are sometimes termed 'quick assets', to current liabilities. The acid-test ratio data for Ratio Co. are set out in Table 3.13.

Table 3.13 Ratio Co. calculation of acid-test ratio

	2001	2000
Quick assets:		
Cash	90,500	64,700
Marketable securities	75,000	60,000
Receivables (net)	115,000	120,000
Total	$280,500	$244,700
Current liabilities	$210,000	$243,000
Acid-test ratio	1.3:1	1.0:1

3.3.5 A thorough analysis of a firm's current position would include the determination of the amount of working capital, the current ratio and the acid-test ratio.

3.3.6 The relationship between credit sales and debtors may be stated as the debtors' turnover. It is computed by dividing net sales on account by the average debtors (see Table 3.14 – note that all sales were made on credit). The increase in the debtors' turnover for 2001 indicates that there has been an acceleration in the collection of receivables, due perhaps to improvement in either the granting of credit or the collection practices used, or both.

Financial analysis and working capital management

Table 3.14 Ratio Co. calculation of debtors' turnover

	2001	2000
Net sales on account	$1,498,000	$1,200,000
Debtors (net):		
Beginning of year	120,000	140,000
End of year	115,000	120,000
Total	$235,000	$260,000
Average	$117,500	$130,000
Debtors' turnover	12.7	9.2

3.3.7 Another means of expressing the relationship between credit sales and debtors is the number of days' sales to collection. This measure is determined by dividing the net debtors at the end of the year by the average daily sales on account (Table 3.15).

Table 3.15 Ratio Co. calculation of number of days' sales to collection

	2001	2000
Debtors (net), end of year	$115,000	$120,000
Net sales on account	$1,498,000	$1,200,000
Average daily sales on account	$4,104	$3,288
Number of days' sales in receivables	28.0	36.5

3.3.8 The number of days' sales in debtors gives a rough measure of the length of time the debtors have been outstanding. A comparison of this measure with the credit terms, with figures for comparable firms in the same industry, and with figures of Ratio Co. for prior years will help reveal the efficiency in collecting debts and the trends in the management of credit.

3.3.9 The relationship between the volume of goods sold and inventory may be stated as the inventory turnover. It is computed by dividing the cost of goods sold by the average inventory (Table 3.16).

Table 3.16 Ratio Co. calculation of inventory turnover

	2001	2000
Cost of goods sold	$1,043,000	$820,000
Inventory:		
Beginning of year	283,000	311,000
End of year	264,000	283,000
Total	$547,000	$594,000
Average	$273,000	$297,000
Inventory turnover	3.8	2.8

Solvency ratios

3.3.10 The improvement in Ratio Co.'s turnover resulted from an increase in the cost of goods sold, combined with a decrease in average stock. The variation in types of stock is too great to permit any broad generalisations as to what is a satisfactory turnover. However, for each business or department within a business, there is a reasonable turnover rate. A turnover below this rate means that the company or the department is incurring extra expenses such as those for administration and storage, is increasing its risk of loss due to obsolescence and adverse price changes, is incurring interest charges in excess of those considered necessary, and is failing to free funds for other uses.

3.3.11 Another way of expressing the relationship between the cost of goods sold and stock is the number of days' sales in stock. This measure is determined by dividing the stock at the end of the year by the average daily cost of goods sold (Table 3.17).

Table 3.17 Ratio Co. calculation of number of days' sales in inventory

	2001	2000
Inventory, end of year	£264,000	£283,000
Cost of goods sold	£1,043,000	£820,000
Average daily cost of goods sold	£2,858	£2,247
Number of days' sales in inventory	92.4	125.9

3.3.12 The number of days' sales in inventory gives a rough measure of the length of time it takes to acquire, sell, and then replace the average stock. Although there was a substantial improvement in 2001 for Ratio Co., comparison of the measure with those of earlier years and of comparable firms is an essential element in judging the effectiveness of the company's stock control.

3.3.13 Long-term notes and bonds are often secured by mortgages on plant assets. The ratio of total plant assets to long-term liabilities provides a solvency measure that shows the margin of safety of the noteholders or bondholders. It also gives an indication of the potential ability of the enterprise to borrow additional funds on a long-term basis (see Table 3.18).

Table 3.18 Ratio Co. calculation of the ratio of plant assets to long-term liabilities

	2001	2000
Plant assets (net)	£444,500	£470,000
Long-term liabilities	£100,000	£200,000
Ratio of plant assets to long-term liabilities	4.4:1	2.4:1

Financial analysis and working capital management

3.3.14 The increase in the ratio at the end of 2001 was due mainly to the liquidation of half of Ratio Co.'s long-term liabilities. The balance sheet of Ratio Co. (Table 3.2) indicates that on 31 December 2001, shareholders' equity represented 72.8 per cent and liabilities represented 27.2 per cent of the sum of the liabilities and shareholders' equity. Instead of expressing each item as a percentage of the total, the relationship may be expressed as a ratio of one to the other (Table 3.19).

Table 3.19 Ratio Co. calculation of ratio of shareholders' equity to liabilities

	2001	2000
Total shareholders' equity	£829,500	£787,500
Total liabilities	£310,000	£443,000
Ratio of shareholders' equity to liabilities	2.7:1	1.8:1

3.3.15 The balance sheet of Ratio Co. shows that the major factor affecting the change in the ratio was the £100,000 reduction in long-term liabilities during 2001.

Typical ratios

3.3.16 When undertaking ratio analysis, the following points should be borne in mind:

- when analysing a set of published accounts, the calculation of the ratios themselves may not always provide answers; however, they will probably identify the line of questioning that one might like to pursue;
- when comparing the trend of ratios for the same company over more than one time period, beware of any inconsistencies in the data – for example, significant asset revaluations;
- when trying to compare the ratios of a company with another or against industry averages, one needs to guard against the following points, any of which could undermine the validity of the comparison:
    - are the accounting policies consistent?
    - is the comparison valid in terms of having two companies with a similar mix of activities?
    - is the industry seasonal, in which case different year end dates may produce totally different results?

3.3.17 In performing ratio analysis on a set of financial statements, it is often difficult to predict the typical ratios that one would expect to see.

Ratios can differ quite extensively across different industry sectors, in addition to varying within that sector. Table 3.20 should therefore be viewed as a general guide to typical ratios, but be prepared for significant deviations.

Table 3.20 Typical ratios by industry sector

Ratio	Manufacturing	Retail	Services	Mining
Return on capital employed (%)	8–12	3.5–7	9–13	3–9
Profit margin (%)	2–3	0.04–0.9	1.8–2.4	3–7
Current ratio	1.1	1.1	1.0	1.0–1.1
Asset turnover (%)	167–169	248–250	174–184	81–94

3.3.18 It is to be noted that the analysis of ratios must also be undertaken with an understanding of the enterprise's operational approach and management style. The application of a just-in-time philosophy, for instance, is likely to produce ratios which may seem out of line with the company's history, or even with industry averages given its impact on stock levels. Likewise, large capital outlays in flexible technologies will alter the asset base mix with attendant effects on ratios and therefore comparability. It is to be noted also that the application of activity-based management (see Chapter **6**) can alter activities and the incursion of cost at different points in the value chain. Some of these effects will alter ratio values and others will have no impact except to change profit potential. There may thus be cost management changes in an enterprise which may only indirectly influence traditional financial analysis. Likewise, companies making extensive e-business process investments operate under different constraints, which may fundamentally alter their financial reports. This is discussed further below.

3.4 Working capital management

3.4.1 Working capital is found by enterprises to be difficult to manage for the following reasons:

- working capital is usually less prominent on the management agenda than profits, sales, products, customers: it seldom receives much attention in board reports;
- managers from a range of functions are involved in managing working capital, and often they have different goals;
- working capital is multi-dimensional, and rigorous attention to detail supported by focused management information is a prerequisite to success.

Financial analysis and working capital management

3.4.2 Working capital management is essential, however, as the costs of not undertaking this include not only interest on funds being tied up but also:

- the opportunity lost by not investing in other profitable projects;
- unnecessary warehousing and manufacturing storage space;
- risk of stock obsolescence, damage and deterioration;
- risk of stock-outs of key products;
- write-offs from bad debts;
- risk of foreign exchange losses;
- risk of penalties for late payment of taxes;
- additional administration through wasteful processes;
- management time sorting out problems;
- adverse impacts on customer relations;
- inability to cost products accurately.

3.4.3 In summary, excess working capital is being used to finance waste and its effective management requires the elimination of non-value-adding balance sheet items.

Working capital management checklist

3.4.4 Businesses need to consider the whole chain from suppliers, through all stages of manufacturing and distribution, to the final sale to the customer and collection of payment. The following extras need to be considered in implementing a proper working capital management policy.

1. *Processes, policy, standards and targets*
    - understand in detail the processes which affect working capital;
    - have a clear statement of policy on how the business will deal with suppliers and customers, and manage foreign exchange exposure;
    - clarify the standards that are expected in terms of customer service, share availability, speed of response and errors;
    - review policies for cash/quantity discounts and use of penalty interest;
    - set targets for eliminating delays and errors in all the steps in the process.

Working capital management

2. *Supply chain issues*

    – raw materials:

    - review costs and effectiveness of acquisition;
    - reduce lead times, reduce stock holding required to support production by synchronising (via JIT etc.);
    - build supply chain partnerships with suppliers, consolidated supplier base, insisting on quality delivered thus reducing inspection costs and need for buffer stocks;

    – work in progress and finished stock:

    - selective policy for each product line to minimise stockholding;
    - eliminate bottlenecks in production and reduce need for work in progress stocks;
    - improve partnership with customers to ensure better order demand information, analyse demand variability and tailor stockholding to suit;
    - review distribution strategy and reduce stocks tied up in delivery chain.

3. *Credit and collection*

    – establish the right terms of trade at the outset and clarify responsibility between sales and finance for communicating terms to customers, credit checking, collection and initiating legal action when all else fails;

    – establish procedures for examining references, visiting customers and clarifying their purchasing and purchase authorisation processes, who signs the cheques, and their monthly cut-off dates. Build relationships with key customer staff.

4. *Financing and treasury issues*

    – develop short-term cash flow forecasts to support investment planning of surplus funds and to minimise use of borrowing facilities;

    – reappraise the adequacy and utilisation of borrowing facilities and their terms and costs;

    – review the preferred currencies for purchasing and selling goods/services;

    – review the dividend policy.

5. *Foreign currency issues*

    – where suppliers or customers are overseas and transactions are in foreign currency, special care needs to be taken to manage exchange rate exposure;

Financial analysis and working capital management

- ensure that open currency positions are recognised and monitored, where possible matching counter-positions;
- establish a policy that defines which risks will be accepted and which need to be covered by options etc., and then ensure that the policy is followed.

6. *Taxation issues*
   - maximise benefit from early utilisation of tax losses, ACT and overseas tax credits;
   - review timing of events which trigger tax payments, such as dividends and interest payments;
   - check that all appropriate tax elections have been made;
   - review VAT and customs duty procedures for opportunities to improve cash flow and take full advantage of postponed payments on imported goods.

7. *Information and costing*
   - set up information systems for monitoring customer queries, working capital levels and delays, not only in aggregate but by product line and customer type;
   - build working capital requirements into product costing and pricing decisions.

8. *Organisation, training and incentives*
   - clarify management responsibilities;
   - train individuals in the importance of working capital management and the procedures for managing it effectively;
   - install incentive schemes for individuals that reflect the importance of working capital to the business.

An example

3.4.5 Company A supplies machines to both developed and undeveloped countries, in addition to providing consumable supplies used on the machines and engineering services to support the machines. Each of these streams poses different working capital issues and the results of an appraisal of the opportunities to reduce working capital are set out below. As can be seen from Table 3.21, Company A recognised the opportunity to reduce working capital by 43

Working capital management

per cent, releasing £2.9 million of funds which would be available for investment elsewhere or could be used to reduce borrowings and hence interest costs. Company A's current working capital performance is shown in Table 3.21.

Table 3.21 Company A's current working capital performance

Total working capital		
Present	£7.1m	14.5% sales
Peak	£8.8m	18% sales
Year end floor	£5.4m	11.1% sales
		(created by withholding creditor payments)
		Make-up of present working capital
Stock (including JIT)		£7.0m
Trade debtors		£4.9m
Trade creditors		£(5.1)m
		£6.8m
Other debtors		£1.8m
Other creditors		£(1.5)m
		£7.1m

3.4.6 The company's current performance (creditors) is as follows:

- creditors paid to terms (or before) other than at year end when payment was deferred for a few days to reflect positively in the balance sheet (see Figure 3.1);

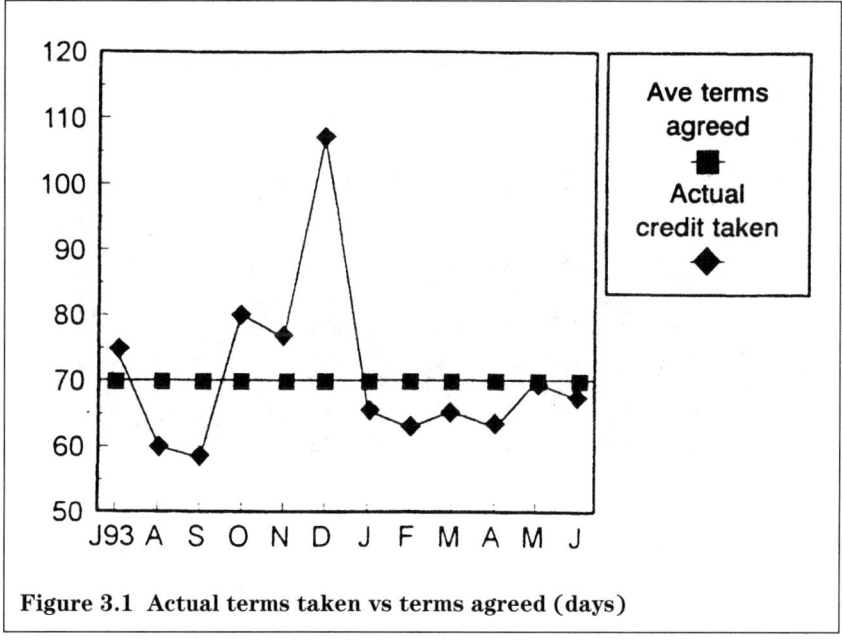

Figure 3.1 Actual terms taken vs terms agreed (days)

Financial analysis and working capital management

- main supplier is on 90 days open account and probably cannot improve this much further;
- some overseas trade is operated on letter of credit which in effect means 30 days' credit;
- some progress could be made with other suppliers to move them from 60 to 80 days.

3.4.7 The company's performance (debtors) is as follows:

- contract terms are settlement 10 days following invoice, but generally these are operated to 30 days. Payments are prompt and monitoring systems effective (see Figure 3.2);
- overall debt position worsened by a developing country's trade debt to over 120 days. This will not deteriorate further as terms have changed and Company A now wants cash up front before trading in that country. The up-front cash compensates for the old debt on the ledger;
- unlikely to be able to reduce terms and, if undertaken unilaterally, such change would have a negative impact on the sales of business.

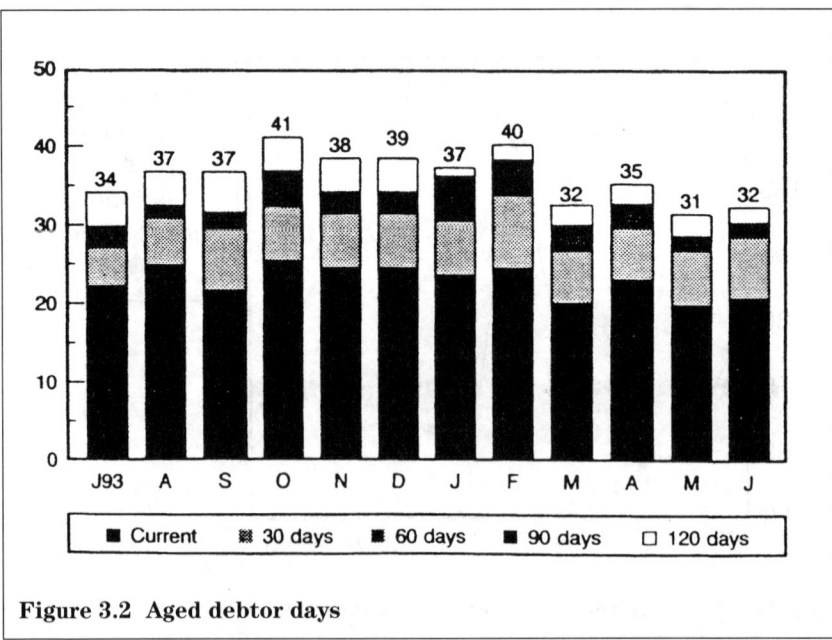

Figure 3.2 Aged debtor days

Working capital management

3.4.8 The company's current performance (stock) is as follows:

- inventory can be categorised into four main groups:
  - machine sales: £3.4 million;
  - developing country trade: £1.5 million;
  - service: £1.5 million;
  - supplies: £1.1 million;
- of the £1.5 million of developing country trade, 25 per cent relates to one line which was bought in 1992 based on an over-optimistic forecast, and little can be done about this in the short term;
- the bulk of inventory is held for the machine sales market for 80-90 days. Safety stock is based on three-month lead time rather than demand peaks. Recently targets of 60 to 75 days have been introduced. Inventory orders are lumpy and are supposedly based on monthly revisions of forecasts (see Figure 3.3).

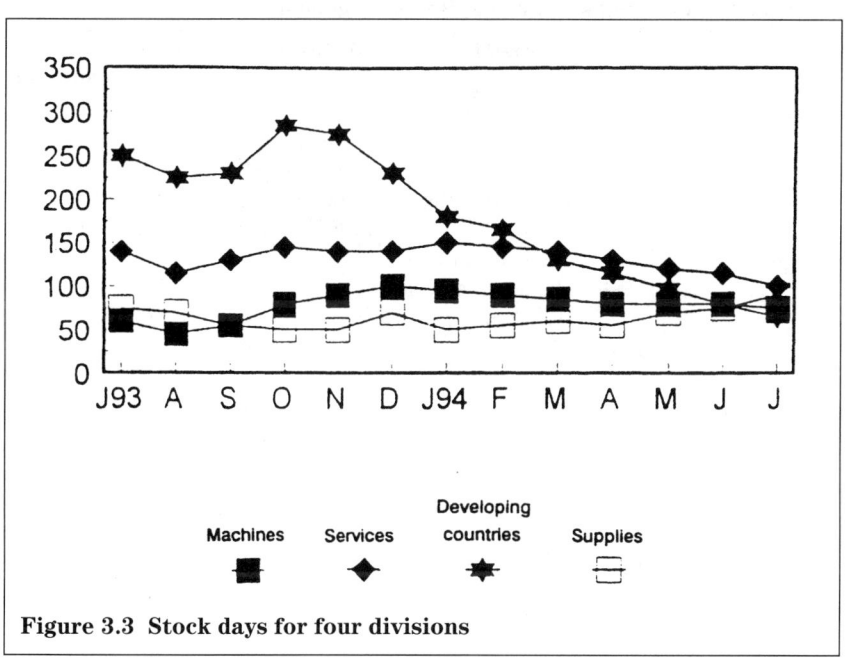

Figure 3.3 Stock days for four divisions

3.4.9 At present, some current initiatives are under way:

- working capital is high on the agenda, targets are established and linked to pay structures;
- however, when the bottom line comes under pressure, working capital takes a back seat in favour of sales and margins;

75

Financial analysis and working capital management

- attempts are being made to reduce service stocks by dropping levels below those suggested by the manufacturers.

3.4.10 The following points should be noted:

- within the business, machines and services, developing country trade and service face different working capital issues;
- as new machines are introduced, older models must be managed out which need to be improved in developing country trade;
- the need to improve sales forecasting and inventory management by employing statistical methods.

3.4.11 If working capital management issues are directly addressed, much improvement can be achieved (see Table 3.22).

Table 3.22 Improving working capital management

	Current	Actions	Future (benchmark)
Creditor days	Less than 60 to 90 days	Improve developing country trade	60 to 90 days
Lead times	2 to 4 months	Negotiate main supplier down	2 months
Range	50 machines 2,000 accessories 3,000 spares	–	No change
Stock over one year	6%	Clear out old stock	3%
Average stock	120 days	Manage supply chain, lower safety and working stocks	90 days
Average debtors	36 days	–	36 days
Average working capital	£6.7m		£3.8m
As % of turnover	14%		8%

3.4.12 Gardiner (1997) identifies problems with comparative ratio analysis. He notes that, in general, a variety of factors evaluated by a financial analyst need to be considered in order to gain a comprehensive picture of a company.

3.4.13 Profitability ratios include profit and loss items such as gross margin and performance measures such as return on assets, on capital employed, and on equity. Since most accounting choices affect profit directly

Working capital management

(e.g., capitalisation of costs) or indirectly (subsequent amortisation), this category is particularly difficult to compare amongst companies in the same country, let alone across borders.

3.4.14 Solvency ratios include the current and acid-test ratios. As noted above, they provide information on how well an enterprise manages its working capital and operating cycle. In the case of the current ratio, Gardiner notes that the benchmark is often said to be around 1.5 but statistics show that for the UK the average is often well below this level. Naturally, the type of industry being considered will alter the magnitude of benchmarks.

3.4.15 Stock turnover, debtor days, asset turnover and similar ratios are also important in evaluating efficiency. Idle or slow-moving assets are to be avoided unless they are justified from a strategic stance. Whilst the ratio values themselves are relevant to consider, so are the trends from year to year. It is important to note that international norms vary – the average invoice payment period in the UK is around 49 days (see Table 3.23 for comparative European data).

Table 3.23 European average payment periods (days)

		Position
Austria	38	4
Belgium	53	9
Denmark	35	2
Finland	29	1
France	65	13
Germany	38	4
Greece	85	17
Republic of Ireland	59	12
Italy	83	16
Luxembourg	56	10
Malta	71	14
Netherlands	45	6
Portugal	58	11
Spain	73	15
Sweden	36	3
Switzerland	49	7
UK	49	7

3.4.16 In the UK gearing levels tend on average to be lower than other countries such as Germany and Japan, where the banks have traditionally provided the bulk of company finance. Relevant accounting and reporting concerns include questions of debt/equity classification, asset valuation, valuation of pension fund liabilities, and the treatment of finance leases and deferred taxes. Investors are often keen to know such statistics as EPS, P/E, dividend

Financial analysis and working capital management

yield, cash flow per share and the total market capitalisation (Gardiner, 1997). Again, international variations exist which are in part explained through accounting standard reporting differences.

3.4.17 Investments in e-business processes can have important repercussions on working capital management opportunities and practices. Business operations in a digitised environment mean that production activities need not take place until an order is placed – and often paid for. This alters the flow of cash *vis-à-vis* traditional bricks and mortar operations. Consider for instance amazon.com's 'float'. A customer purchasing a book through Amazon's site typically pays by credit card, a payment which is collected from the operator within a few days. Yet Amazon's payment to the book publisher may be made after many weeks, giving it the use of the customer's money in the interim. Thus, in 1999 the company's debtors were negligible but its creditors amounted to US$463 million. As Loomis (2000) notes, 'Amazon has a business model that continually generates a golden stream of cash' as new sales are generated.

3.5 Economic value added – EVA®

3.5.1 Hubbell (1996) notes that of the many tools available for measuring shareholder value, one of the most widely accepted is economic value added (EVA®). A company's EVA® is simply its operating profits after tax, less a charge for the capital used in creating the profits. EVA® is related to the profit and loss statement as follows:

Sales

− Operating costs and expenses

= Operating profit before tax

− *Taxes*

= Operating profit after tax

− Capital charge

= Economic value added

3.5.2 The capital charge tends to be a concept of traditional concern to financial economists rather than to accountants. It is calculated by multiplying the cost of capital by the net assets employed (defined as net working capital plus net fixed capital). It is to be noted that the cost of capital includes the cost of both debt and equity.

3.5.3 The cost of equity is best described as the rate of return required by investors to compensate for the risk element that is part of the investment.

Economic value added – EVA®

The cost of equity may be considered an opportunity cost rather than a true cash cost.

3.5.4 The capital asset pricing model developed by finance theorists indicates that an estimate of the cost of equity for a particular company can be derived by adding to the long-term government bond rate (considered to be the risk-free rate):

- a premium for the risk associated with investing in the stock market. This is the 'market risk premium'. Additionally,
- an adjustment associated with the risk of the particular stock, known as the 'beta' of the stock is also made.

3.5.5 Wallace (1998) notes that EVA® is not a new concept. EVA® is essentially residual income modified for today's environment. It addresses what might be considered to be shortcomings of the traditional GAAP measure of earnings in addition to the lack of a charge for equity capital. Stewart (1991) claims that the best practical periodic performance measure is economic value added (EVA®). EVA® has also been described as a measure capable of giving its users, both managers and investors, marked competitive advantages (Tully, 1993).

3.5.6 In the example developed by Hubbell (1996) shown in Table 3.24, the 12.6 per cent cost of equity is calculated as being three times the 4.2 per cent cost of debt. A company with this capital cost structure will find it problematic to create positive economic value by earning a return on capital of 4.2 per cent (i.e., the after-tax cost of debt) or even 7 per cent (the pre-tax cost of debt). Instead, to create positive economic (shareholder) value, the company needs to earn a rate of return on capital exceeding 10.1 per cent, which is the full cost of capital including both debt and equity.

Table 3.24 Weighted-average cost of capital (example of calculation)

Description	Value	Definition
Cost of equity:		
Risk-free rate (Rf)	6%	Current long-term government bond rate
Beta (β)	1.1	Individual stock volatility versus market
Market risk premium (Mp)	6%	50-year average
Cost of equity	12.6%	$= Rf + (\beta \times Mp)$
Cost of debt:	7%	Company's current borrowing rate
After tax cost	4.2%	Assumes 40% marginal tax rate

Financial analysis and working capital management

Capital structure:		
Equity %	70%	Equity % of capital structure
Debt %	30%	Debt % of capital structure
Weighted-average cost of capital	10.1%	(equity %) × (cost of equity) + (debt %) × (after-tax cost of debt)

(Source: adapted from Hubbell, 1996.)

3.5.7 Hubbell (1996) notes that changes in stock prices are most closely related to changes in EVA®. The association of market values with any particular performance measure is measured by the coefficient of determination, or r^2. The results are considered to be statistically significant: 44 per cent of changes in market value are associated with changes in EVA®. Nevertheless, 56 per cent of changes in market value are associated with factors that are not EVA®-related. This is regarded as a stronger predictor of stock prices than a measure such as return on equity (with an r^2 association of only 24 per cent) or growth in earnings per share (with an r^2 association of 15 per cent).

3.5.8 Hubbell (1996a) notes that the strong correlation means that increases in stock prices are closely (but not perfectly) associated with increases in EVA®. This indicates that where a company is with regard to EVA® is not as important as where it is heading. Even though EVA® may be non-positive, the stock market will reward efforts which make EVA® less negative. Efforts to improve EVA® are thus compatible with other continuous improvement efforts which may be adopted by organisations, including total quality management and business process re-engineering efforts in addition to efforts to expand channels via digitisation.

3.5.9 As residual income-based performance measures such as EVA® include a charge on all capital, they are consistent with decision-making rules based on net present value (NPV) criteria (see Chapter **4**). As noted above, residual income represents the annual instalment on a project's lifetime NPV. By deducting the cost of capital, EVA® automatically sets aside a return sufficient to recover the value of capital that has been employed.

3.5.10 Stern, Stewart and Chew (1995) advocate the residual income measure EVA®, as the cornerstone of a total financial management system stressing the need to use a single measure for capital budgeting, goal setting, communicating with investors, and compensating managers. Often, rather than utilising just the one metric, different measures are used within firms for these separate tasks. Examples include discounted cash flow for capital budgeting, market share growth for goal setting, EPS for external reporting, and a variety of measures for performance evaluation of managers.

3.5.11 Wallace (1998) reports that EVA® is claimed to lead managers to act more like owners and therefore to exhibit behaviour consistent with increasing shareholder wealth. As such empirical results from a survey sent to firms that have begun using an EVA®-type performance measure show that senior managers appear to be concerned with not only bottom-line earnings, but also with earning in relation to the capital employed. This is especially true of firms that have more fully embraced the EVA® measure by tying management compensation to performance metrics.

3.6 EVA® versus residual income

3.6.1 In an equity research report published by Morgan Stanley Dean Witter, Massot (2000) reports that, unlike EVA® which considers theoretical taxed earnings before interest and tax, residual income focuses on what will go into the pocket of the shareholder after other stakeholders (debtholders) are paid. As a management tool, EVA® looks at the overall capital efficiency (all assets) whereas residual income focuses the return on what shareholders have invested in the firm. Even if these two approaches rely on the same principles and lead to similar results, Massot (2000) advocates the use of residual income, since it is more accurately focused on equity holders.

3.6.2 Residual income captures value creation for the shareholder. This is seen as the yardstick by which companies ask to be measured. As the model takes on board all exceptional charges and profits, it removes most of the distortions caused by booking 'below the line' exceptional costs. The measure is thus particularly useful in industries in which 'one-off' restructuring charges tend to recur.

3.6.3 Massot (2000) defines residual income (RI) as a multi-period type of analysis that attempts to measure the value created by a company for its shareholders over time. He represents this as:

$$RI = (ROE - COE) \times Equity$$

3.6.4 Simply put, the residual income (RI) in a given year is what is left to shareholders after a cost of equity (COE) charge for capital has been deducted from net profits as return on equity (ROE).

Financial analysis and working capital management

3.6.5 The fair value of a stock (V_0) is then defined as the sum of its latest historical book value (Eq_0) and the present value of all future residual incomes:

$$V_0 = Eq_0 + \Sigma RI_i / (1 + COE)^i$$

3.6.6 To eliminate the infinite series in the valuation formula, a 20-year model, for instance, and a terminal value estimate, which equals the present value of the final RI forecast as perpetuity, would be assumed.

3.6.7 The residual income thus captures a fair value for a stock as a function of a number of parameters, such as earnings growth and interest rates, which have a direct impact on the level of value creation by the company. This contrasts to fair values based on relative price-earning ratios (P/Es), which do not produce adequate results when certain sectors are experiencing structural changes that affect valuations in fundamental terms.

3.7 Accounting ratios and e-businesses

3.7.1 Many Internet companies achieved accelerated stock valuation growth at the turn of the millennium. For instance, in early 2000 amazon.com's market capitalisation exceeded US$22 billion with a share price two and half times higher than it had been 12 months earlier. Yet in 1999, the company reported a loss of US$0.6 billion on revenues of US$1.6 billion. Its bricks and mortar rival Barnes and Noble made US$25 million on revenues of US$2.2 billion but was valued at US$1.3 billion by the market. Stocks valuations have much to do with investors' expectations as to future profitability. But when there are no existing profits to be extrapolated into the future, investment analysts look to a variety of other indicators of future profitability. This can lead to extensive cogitation on the part of accountants on ways to prop up esteemed financial signals of growth to come. Consequently, in the UK, the Urgent Issues Task Force is investigating financial reporting issues relating to computer software, website, database and associated costs. One concern is that the term 'revenue' is not properly defined in UK company law nor is it the subject of a UK accounting standard. Another is that long-standing principles in the fundamental accounting concept of prudence (in SSAP 2) do not provide a standard view on 'cash realisation'. Does this refer to 'reliable measurement' or to 'convertibility to cash'? In the USA, the Financial Accounting Standard Board's (FASB) Emerging Issues Task Force is also addressing the task of developing guidelines for how Generally Accepted Accounting Principles (GAAP) should be applied to Internet companies. The Securities and Exchange Commission (SEC) has likewise tried to specify conditions for revenue recognition which e-businesses need to heed. This is an important issue as, in the absence of

Accounting ratios and e-businesses

positive earnings, investors have looked to the revenue performance of an organisation as a determinant of its stock market value. This has led to questionable ways of maximising the top line in the profit and loss accounts of Internet companies.

3.7.2 A case in point is that of a number of Internet companies which offer their customers introductory sweeteners by way of discounts off the sales price of products and free items such as CD-ROMs or software. Sales are subsequently recorded at the normal level and the discount or free element is recorded as a marketing expense. For instance, an Internet service provider (ISP) may give one month's free service and, in order to maximise the top line, it would book 12 months' revenues and take one month as a marketing expense. This has the effect of enlarging the revenues reported whilst also adding to the marketing expenses line item which is likewise positively perceived as it signals potential future growth.

3.7.3 Rigelsford and Sharp (2000) give an example of an Internet business whose special offers have been so successful that the businesses have been unable to fulfil demand. Consequently, customers have received full refunds. Here, the proposal is that top line revenue should be all those who sought to subscribe for the product/service, regardless of whether or not they were successful and that for those who were unsuccessful the refunds given should be shown as an expense in the profit and loss account. In both of the examples above, UK GAAP requires that the revenue should be shown net. It is not acceptable to have notional income and notional expenses. The second example falls foul of the recognition criteria set out above. No service has been rendered to the potential customers. In the first example, the business has sold the product/service at a reduced amount. This reduced amount represents the economic benefits that will flow to the business and therefore the amount that should be recorded.

3.7.4 Another issue Rigelsford and Sharp cite is that of 'revenue recognition' – in other words, taking income up. For example, an Internet business provides customers with access to a website perhaps to obtain information or to advertise on that website for a period. The business argues that significant work and therefore cost is associated with attracting customers. The cost of maintaining the website and providing access to it are minimal. Furthermore, customers are likely to have paid up-front for the service. Therefore, the income should be recognised in the profit and loss account at the point at which the customer signs up.

3.7.5 But the business has not provided all the services associated with this transaction at the point of sale. It has to ensure that the website continues to

Financial analysis and working capital management

be available for the period of the contract. Accordingly, income should be matched with the period in which it is earned. If those websites were not available for the entire period, then the customers would normally be entitled to a refund either under the specific terms of the contract or if necessary through legal process.

3.7.6 Another revenue recognition problem arises in respect of those Internet businesses that act as aggregators. For example, lastminute.com allows travel companies to advertise late deals on its website. Should aggregators show the gross value of holidays sold or merely the commission that they earn on such sales from the travel companies?

3.7.7 The accounting approaches will depend on whether the aggregator is acting as a principal or as an agent. If the aggregator is acting as a principal, then it has effectively contracted with the travel companies to buy the holiday and then has a separate contract with the customer. As far as the customer is concerned, its arrangements are solely with the aggregator, so if there are any problems with the service then the customer will expect the aggregator to provide the necessary recompense. In such cases, the transactions will be shown gross in the profit and loss account. The aggregator's status should be clear from its website. For example, the terms and conditions on the website of lastminute.com state: 'Your confirmatory notification will inform you with whom your contract is made – in some cases it will be lastminute.com, in other cases it will be a third party where lastminute.com is acting on its behalf'.

3.7.8 If the aggregator is acting merely as agent, it should not reflect the gross value of the holiday in its profit and loss account. It is not incurring the risks and rewards associated with the provision of the service.

3.7.9 In some industries, it has become established practice to provide a memorandum 'gross sales' figure, in other words not a statutory number but the total amount of transactions with which the reporting entity is associated. If aggregators wish to give this information, this should be acceptable, provided the amount is clearly shown as a memorandum number and fully explained in the financial statements. Care should also be taken to ensure that the narrative reports that surround the financial statements do not use this information in a misleading fashion.

3.7.10 In certain circumstances the principal/agent model may not be sufficiently clear. Such transactions will have to be analysed further to determine what aspects of the transaction the Internet business controls, what type of services and value the business is seeking to provide to its customers

Accounting ratios and e-businesses

and whom the customer perceives as the supplier. The fact that the aggregator takes the credit risk is in itself unlikely to be sufficient to support gross revenue treatment, particularly if the credit risk is nominal because payments are made on credit cards.

3.7.11 Kahn and Garcia (2000) likewise report that never before has the way in which companies record their sales mattered so much to investors. For a website trading at 250 times expected sales even a tiny increase in reported revenues can translate into a massive increase in market capitalisation. This factor had, at the peak of the dotcom boom, provided Internet companies with a powerful incentive to inflate sales figures through accounting techniques. Depending on future investment sentiments in this sector, this issue may yet again become cause for concern.

3.7.12 Kahn and Garcia illustrate how Internet firms may 'gross up' their revenues by reporting the entire sales price a customer pays at their site when in fact the company keeps only a small percentage of that amount. This is akin to the lastminute.com issue raised above. For instance, in its last 1999 quarterly SEC filings, Priceline, which was then a stock market darling, reported that it earned US$152 million in revenues, but this figure included the full amount customers paid for tickets, hotel rooms and rental cars. Travel agencies ordinarily call this amount 'gross bookings', not revenues. In common with regular travel agencies, Priceline keept only a small portion of gross bookings – that is, the spread between the customers' accepted bids and the price it paid for the merchandise. The remainder, which Priceline termed 'product costs', were paid to the airlines and hotels that supplied the tickets and rooms. These costs came to $134 million, leaving Priceline just $18 million of what it referred to as 'gross profit' and what most other companies would simply view as revenues. At the time, Priceline traded at about 23 times its reported revenues but at 214 times its 'gross profit'.

3.7.13 Priceline counted gross bookings as revenues because, unlike a travel agency, it considered itself as having assumed the full risk of ownership as the 'merchant of record' and thus to determine the size of its spread.

3.7.14 Kahn and Garcia remark that barter transactions are common in all kinds of media. But for old-media companies such deals tend never to amount to more than 5 per cent of sales. In the on-line world, however, it is not unusual for start-ups to derive as much as half their revenues from barter.

3.7.15 Barter accounted for 6 per cent of all Internet advertising in the second quarter of 1999 according to a survey conducted by accounting firm

Financial analysis and working capital management

PwC for the Internet Advertising Bureau. But that figure fails to take into account barter schemes in which two Internet companies actually exchange cash but simply send each other equal sums. Include those deals, sometimes referred to as the 'revenue merry-go-round' and the real proportion of Internet revenues attributable to barter rises to 15 per cent, according to research firm Jupiter Communications.

3.7.16 GAAP requires that barter transactions be recorded at 'fair value'. But the rules do not explain how fair value should be determined.

3.7.17 Kahn and Garcia further suggest that amazon.com, eToys and 1-800-flowers are among the many e-commerce companies toying with 'fulfilment costs', which are the expenses associated with warehousing, packaging, and shipping products. Offline companies usually record the expense on their income statements as cost of sales but not dot-coms. Many categorise fulfilment costs as a 'marketing expense'.

3.7.18 This is because cost of sales cuts directly into a company's gross profit margin. Also, the practice enables dot-coms to hide operational expenses amid the huge marketing costs that investors believe are a temporary splurge associated with establishing brand recognition. Whilst revenues bolster stock valuations so in some cases high marketing costs will send a signal to the market of a likelihood of future potential profitability.

3.7.19 Greenberg (2000) comments on how accounting figures can further lure investors. Many investors look to earnings before interest, taxes, depreciation and amortisation (EBITDA) as being interchangeable with cash flow. This is acceptable if no major equipment purchase is anticipated or not much money is to be paid for interest on debt. But EBITDA falls where a company uses assets with very short lives and heavily deploys debt leveraging – as is the case with many Internet companies at advanced financing rounds. Cash flow figures tend to be preferable to EBITDA or its variants.

3.7.20 The bottom line is that ratio analysis of financial figures can be useful in making managerial and investment decisions, but that reliance has fed into an industry intent on coupling cosmetics with substance.

A case study: EVA and financial improvement

3.7.21 'I've been hearing a lot lately about something called MVA, which stands for market value added, and I was curious whether it is something we can use at OSI,' Keith Martin said. Keith is president and CEO of OutSource

Accounting ratios and e-businesses

Inc. (OSI). His guest for lunch that day was a computer industry analyst from a local brokerage firm. Keith had invited him to lunch so he could get more information on MVA and its uses.

3.7.22 'Yes,' the analyst replied, 'I've heard a great deal about EVA and MVA. EVA is a residual income approach in which a firm's net operating profit after taxes – called NOPAT – is compared to a minimum level of return a firm must earn on the total amount of capital placed at its disposal. MVA represents the difference between the market and book value of a company over a period of time.'

3.7.23 'Have you seen the most recent issue of Fortune?' he continued, handing Keith a copy. 'It has an article in it updating Stern Stewart's list of the top 1,000 firms ranked by MVA. You will also be interested in an earlier Fortune article on EVA, or economic value added. EVA is closely related to MVA. However, don't be misled by the simplicity of the EVA calculations in that article. The after-tax operating profit and the amount used for capital don't come directly off the financial statements. You have to analyse the footnotes to determine the adjustments that have to be made to come up with those amounts – Bennett Stewart calls them equity equivalents, or EEs, in his book, The Quest for Value.'

3.7.24 'Those articles sound like very interesting reading for me, especially at this point,' Keith said. 'Can you send me copies?'

3.7.25 'Sure,' said the analyst. 'But tell me, what is it about MVA and EVA that piqued your interest in trying them at OSI?'

3.7.26 'In tracking our industry,' Keith replied, 'I see the stock prices of some of our key competitors, like Equifax, increasing. Yet when I compare OSI's recent growth in sales and earnings, our return on equity and earnings per share compare well to those firms, but our stock price doesn't achieve nearly the same rate of increase, and I don't understand why.'

3.7.27 The analyst replied, 'Some of those firms might be benefiting from using EVA already, and the market value of their stock probably reflects the results of their efforts. It has been shown that a higher level of correlation exists between EVA and a stock's market value than has been found with the traditional accounting performance measures, like ROE or EPS.'

3.7.28 'But the MVA 1,000 ranking probably includes only large firms,' Keith observed after looking over the article the analyst had given him. 'Will EVA work in a small service firm like OSI?'

Financial analysis and working capital management

3.7.29 'Most of the largest US firms are in the Stern Stewart MVA ranking,' the analyst said, 'but I've read about EVA being used at smaller firms. And some firms in the ranking are service firms, such as AT&T, McDonald's, Marriott International, and Dun & Bradstreet. I'm not an expert on MVA or EVA, but I don't see any reason why it wouldn't work at OSI.'

3.7.30 'I'd like to find out more about MVA and EVA and how we can use them at OSI. For example, we've talked about a new incentive plan – will EVA work in that area? And, if so, will it help us in deciding how we should organise and manage our operations as we expand and grow? Can you get me more information on these things?'

3.7.31 'An application EVA is touted for is its use in incentive plans,' the analyst replied. 'A team of students from Capital University has been assigned to me this fall to do an industry-related project, and I was looking for something meaty for them to do. This looks like just the ticket. I'll brief them on it and have them come over to get the necessary information and interview you.'

3.7.32 'Great! I look forward to meeting them,' Keith said.

Company information

3.7.33 OutSource Inc. is a computer service bureau that provides basic data processing and general business support services to a number of business firms, including several large firms in their immediate area. Its offices are in a large city in the mid-Atlantic region, and it serves client firms in several mid-Atlantic states. OSI's revenues have grown fairly rapidly in recent years as businesses have downsized and outsourced many of their basic support services.

3.7.34 The CorpInfo Data Service (CIDS) classifies OSI as an information services firm (SIC 7374). This group is composed, in large part, of smaller, independent entrepreneurs that provide a variety of often-disparate services to both corporate and government clients. Market analysts feel a continuously healthy economy translates into strong potential for higher earnings by members of this group. A factor sustaining an extended period of growth is the increased attention of firms to controlling costs and outsourcing their non-core functions, such as personnel placement, payroll, human resources, insurance and data processing. This trend is expected to continue to the end of the decade, probably at an increasing rate. Several firms in this industry have capitalised on their growth and geographic expansion to win lucrative contracts with large clients that previously had been awarded on a market-by-market basis.

Accounting ratios and e-businesses

3.7.35 Although OSI operates out of its own facilities, which include some computing equipment and furniture, the bulk of its computer processing power is obtained from excess computer capacity in the local area, primarily rented time during third-shift operations at a large local bank. To be successful in the long term, however, OSI management knows it must expand its business considerably, and, to ensure full control over its operations, it must set up its own large-scale computing facility in-house. These items are included in OSI's long-range strategic plan.

3.7.36 As OSI's reputation for accurate, reliable, and quick response service has spread, the firm has found new business coming its way in a variety of data processing and support services. The issue has been deciding which services to take on or stay out of, in light of the current limitations on OSI's computing resources, to ensure it can continue to provide high-quality service to its customers. Things are definitely looking up for OSI, and industry market analysts have recently begun to look more favourably on its stock.

3.7.37 In 1993, OSI's board decided to pursue additional opportunities in payroll processing and tax filing services. OSI purchased a medium-sized firm that had an established market providing payroll calculation, processing, and reporting services for several Fortune 500 firms on the East Coast. Now OSI is in the midst of developing a new payroll processing system, called PayNet, to replace the outmoded system originally created by the firm it acquired.

3.7.38 Once PayNet is developed, it will give users an integrated payroll solution with a simpler, more familiar graphical user interface. From an administrative perspective, it will allow OSI to reduce its manual data entry hiring, to speed data compilation and analysis, and to simplify administrative tasks and the updating of customer files for adds, moves and changes. PayNet will serve as the backbone for OSI's service bureau payroll processing operations in the future, but, at present, developmental and programming costs have proved higher than expected and will delay the rollout of the final version of the new payroll engine. Beta testing of the production version of PayNet was delayed from the second to the third quarter of 1996.

Additional accounting information

3.7.39 OSI's financial statements for 1995 appear in Figures 9.34 and 9.35. The following list of information, extracted from the footnotes to OSI's annual report for 1995, is pertinent to calculating a firm's EVA.

- Inventories are stated principally at cost (last in, first out), which is not in excess of market. Replacement cost would be $2,796 more than the 1994 inventory balance and $3,613 more than the 1995 inventory balance.

Financial analysis and working capital management

- Deferred tax expense results from timing differences in recognising revenue and expense for tax and reporting purposes.

- On 1 July 1993, the company acquired CompuPay, a payroll processing and reporting service firm. The acquisition was accounted for as a purchase, and the excess of cost over the fair value of net assets acquired was $109,200, which is being amortised on a straight-line basis over 13 years. One-half year of goodwill amortisation was recorded in 1993.

- Research and development costs related to software development are expensed as incurred. Software development costs are capitalised from the point in time when the technological feasibility of a piece of software has been determined until it is ready to be put on line to process customer data. The cost of purchased software, which is ready for service, is capitalised on acquisition. Software development costs and purchased software costs are amortised using the straight-line method over periods ranging from three to seven years. A history of the accounting treatment of software development costs and purchased software costs follows.

	Expensed	**Capitalised**	**Amortised**
1993	$166,430	$9,585	0
1994	211,852	5,362	$4,511
1995	89,089	18,813	5,111
	$467,371	$33,760	$9,622

Additional financial information

3.7.40 OSI's common stock is currently trading at $2 per share. A preferred dividend of $11 per share was paid in 1995, and the current price of the preferred stock is approximately at its par value. Other information pertaining to OSI's debt and stock follows.

Short-term debt:	$8,889	Rate: 8.0%
Long-term debt:		
Current portion	$18,411	Rate: 10.0%
Long-term portion	$98,744	Rate: 10.0%
Total long-term debt	$117,155	
Stock market risk-free rate (90 day T-bills)	= 5.0%	
Expected return on the market	= 12.5%	
Beta value of OSI's common stock	= 1.20	
Expected growth rate of dividends	= 8.0%	
Income tax rate	= 35.0%	

Figure 3.4 OutSource Inc.'s balance sheet

OutSource Inc. Balance Sheet 31 December	1995	1994
Assets		
Current assets:		
Cash	$144,724	$169,838
Trade and other receivables (net)	217,085	192,645
Inventories	15,829	23,750
Other	61,047	49,239
Total current assets	$438,685	$435,472
Non-current assets:		
Property, plant and equipment	$123,135	$109,600
Software and development costs	33,760	14,947
Data processing equipment and furniture	151,357	141,892
Other non-current assets	3,650	8,844
	$311,902	$275,283
Less-Accumulated depreciation	85,018	57,929
Total non-current assets	$226,884	$217,354
Goodwill	88,200	96,600
	$753,769	$749,426
Liabilities and Shareholders' Equity		
Current liabilities		
Short-term debt and current portion of long-term note	$27,300	$31,438
Accounts payable	67,085	57,483
Deferred income	45,050	32,250
Income taxes payable	19,936	12,100
Employee compensation and benefits payable	30,155	28,950
Other accrued expenses	28,458	27,553
Other current liabilities	17,192	29,769
Total current liabilities	$235,176	$219,543
Long-term debt less current portion	98,744	117,155
Deferred income taxes	6,784	4,850
Shareholders' equity:		
Cumulative Non-Convertible Preferred Stock, $100 par value, authorised 5,000 shares, issued and outstanding 1,000 shares	100,000	100,000
Common stock, $1 par value; 300,000 shares authorised; 219,884 shares issued and outstanding	219,884	219,884
Additional paid-in capital	32,056	32,056
Retained earnings	61,125	55,938
Total shareholders' equity	$413,065	$407,878
	$753,769	$749,426

Financial analysis and working capital management

Figure 3.5 OutSource Inc.'s statement of income

OutSource Inc.	
Statement of income for the year ended December 31	**1995**
Operating revenue	$2,604,530
Costs of services	1,466,350
Gross profit	$1,138,180
Less: Operating expenses	
Selling, general and administrative	$902,388
Research and development	89,089
Other expense (income)	59,288
Write-off of goodwill and other intangibles	13,511
Earnings (Loss) before interest and taxes	$73,904
Interest income	$1,009
Interest expense	12,427
Earnings (Loss) before income taxes	62,486
Income tax provision	21,870
Earnings (Loss)	$40,616
OutSource Inc.	
Statement of cash flows for the year ended December 31	1995
Cash flows from operating activities	
Net earnings (Loss)	$40,616
Depreciation	21,978
Amortisation of software & development costs	5,111
Decrease (Increase) in accounts receivable	(24,440)
Decrease (Increase) in inventories	7,921
Decrease (Increase) in other current assets	(11,808)
Increase (Decrease) in deferred income	9,602
Increase (Decrease) in accounts payable	12,800
Increase (Decrease) in income taxes payable	7,836
Increase (Decrease) in employee compensation and benefits payable	1,205
Increase (Decrease) in other accrued expenses	905
Increase (Decrease) in other current liabilities	(12,577)
Increase (Decrease) in deferred income taxes	1,934
Net cash provided by (used for) operating activities	$61,083
Cash flows from investing activities	
Expended for capital assets	($36,619)
Goodwill amortised	8,400
Net cash provided by (used for) investing activities	($28,219)
Cash flows from financing activities	
Payment of long-term note	($4,138)
Payment of short-term note	(18,411)
Preferred dividends	(11,000)
Common stock dividends	(24,429)
Net cash provided by (used for) financing activities	($57,978)
Net cash flows provided (Used)	($25,114)
Cash at beginning of year	$169,838
Cash at end of year	$144,724

Understanding EVA and MVA concepts

3.7.41 Economic value added (EVA), as noted above, is a measure of financial performance that combines the familiar concept of residual income with principles of modern corporate finance – specifically, that all capital has a cost and that earning more than the cost of capital creates value for shareholders. EVA is after-tax net operating profit – NOPAT – minus cost of capital. If a company's return on capital exceeds its cost of capital, it is creating true value for shareholders. Companies consistently generating high EVAs are top performers that are valued by shareholders.

3.7.42 Key components of EVA are NOPAT and the capital charge – the amount of capital employed times the cost of capital. The capital charge is the cash flow required to compensate investors for the riskiness of the business, given the amount of capital invested. The cost of capital is the minimum rate of return on capital required to compensate debt and equity investors for bearing risk, e.g., a cutoff rate to create value. Capital is the amount of cash invested in the business, net of depreciation. It can be calculated as the sum of interest-bearing debt and equity or as the sum of net assets less non-interest-bearing current liabilities.

In formula form,

$$EVA = (r - c^*) \times capital$$

where

r = rate of return
c^* = cost of capital, or weighted average cost of capital

Then
$EVA = (r \times capital) - (c^* \times capital)$
$EVA = NOPAT - c^* \times capital$
$EVA = $ operating profits $-$ a capital charge

3.7.43 Another perspective on EVA can be gained by looking at a firm's RONA – return on net assets. This acronym has become popular along with the growing interest in EVA. A firm's RONA is calculated by dividing its NOPAT by the amount of capital it employs (RONA = NOPAT/capital), after making the necessary adjustments (EEs) of the data reported by a conventional financial accounting system.

3.7.44 A convenient formulation of EVA is obtained by multiplying the total amount of net assets tied up by the spread between RONA and a threshold or minimum rate of return, like the cost of capital. Thus:

$EVA = $ net investments $\times (RONA - c^*)$

If RONA is greater than c^*, EVA is positive.

3.7.45 Gains in shareholder wealth are driven by gains in EVA. The market price of a stock incorporates the current level of EVA and the expectation of future EVA. To increase the stock price, management must increase the current level of EVA and change the market's expectations of growth in future EVA.

3.7.46 In summary, EVA is essentially simply another definition of earnings – sales less operating expenses – with one more item subtracted, a charge for the use of the capital involved. It is true economic profit consisting of all costs, including the cost of capital.

3.7.47 Market value added (MVA) is a measure of the wealth a company has created for its investors. In effect, MVA shows the difference between what investors put in and what they can take out.

3.7.48 EVA is the fuel that fires up a company's MVA. A company that has a positive EVA year after year will see its MVA rise, while negative EVA year in and year out will drag MVA down, as the market loses faith that the company will ever provide a decent return on invested capital.

3.7.49 MVA is a cumulative measure of corporate performance that looks at how much a company's stock has added to (or taken out of) investors' pocketbooks over its life and compares that amount with the capital those same investors put into the firm. If MVA is a positive number, the company has made its shareholders richer. A negative MVA indicates how much shareholder wealth has been destroyed. Maximising MVA should be the primary objective for any company concerned about its shareholders' welfare.

3.7.50 How is MVA calculated? First, all the capital a company took in over its span of existence is identified, including equity and debt offerings, bank loans and retained earnings, and the amounts are added up. Then, some 'adjustments' (EEs) are made that capitalise certain past expenditures, such as R&D spending, as an investment in future earnings. This adjusted capital amount is compared to a firm's total market value, which is the current value of a company's stock and debt, to get MVA – the difference between what the investors can take out (total market value) and the amount investors put in (invested capital). In formula form, MVA is calculated as follows:

$$MVA = [(\text{shares outstanding} \times \text{stock price}) + \text{market value of preferred stock} + \text{market value of debt}] - \text{total capital invested}$$

3.7.51 MVA tends to move in tandem with the firm's stock market value. Stern Stewart, the consulting firm that developed and promoted EVA in the

Accounting ratios and e-businesses

business community, contends EVA is the sole measurement method that can be correlated with a firm's stock price.

Comparing EVA and MVA versus traditional financial performance measures

3.7.52 How does EVA stack up against the conventional financial measures of performance? Advocates of EVA are quick to point out that financial measures based on reported accounting earnings – earnings growth, earnings per share, and return ratios calculated on either investment, equity or assets – are misleading measures of corporate performance. This opinion is based on their view that accountants place their primary emphasis on placating the interests of a firm's lenders in order to provide a conservative assessment of the firm's liquidation value. Thus, the quality of reported earnings is diminished by various financial accounting rules such as incorporating charge-offs of such value-building capital outlays as R&D and bookkeeping entries that have little to do with recurring cash flow. This group also feels that many investors may be fooled by accounting 'shenanigans', but investors who matter are not misled. They know that stock prices are set by a select group of 'lead steers' who look through misleading accounting results to arrive at true values. Although blissfully ignorant of why the price is right, the rest of the 'herd' is well protected by the lead steers' informed judgements.

3.7.53 One comparison is to the standard accounting return on common equity (ROE), which is generally understood and easily calculated by dividing net income available to common stock-holders by the amount of accounting equity capital. However, ROE suffers from distortions of accounting earnings by, among other things, expensing R&D, or burying recurring cash flows generated from operations in reserves because of accrual accounting methods.

3.7.54 Also, ROE reacts to changes in the debt-to-equity mix a company employs and in the rate of interest it pays on its debts, making it difficult to determine if ROE rises or falls for operating or financial reasons without examining the return on assets and the firm's debt-to-equity ratio. With ROE as its goal, management may be tempted to accept substandard projects that happen to be financed with debt and pass by very good ones that are financed with equity. To avoid such situations, managers shouldn't associate sources of funds with the uses of those funds. Such association distorts the desirability of undertaking a project by mixing operating and financing decisions. Instead, all projects should be thought of as being financed with a target blend of debt and equity no matter how they might indeed be financed. Moreover, by focusing just on ROE, managers may pass up good

Financial analysis and working capital management

(wealth-creating) projects that are safer than the average assets of the firm because the return on the project would lower the firm's ROE. Similarly, managers may take on bad (wealth-reducing) projects that are riskier than the average assets of the firm because the project's return increases the firm's ROE. It should be kept in mind that by focusing on ROE, the manager ignores the risk associated with a specific project and hence the appropriate return needed for that investment.

3.7.55 An alternative measure of performance is return on assets (ROA), but it, too, ignores the cost of capital, which can lead a firm to make decisions that reduce economic value. For example, IBM, in its most profitable year, had a return on assets that was more than 11 per cent, but its cost of capital was almost 13 per cent. Assuming their cost of capital remains at 13 per cent, accepting projects with risks similar to existing assets but with a return below 13 per cent reduces shareholder value.

3.7.56 Another comparison to make is against earnings per share (EPS). In contrast to EVA, EPS tells little about the cost of generating those profits. Since EPS is directly influenced by the amount of earnings relative to the number of shares outstanding, financing new investments through debt capital can increase EPS. Large or rapid earnings growth can be attained by pouring capital into riskier projects; earning an adequate rate of return relative to risk is far more important than growing rapidly. Thus, at best, EPS measures only the quantity of earnings, but the quality of earnings reflected in the price-to-earnings multiple also matters.

Calculating EVA and MVA by the operating and financial approaches

3.7.57 As indicated earlier, EVA and MVA can be calculated using some very simple formulas. But the simplicity of these calculations can be misleading because the after-tax operating profit, NOPAT, and the amount used for capital are not readily available – that is, they do not come directly from the traditional financial statements. The amount(s) of any equity equivalent adjustments (EEs) for certain accounts must first be determined. The footnotes to the financial statements are the primary source of this information.

3.7.58 In *The Quest for Value*, G. Bennett Stewart calculates a firm's EVA in two ways: an operating approach, and a financing approach. The financing approach builds up to the rate of return on capital from the standard return on equity in three steps: eliminating financial leverage, eliminating financing distortions and eliminating accounting distortions. As a result of the first two steps, NOPAT is a sum of the returns attributable to all providers of funds to the company, and the NOPAT return is completely unaffected by the financial composition of capital. What matters is simply the productivity of capital employed in the business. The financial form in which the capital has been obtained does not matter.

3.7.59 The operating approach starts by deducting operating expenses, including depreciation, from sales, but other non-cash-bookkeeping entries are ignored. Next, EE adjustments are made. Interest expense, since it is a financing charge, is ignored, but other (operating) income is added to get pre-tax economic profits, or net operating profit before taxes (NOPBT). In the final step, an estimate of the taxes payable in cash on these operating profits is subtracted, leaving NOPAT at the same amount as in the financing approach. The NOPAT and capital amounts determined by the operating and financing approaches are then reconciled in a summary report.

3.7.60 Before getting heavily involved in preparing the operating and financing approaches, it is important – if not essential – to cover first the concepts of the equity equivalent adjustments, or EEs.

Understanding/use of equity equivalents

3.7.61 Equity equivalents, EEs per Bennett Stewart's book, are adjustments that turn a firm's accounting book value into 'economic book value', which is a truer measure of the cash that investors have put at risk in the firm and on which they expect to accrue some returns. In this way, capital-related items are turned into a more accurate measure of capital that better reflects the financial base investors expect to accrue their returns on. Also, revenue- and expense-related equity equivalent adjustments are included in NOPAT, which is a more realistic measure of the actual cash yield generated for investors from recurring business activities.

3.7.62 Stern Stewart have identified a total of 164 equity equivalent reserve adjustments; however, only about 20 to 25 have to be addressed in detail, and only a portion of them may actually be made in practice. They recommend making an adjustment only in cases that pass four tests.

- Is it likely to have a material impact on EVA?
- Can the managers influence the outcome?
- Can the operating people readily grasp it?
- Is the required information relatively easy to track and derive?

3.7.63 R&D expenditures provide a good example of an equity equivalent adjustment. Under accounting conventions, outlays for R&D are charged off to the income statement in the period when they are incurred.

Financial analysis and working capital management

These immediate charge-offs as operating expenses say there is no future value to be derived from R&D. Thus, the firm's profits are reduced and its capital is undervalued. For EVA purposes, all outlays over the life of successful R&D projects should be removed from the income statement, capitalised into the balance sheet, and amortised against earnings over the period benefiting from the successful R&D efforts. In calculating EVA, R&D is seen as an investment, and amounts spent for it must be included in a firm's capital base to reflect accurately the amount of capital employed. Only the portion of R&D that no longer has future value should be charged to the income statement to reflect properly the costs and profit of a period. The portion of R&D expenditures that has future value should appear as an asset. These equity equivalent adjustments are made in calculating EVA.

3.7.64 The following list of equity equivalents and their effect on capital and NOPAT is derived from G. Bennett Stewart's book, *The Quest for Value*. The asterisked items are equity equivalents in the OSI case.

Add to Capital: Equity Equivalents
Deferred income tax reserve*
LIFO reserve*
Cumulative goodwill amortisation*
Unrecorded goodwill
(Net) capitalised intangibles
Full-cost reserve
Cumulative unusual loss (gain) AT
Other reserves, such as:
Bad debt reserve   Inventory obsolescence reserve
Warranty reserve   Deferred income reserve
Add to NOPAT: Increase in Equity Equivalents
Increase in deferred tax reserve*
Increase in LIFO reserve*
Goodwill amortisation*
Increase in (net) capitalised intangibles
Increase in full-cost reserve
Unusual loss (gain) AT
Increase in other reserves

An overview of the process involved in calculating EVA and MVA

3.7.65 Following is a list of the steps to be completed in calculating OSI's EVA and MVA amounts.

- Obtain a balance sheet and income statement for 1995.

- Obtain the footnotes to those financial statements.

- Analyse the footnotes for information on equity equivalent adjustments.

Accounting ratios and e-businesses

- Obtain information on the firm's stock, debt and interest rates.
- Determine equity equivalent adjustment amounts by analysing the footnotes.
- Calculate the firm's weighted average cost of capital.
- Prepare worksheets of EVA statements for an operating approach and a financing approach and enter data.
- Reconcile operating approach and financing approach EVA amounts to confirm that the calculations are complete, i.e., all amounts are used in their proper place.
- Prepare final operating and financing approach statements of EVA showing amounts calculated for RONA, EVA and MVA.
- Prepare a summary NOPAT and capital statement.

Calculating EVA and MVA using the operating approach

3.7.66 Figure 3.6 contains statements detailing the items included in calculating the capital and NOPAT amounts for OSI for 1995 using an operating approach. Calculation of RONA, EVA and MVA appear in the lower right corner of the statement. Note that two answers appear for the weighted average cost of capital (WACC) and EVA. This is because the weighted average cost of capital is different depending on whether the calculation was based on market or book values. Figure 9.37 shows these two calculations and the financial inputs to them.

Figure 3.6 Balance sheet

OutSource Inc.		
EVA Capital via Operating Approach		
Balance Sheet, December 31,	**1995**	
Assets		
Current Assets:		
Cash and cash equivalents	$144,724	
Trade and other receivables (net)	217,085	
Inventories	15,829	
Lifo Reserve	3,613	(A)
Other	61,047	
Adjusted Current Assets	442,298	
Current Liabilities:		
Accounts payable	67,085	
Deferred income	45,050	
Income taxes payable	19,936	
Employee compensation and benefits	30,155	
Other accrued expenses	28,458	
Other current liabilities	17,192	

Financial analysis and working capital management

NIBCLs (Non-Interest-Bearing Current Liabilities)	207,876	
Net Working Capital	234,422	
Non-current Assets:		
Property, plant and equipment	123,135	
Software and development costs	33,760	
Data processing equipment and furniture	151,357	
Other non-current assets	3,650	
Accum Software Dev. costs Amortisation	9,622	(D)
Capitalise amounts of Software dev.		
costs that have been expensed.	467,371	(D)
Adjusted Property Plant & Equipt.	788,895	
Less-Accumulated depreciation	85,018	
Net non-current assets	703,877	
Goodwill	88,200	
Accum Goodwill Amortisation	21,000	(C)
Gross Goodwill	109,200	
EVA Capital via Operating Approach	$1,047,499	

Income Statement

Net Sales	$2,604,530	
Cost of Goods Sold	1,466,350	
Gross Profit	$1,138,180	
Selling, general and administrative	902,388	
Other operating expenses	59,288	
Lifo Reserve (Increased)	(817)	(A)
Adjusted Operating Expenses	960,859	
Adjusted Net Oper Profit	$177,321	
Other Income	1,009	
NOPBT	$178,330	
Cash Operating Taxes	24,285	
EVA NOPAT via Operating Approach	$154,044	

Analysis of Taxes

Income Tax Provision	21,870	
Less: Increase in Deferred Taxes	(1,934)	(B)
Plus Tax Savings From Interest Expense:	4,349	
Cash Operating Taxes	24,285	

Return on Net Assets (RONA) = NOPAT/Capital

EVA: NOPAT via Operating Approach =	$154,044
EVA: Capital via Operating Approach =	$1,047,499
RONA =	**14.71%**

Calculate EVA – Based on:	Market Value	Book Value
Wgt.Ave.Cost of Capital (WACC) =	12.21%	11.78%
EVA = (RONA – WACC)* Capital =	$26,189	$30,680
Calculate Market Value Added (MVA)		
Market Value of Equity = $2.00 * 219,884 sh=	$439,768	
Less: Economic Value of Equity:		
Common Equity + paid-in Capital + RE=	313,065	
Plus: Total Equity Equivalents=	508,390	
Equals: Market Value Added (MVA) =	($381,687)	

3.7.67 Using the footnote information provided in the case, Figure 9.38 shows the footnotes and the amounts determined for OSI's equity equivalent adjustments for 1995. The alphabetic letter of the footnote is keyed to the related amounts used in the EVA capital and NOPAT calculations.

3.7.68 A special note should be made of the calculation of market value added (MVA) in the box in the lower right corner of Figure 9.36. Only common equity amounts and retained earnings appear in that calculation. Preferred stock and debt are not considered. The market value of the latter two items would normally be included in calculating the market value of a firm; however, for OSI the book value of these items is assumed to be equal to their market value. Since no differences are introduced into the calculation by these two items, they have been excluded to simplify the presentation of the results.

Calculating EVA and MVA using the financing approach

3.7.69 EVA and MVA calculations for OSI in 1995 using the financing approach are detailed in Figure 3.5. Refer to Figures 3.8 and 3.7 for relevant information on the WACC and the equity equivalent adjustment amounts involved in these calculations.

Figure 3.7 Financial data input and calculation of interest rates/expense

	Rate	Interest	
Short-term debt:	$8.889	8.00%	$711
Long-term debt: current portion	$18,411	10.00%	$1,841
Long-term debt: long-term portion	$98.744	10.00%	$9,874
	$117.155	Interest paid =	$12,427
Risk-free rate (90 day T-bills) =	5.0%		
Return on the market =	12.5%		
Beta value of common stock =	1.2		
Tax rate =	35.0%		
Price per share of common stock =	$2.00		
Calculated cost of equity capital:	14.0%		

Financial analysis and working capital management

Common stock dividend/share paid last year =	0.111	per share
Total common stock dividend paid last year =	$24,429	
Calculated current dividend yield (last year) =	5.555%	
Expected growth rate of dividends =	8.000%	
Future dividend yield (next year) =	5.999%	
Common stk dividend/sh. expected-next year =	0.120	
Total common stock dividend to pay next year =	$26,383	
Check: Calculated future dividend yield (next year) =	5.999%	
Preferred stock dividend/share paid last year =	$11.00	per share
Total preferred stock dividend paid last year =	$11,000	
Total preferred stock dividend for next year =	$11,000	

Calculate weighted average cost of capital – based on market

Weights:				% of Total
Long-term note payable			$117,155	17.8%
Preferred stock				
Shares o/s	1,000			
Par value	$100		$100,000	15.2%
Common stock				
Shares o/s	219,884			
Market value	$2.00		$439,768	66.9%
			$656.923	
Weighted average cost of capital				
For Debt =	1.159%			
For Preferred Stock =	1.674%			
Common Stock =	9.372%			
	12.206%			

Calculate weighted average cost of capital – based on book value

Weights:				% of Total
Long-term note payable			$117,155	22.1%
Preferred stock				
Shares o/s	1,000			
Par value	$100		$100.000	18.9%
Common stock				
Share book value	$219,884			
Paid-in capital	$32,056			59.0%
Retained earnings	$61,125		$313,065	
			$530,220	

Weighted average cost of capital

For Debt=	1.436%
For Preferred Stock=	2.075%
Common Stock=	8.266%
	11.777%

Figure 3.8 Outsource Inc. pertinent information extracted from the footnotes to the Annual Report

Footnote

A. Inventories are stated principally at cost (last-in, first-out), which is not in excess of market. Replacement cost would be $2,796 greater than in 1994 and $3,613 greater in 1995.

    $3,613 Add to inventory and capital: amount of the LIFO reserve
    $817 Add to NOPAT: The amount of increase in the LIFO reserve

B. Deferred tax expense results from timing differences in recognising revenue and expense for tax and reporting purposes.

    $6,784 Include as capital: amount of the deferred tax reserve
    $1,934 Add to NOPAT: the amount of increase in the deferred tax reserve

C. On July 1, 1993, the company acquired CompuPay. The acquisition has been accounted for as a purchase, and the excess of cost over the fair value of net assets acquired was $109,200, which is being amortised on a straight-line basis over 12 years. One-half year of amortisation was taken in 1993.

    $21,000 Include as capital: cumulative amount of goodwill that has been amortised to date.
    $8,400 Add to NOPAT: The amount of increase in goodwill amortisation

D. Research and development costs related to software development are expensed as incurred. Software development costs are capitalised from the point in time when the technological feasibility of a piece of software has been determined until it is ready to be put on line to process customer data. The cost of purchased software, which is ready for service, is capitalised. Software development and purchased software costs are amortised using the straight-line method over periods ranging from three to seven years. A history of software development cost items follows:

	Expensed	Capitalised	Amortised
1993	$166,430	$9,585	$0
1994	$211,852	$5,362	$4,511
1995	$89,089	$18,813	$5,111
	$467,371	33,760	$9,622

    $9,622 Include as capital: cumulative amount of software development costs that have been amortised to date.
    $467,371 Include as capital: cumulative amount of software development costs that have been expensed to data.
    $5,111 Add to NOPAT: The amount of increase in goodwill amortisation

Financial analysis and working capital management

Figure 3.9 Balance sheet

OutSource Inc. EVA Capital via Financing Approach Balance Sheet, December 31	1995	
Liabilities & Net worth		
Current liabilities		
Short-term debt and current portion of long-term note	$27,300	
Long-term debt less current portion	98,744	
Total debt	126,044	
Equity equivalents		
Deferred income taxes	6,784	
LIFO Reserve	3,613	
Accum goodwill amortisation	21,000	
Accum software development costs amortisation	9,622	
Capitalise amounts of software development costs that have been expensed	467,371	
Total equity equivalents	508,390	
Shareholders' equity:		
Cumulative convertible exchangeable preferred stock, $100 par value, authorised 5,000 shares, 1,000 shares issued and outstanding	100,000	
Shareholders' equity:		
authorised; 219,884 shares issued and outstanding	219,884	
Additional paid in capital	32,056	
Retained earnings	61,125	
	413,065	
EVA capital via financing approach	$1,047,499	
OutSource Inc. EVA NOPAT via financing approach Income statement	1995	
Income available to common	$40,616	
Deferred taxes (increased)	1,934	(B)
Lifo reserve (increased)	817	(A)
Goodwill amortisation	8,400	(C)
Software development costs amortisation	5,111	(D)
Software development costs expensed	89,089	(D)
Increase in equity equivalents	105,351	
Adjusted income available to common	$145,967	
Add: adjusted interest expense	12,427	
Less: tax benefit of interest expense	(4,349)	
Interest expense after taxes	8,077	
EVA NOPAT via Financing approach	$154,044	

Return on net assets (RONA) = NOPAT/Capital		
EVA NOPAT via financing approach =	$154,044	
EVA Capital via financing approach =	$1,047,499	
RONA =	14.71%	
Calculate EVA – based on:	**Market value**	**Book value**
Weighted ave. cost of capital (WACC) =	12.21%	11.78%
EVA = (RONA – WACC)* Capital =	$26,189	$30,680
Calculate market value added (MVA)		
Market value of equity= $2.00* 219,884 sh=	$439,768	
Less: economic value of equity:		
Common equity + paid-in capital + RE=	313,065	
Plus: total equity equivalents=	508,390	
Equals: market value added (MVA) =	($381,687)	

Reconciling the results in a summary NOPAT and capital statement

3.7.70 Figure 3.10 contains a summary NOPAT and capital statement that reconciles the NOPAT and capital amounts calculated under the operating and financing approaches. Calculations of pertinent items and EVA and MVA amounts are repeated at the bottom of this exhibit.

Other, somewhat similar, performance metrics

3.7.71 This case situation focused primarily on EVA, but other valuation-based performance metrics exist, such as net present value (NPV), cash flow return on investment (CFROI) and residual income (RI). CFROI is a rate of return measure calculated by dividing inflation-adjusted cash flow from the investment by the inflation-adjusted amount of the cash investment. While CFROI does adjust for inflation, it fails to account for risk and the appropriate required return on the project. In a sense, CFROI is similar to the internal rate of return (IRR) after including the EE adjustments; hence it measures the investment's return as opposed to the wealth created or destroyed by the investment.

3.7.72 EVA comes closest in theory and construct to NPV. The information requirements for both techniques are the same. For both techniques you need an appropriate, risk-adjusted cost of capital. To determine the NPV of an investment decision, you need estimates of expected future cash flow. Similarly, to determine the economic value of the decision, you need the present value of expected future EVAs that are based on expected future cash flows of the firm. In other words, the NPV of an asset is simply the present value of the expected future EVA from the asset. Therefore, the notion of increasing or maximising EVA each year is consistent with the goal of shareholder wealth maximisation.

Financial analysis and working capital management

Figure 3.10 OutSource Inc. summary of NOPAT and capital

Operating approach	Financing approach
Sales $2,604,530	Adjusted Current Assets $2,427,209 net working capital $442,298 Debt & Leases $126,044 Interest Expense after tax $8,077
− Operating expenses $2,427,209	
+ Other operating income $1,009	NIBCLs $207,876
= NOPBT $178,330	Adjusted net property, plant Preferred $100,000
	& Equipt $703,877 Common $313,065
	Equity $413,065 + Income available to common $40,616
− Cash operating taxes $24,285	
Net fixed assets $813,077 Gross goodwill $109,200	
Equity equivalents $508,390 + Change in equity equivalent $105,351	
Other assets $0	

Operating NOPAT   Operating capital   Financing capital   Financing nopat
$154,044 $1,047,499 $1,047,499 $154,044
RONA = r =   NOPAT   EVA = NOPAT − c* × Capital
  Capital $1,047,499   =$154,044 $154,044 − $127,855
RONA = r = 14.71% EVA = $26,189
Cost of Capital = c* = 12.21%   Market Value Added (MVA) = Number of Shares × stock price
Shares outstanding = 219,884   − Number of shares × economic book value Per Share
Stock price = $2.00   219,884 × $2.00
Economic book value: 219,884 × $3.74
Common stock (only) = $313,065 $439,768 − $821,455
+ Equity equivalents = $508,390   MVA = ($381,687)
  $821,455
Per share = $3.74

106

Advantages and disadvantages of EVA

3.7.73 All managers basically have the same objective – putting scarce capital to its most promising uses. To increase their company's stock price, managers must perform better than those they compete with for capital. Then, once they get the capital, they must earn rates of return on it that exceed the returns offered by other, equally risky, seekers of capital funds. If they accomplish this, value will have been added to the capital their firm's investors placed at their disposal. If they don't accomplish that goal, there will be a misallocation of capital, and the company's stock will sell at a price that discounts the sum total of the resources employed.

3.7.74 EVA is a financial management system well adapted to this kind of situation because it focuses on creating shareholder value. In using the system, managers and employees focus on how capital is used and on the cash flow generated from it. This idea runs counter to the notion that long-term stock appreciation comes from earnings.

3.7.75 Focusing on EVA growth provides two benefits. (1) Management's attention is focused more toward its primary responsibility – increasing investor wealth. (2) Distortions caused by using historical cost accounting data are reduced or eliminated. As a result, managers spend their time finding ways to increase EVA rather than debating the intricacies of the fluctuations in the earnings reported in their traditional accounting statements.

3.7.76 EVA measures the amount of value a firm creates during a defined period through operating decisions it makes to increase margins, improve working capital management, and use its production facilities efficiently by redeploying under-utilised assets and so on. Thus, EVA can be used to hold management accountable for all economic outlays, whether they appear in the income statement, on the balance sheet, or in the financial statement's footnotes. EVA creates one financial statement that includes all the costs of being in business, including the carrying cost of capital. The EVA financial statement gives managers a complete picture of the connections among capital, margin and EVA. It makes managers conscious of money they spend, whether that money is spent on or off the income statement or on operating costs or on the carrying cost of working capital and fixed assets.

3.7.77 Another very subtle benefit to a firm that adopts EVA is that EVA creates a common language for making decisions, especially long-term decisions, resolving budgeting issues, evaluating the performance of its organisational units and their managers, and measuring the value-creating

Financial analysis and working capital management

potential of its strategic options. An outgrowth of such an environment is that the quality of management also improves as managers begin to think like owners and adopt a longer horizon view.

3.7.78 Why have value added financial measures generated such a high level of interest? Basically, it is due to a growing recognition that a company's market value, its value to shareholders, cannot be properly assessed without focusing on its cost of capital and the timing differences between its investment and the return. In contrast are traditional accounting measures such as earnings per share that do not incorporate these factors but that are affected by write-offs and depreciation schedules that do not reflect the true decline in the value of a firm's assets over time.

3.7.79 However, EVA should not be viewed as the answer to all things. By itself, EVA does not solve business problems; managers must solve them. But having access to such a meaningful measure, strongly linked to share price performance, clarifies a manager's options and, in conjunction with MVA, provides a meaningful target to pursue for both internally and externally oriented decisions.

Using EVA to facilitate the management of the firm

3.7.80 Since managers of EVA-adopting firms know their stock's price is tied to investors' expectations of the company's long-term cash flows, they will explicitly use value added measures in guiding their firm's activities. In this way greater emphasis will be placed on the operating profit needed to justify capital expenditures – or any expenditure, for that matter. It is this awareness of the efficient use of capital that will eventually produce additional shareholder value.

3.7.81 Value added measures can be particularly effective for gauging the performance of subsidiaries, divisions and other business units where a stock price measure is unavailable. By using value added measures at the business-unit level, companies can determine where capital will be most productively invested and the contribution each unit makes to the market value of the company. Unit managers can then be compensated on the basis of those contributions.

3.7.82 In light of 'what gets measured gets managed', EVA concepts can lead to improvements in the overall management of a firm's everyday operations. Incorporating EVA metrics into formal performance measurement systems both facilitates the use of measurements in areas that have been difficult to monitor and adds a degree of precision to measurements that previously have been taken and reported.

3.7.83 With a focus on EVA, managers can do a better job of asset-management, which can free up cash for use in other areas of the business. For example, a good way to boost EVA is to increase inventory turns, which reduces the amount of cash tied up in raw materials. Also, the effects of increasing inventory turns can be readily evaluated against the costs of running out of materials, shipping products late or otherwise failing to satisfy the customer. On a more micro level, manufacturing employees will readily comprehend that by reducing waste they help create economic value.

3.7.84 Companies that adopt EVA find they use it as a basis for decision making at all levels, whether at the strategic level of acquisitions or a new market entry, or thinking about day-to-day trade-offs in the business. In these situations, EVA provides a rather simple means of assessing the alternatives under review because there are only three basic means of raising a company's EVA.

- Raise profit levels without raising the amount of capital spent. The most obvious method is cost cutting, but imaginative managers will always look for other methods.
- Use less capital. That means looking for improvements in the way a business is run, such as streamlining operations.
- Invest capital in high-return projects. Any project should meet the minimum criterion of earning more than the cost of capital invested.

3.7.85 EVA has also been found to be a worthy adjunct to other management change programmes such as total quality management, quick response and total customer development. Rather than being at odds with the aims of those efforts, EVA's quantification of results in financial terms helps to energise them by demanding and getting continuous financial improvement.

3.7.86 With a firm-wide adoption and use of EVA concepts, all employees begin to think, act, and be paid like owners and feel responsible for and take part in the economic value of the firm. Teamwork can be fostered, everyone will care about what goes on and how business progresses on a daily basis.

Managing the implementation of EVA
3.7.87 Making the transition to value added measures is an extensive (and expensive) process. It can require a year or more of planning by internal and external financial and compensation experts. Advocates of value added measures justify the substantial costs by pointing to the benefits of optimising the company's strategy for value creation.

Financial analysis and working capital management

3.7.88 A transition to value added performance measurement must start with a serious commitment of the board of directors and senior executives to use these measures to manage the business. The interests of lower-level managers and the employees they supervise must be cultivated carefully so they buy in.

3.7.89 Success with value added performance measures also requires a massive education and communication effort directed at executives, line managers and hourly employees. Although it will probably require a great deal of training time and money to educate everyone on the basic theory underlying the notion of creating economic value, doing it in a structured, unhurried manner will probably be the most productive way in the long run.

3.7.90 Bennett Stewart outlines five ways that businesses may fall short in implementing EVA.

- They calculate, not inculcate. Estimating a company's EVA is not enough. It has to be a part of every management decision, and it has to be tied to compensation as a way of making it count.
- They try to implement EVA too fast. It has to start with top management and gradually work its way down. The larger the company, the longer it takes to implement.
- EVA should not be expected to apply to every detail of a company, or the cost of administering it may outweigh the benefits.
- EVA may have to be sold to mid-level management, especially if their present compensation works well for them. The best way to sell EVA internally is to tie it to compensation through incentives. If the boss wavers, infighting may well begin as managers battle over turf. They inculcate and forget to calculate. The principle of creating shareholder wealth is important, but many companies become distracted, 1990s style, in endless rounds of discussion about what that means. The bottom line of EVA is that it is good for everyone, and the philosophy will take care of itself.
- Shortcuts in training. To benefit from EVA, it has to be used for all projects – big and small. It is a cultural change. When every member of the company understands that the creation of shareholder wealth is at the top of the pyramid, chances are the company will be too.

Will EVA work in a small service firm such as OSI?

3.7.91 The size and/or the nature of the products provided should not eliminate the use of EVA by a firm; however, a publicly traded stock is probably a bare minimum requirement for valuation purposes. The productive use of EVA will probably revolve around such key characteristics as management's willingness to commit to the 'ideals' of EVA; the acceptance by workers and managers that 'adding shareholder value' is a meaningful enough objective to alter the way they perform their jobs; the accessibility of a set of reliable financial statements; and the availability of historical information on the nature of the firm's significant financial transactions, e.g., footnotes to the financial statements.

Features/benefits of EVA incentive plans

3.7.92 To this point, the emphasis has been on how focusing on EVA may help managers increase shareholder wealth. However, for the metric to help in creating shareholder wealth, managers must behave in a manner consistent with wealth creation. One powerful way to align managers' interests with those of the shareholders is to tie their compensation to output from the EVA metric. In fact, it is not just for managers but may be used for all employees. When implemented correctly, the basic notion of increasing shareholder value will permeate the entire organisation, and employees at all levels will then begin to act in concert with upper levels of management.

3.7.93 Implementing an EVA-based incentive plan is fundamentally a process of empowerment – getting employees to be entrepreneurial, to think and act as owners, to run the business as if they owned it and giving them a stake in the results they achieve.

3.7.94 The overall, firm-wide objective is to generate a persistent increase in EVA. To achieve that, employees must understand the role they play in increasing a firm's EVA. A key factor in sustaining a continuing interest in EVA and in making it work is to revise the compensation system to focus on creating value. It has been shown that one of the critical components in using EVA successfully to improve a company's MVA is tying it to bonuses and pay schemes. Designing an incentive compensation system that pays people for sustainable improvements in EVA, in concert with an understanding of what drives EVA and what drives economic returns, is what transforms behaviour within a company.

3.7.95 A good way to get started quickly is to increase insider ownership of the firm's stock. One way to do this is to turn old profit-sharing plans into employee stock-ownership plans.

3.7.96 If an incentive system is to work, it must have certain distinctive properties.

Financial analysis and working capital management

- An objective measure of performance, one that cannot be manipulated by one of the parties who may benefit. For example, in many existing plans, the budget is a commonly used target for performance – but the manager being evaluated is usually heavily involved in negotiating that budget. If he or she negotiates well, the budget target can be easily beatable.
- It must be simple so even employees far down in the organisation will understand how EVA is tied to economic value, and they can follow it well.
- Bonus amounts have to be large enough for employees to alter their behaviour.
- It must be definitive – which means the target stays fixed and the goal posts will not be moved after the plan gets underway.

3.7.97 Other conditions that are strongly suggested by members of the Stern Stewart organisation, the consulting firm that is the prime mover of EVA, are as follows.

- There should be no limits (caps) placed on the plan. The sky is the limit. Having caps will develop into operating a seasonal business – when the target is reached, slow down.
- Seek sustainable performance by not paying the full bonus amount in one year. This would entail setting up an incentive plan bank account in which the entire bonus is deposited, but some (smaller) portion is paid now and a larger portion is paid later – and the amount to be paid later can be subject to a loss. The objective is to keep EVA positive, and not to achieve that goal only one time. Anyone can do it once.
- Include a cancellation clause. If a person resigns, the banked bonus is lost. But if they retire, the balance is converted into a deferred bonus account.
- For middle and senior people, take a certain amount of each year's cash payment, pay most of it in cash (say, 80 per cent), and the rest in stock options (to get an equity interest). In establishing the ground rules for the plan, the pay-for-performance ratio should be steeply sloped, meaning that a manager's reward is higher on the upside of performance.
- Incorporating a long-term perspective into an incentive plan is another important feature to consider. To get managers to focus on creating real value for the shareholders, a portion of the stock options available to managers can be priced at a premium over the market price on the

Accounting ratios and e-businesses

date of the grant. Thus, managers must first earn the hurdle rate for the shareholders before they can exercise their own options for a gain. Therefore, the manager's financial incentives are aligned with the shareholder's, resulting in the impetus needed to get managers to think aggressively and long term.

- Finally, the structure of the incentive system should be team based, to focus more on individual or small work group results and still capture a larger, longer-term perspective based on the company's performance. The proper weighting of these elements can provide different motivation to different people, depending on their ability to influence the item being measured.

Understanding the EVA and MVA results for OSI

3.7.98 The relationship between EVA and MVA is significant in evaluating the performance of a firm. EVA is indicative of a firm's actual performance during a specific year, while expected performance (by the stock market) is represented in its MVA value, which is a cumulative measure of performance over a number of years.

3.7.99 When a firm's EVA is improving but its MVA is dropping, the market might be sending a signal that should not be ignored. Investors will seek to determine the factors that are driving that situation and, if not satisfied with the answers, they may adjust their expectations and bid less for the firm's stock, leading to further reductions in the firm's MVA. If EVA is stable or declining and MVA is increasing, then the market is reporting that it holds greater future expectations than indicated in the current results.

3.7.100 The picture presented for OSI in the case is that it is a small, fairly young, growing firm that does quality work. It is in an emerging industry segment that is felt to have very promising potential for large future financial returns. However, OSI is currently very heavily burdened with its development, primarily through the acquisition of another firm, and it is struggling with the creation and roll-out of an important new product. OSI appears to have a very promising future; however, in light of its financial performance in recent years it does not appear that the market has valued OSI's future promise as very good (as evidenced by the negative MVA). The key to the fulfilment of its future promise is in the development of PayNet, a new payroll processing system, which is expected to be the future backbone of OSI's service bureau payroll processing operations.

3.7.101 This situation appears to be reflected in OSI's EVA and MVA amounts in 1995. EVA is slightly positive (in the $25,000 to $35,000 range),

Financial analysis and working capital management

and the MVA is negative in six figures (about $400,000), OSI's development and programming costs for PayNet have turned out to be higher than anticipated, and the rollout of the beta version was delayed from the second to the third quarter of 1996. Since OSI appears to be managing its operations satisfactorily, its results offer a small hint of some future promise. However, investors will undoubtedly wait for more convincing evidence of the company's future potential before paying higher prices for OSI stock. Until then, OSI's MVA will probably continue to be negative.

(Source: adapted with permission from Bremser and Dierks, 1998.)

Chapter 4
Investment appraisal in modern enterprises

4.1 Introduction

4.1.1 Enterprises in the manufacturing and services sectors are increasingly facing opportunities to invest in projects requiring large capital resources. This is especially so in sectors that require the deployment of expensive flexible production systems, computerised technologies and sophisticated information systems. A number of traditional 'bricks and mortar' companies are also making inroads into the implementation of Internet-based technologies. As a consequence, many enterprises appeal more heavily to formal investment appraisal mechanisms. Some decision-makers are moving away from accounting return calculations to techniques which take account of the time value of money. Many organisations consider strategic issues in evaluating capital investment decisions.

4.2 The case for discounting cash flows

4.2.1 The instructional literature in financial management and accounting techniques for decision-making has long extolled the virtues of discounting cash flows when evaluating long-term investment projects. The recognition that money has a time value and that, under normal circumstances, future monetary values are worth less than equivalent present ones, has been the guiding principle driving sophisticated investment evaluations. Moreover, in recognition that accounting returns reflect the application of accounting rules over yearly periods, the attention in investment appraisal has been put on the accrual of cash flows to a business over a longer term. In spite of these common sense principles, many executives, consultants, academics and professional accountancy bodies consider that sophistication in discounting cash flows is not sufficient. What is critical is whether the application of discounted cash flow techniques actually captures the broader logic of considering an investment opportunity in the first place. Questions have been asked about whether penalising distant returns on a time value scale in fact also militates against evaluating strategic pay-offs. A net present value (NPV) calculation or an internal rate of return (IRR) value for an investment decision can be applied correctly in theoretical terms, but may leave out the

Investment appraisal in modern enterprises

substance of the project's implication for the firm as a whole. The contemporary view is that for large, longer-term investment options:

- a variety of technical approaches should be used, including simple methods such as return on investment (ROI) and payback time alongside IRR and NPV calculations;
- intangibles can and ought to be evaluated;
- strategic assessment ought to be an essential part of any analysis.

4.2.2 This is particularly true of projects entailing a change in business processes such as investing in sophisticated information technology (IT) or in flexible production technologies.

4.3 From counting to discounting

Return on investment and the accounting rate of return

4.3.1 Return on investment (ROI) has long been an important measure for appraising the performance of individuals, business units or specific projects. ROI is quite straightforward to use but can encompass the effects of a wide array of factors. In considering the use of ROI to appraise capital investments in advanced manufacturing technology, a joint initiative by the Chartered Institute of Management Accountants (CIMA) and the Institute of Professional Engineers (IPE) identified three important factors: cost savings, working capital reductions and market factors.

4.3.2 The accounting rate of return (ARR) seeks to equate the financial data of a capital project with the accrual concept of conventional accounting. It is an attempt to measure the profit and the capital on the same basis as that adopted in preparing the financial accounts of an organisation.

4.3.3 The ARR approach expresses the average return on the investment as a percentage of that investment. As Lefley and Sarkis (1997) explain, the figure for investment may be either the initial cost of the capital project (initial capital method, or return on original investment), or it may be based on the assumption that the cost of the project will reduce to zero or a predetermined residual/scrap value over the life of the project by way of depreciation, and may thus be represented as one half of the capital cost (average capital method, or return on average investment).

4.3.4 In using the initial capital method, the investment figure should be netted after deducting the projected residual/scrap value of the capital asset at the end of the project's life. With regard to the average capital method, the

From counting to discounting

residual/scrap value should be added to the initial cost of the project and, as suggested above, an average figure should be calculated. Whilst this approach is conceptually sound, its effect is to alter the investment figure.

4.3.5 Income can be expressed before or after interest charges and/or tax. There is some preference for the before interest charges and tax figure whilst taking into account depreciation. Some companies treat certain costs that are in effect part of the investment as revenue expenditure. Naturally, this reduces the income generated by the investment and distorts the returns projections.

4.3.6 An investment decision could result in a number of cost benefits. The cost advantage could arise through increases in efficiency and productivity and reductions in staffing levels. Benefits could also accrue from reduced stock. The reduction in the requirement for funds for working capital can reduce the requirement for funds for fixed asset investment. Reductions in stock may also lead to further cost savings, through less space usage and lower indirect labour needs. Profit can be improved by lowering unit costs, or by lowering overheads of all types, but where this is insufficient to improve the ROI to acceptable levels, the capital used will also need to be reduced.

4.3.7 An important consideration is the market impact of new technology investments through the enhanced ability to satisfy customer requirements and achieve higher sales. Production can become influenced by a variety of market factors rather than simply the cost economies of scale, and this will affect the competitive strategy of the firm.

4.3.8 The ROI calculation is easy to perform and managers readily identify with it when comparing investment projects. Where several alternative capital investment proposals are being considered, the proposals can be ranked by their average rates of return. The higher the average rate of return, the more desirable the proposal. For example, assume that management is considering the following alternative capital investment proposals and has computed the indicated average rates of return:

	Proposal A	**Proposal B**
Estimated average annual income	£50,000	£6,710
Average investment	£200,000	£33,500
Average rate of return:		
£50,000/£200,000	25%	
£6,710/£33,500		20%

117

Investment appraisal in modern enterprises

4.3.9 If only the average rate of return is considered, Proposal A would be preferred over Proposal B, based on its average rate of return of 25 per cent.

4.3.10 The primary advantages of the average rate of return method are its ease of computation and the fact that it emphasises the amount of income earned over the entire life of the proposal. Its main disadvantages are its lack of consideration of the expected cash flows from the proposal and the timing of these cash flows. Money has a time value and cash flows are important because cash coming from an investment can be reinvested in other income-producing activities. Therefore, the greater the funds and the sooner they become available, the more income that can be generated from their reinvestment. The definitions of profit and investment are of course subject to arbitrary rules which limit the significance of ROI values. ROI as a performance monitor also suffers from not directly addressing risk or residual values.

4.3.11 The ARR according to Lefley and Sarkis (1997) may be appropriate for the evaluation and comparison of projects which have a similar life span and an even flow of annual profits but, as this is rarely the case, it is problematic as a return measure for the majority of projects. ARR does not fully account for the fact that profits fluctuate from year to year. Moreover, as a measure, it ignores the time value of the flow of funds, and is unsuitable for comparing projects with different life spans. The ARR is simplistic in that it assumes a level of certainty which is not always realistic. It is nevertheless widely used given its ease of calculation and ready comprehensibility. Its reliance on accrual accounting measures mirrors the manner in which managers are often appraised and rewarded. In the same way as almost any measure of performance, ARR can be manipulated given its accrual-based accounting underpinnings.

4.3.12 The accounting rate of return does attempt to assess the profitability of a project. To this extent, it goes beyond the payback approach. It is perfectly possible to modify the standard formula for the calculation of the ARR to include some calculations of the sinking fund approach to account for depreciation, and recognise that retained depreciation funds can earn interest.

4.3.13 Overall though, Lefley and Sarkis believe that the ARR is simplistic and may give incorrect information to managers appraising an investment capital project.

Payback

4.3.14 Many managers like to get a sense not only for the return on investment but also for the return of the investment. One way of approximating the time for an investment to pay for itself is the payback period calculation. For instance, assume that the proposed investment in a plant asset with an eight-year life is £200,000 and that the annual net cash flow is expected to be £40,000. The estimated cash payback period for the investment is five years, computed as:

$$£200,000/£40,000 = 5\text{-year cash payback period}$$

4.3.15 In this example, all the annual net cash flows are assumed to be £40,000 per year. If these annual net cash flows are not equal, the cash payback period is determined by summing the annual net cash flows until the cumulative sum equals the amount of the proposed investment.

4.3.16 The cash payback method is widely used in evaluating proposals for expansion and for investment in new projects. A relatively short payback period is desirable because the sooner the cash is recovered, the sooner it becomes available for reinvestment in other projects. In addition, there is likely to be less possibility of loss from changes in economic conditions, obsolescence and other unavoidable risks when the commitment is short-term. Thus, the cash payback method would be particularly useful to managers whose primary concern is liquidity.

4.3.17 One of the primary disadvantages of the cash payback method as a basis for decisions is its failure to take into consideration the expected profitability of a proposal. A project with a very short payback period coupled with poor profitability would be more desirable under the payback model than one with a longer payback period but with satisfactory profitability. Another disadvantage of the cash payback method is that the cash flows occurring after the payback period are ignored. The major shortfall of the payback method is that it overlooks the time value of money. It has been severely criticised as being at the heart of some of the worst 'short-termist' attitudes in UK industry.

Net present value

4.3.18 The notion of present values is underpinned by a concern that any specified amount of cash to be received at some date in the future is not equivalent to the same amount of cash held at an earlier date. An amount of cash to be received in the future is not as valuable as the same sum in hand today because cash in hand today can be invested to earn income. For example, £100 today would be more valuable than £100 to be received a year from today since, if cash can be invested to earn 10 per cent per year, the £100 today will accumulate to £110 one year from today. The

Investment appraisal in modern enterprises

£100 today can be referred to as the present value amount that is equivalent to £110 to be received a year from today. The NPV method uses present value concepts to compute the present value of the cash flows expected from a proposal. To illustrate, if the cost of capital or the imposed required return for a project type is 12 per cent and the cash to be received in one year is £1,000, the present value amount is £892.86 (£1,000/1.12). If the cash is to be received two years later with the required rate compounded at the end of the first year, the present value amount would be £797.20 (£892.86/1.12).

4.3.19 The rate used is the opportunity cost of capital – that is, the rate the company could earn by the investing of funds in an alternative project of equivalent risk. If the present value of the net cash flow expected from a proposed investment at the selected rate equals or exceeds the amount of the investment, then the proposal is desirable.

An example
4.3.20 Assume a proposal for the acquisition of £200,000 of equipment with an expected useful life of five years and a minimum desired annual rate of return of 10 per cent. The anticipated net cash flow for each of the five years and the analysis of the proposal are shown in Table 4.1. The calculation shows that the proposal is expected to recover the investment and provide more than the minimum rate of return.

Table 4.1 Anticipated net cash flow

Year	Present value of 1 at 10%	Net cash flow (£)	Present value of net cash flow (£)
1	0.909	70,000	63,630
2	0.826	60,000	49,560
3	0.751	50,000	37,550
4	0.683	40,000	27,320
5	0.621	40,000	24,840
Total		260,000	202,900
Amount to be invested			200,000
Excess of present value of amount to be invested		2,900	

4.3.21 When several alternative investment proposals of the same amount are being considered, the one with the largest excess of present value over the amount to be invested is the most desirable. If the alternative proposals involve different amounts of investment, it is useful to prepare a relative ranking of the proposals by using a present value index. The present value index for the previous example is computed by dividing the total present value of the net cash flow by the amount to be invested, as follows:

Present value index = Total present value of net cash flow/Amount to be invested
= $202,900/$200,000 = 1.01

4.3.22 The primary advantage of the discounted cash flow (DCF) method is that it gives consideration to the time value of money. A disadvantage is that the computations are more complex than those for the methods that ignore present value. In addition, this method assumes that the cash received from the proposal during its useful life will be reinvested at the rate of return used to compute the present value of the proposal. As a result of changing economic conditions, this assumption may not always be reasonable. However, expectation as to rate of return fluctuations can readily be incorporated into the NPV calculations.

Internal rate of return

4.3.23 An alternative discounted cash flow method to the net present value model is the internal rate of return (IRR) approach which uses present value concepts to compute the rate of return from the net cash flows expected from capital investment proposals. The IRR method starts with the net cash flows and works backwards to determine the discounted rate of return expected from the proposal. This discounted cash flow method requires a minimum rate of return to be specified. The minimum hurdle rate determines the excess (shortfall) of the present value of the net cash flow over the investment.

An example
4.3.24 Assume that management is evaluating a proposal to acquire equipment costing $33,530, which is expected to provide annual net cash flows of $10,000 per year for five years. If an annual rate of return of 12 per cent is assumed, the present value of the net cash flows can be computed using present values shown in Table 4.2.

Table 4.2 The present value of a stream of cash flows

Year	Present value of $1 at 12%	Net cash flow ($)	Present value of net cash flow ($)
1	0.893	10,000	8,930
2	0.797	10,000	7,970
3	0.712	10,000	7,120
4	0.636	10,000	6,360
5	0.567	10,000	5,670
		50,000	36,050

Investment appraisal in modern enterprises

4.3.25 Since the present value of the net cash flow based on a 12 per cent rate of return (£36,050) is greater than the £33,530 to be invested, 12 per cent cannot be the discounted internal rate of return. In fact, 15 per cent is the rate of return that equates the £33,530 cost of the investment with the present value of the net cash flows (see Table 4.3).

Table 4.3 The present value of net cash flows

Year	Present value of £1 at 12%	Net cash flow (£)	Present value of net cash flow (£)
1	0.870	10,000	8,700
2	0.756	10,000	7,560
3	0.658	10,000	6,580
4	0.572	10,000	5,720
5	0.497	10,000	4,970
Total		50,000	33,530

4.3.26 The primary advantage of the IRR method over payback and ROI is that the present values of the net cash flows over the entire useful life of the proposal are considered. An additional advantage of the method is that by determining a rate of return for each proposal, all proposals are automatically placed on a common basis for comparison without the need to compute a present value index, as was the case for the DCF method. One significant disadvantage of the IRR method is that the computations are slightly more involved than for the other methods. In addition, this method assumes that the cash received from a proposal during its useful life will be reinvested at the discounted internal rate of return. This assumption rarely holds.

4.3.27 Certain items may affect a capital budgeting decision and need to be properly accounted for:

Item	Action
Capital outlay	This must be the net cost of the acquisition (land, equipment, building, etc.).
Tax	All profit returns from the investment must be stated in after tax cash flow terms.
Interest rate	The discount rate used in any DCF calculations reflects the after tax cost of capital.
Risk	The discount rate may be adjusted upwards in line with perceived riskiness of projects.
Inflation	Future cash flows should be stated in real net of inflation terms.
Residual value	If the acquired asset can be sold at the end of the project, this will decrease the net initial capital outlay by the present value of the expected residual value.

Investment life	This should reflect the estimated time period over which the investment will have cash flow consequences.
Discount rate	This is the rate for discounting cash flows reflecting cost of capital, risk and inflation.
Opportunity cost	This is an economic concept indicative of the 'next best thing' – adjustment is subsumed in the chosen discount rate.
Hurdle rate	The desired return which must at least be matched by a project's IRR.

4.3.28 It is not always the case that an enterprise will choose to discount cash flows in appraising an investment. One telecommunications and electronic products company with a turnover of £65 million and a staff of 1,500 made major investments in people affiliated with new product development, but their investment in manufacturing technology was low. Recently, several new products had entered the market and several more were to follow. These were pagers, portable radios, mobile cellular radios and base stations. Many different end products were made to customer order but a considerable degree of component commonality had been achieved.

4.3.29 The company intended to move towards totally integrated computer manufacture in a number of stages, starting with flow-line assembly moving into flexible automated assembly for one of the projects, to be gradually extended into other products at a later stage. The benefits targeted were as follows:

- 96 per cent reduction in lead time and work in progress;
- 80 per cent reduction in rework;
- 20 per cent reduction in space;
- 40 per cent reduction in standard content;
- shop window facility with transfer of manufacturing technology to other product ranges;
- fast introduction of design modifications down to shop floor;
- flexible facility configuration providing invaluable feedback for design for manufacture.

4.3.30 In effect, this medium-sized company aimed at moving its operations towards computer-integrated manufacture in a number of steps: the installation of a flexible assembly system (FAS) for a range of new products resulting in reductions in lead time, inventory, rework, space and standard costs. The project was to serve as a 'shop window' of excellence. Flexibility

Investment appraisal in modern enterprises

and speed of introduction of new products were also important and the 'just-in-time' approach was used as a first step in the investment. As an organisational change with relatively low investment, this first step showed considerably better financial results than the full FAS installation. Justification was based on ROI methods with the analysis set out in Table 4.4.

Table 4.4 Analysis

	Year					Capital expenditure £000	Simple rate of return	
							Total on 5 year %	Rate per year %
Methods	1	2	3	4	5			
Current methods to flowline	(98)	672	1,092	1,512	1,932	557	347	69
Flowline to flexible manufacturing system	(554)	(1,376)	(772)	(561)	(350)	1,707	(20.5)	(4.1)
Combined project	(652)	(704)	320	951	1,582	2,264	67	13.4

4.3.31 Such an approach which does not discount cash flows may be deemed as quite acceptable. Some enterprises believe that the use of a variety of techniques is more appropriate. One company in the sheet metal buildings products industry used a variety of investment appraisal techniques including simple payback, return on assets, internal rate of return, cash flow and sensitivity analysis. The company, an autonomous part of a large group, was faced with a 10–15 per cent growth in sales, and with a greatly increasing variety of styles, shapes and sizes of product which were more costly to make on the traditional equipment used to prepare components. Assembly was also becoming difficult as manual methods were used for all except one size and style of product, for which a dedicated and automated welder was used but for which demand was decreasing.

4.3.32 Two alternative advanced manufacturing technology proposals were planned and evaluated. The first used a cell approach with semi-automated and unlinked equipment and a reduced labour force. The alternative was a fully integrated flexible manufacturing and assembly system, with robotic welding, minimal manual intervention and automated guided vehicle linkages. The target benefits were: reductions in labour and space costs and in the level of stocks and work in progress. In effect, the company was considering:

(1) a fully flexible and integrated manufacturing system using computer-controlled rolls, presses, assembly robots and automated guided vehicles;

From counting to discounting

(2) a lower cost, cell approach using semi-automated and unlinked equipment.

4.3.33 The financial analysis produced the figures set out in Table 4.5. These figures provide more aspects for consideration in reaching the investment decision.

4.3.34 DCF techniques and payback and ROI calculations can only be considered inputs to decisions which will reflect other factors. Typically, one looks for a positive NPV or an IRR which exceeds the hurdle rate. Where quick recovery of initial outlay is important, payback becomes relevant. If liquidity is likely to be a problem at known future stages, positive cash flows at those times will likely be very important and absolute NPV or IRR values may become secondary.

Table 4.5 Financial analysis

Financial results	Fully integrated flexible manufacturing system	Lower-cost alternative (cells)
Cash flow	Positive from year 3	Positive from year 3
Average return on assets	46.71%	53.66%
Internal rate of return (IRR)	25.91%	20.31%
Payback	5.68 years	6.75 years

4.3.35 Booth (1999) identifies some common errors with the use of DCF techniques. He suggests that the scope for error is wide-ranging in terms of the forecasting of cash flows and the selection of the discount rate. In assessing the cash flows, the aim is to achieve expected values. This in turn entails considering different possibilities alongside a set of probabilities. In deciding on the cost of capital, one can under- or over-compensate for risk or inflation.

4.3.36 But Booth suggests that DCF techniques can contribute positively to investment analyses, if performed effectively. Nevertheless, it is worthwhile to consider the appraisal based on real options financial theory.

Real options-based capital budgeting

4.3.37 Seeing investments as real options in the financial sense enables managers to better consider the implications of waiting prior to engaging or continuing with a phase of the investment project. In addition, the possibility of one project leading to other investment options is sometimes an issue.

Real options methodology allows such scenarios to be formally evaluated. What is of essence is that waiting is often a valuable option because risk becomes increasingly resolved, thereby giving managers a better grasp of the trade-offs between acting immediately or waiting for more information.

4.3.38 Peskett (1999) notes that the flexibility provided by real options in investments appears in many guises. Busby and Pitts (1998) have identified the following:

- Timing: options to embark on an investment, to defer it or to abandon it;
- Scale: options to expand or to contract an investment;
- Staging: the option to undertake an investment in stages;
- Growth: options to make investments now that may lead to greater opportunities later;
- Switching: options to switch inputs or outputs in a production process.

4.3.39 Conventional DCF analysis mainly considers whether a project adds value for shareholders. Normally, managers tend not to consider net present values of projects on their own. Investing in a particular project can of course lead to other investment possibilities that DCF analysis may not capture. If a choice is made between projects based only on NPV, a manager may be ignoring options to undertake 'follow-on-investments' that have a value to the business.

4.3.40 Peskett explains that planning a project so that it can be implemented in phases over a time period increases costs, and economies of scale may be less achievable unless the project is phased. As each phase is completed, there exists an option of going no further (the 'staging option'). The added costs of phasing the project plus any foregone economies are akin to the 'premium' paid for a financial or commodity option. One should thus choose to phase a project if the benefit of having the option to discontinue at later stages exceeds this premium.

4.3.41 Peskett also explains that the option to 'wait and see' in the anticipation of gaining further information prior to making a decision is common in investment decisions. But this timing option does not provide the manager with a justification for continued procrastination, since once uncertainty resolves the manager may perceive an acceptable signal to proceed.

Strategic investment appraisal

4.3.42 There is often a time period over which a project can be postponed, corresponding to the time over which the option to invest can be exercised. Even if DCF analysis indicates a positive NPV, there may be a value in delaying before starting on a project to allow time for new information to emerge. Against the value of waiting is the need to consider any cash inflows foregone during the period of the postponement. Likewise, once a project has begun, having the option to abandon it can be of value if the benefits of the project are still highly uncertain.

4.4 Strategic investment appraisal

4.4.1 Factors of strategic relevance cannot be forced into a traditional investment justification exercise. There are now novel approaches to investment justification that attempt to formally extend the methodology for directly assessing strategic issues (Cooper, 1992).

4.4.2 A strategically informed investment justification process can be examined as four interrelated phases: positioning, appraisal, selection and benefits tracking.

Phase one: positioning

4.4.3 Initially, this phase involves defining the relevant investment opportunities and then comparing these opportunities with the strategic objectives of the company. This seeks to ensure that at a high level there is a strategic fit between the investment opportunity and the strategy of the company. The next section identifies the 'principal options' that represent a number of discrete subprojects within the investment opportunity, which either partially or wholly achieve the objectives of the investment opportunity. Finally, an appraisal framework is defined which will form the basis for the appraisal of the principal options. The framework includes a set of 'metrics', which are financial and strategic measures against which the principal options will be appraised.

Phase two: appraisal

4.4.4 In Phase two an evaluation is made of each principal option's costs and benefits (both financial and strategic) against the metrics identified. The main outputs from this phase are a financial and qualitative analysis of each principal option's contribution towards the relevant financial and strategic objectives of the business.

Phase three: selection

4.4.5 In this phase, each principal option is compared with the other principal options in order to rank and select the most appropriate principal option(s). Once this decision has been made, a business case is prepared to justify the principal option(s) selected.

Phase four: benefits tracking

4.4.6 The final phase provides a review process in order to ensure that costs and benefits are delivered to plan. In addition, feedback will be provided to the positioning, appraisal and selection phases in the light of any lessons learned, to ensure that future appraisals take account of previous experience. Nonetheless, each of the phases is discussed in more depth below.

Phase one: positioning the project

4.4.7 The identification of an investment opportunity needs to be clearly defined. The use of a specialised form is desirable at this stage.

4.4.8 In pursuing strategic fit it is essential to consider:

- the corporate strategy;
- the corporate business plan;
- departmental objectives and plans.

4.4.9 The next step is to select principal options. A principal option is defined as a discrete investment that either partially or wholly achieves the investment opportunity identified. For example, the investment opportunity to enhance the financial systems can be broken down into a number of discrete principal options, which may include developing automatic matching facilities and adding real-time data validation capabilities. Each principal option should be sufficiently distinct from other principal options to make its appraisal worthwhile and should not be dependent on the completion of other principal options. Where a dependency exists, the two options should be combined. The principal options should include:

- carrying out the whole investment opportunity as defined (e.g., carrying out all the enhancements to the financial systems);
- carrying out certain specific parts of the investment opportunity (e.g., developing automatic matching facilities but not providing real-time data validation capabilities);

Strategic investment appraisal

- delaying investment in the investment opportunity or specific part, for a certain period of time (e.g., developing automatic matching facilities in one year's time);

- maintaining the current situation, a 'do nothing' option, which will be used as the basis for determining the incremental costs/benefits of the other options. Figure 4.1 gives an example of a principal option definition form.

Figure 4.1 Principal option definition form

Principal option 1	Developing automatic matching facilities
Description	To provide a facility where invoices will be automatically matched to purchase orders
Objectives	A reduction in the cost of manually matching orders
	Improved accuracy in adherence to payment deadlines
Principal option 2	**Real-time data validation**
Description	To move to real time rather than batch update of the system
Objectives	Reduction in time to answer queries
	Substantial reduction in risk of incorrect data being used
	Substantial improvement in data accuracy

4.4.10 Finally, the appraisal framework aims to provide a rigorous assessment of both the financial and strategic benefits of the principal options. This will involve the project team in establishing a set of metrics against which each principal option will be appraised.

4.4.11 A metric is defined as an appraisal measure that is used to determine the relative performance of a principal option towards a financial or strategic objective. Metrics can be financial, for example net present value providing the objective of increased shareholder value, or strategic, for example the level of data security providing the strategic objective of ensuring data security.

4.4.12 However, before this task is undertaken a number of basic assumptions, which will be required in order to perform the appraisal, must be established:

- the life of each principal option (time horizon) over which costs and benefits will occur. For example, the financial systems investment is estimated to have a life of three years before replacement is necessary;

- the discount rate to be used;

- the inflation rate to be used.

Investment appraisal in modern enterprises

4.4.13 The following financial metrics can be used to evaluate the principal options:

- net present value;
- internal rate of return;
- payback;
- present value index.

4.4.14 The strategic appraisal is carried out by defining a framework of strategic subgoals as metrics. The strategic metrics should be identified by a workshop with key operational personnel. Examples of metrics relevant to the financial systems example may include:

- metrics – information and technology
    - quality of systems (ease of change, levels of documentation, robustness of software);
    - security of data;
    - compatibility with existing hardware and operation environment;
    - compatibility with future requirements (growth path, need for total rewrite);
    - impact on implementation of single supplier strategy.
- metrics – organisations/resources
    - compatibility with existing development skills;
    - motivation of users (impact on flexibility, control of own jobs, job interest);
    - impact on IT development staff and structure;
    - efficiency of use of key IT and business knowledge and skills (expert systems).
- metrics – commercial
    - timeliness of development (availability in advance of need);
    - quality of information, and its presentation, for making strategic and tactical decisions;
    - staff productivity;
    - auditability of commercial activities;
    - privacy of commercially sensitive data;
    - quality of service to customers and other group companies;
    - power in negotiations with customers and other group companies;
    - adaptability to changing circumstances;
    - freeing up of skilled staff by removing clerical effort.

Strategic investment appraisal

- metrics – finance
    - net present value of discounted cash flows;
    - impact on P&L account;
    - discounted payback period;
    - profitability index.

4.4.15 Finally, the appraisal framework can be defined.

Phase two: performing the appraisal

4.4.16 The objective of this phase is to identify and appraise all costs and benefits associated with each principal option under consideration and then to present the results in a way that facilitates the selection phase. The main objectives and outputs from each of the above sections are shown in Table 4.6.

Table 4.6 Main objectives and outputs of the appraisal phase

Objective	Outputs
To provide a framework for cost/benefit identification	By principal option, the activities affected by the investment
To identify all types of costs and benefits associated with each principal option	Costs and benefits of each principal option
To identify all intangible costs and benefits and wherever possible quantify them	Additional tangible costs and benefits together with metric statements of intangible items
To assess the potential for underachieving the predicted costs and benefits	Risk score for each metric by principal option Assessment of the level of risk for each principal option
To summarise the information in a way which facilitates the decision process	Cost/benefit analysis

4.4.17 An activity framework is a representation of what the people within the company do. The development of a high-level activity framework will assist in the identification of costs and benefits by providing a better understanding of the impact of the principal options on the activities of the company.

4.4.18 An activity view is significantly different from the traditional view. An activity view enables managers to see not just costs by expense category, but also what people actually do and the associated costs. It is this clear

Investment appraisal in modern enterprises

understanding of the activities performed that enables the project team to assess the impact of each principal option on the activities of the company, together with its resulting cost or benefit. In addition, an activity framework is particularly useful for the identification of costs and benefits because:

- it will measure costs and benefits across traditional organisational barriers;
- it provides a coherent basis for identifying and evaluating all costs and benefits ensuring full inclusion;
- both strategic and investment planning set goals and objectives on a business-wide basis rather than on a vertical organisation basis. An activity framework provides a business-wide view of an organisation.

4.4.19 In this section, the activities affected by each principal option are used as the basis for determining the benefits of each principal option. In addition, all costs – both one-off and ongoing – associated with each principal option are identified and quantified. This information will provide the input to a cost/benefit analysis enabling the project team to assess the relative performance of each principal option. To ensure that, wherever possible, financial values are attributed to costs and benefits, providing a tangible measure, the 'types' of financial cost and benefit set out in Table 4.7 are recognised.

Table 4.7 Types of financial cost and benefit

Type	Description	Example
Tangible	Direct and potentially measurable effect on profit	Reduction in staff
Opportunity cost	Value of resource released to perform other tasks	Time freed up from routine clerical work to perform more valuable tasks
Value	Estimated value, based on a subjective assessment of the investment's benefits	Value of investment as a platform for other projects

4.4.20 However, despite recognising the above 'types' of financial cost and benefit, certain costs and benefits may remain non-quantifiable and are termed intangible costs and benefits. These intangible costs and benefits are, however, often significant to the principal option and cannot be ignored. At this stage they should be recorded; methods for their evaluation are explained in the next section.

4.4.21 Performing sensitivity/risk analysis is essential at this stage. This section aims to assess the risk associated with each principal option by ref-

Strategic investment appraisal

erence to the option's sensitivity to changes in this base assumption. It attempts to quantify the relative risk associated with each principal option to enable the project team to include an assessment of each principal option's associated risk in their decision.

4.4.22 For each principal option, the project team should identify a worst case scenario and calculate a new set of metric scores, in order to evaluate the level of risk. For financial metrics, the worst case scenario should reflect the lowest level of tangible costs and benefits that could be delivered by the principal option. For strategic metrics, the worst case scenario should represent the strategic scores that the project team consider are the lowest possible after the implementation of the principal option. (The risk score is defined as the difference between the expected scenario value and the worst case scenario value.) A metrics performance quadrant can be plotted at this stage to give a quick visual impression of each principal option on the metrics defined.

4.4.23 The company is now in a position to bring together all the work performed to date in a cost/benefit analysis. This provides the major input to the selection phase by comparing each principal option identified in terms of its financial and strategic impact on the business.

Phase three: selecting the preferred principal option

4.4.24 The purpose of Phase three is to ensure that the best principal option(s) is/are selected from a strategic and financial perspective. The main objectives and outputs of this phase are shown in Table 4.8.

Table 4.8 Main objectives and outputs of the selection phase

Objectives	Outputs
To highlight and interpret the difference between the principal options	Detailed comparison of principal options
Identify optimal principal option(s)	A ranked list of principal options for investment
To present the findings and recommendations to management	Business case

4.4.25 The business case gives a summary of the work performed in order to arrive at the principal option(s) selected. The objective of the business case is to provide a single document that summarises the strategic background to the project, defines the principal options for appraisal, the framework used to appraise these principal options and, finally, provides the results and recommendations of the project team.

Investment appraisal in modern enterprises

Phase four: benefits tracking

4.4.26 The objective of Phase four is to ensure that the future net benefits from the principal options selected are maximised and realised. The main objectives and outputs of this phase are shown in Table 4.9.

Table 4.9 Main objectives and outputs of the benefits tracking phase

Objectives	Outputs
To provide information to assess the success of the investment in terms of costs and benefits delivery to date and forecast	Cost and benefit report
To evaluate the delivery of target net benefits	Investment performance report Variance analysis Assessment of suitability of appraisal process Feedback to planning process
To ensure that the future outstanding net benefits are delivered	Detailed action plan including revised targets for next period with identified responsibilities

4.4.27 For smaller investments, this phase is not always essential. Ultimately, what is desired is a basis for making a judgement on an investment decision which is supported by a financially viable methodology which factors in the broader strategic issues facing the enterprise. In using scores to rank investments which include intangible costs and benefits, a strategic planning matrix (see Bromwich and Bhimani, 1991; 1994) may be used.

A case study: capital budgeting in action

4.4.28 Chow, Hwang and Togo (1995) illustrate a capital budgeting case that addresses strategic considerations (adapted with permission). ACE Company is a technology and market leader in the portable electronic games industry. The company is currently enjoying great success with its Model X, which has been on the market for several years. ACE's management believes that as a result of increased competition from other types of entertainment, the demand for Model X will dry up after three more years. The company has forecast Model X's net cash inflows in the next three years to be $400 million, $300 million and $200 million, respectively.

4.4.29 ACE's senior managers are considering the development and introduction of a replacement for Model X, to be called Model Z. According to the engineers, ACE already possesses the technical expertise to develop Model Z. However, the earliest that this product can be introduced into the market is one year from now, as it will take this long to develop and test the

Strategic investment appraisal

new product, co-ordinate with suppliers for parts, set up the production process, and arrange for other related logistic activities. The total cost of these development activities is estimated at £550 million.

4.4.30 All of ACE's top managers agree that Model Z's market potential in terms of net cash inflow would be £200 million in year 2, £400 million in year 3, £300 million in year 4, and £100 million in year 5. They also agree that Model Z would maintain ACE's leadership position in the portable electronic games industry.

4.4.31 Management expects that in addition to developing its own customer base, Model Z also would draw some sales away from Model X. The expected amount of this 'cannibalisation' is £100 million of net cash inflows per year. The following table summarises ACE's prediction of net cash flows (in millions) for the next five years for Model X by itself and with the introduction of Model Z at the end of year 1. Cash outflows occur at the beginning of the year while cash inflows occur at year end. Thus the £550 million development cost in year 1 occurs at the end of that year. The table below shows that net cash inflows of £100 million per year are shifted from Model X to Model Z in years 2 and 3.

Year	Model X only	Introduction of Model Z after one year					
		Model X	+	Model Z	=	Total	
0	£0	£0	+	£(550)	=	£(550)	
1	400	400	+	0	=	400	
2	300	200*	+	300*	=	500	
3	200	100*	+	500*	=	600	
4	0	0	+	300	=	300	
5	0	0	+	100	=	100	

* Reflects £100 cannibalisation of Model X by Model Z

4.4.32 Several members of top management are concerned about Model Z's erosion of Model X sales. They propose that it would be better to spread the development of Model Z over two years and to introduce it at the beginning of year 3 instead of year 2. They suggest that this plan has two major advantages:

(1) it would avoid the £100 million erosion in Model X's net cash inflows in year 2; and

(2) the engineers have projected that extending the time for the development process will yield substantial savings due to efficiencies in scheduling. They have estimated that the two-year plan would reduce Model Z's total development cost to £300 million. Half of this total would be spent in each of the two years.

Investment appraisal in modern enterprises

4.4.33 The table below summarises the estimated net cash flows (in millions) for the two-year plan. Compared to the one-year plan, Model X's year 2 net cash inflow is higher by $100 million. This is due to avoiding cannibalisation by Model Z in year 2.

Year	Model X only	Introduction of Model Z after one year				
		Model X	+	Model Z	=	Total
0	$0	$0	+	$(150)	=	$(150)
1	400	400	+	(150)	=	250
2	300	300	+	0	=	300
3	200	100*	+	500*	=	600
4	0	0	+	300	=	300
5	0	0	+	100	=	100

*Reflects $100 cannibalisation of Model X by Model Z

4.4.34 Proponents of the two-year plan acknowledge that delaying Model Z's introduction by one year would require foregoing its year 2 $300 million net cash inflow. But they emphasise that this sacrifice is more than made up by the additional $100 million cash inflow from Model X in year 2 and the $250 million savings in Model Z development costs.

4.4.35 Supporters of the one-year plan argue that proponents of the two-year plan have overlooked a major factor: that the timing of Model Z's introduction could have an impact on competitors' actions. They maintain that if ACE does not introduce Model Z as quickly as possible, ACE's major competitor would most certainly come in with a comparable product. In response to a query from these managers, ACE's engineers have conducted a study of the competitor's current capabilities. They have reported that due to the competitor's less sophisticated technologies, it will require two years to develop a comparable product for market introduction.

4.4.36 The nature of the industry is such that there is a significant first-mover advantage. Similar products that reach the market at the same time tend to get equal shares of the market. But once a product is introduced, it tends to get so entrenched that comparable products introduced subsequently can gain only inconsequential market shares.

4.4.37 Table 4.10 shows the NPV computations for the status quo as well as the one-year and two-year plans. Both Model Z introduction plans have substantially higher NPVs than the status quo. The two-year plan's NPV exceeds that of the one-year plan by $98.355 million ($1,042.965 versus $944.61 million). Based on these comparisons, the two-year plan should be supported.

Strategic investment appraisal

Table 4.10 Net cash flows and net present value analysis of alternatives in the absence of competing products

Panel A (Status quo: Model X only)			
Year	Net cash flow from Model X	PV factor	PV
1	£400	0.9091	£363.64
2	£300	0.8264	£247.92
3	£200	0.7513	£150.26
		NPV	£761.82

Panel B (One-year plan)						
	Net cash flow from					
Year	Model X	+ Model Z	= Total	PV factor	PV	
0	£0	+ £(550)	= £(550)	1.0000	£(550)	
1	400	+ 0	= 400	0.9091	£363.64	
2	200	+ 300	= 500	0.8264	£413.20	
3	100	+ 500	= 600	0.7513	£450.78	
4	0	+ 300	= 300	0.6830	£204.90	
5	0	+ 100	= 100	0.6209	£62.09	
				NPV	£944.61	

Panel C (Two-year plan)						
	Net cash flow from					
Year	Model X	+ Model Z	= Total	PV factor	PV	
0	£0	+ £(150)	= £(150)	1.0000	£(150)	
1	400	+ (150)	= 250	0.9091	£227.275	
2	300	+ 0	= 300	0.8264	£247.92	
3	100	+ 500	= 600	0.7513	£450.78	
4	0	+ 300	= 300	0.6830	£204.90	
5	0	+ 100	= 100	0.6209	£62.09	
				NPV	£1042.965	

4.4.38 Table 4.11 provides the annual cash flows and NPVs for the three added outcomes

4.4.39 Panel A of Table 4.11 shows that even if ACE does not introduce Model Z, it still cannot count on Model X's net cash inflows remaining intact in its remaining market life. Compared to Panel A of Table 4.10, Model X's net cash inflow in year 3 is lower by £100 million due to the competitor's entrance at the end of year 2. Panel B of provides the annual cash flows Table 4.11 on the other hand, is identical to the corresponding panel in Table 4.10.

Investment appraisal in modern enterprises

This is based on the assumption that even if the competitor were to enter the market at the end of year 2, Model Z would still have an overwhelming first-mover advantage from having been introduced one year earlier. This assumption is aimed at simplifying the numerical aspects of the case.

4.4.40 Finally, Panel C of Table 4.11 shows that Model Z's net cash inflows in years 3, 4 and 5 are only half of those in Panel C of Table 10. This reduction reflects the expectations that Model Z and the competing product would each get half of the market since they would be introduced simultaneously.

Table 4.11 Net cash flows and net present value analysis of alternatives assuming entry by competition

Panel A (Status quo: Model X only)						
Year	Net cash flow from Model X			PV factor		PV
1	£400			0.9091		£363.64
2	£300			0.8264		£247.92
3	£100			0.7513		£75.13
				NPV		£686.69

Panel B (One-year plan)						
	Net cash flow from					
Year	Model X	+	Model Z	=	Total	PV factor	PV
0	£0	+	£(550)	=	£(550)	1.0000	£(550)
1	400	+	0	=	400	0.9091	£363.64
2	200	+	300	=	500	0.8264	£413.20
3	100	+	500	=	600	0.7513	£450.78
4	0	+	300	=	300	0.6830	£204.90
5	0	+	100	=	100	0.6209	£62.09
					NPV	£944.61

Panel C (Two-year plan)						
	Net cash flow from					
Year	Model X	+	Model Z	=	Total	PV factor	PV
0	£0	+	£(150)	=	£(150)	1.0000	£(150)
1	400	+	(150)	=	250	0.9091	£227.275
2	300	+	0	=	300	0.8264	£247.92
3	100	+	250	=	350	0.7513	£262.955
4	0	+	150	=	150	0.6830	£102.45
5	0	+	50	=	50	0.6209	£31.045
					NPV	£721.645

Strategic investment appraisal

4.4.41 Computing expected values requires values for probabilities. Under the two-year plan, the probability of ACE's major competitor introducing a comparable product simultaneously can be labelled 'p'; thus the probability that it will not enter the market is $(1-p)$. Using these labels, the two-year plan's expected NPV can be represented as $\{\$721.645 \times p\} + \{\$1042.965 \times (1-p)\}$. Since the one-year plan involves no uncertainty, its expected NPV is simply $\$944.61$. As p is the relative weight of the two-year plan's less profitable outcome, the higher the value of p, the smaller would be this plan's expected NPV. Thus, which plan has a higher expected NPV depends on the value of p.

4.4.42 For ACE's decision problem, the key number for defining this range is the break-even value of p: that which would make the expected NPVs of the one- and two-year plans equal. This value is obtained by solving the following equation:

$$\$944.61 = \{\$721.645 \times p\} + \{\$1042.965 \times (1-p)\}$$

4.4.43 The break-even value of p is:

$$(\$1042.965 - \$944.61) / (\$1042.965 - \$721.645) = \$98.355 / \$321.32 = 0.3061$$

If there is less than a 30.61 per cent probability that ACE's major competitor would introduce a competing product at the end of year 2, then ACE would maximise expected NPV by choosing the two-year over the one-year plan, and vice versa. Thus, ACE can focus on ascertaining whether p is above or below 0.3061, rather than the much more difficult task of generating a precise point estimate.

4.4.44 Table 4.12 presents the competitor's predicted cash flows and NPVs from introducing a competing product at the end of year 2 (the earliest it is able to do so) depending on whether ACE develops Model Z and, if it does, whether it adopts the one- or two-year plan.

4.4.45 Panel A of Table 4.12 shows that if ACE does not develop Model Z, then after investing $150 million in each of years 1 and 2, the competitor would reap the net cash inflows that would otherwise have gone to Model Z (including the $100 million captured form ACE's Model X in year 3). Panel B assumes that if the competitor invests $150 million in year 1 and then finds ACE introducing Model Z at the end of year 1, it would abandon the project since ACE would garner an insurmountable first-mover advantage. Developing the figures for this panel affords the opportunity to discuss the irrelevance of sunk costs. Panel C assumes that the competitor and ACE would each gain 50 per cent market share by introducing comparable products simultaneously.

Investment appraisal in modern enterprises

4.4.46 Figure 4.12 presents a decision tree from the competitor's perspective. It shows that product development has a positive expected NPV if ACE either does not develop Model Z or it does so over two years. Overall, the competitor's expected NPV from product development would depend on its assessment of the probability that ACE would select each of its three options.

Table 4.12 Net cash flows and net present value analysis of entering the market from the competitor's perspective

Panel A			
ACE does not introduce Model Z			
Year	Net cash flow from new product development & introduction	PV factor	PV
0	£(150)	1.0000	£(150)
1	£(150)	0.9091	£(136.365)
2	£0	0.8264	£0
3	£500	0.7513	£375.65
4	£300	0.6830	£204.90
5	£100	0.6209	£62.09
		NPV	£356.275
Panel B			
(One-year plan)			
ACE introduces Model Z at the end of year one			
Year	Net cash flow from new product development & introduction	PV factor	PV
0	£(150)	1.0000	£(150)
1	£0	0.9091	£0
2	£0	0.8264	£0
3	£0	0.7513	£0
4	£0	0.6830	£0
5	£0	0.6209	£0
		NPV	£(150)
Panel C			
(Two-year plan)			
ACE introduces Model Z at the end of year two			
Year	Net cash flow from new product development & introduction	PV factor	PV
0	£(150)	1.0000	£(150)
1	£(150)	0.9091	£(136.365)
2	£0	0.8264	£0
3	£250	0.7513	£187.825
4	£150	0.6830	£102.45
5	£50	0.6209	£31.045
		NPV	£34.955

Chapter 5
Changing technologies and cost management

5.1 Technology, processes and accounting

5.1.1 In a constantly changing business environment, management is under tremendous pressure to make continuous improvements in all aspects of organisational infrastructure including internal accounting control systems. Change was slow during the first half of the twentieth century partly because production technologies were slow to change. During the 1920s, production processes in most Western enterprises tended toward the repetitive manufacturing of homogeneous products. Although investments in heavy machinery, which were essential to such processes, were high, the emphasis on specialised production equipment for mass production coincided with an increased demand for focused labour. High direct labour costs constituted a significant portion of direct costs. This meant that calculation of a full average cost per production unit had a relatively clear meaning and that little distortion of cost was introduced by allocating manufacturing overheads across a portfolio of relatively similar products (Bromwich and Bhimani, 1996).

5.1.2 Over the second half of the twentieth century, direct labour costs in manufacturing organisations declined in relation to total production costs. As companies adopted advanced manufacturing technologies (AMTs), such as numerical control machines, computer-aided design and manufacturing systems and other forms of flexible production technologies, the need for direct labour input diminished rapidly (Bromwich and Bhimani, 1994). By contrast, as investments were made into AMTs, overhead costs and support activities quickly expanded. This trend continues today as organisations invest in AMTs and web-enabling technologies. The expansion in overhead costs arises not only from the attendant depreciation, insurance and maintenance costs, but also from a new category of costs which is associated with servicing the new technology and which reflects indirect support activities. Flexible forms of production technologies and digitised operating platforms within organisations require computer expertise, software updates, personnel training, scheduling systems and integrative information networking to link and co-ordinate automated production and processing activities. As a

Changing technologies and cost management

result, overhead costs rise quickly while direct labour costs continue to decline rapidly.

5.1.3 The growth in overhead costs has also been intensified by the application of innovative work approaches, such as total quality management and just-in-time production systems, which help contain certain costs but require additional overhead costs to be met. From the perspective of traditional costing logic, such changes in the manufacturing cost mix can be particularly problematic. Conventionally, direct labour has served as the principal application base for indirect costs, which have tended to be low. However, where the overhead rate's numerator grows at a pace not dissimilar to the swiftly diminishing direct labour denominator base, an inappropriately leveraged burden rate results (sometimes of the order of 2,000 to 3,000 per cent). Also, the demand for resources by different products is often not reflected accurately by a labour allocation base within emerging organisational environments.

5.1.4 The managerial logic, which identifies the potential benefits that can be derived from economies of scale through mass production, continues to see changes in concert with the implementation of AMTs, flexible work organisation methods and the use of digitised business technologies. There is now seen to be considerable merit in satisfying a greater diversity of customer needs by developing and producing a larger range of quality products and by providing a custom-made product within a minimal timeframe. However, the availability of flexible and digitised technologies to achieve this goal is not always the main motivating element. Rather, new customer relationship options, product diversity and multi-channel product offerings are sometimes the only strategic option a company can take in a dynamic and competitive market environment. The fast pace of change in business pressures companies to be pro-active rather than reactive. The adoption of altered production technologies, work organisation approaches and digitised business operating platforms rests on transformed philosophies about 'best' business practices. New managerial thinking must now accompany enhanced product diversity, technological complexity and operational flexibility. One consequence of this is the reorientation of accounting practices for both operational activities and decision-making.

5.1.5 This chapter discusses technological and processional changes in the light of their implications for management accounting practices.

5.2 Just-in-time systems

5.2.1 The logic of just-in-time (JIT) systems for guiding operational processes has affected a wide array of enterprises in the West. Although JIT

Just-in-time systems

originated in Japan, it is now widely believed that the basis for this work methodology can be applied in one form or another in Western companies. Just-in-time systems operate a logic whereby production is initiated as a reaction to present demand. The systems in effect comprise two separate sets of activities:

- JIT purchasing, which attempts to match the acquisition and receipt of material sufficiently closely with usage such that raw material inventory is reduced to near-zero levels;
- JIT production, whereby production takes place only through a pull-system driven by the demand for finished products.

5.2.2 Just-in-time production's aim is to obtain low-cost, high-quality production and on time to order by minimising stock levels between successive processes and therefore idle equipment, facilities and workers.

5.2.3 Some benefits of just-in-time purchasing include raw material stock reduction, control over delivery timing, close working relations with fewer suppliers, long-term contracts, quality assurance and raw material/subcomponent specifications. Just-in-time production, on the other hand, stresses work in progress and finished goods inventory reductions, decreased lead and set-up times, zero defects, a flexible workforce, continuous improvement and quality control as part of the production process and producing to order. Like total quality management, just-in-time emphasises the detection of production problems as they occur rather than establishing procedures for dealing with problems after production has taken place and setting aside facilities for further processing.

5.2.4 The *kanban* process can also support just-in-time production by acting as an information system through cards which relay information about type and quantity of inputs withdrawn from a container. Under *kanban*, a card is sent from a subsequent process to the preceding one when an item is withdrawn. *Kanban* therefore connects all aspects in the flow of manufacturing within an organisation through the provision of information about the category and quantity of materials going through the system by linking one process to the prior process. It can extend from vendors and subcontractors to the parent manufacturing firm.

5.2.5 A just-in-time system converts the structure of production into a process operation. Process costing methods may therefore be used to trace costs where production lines are treated as cost centres and unit costs are calculated by dividing costs of a period or an order over the units processed in that period. Direct labour may be treated as fixed and merged with over-

Changing technologies and cost management

head in the form of period costs. Organisation-wide cost pools may be abandoned in favour of activity-linked bases for allocating overheads. In this respect, just-in-time is appealing as it enables the identification of cost drivers by highlighting non-value-added activities. Price variances should no longer be determined where long-term contractual links with suppliers exist. Performance evaluation under a just-in-time system becomes altered as actual, rather than standard, costs are stressed and variance analysis is likewise changed as attention is directed towards material quality, supplier service, zero defects and throughput performance. The demand-pull emphasis on the physical flow of goods across the factory floor, which underlies just-in-time production, can be complemented by costs being determined retrospectively through an accounting record-keeping technique called *backflushing*. Any significant change in underlying operations is likely to justify a corresponding change in accounting. For just-in-time systems, backflush accounting has been highlighted as a natural consequence.

5.2.6 A just-in-time system enables more direct traceability of certain costs, which raises new possibilities for more comprehensive reporting. For instance, materials handling facilities are often dedicated to a single retail area or a single production line. Such operational costs can therefore be classified as direct costs of individual retail areas or production lines. In effect, many activities which previously would have been classified as indirect costs would be considered direct costs under just-in-time (see Table 5.1).

Table 5.1 Classification of costs in traditional and just-in-time environments

	Traditional	Just-in-time
Materials handling	Indirect	Direct
Repair and maintenance	Largely direct	Direct
Energy	Indirect	Direct
Operating supplies	Indirect	Direct
Supervision	Indirect	Direct
Production support services	Indirect	Largely direct
Depreciation	Indirect	Direct

5.2.7 Just-in-time can allow accounting records to be simplified through backflush accounting whereby the level of detail with which product information is recorded is greatly reduced. A backflush costing system focuses first on the output of the organisation and then works backwards when applying costs to units sold and to stock. In contrast, conventional product costing systems track costs through work in progress, beginning with the introduction of raw material into production.

Just-in-time systems

5.2.8 Backflushing focuses first on output and then works backwards when allocating costs between cost of goods sold (CGS) and inventory with no separate accounting for work in progress (WIP).

An example

5.2.9 JIT Co. manufactures calculators and uses a backflush cost accounting system. The standard material cost per unit is £4.00 and the standard conversion cost (CC) is £3.00 per unit. Ten units are manufactured during its first month of operation and six units are sold. During the month £48.00 of raw material (RM) are purchased on credit.

5.2.10 Under a backflush accounting system, the point at which a sale occurs can be taken also to be the point at which accounting entries are made. Tables 5.2 and 5.3 depict the journal entries that would be made for the six units sold under a backflush system and a traditional cost accounting system respectively.

Table 5.2 JIT Co. entries made under a backflush accounting system

Cost of goods sold (6 units * £7)	£42	
Conversion cost (6 units * £3)		£18
Creditors (6 units *£4)		£24

Table 5.3 JIT Co. entries made under a traditional cost accounting system

1.	To record purchase of raw material (RM) on credit:		
	Material stock	£48	
	Creditors		£48
2.	To record application of RM to WIP for 10 units:		
	Work in progress (10×£4)	£40	
	Material		£40
3.	To record the application of conversion costs to WIP:		
	Work in progress (10×£3)	£30	
	Conversion costs		£30
4.	To record transfer of finished goods to warehouse:		
	Finished goods	£70	
	Work in progress		£70
5.	To record the sale of 6 units:		
	Cost of goods sold (6 units×(£4+£3))	£42	
	Finished goods		£42

5.2.11 The example above indicates the potential for cost reductions which can result from using a simplified and less extensive accounting record-keeping system such as backflushing. The backflush entry for creditors (£24) of course does not reflect legal transfer of material and therefore

145

ownership (£48). Thus, for final financial reports an adjustment is still required. As it stands, the backflush entry accounts only for resource inputs for sales rather than full receipt of inputs from suppliers. A just-in-time system implies that physical material moves along the production line as sales are made rather than being pushed into production only to be stored in warehouses. Backflush accounting reflects the nature of this physical production flow by making accounting entries only as the demand-pulled production process takes place, thereby reducing book-keeping entries and their associated costs as shown above.

5.2.12 Just as just-in-time generates new accounting needs, it also alters the costing system, making certain traditional practices redundant. For instance, an organisation may ordinarily collect information on purchasing, warehouse and raw material inspection activities. These costs are subsequently placed into a cost pool along with others and a base such as warehouse space is used to allocate costs. Under just-in-time, long-term purchase contracts are used and the number of suppliers is typically reduced, thereby decreasing purchasing costs. Likewise, the goal of 'zero-stock' manufacturing eliminates warehouse storage requirements, and quality and quantity inspection procedures as well as working capital are greatly diminished. Such changes mean cost pools may alter considerably and allocation bases consequently have to be redefined.

5.2.13 Furthermore, under just-in-time purchasing, factors such as quality of raw materials, availability of subcomponents and reliability of supplies often take precedence over short-term price advantages. Price reductions of raw material and bought-in parts are often achieved by deploying long-term agreements with suppliers. Consequently, data on purchase price variances, which may have constituted an important part of accounting-based performance measures, lose relevance in a just-in-time environment. What is of essence is not to judge the performance of the purchasing manager as an isolated activity but to evaluate the production process as an integrated and complex set of interrelated functions. Likewise, recognising that just-in-time production entails a far-reaching form of decentralisation – whereby each individual factory worker can halt the production process when a problem arises – renders the relevance of labour efficiency variances doubtful.

5.2.14 Performance evaluation indicators other than variances are affected by the application of just-in-time principles. Traditionally, the management accounting system reports an array of financial monitors on a periodic basis, many of which are of little use given the growing importance of real-time information in many enterprises. In this context:

Just-in-time systems

'a feed forward system which would predict a deviation thus allowing the process to be corrected before it occurred, would be preferable in a JIT company.' (Source: Cobb, 1991.)

5.2.15 While there is little documentation of companies which have moved towards such a system of internal reporting, many firms report the enhanced use of non-financial monitors tied to quality objectives, reduction of stock, co-operation with vendors, on-time deliveries and process cost reduction. More specifically, measures including elapsed time, distance moved, space occupied and number of parts are used alongside metrics concerned with quality, cycle time and product complexity.

5.2.16 McHilhattan (1987) has contrasted some performance measures under traditional and just-in-time environments. These are set out in Table 5.4.

Table 5.4 Contrasting performance measures under traditional and just-in-time environments

Traditional	Just-in-time
Direct labour (efficiency, utilisation, productivity)	Total head count productivity
Machine utilisation	Days of inventory
Stock turnover	Group incentives
Cost variances	Customer service
Individual incentives	Knowledge and capability-based promotion
Promotion based on seniority	Ideas generated and implemented customer complaints

A case study: work reorganisation and cost effects

5.2.17 Ken Lutz, a creative engineer, founded Kenco Engineering in Bangor. The business is built around proprietary processes and custom designs that extend the wear life of parts on heavy equipment. (Blade edges are like gloves that fit on expensive larger pieces of equipment. They cover the abrasive parts of equipment that suffer damage in use. The $500 to $2,000 blades are worn out and replaced, rather than the $50,000 to $200,000 equipment parts.) The key manufacturing process melts steel blade edges and impregnates them with tungsten carbide. Kenco adds value to original equipment manufacturers' (OEMs') products. Such equipment includes road graders and buckets on earth-moving tractors for roadbuilding, mining and construction.

Changing technologies and cost management

5.2.18 Also, Kenco outsources the manufacture of foundry castings that it custom designs. An example is hammers in grinding machines. It then wholesales the castings. As with its steel-blade tungsten-impregnating business, Kenco emphasises castings that wear out. It competes by extending wear cycles with longer lasting products.

5.2.19 The firm is family-owned and small with $4–6 million in sales. It has sought OEM relationships, but primarily bids for jobs with blade or parts end-users. Lot sizes for steel blade impregnating are one to ten units. The norm is single-unit orders.

5.2.20 Kenco was profitable from the beginning. However, in 2000 it suffered a loss of $350,000 (about a third of its equity). From 1996 to 2000 the second generation of family management oversaw a marked change in product mix. The mix of steel-blade impregnating business versus castings-wholesaling moved from $0.6 and $1.6 million, respectively, to $3.6 and $1.4 million. Thus, Kenco moved from being primarily a castings wholesaler to predominant activity in tungsten carbide impregnating. Tungsten carbide impregnating is variously termed TCing or steel blade impregnating.

5.2.21 The business's growth unexpectedly resulted in the large, clearly unacceptable loss. With the move to more in-house manufacturing (TCing), profits had suddenly fallen. Stock for the TCing business had grown to average as much as $80,000. (Average inventories have since been brought down to $6,000.) Ken Lutz's sons understood the need for change.

5.2.22 Responding to the situation, the Lutz brothers created a new position of accountant. They hired Vern Hughes whose background included five years in auditing and nine years in manufacturing. Hughes had in-depth knowledge of costing systems and significant large-firm experience implementing just-in-time (JIT) production systems. At Kenco, Hughes accomplished major changes in operating systems, product costing and cost control.

Previous purchasing/inventory management

5.2.23 Each day three or more suppliers bid for TCing's steel requirements. Steel blades are impregnated in job-lots, so steel was purchased in quantity at lowest-bid maximum-discount prices. The *de facto* operating rule of 'sell one make 12; somebody will buy the inventory' resulted in increased steel and finished blade inventories. Hughes found that 50 per cent of the finished parts did not turn in 12 months. One part, purchased at a large discount, had a 12-year supply at its current usage rate.

Just-in-time systems

5.2.24 Kenco also received bids from three foundries for 95 per cent of its outsourced castings. It bought at the lowest-price quantity discount. Consistent with this rule, the firm contracted with overseas suppliers and received large (one or two container car) deliveries. Resulting problems centred on Kenco's inability to meet delivery dates. This denied customers time to refurbish their equipment. Many customers had seasonal demand, with delivery required in a January to March 1 window. While saving money, late delivery of container cars (due to customs or offshore problems) lost a lot of business.

5.2.25 Kenco's inventory records for castings were less than 25 per cent accurate. For important new orders, clerks had to recount and tag parts. Split lot deliveries were common and added to overhead. Clerks found that they constantly ran out of stock on fast-moving seasonal items. Supplier foundries constantly rescheduled and rushed Kenco's orders.

Previous TCing (production) environment

5.2.26 Kenco's steel-blade production system had functional work centres, job lots and high inventory levels. Figure 5.1 shows the shop-floor layout for this traditional job shop. Production was complex with many steps and unique activities. Long cycle times averaged eight weeks. Cranes and fork-lift lorries moved heavy materials through production.

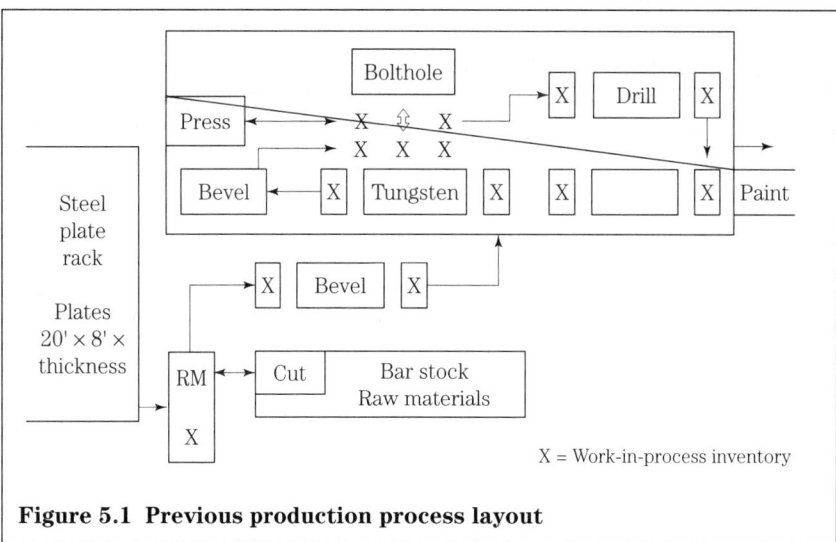

Figure 5.1 Previous production process layout

5.2.27 First, suppliers delivered steel plates weighing tons to the cutting station's incoming inventory rack. An overhead crane moved the huge

Changing technologies and cost management

plates with a lot of physical effort and danger. Workers cut the plates to rough dimensions and placed them in an out-going rack. Fork-lift lorries moved them to bevelling's incoming inventory rack. Bevelling then placed its output on an out-going rack and so on throughout the production process.

5.2.28 Each workstation's use of incoming and out-going inventory racks lengthened set-up times. Combined with the effects of expediting, this caused high in-process inventories and wasted time. The average job used 80 per cent of labour time in set-up. Hunt-and-peck was required to sort through incoming inventory and find the next job.

5.2.29 Rework was high with 50 per cent of boltholes out-of-specification. Workers positioned materials by hand at each station, making the work physically demanding and dangerous. Fingers were not just broken, they were crushed. As a result, very high worker compensation rates exceeded £11,000 per month. (After process redesign, this cost fell to £4,000 per month.)

Key success factors

5.2.30 In order of importance, Kenco's key success factors are quality, on-time delivery and cost. With quality defined as wear life and custom specifications, Kenco's products have no problems. Its products' lives are several times those of standard replacement parts.

5.2.31 Delivery is a problem. Kenco's markets are very sensitive to lead time and Kenco had long lead times. Sales would increase until lead time got to eight weeks. Then orders dropped off. When lead time returned to five weeks, sales again increased. With its previous systems design, Kenco was in a constant cycle of losing and gaining sales as lead times stretched and shrunk.

5.2.32 An asphalt plant in Chester discontinued Kenco's products because Kenco could not deliver on time. The failure to deliver one part idled the customer's entire plant. A part costing £2,000 idled a plant that cost £20 million! Kenco temporarily reduced leadtime by opening a second plant in the Midlands. However, when this plant's pipeline filled, the old cycle resumed. Still, Kenco produced and sold 100 per cent of its capacity. There was no alarm until the £350,000 loss in 2000.

5.2.33 Kenco wholesaled castings at minimum bid prices determined by a formula: materials cost times 181 per cent. Thus, a casting with materials that cost £400 was sold for a minimum of £724. Kenco's managers viewed these numbers as implying a large gross profit for the product.

Just-in-time systems

5.2.34 Managers based steel impregnating job bids on their judgement of competitive market conditions. For TCed products, the wholesale markup (181 per cent) was used to estimate gross profits. For example, Kenco sold a steel-impregnated product for £905 at an estimated gross profit of £405.

5.2.35 Management thought, product-by-product, that it was making a lot of money. Market prices often greatly exceeded minimum bid prices and material costs. For example, a product with material costing £75 might sell for £350 – far above £75 multiplied by 181 per cent. Kenco was making so much money a few years earlier that management did not think more accurate product-profitability reporting and a better bidding system were necessary. However, the company's reported net income was much lower in 2000.

New purchasing/inventory management

5.2.36 The new accountant, Vern Hughes, developed some key total quality management (TQM) ideas. They focused on value added to the customer and process simplification. Hughes focused quality on designing custom products and emphasising Kenco's competitive advantage in TCing. Delivery strategies were related to cycle time and the influence of lead times on sales demand. Finally, Hughes evaluated bidding effects of product cost accuracy and reported product profitability.

5.2.37 Consistent with a belief in simplicity, Hughes thought many of the firm's practices only obscured the management process. He sought ways to simplify management and better control costs. He also looked for ways to improve purchasing, increase control of inventory and reduce cycle time. Hughes proposed mutually helpful linkages to Kenco's major suppliers of steel (for manufactured blades) and castings (for wholesaled parts).

5.2.38 The plan was to source specific parts 100 per cent from one supplier and end rush orders. All purchases of a given material were at an annually negotiated price, regardless of individual orders' unit volume. Suppliers gave blanket discounts based on annual purchase volumes and average materials' prices dropped 15 per cent. They delivered steel precut to job specifications, eliminating Kenco's cutting operation. All steel deliveries were in a three-day window, and foundry castings received four-week delivery.

5.2.39 Most of Kenco's suppliers could not perform according to these arrangements. However, one supplier met them after some arm twisting.

5.2.40 To improve inventory accuracy, Hughes introduced cycle counting. Kenco now counts 100 items making up 80 per cent of the wholesaled-castings sales volume every four weeks. It scraps or deeply discounts and sells all inventory not turning in 12 months. Wall-to-wall inventory counts are made every 90 days. Count accuracy improved rapidly. Additionally, Kenco reduced 5,000 castings part numbers to 1,200 stockable items. All other items are purchased only when sold. Hughes successfully rid the company of many of its management headaches, while saving money.

New TCing (production) environment

5.2.41 Aware of cycle time's importance to market demand, Hughes, the accountant, moved to change the manufacturing process. A central objective was to simplify management of Kenco's value-added TCing process. Hughes investigated ways to improve steel impregnating production. Based on JIT and TQM, he guided redesign of the manufacturing process. Kenco moved from a traditional functional layout to what Hughes called an 'in-line' (straight-line, single-unit flow) system. With inventories reduced and many part numbers outsourced, manufacturing labour fell 40 per cent. Operating system simplicity, timeliness and continuous improvement were key elements for success.

5.2.42 To improve process management and costing, Kenco regrouped its many production activities into two activity centres. These are: tungsten crushing and conversion processing. The cutting operation was eliminated by vendors supplying steel precut to specification. Using a proprietary process, tungsten is crushed from scrap parts. Merging tungsten chips with a steel blade occurs in conversion processing.

5.2.43 A single building houses conversion processing, which works as one JIT manufacturing cell. Figure 5.2 shows the factory layout after the change. The conversion processing cell combines five of the previous activities: (1) bevelling, (2) bolthole cutting, (3) tungsten impregnating (TCing), (4) steel blade straightening and (5) drilling.

5.2.44 This cell focuses on TCing, the critical proprietary process. The other four activities have excess capacity and do not limit conversion processing throughput. Thus, the cell is unbalanced. In many ways it is designed following a Theory of Constraints philosophy (see Chapter **7**). Tungsten impregnating is the constraining process, and the JIT cell serves this process. The TCing machine runs at 80 per cent of maximum capacity. This is average available capacity or maximum capacity net of average downtime for maintenance and repairs.

5.2.45 The conversion processing flow uses conveyors for a single-unit production line through five activities. Achieving this sequential layout required extensive process redesign and added materials-flow equipment.

Just-in-time systems

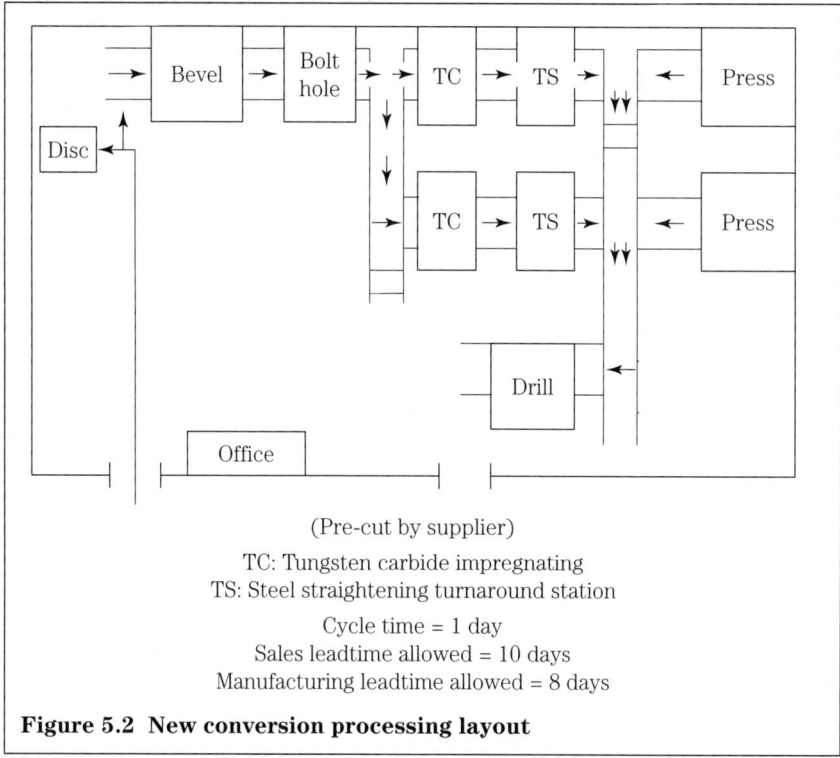

Figure 5.2 New conversion processing layout

The new design allows the operator at each process to receive and mechanically position each job. There is no more manual raising and lowering of heavy steel plates. This production flow lessens set-up time, cuts inventory racks and in-process inventory, and stops the hunt-and-peck of looking for the next job. Forklifts now only bring steel to the beginning of the line and remove finished product at the end.

5.2.46 The savings were dramatic. Three shifts decreased to one. Headcount fell from 40 to 20 people. Cycle time dropped from eight weeks to eight days. Manufacturing defects fell from 25 per cent to one per week. Monthly worker compensation savings of £7,000 paid for the additional new production equipment.

Implications for costing systems

5.2.47 Figure 5.3 depicts Kenco's product cost flows. Each work-in-process account has the materials flow shown. Additional charges include other direct materials, direct labour and one overhead cost pool. Each account's overhead cost pool includes stage I allocations caused by activities

Changing technologies and cost management

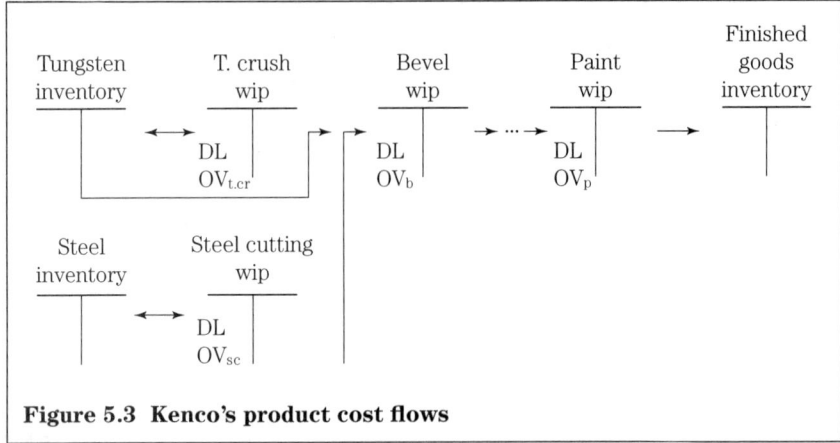

Figure 5.3 Kenco's product cost flows

such as materials movement. Direct labour hours is a traditional stage I allocation basis.

5.2.48 Example drivers for the stage II overhead cost pools are: cutting (length of cuts), crushing (pounds crushed), bevelling (set-up time or length of steel plate), TCing (length of steel plate), press straightening (steel thickness), boltholes (hole size) and drilling (number of holes). Actual or standard costs may be used. The discussion assumes actual materials and labour. Overhead costs are applied using predetermined rates. At Kenco, product volume and margins were very good, therefore management felt little need to control costs until a major loss occurred. The accounting system was designed to report financial activities externally. Kenco was only concerned with getting clean audit opinions. Little information was available for product costing and cost control.

5.2.49 Figure 5.4 depicts a system based on backflush and product costing designs. These are for the new manufacturing system where the cutting operation has been eliminated. The following design's transaction entry

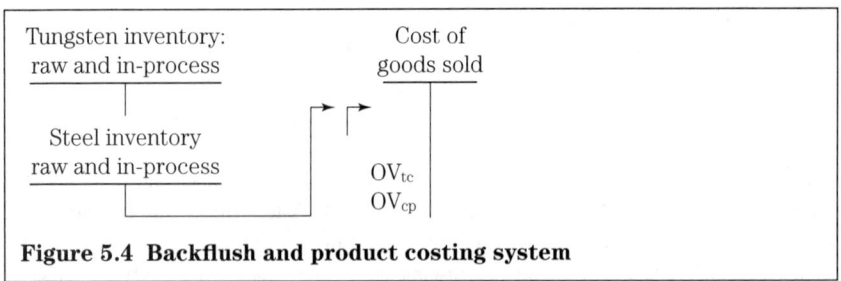

Figure 5.4 Backflush and product costing system

Just-in-time systems

(trigger) points are at the time materials are purchased and product is sold. The design has close to the least possible complexity.

5.2.50 To avoid requirements for specific-materials identification, a backflush design requires standard or predetermined costs.

5.2.51 A charge for tungsten crushing isolates costs in support of outsourcing decisions. An easy-to-get driver is pounds crushed (or the driver used in the hybrid design).

5.2.52 A second charge combines all conversion costs in conversion processing. The driver could be conversion-processing cycle time and steel blade length in inches. Cycle time is typical for a just-in-time (JIT) manufacturing cell.

5.2.53 Account entry need not mirror physical manufacturing events when they occur. Computer-controlled production or laser reads of barcoded material movement are needed to make real-time systems cost-feasible. The obvious alternative is to make periodic (weekly for Kenco) batch entries. Managers can estimate work-in-process and count other end-of-period inventories.

5.2.54 Traditional hybrid, job, and process costing systems require a lot of detail. In terms of materials, labour, overhead, department and inventory cost records. A key point is the cost of detail. Effects are felt in underlying information systems, accountants' time and the loss of worker productivity in recordkeeping.

5.2.55 Backflush costing exploits an effective JIT manufacturing system. Reduced need to track work through the production cycle enables dropping detailed materials requisitions and labour time distributions. Products are assigned standard costs. Trigger points can be materials purchase, product sale or product completion. Fewer trigger points remove the need for separate work-in-process and possibly finished goods accounts.

5.2.56 Kenco's JIT production is unbalanced with the TC-machine constraining throughput. However, push-button control, single-unit flows and fast throughput produce low and stable inventory balances. This supports backflush costing for external financial reporting. It also makes the detail of a hybrid costing system unnecessary.

5.2.57 However, both backflush and hybrid costing are compatible with Kenco's new manufacturing system. Either design combined with effective operating systems would satisfy external reporting requirements.

Changing technologies and cost management

5.2.58 In contrast, the previous production system required more detailed costing (a job or hybrid design). Kenco experienced large and unstable inventories and uncontrolled production costs. Backflush costing in this environment would produce material inaccuracy in externally reported inventory balances.

5.2.59 Product costs are substantially accurate when product variety is small. Kenco's jobs do not exhibit much resource consumption variety unaccounted for by the costing system. The basic activities assign most significant costs to products with good accuracy.

5.2.60 At Kenco, set-ups were long and required searching through incoming and out-going inventory racks. Job lots were one to ten units, with a norm of single-unit orders. Set-up costs were significant. The average job used 80 per cent of its basic-activities labour in set-up. Implicitly, direct labour charges accurately assign their portion of set-up costs to jobs.

5.2.61 The materials-movement portion of set-up costs includes other costs such as indirect labour and forklift operations. The hybrid design allocates these costs to the work-in-process accounts. These stage I allocations are based on basic-activity direct labour hours. Stage II allocations to products are based on drivers such as length of cuts (steel cutting) and hole size (bolthole cutting). Both allocations create product miscosting. The costs are not cause-effect related to the allocation bases or drivers. Batch-level allocations would reduce this inaccuracy. Cycle time through conversion processing is a satisfactory driver for an activity accounting system (see Chapter 6). The JIT, push-button, single-unit-flow production system is effective. Thus, costs for set-up, materials movement, and holding inventory are minimal. Cycle time appears effectively to capture work driving the basic-activity costs. Also, it is cost-effective to use a single pool and driver when accounting primarily for external reporting.

5.2.62 Kenco does not have significant batch-level or higher costs. However, it does have some engineering and product design costs. For other companies, these costs are more significant and may be assigned to products. For these companies, a single cost pool assigned by cycle time may not achieve costing accuracy. Multiple pools, better drivers, hierarchical costing, and full-product costing (covering the value chain) may be needed.

5.2.63 For product costs used in decision-making, accounting can develop activity standards or cost-load factors. Periodic ABC can use this information. The size and frequency of changes in resource costs, product design and process technology determine the timing of ABC cost revisions.

Just-in-time systems

5.2.64 In the current environment, prices are market-driven. Nevertheless, reported product costs and job profits affect bidding-formula revisions. Obviously, more product costing accuracy increases the accuracy of reported profits. These profits influence decisions about product mix, job and customer emphasis, and the structure of customer relationships.

5.2.65 For example, the hybrid design for the old production system inaccurately allocates some stage I and II materials movement costs. To this extent, product costs do not correctly reflect cause-effect relationships between costs and activity. The process costs assigned to a job are disproportionate to materials movement costs caused by the job.

5.2.66 Suppose a short (light-weight) blade requires a large number of drilled holes. There is no correspondingly large effort to move the blade. Overhead charges based on the number of holes drilled tend to be disproportionately high. Management may emphasise more standardised blade fittings with fewer holes drilled. Given the market price, this product-mix strategy appears to increase profits. In fact, the original profit is understated and does not support the decision.

5.2.67 An example of product miscosting can also be constructed for the backflush design with the new production system. A customer may need greater-than-average design help to position tungsten strips on steel blades. Assume the product uses a below-average amount of cycle time in conversion processing. The product is under-costed when costed on cycle time. Engineering costs are disproportionately allocated to the customer's job.

5.2.68 In this case, managers may be satisfied with the reported job profit. They may not restructure the customer relationship. Restructuring might have included a higher volume of business with the customer, a longer-term relationship or negotiating a price that unbundles the design value added.

5.2.69 The original costing design has less detail for cost-benefit reasons. However, it has some activity-based costing elements. Engineered standards or continuous improvement targets are not cost effective for Kenco's scale of operations. The work-in-process accounts capture actual direct and applied overhead costs.

5.2.70 The hybrid design provides data for vertical cost control. Managers can compare actual costs to flexible budget and applied costs. Variances signal the need for investigation and possibly corrective effort.

5.2.71 Coverage of traditional variances' strengths and weaknesses include the following. Strengths are: the control information has a profit

Changing technologies and cost management

focus. It bears the hallmark of accounting's real scorecard for the business game. Financial variances are communicated to top management. They isolate cost behaviour by responsibility centre. Examples are materials spending in purchasing and labour efficiency in tungsten crushing.

5.2.72 Possible weaknesses exist, particularly without offsetting controls or continuous improvement targets. Normal levels of inefficiency tend to be accepted. Dysfunctional behaviour can be promoted. An example is low-bid purchasing without enough regard for quality and delivery. Specific resource efficiency can be promoted to the detriment of total cost control. An example is fully using capacity to produce excess inventory.

5.2.73 Examining backflush costing and control calls for some understanding of new manufacturing environments.

5.2.74 The backflush approach uses standard or predetermined costs. Conversion costs are applied separately for tungsten crushing and conversion processing. The drivers for these activities are pounds crushed and cycle time. Trigger points are materials purchases and finished unit sales.

5.2.75 The backflush costing and control system underpins how effective JIT can affect cost-variances. It may make these controls obsolete and dysfunctional. Traditional variances often encourage behaviour that is the opposite of what JIT requires. For example, they focus on low-cost purchases rather than timely delivery of defect-free materials. Therefore, backflush costing's failure to track actual costs through manufacturing does not force control weakness.

5.2.76 Backflush costing does not directly support cost-performance analysis by responsibility centre or activity. However, loss of control is offset by underlying JIT controls. JIT offers line-of-sight management, physical controls such as *Kanbans* and balanced production, and elements of total quality management (TQM) (see Chapter **8**). Book entries made after the completion of production are not timely for control of intermediate processes. However, fast cycle times reduce the significance of this delay. Timely materials price variances can be computed.

5.2.77 With effective JIT systems, operating controls and physical measures can be effective for total cost control. An example physical measure is the percentage of on-time deliveries.

5.2.78 Backflush costing does generate conversion cost variances (actual minus applied). Under- and over-applied costs do not effectively signal the

Just-in-time systems

need for investigation, but rather aggregate costs and tend to be untimely. However, budget estimates used to develop overhead rates can be separately compared to detail on actual costs. Managers can use these data to reconcile costs with their intensive knowledge of operating problems. This information provides a profit focus for physical activity. It helps identify and prioritise the cost significance of specific conversion activity problems.

5.2.79 Overall then, backflush costing shifts the control emphasis to other systems. Managers rely on underlying JIT systems, TQM and their intensive knowledge of daily operations for activity and cost control.

Focusing on profits and cost control
5.2.80 Kenco's falling profits led the company to hire Vern Hughes for the new position of accountant. Many organisations become more accounting intensive when facing financial woes. Hughes thinks that non-value added activities obscure business decisions. A small company should keep it simple. Also, he is a Pareto type manager, believing that a few key factors drive most of the profits.

5.2.81 Hughes directed major strategic changes in Kenco's purchasing, inventory management and steel blade impregnating (TCing) systems. While the case so far addresses these changes and accounting systems that might be matched to them, of relevance is the more strategically and market-economics focused accounting system the company actually adopted. This system reflects key linkages between market demand and manufacturing strategy. Market demand defines the company's production cycle time. Cycle time drives cost structure.

5.2.82 Dave Lutz (one of the founder's sons) designed the sales bidding sheet (Figure 5.5). This isolates factors expected to create market value for the product. It shows the various factors affecting production cost: tungsten crushing, set-up, number of edges, bolthole cutting, etc.

5.2.83 Hughes first determines the market values of activities required by a job. He then lists them on the bidding sheet to explain price. The bidding sheet gives a market-value, not a cost-plus, price justification. It signals unusual job specifications requiring price negotiation. It communicates to customers that product prices are based on value delivered. Customers see prices as market-driven, rational and fair.

5.2.84 Management receives weekly job cost and profitability reports (Figure 5.6). However, due to small jobs and fast cycle times, this information is usually delivered after production. With no contract renegotiation,

Changing technologies and cost management

Bidding Sheet
Front End Loader Edges (FEL) A-36

Customer:
Dist.:
Date: 10/2/91
Calc. by: RHM

Remarks:
Item No. 1   DWG NO.   N/A

Type (DE/SE)	SE		Set up chrg	Single edge	Double edge
Thick	1.00		0"-35"	$10.00	$12.00
Width	12.00		36"-71"	$15.00	$17.00
Length	53.00		72"-107"	$20.00	$22.00
Hole qty	12		108"-131"	$22.00	$24.00
TC passes	4		132"-155"	$24.00	$26.00
Single passes	0		156"-up	$30.00	$32.00
SU	$17.00				
SQ in TC	0.00		Sq in TC	0.00	
List price	$407.19		Weight	178.08	
Dist price	$325.75		Pin TC	212	
			SPINTC	0	

SET UP	STEEL	TC	Single TC	BOLTS	Sq in TC
$17.00	$106.85	$225.14	$0.00	$42.00	$0.00

Remarks:
Item No. 2   DWG NO.   N/A

Type (DE/SE)	SE		Set up chrg	Single edge	Double edge
Thick	1.00		0"-35"	$10.00	$12.00
Width	12.00		36"-71"	$15.00	$17.00
Length	53.00		72"-107"	$20.00	$22.00
Hole qty	12		108"-131"	$22.00	$24.00
TC passes	4		132"-155"	$24.00	$26.00
Single passes	0		156"-up	$30.00	$32.00
SU	$17.00				
SQ in TC	0.00		Sq in TC	0.00	
List price	$407.19		Weight	72.24	
Dist price	$325.75		Pin TC	86	
			SPINTC	0	

SET UP	STEEL	TC	Single TC	BOLTS	Sq in TC
$12.00	$39.73	$91.33	$0.00	$14.00	$0.00

Figure 5.5

Kenco bears all cost risk. Thus, managers evaluate past job information looking toward future contracts with product similarities. They must bring future costs into line with value added.

5.2.85 Hughes uses bid price and product cost to compute job gross profit. The target profit is 50 per cent. In weekly meetings, managers review in detail all products with profits below 30 per cent. Products with negative

Just-in-time systems

Org. qty	Qty. good	Sta. #	Date	Unit price	T.C. in	Steel cost	Avg. time	T.C. cost	Conv. cost	Unit cost	Unit profit	Gross profit
17	17	3	09-28-1995	$27.50	23	$0.00	0.202	$3.95	$34.50	$38.45	($10.95)	-39.81%
48	48	D	09-26-1995	$13.20	5	$2.60	0.097	$0.86	$7.44	$10.90	$2.30	17.41%
2	1	D	09-25-1995	$247.00	90	$86.39	0.699	$15.46	$53.63	$155.48	$91.52	37.05%
2	2	D	09-25-1995	$247.00	90	$86.39	0.654	$15.46	$50.18	$152.03	$94.97	38.45%
8	8	3	09-27-1995	$46.58	8	$17.58	0.049	$1.37	$8.37	$27.32	$19.26	41.34%
80	68	3	09-26-1995	$27.81	10	$5.44	0.048	$1.72	$8.20	$15.36	$12.45	44.78%
2	2	4	09-26-1995	$752.73	363	$95.73	1.375	$62.37	$234.82	$392.92	$359.81	47.80%
4	4	4	09-26-1995	$411.56	231	$101.22	0.42	$39.69	$71.73	$212.63	$198.93	48.34%
80	80	4	09-28-1995	$27.81	10	$5.40	0.042	$1.72	$7.17	$14.29	$13.52	48.61%
1	1	4	09-26-1995	$1,390.79	655	$384.94	1.144	$112.54	$195.37	$692.85	$697.94	50.18%
64	34	4	09-28-1995	$50.04	23	$3.45	0.102	$3.95	$17.42	$24.82	$25.22	50.40%
80	80	4	09-27-1995	$20.36	8	$4.34	0.021	$1.37	$3.59	$9.30	$11.06	54.32%
80	40	D	09-29-1995	$38.88	16	$6.82	0.101	$2.75	$7.75	$17.32	$21.56	55.46%
64	64	D	09-27-1995	$35.03	10	$6.50	0.096	$1.72	$7.37	$15.58	$19.45	55.51%
1	1	4	09-27-1995	$3,697.00	1388	$905.48	2.887	$238.49	$493.03	$1,637.00	$2,060.00	55.72%
4	4	D	09-25-1995	$205.18	47	$52.92	0.341	$8.08	$26.16	$87.16	$118.02	57.52%
2	2	4	09-25-1995	$226.74	119	$31.57	0.251	$20.45	$42.86	$94.88	$131.86	58.15%
80	40	D	09-27-1995	$27.04	10	$5.44	0.05	$1.72	$3.84	$10.99	$16.05	59.34%
1	1	4	09-25-1995	$3,328.26	1248	$809.38	1.88	$214.43	$321.06	$1,344.87	$1,983.39	59.59%
4	4	4	09-26-1995	$502.42	242	$88.26	0.422	$41.58	$72.07	$201.91	$300.51	59.81%
2	2	4	09-27-1995	$560.20	160	$49.05	0.768	$27.49	$131.16	$207.69	$352.51	62.93%
1	1	4	09-26-1995	$281.31	139	$35.30	0.257	$23.88	$43.89	$103.07	$178.24	63.36%
2	2	4	09-25-1995	$336.42	170	$50.03	0.256	$43.72	$43.72	$122.96	$213.46	63.45%
4	4	4	09-25-1995	$280.83	155	$17.68	0.317	$26.63	$54.14	$98.45	$182.38	64.94%
1	1	4	09-25-1995	$715.52	361	$92.34	0.525	$62.03	$89.66	$244.02	$471.50	65.90%
40	40	3	09-28-1995	$23.09	6	$3.41	0.017	$1.03	$2.90	$7.34	$15.75	68.19%
4	4	4	09-26-1995	$143.34	70	$11.88	0.109	$12.03	$18.61	$42.52	$100.82	70.33%
Run time 86.304				Total sales $50,798.68 $50,798.68	Total TC inches 20082 20082	Total TC cost $3,450.52 $3,450.52	Total steel ext. $10,036.95 $10,036.95	Total labor/OH $10,617.67 $7,488.00	Total cost $24,129.31 $20,975.47	Total profit $26,669.37 $29,823.31		Gross profit 52.50% 58.71%

Figure 5.6 Weekly production and cost report

profits receive priority attention. Looking to future jobs, managers consider production process changes and product redesign. They may also consider bidding formula changes or price increases as a last option.

5.2.86 For example, one product for a completed contract had required a series of tungsten strips. Impregnating these strips onto the steel blade used several passes on the TCing machine. The job profit was negative. The problem was that repeated passes on the TCing machine wasted its bottle-neck-capacity time. Looking to future contracts for this product, Kenco worked with the customer to redesign the product. In the future it would use fewer and more critically placed tungsten strips. The product then became profitable and the price remained competitive.

5.2.87 Kenco's owners and Hughes understand that the market sets the value of its critical competency – TCing. They designed TCing as the constraint in a just-in-time (JIT) cell. Other cell activities carry excess capacity to assure the critical resource (TCing) is fully used. Hughes loads all conversion-processing costs on the TCing machine. Thus, he aligns cost with the core competency that the market pays for – TCing. By measuring this cost burden against market prices, Hughes assesses the value his costs create. Costs that do not add value should be reduced. This analysis is critical to Kenco's profitability.

Profitability and key performance indicators

5.2.88 Product (steel-blade) cost is the sum of steel, crushed tungsten and conversion-processing costs. Steel costs are from outsourced materials. Crushed tungsten cost is the sum of tungsten and the crushing process. Conversion-processing cost is from the JIT cell. Average available run time for the TCing machine is 80 per cent of maximum capacity.

5.2.89 A basic purpose of contemporary management accounting and operations systems is to focus areas for performance improvement. Kenco focuses attention on use of the TCing machine. This is where change will be most beneficial. Since the TCing machine sets capacity for the JIT cell, it is the only constraint. Figure 5.6 presents Kenco's weekly production and cost report for TCing. The report gives product unit costs and gross profits. It also shows job run time on the TCing machine and total percentage use of this capacity.

5.2.90 The 80 per cent TCing machine capacity is maximum capacity net of average downtime for maintenance and repairs. Actual run time signals profitability because it focuses on use of Kenco's key revenue-producing and constraining resource. Run times below 80 per cent mean that profits are

Just-in-time systems

below what is possible. Critical-process run time signals productivity for the entire conversion processing cell.

5.2.91 Kenco derives significant benefit from its capacity run time indicator. Market forces direct continuous improvement through competitive prices. In the short-term, market prices drive profit. Management focuses on these market-driven profits to identify the need for process and product design improvement, cost reduction and margin improvement. This is an application of the target costing concept (see Chapter **10**). The sales force helps implement market-driven improvement. Sales people participate with the customer and Kenco engineers in product design.

5.2.92 Kenco stresses timely continuous improvement driven by market prices. The prices that customers accept signal the efficiency of Kenco's processes versus competitors. Management must decide if these prices reflect value added or a special circumstance. When the price reflects value added and projected profits are below target, management investigates whether costs can be reduced. Value added rather than the costing system drives this analysis.

5.2.93 For Kenco, a costing system relevant to market economics (demand for value added) provides competitive advantage. The company can bid competitively and with the confidence that it will make a profit. The costing system with bid prices adds value to Kenco by identifying opportunities for market-driven efficiency. Market prices motivate improvements in production processes and product design.

5.2.94 Other weekly reports track three additional broad performance trends. The measures are: gross profit percentages, tungsten-steel inches impregnated and customers served within eight days (see Figure 5.7). These measures are highly correlated with the critical success factors of cost, quality (value-added TCing) and delivery.

Product costing

5.2.95 Kenco's accounting system computes timely product costs and the information is reported weekly. Hughes designed the costing system to be simple and easily understood. The sales force and managers at all levels have no difficulty working with cost information. It is timely and useful for decision-making.

5.2.96 The system costs TCed blades as crushed tungsten, steel and conversion-processing costs. Kenco crushes tungsten from scrap parts, but could outsource crushed tungsten. The decision to purchase crushed tungsten on

Changing technologies and cost management

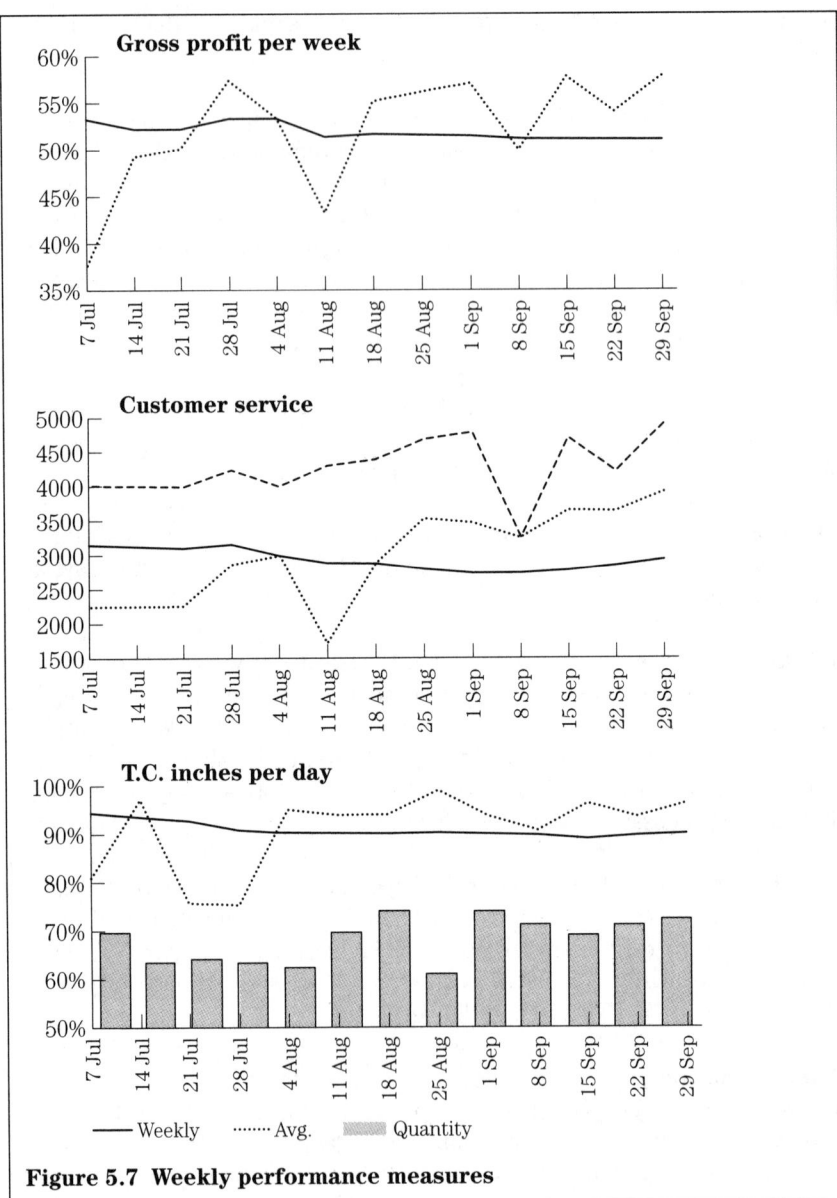

Figure 5.7 Weekly performance measures

the open market is continually reviewed. Hughes closely watches the costs of scrap materials and operating the tungsten-crushing machine. For product costing, these costs are directly assigned to steel-blades processed.

5.2.97 Steel costs are drawn from invoices. Steel is delivered precut, so this activity is outsourced. It is costed directly to products.

5.2.98 The system develops conversion-processing cell costs, which is unlike many other JIT applications. Kenco adds value to blades for earth-moving and other heavy equipment. It impregnates the steel blades with tungsten carbide. The proprietary process and product handling characteristics (including weight) prohibit outsourcing. Thus, the existence of any production requires all conversion-processing activities.

5.2.99 Accordingly, Kenco treats conversion-processing as a JIT cell. However, it is focused on the proprietary TCing process. Non-TCing activities have excess capacity. Labour is fixed at a single-shift. Thus, non-TCing activities are not a focus for incremental cost control. To illustrate, the TCing machine has bottleneck capacity and bevelling has excess capacity. Bevelling's single-shift labour is a fixed cost. Thus, managers cannot realise labour cost savings by marginally reducing bevelling set-up time. Bevelling conversion cost per bevelling hour would not be useful for cost control.

5.2.100 Kenco's costing system applies all conversion-processing costs to steel blades based on TCing time. It identifies total cell cost per TC-machine hour. (Conversion cost per TC-machine hour equals total cell cost divided by 80 per cent of maximum TC-machine time.) This is not well-designed for conventional cost control since TCing time does not drive all costs. However, the bulk of the cell costs are fixed per period. They vary rarely with extreme volume fluctuations. While incremental cost-assignment errors occur, the costing system is well-designed to focus on TCing time management.

5.2.101 Kenco's costing supports value added assessments and helps target products for design improvement. Each TCing hour consumes Kenco's proprietary revenue and profit-generating potential. TCing time is what Kenco sells – the basic value added to customers' equipment. Multiplying cell cost-per-hour by product time-used gives a surrogate for critical resource value consumed by products.

Rethinking product costing at Kenco

5.2.102 Kenco's managers use accounting information for a number of decisions. These include strategic resource (TCing machine) management, value added analysis, process and product design improvement and bidding.

Changing technologies and cost management

Given the competitive and strategic environment and the information specifically designed for decision support at Kenco, one might rethink the backflush costing design for Kenco and devise a more economically useful and strategically focused accounting system for the new manufacturing environment.

5.2.103 Accounting can be a strong force in managing the enterprise. Hughes shows this in Kenco's profit turnaround. Kenco's costing system differs from designs typically encountered. Kenco's system is not necessarily the best one possible. It works and adds value. However, a better system may be possible – now or as Kenco's needs change.

5.2.104 Hughes uses pounds crushed as a driver to apply tungsten-crushing conversion costs. He uses TC-machine time to apply conversion costs for the conversion-processing cell. Actual invoice materials costs go into the accounts. Conversion costs are assigned using predetermined overhead rates. Hughes does not need to develop standard costs because the bulk of conversion costs are fixed, cycle times are fast and accounting is timely.

5.2.105 The costing system gives management weekly tungsten-crushing costs. Hughes compares these costs to outsourcing prices to assess the ongoing decision to make. Thus, the costing system should assign only dedicated overhead to tungsten crushing. The activity is the sole cause of this overhead and outsourcing eliminates it.

5.2.106 One technique that can aid capacity management is biased cost measurement to focus management's attention. Biased costs may be incremental costs that are not assigned by a driver (on a cause-effect basis). Also, they may be capacity (fixed) costs that are not assigned on a resources-consumed basis. An example is dividing fixed batch (equipment set-up) costs across jobs and then allocating to products within jobs. A second technique for capacity management is the Theory of Constraints (see Chapter **7**).

5.2.107 One might ask: how does Kenco's use of the 80 per cent run time goal differ from some larger companies' management of capacity?

5.2.108 Eighty per cent of the scheduled shift time (machine maximum capacity) is usually the available capacity. This is the average TCing capacity available to generate revenue. Bottleneck-process run time signals productivity for the entire conversion processing cell. Thus, TCing must run at 80 per cent of maximum capacity to achieve the maximum available output and profit.

Just-in-time systems

5.2.109 Inherently, capacity fixed costs per product unit vary inversely with output. Idle capacity increases assigned product costs. When the market will not pay higher prices to cover these costs, product and company profits decrease.

5.2.110 Kenco, however, does not manage capacity through a cost focus. It does not use the 80 per cent run time goal to target minimum fixed cost per product unit. Targeting costs can imply a cost-plus pricing and profit management focus. However, some larger companies do focus on per unit costs to co-ordinate capacity with prices and required profits. They typically have a complex set of capacity resources. Kenco has only one TCing machine and runs a single shift.

5.2.111 Instead then, Kenco uses market prices to drive management of capacity costs. The 80 per cent indicator is a physical measure used to exploit full TCing capacity. It can be thought of as Kenco's revenue-generating potential. Value added as measured by market-driven prices signals the need to assess opportunities for capacity cost restructuring. Kenco begins with market price and product profitability as the focus of analysis. It then assesses whether process redesign can bring costs into line with market demands and desired profit.

5.2.112 Besides seeing alternative ways to manage capacity costs, one should understand the central goal. It is to have capacity meet external demand at a satisfactory profit. Vern Hughes believes that beginning with the market rather than cost best achieves this goal. Using either approach, downsizing or other changes in capacity cost structure can bring product costs into line with target profits. Beginning with what the market will pay may achieve better management focus.

5.2.113 Of course, downsizing or outsourcing conversion-processing is now inappropriate for Kenco. It is a small, single-shift firm with a proprietary process. Kenco can, however, change its cost structure through process redesign.

5.2.114 How does applying all of conversion processing's use of the TC-machine help increase profitability?

5.2.115 The market drives prices, demanding a level of efficiency. Kenco uses JIT and TQM-focused operations to raise productivity to this level. These principles are used to enhance value added and cut non-value added. Also, Kenco works to manage the profitability of its core competitive advantage – the TCing process. Maximising the profit potential of the TC-machine is a problem in bottleneck capacity management. Kenco manages TC-machine time to cut wasted use of proprietary value. This maximises product profitability. It increases throughput and frees capacity for added volume.

5.2.116 Conversion-processing activities (bevelling, drilling, TCing, etc.) occur within one building. Accounting forms a single conversion cost pool for these activities (a 'four wall' costing system). Dividing by 80 per cent of the TC-machine hours available gives a rate used to assign conversion costs to steel blades. A single pool is appropriate because most conversion costs are fixed for a single shift. Incremental costs caused by alternative drivers are not significant. Also, activities supporting TC machining have excess capacity.

5.2.117 Using TCing time to assign this cost pool reflects elements of the Theory of Constraints. Each TCing hour consumes Kenco's proprietary revenue and profit-generating potential. TCing time is what Kenco sells – the basic value added to customers' equipment. Cell cost per TCing hour multiplied by product time-used measures resource consumption. This is a surrogate for critical resource value consumed by the product.

5.2.118 Since TCing time drives profit and constrains production, performance improvement should focus on its productive use. The unbalanced cell ties other activities' productivity to the TCing machine. Improving their productivity and profitability requires first improving the bottleneck machine's productivity. Cell conversion cost per TCing hour focuses product profitability on the critical resource.

5.2.119 The product redesign had required too many tungsten strips and multiple TCing machine passes. The blade's high time-use and processing cost lowered its profit margin. This signalled a potential loss of greater sales volume. The assigned cost made the product's overuse of critical TCing capacity highly visible.

5.2.120 Another costing design might not have made the extent of the problem visible. Using activity-based costing (ABC) (see Chapter **6**), Hughes could have designed a homogeneous cost pool for TCing and other pools for bevelling, etc. However, the product's cost would have been less. It would not have as clearly signalled the capacity-management opportunity.

5.2.121 Kenco's accounting system accurately assigns tungsten, tungsten crushing and steel costs. Pounds crushed and invoices drive all of these conversion and materials costs.

Just-in-time systems

5.2.122 But how does the costing system inaccurately assign conversion costs in the conversion-processing cell?

5.2.123 Kenco allocates all cell conversion costs on TCing machine time. However, this basis has a cause-effect relationship only to TCing-process costs. The costing design intends this. Vern Hughes' design allows some cause-effect inaccuracy when cell costs are allocated to products.

5.2.124 The following contrived data may be useful to consider in terms of product miscosting alternatives and effects at Kenco.

Table 5.5 Product miscosting alternatives and effects

	Product	TCing machine minutes used	Conversion processing costs other than for TCing	
			Actual support costs	Applied support costs*
Case no 1:	A	60	$900	$600
	B	120	900	1,200
Case no 2:	A	60	$800	$600
	B	120	1,000	1,200
Case no 3:	A	60	$1,000	$600
	B	120	800	1,200
Case no 4:	A	60	$800	$900
	B	120	1,900	1,800

*($1,800 ÷ 180 total TCing minutes) = $10 per TCing machine minute used
($2,700 ÷ 180 total TCing minutes) = $15 per TCing machine minute used

5.2.125 In cases nos 1–3, product A incurs a higher percentage of total actual support costs [50 per cent = $900 ($900 + $900), 44.4 per cent = $800 ($800 + $1,000) and 55.6 per cent = $1,000 ($1,000 + $800)] than TCing time [33.3 per cent = 60 (60 + 120)]. Applying cost on TCing time under-costs product A. Its proportion of total TCing time is always less than its proportion of total actual costs. Conversely, product B is always over-costed. Product B has a disproportionately high use of TCing time compared to actual cost.

5.2.126 In case no 4, product A is over-costed. It incurs a percentage of total actual costs [29.6 per cent = $800 ($800 + $1,900)] that is less than its percentage of total TCing time [33.3 per cent = 60 (60 + 120)]. Product B is under-costed. It has a disproportionately low use of TCing time compared to actual cost. In all cases nos 1–4, TCing time inaccurately assigns costs to products A and B.

5.2.127 All products influence the bias in costing any one product. Under- or over-costing of one product depends on other products' actual support costs and TCing time-used. Thus, the one product is randomly miscosted.

5.2.128 For example, a customer may use an earth-moving bucket in loose, rock-free soil. Its blade will have comparatively low TCing support costs and require little tungsten impregnating. This is illustrated by product A in cases no 2 and no 4. Given product A's resource requirements, its under- or over-costing depends on other products' resource requirements.

5.2.129 Using product B on an earth-moving bucket in rocky soil requires more tungsten impregnating (TCing time). Added production support (caused by larger boltholes, a thicker piece of steel, etc.) might cost $1,000 or $1,900. Cases no 2 and no 4 illustrate these facts. In case no 2, product B's requirements raise its support costs to 125 per cent ($1,000,800) of product A's. In case no 4, product B's costs are 237.5 per cent ($1,900,800) of product A's costs. In both cases, product B's TCing time and applied costs ($1,200, $600; $1,800, $900) are 200 per cent of product A's.

5.2.130 Allocation on TCing time overstates product B's cost in case no 2 (understating A's). It understates B's cost in case no 4 (overstating A's). Thus, changes in product B's resource use determine the direction and degree of product A's costing error.

5.2.131 Managers may be authorised to adjust for product cost bias in making decisions. A problem with random miscosting is that they do not know the bias's direction and size. For example, Kenco's costing system misstates the cost of resources consumed by using TCing time. This is done for a good reason – to target productivity improvement. However, there is a good reason to know the nature of over- or under-costing. This information enables managers to avoid uncompetitive responses to customers' manufacturing and price demands.

5.2.132 Kenco's accounting system always overstates TC-machining's cost per hour. By assigning all cell conversion costs on TCing time, it overstates the cost of providing the TCing activity. This has implications for cost control. However, the system does not systematically overstate cost assigned to a product. Costs allocated to products measure their consumption of total-cell resources relative to other products.

5.2.133 A single, heterogeneous cost pool allocated on TCing time yields inaccurate product costs. Thus, Kenco's managers make cost-related decisions without precise cost information. They do not precisely know cost-driver relationships and resource costs consumed by products. They do not

Just-in-time systems

know the direction or degree of individual product cost-bias. Products use different amounts of TCing time and other cell-activities, but there is no analysis of these relationships.

5.2.134 However, Hughes and Kenco's managers see no problems caused by the absence of marginal cost information. This is true for activity as well as product decisions. Process improvement, cost control and pricing decisions are made effectively at Kenco with the information available. A major reason is that incremental costs (for bevelling, etc.) are immaterial. Most cell conversion costs are fixed. Also, single-shift operations have excess capacity.

5.2.135 Kenco has designed inaccuracy into the costing system, but product cost inaccuracy is immaterial. Random bias designed into product costs can lead to problems, but it does not for Kenco.

5.2.136 Kenco's differentiated products can earn above-average margins. However, they must stay price competitive at the market's perception of value added. Also, substitute (though inferior) products give Kenco's market-based prices some cost sensitivity.

5.2.137 This argues for accurate product costing. Without accurate cost information, Kenco may be sacrificing, rather than optimising, its profit potential. Unseen opportunity losses could exist with under-costed products sold below achievable prices. Better cost justification to customers could bring higher prices.

5.2.138 Kenco uses its bidding-sheet cost breakdowns and list prices to justify its bid prices. Customers are satisfied with prices as measured against perceived value added, substitute products and the bidding-sheet information. Kenco has premium prices that are successfully communicated to customers as fair. By these criteria, it has selected an appropriate cost system.

5.2.139 Vern Hughes sees no cues to suggest that any product cost errors are material. Any bias does not result in significantly adverse price or profitability effects. Also, Hughes sees no customer relationships that might be suboptimally structured because of inaccurate costs.

5.2.140 The costing system (product cost inaccuracy) helps manage TCing machine time. It focuses on fully using Kenco's most critical profit-generating resource. The TCing machine is Kenco's primary source of value added and its capacity bottleneck. The costing system improves management of this machine's time.

Changing technologies and cost management

5.2.141 Assume Hughes used activity-based costing to compute product profits. How could Kenco use this profit to manage TCing capacity? One method measures profit per unit of scarce resource. Product indices are ranked to target improvement. An example index is: ABC product profit, TCing time = profit/hour of scarce resource use.

5.2.142 In broad terms, Vern Hughes has chosen a costing design that has costs. These are: small cost inaccuracies, unknown biases and suboptimal decisions that are theoretically possible. However, the design also has benefits. These are: support of management's decision focus, economic relevance, timely information and low system cost. Hughes has sought to favour a system that corresponds to Kenco's specific situation and emphasises management's agenda.

Non-financial metrics

5.2.143 What has Hughes done to give continuous improvement a financial focus? Kenco relies heavily on market prices to reflect competitor and market-demanded efficiency and value added. Given these price attributes, product profits signal the adequacy of Kenco's efforts.

5.2.144 Gross profits prioritise products for analysis. Managers look for improvement in product design, manufacturing processes and the bidding formula. Products with negative profit receive priority attention. Weekly reporting of product profits makes this a continuous improvement program. Of course, managers must determine if market prices legitimately reflect value added and efficiency. There may be only special negotiating circumstances.

5.2.145 Conversion-processing costs significantly affect product profit. Thus, biased costs can incorrectly signal improvement needs. Products with low TC-machine time tend to report upwardly biased profits. They are not targeted, but may have potential for improvement. Highly TCed products tend to report downwardly biased profits. They are targeted for improvement.

5.2.146 Is the bias in the costing system a design weakness for control and continuous improvement?

5.2.147 The bias is a design weakness that can affect cost control and continuous improvement. However, it is not a significant weakness in Kenco's environment. Kenco is a small firm whose accountant thoroughly knows and participates in operations. Hughes watches several key variables for abnormalities. Also, physical controls are JIT and TQM-focused. Production is substantially efficient and managers are likely to be aware of operating inefficiencies and non-value added. Finally, managers and engineers work

Just-in-time systems

closely with the sales force to meet customer demands and identify areas for improvement.

5.2.148 What does Kenco's costing system uniquely achieve for control and continuous improvement? Weekly reports of product profitability focus these efforts around the profit objective. Product profitability is understood by everyone. Therefore, it effectively integrates efforts to analyse value added and efficiency.

5.2.149 Also, product profitability signals competitor efficiency. It signals market recognition of value added by Kenco's unique production technology. Product profits should reconcile with other, more internally based, control systems. Targeting highly TCed products for improvement implements Kenco's belief that the value it adds is TCing. By not wasting TCing time, Kenco more fully exploits its core profit-generating resource. Higher prices cannot recover the wasted resource's profit-potential. This is a non-value added that is not recognised by the market.

5.2.150 Kenco's system isolates this activity's costs so they are directly comparable to external-sourcing prices. Hughes watches these market prices as benchmarks for cost control and appraisal of the make-buy decision.

Management response
5.2.151 Kenco's AIS system is designed to support a relevant costing or decision focused concept. The basic justification is the use of different costing systems for different purposes. Kenco's AIS is designed to support a specific management approach that has shaped the design of the manufacturing process, marketing and management strategies. To fit the relevant costing analogy, the existing cost structure is like a sunk cost. These sunk costs reflect the company's philosophy and game plan.

5.2.152 The physical layout was redesigned to fit the company's key strategic needs of flexibility, custom design, short cycle times, TCing and bidding.

5.2.153 To achieve the needed flexibility and throughput, out-sourcing contracts and a JIT cell were set up. To give the cell the required flexibility (lot sizes of one are common), Kenco chose to build excess capacity at each station except for the key proprietary process (TCing).

5.2.154 The old production system used a traditional manufacturing strategy. Under this type of management philosophy, groups of identical

Changing technologies and cost management

machines (or a machine) were separated by WIP so that they all could be active regardless of the balance of the product mix with machine capacity. Excessive WIP allowed the company to keep machines running relatively independent of each other. This allowed them to utilise fully the capacity of each machine group. Thus, in theory, unit costs could be reduced by spreading fixed costs over more units.

5.2.155 With Kenco's variety of products and low lot sizes large levels of WIP would be necessary to ensure that all fixed machine capacity would be fully utilised. This production variation forced long lead times on this 'push' manufacturing system.

5.2.156 On the other hand, the new JIT cell is unbalanced by design. TCing is meant to be the constraint. The constraint sets the capacity for the cell and, given the simplicity of the manufacturing system, for the company as a whole. The key design tradeoff between the before and after systems is between excess capacity versus excess WIP.

5.2.157 The efficiency tradeoff between the two systems is to spend money on excess capacity that may not be fully used in exchange for limiting the level of WIP required to balance the capacity of each station. The JIT design, in turn, allows the flexibility and cycle times generated by a pull system. Even so, Hughes has mitigated this JIT inefficiency by cross-training his personnel as much as possible.

5.2.158 In the new JIT cell, the fixed capacity costs (including labour) are sunk. In this case, product variation has little impact on costs as long as no new constraints occur. In an unbalanced cell, the bottleneck or constraint's value is set by the opportunity cost of its capacity.

5.2.159 The weekly reports on product profitability are estimates of the opportunity cost of TCing capacity. For this purpose, the decision focused AIS system is perfectly accurate. It provides a ranking of the relative profitability of the products in the cell as management designed it to work. All the manufacturing costs, other than steel and tungsten, are treated as sunk.

5.2.160 The problem seems to occur when the constraint or bottleneck floats. That is, the capacity of the cell is set by some activity other than the TCing machines. The relevant cost of the cell now shifts to the opportunity cost of the new activity. The existing system is inaccurate when the costs are assigned to the wrong (i.e., non-constraint) activity. Before changing the AIS, however, Kenco must determine whether or not the constraint is a permanent condition signalling a basic shift in the market place.

Just-in-time systems

5.2.161 Suppose the company invested in purchasing additional machine and labour capacity to move the constraint back to the TCing machine. The traditional argument suggests that inaccurate bidding has created a demand for products that signals the need for the additional capacity. However, this expansion would *not* necessarily be efficient. The need for greater capacity is created by a bidding system that literally assigns no cost to the use of non-TCing resources. But why has this not happened to Kenco?

5.2.162 Perhaps it is because the competitive market sets the price, not the company. Costs are the constraint used for rejecting, and not accepting, orders. Most orders are based on what is the best price Kenco can get.

5.2.163 However, the bottleneck may change because of a large order. For example, Kenco bid on a large order (about 100 units) that shifted the constraint temporarily. This does not occur frequently. However, when it does occur, a detailed analysis is made to see if the cell can be balanced to handle this special order. Because management can focus on simple visible manufacturing cost relationships in the JIT cell, they can make an accurate evaluation of the need for additional capacity investments. However, since these decisions are rare they do not need a formal data system to support them.

5.2.164 In conclusion, Kenco's system has two features to limit the unsatisfactory effects of a 'biased' costing system.

(1) Only products that are marginally profitable are evaluated with respect to cost. Pricing is based on what the market will bear – market-based pricing. Using a market-based bid sheet that prices the features the customer demands based upon some evaluation of the market value of these features is crucial. The 'traditional machine and labour costs' to make the products are not relevant since they are sunk. They are not used to value the benefits of additional capacity except in a special analysis. Costs are not used to 'signal' the need for additional capacity.

(2) Products in larger volumes can shift the constraint away from the TCing machine. These are subject to special analysis. Special analysis is made easy by the simplicity of the system.

5.2.165 This is a relatively common situation for costing systems. The key is that the weaknesses are known and understood by management and hence can be avoided through the implementation of appropriate management policies.

(Source: case adapted with permission from IMA (1997).)

5.3 Enterprise resource planning

5.3.1 Total quality management (TQM) and just-in-time systems can be viewed as work philosophies rather than technological advances. Conversely, enterprise resource planning (ERP) systems, which offer a means of integrating and servicing all the different functions of an organisation by interlinking information bases and exchanges, appeal to innovative computerised technologies. The precursor to ERP for many enterprises was materials requirement planning (MRP) which, for production environments, concerned itself with maximising efficiency in the timing of raw material orders placed with vendors and with scheduling the machining and assembly of the final manufacturing product. It makes available components and subassembled parts just before they are needed by the next stage of production for dispatch. MRP systems were implemented as production and planning tools in traditional manufacturing contexts as they entailed only a basic level of automation by way of computer software for back-scheduling the major production processes given the required date for delivery of the final products to a customer. Early MRP systems depended on information based on weekly predictions, whereas later manufacturing resources planning (MRP II) systems, which linked medium- to long-term production plans with existing and planned capacities, needed daily updating. The objectives of MRP II systems included minimising stock levels, production run disruptions, storage costs and the extra expenses incurred in accepting rush orders. MRP II systems also provided forecasts of the production status of specific products and thus enabled the preparation of proforma statements of all categories of stocks by aggregating individual product forecasts. MRP II systems made evident the need to rate vendors on price, quality and delivery. An example of a quality measure could be:

> No. of parts inspected and passed/No. of parts inspected = Quality performance rating

5.3.2 Such a measure would be stored in the vendor master file MRP II database and viewed on-line periodically. Over time, movement to just-in-time could eliminate incoming inspections which add no value and the rating measure could help identify the best vendor for contracting under just-in-time.

5.3.3 An important drawback identified by MRP II systems is the reliance on the batch processing of data to generate 'what was' rather than 'what is' analyses. To overcome the paper-based batch record processing associated with MRP II, a partial solution was viewed as moving to 'paperless' processing. More problematic was the difficulty in integrating MRP II functions with marketing, sales and accounting functions. One approach adopted by many organisations desiring to break down business processes into smaller manageable subparts has been object technology whereby building blocks can be mixed and matched to allow new business processes to be affected. Breaking systems into smaller, manageable objects has a number of distinct advantages:

- systems development projects can be split into manageable blocks with different teams given responsibility for developing and testing the various elements of the project;
- common processes or objects can be shared between different application systems. This concept is often referred to as object reuse;
- changes and enhancements to business processes are easier to isolate and implement;
- testing business processes is more thorough and is easier as each object is tested before all the objects are put together and the system is tested as a whole;
- business processes are more easily understood if they are broken down into smaller component parts which in turn allows the optimum design to be achieved;
- enabling increased productivity by systems development teams by focusing developers on business issues not the underlying technology.

5.3.4 The object-oriented approach is not confined to systems development and the IT department as the concept can be used anywhere that solutions to business problems are required. The concept of breaking a process into component parts can be applied to company organisation structures, customer service functions, inventory ordering and control, etc. In addition, combined with business process re-engineering, the object-oriented approach can provide the basic tools for enhancing and developing new business functions for an organisation.

5.3.5 Designing a system using object technology techniques requires the designer to think about the business process rather than consider the technical detail. During the design process it is likely that a number of different object categories will be identified, including:

- *Business objects* – high-level business functions. The order processing cycle can be considered a business object which in turn is broken down into lower-level business objects such as customer set-up, stock enquiry, etc.

Changing technologies and cost management

- *Technical objects* – computer programs performing specific low-level functions. A particular application will be made up of many technical objects or computer programs.

- *Wrapper objects* – allow new processes to be integrated with existing application systems (often referred to as legacy systems).

- *Distributed objects* – provide integration between remote objects and allow true distributed computer systems to be implemented.

5.3.6 According to Armstrong (2000), a system developed using object-oriented techniques will usually result in the separation of the following:

- *Data* – which will be maintained within an appropriate database manager;

- *Business functionality* – which will be maintained in the actual programs;

- *Presentation of business functionality* – which will be viewed by the user via appropriate GUI tools.

5.3.7 In summary, the object technology approach enables an organisation to break down its business into component parts which can be quickly reorganised in response to changes to the business and to meet new opportunities without the need for major redesign of the underlying processes.

5.3.8 During the 1990s many organisations moved to ERP systems. ERPs are software systems which enable the 'enterprise-wide integration of commercial and technical functions'. ERP aims to provide instant access to data of all sorts generated by widely scattered and functionally diverse sites.

5.3.9 Historically, departments within most organisations have been responsible for defining their specific IT application requirements. The finance department would specify the accounting systems needs, operations would outline the distribution and logistics systems, and manufacturing the MRP and related solutions. The result was that organisations ended up with different applications from different vendors with little or no integration and a high level of data duplication.

5.3.10 Armstrong (2000) notes that software and application suppliers have recognised this situation and have started to extend the range of software solutions to cover the functions found in typical organisations. Where software authors traditionally specialised in accounting ledgers they have extended their software offerings by adding manufacturing and distribution modules. Likewise, specialists in distribution and logistics have started to add accounting and manufacturing solutions. This results in ERP solutions that are meant to cater for all the requirements of an organisation and allow customers to buy solutions from a one-stop shop.

5.3.11 Vendors generally supplying the high-end and corporate market place have enthusiastically taken up the ERP approach. Organisations such as SAP, Baan, Oracle and JD Edwards promote their products under the ERP banner. However, ERP is not restricted to these large organisations: some of the suppliers serving smaller organisations also have ERP offerings. Examples include Great Plains, Navisions and Exact.

5.3.12 The need to supply an extended set of applications quickly has proven to be problematic for software suppliers. Some suppliers have extended their range of applications by writing the applications in-house, allowing them to provide a high-level of integration between their application areas. Other organisations have chosen either to acquire or to form partnerships with other suppliers who have complementary software products.

5.3.13 Some software suppliers have recognised that they cannot compete in the ERP arena and have decided to maintain a niche presence providing best-of-breed applications in their area of specialisation. Customers deciding to purchase best-of-breed applications rather than totally integrated solutions are not necessarily excluded from achieving an ERP solution. The advent of middleware now makes it much easier for applications from different vendors to be integrated, although the customer will normally need appropriate IT resources or a reliable third party supplier to assist in making this possible according to Armstrong (2000).

5.3.14 During the 1990s many organisations moved to ERP systems to enable the enterprise-wide integration of commercial and technical functions. Smith (1999) notes that there has been immense growth in the ERP market over the last few years. Worldwide sales exceeded $24 billion in 1999. As ERP systems expand their compatibility with digitised e-commerce business processes, the organisational information systems integration market is set to continue to expand.

5.3.15 The adoption of integrated information systems in some companies has suffered setbacks. Smith (1999) observes that some enterprises failed to reap the benefits that investments in ERP should have yielded. He notes that the current consensus seems to be that ERP projects have:

Changing technologies and cost management

- represented very large investments for some organisations;
- been very painful to implement and left these organisations drained and resistant to launching further projects;
- delivered limited business benefits over and above the installation of new base systems infrastructure.

5.3.16 Ultimately, some organisations have failed to address the fact that business change is essential to generate value. Simply altering the technology that underpins particular ways of doing business is insufficient to reap the full scale of potential benefits. It is important to develop an exploitation strategy relating to systems change as well as to pinpoint the desired benefits. Subsequently, a programme to adopt systems to extract such benefits and to monitor their delivery must be developed.

5.3.17 Scapens *et al.* (1998) note that there are important implications for management accountants within organisations implementing the ERP system, 'Systems, Applications and Products' (SAP). SAP uses relational database technology to integrate the various elements of an organisation's information system. SAP packages provide a number of separate, but integrated modules, which can be configured for any organisation. The SAP 'R/2' version which focuses on mainframe environments is largely intended for batch operations whereas 'R/3', the more common version is primarily designed for client/server environments.

5.3.18 Scapens *et al.* (1998) note that as well as many other benefits of integrating information systems, such as overcoming the problems of interfacing many different systems, the use of an ERP system avoids the costs of maintaining many separate legacy systems. Scapens *et al.* (1998) note that SAP must be customised to fit the particular needs of the business through a process of configuration. But since SAP is organised around business processes, rather than traditional functional areas (such as production, sales, accounting and so on), it is important to review these business processes prior to implementation. An ERP system like SAP promotes cross-functional co-operation and team working, aside from possible changes to business processes. SAP implementation must consider how far existing business processes require modification and at what stage, i.e., before, during or after the implementation of SAP R/3 for instance. Any systems implementation must consider whether the generic capabilities meet particular businesses' needs or whether extensive customisation is essential.

5.3.19 Scapens *et al.* (1998) note that ERP systems are changing the relationship between accounting systems and other management information

Enterprise resource planning

systems. SAP integrates a variety of separate functions and business processes within the one system for the whole company. Consequently, its development and co-ordination is usually undertaken centrally by a group of specialists responsible for both the implementation and operation of the system. A consequence of such centralisation is the possible loss of control which operational units at the local level may perceive.

5.3.20 Concurrent with the centralisation of the information system, development and implementation there will likely be decentralisation of data, information and knowledge. Individual managers may, following systems implementation, directly access the information they desire. They can bypass management accountants and other information specialists for information. Budgets, variance reports, performance metrics and other cost and revenue information for different parts of the enterprise can be accessed directly by individual managers. If functional support specialists were previously in charge of providing such information to managers, the information is now readily available in the absence of the 'intermediary'. Managers need to know what is available and how to access it. In such cases, the management accountant and other information specialists may have to develop an educational role. This role may be temporary or continuous depending on the business environment. Integrating information systems like SAP which focus on business processes and which can cut across many established functions requires an understanding not just of organisational processes and functions but also of the organisation.

A case study: integration through ERP

5.3.21 Tompkins (1997) provides an example of SAP implementation at the Hibernia Management and Development Company Ltd. Hibernia is the fifth largest discovered oilfield in Canada. An important cornerstone of Hibernia's business strategy has been to enter into long-term performance-based relationships with a variety of strategic alliances, which assume a high degree of people and process integration. The commercial and operating strategies of the alliances necessitate high integrity of business and financial systems. This ensures that operating processes and their related performance measures are applied and assessed in line with regulations established by the Canada-Newfoundland Offshore Petroleum Board (CNOPB), a certifying authority.

5.3.22 Tompkins (1997) notes that the project has three levels of activity (see Figure 5.8 on page 182). During the Level 1 effort, the first level of processes was defined in terms of each core process area. Tompkins (1997) explains that the following comprises the target deliverable for Level 1:

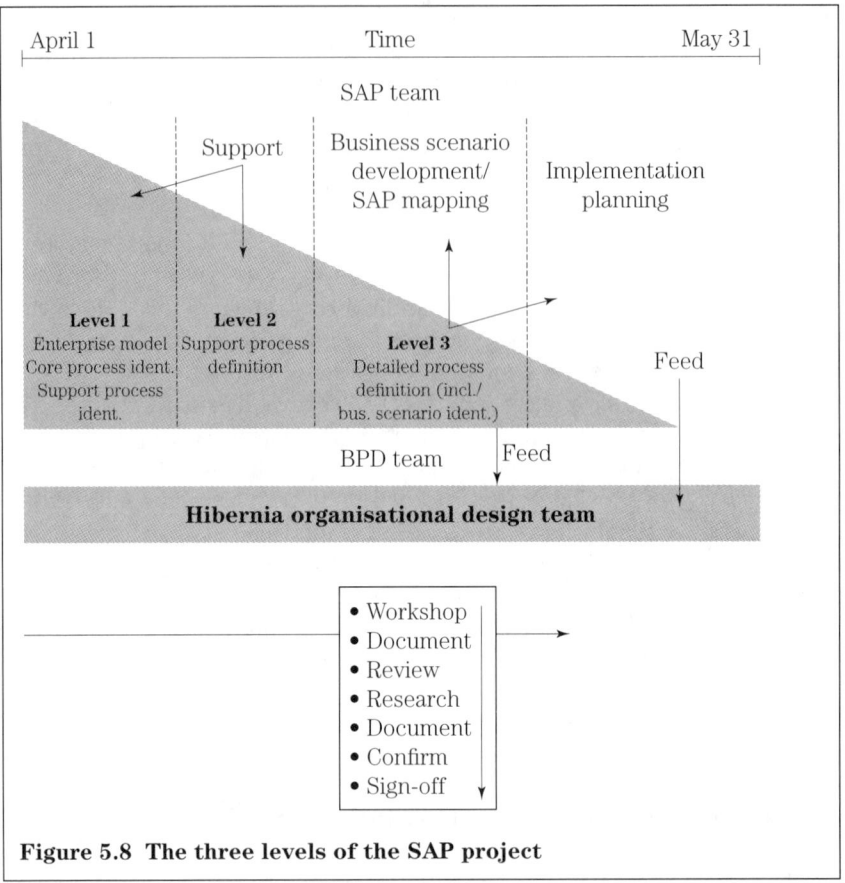

Figure 5.8 The three levels of the SAP project

(1) A short and concise definition of the core process;

(2) General processes that are included within this core process;

(3) Processes that support the above process;

(4) Entities that participate in this process (e.g., vendors, materials, supply base, etc.).

5.3.23 The above information was recorded as part of the Level 1 documentation.

5.3.24 The aim of Level 2 was, as Tompkins (1997) notes, to map the process sequences identified during the Level 1 effort onto a process-flow diagram.

Enterprise resource planning

5.3.25 The Level 3 entailed 'drilling down' processes to the appropriate level of detail so as to differentiate variations in the process flow. These variations were charted in a process-flow diagram, with qualitative information in corresponding documents. Each process variation depicted on the diagram provided details of what constituted the business scenario. Process flows gave users an in-depth understanding of each process and were utilised to compile the business scenario listing.

5.3.26 The objective of Level 3 activity according to Tompkins (1997) was to take the process flows documented in Level 2 and create flows at a more detailed level for some of the processes. The principal difference was that each Level 3 flow related to only one step in a Level 2 process. A Level 2 process could have multiple Level 3 process flows which depict different variations of the process. These process variations represented different business scenarios. These scenarios would subsequently be utilised in the next phase of the project to conduct what Tompkins (1997) calls a 'gap-fit' analysis against SAP functionality. These prioritised 'gaps', along with basic SAP functionality in support of the designed processes, would form an important cornerstone of the implementation plan.

SAP implementation

5.3.27 The above phases of implementation took four weeks and were within budget. This produced a listing of about 500 process variations. The next step was to determine how well they would fit against standard SAP functionality. To make this determination, the elements of the process against SAP were mapped and gaps identified. These gaps were prioritised based on the critical nature of their contribution towards obtaining 'first oil'. Some gaps were fixed after minimal changes to the process. There were instances where no functionality was evident to support the process, thus manuals were developed to provide guidance.

These activities allowed the SAP implementation plan to emerge. The methodology was as follows:

(a) Build processes in an integrated rather than sequential manner;

(b) Test processes in an integrated fashion with individuals who were not involved in building the processes;

(c) Implement processes concurrently.

5.3.28 A model for making decisions (see Figure 5.9) was developed. The model aligned with team-based culture and enabled 'rules' to be operationalised early in the project. The essence of the model was that 80 per cent

Changing technologies and cost management

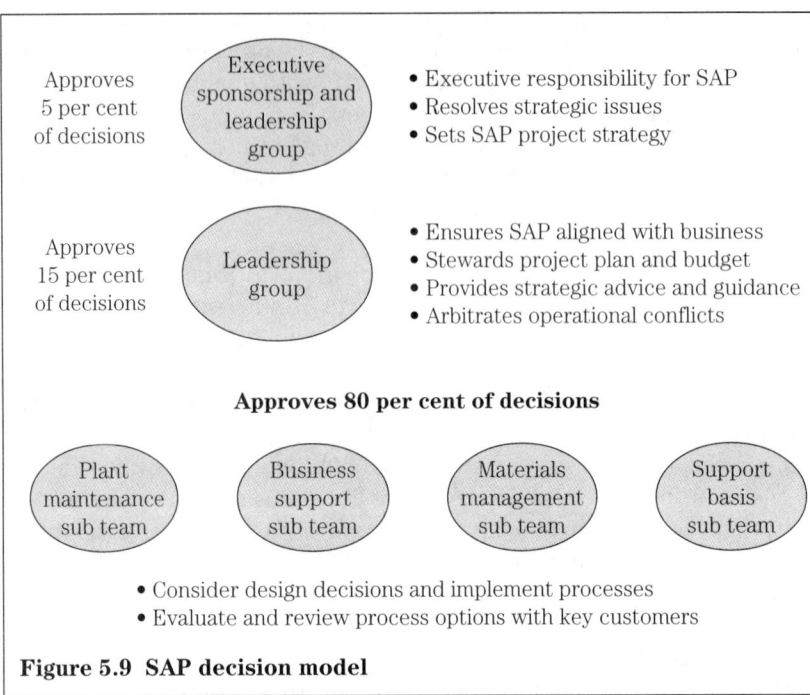

Figure 5.9 SAP decision model

of the decisions would be made by the work teams, 15 per cent would be made by the 'leadership group', and 5 per cent by the 'executive sponsor' and the leadership group. Communication was encouraged, if not required, at all points in the model. The model promoted 'ownership' according to Tompkins (1997).

5.3.29 Tompkins (1997) identifies the following as useful points for project managers:

- Establish a 'bullet-proof' acceptance/quality assurance testing process;
- Architecture constraints will become evident;
- Do not try to become a functional expert;
- Get a planner! Focus on planning analysis;
- Most of the re-engineering performed will be human;
- Only full-time people from the business should be involved;
- Partner with a consulting firm that fits the business culture of the enterprise;

- Worry about master data first;
- Involve senior management frequently.

5.4 Numerical control machines

5.4.1 Numerical control (NC) machines are traditional manufacturing tools which may be programmed with a set of instructions for guiding desired processes within predefined performance criteria. Although NCs have been superseded in many organisations by more advanced forms of flexible technologies, the availability of computer power has permitted enhanced flexibility of machine controls by computerising numerical controls. The principal aim of an NC machine is to shorten production times by reducing set-up activities which do not add value to the processing function. Other benefits which may accrue from NC technologies include improved quality and reduced variability of output, decreased scrap and rework levels, substantial reductions in the number of direct labour workers required to achieve a desired output level and overall productivity gains.

5.4.2 The decision to acquire NC technology can be problematic in that benefits such as decreases in direct labour costs, lead times, inventory levels and increases in quality, capacity and manufacturing flexibility are difficult to evaluate quantitatively. The problem of separating cash flows from different machines used together in the production process also makes performance measurement a difficult exercise.

5.4.3 Undertaking cost control poses a challenge in that NC machines replace direct labour costs with depreciation and machine-related costs which are not readily captured and controlled by conventional cost accounting systems. Differentiation between controllable versus uncontrollable costs is not easy and may be impossible. The use of NC machines can make product costing increasingly arbitrary as the cost behaviour of machine operator wages is altered but does not become categorically direct or indirect. Overhead rates which are based on direct labour costs or hours become volatile and distort product costs to the extent that product line profitability figures may mislead decision-makers when judging the returns from individual product lines. Table 5.6 highlights some accounting problems (together with possible solutions) posed by NC actions.

Changing technologies and cost management

Table 5.6 NC machines: problems and solutions

	Problem	Solution
1.	Benefits, even direct labour cost savings, are difficult to quantify	Proper consideration of subjective factors
		Avoid excessive optimism
		Do not over-quantify
		Improve quantification of direct labour cost savings
2.	Costs are less controllable	See discussion below on flexible manufacturing systems
3.	Product costing:	
	(i) overhead base: direct labour is not related to overhead	Use a machine-hour base \ runtime, engineered time or actual machine-hours
	activity-level: errors in annual forecasts of activity cause fixed overhead allocations to be inaccurate	Use variable costing, or adjust activity levels more frequently than every year
	overhead costs are not relevant: future costs are not recorded, and recorded overhead is irrelevant	Use variable costing
	plant-wide and company-wide rates cause inaccurate allocations	Use departmental rates
		Use different overhead bases and rates for different overhead costs within a department

	(ii) identification of machine operator wages as direct or indirect is difficult:
	   * satellite work
	   * second-job idle time
	   * number of machines exceeds number of operators
		Treat all machine operators' wages as indirect, or review all machine operator wages and reclassify as indirect wages (including idle time) that are hard to trace to the product

4.	Performance measurement on NC machines is difficult:	New measures of productivity should be developed, but judgement should not be eliminated
	(i) benefits are difficult to quantify	Consider all labour to be fixed, or
	(ii) cash flows are difficult to separate	classify these wages as variable or fixed on a case by case basis
	(iii) measures intended to evaluate direct labour are used	Less emphasis on net income, more emphasis on long-run goals, promotions, alternative valuation bases, and so on
	(iv) machines are evaluated on the local goal of efficiency rather	

	than the broader goal of productivity	
5.	Cost behaviour: wages of machine operators are often a fixed cost	Treat as fixed cost or part of indirect labour costs
6.	Over-emphasis on the short run to the detriment of the long run is caused by the use of financial accounting information:	See 4 above
	(i) efficiency versus productivity	
	(ii) over-emphasis on net income	
	(iii) excessive pressure to control costs	

(Source: adapted from Bennett *et al.*, 1987.)

5.5 Computer-aided design and computer-aided manufacturing (CAD/CAM)

5.5.1 CAD/CAM refers to a blending of mechanical and computer technology to facilitate the designing and manufacturing of a product. CAD/CAM systems can potentially take an engineer's vision of a new product from the idea phase to actual product in a fraction of the time required previously. Specifically, computer-aided design entails the use of computers in the course of developing, analysing and modifying the design for a product. A typical system capable of performing the tasks required includes hardware elements such as computer, keyboards and graphics monitors. The software required includes a graphics package and the applications programs. Computer-aided manufacturing refers to the use of computers to plan, implement and control the production of a product through the utilisation of manufacturing facilities and resources. Such systems range from those that generate plans that people must implement and control to those that develop the manufacturing plans and implement and control the operations according to those plans while, at the same time, reacting to variations between planned and actual performance.

5.5.2 The decision to use CAD/CAM technology is difficult to analyse using conventional financial capital appraisal techniques because of the wide array of intangible benefits which are not easy to quantify (for instance, improved design drafts, better customer perception of products, increased productivity of draughtsmen and enhanced product quality). Cost control in CAD/CAM settings is also problematic because of the difficulty of setting labour standards for activities such as drafting and design. Moreover, with experience, these activities result in increased productivity and reduced

Changing technologies and cost management

operational time which generates the need to update standards continuously. Product costing is simplified when engineering and design costs can be ascribed to the production of a specific order. This is not always feasible, however, and it is easier simply to include costs in total departmental overheads with the attendant drawbacks of arbitrariness when costs are consequently assigned to individual products. Performance measures can be tied to improving set-up times, materials usage and manufacturing time, defect rates, product versatility and quality for which no simple measures exist but need to be custom-made for different production contexts.

5.5.3 Problems and potential solutions in the use of CAD/CAM systems are set out in Table 5.7.

Table 5.7 CAD/CAM: problems and solutions

Problems	Solutions
(1) *CAD/CAM system acquisition:*	
(i) initial system acquisition	Use discounted cash flow capital budgeting techniques. Take particular care to include estimated cash flows associated with both the tangible and intangible elements of CAD/CAM system performance. Management judgement is particularly critical in this acquisition decision
(ii) subsequent expansion and upgrading of CAD/CAM systems	Identify systems performance measures during planning and implementation of the original CAD/CAM system. Provide for capture and reporting of these measurements as a basis for justification for expansion or upgrading of the system
(2) *CAD/CAM system cost control:*	Identify CAD/CAM system cost centres (by the activity driving the incurring of cost) and control cost by these cost centres
	Use flexible budgets and performance reports distinguishing between controllable and uncontrollable costs
	Develop and use standards to control spending and utilisation of CAD/CAM system inputs in designing products and programming manufacturing
(3) *Product costing:*	
(i) defining CAD/CAM cost centres	Define individual CAD/CAM cost centres, and develop overhead rates for

	each centre based on specific activities driving the cost incurrence. If a single driver exists, then an overall rate may be developed for the CAD/CAM system
(ii) accumulating CAD/CAM system costs: – direct costs	Identify all costs that can be traced directly to the CAD/CAM system cost centres and those that can be traced to the jobs or products. Charge these costs directly to the cost centres and/or the products
– indirect costs	CAD/CAM system costs recognisable as system costs but not traceable to specific system cost centres should be assimilated in system overhead pools and subsequently allocated to the cost centres or to the products using an appropriate allocation base. The preferable base is one reflecting cause/effect or cost/benefit relationships
(iii) CAD/CAM cost allocations	Develop cost centre allocation rates based on activities driving the costs incurred, and allocate the costs on this basis
	Develop system overhead pool allocation rates for system costs not traceable to system cost centres, and allocate these costs using an appropriate allocation base. The preferable base is one reflecting cause/effect or cost/benefit relationships
(4) *Performance measurement:*	
(i) measuring CAD/CAM system productivity	Develop specific performance measures for each relevant CAD/CAM system activity. Provide for capture and reporting of these measurements as a basis for evaluating the performance and productivity of the system, i.e., number of designs, number of NC programs, time to perform design analysis, quality monitors, and so on
(ii) measuring manufacturing productivity enhancement related to the CAD/CAM system	Changes in manufacturing productivity attributable to CAD/CAM may be measured by traditional performance measures such as budgets and standards. The changes in performance attributable to CAD/CAM are evident in the difference between standard performance before CAD/CAM and that of the CAD/CAM system standard performance

Changing technologies and cost management

(iii) measuring quality of CAD/CAM system performance	Develop quality measures for the CAD/CAM system. Provide for capture and reporting of these quality measurements as a basis for measuring the quality of system performance, for example reduction in defects and spoilage, improved quality of design, versatility of tools and fixtures, and so on

(Source: adapted from Bennett *et al.*, 1987.)

5.6 Flexible manufacturing systems

5.6.1 A flexible manufacturing system (FMS) refers to a computer-controlled production system intended to produce a family of parts. In an FMS, workpieces of different types travel between and are processed at various programmable, multi-purpose machine tools and other workstations. Parts flow through the system according to individual processing and production requirements. A number of companies utilise computer-controlled FMSs running unattended on night-shift operations.

5.6.2 Production technologies such as CAD, CAM and robots are used to partially computerise factory environments so that FMSs contribute to 'islands of automation' (IA) buffered by intermediate storage of semi-finished/assembly products. IAs can be integrated so as to automate fully the production process under total computer integrated manufacturing (CIM). The main advantages of an FMS over a traditional factory organisation structure include the ability to produce differing varieties and volume levels using the same technology, quick customer response, and reduced labour costs as materials-handling systems and automated storage and retrieval systems replace labour. In addition, there are savings from the actual automation of manufacturing processes which themselves cut down on human operators. Furthermore, product quality, set-up times, machine utilisation, low inventory levels, space and enhanced information on production are all affected favourably by an FMS. It is impossible to evaluate all these benefits in quantitative form, which makes it difficult to justify FMS expenditures in purely financial terms. Cost control, product costing and performance measurement problems arise principally from the reduction in indirect labour utilisation and the high capital cost components of an FMS.

5.6.3 Table 5.8 identifies some potential accounting problems and solutions relating to FMS use.

Table 5.8 FMS: problems and solutions

Problems	Solutions
(1) Expected benefits, operation costs and useful life are difficult to quantify	Use discounted cash flow capital budgeting techniques and quantify future benefits, costs and useful life to the best extent possible
(2) Fixed costs not controllable by the FMS supervisor comprise a large portion of FMS costs. This problem and its solutions also apply to NC machines	Use flexible budgets and performance reports delineating controllable and uncontrollable costs
(3) Product costing:	
(i) defining the cost centre – plant-wide or company-wide overhead rates are inaccurate	Define the FMS as a separate cost centre with its own overhead rate
(ii) aggregating costs related to the FMS:	
– direct costs – inaccurate product costs will result if all costs directly identified with the FMS are not specified	Specify all costs that can be directly identified with the FMS
– indirect costs – many fixed overhead costs must be allocated to the FMS cost centre	Allocate to the FMS all appropriate costs not directly identified with the FMS using an appropriate allocation base
(iii) determining the overhead application base – inaccurate products costs may result if an inappropriate base such as direct labour is used	Use units of production, total time in the FMS, engineered machine hours or actual machine hours. The last two bases will probably be most suitable and implementable for most companies
(4) Performance measurement – many cost systems are designed to measure direct labour, which is insignificant in an FMS, and are not designed to measure the factors that are critical to successful performance of the FMS	Develop performance measures for the critical success factors related to the FMS. Accountants will need to work closely with manufacturing managers and engineering personnel to develop new performance measures

(Source: adapted from Bennett *et al.*, 1987.)

Material handling systems

5.6.4 Material handling systems (MHS) include those that store and warehouse raw materials and purchase parts inventory and in-process stock

Changing technologies and cost management

between operations or manufacturing functions and those that move inventory within and between manufacturing, assembly or shipping functions. The systems that store and warehouse stock between operations or manufacturing functions are represented by conventional stockrooms located in the middle of many manufacturing operations. The systems are characterised primarily by manual operations for moving the inventory to, within and from the storage area, and the handling of paperwork to keep track of inventory quantities and locations. These systems are being replaced by automatic storage/retrieval systems (AS/RS) which store and receive parts and products and can be integrated into a computerised manufacturing operation to keep accurate track of inventory and deliver required parts at just the right moment. AS/RS systems increase the speed and accuracy of inventory storage and retrieval in the automated factory.

5.6.5 FMSs can be fully compatible with the use of AS/RS system. Table 5.9 highlights some accounting problems and solutions relating to material handling systems.

Table 5.9 AS/RS: problems and solutions

Problems	Solutions
(1) Benefits and labour cost savings are difficult to quantify	Proper consideration of: (i) stock reduction savings (ii) space reduction savings (iii) increased accuracy of inventory data
(2) Costs are shifted to fixed costs and are less controllable	Establish separate cost centres for identification of controllable and non-controllable costs and reporting of controllable costs to cost centre supervisors for performance measurement
(3) Performance measurement of AS/RS must be based on: (i) system operating time (ii) computer operating time (iii) computer picks per worker hour	Develop methods for monitoring the up-time for the system Develop methods for monitoring the up-time for the computers Identify productivity measurements which can be used to count the picks per worker hour
(4) Acceptable stock accurate percentage	Monitor errors discovered by operators when picking and those discovered by cycle stock count procedures

(Source: adapted from Bennett *et al.*, 1987.)

Flexible manufacturing systems

A case study: rethinking plant layout

5.6.6 Morse (1990) provides an excellent study of an organisation (Rantoul Tool Ltd) which must deal with the need for accurate product cost information within the parameters set by the manufacturing process and plant layout. The following is based on the case described by Morse (1990) (adapted with permission).

5.6.7 Rantoul Tool Ltd is a medium-size producer of custom machine tools. The company's single production facility is located just west of Manchester. Last year's sales totalled £93 million. Rantoul's 115 employees include seven sales representatives, four industrial and mechanical engineers, 16 office employees (order entry, accounting, scheduling, secretarial services and health), five corporate officers, and 83 plant employees (supervisors, expediters, machine operators, material handling and maintenance).

5.6.8 Rantoul's products are used as manufacturing supplies by large manufacturers. Products vary considerably in their raw materials and manufacturing requirements. Because of competitive pressures, management considers that accurate product cost information is required for pricing and cost control. Until about five years ago, Rantoul's factory contained a total of 35 machines of eight different types, distributed as follows:

Type	Number	Type	Number
A	5	E	8
B	6	X	1
C	4	Y	1
D	9	Z	1

5.6.9 The machines differed significantly in their original cost, operating life, power consumption and maintenance requirements.

Production flows: plant layout

5.6.10 Rantoul's machines were laid out and organised into departments by machine type with a supervisor in charge of each department. Although each was unique, the three specialty machines (X, Y and Z) were placed in one department. Hence, there were a total of six departments. The layout of the 35 machines is detailed in Figure 5.10. Each department's work area is enclosed in dashed lines.

5.6.11 The firm's products, produced in batches of identical units referred to as a *job*, were quite heterogeneous. Some required work on only three

Changing technologies and cost management

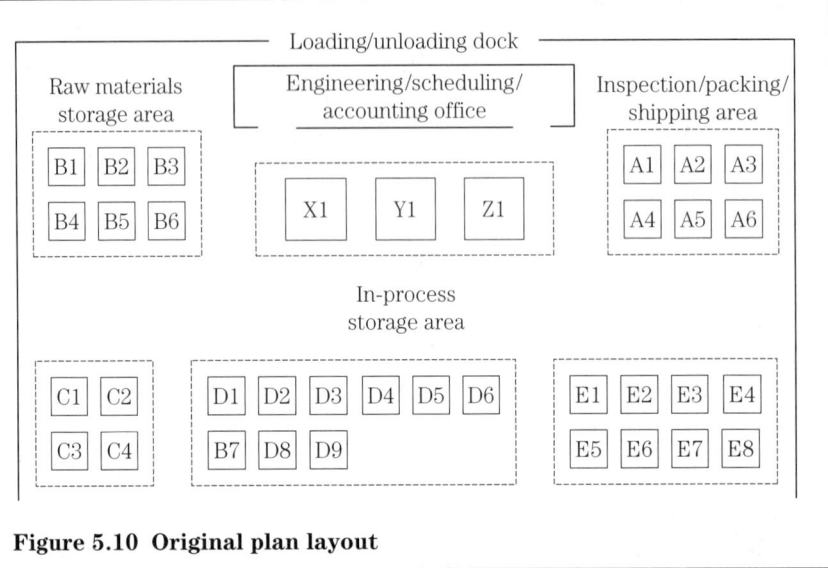

Figure 5.10 Original plan layout

machines but others required work on as many as seven machines. Nor was there a consistent flow of work among machines. Some jobs, for example, went from a B to a D to a Z while others went from an A to a Z to a D to a C, and so forth.

5.6.12 A work team of one or more employees was assigned to each machine centre. In general, each operator worked only on the machine to which he or she was assigned and worked on only one job at a time. A worker would occasionally help another operator who was having difficulty.

5.6.13 At the start of each morning and afternoon, each department supervisor received information on job assignments for the next four hours. Employees obtained materials for jobs from either the raw materials storage area or the in-process storage area, located as shown in Figure 5.10. After performing the required operation, employees placed the job in either the in-process storage area or the inspection/packing/shipping area.

Systems redesign: dedicated production lines

5.6.14 The production system described above served management well for many years. But with growing competitive pressures, management became concerned about the high storage cost of in-process stock and the amount of time production employees spent on activities that did not add value to the final product.

Flexible manufacturing systems

5.6.15 Several years ago management instituted a special study of work flows with the goal of reducing in-process inventories and non-value added activities. Only activities that physically changed materials were classified as value added. All other activities, including receiving instructions, moving inventories, looking for jobs in the in-process storage area, and setting up machines to work on jobs, were classified as non-value added.

5.6.16 The study revealed that although the products were heterogeneous, approximately 50 per cent of the company's products could be placed in one of two homogeneous categories. Products in each of these categories required work on the same types of machines, in the same sequence, and with the same proportion of work time on each machine in the sequence. In addition, the machine settings for products in each category were similar, so virtually no additional set-up time was required in the changeover from one job to another within the same product category.

5.6.17 Management believed that significant improvements in productivity and reductions in stock could be obtained by changing the plant layout so the jobs in these two homogeneous categories would never enter the in-process storage area. Instead, employees would move the units in each job directly from one machine to the next.

5.6.18 Management anticipated that shorter production times and reduced selling prices, made possible by increased productivity, would result in an increase in sales. Consequently, management elected to maintain the current number of machines. Management also anticipated a reduction the complexity of machine set-ups and the need to expedite orders. This made possible a reduction in the number of departments and production supervisors from six to five. The new departments were: Category 1 products; Category 2 products; Machine Groups B, E and C; Machine Group D; and Machine Groups X, Z and A.

5.6.19 The number of machines placed in the first two departments was selected to achieve balanced flows within the departments, given the varying speeds of individual machines. The redesigned plant layout is presented in Figure 5.11. Each department's work area is enclosed in dashed lines.

The flexible manufacturing system
5.6.20 Rantoul's management was delighted with the results obtained from the plant reorganisation. As a result of reduced materials movement and less in-process stock in storage, manufacturing and storage costs fell while production times decreased. Even more welcome was a decline in the percentage of Category 1 and Category 2 products identified as defective.

Changing technologies and cost management

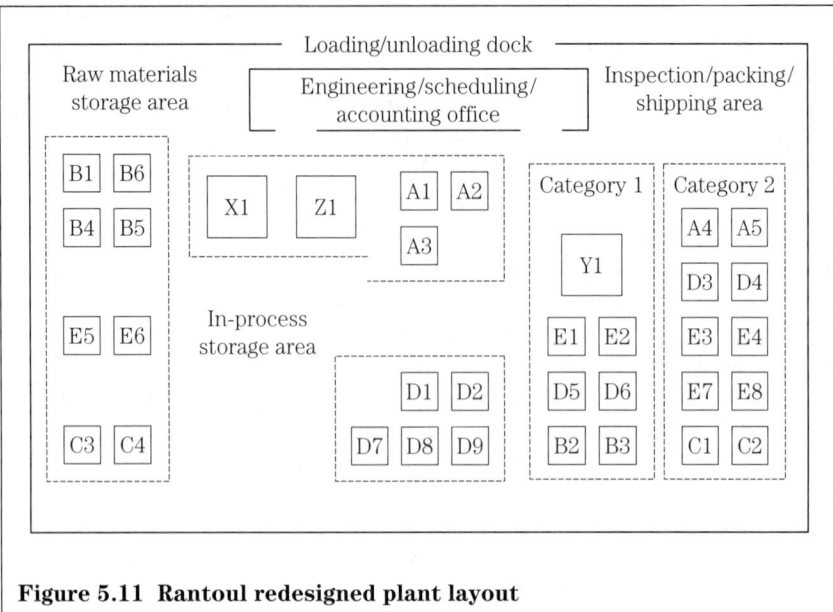

Figure 5.11 Rantoul redesigned plant layout

The increase in quality appeared to result from:

(1) an increased ability to spot quality problems when there is less stock with which to deal; and

(2) the immediate identification of quality problems by subsequent machine operators. This facilitated corrective action before many units were spoiled.

5.6.21 Management has now turned its attention to correcting the problem of high set-up costs and in-process stock of products not in Categories 1 or 2. These products are now called Category 3 products. In an attempt to reduce the cost of Category 3 products, management has decided to replace all machines used to manufacture them, installing in their place a flexible manufacturing system. The lines for Category 1 and Category 2 products will not be changed. As before, each Category 3 product will follow its own production path; each will require its own combination of operations.

5.6.22 In the new FMS line for Category 3 products, jobs will be subdivided into individual units. Employees will place all materials for each unit on a portable platform. Subsequent movements to appropriate machines and all machine work will be automatic and computer controlled. Because each of the new machines will be highly flexible, labour set-up time will be virtu-

Flexible manufacturing systems

ally nil. The work platforms will be of identical size. Each platform will contain coded information about the operations to be performed at each workstation and the materials or partially completed units required for those operations. As the platform arrives at a machine, the coded information will be used to verify the job and the specified work will be performed. If materials are misplaced or the coding is incorrect, a call for manual assistance will be sent automatically.

5.6.23 Computers will monitor all operations and keep detailed records on job status and the amount of time each unit spends on each machine. Maintenance employees will continually inspect machines and make needed adjustments. As units are completed, employees will remove the units from the portable platforms, inspect the units, assemble the units by job and pack the jobs for shipment. The in-process storage area will be eliminated.

The redesigned plant layout, with the FMS line, is presented in Figure 5.12.

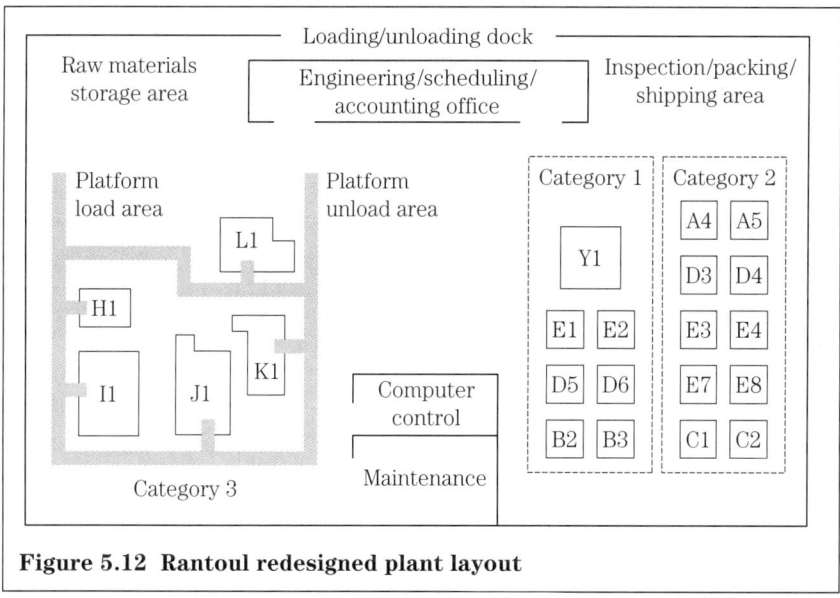

Figure 5.12 Rantoul redesigned plant layout

5.6.24 The computer controlled machines in Category 3 are identified as H1 through L1. There is only one machine of each type, and the operating costs of each machine differ significantly. The broad lines around and to the machines represent the computer controlled movement system.

5.6.25 The redesigned factory will have only three production departments for Category 1, 2 and 3 products. The number of direct labour employees has

Changing technologies and cost management

been significantly reduced, but their responsibilities have been increased. Support activities will have been expanded to include two new service departments, computer control and maintenance.

Cost system for the original plant layout

5.6.26 The basic records required to plan and initiate production for a job-cost system are the bill of materials, operations list and production order. The basic records required to accumulate information for product costing purposes are the job cost sheet, materials requisition and work ticket. Although some of these records might have a physical existence on paper, they are more likely to exist as part of a computer database. Although data entry may involve writing information on paper, it is as likely to involve entering information into a computer terminal. The entry into a computer terminal might involve keying data or optical scanning.

5.6.27 The situation presented above represents a traditional job-shop environment. For Rantoul's original plant layout each job could be assigned a specific number and a job-cost sheet. There should be a total of eight cost centres, one for each machine type. As employees work on a job, they should complete a work ticket, which serves as the basis for assigning direct labour costs to the job. Because of the differences that exist among different machine types and product heterogeneity, the use of a plant-wide rate for overhead cost assignment is not appropriate. Accurate product costing requires the use of eight cost centres, one for each type of machine. In this problem, labour hours and machine hours are approximately equal (and the machines are idle while employees are moving stock or receiving instructions). Hence, either is an acceptable basis of overhead application. Because labour hours are currently accumulated, this is a reasonable basis of overhead application. Finally, a predetermined overhead rate could be recommended. Because of the high correspondence between machine and labour hours, the cost system throughout the plant can be simplified if direct labour and overhead costs are combined into a single category of conversion costs. In each cost centre, conversion costs may then be assigned to jobs on the basis of direct-labour hours or machine hours.

5.6.28 Note that some departments contain only one cost centre but others contain up to three cost centres. Although departments are often regarded as cost centres, if a department contains several activities with different cost structures, it may be desirable to divide the department into two or more cost centres. The relative costs and benefits of more accurate information could be considered in making this decision.

Flexible manufacturing systems

Cost system for the redesigned layout with dedicated production lines

5.6.29 The situation presented still represents a traditional job-shop environment. Each job should be assigned a specific number and a job-cost sheet. The products in Categories 1 and 2 are homogeneous, with proportional distribution of work time on the same type of machines. Hence, each category can serve as a single cost centre, with conversion costs assigned to jobs on the basis of throughput time. Accurate product costing in the balance of the plant will require a total of seven additional cost centres, one for each machine type.

5.6.30 Note how a simplification in the organisation of production can also result in a simplification of accounting procedures. With the revised system, approximately 50 per cent of the firm's products (those in Categories 1 and 2) will have only one work ticket for each product. Hence, the complexity and operating cost of the cost system will be reduced.

5.6.31 Also note that product costs would be accurate even if the cost system designed for question 2 were not modified. That cost system design was, however, more complex and costly to operate.

5.6.32 On the negative side, the revised cost system does not provide detailed operating cost information for machines in Categories 1 and 2. Hence, a special study would be required to obtain financial information needed for decisions pertaining to individual machines in each category.

Cost system with dedicated production lines and FMS

5.6.33 Each job should be assigned a specific number and a job-cost sheet. Because the products in Categories 1 and 2 are homogeneous, with proportional distribution of work time on the same types of machine, each of these categories can serve as a separate cost centre, with conversion costs assigned to jobs processed in them on the basis of time.

5.6.34 Because the jobs in Category 3 are heterogeneous and do not require work on all machines, they must be assigned costs on the basis of the time spent in each machine centre. Hence, the new plant will require a *minimum* of seven cost centres: Category 1 machines; Category 2 machines; and Machines H1, I1, J1, K1 and L1.

5.6.35 Because Category 3 involves virtually no direct labour, except perhaps for loading and unloading, all conversion costs may be assigned on the basis of machine hours. Differences in operating costs would likely necessitate different rates for each machine.

Changing technologies and cost management

5.6.36 The costs of loading, unloading and assembling the units in a job could be assigned on the basis of labour hours. However, the benefits of more accurate product costs may not be sufficient to justify the paper work involved. Perhaps these costs could be treated as an additional cost category and assigned on the basis of the number of units in each job.

5.6.37 No doubt, significant costs are associated with the computer-controlled movement system. These costs might be treated as an additional cost centre. It likely would be difficult to determine the time each unit spends being moved. Moreover, the usefulness of cost assignments based on movement time would be questionable if there were significant waiting time between machines. Movement centre costs might reasonably and easily be assigned on the basis of the number of units in the job or, perhaps, on the basis of the number of machine-units in a job (i.e., units in job multiplied by the number of machines that process each unit). Once sufficient actual cost and activity data are available, the relationship between movement system costs and alternative bases of cost assignment may be examined statistically. Perhaps one of the alternatives, having a high correlation with movement system costs, would be a logical cost driver and be relatively easy to use as a basis of cost assignment.

5.6.38 It is difficult to associate the costs of the computer centre and the maintenance centre with individual jobs. The same is true for the costs of scheduling, accounting, unloading and so forth.

(Source: adapted with permission from Morse, (1990).)

A case study: investing in AMT

5.6.39 The East River Manufacturing case provides an excellent exposition of factors at stake in AMT investments.

5.6.40 Power Services Industries has been in business since 1907. PSI's principal business is the design, manufacture and erection of steam generation equipment for utility and industrial customers. PSI also serves the after-parts market, which includes individual boiler components and loose tubes for repair and replacement. Their primary product, coal-fired boilers, burns fossil fuels to heat water, which turns to steam and is used either for electrical generation or industrial process. Boilers are highly engineered products which can take anywhere from six months to five years to complete from the design stage through manufacturing and erection phases.

5.6.41 The East River, Illinois plant is one of three manufacturing facilities of the Services Division of the Energy Group. The East River plant has over 503,000 square feet of fabrication area, nine fabrication bays and a practical capacity load of 1,345,000 man hours. There are over 500 hourly and salaried employees at the East River plant.

Market and competitive environment

5.6.42 Throughout the post-World War II period and up until the mid-1970s, the demand for power-generating capacity increased steadily. PSI was a prime beneficiary of this growth in demand for electricity. They were awash in orders for original equipment. Backlogs of orders for 40 or more radiant boilers were common and when measured in man hours, were equivalent to over five years of work. The typical order for original equipment boilers averaged $30 million. Prior to the 1980s, the original-equipment market (OEM) made up more than 60 per cent of East River's revenues. Throughout this period, PSI earned a very respectable return on its investment.

5.6.43 As a sideline to the OEM, East River also serviced the replacement parts (known as loose tubes) market. Tubes wear out in a hostile environment (e.g., coal-fired boilers generate fly ash which is very corrosive when it continually beats against a tube wall) and need to be replaced. However, demand for service work (replacement parts and components or subassemblies) is extremely difficult to project. Replacement parts business requires short lead times, on-time shipments and competitive prices. Service work is made more demanding because customers want made-to-order replacement tubes in small quantities. The typical replacement parts order was $50,000 and usually had to be delivered in less than ten days, although the need to expedite an order overnight was not unusual. Replacement orders made up about 40 per cent of revenues. And while the reported gross profit margins on individual loose tubes were high, the absolute size of and total returns on OEM projects made that market more attractive.

5.6.44 In the early 1980s, a combination of fuel price increases, high interest rates and global recession hit and the bottom fell out of the OEM. In the past, this was normally a temporary setback and orders always picked up once the economy recovered. But this time it was different. The steady growth in electricity consumption, which had been predictable for so long, levelled off and OEM orders plunged. A number of factors led to a permanent drop in demand by the OEM, including the sharp increase in the cost of energy, unsympathetic utility regulatory agencies, uncertainty related to deregulation, environmental concerns about acid rain and improved capabilities to transmit excess energy across markets.

5.6.45 This new environment was marked by wide swings in business and fluctuating manning requirements. OEM business picked up again in the

Changing technologies and cost management

mid-1980s, but total OEM business and profits never returned to their former high levels and the total workload at the East River facility continued to drop. The inevitable profit squeeze caused by excess capacity and by ever-rising costs led PSI to look to the replacement parts business to offset the declining OEM business.

5.6.46 Demand for replacement parts expanded as orders for original equipment declined. The principal reason was that utility and industrial customers wanted to maintain and prolong the useful life of power-generating equipment by replacing worn out parts rather than build new capacity. In addition, PSI engineers worked closely with customers to achieve greater efficiencies and enhance the power output of existing power sources by redesigning components or adding additional parts.

5.6.47 The determinants of successful management of large and complex OEM projects are very different from the key success factors in the replacement parts market. Critical market drivers in the loose-tube replacement market are:

- increased flexibility;
- reduced lead time;
- low price;
- on-time delivery;
- high quality.

5.6.48 Except for high quality, these factors did not carry the same weight in the OEM. As a result, PSI had to adapt quickly. For example, fast turnaround of worn or damaged parts is crucial once a boiler is in operation. Replacement parts availability is critical to a pulp and paper customer like Weyerhaeuser. Customers can suffer losses in the tens of thousands of dollars daily if their boilers are shut down as a result of part failure. East River always tried to accommodate customers' needs for replacement parts. But East River was structured to capitalise on the returns to be made on large-scale OEM projects. Primary considerations on OEM projects were to complete the boiler on time, within budget and according to contract specifications.

5.6.49 The urgency of meeting contract lead times and completion dates on new equipment was not as critical as it was for replacement parts. But now, replacement parts were the primary source of revenues. And while new boilers were still being sold, replacement parts for existing boilers now made up 70 per cent of East River's workload. Since PSI's major competitors (e.g.,

Flexible manufacturing systems

Asea, Brown, Bovari/Combustion Engineering; Babcock & Wilcox; Riley, Foster, & Wheeler; and Zurn) were suffering from the same drop in OEM orders, they too started to compete aggressively for the growing replacement parts business. The field was crowded with competitors. But the expanding replacement parts business was not large enough to offset the lost OEM orders. By the early 1990s, total OEM and replacement parts business was significantly less than it was in the early 1980s. There was now a glut of industry-wide capacity. By 1989, the industry was over-capitalised and demand from the OEM and replacement parts markets was running at a level which utilised only 45–50 per cent of East River's capacity. The inevitable outcome was constant pressure on prices, margins and market share.

Major products
5.6.50 The East River plant manufactures a wide variety of components for boilers including wall panels – a collection of steel tubes (carbon steel, stainless, or composites) which are welded together with membrane bars in between them; loose tubes that have a number of bends in them or studs applied to them for heat transfer capability; burners which can burn coal, oil, or gas; structural members which contain the tubes that make up the walls of the boiler; expansion joints; dampers; economisers; risers and supplies tubes.

5.6.51 The Bay 7 facility was configured and equipped to process straight lengths of loose tubes into various shapes and lengths, suitable for the repair and replacement parts market or needed as component parts of other assemblies completed at East River. Replacement parts and components are custom-made from unique materials compositions and configurations so that the parts can function reliably in a power-generation environment where steam may be generated by burning any one of hundreds of different kinds of coal or other fossil fuels. Many of the tubes manufactured have difficult welds and intricate bends in several different planes. All of these bends are engineered to a certain size, dimension and location on the tube. Quality has to be right the first time. Once parts are in the field, they have to fit exactly. There is no reworking on the line.

Engineering and production process
5.6.52 Customer orders for individual boiler components and loose tubes to be fabricated in Bay 7 are initially processed at PSI's Dallas, Texas headquarters. Since there are no off-the-shelf parts, preliminary tube designs are prepared by product design engineers from historical data. Cost estimators use these preliminary tube designs to prepare estimates of the tube's manufacturing and material cost. The base estimating data used by cost estimators was developed from industrial engineering time studies completed in

the early 1970s. There are enough similarities to previously-fabricated tube variations that customer requested quotes can be developed on a timely basis by querying the parts database. If the proposal is accepted and becomes a contract, the proposal becomes the base-line or 'as-sold' estimate (i.e., the budgeted cost) for cost monitoring and measuring actual performance.

5.6.53 Once a proposal is accepted, product design engineers 'start from scratch' and prepare detailed part and component designs on computer-aided design (CAD) systems. They also determine the materials composition for all tubes. This product structure and tube geometry, which describes the physical characteristics of the tube, is then transferred to draftsmen who transform the product structure into detailed graphics (blueprints). Draftsmen manually load information on the tube's geometry into three different computer systems: (1) the Bill of Material system; (2) the CAD drawing system; and (3) the Tube Detail file which converts tube geometry along with design, process, machine and tooling constraints data into process plans. This information is downloaded to East River's mainframe computers.

5.6.54 Purchasing places orders for all stock and non-stock items, many of which have long lead times. The process engineering group uses the Tube Detail file to generate the route sheet generation program or RSGP. RSGP creates a routing for each part with specific work centres, operations descriptions and estimated process times. Customer order information is entered into MAPICS II (Manufacturing Accounting Production Inventory Control System), an IBM MRP II system. MAPICS generates bill of materials, routing sheets, order quantities and required delivery dates. Manufacturing orders released by MAPICS were hand delivered to their respective work centres. Figure 5.13 shows the sequential flow of a contract from the preliminary proposal through shipment to the customer.

5.6.55 The East River plant has nine manufacturing bays. By 1990, the average age of equipment in Bay 7 was greater than 29 years. Bay 7 has practical capacity of 160,000 man hours. Tubes were received by truck and unloaded by a radio-controlled overhead crane with the assistance of two workers. Tubes moved through the shops by a series of overhead cranes, jib cranes hung from building supports, forklifts and transfer cars.

5.6.56 Tubes were shotblasted, cut to length and machined as required. Tubes may be welded together prior to moving to the stencil/layout table, where the tubes were paint marked for a variety of studding and bending patterns. Tubes were then moved to a staging area near the stud welders and

Flexible manufacturing systems

benders. Tubes were processed through a series of stud welding and bending stations, which were machine-assisted but still highly labour-intensive. Bending dies were stored outside Bay 7 and, when needed, transported by forklift to the proper bending station. Tube bundles were moved from station to station through Bay 7 by a series of pendant operated overhead cranes. Tubes were then checked, inspected, finished and cleaned prior to shipment to the customer or transferred to another bay where they were assembled into boiler components. Average throughput time in the bay was approximately 3–4 weeks with high work-in-process. About 40 per cent of the man hours in Bay 7 were attributable to material handling at the workstations or movement between workstations. Figure 5.15 shows the process flow for Bay 7, including machine count and headcount.

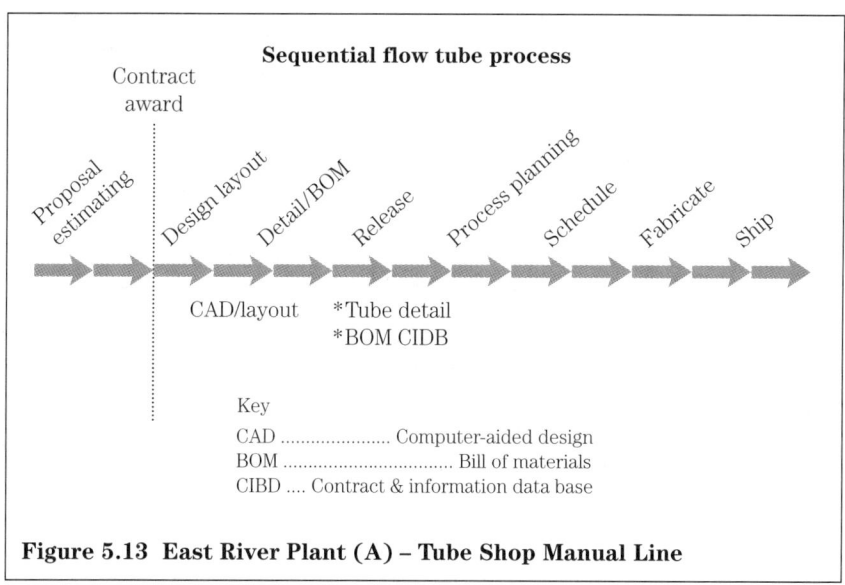

Figure 5.13 East River Plant (A) – Tube Shop Manual Line

5.6.57 It was not unusual for bottlenecks and scheduling difficulties to arise during processing. Work-in-process was stored adjacent to workstations to alleviate any disruptions which might occur in upstream operations. There was approximately $7 million worth of inventory at East River at any given time.

5.6.58 Over the years, maintenance expenditures were kept at levels sufficient to sustain current operations. Competing on cost meant that operations management focused on high levels of equipment utilisation. However, machine downtime and costs to repair equipment were now rising rapidly. In addition, depreciation expenditures were not reinvested in new equipment.

Changing technologies and cost management

5.6.59 Furthermore, the collective bargaining agreement with the union did not allow workers to be cross-trained to run multiple machines and perform a variety of functions. Part of the difficulty was that over the years the collective bargaining unit negotiated 15 different job levels along with several classes within each level. But now competition was placing a premium on flexible work rules and East River was saddled with a labour agreement which made it difficult to respond quickly.

5.6.60 With so much to disrupt shop floor control, it was hard consistently to maintain contract work schedules and meet customers' requested shipping dates.

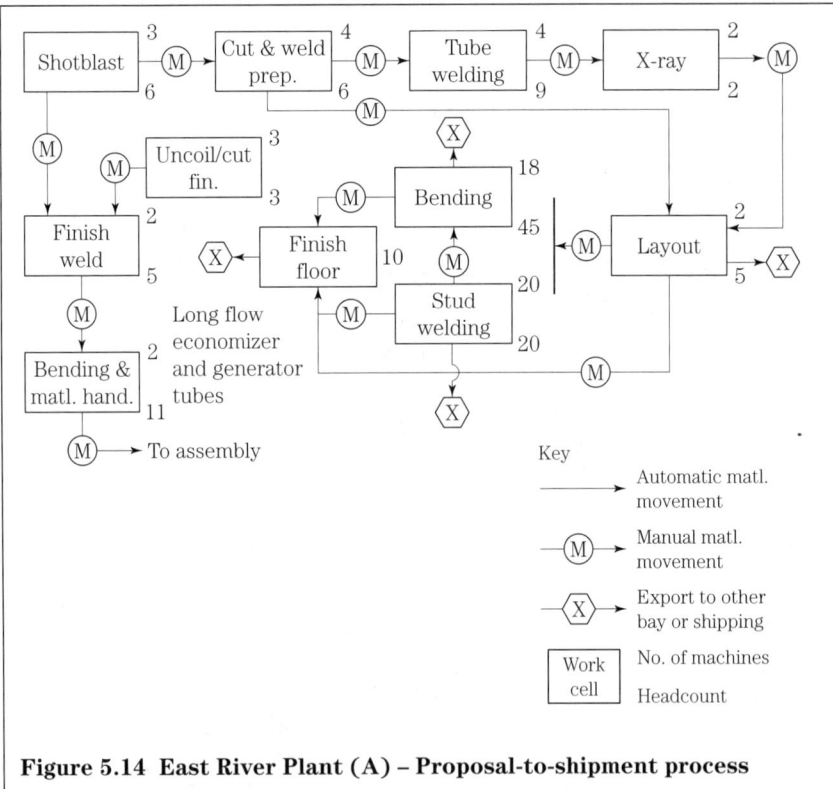

Figure 5.14 East River Plant (A) – Proposal-to-shipment process

Existing cost system

5.6.61 Traditionally, throughput in East River's labour-intensive shops was measured by man hours. The East River facility is on a job cost system. The same job cost system was installed in all plants built during the 1950s.

Flexible manufacturing systems

In the case of East River, the job cost system was installed in 1951 and remained virtually unchanged until 1992, with two exceptions: (1) practical capacity replaced a three-year average of expected actual capacity for determining burden rates in 1982; and (2) a material burden rate was developed in the late 1980s. A job or contract cost system is necessary since PSI does not make a standard product. End products are manufactured to customers' specifications. The entire project is designed and engineered at PSI's Dallas, Texas headquarters. Materials composition and product structure are based upon the type of fossil fuel that will be used by the power generator and other environmental variables.

5.6.62 The contract is the primary cost object. Orders are grouped by contract, and costs are accumulated for purchase orders as well as manufacturing orders. The cost system charges materials and labour costs directly to the contract and to the part. Product design engineering, drafting or graphics, machine set-up and material handling costs are also directly charged to contracts. Burden rates are based upon practical capacity. A material burden rate of 5 per cent of material cost covers the cost of purchasing and material control costs. Pressure Shop 415's overhead for three bays includes indirect labour and fringes, equipment-related costs, maintenance and repairs, and supplies. Shop 415 overhead was charged to contracts and other cost objects at 150 per cent of direct labour cost. Plant support services, known as works-general costs, consist of production control, plant engineering, quality assurance, payroll, accounting, and other support services and are charged to contracts at the rate of 40 per cent of direct labour cost. In addition, operating-all-works (OAW) costs associated with Dallas support services are charged to contracts at the rate of 15 per cent of direct labour cost. OAW consists of manufacturing engineering support and the resource allocation group which plans and monitors plant loads, product mix and production volume. These costing procedures were more than adequate given market conditions and the focus on large OEM projects throughout most of the post-war period.

5.6.63 In addition to costing the contract at practical capacity, the cost system was also capable of providing operating personnel with contract-related performance information. One of the most critical performance indicators was the monthly ratio of Estimated Man Hours to Actual Man Hours (E/A). Given that contracts could easily extend over a period of years, operating management could not wait until the project was completed to determine whether the contract was coming in over budget. It was essential to have some basis for monitoring progress on each project on an ongoing Percentage-of-Completion basis. Using information supplied by process engineering, accounting staff estimated time for every task that had to be performed. As tasks were completed, comparisons of estimated man hours with actual man hours resulted in an E/A performance percentage. If performance was at 100 per cent or better, the contract was going well and the plant would earn a respectable profit. If performance was below 100 per cent, say 75 per cent, contract performance was not going very well.

5.6.64 The relationship between equipment age and equipment tolerances is an example of how E/A could gradually worsen over long periods of time even when no changes were made in the tube design. One study of studding machines revealed that time and cost overruns were occurring with increasing frequency. Studding machines spot weld studs to the tubes. These machines were some of the oldest equipment in the Tube Bay. Therefore, controls on the stud welders were old and not as effective as they were when the equipment was newer. The welds did not always achieve the degree of penetration on a weld necessary to pass quality specifications. Studs which were not welded correctly could break off. These studs had to be manually rewelded because the number of studs on the tube precluded it from being rewelded on the studding machine.

5.6.65 Periodic monitoring of actual contract costs against the original bid or as-sold estimate assisted plant management in managing costs on a contract. The contract cost accounting system provides reports which show actual costs incurred for the contract to date, as well as reports which show the actual costs incurred for a contract during a specific period. All reports provide variances between actual costs and as-sold estimated costs and the engineered standards. This information was reviewed informally on a weekly basis and underwent a thorough, formal review each quarter (Figure 5.15).

5.6.66 From a customer's perspective, there are two other critical performance indicators: (1) on-time delivery – meeting the customer-requested delivery schedule; and (2) quality. Often, customers have planned outages and want replacement parts delivered during a certain outage window – a specific date and time. If this window is missed, at the very least customers lose confidence in suppliers. In some cases, there are substantial liquidating damages associated with a missed delivery date.

5.6.67 Quality Assurance reports defects. If a defect will cost more than $1,000 to repair, a separate sub-account is established for the contract, called a C-order, and all costs of reworking the part(s) are charged to this account. Accounting supplies the cost information to QA, which then identifies what the problem was, where it occurred, what the root cause was and who had primary responsibility for correcting it. Some defects are due to design errors, referred to as a D-orders. Design flaws can be identified when

Flexible manufacturing systems

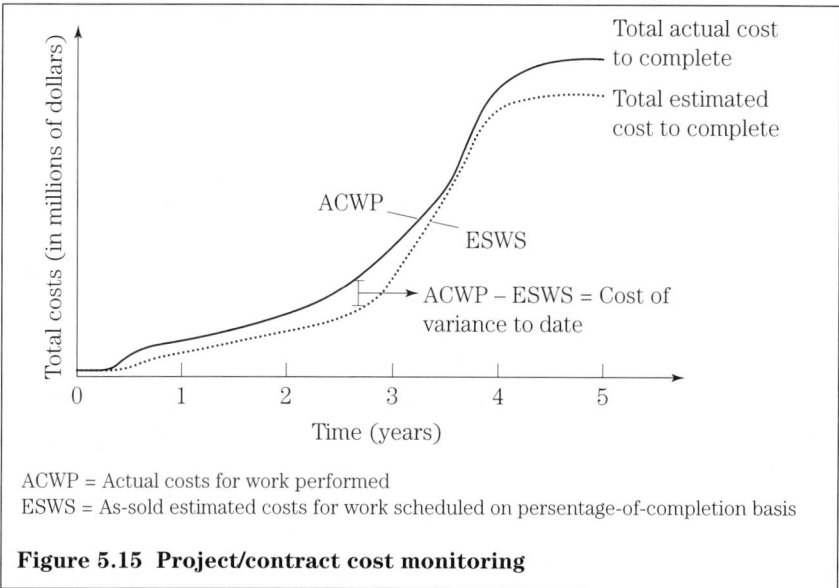

ACWP = Actual costs for work performed
ESWS = As-sold estimated costs for work scheduled on persentage-of-completion basis

Figure 5.15 Project/contract cost monitoring

parts do not assemble properly. It is important to determine the cause of design errors so that they do not repeat these mistakes on future contracts of a similar nature or, if the error is the result of a flaw in the manufacturing process, the process gets corrected. Guarantee-orders or G-orders accumulate the cost of corrective work on a unit in the field that doesn't meet its warranted performance. Reserves are set up for C-, D-, and G-orders to cover the estimated cost or liability. These costs are built into the base estimating data used for proposals and establish allowances for contract cost.

Understanding the environment

5.6.68 Before a cost management solution can be developed, the plant manager must understand the context within which it must be implemented. First it needed to be recognised that the competitive environment was rapidly changing.

5.6.69 The pre-1980s competitive environment for steam generation equipment manufacturers was typical for US industry in general during the post-World War II era. A combination of factors including lack of competition, pent-up demand, rising standards of living and a population explosion fed by the baby boom from 1946–1964 drove business demand to unprecedented levels for 25 years after the war. The prime beneficiaries of this boom were the utility and industrial process firms whose power generation needs were met by PSI and its OEM competitors. However, for a variety of reasons

– some economic, some technological, some regulatory and some demographic – the long expansionary period after World War II came to an abrupt end by the late 1970s.

5.6.70   The competitive structure and the economics of the power business were changing rapidly. Utilities and process-intensive industries experienced dramatic cost increases. OEM orders dried up and the once-predictable growth in demand for power-generation equipment vanished almost overnight. What evolved was a highly competitive market fueled by new players, including mature foreign suppliers like Mitsubishi. Beginning in the early 1980s, the industry was to undergo a dramatic shift away from OEM toward the replacement parts business. But with overall demand down, the industry was suffering from severe over-capacity. It was inevitable that a shakeout would occur, during which there would be severe dislocations within the industry. The economies of scale enjoyed by the OEM manufacturers dissipated as the market shifted to the low-volume, made-to-order replacement parts business. The key factors of success for the replacement market were, for the most part, quite different from those for the OEM market.

5.6.71   Plant management, together with marketing, product engineering and process engineering, needs to develop strategies to:

- Reduce cost;
- Increase flexibility to produce small orders;
- Shorten lead time;
- Improve on-time delivery;
- Produce more consistent quality;
- Increase market share.

5.6.72   Prior to 1992, the Tube Shop's manufacturing process had high manpower requirements, high in-process inventories and high maintenance costs. East River and the other OEM manufacturers were not structured to meet the demands of serving the replacement parts market – short lead times, diverse tube designs and competitive cost. Changes in the cost of generating power in the late 1970s led to a rapid shift in demand for power-generation equipment away from huge OEM contracts toward low-volume, highly specialised repair and replacement business. The economics of production for repair and replacement parts place a premium on cost-efficient flexibility and fast turnaround. Traditionally operated plants targeting the OEM market were not configured to produce a low-volume order efficiently.

5.6.73 Another disadvantage was that these plants often lacked the manufacturing flexibility needed to meet customers' demands for quick response to tailor-made orders for repair parts. The East River plant was no exception. Customers cannot afford to have equipment costing millions of dollars down for any length of time. They need a reliable source of replacement parts – one which can expedite an order immediately at reasonable cost. Given the equipment changeover requirements all along the tube line, normal throughput times were 3–4 weeks. While East River always tried to accommodate customers' immediate needs, they did so at considerable cost and disruption to production schedules.

5.6.74 Furthermore, productivity and product quality were suffering for several reasons. As product variety increased, the workload was more complex and rework was more frequent. Also, relations among management, first-line supervisors and the union workforce were not on the best of terms, which probably had a residual effect on product quality.

5.6.75 Whatever the solution, East River would continue to face heightened competition for a decreasing number of orders. Survival was dependent upon their success at reducing cost, improving response time and making further inroads into the replacement parts market.

5.6.76 Whilst marketing felt every job they bid on was a competitive quote the loss of bids indicated that the main problem with the Tube Shop manufacturing process was that costs were out of line and that it was difficult to predict with any consistency which bids would be won and which would be lost. In part, this was documented in situations of open public bids, discussions with sales personnel from competing firms and other information sources.

5.6.77 After study, there were a number of causes cited for excessive costs. The process had not changed much since Tube Shop was opened in 1970. The prevailing technology consisted primarily of labour-intensive, electromechanical equipment which was now more than 29 years old, on average. So, technologically speaking, most equipment was not on par with modern welding, studding and bending equipment. After 30 years of use, the capabilities of the equipment were no longer as precise as when the equipment was new (e.g., when equipment is new, tolerances are tighter and there is less variation in the controls). Also, because of age, the equipment was becoming burdensome: breakdowns occurred more often, preventive maintenance was needed with increasing frequency and, in general, annual expenditures on maintenance and repairs were increasing.

5.6.78 In addition, the existing process required that machine operators and tenders spend considerable time handling and moving batches of tubes from one workstation to another by pendant-controlled overhead cranes. The portion of time spent on materials handling was high (greater than 40 per cent). Material movement was a direct charge to the contract. Another major cost driver was machine set-up. All equipment required set-up but certain machines such as tube benders, which require manual changing of dies, could take hours to set-up and adjust, especially when dies had to be transported from a central storage shed. Machines were manually loaded and offloaded to racks after welding, studding or bending. All of this involved considerable time and effort which, while necessary under the existing production process, was not a productive use of operator time and was not adding any value to the product.

5.6.79 Because of bottlenecks and scheduling difficulties, workers were frequently waiting for materials. Work-in-process was stored adjacent to workstations creating buffers which helped alleviate any problems upstream. However, this protection against machine breakdowns and other disruptions came at considerable cost when you consider the $7 million investment in inventory and related expenses.

5.6.80 Furthermore, the replacement business favoured speed and product customisation. Yet, as low-volume orders increased, less time was spent processing tubes and more orders were expedited in order to meet customers' delivery requirements. The cost penalties attributable to all the operator and machine downtime when nothing was being processed were magnified.

5.6.81 Different courses of action might be appropriate for the plant manager in order to reverse the decline in market share and capacity utilisation.

Alternative no. 1: Maintain the present facility

Advantages:

(1) Minimum capital outlay;
(2) Least amount of technical risk as the current operation is a known commodity.

Disadvantages:

(1) Current operation is not gaining market share in the parts business due to demanding price and delivery requirements;

Flexible manufacturing systems

(2) Continued high maintenance costs with frequent outages;

(3) Continued fluctuation in manpower requirements with business swings.

Alternative no. 2: Islands of automation

This alternative considers taking a piecemeal approach to the automation of Tube Shop by adding improvements incrementally over time.

Advantages:

(1) Lower capital expenditure;

(2) Reduced risk exposure from a technical production standpoint;

(3) Some replacement of aging equipment and productivity improvements could occur;

(4) Phased implementation.

Disadvantages:

(1) Integration of the work cells would prove more difficult through a lack of continuity of a dedicated project team;

(2) Substantial saving occur when material handling, scheduling, job set-ups, etc. are all in place. Until that time, cost reductions only affect a portion of the shop's operations;

(3) A stretchout could result in a steadily deteriorating competitive position.

Alternative no. 3: Complete modernisation of Tube Shop

This alternative calls for replacing most of the manual machines in the Tube Shop with computer numerical control (CNC) machines, installing automated material handling equipment and implementing computer systems to schedule and control the entire operation.

Advantages:

(1) Highest level of savings relative to the other alternatives;

(2) Increased market share based on improved cost, price and delivery capabilities;

(3) Less machine downtime and lower maintenance and repair costs;

(4) Reduced product throughput time;

(5) An integrated modernisation effort.

Disadvantages:

(1) Highest capital outlays among the various alternatives.

5.6.82 The project team recommended alternative no.3, full modernisation of the Tube Shop. Interestingly, the existing process was actually more flexible in some sense than the newer CIM technology. For example, flexible manufacturing systems have certain machine constraints related to tube length – tubes of more than 40 feet in length could not be processed on certain equipment. The manual process was highly dependent on the experience of the machine operators, whose skills, when matched with the general-purpose machines, were adaptable to almost any set of tube specifications and configurations. The manual line was kept intact and moved to another area of the Tube Shop. Therefore, tube orders which could not be processed through certain automated operations on the CIM line could be offloaded and shifted to the manual line, then transferred back to the CIM line for completion.

5.6.83 Nonetheless, the CIM line was faster, less costly, more precise and, within the system's constraints, more flexible than the manual line.

Modernisation of the Tube Shop and the impact on the workforce

5.6.84 There is a human impact to consider that extends beyond analysing the financial consequences of a decision. How is management going to deal with the consequences of automation on the workforce? Change to an automated facility can be very threatening for several reasons. First, the workforce's present set of job skills and experience would be outdated and largely irrelevant if the Tube Shop was automated. Second, major workforce reductions are usually associated with automation. In fact, approximately one-third of the cost savings from automating the Tube Shop would come from cutting the manpower requirements by half. These and other issues present management with challenges every bit as difficult as analysing and implementing the computer-integrated manufacturing system.

5.6.85 The operations in the Tube Shop support the lucrative replacement parts business and tube fabrication activities for new boilers. One way to meet the pressures of an increasingly competitive market was to cut material movement, equipment maintenance, inventory carrying costs, lead times and improve quality. The Tube Shop had practical capacity of 160,000 man hours. About 40 per cent of the man hours related to material movement. Time lost because of machine breakdowns and costs to repair equipment was rising rapidly. Furthermore, WIP buffer stocks were excessive due to a combination of poor scheduling and the uncertainty of equipment availability.

Flexible manufacturing systems

5.6.86 In 1989, a project team consisting of engineers, plant personnel, marketing people plus an accountant performed an economic analysis of the costs and benefits of modernising the Tube Shop. The project team recommended committing over $13.1 million to a computer-integrated, automated tube line, while maintaining certain manual capabilities (see Figures 5.16 and 5.17). The $13.1 million modernisation of the Tube Shop is broken down as follows:

	$ million
Equipment	8.307
Control System	2.138
PSI and Subcontractor Services	0.543
Training	0.250
Implementation Team	0.380
Technical Support	0.300
Contingency	0.982
Relocation of Existing Equipment	0.200
Total	13.100

		FY 91	FY 92	FY 93	FY 94	FY 95
I.	Reduction of manpower	$2,355	$2,444	$2,517	$2,593	$2,671
II.	Productivity gains	1,124	1,168	1,203	1,239	1,277
III.	Maintenance savings	164	126	90	55	20
IV.	Replacement parts	3,500	3,605	3,713	3,825	3,940
V.	Finished bar relocation	260	269	277	286	293
		$7,403	$7,612	$7,800	7,998	$8,201

For financial analysis, savings are not recognized until implementation is complete. Assume tax rate = 40%.

Figure 5.16 CIM Line Savings Summary ($US)

5.6.87 The CIM line should reduce the cycle of downtime, material handling and instock associated with the manual process. It would reduce costs and lead times and be flexible enough to manufacture made-to-order boiler components in a variety of configurations and batch sizes. Benefits from the automated tube line will be realised in five areas: reduction in personnel, productivity gains, reduced maintenance costs, relocation of the finished bar

Changing technologies and cost management

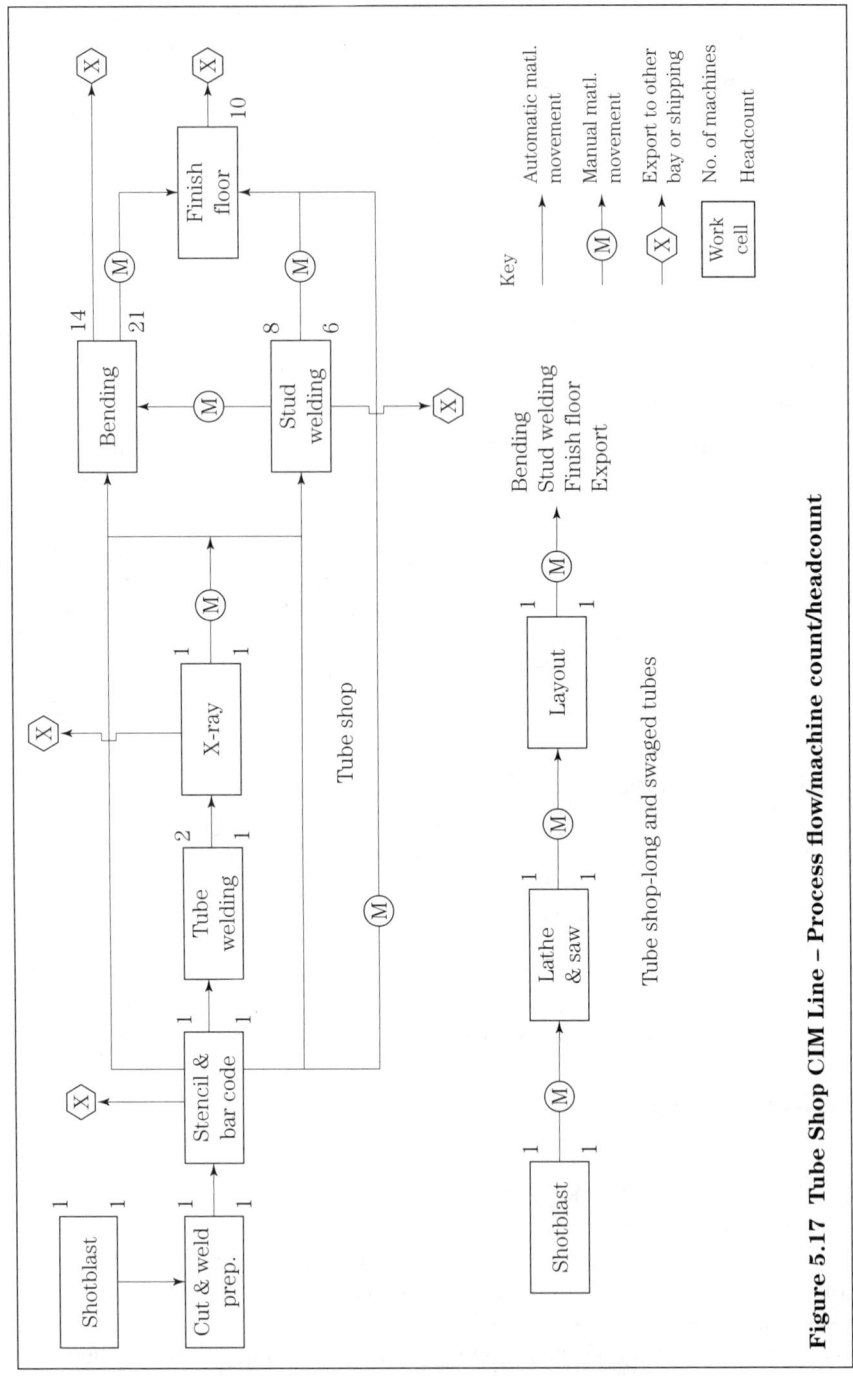

Figure 5.17 Tube Shop CIM Line – Process flow/machine count/headcount

Flexible manufacturing systems

line and increased profits from capturing additional replacement parts business. An explanation of the benefits from implementing the project is provided below.

- Increased throughput. If marketing could generate the increased number of orders which the Tube Shop would now be capable of processing, the output per worker would increase dramatically. Given the flexibility of the automated line, the Tube Shop could now respond to the diversity of orders characteristic of the replacement market, without experiencing a dropoff in output.

- Increased quality. CIM, advanced x-ray vision systems and automated testing equipment will allow greater control over quality. First, automated processes produce more consistent quality and, therefore, fewer defects. Second, the sooner a defect is identified, the lower the cost of fixing it. Quality control checks are built into every step of the process. Defects should be spotted immediately. The intangible benefits associated with a reputation for higher quality can result in a competitive edge which is reflected in increased market share.

- Reduced lead time. One of the major goals is to improve customer service by reducing the time required to deliver new orders or respond to 'hot tagged' orders. Equipment set-up time has been cut dramatically except for two workstations, thereby reducing the cycle time to produce an order. Tube Shop now has the capability of handling a wide range of tube variations without costly set-ups. This should also favourably affect market share.

- Reduced equipment maintenance costs. Newer equipment requires much less maintenance and repair work than older equipment.

- Reduced WIP. Product flow will pull a part through the Tube Shop, completing all fabrication steps without undue build-up of WIP between workstations.

- Reduced material movement. Most material handling will be by V-roll conveyors and cascades (a buffer storage in front of a workstation). When a part has been studded or bent, the batch will be transported by a radio-operated crane.

- Reduced manpower. Manpower requirements were reduced by half from 129 to 63 employees. The remaining employees were grouped into three teams and each team member received intensive training on the equipment, equipment set-up (if necessary), maintenance procedures and the control system so they could perform every task in their area.

Changing technologies and cost management

5.6.88 The automated tube line could handle 90 per cent of the workload. However, the manual line was still necessary to process tubes over 40 feet in length or to apply studs to tubes with intricate bends or a large number of bends. The Tube Shop needed a common scheduler that would both integrate and schedule the products across both lines. It had to work as if there was only one line. In addition, to be most effective, the manufacturing system required a common computerised control system that would control the entire bay.

5.6.89 Enlisting employees' support was also important in upgrading production. Employees and the union needed to understand that their jobs were best protected by their own productivity, modern work skills and product quality. However, the productivity gains from the CIM equipment would enable plant management to shrink the headcount in the Tube Shop, something employees were likely to resist. Also, new work relationships had to develop based upon trust and teamwork. In the Tube Shop, self-managed teams would be used for most jobs, thereby eliminating the need for supervisors. Workers would feed the machines, inspect the tubes and determine when something was amiss.

5.6.90 Because of the collaborative efforts of everyone involved, this transition ended up being a win-win situation. Plant management smoothed the transition by avoiding layoffs. Although management and union relationships had been somewhat adversarial at times in the past, there is now a much more co-operative work climate. Through a co-operative effort with the State of Illinois and the International Brotherhood of Boilermakers, East River management assessed employees' educational and skill levels in relation to the knowledge required to perform a variety of functions within a highly automated system. Maths and computer skills stood out as notable deficiencies. Each employee went through a training programme tailored to her/his deficiencies. Better trained and more knowledgeable workers are crucial to the success of the computer-integrated technology. Workers who once performed just one or two tasks would now be trained to perform a dozen or more.

5.6.91 The new process was totally dependent on a team concept. This is in sharp contrast to the previous structure of specialised job classes which had developed over the years as part of the collective bargaining agreement. There were 13 different job classes which had different pay rates and contractual limitations on the tasks a particular job class was permitted to perform. Flexible skills were critical given the type of sophisticated, computer-controlled equipment utilised in the Tube Shop. By management working with the collective bargaining unit, management was able to reduce the 13 different job classes to three job classes without all the contractual limitations on work tasks under the old contract. This flexibility allowed a reduction in work force from 129 to 63 employees in just this one area. None of these employees was displaced; jobs were found in other areas of the plant as demand increased. Team 1, Prep Operators, reduced four different job classes down to one and headcount went from a two-shift total of 42 to 14. The second team, Bender General, replaced five job classes with one job class and headcount went from 71 to 33. The last team, Tube Fitter/Welder, compressed four job classes into one job class. However, because this process contained many highly labour intensive operations, staffing levels remained nearly the same.

As-sold cost estimates versus the actual contract cost
5.6.92 Part of the problem is endemic to the business. Cost estimators need to generate expedient bid proposals. Under the 'Proposal Front-end' system, product design engineers and cost estimators consult historical data bases for information on previous orders – tube geometry, bill-of-materials, routings – to develop a tube design scenario and estimate the tube's manufacturing and material cost. There may be little or no passing of information to the contract stage if the proposal is accepted.

5.6.93 If the proposal becomes a contract, product design engineers create detailed product structures. The as-sold estimates may differ from the actual engineering design in significant respects. The contract cost accounting system had the capability to query the system to identify where engineered standards differed from the base estimating data used to develop the proposal.

5.6.94 There was also a problem with the information used to develop bids. Base estimating data used had been developed in the early 1970s when the equipment was newer and equipment controls were tighter. These standards had not been updated in large part because it costs several million dollars to create all new data from time studies. And since the process had not changed, the base data had not been changed since then. One study of contract cost overruns described in the case revealed that the performance of the stud welding machines was not always meeting detailed engineering estimates. Actual man hours were overrunning estimated man hours on studding machines with increasing frequency, even though no changes had been made in the tube design. It was determined that when studs were spot welded to tubes, frequent rewelding had to be done because tolerances were not always being met the first time. Age and wear and tear on the stud welders' controls had caused tolerances to loosen and deteriorate over time, thereby causing more man hours to reweld some spot welds manually off line.

Changing technologies and cost management

5.6.95 The primary cost object is the contract. The as-sold estimate (ASE) for a job served as the bid on a customer's request for a quote (RFQ). If the bid was accepted, the ASE became the budget for the contract and was used for monitoring costs and evaluating performance. Regardless of the accuracy of the cost assignment methodology, using ASE as the contract budget had major implications.

5.6.96 Cost estimators prepare ASEs based upon specifications supplied by the customer and from parts and cost records of similar parts and assemblies on past contracts. However, once a quote was accepted, a more detailed product design process began. (Design work was not necessary for replacement tubes on PSI original equipment.) Design decisions affected materials composition, process routings and resources used. Design engineers did not feel obliged to stay with the original ASE specifications. Their motivation was to design and build the best component/part for the situation (see Figure 5.18).

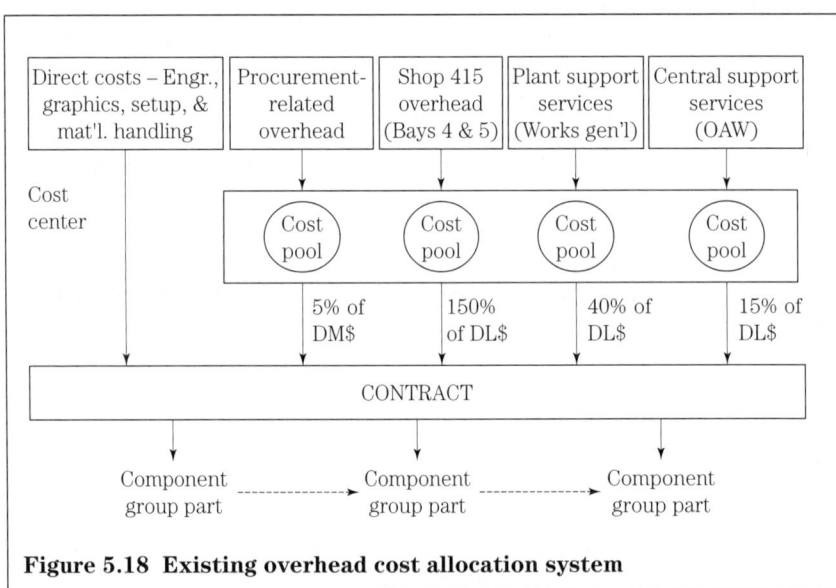

Figure 5.18 Existing overhead cost allocation system

5.6.97 However, the cost system provided no incentive for design engineers to consider the long-term consequences of engineering so many unique parts. If there was a significant cost overrun on a project and actual man hours were running ahead of estimated hours, it could just as easily be due to differences between ASE and actual product design decisions as to difficulties associated with actual production of the order. This may not be a major issue on a single replacement part or component but could result in cost discrepancies in the hundreds of thousands of dollars or more on major OEM projects.

5.6.98 As to the cost assignment process itself, the system for charging costs to contracts was both unique and conventional. Since boiler components are highly engineered, there is significant design engineering and graphics effort which goes into designing components. Therefore, design engineering and graphics time was accumulated and charged directly to the contract. However, it is unusual to see machine set-up and material handling costs directly charged to a contract, component or part as they are under this system.

5.6.99 Nonetheless, the cost system was prone to some of the same cost distortions typical of cost systems of this time period. Every project bore some of the costs of every resource – all shop supervision, all direct overhead, all depreciation, all repair costs of every piece of equipment in the Tube Shop. This system is a shotgun approach to contract and component costing. All resources were charged to the contract through the man hour rate, regardless of the actual resources used in processing parts and components. The system averaged all costs across contracts in proportion to man hours consumed and did not address the different processes utilised for a contract. However, since the old electromechanical technology was labour-paced, there was a correlation between man hours and equipment-related costs. Therefore, cost distortion was not as great as it would be in more automated environments.

5.6.100 Within the company, there was some dissatisfaction with the cost system prior to implementation of the CIM line. The overall cost competitiveness of the pre-1992 manufacturing process was the main concern. For instance, marketing was frequently dissatisfied because they often felt costs were too high to allow a competitive price. Most of the dissatisfaction was directed at the overall level of costs assigned to a contract and not with the cost system *per se*.

5.6.101 Since the primary cost object is the contract or project, then the adequacy of the cost system should be judged in that context. Successfully managing long-term OEM projects requires an understanding of costs across the entire design-build-ship-erect cycle. Management should have an understanding of what impact decisions throughout the value chain will have on costs and profits at the project level. Given the number and size of OEM projects, it may not be important that individual loose tubes be costed correctly so long as any distortions at the part level average out at the project level. If that was the case, the labour-based system was probably adequate when the majority of the workload related to 20 to 30 large OEM projects being processed at any given time.

5.6.102 Today, the majority of the Tube Shop's orders are for replacement parts. These typically consist of orders ranging anywhere from a single tube to a batch of 15 tubes to an entire replacement component. Understanding costs at the part and component level takes on much more importance in the current environment. Shop overhead, plant support services and operating-all-works are assigned to contracts at almost twice the direct labour cost. Under the job cost system which existed prior to 1992, there was very little of a cause-and-effect relationship between these support costs and direct labour. Even if the Tube Shop process had not been automated, more accurate cost estimating at the individual part and component level would be necessary. With the automation of the Tube Shop line, direct labour has even less of an association with activities performed on the CIM line. It would be more meaningful for cost estimation and cost management purposes if cost assignment procedures were developed which recognise the cost of activities performed throughout the Tube Shop.

5.6.103 Whether the pre-1992 labour focused cost system was adequate or not is no longer the issue. Given the nature of the CIM system, clearly there is no longer much of a relationship between direct labour and work performed by CNC machines. A new cost assignment process was needed to accommodate the new production process. Since elements of the old manual line were still needed to process tubes which exceeded the machine constraints on the CIM line, the activities chosen to assign costs should relate to both lines. Otherwise, it would be difficult to integrate and compare activities and costs on the two parallel lines.

Concerns with the labour-focused costing system
5.6.104 The Tube Shop's manual production process had been redesigned and full operational implementation of the new $13 million computer-integrated manufacturing line (CIM) was complete. The bay's fabrication operations were automated in order to cut costs, reduce raw tube to finished product time by up to 80 per cent, provide superior quality and ship orders on schedule. 'In today's highly competitive arena we must become the front runner of innovation, quality, cost/value, delivery and service,' according to Wayne Dreher, manager, Manufacturing/Process Engineering, Tube Shop.

5.6.105 As mentioned above, prior to installation of the CIM system, the major concern was the efficiency of the manual production process. Marketing often complained that contract cost proposals were excessive and led to uncompetitive quotes. On occasion, their concerns could be documented by evaluation of open public bids or other information gathered by sales personnel. Manufacturing was frequently dissatisfied because a key performance indicator, E/A (estimated man hours/actual man hours), was often unfavourable and there were frequent cost overruns on contracts, even though no changes had been made in the detailed engineering design. And engineering was looking to improve their ability to evaluate numerous design and manufacturing alternatives (tooling, machine constraints and cost) at the tube and feature level, early in the design cycle.

5.6.106 While there had been some question about the adequacy of the labour-focused cost system in place before automation of the Tube Shop, the plant accounting staff felt the system was acceptable and did not see any pressing need to change it as long as the labour-paced manual line was still in place. Recently however, the cost system was beginning to come under greater scrutiny. There was now concern that the labour-based overhead allocations did not reveal important differences in the cost of projects, some of which could take three to five years to complete and run into the millions of dollars. With implementation of the CIM line, there was little doubt that the prior labour-based cost system would be incapable of providing the kind of reliable cost information that engineering, marketing and operations would need.

Cost estimation and product engineering

5.6.107 Sales personnel generate requests for quotations (RFQs) for entire steam generation systems, replacement boiler components and loose tubes from potential customers. As mentioned, RFQs are initially processed at PSI's Dallas, Texas headquarters. If the order is for replacement parts on a power system originally designed and built by PSI, then detailed blueprints are available and cost estimators can prepare their bids from these blueprints. However, if the customer wants a new power generation system or has equipment made by another manufacturer and wants to replace a component (a complex subassembly consisting of many parts), then product engineering will prepare preliminary tube designs from historical data on similar products produced before by PSI. There are enough similarities to previously-fabricated tube variations that customer RFQs can be developed on a timely basis by querying the parts database. Cost estimators use these preliminary tube designs to prepare estimates of the tube's manufacturing and material cost.

5.6.108 There are several problems associated with the manner in which cost estimates are prepared. First, preliminary engineering designs of new systems and, to a lesser degree, replacement components can only be described at a fairly general level of detail. Firms bidding on projects must prepare quotes without knowing the final design of the project or what demands it will place on the production process. Second, the base estimating data used by cost estimators was developed from industrial engineering time studies completed in the early 1970s. Mistakes in estimating projects of this magnitude can prove to be very costly. If a project's cost is underestimated, then sizable cost overruns can occur and the contract will be unprofitable. If a project's cost is overestimated, the contract will likely be won by a competitor.

5.6.109 If the proposal is accepted and becomes a contract, the proposal becomes the base-line or 'as-sold' estimate (i.e., the budgeted cost) for cost monitoring and measuring actual performance. Once a proposal is accepted, product design engineers 'start from scratch' and prepare detailed part and component designs on computer-aided design (CAD) systems. They also determine the materials composition for all tubes. This product structure and tube geometry, which describes the physical characteristics of the tube, is then transferred to draftsmen who transform the product structure into detailed graphics (blueprints). Draftsmen manually load information on the tube's geometry into three different computer systems: (1) the Bill of Material system; (2) the CAD drawing system; and (3) the Tube Detail file which converts tube geometry along with design, process, machine and tooling constraints data into process plans. This information is downloaded to East River's mainframe computer.

Computer-integrated manufacturing process

5.6.110 Benefits from implementing the CIM system were expected to result in:

- Reduction of manpower;
- Increase in throughput;
- Decrease in work-in-process inventory;
- Reduction in maintenance costs;
- Shortening of lead times;
- Increased quality;
- Increased capacity;
- Increased market share.

5.6.111 Complete automated operations commenced with the integration of all work cells with the Tube Shop controller and plant mainframe computer in April 1992. Product flow philosophy is to pull a part through the

Tube Shop without undue build-up of work-in-process inventory between workstations. Most material handling will be by V-roll conveyors and cascades (a buffer storage in front of a workstation). Once a part has been studded or bent, it will be transported by radio-operated crane.

5.6.112 An automatic storage and retrieval system is the first stop for tubes entering the Tube Shop. The system orders and stores tubes in bins until they are needed. When the schedule calls for them, the automatic storage and retrieval system locates the required tubes and transports them directly into the Tube Shop and through the automatic shotblast, which cleans the tubes. From the shotblast, the tubes are fed directly onto an automatic conveyor and cascade system. These systems are used to perform materials handling wherever possible.

5.6.113 Tubes are then routed to the Bardons & Oliver, a new double-end milling station where tubes are weld prepped and cut to length. A probe automatically inspects the dimensions of the tube, compares the readings to the programmed dimensions and either accepts or rejects the part. This machine also automatically bar codes each end of the tube with its own unique identification marking its shop order, part number and manufacturing process information. Bar code readers located at each work cell continuously update the Tube Shop controller as to the status of each tube in the system. This machine also applies the layout lines for stud patterns and bend tangents. Although much of the work downstream will be performed automatically, the layout lines help operators to verify subsequently that bending and studding equipment is performing to specifications.

5.6.114 Tubes discharged from weld prep will move onto either the tube-to-tube weld line or the line that feeds the studding and bending machines. Tubes that require bending or studding transit down the main line where they will go to either a flat studder, pin studder or a bender. Once all the studding is complete, the tubes are sent via conveyor to the end of the line, where they are deposited in a drop rack until they are needed. Tubes that need to be welded to one or more other tubes travel to the new tube-to-tube welding system where it may take anywhere from 50 seconds to 150 seconds to weld two tubes. Next, they go to the NDE (non-destructive examination) station where the welds are x-rayed to ensure product integrity. Tubes that pass inspection are then conveyed to a drop rack to await manual handling.

5.6.115 The only manual handling or set-up required is with the stud welders and certain types of bending machines. This involves changing of the dies and cleaning of feeder systems. Tool and die changes have been made more efficient by locating tooling near machines, staging in the order needed and by eliminating the need to bolt dies in place.

5.6.116 The CIM control system is the heart of the Tube Shop automation. It integrates the information flow within the shop. The control system has an internal model of the shop floor with its machines, queues, material, tooling, consumables and personnel. In addition, it has a list of the work performed, work currently underway and completed work. The control system is responsible for downloading all the information required to process tubes to each machine's computer-numerical control (CNC) system. It ties together all the information for a given work order, from staging of the raw material through completion of all manufacturing processes and inspection. Each order is tracked in real-time with the use of the advanced bar coding system described above which provides critical monitoring and control information and detects costly errors before they impact on product integrity or scheduled shipments. All individual machine control systems serve as shop floor data collectors and upload information on an order's status to the Tube Shop supervisory controller. Factory Link, the systems application software, is used to manage shop floor activities for each manufacturing order.

5.6.117 The Tube Shop utilises an IBM Manufacturing Resource Planning System (MAPICS II), a computer-based resource planning and control system which generates bills of materials, process routings, order quantities and required shipping dates from customer order information entered into East River's mainframe. As part of the CIM system investment, the archaic and inefficient manual scheduling system was discarded and a computerised production floor scheduler, known as FACTOR, was integrated into the computer-integrated manufacturing system. FACTOR creates a detailed shop floor schedule. Both the CIM control system and FACTOR feed information into the higher-level MAPICS II system. Orders are produced on a priority basis. Tubes are run in batches of ten to facilitate any emergency orders which must be immediately interjected into the process. Bar coding is an integral part of the computer-controlled process, providing not only routing and processing instructions but also allowing other systems, including accounting, to capture real-time data on an order's status as it moves through the Tube Shop. In this way, timely, reliable and inexpensive analysis can be performed and feedback provided.

5.6.118 The production schedule developed by FACTOR, plus the engineering design requirements from the Tube Detail file and loose tube fabrication program are transferred to the CIM Control/Integration System where Factory Link manages an order through the factory. The control system should keep material flowing through the Tube Shop in as close to an

Flexible manufacturing systems

optimum manner as possible and consistent with meeting production schedule and cost objectives. Scheduling is accomplished in five to ten minutes, enough time to allow enquiries and subsequent rescheduling. Examples of enquiries include: the effect of adding overtime or a second shift; the result of adding a high priority order; or the result of totally dedicating a particular machine to one large order until it is completed. Output will include not only the schedule impact of these changes but also the cost implications.

5.6.119 Electronic Data Interchange (EDI) is utilised to provide a paperless data flow through all operations. 'These high-tech computer systems virtually eliminate the need for paperwork within the Tube Shop', noted Kitchen. 'They also give us better control. They allow us to predict the impact of rush orders and plan them through without having to put buffers in (the schedule). They let us run the business better and smarter', he said.

5.6.120 The Tube Shop was restructured to provide for two modes of operation in the processing of loose tubes. The first mode is the CIM line which processes the loose tubes required for repair and replacement parts and the fabricated tubes needed as component parts of other assemblies completed at East River. The second mode is a smaller manually operated fine which can accommodate unique configurations which cannot be processed on the automated fine.

5.6.121 To make the transition successful, management had to have the acceptance and participation of employees and their union. A co-operative effort between the state, the union and East River management resulted in extensive training to enhance the computer and mathematics skills necessary for operating the sophisticated computer-controlled equipment in a particular area. The number of job classifications was reduced from thirteen to three and workforce requirements were reduced by half. Workers no longer needed in the Tube Shop were reassigned to other parts of the plant.

5.6.122 With the change to self-managed teams and the introduction of automation to the tube line, John Phillips, Manager of Manufacturing Accounting at PSI's Dallas, Texas headquarters knew there would be even less assurance that the numbers coming out of the existing cost system would be reliable. A different cost system would be needed to accommodate the new process and more accurately measure the costs of activities on the manual line if the cost system were to provide operating personnel with more reliable contract cost estimates and performance data. Plus Phillips was aware that the plant-wide assignment of overhead costs created cross-subsidies for unprofitable components. With automation, the

Changing technologies and cost management

labour-focused cost system would be all but irrelevant to bid proposals and project management. Phillips had the additional assurance of high level support from Dan Stevens, President of PSI, who understood the need to change the cost accounting system to accommodate the new manufacturing system.

Activity-based costing project team

5.6.123 The makeup of the activity-based costing (ABC) team would prove to be critical to acceptance of the ABC system throughout its design and implementation phases (see also Chapter **6**). It was important that the ABC system be perceived as a system designed by operating personnel to improve decisions with respect to product design, the production process and marketing strategy. It would be a mistake if the ABC system was designed by accounting staff only. Therefore, the ABC project team would have a strong operational orientation and a good understanding of the new automated process.

5.6.124 The ABC team was chosen from members of the CIM implementation team and consisted of a mix of accounting, information systems, engineering, manufacturing and cost estimating people knowledgeable of East River's products and processes. For example, a cost estimator was part of the team since it was crucial to be able to prepare cost estimates for a contract the same way that accounting would accumulate costs for the contract. If a conflict arose, operational considerations took precedence over standard accounting practices. Prior to the actual start of system design, Phillips held an on-site seminar which outlined the limitations of the labour-based system, described ABC systems, enumerated the objectives and information requirements for implementing ABC at East River and proposed an implementation plan.

5.6.125 At all times during the design phase, engineering, production and marketing personnel were kept informed of what the ABC team was doing. The team wanted to improve the chance that the ABC system would play an integral part in decisions affecting marketing strategy, product design and the production process. They were not about to let communication breakdowns undermine the credibility of the ABC system. If the channels of communication were kept open and the team could get users to buy in throughout the design and implementation stages, then the likelihood that ABC information would be viewed as essential to project management and future improvement initiatives would be greater. Throughout the CIM/ABC analysis, design and implementation, a major effort was made at cooperating with and satisfying those who would be using the output of the ABC system.

Activity-based costing design objectives

5.6.126 The goal of the ABC project was to design a system which could function as a management tool by providing timely and accurate measurements of which resources were used how resources were used and how much it cost to use those resources. The ABC system would provide more accurate measures of resources consumed by each contract and could be used to 'drill down' to the component and part level for more detailed costing information. This would satisfy the concerns of marketing people and cost estimators for more reliable product/component information. But the intention was to make it more than just a better part or contract costing system. Phillips recognised that engineering and manufacturing personnel had little interest in product cost data. They were more interested in identifying the cost of various design alternatives, opportunities for cost reduction and permanent cost savings.

5.6.127 Specifically, the following objectives were expected from implementing ABC:

- Identification of high-cost activities throughout the manufacturing process;

- Highlighting of high-cost activities whose cost could be reduced by,
  - reducing the need for an activity (e.g., reducing the number of moves), or
  - reducing the time to perform an activity and, therefore, increase throughput;

- Identification of the costs of low-value and waste activities and establishment of priorities for improvement or elimination;

- Use of the activity reports as a basis for establishing ongoing cost reduction programs in engineering, purchasing and manufacturing;

- Provision of more accurate cost data to Dallas Marketing/Estimating personnel so they could quote projects with better, more reliable cost numbers;

- Building of a file of historical data to load into a simulation model for scheduling and manpower forecasting;

- Expansion of the study to include plant support costs not included in this phase.

5.6.128 Ultimately, the usefulness of ABC information would be judged on its ability to provide reliable *ex ante* as well as accurate *ex post* information.

Changing technologies and cost management

ABC objectives were equally focused on achieving cost estimating, cost reduction and contract cost control goals by linking the ABC system to the automated collection of activity information. The new cost system was designed to place a premium on generating timely information. The CIM system made this possible. The intention was for the cost system to function in more than a scorekeeping or attention-directing capacity. The hope was that by integrating ABC into engineering and production systems, ABC would be flexible enough to be an integral part of product design and process-related decisions.

ABC direct and indirect costs

5.6.129 Because the cost system of the Tube Shop was so closely tied to that of the other four bays, where operations were still largely labour intensive, Phillips decided not to expand the scope of the project to include East River's or Dallas's support services. Instead, the ABC team focused on the Tube Shop direct costs – labour, fringe benefits, set-up, repairs and maintenance, depreciation and supplies – plus support costs allocated from works-general (i.e., plant support services) and operating-all-works (i.e., central support services located in Dallas).

5.6.130 The contract is the primary cost object in a project management environment. The cost system charges materials directly to the contract and to the part. Product design engineering and drafting/graphics costs are also directly charged to contracts. Burden rates are based upon practical capacity. A material burden rate of 5 per cent of material cost covers the cost of the purchasing and material control costs. Works-general overhead consists of production control, maintenance, quality assurance, payroll, accounting and other support services charged to contracts at the rate of 40 per cent of labour cost. In addition, operating-all-works (OAW) costs associated with Dallas support services are charged at the rate of 15 per cent of labour cost. OAW consists of manufacturing engineering support and the resource allocation group which plans and monitors plant loads, product mix and production volume. In total, the combined works-general and OAW costs allocated to the Tube Shop amount to less than 30 per cent of the Tube Shop's direct costs.

5.6.131 The Tube Shop's direct costs can be clearly identified with one of 22 process-related cost pools associated with the automated line, the manual line and labour-intensive activities. Figure 5.19 lists these 22 processes or operations and their associated cost drivers. A cost driver rate is determined for each activity cost pool and serves as the basis for charging contracts and components with the Tube Shop's direct and allocated costs. The Tube Shop costs and cost rates are provided in Figure 5.19.

Flexible manufacturing systems

Activities & activity cost pools:	Cost driver description	Budgeted annual cost driver	Bay 7 direct cost of activity	Bay 7 direct cost per activity	Wks gen. allocated cost	Wks gen. cost per activity	OAW allocated cost	OAW cost per activity
Automated line								
Retrieval	No. of lifts	28,080	$127,200	$4.530	$0	$0.000	$0	$0.000
Shotblast – auto	No. of lineal feet	4,193,280	177,500	$0.042	16,200	$0.004	$6,100	$0.001
Mill B&O – auto	No. of end mills	149,760	318,600	$2.127	16,200	$0.108	$6,100	$0.041
(Weld prep. and bar code)								
Layout – auto	No. of layout lines	1,198,080	184,300	$0.154	16,200	$0.014	$6,100	$0.005
Weld – STW – auto	No. of joints welded	88,750	402,600	$4.536	48,600	$0.548	$18,200	$0.205
Weld – auto pin	No. of studs	5,990,400	312,100	$0.052	48,600	$0.008	$18,200	$0.003
Weld – auto flat	No. of studs	5,990,400	312,100	$0.052	48,600	$0.008	$18,200	$0.003
CNC bend – auto & check	No. of bends	59,900	306,600	$5.119	48,600	$0.811	$18,200	$0.304
			2,141,000		$243,000		$91,100	
Activities & activity cost pools:								
Manual line								
Shotblast – manual	No. of lineal feet	1,048,320	100,300	$0.096	$24,300	$0.023	$9,100	$0.009
Mill B&O – manual	No. of end mills	68,380	97,800	$1.430	$24,300	$0.355	$9,100	$0.133
(Weld prep. and bar code)								
Lathe – manual	No. of end mills	12,780	41,900	$3.279	12,200	$0.955	$4,600	$0.360
Saw in shop – manual	No. of cuts	11,810	48,300	$4.090	12,200	$1.033	$4,600	$0.390
Layout – manual	No. of lines	427,890	98,000	$0.229	24,300	$0.057	$9,100	$0.021
Tube weld – STW – manual	No. of joints welded	11,070	108,900	$9.837	24,300	$2.195	$9,100	$0.822
Weld – manual stud	No. of studs	3,010,180	215,200	$0.071	48,600	$0.016	$18,200	$0.006
Bend – press	No. of bends	14,530	152,800	$10.516	48,600	$3.345	$18,200	$1.253
Bend – #2 pines	No. of bends	40,860	372,500	$9.116	145,800	$3.568	$54,700	$1.339
Bend – #4 pines	No. of bends	57,410	480,300	$8.366	194,400	$3.386	$72,900	$1.270
Bend – conventional	No. of bends	14,190	251,700	$17.738	72,900	$5.137	$27,300	$1.924
Swage	No. of reductions	93,210	160,500	$1.722	24,300	$0.261	$9,100	$0.098
			2,128,200		$656,200		$246,000	
Non-machine activities & activity cost pools:								
Labor driven operations								
Bend – hot	No. of bends	4,860	$56,400	$11.605	$18,200	$3.745	$6,800	$1.399
Tube finish	Minutes	1,573,730	836,500	$0.532	249,100	$0.158	$93,400	$0.059
Hand operated			$892,900		$267,300		$100,200	
Total			$5,162,100		$1,166,500		$437,300	

Figure 5.19 East River Plant (B) – Bay 7 Manufacturing – Major activities and cost drivers

Changing technologies and cost management

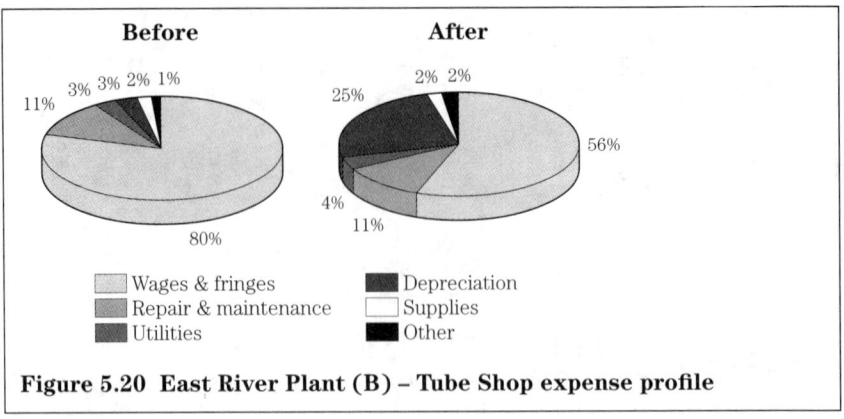

Figure 5.20 East River Plant (B) – Tube Shop expense profile

Computer simulation of major activities

5.6.132 The ABC project team used now-familiar interviewing techniques to gather activity-based costing information about the manual line. But interviewing was of limited use for organising cost pools and determining cost drivers for the new CIM process. The first step was to identify major activities at each workstation and work cell. Many of the activities performed in the Tube Shop, the human and technology-related resources that would ultimately perform the activities, and the cost of these resources, particularly for the manual line, were well-known to operating personnel. For the CIM line, manufacturing engineers had carefully assessed the performance capabilities of the new equipment during the project's evaluation stage. With this information in hand, the ABC team consulted with the Operations Research Group in the Fort Worth Research Division in order to determine the capacities of the major activities. The research group ran an off-the-shelf computer simulation of the automated line which incorporated known constraints of the automated line, inputs required, outputs that would be generated and the constraints of each part. Utilising a typical 12-month product mix, engineering provided part geometry data – size of the tube, inside diameter, wall thickness, the number of bends, the type and number of studs applied and any other activities which would be performed on a particular tube.

5.6.133 The simulation was a computerised miniaturisation of the entire automated line. It clearly identified each machine, all conveyors connecting the different machines, any cascades where the tubes could be off loaded, all manning requirements and other elements of the CIM line. As a tube progressed down the line, calling on the different resources needed according to the hypothetical production schedule and tube geometry, the simulation identified unanticipated bottlenecks where tubes started to build up and machines could not operate fast enough to meet the throughput target. For example, if set-up for a tube bender could require from one-half hour to four hours of set-up time. Changing over from one set of dies to another set in order to make a different type bend, even in an automated line, would severely restrict the throughput on the line. That was unacceptable. Plus, it would be extremely costly to correct such a deficiency once the automated line was in place since the equipment and transfer lines were so tightly wedded together. So, in addition to identifying major activities for the ABC study, the simulation provided information about where additional equipment was required before the CIM capital investment decision was finalised.

5.6.134 Information from the simulation was supplemented with information gathered from interviews of hourly people and supervisors to identify their activities further – what they did, how the process worked, some of the process drawbacks and constraints and an initial determination of the non-value-added and value-added activities involved in the Tube Shop operations. After several months, a complete list of activities and their appropriate cost drivers was developed.

5.6.135 The ABC team wanted to utilise the computer-integrated control system to supply all the data for the cost drivers which would serve as surrogates for the activities previously identified. Each cost driver had to be measurable, readily available and easily understood. The information was going to be used as much for cost management purposes (e.g., evaluating alternative routings) as it was for product design for manufacturability evaluations and component costing purposes. Therefore, fast communication to decision-makers was critical. If it was not in the control system then it was eliminated from the list of potential cost drivers. Information from the computer simulation, the interviews and historical engineering data available in the control system was very helpful in this stage of the analysis.

5.6.136 Also, automated collection of activity data during production by means of the integrated shop floor control system permits timely measurement of operating performance and signals operators when to intervene and make necessary corrections. Work cell schedulers automatically collect feedback on process activities (e.g., number of studs applied, number of bends made and other activity-related data) and compare this data with information generated by the computer-controlled production scheduler, which maintains data on each product's requirements. Accumulating actual cost driver data at cost driver rates allows shop supervisors to make frequent

Changing technologies and cost management

contract-progress (cost-to-date) comparisons to evaluate how well the contract is progressing against promised delivery dates and as-sold cost estimates (the original bid prices accepted by customers). Any deviations are spotted almost immediately.

5.6.137 The ABC team tried to maximise the amount of the Tube Shop resource cost which could be identified with the major activities. Labour, fringes, welding supplies, repairs and maintenance and depreciation became activity cost pools. Traditional labour-based methods were used to charge a portion of cost allocated from the general plant overhead pool (works-general) and the OAW pool to the new activity cost pools. A cost profile of the Tube Shop before and after implementation of the CIM is provided in Figure 5.21. As anticipated, not only was the absolute dollar cost down significantly, but the mix of costs had changed drastically. The Tube Shop line headcount was reduced from 129 to 63, labour cost was cut in half from $5.5 million to $2.8 million and conversion cost decreased from $7.3 million to $5.2 million. While labour cost had been largely variable before modernisation, the demands of the CIM system required manning with relatively fixed teams of workers, regardless of output. Each operator was trained to perform a wider variety of activities than before, including interpreting engineering data and running multiple machines. Conversion costs were now relatively fixed.

Customer	Contract	ABC estimate	Actual cost	VAR	Labor-based estimate	Actual cost	VAR
Amer Paper Products	100-112345	$742	$999	($257)	$1,680	$999	$681
Amer Paper Products	100-112298	58	36	22	490	36	454
Midwest Electric	200-163113	$271	$234	$37	$471	$234	$237
American Power	100-177819	572	402	170	560	402	158
General Pulp	200-243654	802	665	137	1,120	665	455
Pittsburgh Steel	100-211105	12,569	11,852	717	16,520	11,852	4,668
Total		$15,014	$14,188	$826	$20,841	$14,188	$6,653

Figure 5.21 East River Plant (B) – Bay 7 Automated line – Conversion cost estimate comparison on selected contracts

How would the ABC system be used?

5.6.138 There were two overriding objectives in the design of the ABC system. First, ABC should provide a more accurate assignment of costs to contracts, components and parts. The combined benefits of lower costs attributable to the automated fine and more reliable ABC cost estimates should result in more competitive bids and an increase in market share for the replacement parts business unit. Plus, they could be more confident that

Flexible manufacturing systems

contracts accepted would result in a positive impact on the unit's P&L statement. Also, proposals lost could be analysed to determine where costs were not competitive.

5.6.139 In turn, cost estimators would need to develop cost estimates which emulated the new cost system. It was important that cost estimators' jobs were not made more difficult. With an estimator on the ABC team, the team was able continually to review the new set of cost drivers and how activities were going to be costed. In most cases, ABC estimates of the cost to produce a job on the CIM line were significantly less than what it would have cost to manufacture on the old manual line.

5.6.140 The second, more difficult, objective for ABC was to improve East River's ability to better manage the overall process from product design through product delivery. That meant using ABC data to evaluate and select the best designs and processes. Engineers and operating personnel could see the potential for using activity management and activity costing to improve both the design process and the production process. In addition, through the CIM system, East River is extending the existing database of operational information so that it can be utilised to develop new evaluative capabilities and performance measures. By keeping ABC's design and operational uses foremost in mind, management hopes to create an environment where informed decision-making can be accomplished with confidence through the use of ABC feedback.

The perceived need for an ABC system
5.6.141 As suggested above, for East River to grow its repair and replacement parts and services business, it has to please a market which demands strict attention to product integrity and immediate service. Neither utilities nor industrial processors can afford costly shutdowns for any length of time. Equipment breakdowns can cost hundreds of thousands of dollars daily. Losses of that magnitude place demands on manufacturers to provide quick turnaround of orders. PSI automated its tube fabrication operations, the Tube Shop, with these requirements in mind. This enabled East River to cut its raw tube to finished product time by up to 80 per cent, increase quality and improve on-schedule shipments dramatically. All this had to be done while competing for business in a very price-sensitive market and in an industry plagued by excess capacity.

5.6.142 Internationally, the market for original equipment purchases in the developing nations like China shows great promise. These nations are just now building the infrastructure necessary to supporting their expanding industrial capability. However, while the outlook is encouraging, there is no lack of willing global competitors such as the Japanese to challenge for every order in these advancing markets.

5.6.143 Timely access to information is indispensable to some managers. With implementation of the CIM system, high quality and timely manufacturing information is now readily available, which had not previously been the case. The prior labour-based, job cost system was never capable of providing accurate cost information at the part or component level. In fact, every part and component was allocated a proportionate amount of all indirect resources such as equipment and production support services, regardless of the mix of resources actually used. At the time of its implementation during the 1950s, accurate component costs were not much of a concern. However, in the fiercely competitive environment of the 1990s, accurate cost estimates were an absolute prerequisite.

5.6.144 One of the problems in securing contracts in the past was that the data cost estimating and marketing used was not always reliable. Product design engineers prepared preliminary tube designs at a fairly high level (i.e., designs were not very detailed) based upon historical data on similar products produced by PSI. Cost estimating personnel drafted bids using the broad designs and cost estimates prepared from base estimating data developed back in the early 1970s. (Another industrial engineering study to revise these standards would cost in excess of $1 million.) Then a proportionate share of all manufacturing overhead was allocated to each proposal based upon the estimated number of man hours that would be utilised on a project. These overhead resource allocations were misleading since the cost system was not capable of identifying which manufacturing resources would be used by each project. Given the size of many contracts – OEM projects typically cost $2 to $10 million and replacement components usually cost more than $150,000 – the risk of misestimating quotes was considerable. If a proposal was underestimated and the bid was accepted, the contract might very well be unprofitable. An unprofitable contract on jobs of this magnitude could be very costly. On the other hand, if a proposal was overestimated, the job might be lost to a competitor and PSI's profits would suffer accordingly.

5.6.145 Second, a CIM-driven line would make man hour data all but irrelevant for project proposals and project costing, since direct labour hours would no longer represent the demands which each project would place on overhead resources. With the newly-installed CIM line, man hours were cut in half. The production line is controlled by a central controller as opposed to machine operators. Manpower necessary to operate the line consists of self-managed teams of highly trained workers whose skills are needed regardless of the number of units scheduled for production. The change to

Flexible manufacturing systems

CIM technology meant that the manning requirements were largely fixed and unrelated to actual production volumes.

5.6.146 Therefore, John Phillips saw the need to develop a link between the activities and operations performed on the CIM line and on the automated materials handling system and the costs of these resources. If a plausible set of cost drivers could be determined, ABC would provide more accurate measures of manufacturing resources consumed for purposes of preparing contract proposals and controlling costs on projects won.

5.6.147 Another reason for implementing an ABC system was the likelihood of further cost reduction opportunities. Prior to installing the CIM system, East River's primary competitive problems were high cost and long lead times. The CIM system had an immediate impact on both. It reduced the costs associated with materials movement/handling, equipment changeover, machine maintenance, rework and manpower, while increasing productivity and shortening lead times. Beyond the immediate cost savings inherent in automating the Tube Shop, ABC information should provide product design engineers and manufacturing managers with more reliable information about the cost of different design decisions and alternative routings. Long term, ABC should help generate additional cost reduction opportunities by identifying high-cost, low-value activities where favourable cost trade-offs could be made without sacrificing quality. For example, if supply costs are going up on the shotblast, perhaps they could renegotiate selling prices with vendors or consider a recycling process.

5.6.148 One dilemma faced by the accounting group was that the rest of the plant was still using man hours to allocate corporate and plant overhead down to the individual bays. The Tube Shop had to supply a man hour figure to plant management so that the Tube Shop could be allocated its 'fair share' of overhead, even though man hours were almost totally irrelevant when it came to understanding cost cause-and-effect relationships in the Tube Shop.

The objectives of the plant's activity-based costing system

5.6.149 The intention was to make the ABC system a flexible, process-based cost system. Cost estimators and marketing needed more reliable information about component and contract costs for bid preparation purposes. Engineering and operations needed information about process costs and activities in order to evaluate numerous design and manufacturing process alternatives. The following objectives were expected from implementing ABC:

- Identification of high-cost activities throughout the manufacturing process;

- Highlighting of those high-cost activities whose cost could be reduced by:
  - reducing the need for an activity (e.g., reducing the number of moves), or
  - reducing the time to perform an activity and, therefore, increase throughput;
- Identification of the costs of low-value and waste activities and establishment of priorities for improvement or elimination;
- Use of activity reports by engineering, purchasing and manufacturing as a basis for establishing ongoing cost reduction programs;
- Provision of more accurate cost data to Dallas Marketing/Estimating personnel so they could quote projects with better, more reliable cost numbers;
- Building of a file of historical data to load into a simulation model for scheduling and manpower forecasting;
- Expansion of the study to include plant support costs not included in this phase.

5.6.150 It is helpful to keep in mind that in a project management environment, a contract for a steam generator or replacement component is the project or product. Therefore, cost pools are organised according to whether the costs can be directly identified with a contract/component or, if not, can be included in one of several process-level or support-level cost pools. The following bullets give a brief explanation of each cost pool.

- A contract pool accumulates all costs such as raw materials, design engineering and detail graphics which can be directly traced to a specific contract or replacement component.
- A materials-procurement pool, which was first developed in the late 1980s, includes costs, other than raw materials, associated with materials acquisition, storage and movement.
- In production, there are 22 process-level cost pools which summarise costs of a specific work cell or other value-adding operations such as tube finishing. There are eight process cost pools and seven cost drivers for the automated line and another 12 process cost pools and eight cost drivers for the manual line. Labour-intensive finishing work is separated into two cost pools, each with its own cost driver.
- Two support-level cost pools, works-general and operating-all-works, help sustain the plant's overall manufacturing process.

Flexible manufacturing systems

5.6.151 In designing the process-related cost pools, it made sense to use the information that would already be generated by the automated manufacturing system. The CIM system creates a wealth of operational information, including data on cost driver activity which is used to cost parts, components and entire contracts. Therefore, the functionality of the ABC system for manufacturing engineering and production decisions can be credited to the timely delivery of production information fed to it by the CIM system.

5.6.152 In reviewing the cost drivers used to allocate process-related costs (e.g., the number of lifts, bends, studs, lineal feet, minutes, etc.), it is clear that they are all unit-based. An appropriate cost driver is identified with each process-level cost pool within the Tube Shop. In this sense, there is a far more accurate assignment of the cost of production operations based upon the demands that a process quantity places on the resources (labour and machine) of that manufacturing operation than there was under the previous labour-based overhead allocation system. In defence of this emphasis on unit-level or volume-related activities, it should be emphasised that 76 per cent ($5.162 million/$6.766 million) of the process-level costs assigned to components and contracts are the result of direct processing activities of the Tube Shop.

5.6.153 There are several reasons for this emphasis on unit-level activities. First, the lack of batch-level cost pools can be attributed to the significant reduction in batch-related activities and costs. The advanced manufacturing and information technology used in the Tube Shop and the physical layout of the bay significantly reduces such batch-level activities as production scheduling, material movement, equipment changeover and quality inspection and testing. Second, batch-level activities are less important in this environment given that batches of ten tubes are processed at a time. The manufacturing system is designed to place a premium on flexibility to meet unexpected conditions. If a customer has an emergency shutdown, then the production schedule is flexible enough to allow easy integration of the emergency order without disrupting normal operations. In this business, the unexpected is the norm and emergency orders are not unusual and definitely a priority.

5.6.154 Third, product-sustaining activities associated with engineers designing replacement components or entire steam generation systems are charged directly to the component and contract, unless they are insignificant.

5.6.155 The two support-level or process-sustaining cost pools assigned to the Tube Shop and to the process pools from works-general and operating-all-works are assigned more or less arbitrarily by man hours. Some production

Changing technologies and cost management

support activities, like expediting, could be directly identified with a specific process, contract, component, or part, while other production support activities, like production control, manufacturing engineering and the resource allocation group are performed to maintain the plant's overall production process. Though these latter activities are necessary to production, they are difficult to identify with the production of individual parts and components. They are the joint or common costs of different products.

Determining the cost drivers

5.6.156 The need for timely data was seen as paramount. Also, much of the manual line has been retained. In order to process certain tubes which exceed the constraints of the automated line, tubes are offloaded to the manual line for processing the constraint operation and then returned to the automated line for completion. It is important for both lines to be costed on the same set of cost drivers. This allows manufacturing engineers to use the ABC information database to determine the most efficient routing for each tube.

5.6.157 Production personnel were consulted about the major activities or operations necessary to process structural steel into finished tubes on the manual line. In the case of the CIM line, manufacturing engineering and the Research Group in Fort Worth analysed the new technology and determined the appropriate activities, the capacity of each activity at each work cell and the cost drivers which would be used to set ABC rates. Most of the activities are the same on both the manual line and the new CIM line.

5.6.158 The issue of processing time versus activities undertaken was addressed by the ABC project team. Product design engineers tend to think in terms of tube features – number of bends, geometry of each bend, number and type and number of studs applied, number of swaged ends, etc. – many of which relate to the number of times an activity is completed. Manufacturing engineers focus more on time to complete an activity, operation or entire process. Substituting the number of times an operation or activity (feature) is performed for the span time of that operation is based upon the assumption that there is a linear relationship between the two. For most operations completed on the automated line, the time differences within a particular process are not usually worth accounting for at this stage of the development of the ABC system.

5.6.159 In the case of operations completed on the manual line, there can be greater variations in set-up time, time to bend pipes to different angles, or the elapsed time to complete a tube-to-tube weld (from 50 seconds to 150 seconds). Here averaging time across the quantity of the cost driver does

Flexible manufacturing systems

create cost distortion. One of the major strengths of the ABC system was to reveal the cost differentials of performing different operations on the two lines. Most operations completed on the CIM line are less expensive than those same operations completed on the manual line (see Figure 5.21).

5.6.160 The project team discussed these issues and recognised that certain trade-offs were necessary. They believed that using cycle times for each activity, while more accurate and more useful for manufacturing engineering and process improvements, would unnecessarily complicate the process of assigning costs at this time. The project team wanted to ensure that a broad range of people had access to ABC information, would experiment with it and get timely feedback on their decisions. This process seemed to offer the greatest chance of evaluating the use of ABC information and increasing knowledge of Tube Shop operations.

5.6.161 Furthermore, a more complicated cost system would run the risk of not being as well received by the design engineers, cost estimators and marketing people whose understanding, acceptance and use of the ABC system was so critical to its success. The near-term objective was to get them to use the new cost numbers in their product design, project cost estimation and pricing decisions. The thinking was that if they found the information useful, the news of ABC's usefulness would accelerate its spread to other areas like manufacturing engineering. If that meant achieving 60–70 per cent of the project's objectives initially, that was acceptable. Given time, the new system could evolve into a tool for cost reduction and continuous improvement. But an unnecessarily complicated system would create confusion and require continual explanation and clarification, thereby offsetting the build-up of genuine enthusiasm and insight that had occurred during the ABC analysis and design phases.

The computer-integrated manufacturing system and efficiency

5.6.162 Many of the benefits expected from investing in the new technology resulted in significant cost savings. The flexibility of the new technology further complements these cost savings. The Tube Shop is now more productive because it can produce smaller, replacement orders nearly continuously.

5.6.163 Many of the benefits of the computer-aided process planning and production system were realised when batch-level activities were minimised. A number of high-cost, low-value activities were an inherent result of the prior manufacturing process. Several of the more costly activities highlighted in the CIM analysis included manual scheduling of orders, materials movement and handling into and out of the raw materials storage area

Changing technologies and cost management

and within the shop, machine set-up including die retrieval and placement, line layout and manual inspection and testing of parts all along the line. These activities were largely batch-related activities. The time to perform these activities was significantly reduced when the automated storage and retrieval system and CIM system were introduced. For example, computerised quality control and real-time tracking of parts were incorporated throughout all phases of tube fabrication, providing not only more timely monitoring and control information but eliminating the manual tracking, checking and inspecting endemic to the old manual system.

5.6.164 With quality checks built into every step of the manufacturing process, quality problems are spotted immediately instead of at final inspection. This not only reduces the cost of scrap but also eliminates most of the extra workers, rework and overtime spent reacting to quality problems.

5.6.165 One goal of the CIM line and automated material handling was to limit the amount of work-in-process in transit or waiting to be processed. Additional savings were accomplished by reducing the excessive inventories on the shop floor and in production queues around machines. Although intrinsic to the manufacturing processes of that day, carrying large inventories was very costly.

5.6.166 Also, given that boilers are highly engineered products which can take months to design, product design engineers were already using the latest computer-aided design and engineering technologies to shorten overall lead time from concept-to-part cost. Therefore, many of the engineering-related processes had already been streamlined and automated long before any consideration was given to modernising the Tube Shop or implementing an ABC system. Further, the new equipment would be less costly to maintain. Equipment breakdowns would occur less often, thereby saving the costs of repair and downtime while the equipment is being fixed.

5.6.167 One other major source of cost and time savings which was generally invisible under the prior manufacturing system was the large amount of paper work and paper flow associated with the manual line. The CIM system utilises electronic data interchange to provide a nearly paperless data flow through all operations in the Tube Shop. And while the savings of all the paper processing could not be documented, everyone knew it was a substantial time consumer.

5.6.168 ABC theory is based on the notion that activities create costs (see Chapter **6**). The cost of a part, component or product should not change as a result of under-utilising or over-utilising available capacity. In fact, adding

Flexible manufacturing systems

capacity or eliminating existing capacity should not affect the cost of the item unless the mix of resources used to make that part changes. The assignment of fixed and semi-fixed capacity-related costs to actual or anticipated production volumes would cause product costs to fluctuate, sometimes wildly, from period to period. If the costs of producing a replacement part are thought to be a function of the activities and resources actually consumed or used in its processing (not to be confused with resources available or spent), then fluctuations in actual capacity utilisation levels would not cause product costs to change. While this may not be the usual manner in which conventional accounting systems cost products, it is a more economically plausible way to cost products. A more reliable measure of the underlying economics of product cost is the basis of activity-based product costing systems. Acquiring, eliminating or under-utilising resources (capacity) should have no impact on product costs unless the resources are used to produce a product change.

5.6.169 The way this is achieved in practice is to base resource consumption rates on a fixed resource usage level, usually practical capacity or some other efficient level of usage of the available capacity of a resource. Back in the early 1980s, East River changed the budgeted activity or denominator volume used to compute its factory burden rate from a three-year running average of actual production to practical capacity. While this may seem like a subtle change, it is very important to a business whose quotes are based on cost estimates. If a firm bases product costs on actual capacity utilisation levels and prices products on a cost-plus basis (as most job-order companies do), then low levels of capacity utilisation could result in a perverse and destructive bid-setting procedure which could jeopardise the firm's long-run viability. Otherwise, given the continued slack demand, East River risked aggravating its loss of business and repeating the 'death spiral' experienced by so many other firms whose costing practices placed a priority on fully absorbing overhead.

5.6.170 Unfortunately, capacity utilisation remains stuck at a low level because the market for power generation equipment remains depressed. One of the projected benefits from automating the Tube Shop was that East River would gain market share. They have. The problem is that forecasts for an increasing market as the American economy pulled out of the recession of the early 1990s have not materialised.

5.6.171 Other areas of project design, marketing or manufacturing could be reviewed for continuous process improvement

5.6.172 For some companies, ABC has become an important tool for driving down costs and achieving additional productivity gains. Given that all

Changing technologies and cost management

products – individual tubes, components and entire boilers – are highly engineered and made-to-order, design and process engineering for new parts would be an especially fruitful area for the company's continuous process improvement (CPI) program.

5.6.173 Various studies have indicated that 80–90 per cent of a product's costs are locked in during the design stage. If that is the case, design decisions made up-front can make or break a project. Could ABC information be used to evaluate all the engineering and manufacturability alternatives in the proposal stage? PSI needs the ability to generate an accurate and timely tube proposal estimate. The proposal needs to evaluate numerous designs for manufacturability alternatives (tooling, machine constraints and cost) for the Tube Shop's automated and manual lines. This would allow engineering, cost estimating and detail graphics personnel to evaluate more cost and manufacturability comparisons at the tube and feature level early in the design cycle. An ABC unit cost for each feature on the tube would be available as it is created so that the feature and process alternatives could be evaluated. The ABC tube cost will be accurately estimated after the design and process plan have been completed.

5.6.174 Concurrent with the design for manufacturability analysis, design engineering would run an analysis of the resource trade-offs. Also, given the operational focus of an established business like boiler parts/components manufacturing, plant functions like manufacturing engineering, manufacturing and production control focus on making the process run as efficiently as possible. They are constantly looking for ways to remove cost from the process or to determine a more efficient routing for a part. Since all parts are made in the Tube Shop, ABC can evaluate the consequences of different decisions on overall costs of a part. This is made possible because the Tube Shop's CIM line and manual line are fully integrated and the ABC numbers are based upon real-time machine data. Therefore, it is possible to look at the impact of one decision on the overall cost rather than focusing on its impact on just the cost of a single operation or activity. ABC helps to determine the optimal relationship among all the factors which go into making a part in the Tube Shop.

5.6.175 The objective of an ABC system might be first to create an environment where informed decisions are made with confidence. The ABC system can prove to be a valuable tool for highlighting high-cost processes and parts, allocating resources, and instilling a cost awareness among labour and plant support staff. Under the prior job cost system, detailed product and process information was not available. Without the ABC numbers, the problem-solving process would not function as well as it does. ABC helps identify problems and the potential savings from improvement projects. In this way, ABC serves as a priority-setting mechanism. However, ABC is not a diagnostic tool. ABC has limited ability to identify the underlying cause of problems or suggest corrective actions. Armed with ABC information, engineers and operations personnel analyse the problem and determine its source. After changes are made, accounting can document the savings from the improvement project.

5.6.176 Why was an ABC system not developed for the entire plant? There was no mandate to develop an ABC system for the entire plant. More likely, there would have been considerable resistance to any efforts to impose a different accounting system where none was requested. The plant manager had not asked for a new cost system and may very well have resented any efforts by the accounting staff or Dallas to impose one on the entire plant. Further, John Phillips and the accounting staff were not convinced that ABC was necessary for the rest of the plant at this time. The remainder of the facility was still labour-intensive and there was a significant relationship between labour and the electromechanical equipment operated by the workforce.

5.6.177 However, the Tube Shop was a key area for a number of reasons. First, CIM was introduced in order to reduce the cost and lead time of orders, while being able to satisfy customers' demands for high quality, made-to-order products. Once CIM was introduced, there was very little relationship between costs incurred in the Tube Shop and the existing labour-based overhead allocation system. All were in agreement that a new cost system was needed for this reason alone. (It did not hurt that PSI's president thought changes in the cost system were necessary.) Second, the Tube Shop was relatively autonomous from the rest of the fabrication area. It was the front-end of manufacturing at East River. All orders began here. Since the plant's workload was now heavily dependent on repair and replacement orders, more volume and product variety were involved than at any time in the past. Intuition told Phillips and his staff that whatever merits the old labour-based cost system once had, the demands of today's market place made it irrelevant if not misleading.

5.6.178 The immediate objective of the ABC system was to be able to provide cost estimating and marketing with more accurate information for project proposals. Another objective was to design a cost system that would be used by design engineers to develop more efficient product designs and by manufacturing engineers to reduce costs while improving service and quality. By integrating the ABC system with the CIM system, management would have timely access to the financial consequences of engineering and manufacturing decisions.

Changing technologies and cost management

5.6.179 A multi-disciplinary team consisting of personnel from engineering, production, information systems and cost estimating, as well as accounting, was chosen from the CIM project-analysis team. Phillips felt that familiarity with the existing cost system was not considered crucial to team membership. Phillips was the only member who had in-depth knowledge of the East River accounting system. The non-accounting members of the team were excited about the opportunity to design a cost system shaped to their needs, rather than one designed to fulfil accounting reporting requirements. In summary, the intention was to have operating personnel design the new ABC system and champion its cause. If they viewed it as their system, they would have a greater sense of ownership in it and would use the information to make decisions.

Resistance to the new ABC system
5.6.180 While it is not unusual to have a fair amount of resistance and scepticism when designing and implementing an ABC system, the implementation process at East River went smoothly and encountered minimal antagonism. Probably the most important reason was that East River was under pressure throughout the 1980s and on into the 1990s. Demand for original equipment boilers remained slack. Capacity utilisation was half of what it was in the halcyon days of the 1960s and 1970s. The plant was caught in a profit squeeze between the high costs of operating the manual line and aggressive pricing by rivals brought about by the glut of capacity in the industry. Everyone understood that major changes were necessary to secure East River's future. By investing $13 million in a state-of-the-art facility and upgrading the skills of the work force, management showed its willingness to make a major commitment to East River. If the plant was going to survive, the modern, computer-controlled tube facility seemed like a good bet.

5.6.181 Management assured the union work force that there would be no job losses. Workers made redundant by the CIM line were reassigned to other areas in the plant. The remaining workers received extensive cross-training on the computer-controlled equipment. Each worker was trained to operate all the machines in their area. Their jobs were enriched and their skills broadened. Further, the team concept is used widely throughout the Tube Shop. Hourly employees share in decision-making and problem-solving. Management and the work force have developed stronger working relationships. Employees can see that management wants the plant to succeed.

(Source: adapted with permission from Carr (1997).)

Chapter 6
Activity accounting

6.1 Introduction and background

6.1.1 Among the many novel cost management techniques which emerged during the 1980s, activity-based costing (ABC) has received much attention. ABC entails the examination of activities across the entire chain of value-adding organisational processes underlying causes of cost. It attempts to overcome cost distortions by addressing cost behaviour parameters, which include non-volume cost drivers reflective of production complexity and product diversity in addition to volume-linked drivers of cost. Although one output of ABC calculations is costs based on resource consumption, the actual process of deriving such costs offers a number of monitors which may be useful for a variety of managerial purposes. These include novel performance measures, altered budgeting techniques and a large amount of decision-making information tied to the broader concept of activity-based management. Activity accounting is the term used here to refer to activity-based costing, activity-based management and their variants.

6.1.2 The literature on activity accounting has developed considerably since the late 1980s. Whereas the early proponents of ABC tended to be consultants and distinguished accounting scholars, it was promoted in the absence of extensive empirical evidence of ABC's consequences. There is now much more evidence which indicates that major enterprises across the Western world are exploiting ABC's offerings (see Bhimani 1996). Yet it is also true that many organisations – which for a number of years have acknowledged the necessity of investing in accounting resources that reflect the ideas encompassed by ABC – have not insisted on deploying ABC systems. Moreover, many organisations have abandoned their usage of ABC. Innes, Mitchell and Sinclair (2000) report that the ABC/M phenomenon was arguably the biggest management accounting issue of the 1990s. They investigated how important ABC became in practice via surveys carried out in 1994 and again in 1999. The 1994 survey of UK companies indicated a 19.5 per cent rate of adoption with another 27.1 per cent of firms actively considering ABC. However, 13.2 per cent rejected ABC after assessment. Firms which deployed the technique used it in product costing, cost reduction, budgeting, decision making or performance measurement.

Activity accounting

6.1.3 In 1999, these authors' survey revealed a 17.5 per cent adoption rate with 20.3 per cent actively considering ABC and 15.3 per cent rejecting the approach. In considering the responses of companies which took part in both surveys, one third of companies using ABC in 1994 no longer did so in 1999. This same level rejected ABC after considering it in the earlier survey, whilst one third adopted it and the remaining third were still considering it. What is evident is that ABC continues to influence costing practices in a very large number of UK and other Western enterprises.

6.2 What drives costs?

6.2.1 During the first half of the twentieth century, production processes in most Western enterprises tended to be geared toward the repetitive manufacturing of homogeneous products. High direct labour costs constituted a significant portion of direct costs. As such, little distortion of cost was introduced when manufacturing overheads were allocated across a portfolio of relatively similar products.

6.2.2 During the second half of the twentieth century, direct labour costs in manufacturing organisations declined in relation to total production costs. As companies adopted advanced manufacturing technologies (AMTs), such as numerical control machines, computer-aided design and flexible manufacturing systems and other forms of automated production technologies (see Chapter **5**), the level of direct labour input diminished rapidly (Bromwich and Bhimani 1994). By contrast, as enterprises invested in AMTs, overhead costs and support activities quickly grew. This was not only caused by depreciation, insurance and maintenance costs, but also from a new category of costs associated with servicing the new technology, and which reflected indirect support activities. Flexible forms of production technologies can, for instance, require computer expertise, software updates, personnel training, scheduling systems and integrative information systems to link and co-ordinate automated production activities. As a result, overhead costs can quickly rise while direct labour costs continue to decline rapidly.

6.2.3 The growth in overhead costs was also intensified during the 1990s by the application of innovative work approaches, such as total quality management and just-in-time production systems, which help contain certain costs but which require additional overhead costs to be incurred. From the perspective of traditional costing, such changes in the manufacturing cost mix can be quite problematic. For many firms, direct labour has served as the principal application base for indirect costs, which have tended to be low. However, where the overhead numerator grows at a rate matching the swiftly diminishing direct labour denominator base, an inappropriately leveraged burden rate results. The demand for resources by different products is likewise no longer reflected accurately by a standard labour allocation base.

6.2.4 The managerial logic which identifies the potential benefits that can be derived from economies of scale through mass production continues to change alongside the implementation of AMTs. There is now seen to be considerable merit in satisfying a greater diversity of customer needs by developing and producing a large range of quality products and by providing a custom-made product within a minimal timeframe. However, the availability of flexible advanced technology needed to achieve this goal is not always the main motivating element. Rather, product diversity is sometimes the only strategic option open to a company in a dynamic and competitive market environment. The rapid pace of change in commercial markets and ongoing technological advances force corporate rethinking. The adoption of altered production technologies and work organisation approaches rests on transformed philosophies about 'best' business practices. New managerial thinking is accompanied by product diversity, technological complexity and operational flexibility. One consequence of this is the possibility of a reorientation of accounting practices.

6.3 The logic of activity accounting

6.3.1 Conventionally, organisations have attempted to achieve profitability by managing costs which do not necessarily translate into measures of resource-consuming activities. Costs are reported on the basis of responsible organisational units and the objective has been to ensure that business decisions deliver value to the customer in excess of the costs required to produce that value. Consequently, costs are often regarded as generating value and measuring production activities rather than merely representing in accounting terms the utilisation of resources by organisational activities. Using cost as a substitute for activity does not pose any difficulty where the manufacturing process is relatively simple and produces homogeneous products. Here, production costs may be readily traced and allocated to product units. In more sophisticated manufacturing environments, however, product quality, diversity and complexity have been viewed as critical in maintaining competitiveness and dictating how resources are used. In these contexts, activity-based information has been argued to be more useful than traditional costing data, as it attempts to capture cost causality factors more effectively. Accordingly, The Chartered Institute of Management Accountants (CIMA, 2000) defines ABC as 'an approach to the costing and monitoring of activities which involves tracing resource consumption and

Activity accounting

costing final outputs. Resources are assigned to activities and activities to cost objects based on consumption estimates. The latter utilise cost drivers to attack activity costs to outputs'. Activity-based management produces information that focuses employee efforts on continuously improving quality, time, service, cost, flexibility and profitability. In this light, CIMA defines activity-based management as a 'system of management which uses activity-based cost information for a variety of purposes including cost reduction, cost modelling and customer profitability analysis' (CIMA, 2000).

6.3.2 The foundation of all ABC systems is the view that the organisation is made up of activities: activities consume resources and cost objects (usually products) consume activities. This is in contrast to traditional accounting where costs are consumed by cost objects (mainly products). With ABC, the focus is not on the amount of each type of general ledger costs, such as wages, equipment, power and supervision, incurred by a department, but on the costs of the activities undertaken in the department. Thus, the conventional costs of a department would be assigned to the activities contributed to by the department.

6.3.3 Activity-based information may be non-financial or of a strategic cost nature (Cooper and Kaplan, 1999) and comprise any relevant data about activities across the entire chain of value- adding organisational processes, including design, engineering, sourcing, production, distribution, marketing and after-sales service. Information of this kind focuses managers' attention on the underlying causes (drivers) of cost and profit on the premise that individuals cannot manage costs but they can manage activities which cause costs to be incurred.

6.3.4 The manufacture of a product entails many processes which add cost to the product, but not all such activities necessarily add value to the product. It is therefore possible, in principle, to differentiate in cost management between value added and non-value added activities, according to whether or not the elimination of an activity from the operational process would result in a deterioration of product attributes such as performance, function, quality and perceived value, and thus reduce the value perceived by the customer.

6.3.5 Production approaches such as just-in-time systems, flexible production technologies and ERP systems place emphasis on eliminating waste, delay, excess and unevenness of product whilst integrating information relating to functional processes. It is potentially useful for managers to attempt to identify activities that waste organisational resources since they do not augment the customer's perception of a product's value. Such a perspective highlights a key aspect of what activity-based management systems attempt to do.

6.4 Scope versus scale

6.4.1 Problems may arise where traditional cost accounting systems, designed to value stock for financial reporting purposes, are assumed to provide a measure of the organisational resources used up in their production. One reason for this is that overhead cost growth can be due to increased diversity (or scope) of output rather than the volume (or scale) of output. A traditional cost accounting system which allocates overhead on the basis of scale of output rather than scope of output will tend to 'over-cost' high volume products and 'under-cost' low volume products relative to allowing for economies of scope (Bhimani and Bromwich, 2001). The resulting potentially 'distorted' cost information can encourage managers to proliferate low volume product lines which may, indeed, be loss-makers even though they may seem profitable under conventional management accounting. As Cooper and Kaplan explain:

> 'Low volume products create more transactions per unit manufactured than their high volume counterparts. The per unit share of these costs should therefore be higher for the low volume products. But when volume related bases are used to allocate support-department costs, high volume and low volume products are not treated differently because each individual unit produced represents the same volume of production . . . high volume products receive an excessively high fraction of support-department costs and, therefore, subsidise the low volume products'. (Source: Cooper and Kaplan, 1987.)

6.4.2 Most cost systems in manufacturing firms use a two-stage cost-tracing procedure for non-direct cost, whereby the first stage assigns resources to specific segments of the production process (departments). The second stage traces costs to products by using some measure of the quantity of resources consumed by each product. It is the choice of overhead application measure in this second stage which is seen as being able to distort costs if it is not chosen carefully (Cooper, 1987).

6.5 Long-term versus short-term cost behaviour

6.5.1 Conventional accounting has differentiated between costs which remain constant per unit but vary in total with production volume (variable costs) and those costs which remain constant irrespective of the total actual volume over a relevant range of production (fixed costs). Certain fixed costs

Activity accounting

are viewed by critics of conventional management accounting as being long-term variable costs which vary with measures of activity (other than production volume) but which do not vary concomitantly with such. These have traditionally been thought of as fixed costs and have been apportioned on the basis of arbitrary allocation rules devoid of any apparent cause-and-effect link. Commonly used traditional volume-based 'cost drivers' for allocating short-term variable costs include direct labour hours, machine hours and material costs (all of which are volume-based). The same bases are also used to allocate long-term variable costs by traditional cost accounting systems, resulting in cost tracing, which is regarded as inaccurate.

6.5.2 ABC methodology is founded on the view that long-term costs which vary with activity but not production volume are related to complexity. Increasing the volume of production does not increase the utilisation of support services (such as set-ups, expediting, inventory movements and scheduling activities), whereas augmenting the range of products will increase such support costs rapidly. For example, increased product diversity may increase the documentation and record-keeping activities associated with set-ups, since the number of set-ups increases when production lines utilising flexible technology switch from one product to another to increase the range of production. Under a conventional costing system, these increased record-keeping costs become part of overhead and are allocated to products using an application base such as direct labour.

6.5.3 It is not direct labour utilisation or production volume that is responsible for the increased record-keeping costs, but another measure of activity, which represents increased product diversity. The cost drivers underlying increased record-keeping costs mirror transactions which increase the scope of output rather than the scale of output. As such, the choice of cost drivers for activity-based costs should be based on factors which capture units or transactions and activities, such as inspection hours, number of inspections undertaken, production lots manufactured, set-ups, shipments, orders and even the number of vendors.

6.6 What is an activity?

6.6.1 The first step in determining an activity's cost is to ascertain which factors determine the amount of resources required by the activity. The aim is to make the pattern of costs reflect the usage of resources on activities. The technology used in the activity may be seen to determine the amount of resources used in the activity and therefore the demand for the activity's output and the size of the activity's cost pool. Thus assessing an order for creditworthiness may involve a certain amount of staff time, data and paper processing and the use of telecommunications. It is the technical operations required which determine the resource requirement of the activity. Ideally, the attribution of costs to activities should reflect this technology by tracing costs empirically on the basis of the activity's resource driver. Often judgement, interviews, diaries and informal records are used in estimating the resource requirements of an activity.

6.6.2 An activity should be capable of being viewed as separate from other activities and the output of the activity should be capable of being explained, ideally by only one factor (the cost driver). This will demonstrate how costs change with variable demands for the activity's output. The driver chosen should be deduced using empirical evidence and may be specific to the firm. There are two usual types of drivers (Bhimani and Bromwich, 2001).

(1) The volume or activity output. Examples include the number of set-ups and the number of quality inspections.

(2) Activity complexity. For example, creditworthiness checks may depend not only on order size but on the type of credit arrangement required by the customer; they may be influenced by the customer or by the total size of likely demands – such as the number of products, customers and suppliers – and by the technology and the organisational structure.

6.6.3 The costs derived from ABC are of a different nature to traditional costs. They are argued to represent the costs of activities as seen at a time when the firm is able to rearrange its operating activities (Cooper and Kaplan, 1999). In a shorter time-period, such factors as labour contracts or indivisible capacity (which technically cannot be reduced in the short run) may prevent any reduction in activity costs. Another factor preventing the rearrangement of operating activities relates to managerial decisions about activities, which may reside with functional managers not directly responsible for the activities under consideration. For example, halting production of some product which is expensive in activity cost terms will not automatically lead to cost reductions. The case in Section **6.8.8** shows how product costs may be distorted by conventional product-costing exercises and how an activity accounting approach can assist in assigning costs more equitably.

6.7 When to replace your costing system

6.7.1 The idea that an understanding of activities is necessary to manage costs was initially limited to a concern to better understand costs through activity-based costing. A number of signals may suggest the need to modernise a company's costing system:

Activity accounting

- Functional managers want to drop seemingly profitable products;
- Profit margins are hard to explain;
- Hard to make products show big profits;
- Functional departments have their own costing systems;
- The accounting department spends a lot of time on special projects;
- The company maintains a high-margin niche;
- Competitors' prices are unrealistically low;
- Customers do not mind price increases;
- The results of bids are hard to explain;
- Vendor bids are lower than expected;
- Reported costs change because of new financial accounting regulations.

6.7.2 An obsolete cost system can be demonstrated in terms of the cost of errors *vis-à-vis* accuracy: a cost system need not measure absolutely everything down to the finest degree. Taking infinitesimal measurements of each bit of material and each second of direct labour can be expensive and time-consuming. The expense is necessary only when the consequences of relying on inaccurate information are severe. When, for instance, margins are paper thin and the market moves quickly, basing decisions on inaccurate cost data can put a company out of business in next to no time. In other situations, highly accurate numbers are less important, and the company should not spend a lot of money to get them.

6.7.3 A good cost system trades off the cost of measurement and the cost of errors from inaccurate information in a way that minimises total cost (see Figure 6.1). As an economist would put it, the optimal system exists at the point where the marginal cost of improving the system's accuracy exactly equals the marginal benefit. An optimal cost system is a moving target. Competitive conditions are dynamic, so the cost of errors changes. Similarly, as information-processing technology changes, so does the cost of measurement.

6.7.4 It is important to remember that as product diversity increases – as high volume is mixed with low volume, or labour intensity is mixed with automation – costs are more likely to be skewed. To achieve the same level of accuracy, companies will have to spend more on measurements than when

When to replace your costing system

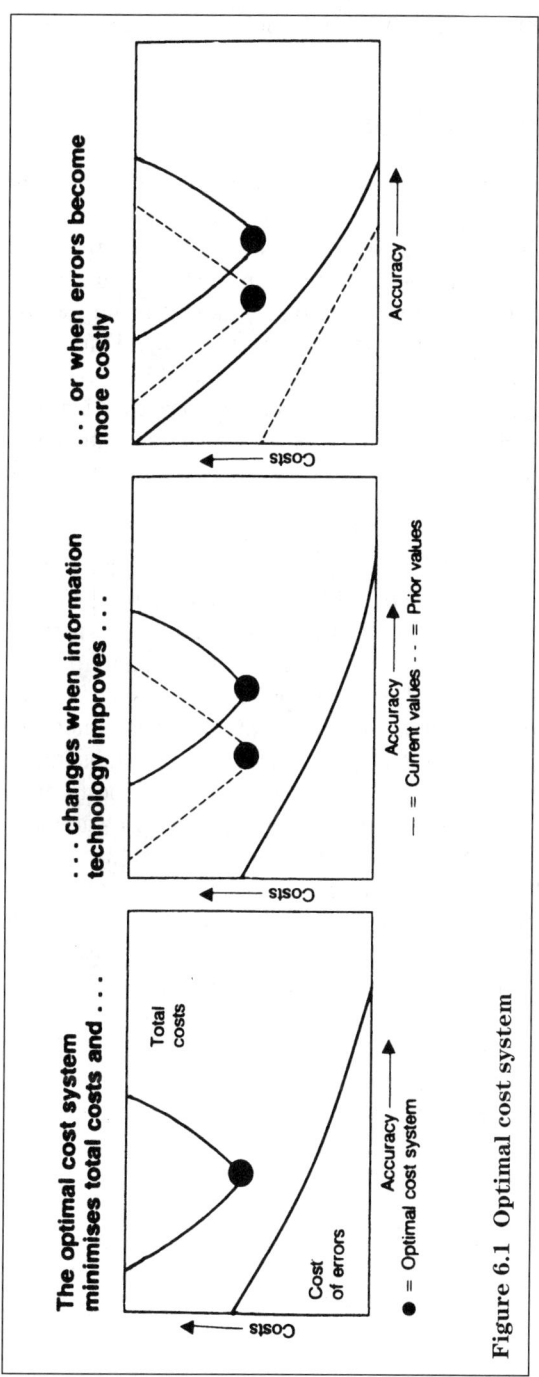

Figure 6.1 Optimal cost system

Activity accounting

products were more homogeneous. If they do not, their cost systems will be obsolete.

6.8 Determining cost drivers

6.8.1 The increasingly widespread deployment of advanced manufacturing technologies alongside the growing application of altered work organisation techniques and management approaches is considered to have significant implications for cost management. The product cost mix comprising material, overhead and labour (if any) can undergo an important transformation. Likewise, changes in product diversity, variety and life-cycle can give rise to a range of costing repercussions. The adoption of flexible production technologies entails training, maintenance, service expertise and automation costs which, coupled with changes in organisational management practices, can induce an altered conception of the economics of production.

6.8.2 Traditionally, production processes tended towards the repetitive manufacturing of homogeneous products. Although investments in heavy machinery to enable this were high, the emphasis on specialised production equipment for mass production coincided with an increased demand for specialised labour. The net consequence of this was high labour costs comprising a significant portion of direct costs. More recently, direct labour costs have declined in relation to total manufacturing costs. As companies adopt advanced manufacturing techniques (AMT), the need for direct labour input rapidly diminishes whilst overhead costs expand quickly. This arises not only from the attendant depreciation, insurance and maintenance costs, but also from a new category of costs associated with servicing the new technology (computer expertise, software updates, personnel training, scheduling systems and integrating information systems to link and co-ordinate automated production activities). From the perspective of costing logic, such rapid changes in the manufacturing cost mix (rising overheads and declining direct labour costs) can be particularly problematic. Conventionally, direct labour has served as a principal application base for indirect costs which tended to be low. However, where the overhead numerator grows at a pace not dissimilar to the swiftly diminishing direct labour denominator base, an inappropriately high overhead burden rate results.

6.8.3 The idea that an understanding of activities is necessary to manage costs was initially limited to a concern to better understand costs through activity-based costing. Activity-based information may be non-financial or of a strategic cost nature and may comprise any relevant data about activities across the entire chain of value-adding organisational processes including

Determining cost drivers

design, engineering, sourcing, production, distribution, marketing and after-sales service. This information focuses managers' attention on the underlying drivers of cost and profit. The manufacture of a product entails many processes which add cost to the product, but not all such activities necessarily add value. ABM enables a company to differentiate between value added and non-value added activities according to whether the elimination of an activity from the manufacturing process would result in a deterioration of product attributes such as performance, function, quality and perceived value and thus reduce value to the customer.

6.8.4 Management systems and approaches such as enterprise resource planning (ERP), just-in-time (JIT) and forms of AMTs place emphasis on eliminating waste, causes of delay, excess and unevenness of product. It is potentially useful for managers to attempt to identify activities which waste organisational resources in these ways and to view these non-value adding activities as undesirable since they do not augment the customer's perception of a product's value.

6.8.5 Long-term costs which are variable with activity but not production volume are related to complexity, and increasing the volume of production does not increase the utilisation of support services such as set-ups, expediting, inventory movements and scheduling activities, whereas augmenting the range of products will increase support costs rapidly. Increased product diversity may increase the documentation and record-keeping activities associated with set-ups since the number of set-ups increases when production lines utilising flexible technology switch from one product to another to increase the range of production. Under a conventional costing system, these increased record-keeping costs become part of overhead and are allocated to products using an application base such as direct labour. Yet it is not direct labour utilisation or production volume which is responsible for the increased record-keeping costs but some other measure of activity which represents increased product diversity. The cost drivers underlying increased record-keeping costs mirror transactions which increase the output rather than the actual volume of output. The choice of cost drivers for activity-based costs should thus be based on factors which capture transactions, such as inspection hours, number of inspections undertaken, production lots manufactured, set-ups, shipments, orders and even the number of vendors.

6.8.6 The identification of cost drivers is essential for the implementation of an activity-based cost system. What is required is to identify activities essential to enabling the enterprise to function. Activities may relate to organisational sub-units and will often bypass organisational boundaries. As

Activity accounting

a rule of thumb, an activity unit might consist of between five and 20 people. The expenditure levels may be over £20,000. Any of the following may be useful in defining activities:

- Analysis of historical records;
- Analysis of organisational units;
- Analysis of business processes and functions;
- Carrying out industrial engineering studies.

6.8.7 These may yield activity categories which will suggest the appropriate cost driver. Table 6.1 identifies some possibilities. It must be borne in mind that no two enterprises will have identical cost drivers for particular activities. Different organisations will opt to deploy different resources for similar tasks. This makes cost driver analysis highly organisation-specific.

Table 6.1 Cost drivers appropriate to activity categories

Activity	Cost driver
Scheduling	Number of works orders
Picking	Number of parts
Inspection	Number of inspectors
Set-up	Number of batches
Promotion	Number of advertisement runs
Record-keeping	Number of clerical hours

A case study: cost-based decisions

6.8.8 A case study to illustrate the promise that ABM can offer in a particular enterprise is provided in following illustration. Henry Hillberry, managing director of the Titanic Automobile Production Co. (TAP), is quite concerned as he arrives at the office one morning. He has spent the past two days at a seminar entitled 'Manufacturing strategies for the next decade' and was particularly interested in one session on cost management. He was convinced that he and the TAP board of directors were simply not getting the information they needed to make important decisions. Among the important issues they faced were:

- The pricing of one particular auto model;
- The relative profitability of TAP's three product lines;
- The possibility of further automation;
- The overall ability of TAP's managers to control the business.

6.8.9 As a result, Hillberry decided that he had to look beyond the monthly reports he had been receiving.

6.8.10 At the recent TAP annual meeting, Hillberry presented the financial statements for 2001. As shown in TAP's balance sheet and income statement (see Tables 6.2 and 6.3), TAP had gross sales revenue of $66.5 million on assets of $56 million at year-end. After-tax income of $4.9 million (up from $4.6 million in 2000) amounted to 7.4 per cent of sales, 8.8 per cent of assets, and a return on equity of 19.9 per cent.

Table 6.2 TAP Co. balance sheet as of 31 December 2001

	$m		$m
Cash, etc.	3.1	Current liabilities	18.1
Receivables	9.4	Long-term debts	13.3
Inventory	12.7	Ordinary shares	7.2
Net fixed assets	30.8	Retained earnings	17.4
Total	$56.0	Total	$56.0

6.8.11 Although these profitability numbers were well received at the annual meeting, Hillberry is not sure how TAP compares with other firms in the automotive industry. He is also not sure what changes, if any, should be made to TAP's product line and marketing strategy to remain competitive in the years ahead. To answer these questions and to learn more about TAP's cost management system, Hillberry requests a meeting with TAP's accountant Bradley McKinnis.

6.8.12 McKinnis brings breakdowns of sales and profitability for each of the three automobiles that TAP produces (compact, midsize and luxury). Table 6.3 shows that total volume reached 10,000 autos in 2001, an increase of almost 650 over 2000.

Table 6.3 TAP Co. schedule of sales revenues by model for the year ended 31 December 2001

Model	Volume	Price $	Revenue $m
Compact	7,000	5,000	35.0
Midsize	2,900	10,000	29.0
Luxury	100	25,000	2.5
Total	10,000		$66.5

6.8.13 Although sales volume increased for all three models, most of the increase was accounted for by compacts. Management has been pleased with

Activity accounting

the results of the vigorous advertising programme for compacts that led to that increase. Profitability, though, is another matter. Compacts lost almost $2.3 million (see Table 6.4). Manufacturing overhead totalling $25 million is allocated by the conventional method, on the basis of direct labour hours at the rate of $25 per hour. Midsize product line was by far the largest contributor to TAP's gross margin in 2001. McKinnis explains that TAP's corporate overhead of $1.2 million in 2001 must be subtracted from the gross margin of $8.2 million to obtain the firm's before-tax income of $7 million.

Table 6.4 TAP Co. schedule of profitability by model: conventional cost management system for the year ended 31 December 2001

Model	Sales revenue $m	Material $m	Direct labour $m	Overhead $m	Total cost $m	Gross margin $m
Compact	35.0	14.0	6.65	16.62	37.27	(2.27)
Midsize	29.0	8.7	3.19	7.98	19.87	9.13
Luxury	2.5	0.6	0.16	0.40	1.16	1.34
Total	$66.5	$23.3	$10.00	$25.00	$58.30	$8.20

6.8.14 Under a conventional cost management system, TAP loses $325 on each compact sold (see Table 6.5). In contrast, TAP earns $3,150 on each midsize and $13,400 on each luxury automobile sold.

Table 6.5 TAP Co. schedule of profitability by vehicle: conventional cost management system for the year ended 31 December 2001

Model	Sales revenue $m	Material $m	Direct labour* $m	Overhead $m	Total cost $m	Gross margin $m
Compact	5,000	2,000	950	2,375	5,325	(325)
Midsize	10,000	3,000	1,100	2,750	6,850	3,150
Luxury	25,000	6,000	1,600	4,000	11,600	13,400

* Direct labour is charged at $10/hour.

6.8.15 Despite TAP's favourable aggregate results in 2001, Hillberry and McKinnis agree that they need to reconsider the emphasis previously placed on particular models. In particular, it seemed doubtful that TAP should continue its aggressive advertising of compact automobiles.

6.8.16 Hillberry shares with McKinnis what he learned from the recent seminar and asks McKinnis to apply some of the newer thinking on cost management to TAP, especially the concept of activity-based management. Two weeks later, Hillberry and McKinnis have a second meeting to continue their discussion of the relative profitability of the TAP automotive products. Hillberry has time for only a summary of the recent work, so McKinnis decides to present just the chart shown in Table 6.6.

6.8.17 The comparison between the results reported by the conventional cost system versus the costs reported by the activity-based cost accounting systems is striking. In particular, note that the results have almost totally reversed: the activity-based cost system indicates that compacts make money, while luxury cars lose money. Meanwhile, midsize automobiles continue to generate the largest part of gross margin. Both Hillberry and McKinnis express surprise at these results. At the end of the meeting, Hillberry asks for further explanations at their next meeting of why activity-based cost accounting leads to such different results.

Table 6.6 Comparison of accounting systems on gross margin for the year ended 31 December 2001

		Gross margin	
	Sales revenue	Conventional cost system	Activity-based cost system
Model	$m	$m	$m
Compact	35.00	(2.27)	2.00
Midsize	29.00	9.13	8.79
Luxury	2.50	1.34	(2.59)
Total	$66.50	$8.20	$8.20

6.8.18 Ten days later, McKinnis provides the necessary back-up information to justify the numbers he had presented. He explains that TAP has four distinct overhead functions and that it is necessary to examine each individually. The four overhead departments are:

- Purchasing;
- Production planning and control;
- Quality control and inspection;
- Inventory control.

6.8.19 Analyses of these four overhead departments are presented in Tables 6.7–6.10 (rounding errors may mean that totals do not add up). For each overhead department, it is necessary to define the particular activities that drive the functions within that department. For example, in 2001 the purchasing department incurred total costs of $5 million. Major activities (i.e., cost drivers) were the purchasing of raw materials, the purchasing of

Activity accounting

components and vendor relations. Appropriate allocation measures for those activities are number of orders for purchasing (i.e., of both materials and components) and number of vendors for vendor relations. Levels of those activities for each model are indicated in panel B. In turn, those levels lead to the total allocated costs for each auto model in panel C.

Table 6.7 Activities and costs for purchasing for the year ended 31 December 2001

Panel A: Analysis				
Activity	No. of employees	Total cost £m	Allocation measures	Unit cost £
Purchasing materials	20	2.0	No. orders	2,000
Purchasing components	5	1.0	No. orders	250
Vendor relations	10	2.0	No. vendors	20,000
Total		£5.0		

Panel B: Activities No. of purchase orders			
Model	Materials	Components	No. of vendors
Compact	500	2,000	25
Midsize	300	1,500	30
Luxury	200	500	45
Total	1,000	4,000	100

Panel C: Costs				
Model	Purchasing materials £m	Purchasing components £m	Vendor relations £m	Total costs £m
Compact	1.00	0.50	0.50	2.00
Midsize	0.60	0.38	0.60	1.58
Luxury	0.40	0.13	0.90	1.43
Total	£2.00	£1.00	£2.00	£5.00

Table 6.8 Activities and costs for production planning and control for the year ended 31 December 2001

Panel A: Analysis				
Activity	No. of employees	Total cost £m	Allocation measure	Unit cost £
Developing mfg. plan	10	1.0	No. units produced	100
Controlling mfg. plan	10	1.0	No. units product	100
Expediting mfg. plan	10	1.0	No. units expedited	500
Total		£3.0		

Determining cost drivers

Panel B: Activities Model	No. of units produced	Expedited
Compact	7,000	1,500
Midsize	2,900	450
Luxury	100	50
Total	10,000	2,000

Panel C: Costs Model	Developing mfg. plan £m	Controlling mfg. plan £m	Expediting mfg. plan £m	Total cost £m
Compact	0.70	0.70	0.750	2.150
Midsize	0.29	0.29	0.225	0.805
Luxury	0.01	0.01	0.025	0.045
Total	£1.00	£1.00	£1.000	£3.000

Table 6.9 Activities and costs for inventory control for the year ended 31 December 2001

Panel A: Analysis Activity	No. of employees	Total cost £m	Allocation measure	Unit cost £
Receiving parts	25.0	5.0	No. of shipments	1,250
Receiving materials	12.5	2.5	No. of shipments	2,500
Disbursing materials	12.5	2.5	No. of production runs	50,000
Total		£10.0		

Panel B: Activities Model	Parts	No. of shipments Materials	No. of production runs
Compact	2,000	500	10
Midsize	1,500	300	15
Luxury	500	200	25
Total	4,000	1,000	50

Panel C: Costs Model	Receiving parts £m	Receiving materials £m	Disbursing materials £m	Total cost £m
Compact	2.500	1.250	0.500	4.250
Midsize	1.875	0.750	0.750	3.375
Luxury	0.625	0.500	1.255	2.375
Total	£5.000	£2.500	£2.500	£10.000

Activity accounting

Table 6.10 Activities and costs for quality control and inspection for the year ended 31 December 2001

Panel A: Analysis				
Activity	No. of employees	Total cost £m	Allocation measure	Unit cost £
Inspecting materials	15	3.0	No. of shipments	600
Inspecting autos	20	4.0	No. of inspection points × No. of autos	12.50
Total		£7.0		
Panel B: Activities				
Model	No. of shipments	No. of inspection points/auto	Total no. of points	
Compact	2,500	28	196,000	
Midsize	1,800	41	118,900	
Luxury	700	51	5,100	
Total	5,000		320,000	
Panel C: Costs				
Model	Inspecting materials £m	Inspecting autos £m	Total cost £m	
Compact	1.500	2.450	3.950	
Midsize	1.080	1.486	2.256	
Luxury	0.420	0.064	0.484	
Total	£3.000	£4.000	£7.000	

6.8.20 The other overhead departments for TAP are: £3 million for production planning and control, £10 million for inventory control and £7 million for quality control and inspection.

6.8.21 Activity and cost analyses provide improved overhead allocations that can be used to understand better the relative profitability of each of the TAP auto models. The results are included in the revised profitability schedule shown in Table 6.11. As the following sections show, this information proves useful in making decisions about product pricing, investment justification and performance measurement.

Determining cost drivers

Table 6.11 Revised schedule of profitability by model: activity-based cost management system for the year ended 31 December 2001

Model	Sales revenue $m	Material $m	Direct labour $m	Overhead $m	Total cost $m	Gross margin $m
Compact	35.0	14.0	6.65	12.35	33.00	2.00
Midsize	29.0	8.7	3.19	8.32	20.21	8.79
Luxury	2.5	0.6	0.16	4.33	5.09	(2.59)
Total	$66.5	$23.3	$10.00	$25.00	$58.30	$8.20

Product pricing

6.8.22 Recently, Simon Stavreff, senior manager of TAP's compact product line, suggested that the price of compacts should be increased by 10 per cent in the next model year (i.e., from $5,000 to $5,500). According to Stavreff, if sales remain at the current level of 7,000 units, both revenues and costs would increase but the gross margin would improve from a loss of $2.27 million to a profit of $1.2 million.

6.8.23 It seems more realistic, however, to think that a price increase of 10 per cent would cause sales volume for compacts to decrease, especially since the compact model competes in a price-sensitive segment of the market. Stavreff, therefore, forecasts a reduced sales volume of 5,500 units as a result of the 10 per cent price increase. He and his management colleagues believe that the sales of midsize and luxury automobiles are likely to remain the same during the next model year. A comparison of direct labour utilisation is shown in Table 6.12.

Table 6.12 Revised schedule of direct labour utilisation: conventional cost management

	Before price change			After price change		
Model	Volume	Labour hours		Volume	Labour hours	
Compact	7,000	665,000	(66.5%)	5,500	522,500	(61%)
Midsize	2,900	319,000	(31.9%)	2,900	319,000	(37%)
Luxury	100	16,000	(1.6%)	100	16,000	(2%)
Total	10,000	1,000,000		8,500	857,500	

6.8.24 Total overhead of $25 million remains the same – at least in the short run – and hourly costs thus increase from $25 per hour before the price increase to $29.15 per hour after the price increase (i.e., $25 million/857,500 hours). A recalculation of overhead allocations on model profitability using

Activity accounting

the company's conventional cost system is presented in Table 6.13. McKinnis notes that sales revenue for compacts would be expected to decrease from $35 million to $30.2 million as a result of the lower volume. The gross margin for compacts improves from a loss of $2.27 million (before the price increase) to a loss of $1.28 million after the price increase. Note that gross margins of both midsize and luxury models decrease: they are penalised by having to absorb more of the total overhead.

Table 6.13 Revised schedule of profitability by model: conventional cost management system for the next model year

Model	Sales revenue $m	Material $m	Direct labour $m	Overhead $m	Total cost $m	Gross margin $m
Compact	30.2	11.0	5.23	15.25	31.48	(1.28)
Midsize	29.0	8.7	3.19	9.25	21.14	7.86
Luxury	2.5	0.6	0.16	0.50	1.21	1.29
Total	$61.7	$20.3	$8.58	$25.00	$25.00	$7.82

6.8.25 Under the conventional cost management system, after looking at the decreased gross margins for the midsize and luxury models, management might propose price increases for those products as well. In other words, conventional cost management systems give incorrect signals that are not in the best interest of the firm and its owners.

6.8.26 If TAP were to utilise an activity-based costing system, Stavreff probably would not have proposed a price increase, since compacts were already making a $2 million contribution to the overall profitability of TAP. Under the activity-based costing system, the difficulty caused by lower volume can be avoided by treating the cost of idle capacity as a period cost rather than attributing it to individual products. This is illustrated in Tables 6.14 and 6.15.

6.8.27 The Stavreff proposal would cause the gross margin of compacts to increase from $2 million to $4.01 million. However, that improvement would be more than offset by the $2.39 million cost of idle capacity, so the project should be rejected. Moreover, note that the activity-based cost system suggests that TAP's problem is not with the compact line but with the luxury line of automobiles. Specifically, either the price of the luxury automobiles should be increased substantially or costs for the luxury automobiles should be drastically cut. Indeed, perhaps TAP should consider abandoning that segment of the market.

Table 6.14 Comparison of direct labour utilisation for the next model year

Model	Conventional cost	Activity-based cost
Compact	522,500	522,500
Midsize	319,000	319,000
Luxury	16,000	16,000
Idle capacity	0	142,500
Total	£857,500	£1,000,000

Table 6.15 Revised schedule of profitability by model: activity-based cost management system for the next model year

Model	Sales revenue £m	Material £m	Direct labour £m	Overhead £m	Total cost £m	Gross margin £m
Compact	30.2	11.0	5.23	9.96	26.19	4.01
Midsize	29.0	8.7	3.19	8.32	20.21	8.79
Luxury	2.5	0.6	0.16	4.33	5.09	(2.59)
Subtotals	61.7	20.3	8.58	22.61	51.49	10.21
Cost of idle capacity				2.39	2.39	(2.39)
Total	£61.7	£20.3	£8.58	£25.00	£53.88	£7.82

Investment justification

6.8.28 Soon thereafter, the TAP board of directors heard a presentation from a firm that manufactures high-technology industrial equipment. Specifically, the firm makes a new machine that performs a variety of inspection activities with great precision and considerable flexibility. The president of the firm argues that the new machine would be ideally suited for relatively low-volume, high-quality manufacturing, like TAP's midsize automobiles. The new machine costs £2.2 million, has an expected useful life of six years, an estimated salvage value of £400,000, and is expected to reduce the manual inspection of midsize automobiles by two-thirds.

6.8.29 The TAP board was impressed by the presentation. Some members believe that the proposed new machine would increase the profitability of the midsize line. As a result, Hillberry asks McKinnis to run the numbers, factor in other relevant considerations and make a recommendation. McKinnis wonders if his new data that use an activity-based cost analysis will have any impact on his eventual recommendation.

6.8.30 McKinnis works hard to understand the full implications of the proposed machine for automated inspection of midsize automobiles. He

Activity accounting

wonders what incentive there might be for management of the midsize line to adopt such a cost-savings device, since under the conventional cost management system the savings would reduce that portion of total overhead attributable to quality control and inspection, which is then allocated to all three TAP product lines. Consequently, the midsize product line would not receive the full benefit of the new inspection equipment. To understand the implication of this, McKinnis decides to prepare an analysis of the potential savings from the proposed equipment under both cost management systems.

6.8.31 The conventional cost management system cannot even tell TAP management how many hours currently go into inspection. In a sense, this information is not important to the conventional system because total overhead expenses are allocated on the basis of direct labour hours. McKinnis proceeds as follows for his analysis of the midsize product line:

- 20 employees × 32 effective hours per week × 50 weeks = 32,000 hours per year;

- 320,000 inspection points / 32,000 hours per year = 10 inspection points per hour;

- Each midsize auto has 41 inspection points, hence 4.1 hours of inspection time per auto;

- 2,900 autos × 4.1 hours = 12,000 hours of inspection reduced by two-thirds (i.e., from 12,000 to 4,000 hours), hence savings = 8,000 hours, or 5 employees;

- 5 employees × (£10 wages + £2 benefits) × 40 hours per week × 52 weeks = £125,000 per year.

6.8.32 Since this is a permanent reduction in the number of employees, the fixed overhead attributed to each employee is also eliminated, for a saving of £1 million.

6.8.33 Assuming overhead percentages among the three product lines remain the same, under conventional costing the midsize line would have an overhead reduction of £1 million × 31.9 per cent = £319,000.

6.8.34 Total quality control and inspection overhead of £7 million would be reduced by £125,000 in labour saved and £875,000 of fixed overhead to become £6 million. The saving by product line is shown in Table 6.16.

Determining cost drivers

Table 6.16 Saving by product line

Model	Before	After	Saving
Compact	4,655,000	3,990,000	665,000
Midsize	2,233,000	1,914,000	319,000
Luxury	112,000	96,000	16,000
Total	£7,000,000	£6,000,000	£1,000,000

6.8.35 McKinnis is puzzled by the result. Under the conventional cost management system, the primary beneficiary of the proposed inspection equipment for midsize automobiles is the compact line even though that part of the business has nothing to do with the proposed new equipment. Management of the midsize product line would therefore have little incentive even to propose the project, since they would be charged the entire £2.2 million cost of the new machine and yet would receive credit for only part of the potential savings. In fact, under conventional costing, the project would actually reduce the return on investment of the midsize line even though the project would help the corporation overall.

6.8.36 McKinnis proceeds to analyse how the proposed new equipment for midsize inspection would look under an activity-based cost management system. His calculations are shown in Table 6.17.

Table 6.17 Activities and costs for quality control and inspection for the year ended 31 December 2001

Panel A: Analysis				
Activity	No. of employees	Total cost £m	Allocation measure	Unit cost £
Inspecting materials	15	3	No. of shipments	600
Inspecting autos	15	3	No. of inspection points × no. autos	12.50
Total		£6		

Panel B: Activities			
Model	No. of shipments	No. of inspection points/auto	Total no. of points
Compact	2,500	28	196,000
Midsize	1,800	½ × 41 = 14	40,600
Luxury	700	51	5,100
Total	5,000		241,700

Activity accounting

Panel C: Costs

Model	Inspecting materials £m	Inspecting autos £m	Total cost £m
Compact	1,500	2,450	3,950
Midsize	1,080	500	1,580
Luxury	420	64	484
Total	£3,000	£3,000	£6,000

6.8.37 The results are striking. Under an activity-based system, the £1 million saving per year is fully attributed to the midsize product line. If TAP has a tax rate of 30 per cent and an annual after-tax cost of capital (i.e., required rate of return) of 15 per cent, then the net present value of the six-year investment would be as follows.

	£
Present value:	
Savings: 3.784 × £1,000,000	3,784,000
Tax shield: 3.784 × £2,200,000 − £400,000 / 6 years	340,560
Salvage: 0.432 × £400,000	273,800
	£4,297,360
Cost of the inspection equipment	2,200,000
Net present value	£2,097,360

6.8.38 This, of course, looks good for TAP – and is a direct result of a proposal appropriately attributable to the midsize product line.

Performance measurement

6.8.39 Soon after McKinnis completes his analysis of the inspection equipment, he receives another proposal from the compact division. The head of the compact division proposes a £2 million automation project that is expected to reduce direct labour from 95 to 90 hours per auto. He wonders how this proposal will look under different cost management systems.

6.8.40 McKinnis proceeds to analyse the new proposal. The automation project will result in the reduction of direct labour from 95 to 90 hours per auto. That would represent an annual savings of:

$$5 \text{ hours} \times 7,000 \text{ autos} \times £12 \text{ per hour} = £420,000$$

6.8.41 The new automated process costs £2 million, has an expected life of five years and an estimated salvage value of £300,000. The annual tax shield would be:

$$(30 \text{ per cent} \times (£2 \text{ million} - £300,000)) / 5 \text{ years} = £102,000$$

6.8.42 The present value calculation would be:

	£
Present value:	
Savings: 3.352 × £420,000	1,408,260
Tax shield: 3.353 × £102,000	342,000
Salvage: 0.497 × £300,000	149,100
	1,899,360
Cost of investment	2,000,000
Net present value	(£100,640)

6.8.43 Because the net value is negative, the proposal should not be accepted using the traditional approach.

6.8.44 Suppose, however, that the new equipment would also improve the flexibility of TAP to offer additional options for the component whose production is being automated. For example, the machine might be able to perform certain manufacturing steps in very short times that are economically unfeasible using the current production process. This ability to offer additional variations of the component might be expected to be valued by consumers. Thus, TAP would be able to charge more for compacts with the new options. Assume that 2,000 compacts per year would be sold with the more expensive option at a price of £5,070 (i.e., £70 higher). Added material cost for the option would be £10. Hence, TAP would benefit each year by the after-tax amount of:

$$2{,}000 \text{ autos} \times (£70 - £10) \times (1 - 30 \text{ per cent}) = £84{,}000$$

The present value of this is:

$$£84{,}000 \times 3.353 = £281{,}650$$

6.8.45 The net present value of the proposal becomes £181,010. Therefore, the project would be accepted.

(Source: adapted with permission from Smith and Leksan, 1991.)

6.9 Activity accounting design issues

6.9.1 As suggested by the above example, activity accounting extends the variable costing rationale in an attempt to render cost determinations more useful for managerial purposes. Whereas variable costing focuses on short-term volume-related costs, an ABC cost determination includes

Activity accounting

long-term variable costs, which traditionally are grounded in overhead cost pools. ABC nevertheless goes beyond a contribution margin analysis in that it addresses cost behaviour quantitatively in terms of both short-run volume changes and longer-term cost trends that are independent of scale changes. This approach offers an element of rationality and compelling logic which managers often readily identify with (Bhimani and Bromwich, 2001).

6.9.2 The search for appropriate cost drivers forces managers and accountants to reconsider operational processes in a comprehensive manner and within an economic and strategic management frame of reference. The identification of value added and non-value added activities required for the implementation of an activity accounting system is important. Costing-based accounting information can help identify more desirable production strategies, such as the design of products with common parts, the discontinuance of low volume products necessitating complex manufacturing processes, and the identification of cost drivers which can lead to the adoption of altered production technologies. Activity accounting can offer an enterprise information not only about the profitability of its output, but also about the gains that may emanate from altering organisational processes. In budgeting, activity-based budgets can usefully point to significant planning and control dimensions. Budgets can appear as matrices for different departments, whereby activities are represented in columns and required or expected resources are placed in rows. Naturally, the representation of activity accounting information can be formatted so as to fit the organisational context and its idiosyncratic deployment of financial information (Bhimani, 2001).

6.9.3 It has been said that an additional benefit of ABC is that it provides non-financial managers with data that is more useful than traditional product-costing information. By linking overheads to activities rather than products or periods, ABC provides the benefit of making them more transparent. This enables non-financial managers to carry out inter-unit cost comparisons. Improvements between plants can thus be made and subsequent inter-temporal comparisons for effective cost control over time.

According to Cooper (1996), ABC systems provide three categories of benefits:

(a) more accurate product costs;
(b) an improved understanding of the economics of production;
(c) a picture of the economics of the activities performed by a company.

Activity accounting design issues

ABC and lean enterprises

6.9.4   Cooper (1996) notes that an ABC system can support a company's transition to a lean enterprise which he sees as characterised by:

- Adoption of just-in-time (JIT) production;
- Total quality management (TQM);
- Team-based work arrangements;
- Supportive supplier relations;
- Improved customer satisfaction.

6.9.5   Cooper (1996) believes that for ABC in fact to hinder the spread of the 'lean enterprise', the information it generates must be sufficiently contrary to the basis of the lean enterprise that it forces managers to re-adopt mass-production practices (i.e., batch size greater than 1 and defects effectively greater than 0) rather than lean-enterprise practices (i.e., batch size approaching 1 and defects approaching 0).

6.9.6   Cooper (1996) believes that ABC supports the shift to TQM and JIT. Since both ABC and the lean enterprise lead to reduced defect levels, there is no obvious conflict between the two levels. ABC systems report much higher costs of defects than traditional cost systems. This helps managers begin to pursue a policy of zero defects.

6.9.7   Cooper (1996) considers that the relationship between ABC and JIT is complex. ABC and the move to the lean enterprise can appear to be in conflict, because ABC systems suggest the need for larger batches while lean manufacturing calls for smaller ones. The apparent conflict stems from the EOQ model which defines a simplistic relationship between carrying and order costs. Given a holding cost of X and an order cost of Y, the EOQ model will identify the optimum batch size and hence the number of batches to be produced. The problem lies in the managerial assumption that the cost of batch-level activities cannot be altered. EOQ models were not designed to encourage the elimination of costs, so they do not challenge whether the costs of activities could be changed. Consequently, the application of a cost-minimising EOQ model leads to manipulations of the size of the batch rather than the elimination of batch-related costs.

6.9.8   Cooper (1996) notes that ABC can play a significant role in the successful spread of the lean enterprise. Its superior ability to trace costs of products, services, customers and production activities provides more

Activity accounting

favourable insights into the premises of business management than a traditional cost system.

6.9.9 Clearly, the activity accounting methodology has relevant implications for quality, management, just-in-time systems and the adoption of flexible production technologies. But over the past few years, activity accounting techniques have been documented to have other widespread implications. Bjornenak and Mitchell (2000) identify links between the ABC literature and throughput accounting, business process re-engineering, economic value added, transfer pricing, life-cycle costing, zero-based budgeting, functional analysis, benchmarking, capital budgeting and target costing among others. Perhaps for this reason, there are about as many distinct ABC/M systems in operation today as there are companies deploying them.

6.9.10 Shields and McEwen (1996) report that although many companies prefer activity-based costing to traditional cost accounting systems for measuring resource consumption, little has been documented as to companies that have experienced problems with ABC. Shields and McEwen (1996) report on the results of a survey they carried out. Of 143 large US companies responding to the survey, 75 per cent reported that their company had received a financial benefit from ABC, while 25 per cent indicated that they had not. They point out that one important reason for unsuccessful implementations of ABC is that many companies have over-emphasised architectural and software design issues of ABC systems and failed to pay sufficient attention to organisational issues.

Top management support

6.9.11 The survey results show for instance that top management support is the most important factor in determining how successful an ABC implementation is.

6.9.12 Shields and McEwen (1996) state top management support for ABC is important because:

(a) top management can focus resources (e.g., money, time and talent), goals and strategies on those innovations they deem worthwhile and deny resources for innovations they do not support;

(b) they can provide the political resources to offset or motivate employees who try to hinder innovations they want to succeed; and

(c) since ABC maps the internal economics of a company's resources, products, activities and organisational units, it plays a principal role in the development of organisational goals and strategies.

Activity accounting design issues

6.9.13 They note that top management must show a commitment to ABC by using it as the basis for decision making. It is especially important for top management to deploy ABC information in communication and agreements with other employees to encourage (or force) them to use such ABC information.

6.9.14 Information can be useful in assessing competitive strategy. The Shields and McEwen (1996) survey results indicate that level of linkage of ABC to competitive strategy is an important determinant of the success of an ABC implementation.

6.9.15 According to Shields and McEwan (1996) ABC should be linked to a firm's competitive strategy regarding organisational design, new product development, product mix and pricing and technology. They give some examples as follows.

- Competing based on cost or custom design: if a company chooses to compete based on the design of custom or low-cost products, its ABC systems should provide designers with accurate estimates of product or process costs. These costs should be available both before and during the design process. Designers should also know the costs of customisation.

- Competing based on scale economies: if a company competes on the basis of manufacturing scale economies and efficiencies for commodity products, its ABC systems should focus on measuring the costs of manufacturing activities and plant capacity.

- Competing based on distribution and logistics: if a company competes based on superior distribution and logistics, its ABC systems should focus on measuring the costs of those activities rather than manufacturing costs.

- Linkages to continuous improvement: especially important is the link of ABC to continuous improvement of quality and time.

6.9.16 The Shields and McEwan (1996) survey indicates that the degree of linkage between ABC and performance evaluation and compensation is an extremely important determinant of a successful ABC implementation. This is because employees pay attention to those things that affect their well-being. Most employees are concerned and affected by the system used to evaluate and compensate them. Therefore, where ABC is linked to performance measurement and compensation – and provided that employees believe that the resulting system fairly represents their performance – they will be motivated to help it succeed.

Activity accounting

ABC training

6.9.17   ABC can be linked to competitive strategy, continuous improvement programmes and performance evaluation and compensation through: readings, lectures, hands-on projects and on-the-job training.

6.9.18   Training in the logic and operation of ABC is important according to Shields and McEwan (1996) because it helps people understand how ABC differs from traditional cost accounting and why ABC provides a superior economic measurement and information system. If individuals do not understand why or how ABC works, they are likely to disregard or misunderstand it.

6.9.19   The survey found that non-accounting ownership of ABC was an important determinant of ABC success, while accounting ownership was unimportant.

6.9.20   According to Shields and McEwan (1996) a broad cross-section of employees should be involved in decisions about the initial decisions to invest in ABC, the design and implementation of ABC systems, and the use of ABC information for analysis and action.

6.9.21   ABC can generate important economic information about different parts of an enterprise: broad ownership raises the chances that non-accountants will support and promote ABC and be committed to its use and success.

6.9.22   When ABC is owned only by accountants, there is the danger that it might be used only to satisfy their needs, which often relate to status within the accounting profession and the departmental culture of the accounting, rather than the operational, managers. The survey shows that some companies have not had good implementation experiences because accountants have retained ownership or have not succeeded in sharing ownership or have not succeeded in sharing ownership with non-accountants. The consequence can be a repeating cycle of ABC designs without corresponding management action.

ABC and consultants

6.9.23   The use of external consultants can be important according to Shields and McEwan (1996) where companies have little internal expertise with ABC. Using external consultants can provide benefits to the design of an ABC system and in providing training about ABC.

6.9.24 But there is also a potential danger in relying too much on external consultants. Consultants cannot substitute for the support of top management and the linkage of ABC to competitive strategy, continuous improvement, performance measurement and compensation. Successful implementations of ABC require the presence of these factors. The implementation process must create internal ownership, knowledge and action according to Shields and McEwan (1996). Ideally, an external consultant should be used to facilitate an ABC initiative. A consultant is a source of knowledge that should be used to increase the knowledge and expertise within a company for selling, designing, implementing and using ABC.

Clarity of objectives

6.9.25 Finally, the survey found that consensus and clarity of objectives for ABC are important determinants of ABC success. The clarity of purpose and consensus about the objectives of ABC are often not what they should be. To clarify objectives, the following questions might be asked:

- What are the cost objects?
- What resources in a company should be included?
- How accurate should the measurements be?
- How frequently should the measurements be made?
- Who is the information intended to be used for?

6.10 Achieving the right fit

6.10.1 McNair (1996) considers that fitting a cost system to an organisation must go beyond simply implementing activity-based costing (ABC) or deploying quality costing for instance. Rather, a careful analysis of the following is preferable:

(a) the relationship between resources and activities;

(b) the ways in which changes in activities create changes in the economics of the business; and

(c) identifying where opportunities lie for managers to take actions that will enhance the performance of the company in the near and far term.

6.10.2 McNair (1996) offers six tenets which can be used to achieve 'fit' in the design of actionable, relevant cost management systems.

(1) Cost management systems ought to be designed from the bottom up, rather than from the top down.

Activity accounting

(2) Processes which underlie value creation and reports need to be included.

(3) The cost management system must be integrated with the operational, non-financial, measures and management methods used by the organisation.

(4) The basis of the cost management system should be a comprehensive set of estimates of costs relating to the key activities of the organisation.

(5) The measures used by the cost management system should move beyond a concern with the mean cost to capture the impact of variation, or change, on the organisation and its results.

To identify opportunities for improvement, measures should start with theoretical capacity or 100 per cent of the potential value-creating ability of a set of resources.

(Source: Cooper and Kaplan 1987.)

6.11 Why ABC can fail

6.11.1 Roberts and Silvester (1996) state that many ABC implementations fail. They suggest that this often has less to do with technical flaws in ABC or the way the theory is applied than the structural barriers managers encounter when attempting to implement ABC. They offer the following scenario prior to elaborating on the nature of possible structural barriers.

6.11.2 The Zebra Company has just completed an ABC analysis for a division with two major product lines: Widgets and Fidgets. According to Zebra's ABC analysis, Widgets have been over-costed by 20 per cent, while Fidgets have been under-costed by the same amount. As a result, Fidgets (which were previously considered reasonably profitable) are now marginal products at best, which is of concern to the Fidget product manager. The product manager of the Widget product line, by contrast, is content to see the suddenly increased profitability of Widgets – which required no expenditure of effort!

6.11.3 To address the situation, the Fidget Product Manager has three possibilities (see Figure 6.2).

(Source: adapted from Roberts and Silvester, 1996.)

6.11.4 To accept the data and take appropriate action leads to significant barriers, according to Roberts and Silvester (1996). The attempt to improve profitability can proceed in three possible ways (see Figure 6.3). Increase

Why ABC can fail

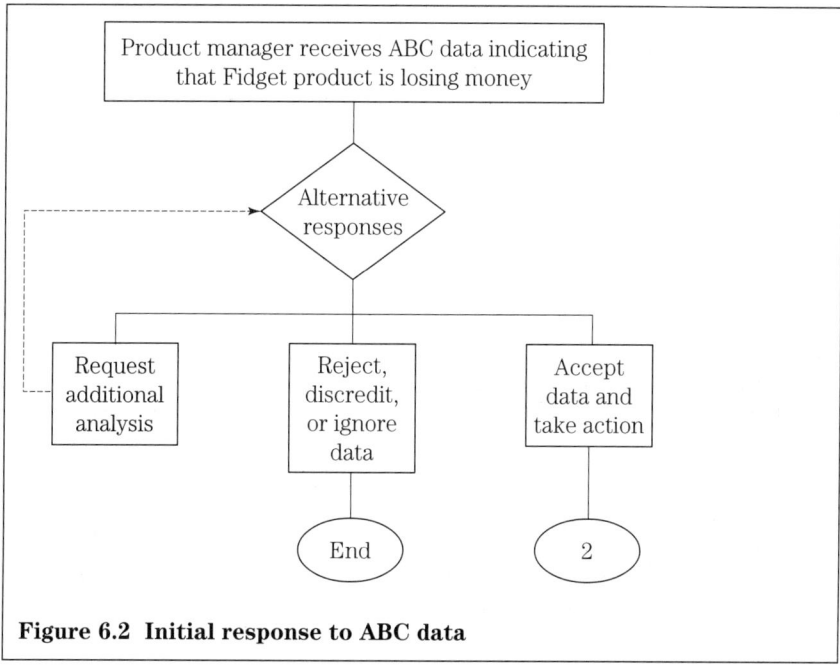

Figure 6.2 Initial response to ABC data

Fidget revenue while maintaining or reducing cost; or reduce Fidget costs; or eliminate the Fidget product line.

(Source: adapted from Roberts and Silvester, 1996.)

6.11.5 These three alternatives identified in Figure 6.3 raise important issues.

Increasing revenue

6.11.6 An increase in revenue might be accomplished by increasing the sales price, the unit volume of Fidgets, or both (see Figure 6.4). Naturally sales price and unit volume are constrained by external market conditions.

6.11.7 If the product manager raises the price of Fidgets, customers may seek alternative sourcing and volume of sales may be lost to lower-priced competitors. If prices are lowered in the hope of increasing unit volume, competitors may respond by reducing their prices. This will result in a no-win situation whereby no volume increase takes place and profits will no doubt further decline.

(Source: adapted from Roberts and Silvester, 1996.)

Activity accounting

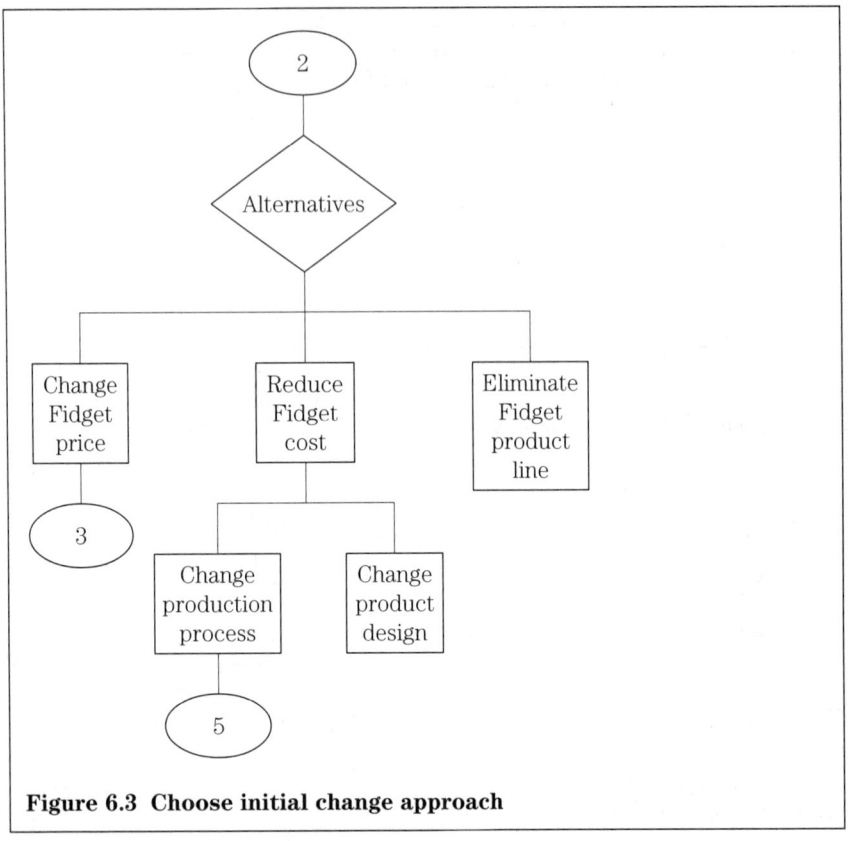

Figure 6.3 Choose initial change approach

Reducing cost

6.11.8 A cost reduction exercise is less problematic than price increase options. But cutting product costs significantly is not straightforward.

6.11.9 Product costs can be reduced by altering the production process and/or the design of the product. As Roberts and Silvester (1996) note, this requires considerable co-ordination and resource deployment at a cross-functional level. The cross-functional nature of the efforts can lead to ABC implementation problems. An enterprise that operates hierarchically will have functional barriers across organisational sub-units. Achieving cross-functional co-operation and effective communication exchange can require fundamental changes in organisational participants' mindsets.

(Source: adapted from Roberts and Silvester, 1996.)

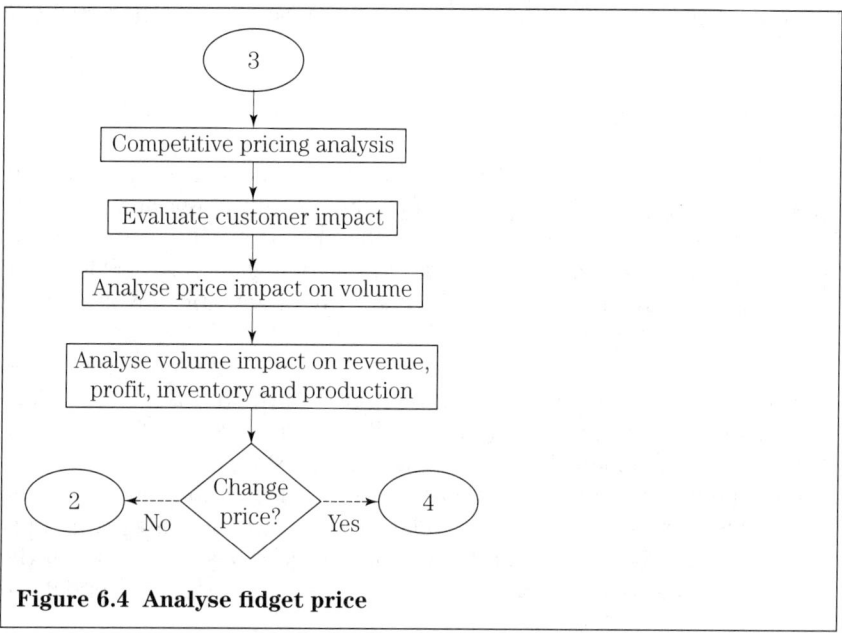

Figure 6.4 Analyse fidget price

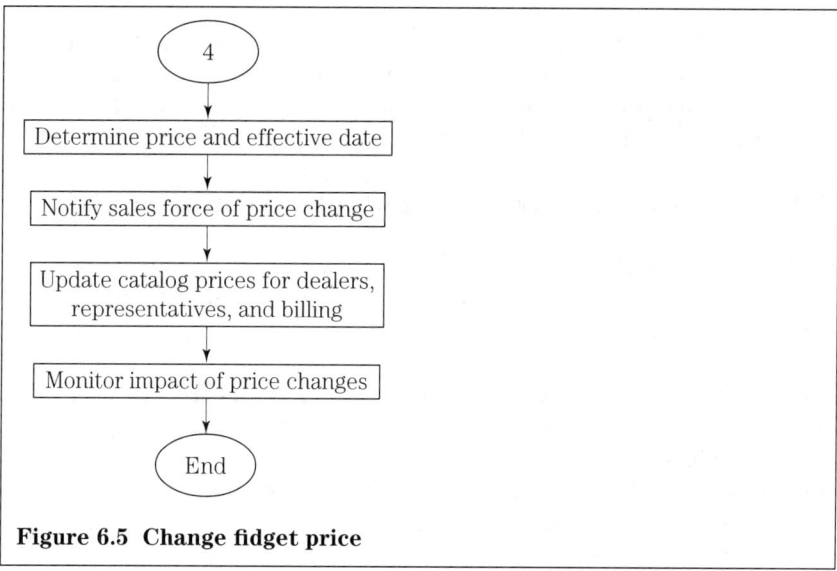

Figure 6.5 Change fidget price

6.11.10 Altering the production process: it may be that if attempts are made to reduce processing costs, an ABC analysis may suggest that high cost sub-components and assembly operations should be focused upon first. An organisation may target specific processing activities for cost reduction

Activity accounting

which requires some investment of time and resources in understanding such activities.

Product redesign

6.11.11 Any attempt at redesigning a product must meet market tests entailing the customers' acceptance of product modifications and the viability of supply chain ramifications. Naturally, new cost will also emerge in terms of product development efforts and scheduling and logistics issues of resources redeployment. Financially, the array of activities involved must make sense.

6.11.12 Eliminating the product line. As Roberts and Silvester (1996) note, any product elimination decision will affect many areas of an organisation – strategic planning, human and marketing resources, financial analysis and production and operations. Clearly, product elimination may wound the status of some individuals who have played a role in sponsoring the product line in the first place or in managing it. Some key issues to consider at the decision-making stage are market reactions, cost containment potential and enhancement of profits.

6.11.13 What is important to note is that the organisational tensions and behavioural difficulties posed by possible product line eliminations often predispose enterprises to retain the status quo even in the face of analytical judgement suggesting that this is an economically unviable option.

6.12 Economics versus organisational reality

6.12.1 There are internal as well as external barriers to change. The economics of the situation are often (wrongly) assumed to take precedence over fundamental aspects of organisational action.

6.12.2 Roberts and Silvester (1996) state that traditional economic models assume that a company engages in production to meet market requirements so as to enhance profits. The missing element is that individuals do not operate on the basis of conceptual economic models. Their behaviour as individuals and in groups tends to suggest an element of erring which is not readily subsumed in economic conceptualisations of enterprise processes.

6.12.3 Little recognition is given to the processing of information, executive idiosyncrasies, internal dynamics and the play of social interaction in classical economics. Since many 'rational' management tools, including the economic logic ascribed to particular ABC systems, conform to the classical economic perspective, implementation issues at the organisational level are bound to arise. Roberts and Silvester (1996) note that it is precisely the structure of a company that can produce a barrier to effective ABC implementation.

6.12.4 Transaction-based economics offers a departure from traditional economic theory in that it gives primacy to organisational form in attempting to address issues of a broader conception of organisational costs. For instance, this perspective recognises that executives live by behavioural rules of thumb, sometimes of their own making, to deal with complex and risky situations. A situation's complexity and uncertainty will dictate reliance on such rules. What is especially important to recognise is that idiosyncrasies can become embedded in the structure of an organisation. They can ossify within the enterprise's systems of operations. Thus any subsequent attempt to deal with the implementation of externally conceptualised logics of operating or of making decisions will face elements of such institutionalised idiosyncrasies. Consequently, tensions, resistance and dysfunctions can arise.

The legacy of bygone rationalities

6.12.5 Another problem faced in the implementation of novel cost management approaches relates to shifts in the logic of production. For example, the management of vast amounts of information concerning specific functional activities can lead to organisations investing in information systems which accord with such information processing needs. When the dynamics of operating processes alter so as to require greater interdependence and integration of organisational activities, such 'legacy' systems are ill-prepared to face the altered environment and resistance to change emerges.

6.12.6 Roberts and Silvester (1996) thus note that many enterprises facing greater complexity and interdependency adopt accounting in an attempt to deal with their interdependent processes. Organisations with the greatest level of cross-functional activities may be ones that can benefit most from ABC. Nevertheless, many such companies have retained their traditional organisational forms and procedures. Such highly developed traditional structures – which may have been cost efficient in the past – now raise important barriers to the implementation of cross-functional change. Consequently, ABC tends to be more difficult to implement in these enterprises than might be assumed.

6.13 Change strategies

6.13.1 Roberts and Silvester (1996) suggest some key success factors for the implementation of change strategies.

Activity accounting

- Interdependent environment: a most important characteristic of implementations deemed successful appears to be prior engagement in an ongoing process-oriented improvement initiative. Many enterprises which consider themselves successful ABC implementors had beforehand embarked on significant process changes (e.g., computer-integrated manufacturing, flexible productions, just-in-time processes or statistical process control). Many ABC implementors incorporate their ABC implementations within ongoing total quality management programmes. This reinforces the desirability to tackle head-on any resistances embedded in legacy systems.

- Security: ABC information can point to decisions which senior executives may find unsavoury. Achieving organisational welfare may contradict personal pursuits. Systems must be put into place to delineate outcomes from an ABC exercise to the extent possible and make the potential for painful decisions more transparent, beforehand.

- Legitimacy: many studies confirm that for ABC to be successfully implemented, support for the changeover must be seen to exist, and perhaps to emanate, from senior management as suggested above.

- Timing: availability of any information is key to altering the perception of its usefulness. An ABC implementation must take into consideration both the nature and the timing of information provision.

6.13.2 Roberts and Silvester (1996) believe that the success of any initiative (ABC or otherwise) rests on managers analysing the types of changes likely to be needed to alter activities and processes prior to implementation. Moreover, some assessment must be made of the structural barriers to change. Dealing with the challenges of change is important to realising the potential benefits from activity accounting systems.

(Source: Roberts and Silvester 1996.)

A case study: ABC implementation success

6.13.3 A case study of a successful ABC implementation by Harris Semiconductors Sector (HSS) is discussed by Dedera (1996). In the 1990s, HSS operated in a market which required semiconductor companies to compete on delivery, time, quality and cost. HSS had five product lines with 40,000 part numbers. It competed in multiple markets – from the commodity markets of power and logic to niche markets in analog and digital products. In the semiconductor industry price decreases are expected every year. As a product goes through its product life-cycle, its price will be taken to reduce rapidly.

6.13.4 Dedera (1996) notes that the cost of building a new semiconductor plant can run from hundreds of millions to billions of pounds. Major equipment in fabrication plants can readily cost a million pounds or more. Moreover, it generally takes more than a year before the first saleable product can be produced. The time can extend to two years for a new plant to reach peak production levels from newly added capacity.

6.13.5 In the early 1990s, HSS deployed a traditional standard cost system that used direct labour as the allocation base. Industrial engineers spent long time periods attempting to determine the operating efficiencies of critical equipment in the process. This information was fed into the standard cost system to derive labour rates at each operation. These labour rates were then applied to allocate overhead to individual products.

6.13.6 Overhead allocations were calculated on the basis of a percentage of direct labour. The overhead for an area was divided by the direct labour costs for that area to derive the overhead percentage. This overhead rate ranged from 800–1,800 per cent of the direct labour costs. As such, 90–95 per cent of all costs were allocated on the basis of a 5–10 per cent (direct labour component) of the cost base.

6.13.7 Managers at HSS thought that this cost allocation method produced inaccurate product costs and rendered little information of value to operations personnel. Marketing and sales managers did not use the product costs to make pricing decisions on a day-to-day basis. They did however rely on the cost data to question or reject key orders which indicated low margins. Marketing and cost accounting managers spent long time periods discussing the cost information on these key orders in seeking to make correct decisions.

6.13.8 Manufacturing employees paid little attention to the cost data. The cost accounting department considered costs as being valid mainly for stock valuation and that using the cost data to make individual decisions would be a mistake. Thus, even the accountants considered cost data to be suspect for decision making.

6.13.9 The new ABC cost system at HSS attempted to address management's concerns about the lack of decision-making usefulness of the standard cost system. The new ABC system attempted to trace all manufacturing costs to activities following which activity rates could be developed. These

Activity accounting

activity rates would then be input into the existing standard cost system so as to trace the activity costs to cost objects. The old standard cost system would continue to be used to determine the cost of sales on the company's profit and loss statement.

6.13.10 Dedera (1996) notes that HSS's ABC system provides marketing and sales personnel with valuable data about new orders. Likewise, manufacturing employees understand the ABC data and its relation to their operational processes. A significant change in cost discussions followed at HSS after the ABC system was put into place. Rather than discussing the propriety of cost calculations, managers instead focus on their causes.

The process of implementation

6.13.11 To depict basic ingredients of ABC implementation success at HSS, Dedera (1996) discusses the way in which the process was structured. To guide the ABC project, the executive committee formed a steering committee. The controller became the project 'champion' and a member of the steering committee. Other members of the steering committee came from various functions.

6.13.12 The MIS director was appointed chairman of the steering committee. Members for the different functions included:

- Finance: the controller of manufacturing, the controller of general accounting and the cost accounting manager;
- Operations: a plant manager and a fabrications manager;
- Product line management;
- Marketing managers;
- Product engineers;
- Consultants.

6.13.13 The steering committee collated a project team responsible for mapping, developing and following through the implementation plan.

6.13.14 Upon completion of the first two sites, the third domestic site would be completed. Finally, the overseas locations in the Far East would be completed.

6.13.15 As part of its remit, the project team carried out plant visits to:

(1) project planning;
(2) interview sessions;

(3) data gathering;

(4) modelling;

(5) validation;

(6) analysis; and

(7) presentation to the steering committee.

6.13.16 Dedera (1996) remarks that ABC data altered the corporate culture at HSS. Although some individuals resisted the change, the majority recognised the benefits of ABC. This view was facilitated by top management's support of ABC implementation. Two factors were key in the success of ABC implementation: people and communication.

Key lessons

6.13.17 Some key lessons could be identified from the implementation of ABC at HSS:

- define the problem before developing the solution;
- include top performers on the project team including an ABC 'champion';
- identify the objectives of the ABC project before starting;
- obtain top management support for ABC;
- keep decision-makers informed and involved through the project;
- assign responsibility for open issues throughout;
- allow extra time for data-gathering over and above that planned initially;
- anticipate that system integration will entail more issues than can be predetermined;
- the systems group must be an active participant not an observer of the implementation;
- the project team will need project management expertise;
- the project team will require cross-functional oversight and staffing.

(Source: Reprinted with permission from Dedera, 1996. For more information, visit www.wglcorpfinance@riag.com)

Activity accounting

A case study: ABC in a service context

6.13.18 Shanahan (1995) has described how the Australian Postal Corporation (APC) implemented ABC. This provides an important contrast to the manufacturing context of ABC adoption described for HSS.

6.13.19 The APC has six divisions, over 45,000 employees, and nearly A$2.5 billion in revenue. A significant reason for ABC was the 1989 Postal Services Amendment Act which specified a new corporate structure on the organisation. Information for budgeting decisions and financial performance measurement was to change. Basically, as Shanahan (1995) notes, the cost of carrying out the community service obligations of the Act had to be considered in setting financial targets and reported in APC's annual report.

6.13.20 Aside from the Act, APC was also the subject of an inquiry by the Industry Review Commission which sought to assess the efficiency and cost of the APC and its competitors in providing communication services. Information was sought on the cost of delivering inland letters and delivery performance criteria, among other aspects of APC's functioning.

6.13.21 From within APC, there were also influencing factors on the decision to adopt ABC. New product manager positions had been created and given responsibility for the profitability of broad product groups. Product managers sought information on the origins of overheads on specific product or service areas. Such information was not available under the traditional costing system.

Why ABC at APC?
6.13.22 Shanahan (1995) quotes an employee who had overall responsibility for the ABC project on why APC implemented ABC: 'The manager of product and service costing was given a trip around the world with the consultants to investigate it (ABC) . . . so we had to run with it'. Whilst the consulting firm was experienced and reputable 'the employees ended up doubting whether the process was worthwhile'. Whilst ABC is better suited to situations where overhead costs are considered high relative to direct labour costs, at APC almost 70 per cent of costs were driven by labour which made the implementation of ABC questionable.

6.13.23 Shanahan (1995) notes that APC did not clearly identify beforehand what decisions ABC would seek to improve. The objectives for ABC lacked clarity. Conversely, there were potential benefits to be derived from activity-based management (ABM) as opposed to ABC. As Shanahan (1995) states, ABM refers to the use of ABC information to focus attention on continuously improving the cost, time and quality fundamentals of activity. Improvement may be attained through reduction of the time and effort required to perform activities, removing unnecessary activities and identifying the lowest-cost alternative to carry out an activity.

6.13.24   Just as many commentators on activity accounting methods have noted, Shanahan (1995) remarks that 'when modernising a cost system, the real problem and challenge lies not in the technical aspect, but in the human element of the management system'.

6.13.25   At APC, little effort had been made to show employees what the ABC system was intended to do and how. It was simply seen as a precursor to cost cutting. Likewise, to obtain ABC effectiveness, different individuals must co-operate in identifying cost pools, cost drivers and key performance indicators. This was not achieved at APC. Moreover, ABC implementation was imposed from the top. There were no 'champions' at the grass root level.

More lessons

6.13.26   Shanahan (1995) believes that despite the pitfalls, ABC can be successfully implemented in various types of organisations. Just like Dedera (1996), Shanahan (1995) identifies some important lessons from the ABC implementation experience at APC: a sound reason must be identified for implementing ABC.

- Determine the magnitude of the indirect overhead in total costs to determine the potential benefits of implementing ABC.
- Involve the entire workforce in implementing ABC to facilitate acceptance of ABC and encourage its use after implementation.

6.14 ABC and the 'death spiral'

6.14.1   An ABC system can potentially help companies avoid dropping products erroneously because of misleading product costs. Radhakrishnan and Srinidhi (1997) use an example to show that since traditional costing systems have a tendency to report lower profits for larger-volume products that consume more of the cost driver, these products will likely be the first to be deleted.

6.14.2   Subsequently, low profits for the remaining smaller-volume products which consume more of the cost driver will also cause their elimination

Activity accounting

from product offerings. Radhakrishnan and Srinidhi (1997) explain that incorrect product discontinuance decisions inevitably lead to more product discontinuance and/or outsourcing. Ultimately, very few products are left which imperil the viability of the enterprise. They term this process a 'death spiral'.

6.14.3 Radhakrishnan and Srinidhi (1997) provide a graphic illustration of the role of ABC in avoiding the death spiral. Suppose that each year one big assembly manufacturer requires four products:

- 6,000 units of A;
- 3,000 units of B;
- 15,000 units of C; and
- 12,000 units of D.

6.14.4 Three competitors – Companies L, M and N – produce these products. These companies use the same technology and incur identical costs for the same activity levels. They use different costing systems that report different product costs. The price is specified by the customer, and the annual requirement is split evenly among those companies that are willing to supply at the specified price.

6.14.5 The manufacturing process for the products requires certain activities that are organised as cost pools. The cost pools, activities, and cost drivers are shown in Table 6.18.

6.14.6 All three competitors trace material costs directly to the products; other costs are treated as indirect costs. Company N traces all indirect costs to each cost pool and uses the appropriate activity drivers in applying the indirect costs to the products. Companies L and M, on the other hand, do not accumulate costs for each activity. Instead, Company L uses direct labour hours as the sole cost driver for assigning indirect costs to the products, while Company M uses machine hours for cost tracing.

Table 6.18 Cost pools, activities and cost drivers

Cost Pool	Activities	Cost Driver
1.	Purchase, storage, material handling and production scheduling	Number of items input
2.	Machining shop	Machine hours
3.	Assembly shop	Direct labour hours
4.	Packaging and shipping	Number of packages

ABC and the 'death spiral'

Table 6.19 Product, cost and market characteristics

Per Unit Resource Requirements				
	Product A	Product B	Product C	Product D
Direct materials	1 unit	2 units	8 units	10 units
Labour time	10 hours	5 hours	30 hours	20 hours
Machine time	5 hours	7 hours	15 hours	30 hours
Packaging	1 unit/pack	2 units/pack	2 units/pack	1 unit/pack
Direct material unit cost	£50 per unit	£20 per unit	£10 per unit	£7 per unit

Cost Data			
Cost category	Long-term	Short-term (Variable)	Cost Driver
Assembly	£5,000	£10/direct labour hour	Direct labour hours
Purchase	£4,000	£2/item input	Number of items input
Machining	£20,000	£1.50/machine hour	Machine hours
Packing	£0	£15/pack	Number of packages

Customer requirement				
	Product A	Product B	Product C	Product D
Price	£180	£180	£450	£420
Total requirement	6,000	3,000	15,000	12,000

6.14.7 Product A and B consume fewer machine and labour hours than products C and D. Products A and C require two labour hours for each machine hour (i.e., 10/5 for A and 30/15 for C). Product B requires 0.71 labour hours for each machine hour, while product D requires 0.67 labour hours for each machine hour. Because products A and C require more labour hours than machine hours, they are relatively more labour intensive. Similarly, since products B and D require more machine hours than labour hours, they are relatively more machine intensive. The long-term costs represent committed costs such as depreciation and rent.

6.14.8 In the first year, all companies are willing to supply all products. In the second year, based on the information provided by their respective costing systems (i.e., reported costs, contribution margins, and profits), each company decides to discontinue products with negative contribution margins. This pattern of product discontinuance decisions is repeated in the third year.

The outcome – year one

6.14.9 In the first year, each company gets an order for a third of the requirements of the customer for each product. At the end of the year, each company uses its own costing system to evaluate the relative performances of each product.

Activity accounting

6.14.10 Company M finds that product D has a negative unit contribution margin of £98.73, and Company L finds that product C has a negative contribution margin of £3.06. This occurs because product D is relatively more machine intensive while product C is relatively more labour intensive. Hence, Company L's costing system based on labour hours over-costs C, while Company M's costing system based on machine hours over-costs D. The ratios of resource consumption patterns for products A and C are equivalent – i.e., for each machine hour, both products consume twice as many labour hours. However, Company L does not show a negative unit contribution margin for product A in the first year because the total of labour and machine hours consumed by product C is greater than the total of labour and machine hours consumed by product A. Similarly, Company M does not show a negative unit contribution margin for product B. Company N, using ABC, shows a positive contribution margin for each product.

The start of the death spiral – year two

6.14.11 The companies use the costs reported by their respective costing systems to evaluate each product. Due to negative unit contribution margins, Company L incorrectly decides to discontinue product C, and Company M incorrectly decides to discontinue product D.

6.14.12 Company M finds that product B has a negative contribution margin of £17.62, and Company L finds that product A has a negative contribution margin of £8.00. For Company M, product B is the most machine-intensive product because it produces only products A, B and C. Hence, the costing system based on machine hours over-costs product B. Similarly, because Company L only produces products A, B and D, product A is the most labour-intensive product. Hence, the costing system based on labour hours overcosts product A. Therefore, in the second year a labour-based cost system reports a negative unit contribution margin for product B. Company N, using ABC, reports unit contribution margins for the second year that are the same as that reported for the first year.

The progress of the death spiral – year three

6.14.13 After the second year's operations, Company L's costing system reports a negative unit contribution margin for product A, while Company M's costing system reports a negative unit contribution margin for product B. Consequently Company L incorrectly decides to discontinue product A, and Company M incorrectly decides to discontinue product B.

ABC and the 'death spiral'

Table 6.20 Year 3 operating results

	Company L	Company M	Company N
Order quantities			
Product A	Discontinued	3,000	3,000
Product B	1,500	Discontinued	1,500
Product C	Discontinued	7,500	7,500
Product D	6,000	Discontinued	6,000
Unit cost			
Product A	Not applicable	£167.55	£174.99
Product B	£111.25	Not applicable	£112.58
Product C	Not applicable	£432.65	£427.63
Product D	£355.02	Not applicable	£352.53
Unit contribution			
Product A	Not applicable	£13.59	£5.50
Product B	£69.88	Not applicable	£68.00
Product C	Not applicable	£20.76	£24.00
Product D	£69.53	Not applicable	£70.00
Profits	£458,059	£153,912	£675,000
Product discontinuance/Outsourcing decision			
Company L	None		
Company M	None		
Company N	None		

6.14.14 The product discontinuance decisions of Company L lead it to manufacture only products B and D, both of which are relatively more machine intensive. On the other hand, the product discontinuance decisions of Company M lead it to manufacture only products A and C, both of which are relatively more labour intensive. Company N, using ABC, is the only company that continues to manufacture all products.

6.14.15 As a consequence of the discontinuance decisions, Companies M and N supply products A and C in the third year, whereas Companies L and N supply products B and D. The unit costs, unit contribution margins, total contribution margins and profits for the third year are provided in Table 6.20.

6.14.16 In the third year, all three competitors make positive contribution margins for each product that they manufacture, and therefore no further product discontinuance decisions are made. However, Company M under-costs product A and over-costs product C, while Company L under-costs product B and over-costs product D. Products C and D are high-volume products and are overcosted by traditional costing systems. This is referred to as the volume effect. In this illustration, the mis-estimation of costs due

293

Activity accounting

to the volume effect does not lead to further product discontinuance decisions. However, increased competitive pressures which lead to lowering of the price could lead to further product discontinuance decisions. For instance, if the price for product C drops by £20, then Company M would have a negative unit contribution margin reported for product C. This could lead Company M to drop product C.

The effects on profits

6.14.17 Table 6.21 captures the adverse effects on profits that using the traditional costing systems has, due to product discontinuance decisions. It shows the profits of the three companies over time. Company N does not discontinue any product and therefore remains in all product markets. Company N's increase in market share due to the wrong decisions made by the competitors demonstrates a long-run benefit of using ABC. In contrast, companies with traditional costing systems are more likely to make incorrect product discontinuance decisions by pulling out of profitable product markets. As Radhakrishnan and Srinidhi (1997) note, in the long run, these companies could lose market share and suffer decreases in profits.

Table 6.21 Profits over three years

	Year 1	Year 2	Year 3
Company L	£450,000	£470,000	£458,059
Company M	£450,000	£230,000	£153,912
Company N	£450,000	£675,000	£675,000

The long run

6.14.18 Radhakrishnan and Srinidhi (1997) conclude that the long-run benefit of using ABC could vary depending on the following factors.

6.14.19 Volume effects: when a common facility is used to manufacture both large-volume and small-volume products, large-volume products that use more resources will be over-costed by the traditional costing system. This is the case even when both the large-volume products and the small-volume products use the same proportion of all resources. Thus, large-volume products can appear to be more unprofitable than they actually are.

6.14.20 Resource utilisation effects: the usefulness of ABC increases if products use different resources with varying relative intensities. But if all products consume resources proportionately, then a costing system based on any one cost driver will suffice. Therefore in deciding on cost pools, one needs to look at whether products have similar or contrasting resource usage intensity.

6.14.21 Competitive pressures: the impact of incorrect product discontinuance decisions resulting from traditional costing systems becomes more pronounced with increased competitive pressures. Increased competitive pressures result in lower contribution margins. The value of ABC is thus a function of competitive pressures. Naturally, companies that strategically compete on high asset turnovers and low profit margins will perceive the value of ABC to be higher.

(Source: adapted from Radhakrishan and Srindhi, 1997.)

6.15 Gap between theory and practice

6.15.1 Ruhl (1995) has noted that many firms have reported problems in implementing ABC and ABM. Some managers have invested significant time and resources to attempt to implement ABC, with little success. In part, this is because there are gaps between the theory of activity accounting and practice.

6.15.2 Player and Keys (1995a, 1995b, 1995c) provide approaches to bridge such gaps through their research on ABM. They define ABC as the cause-and-effect assignment of costs to cost objects, such as activities, products and customers, while they reserve the term ABM to refer to the use of ABC information for decisions about activities, products, customers and other cost objects.

6.15.3 Player and Keys (1995a) outline the following pitfall: when top management is not fully supportive of an ABM effort, the exercise is likely to falter. Naturally if there is no 'buy-in' or ownership, then managers will not give the initiative time, nor any other scarce resource.

6.15.4 Player and Keys (1995a) believe that, ideally, top management support should be in place before ABM is started. If it is accepted that cost management systems serve financial, operational and strategic purposes then it must be recognised that an activity accounting system is unlikely to be able to satisfy all three at the outset. Indeed, Player and Keys (1995a) believe that 'an ABC/ABM system can serve all three purposes, but it cannot do them all simultaneously'. Thus it is important to understand how information from a new cost system is likely to be used. This in turn can guide project design issues.

Activity accounting

Strategy versus finance

6.15.5 It is important to recognise that costing for strategic decision making, as opposed to financial reporting, differs. Strategic product costs may, for instance, include some costs which are not recognised under generally accepted accounting principles (GAAP). Likewise, strategic product costs may exclude certain factory overhead costs if they are not deemed assignable to individual products. Moreover, strategic product costing may defer certain costs to future periods, and recognise other costs currently counter to the matching principle. Consequently, strategic product costs need to be altered at the end of each period if they are to be used for financial reporting. This can act as a deterrent to using activity accounting methods.

Clarifying business objectives

6.15.6 Player and Keys (1995a) also suggest that a need for a clear business objective exists for an activity accounting initiative. The following questions and answers make the point.

(a) Why is this project being performed?
'Because it will make us a better company.'

(b) Why will it make us a better company?
'Because we will better understand product costs.'

(c) Why do you need to understand product costs?
'Because we do not understand what causes costs.'

(d) Why do we need to understand what causes costs?
'Because we have to understand how we can reduce and avoid costs.'

(e) Why is reducing and avoiding costs important?
'To meet our strategic objective of being the low cost provider.'

These questions should clarify the business objectives.

Heading ABM: don't choose an accountant

6.15.7 A principal point noted by Player & Keys (1995a) is that 'a financial person should not head an ABM project, nor should the ABM teams be made up only of financial people'. This is because the project should not be viewed as an accounting project. It is preferable to place a marketing, operations or engineering person at the head of the initiative. Consequently, ABM will be perceived as a management tool to serve management decision making.

Gap between theory and practice

6.15.8 Additionally, it is important to involve other staff members, with the identification of activities and cost drivers to be undertaken primarily by non-accountants. This is so that those most knowledgeable about the work identify what drives processes.

6.15.9 It is found that when non-accountants are involved in creating an activity accounting system, they can be more likely to use the information it generates (Bhimani and Pigott, 1992).

6.15.10 Player and Keys (1995a) suggest that it is worthwhile ensuring that the activity accounting project has adequate funding and that relevant employees receive proper training. They warn that some consultants may want to impose the same answers that they have used in previous engagements rather than find answers that are company specific. It is important that an activity accounting system reflect the 'worldview' of management and the culture of the organisation to the extent possible. Extra-organisational solutions may not sit in with an enterprise's specific culture.

6.15.11 Whilst many managers may be familiar with activity accounting, Players & Key (1995a) deem it essential that at least one permanent employee in the company should become an ABM expert.

6.15.12 Finally, they suggest that there must be linkage between activity accounting and JIT, TQM, BPR or other management initiatives.

The usefulness of a pilot system

6.15.13 Player and Keys (1995b) believe that it is extremely difficult to implement a comprehensive activity accounting system without undertaking a pilot project first. This is because the pilot can be structured to enhance the chances that the activity accounting system gains greater support.

6.15.14 This also ensures that the consequences of any mishaps are isolated to that part of the organisation where the pilot exercise is taking place. A pilot project is essentially also a training programme – i.e., through the pilot, ways of improving can be developed. Moreover, pilot projects can be completed over short periods of time, and feedback on successes and problems can be derived more quickly.

How much complexity?

6.15.15 Sometimes, AA systems reflect the predilection of operating and financial personnel who seek the ability to view cost in multiple dimensions

Activity accounting

and minute detail. Project teams may want ABC to include product costing with detailed activity levels, customer costing and distribution channel costing. They may want AA to include process costing, value-added analysis and cost of quality. Information may also relate to variable, semi-variable and fixed cost differentiations and there will be categorisation in terms of unit-level, batch-level, product-level, process-sustaining, facility-sustaining, customer-sustaining and decision-levels of costs. Such pursuits can be costly and over-detailed. It is essential to match the complexity of AA information to its relative ease of digestibility by its users. Whilst too much information may be problematic, so may too little detail. Thus, investigating users' needs and the activity accounting system's intended role is important at the outset.

6.15.16 Some AA projects are hindered by problems relating to activity data collection. There may be problems in terms of definitions of individual activities; the level of reliability that the activity data has; and the methods of collecting the activity information. In terms of data reliability, it is important to note that data gathering may suffer from intentional bias. When a member of staff is questioned about how their time is spent, it is important to ensure that the most recent time frame does not reflect 'seasonality of activities'.

6.15.17 Moreover, some individuals may fear the loss of their jobs, while others may bias data to make favourite products, activities or functions look like they are performing better than they actually are. Idle time or non-value added tasks can be masked. It must be recognised that budgeting systems and some accounting initiatives have always assumed that slack build-up and padding is a necessary and, indeed, desirable cost to enable an organisation to work better under some circumstances. Management based on brute economic logic can lead to employee turnover and other consequences while having a negative impact on the financials.

6.15.18 The issue of data collection is important. When selecting activity bases and cost drivers, some companies may give preference to drivers that are already being gathered or drivers that will be easier to collect.

6.15.19 Software specifically designed for activity accounting systems may alter the computing cost of keeping detailed information. But the time required to generate and understand the information may be an issue as some software vendors attempt to build in as many options as possible. It is important for the user to decide exactly which features are needed to meet the business objective and not to use all features available.

6.15.20 Players & Keys (1995b) hold that activity accounting implementation is similar to any large-scale improvement project in that the pilot effort may not survive poor project management. The leader of the project team should understand the business, and work well with people from many functional areas. The projected stature and attitude of the project leader will affect the rest of the organisation's perception of whether management is serious about this effort and of the potential payoffs.

6.15.21   Project teams often have problems with communication. Activity accounting can be a major change initiative and, possibly, it should deploy a formal communication plan. Project objectives should be written down and compared to expectations. Expectation gaps should be identified early so that objectives can be altered or the work plans modified.

A case study: achieving balance

6.15.22   There are critical times in the growth of a company; times when the way work is defined, managed, measured and evaluated is changed to meet new challenges from the market place. The period from 1989–1993 was such a period for Standard Soap Ltd. Having reached the growth threshold, this family-owned business has turned to Total Quality Management (TQM) and an Activity-Based Management (ABM) system to smooth its transition from a small job-shop making private label soaps and speciality chemicals to one of the most successful, and innovative, international producers of speciality soaps. The path these implementations has taken has not been without its bumps and dangers for the company.

'We're out of control'
6.15.23   The gloom of a cold winter morning matched the mood of the four people huddled around the small conference table in the Standard Soap Ltd business office. For the past hour company managers (Joe, Plant Manager; Fran, Treasurer; Bob, Accountant) had been describing Standard Soap's history, product line focus and current status to a lecturer from a local business school (K.T.). The problem facing the firm was well-documented: it had reached the growth threshold, a gap that separated this small 'soaper' from the ranks of large, established corporations. The symptoms of the stress the firm was experiencing were everywhere: inventories were growing faster than production volumes, orders were often late, product was being returned at an alarming rate due to defects and other problems, and individual managers were finding it harder and harder to control, let alone predict, the outcome of operations.

6.15.24   Joe put his feelings in graphic terms, 'We're out of control – I simply can't manage the plant anymore. I'm practically living here, but it isn't doing any good at all. We're blowing our schedules, missing ship dates, and

Activity accounting

turning out bad product. I simply can't handle the system anymore'. As this 'true confession' was revealed, the room fell silent. Bob looked down, saying little. Fran, a family member just returning to active involvement after a year-long leave, looked puzzled. As with all true confessions, Joe's comments were not greeted with cheers. He had violated a taboo by opening the kimono of this staid firm to an outsider.

Background information

6.15.25 Standard Soap Ltd is a £30–35 million producer of private label soaps. Owned by the Janssen family since the mid 1960s, the firm has been in continuous operation since its founding in the late 1800s by two immigrants from Warwick, England. The company occupies an old mill building in West Warwick that abuts a local river used in earlier days for power. It currently employs over 500 people in this plant, operating three shifts a day, six days a week.

6.15.26 In any year, Standard Soap produces over 5,000 different varieties of bar soap. Over 40 per cent of these orders represent new business or new products for the firm. The high level of variety and the fact that the source and characteristics of future business is always a question mark, makes effective, efficient management of the plant a challenge.

6.15.27 Figure 6.6 details the process of soap-making at Standard Soap. Raw materials are transformed into natural and synthetic base soap in the kettle room. Still as much of an art as a science, the production of base soap is one of Standard Soap's competitive advantages. It can control the supply and quality of the key raw material going into bar soap. In addition, Standard Soap has been able to use its soap-making expertise to develop new soap formulations that competitors cannot match. It is this soap-making expertise that lies at the heart of its recent growth.

6.15.28 Bulk soap is dried and stored for later use in bins and containers on the plant floor. When an order is received, the required bulk soap and additive packages are moved to the amalgamators at the head of the production line. There, a master soap-maker measures the ingredients per the instructions on the product's formulation card, mixes the batch and then signals the line supervisor that the soap is ready to run.

6.15.29 Soap is extruded as it passes from the amalgamator, forming into a solid block of soap. This unending flow of soap slides down a metal chute to a press where metal dies transform the soap into bars that meet the size and shape requirements set by the customer. After pressing, the bars move down a conveyor belt where visual inspection of each bar takes place. Good

Gap between theory and practice

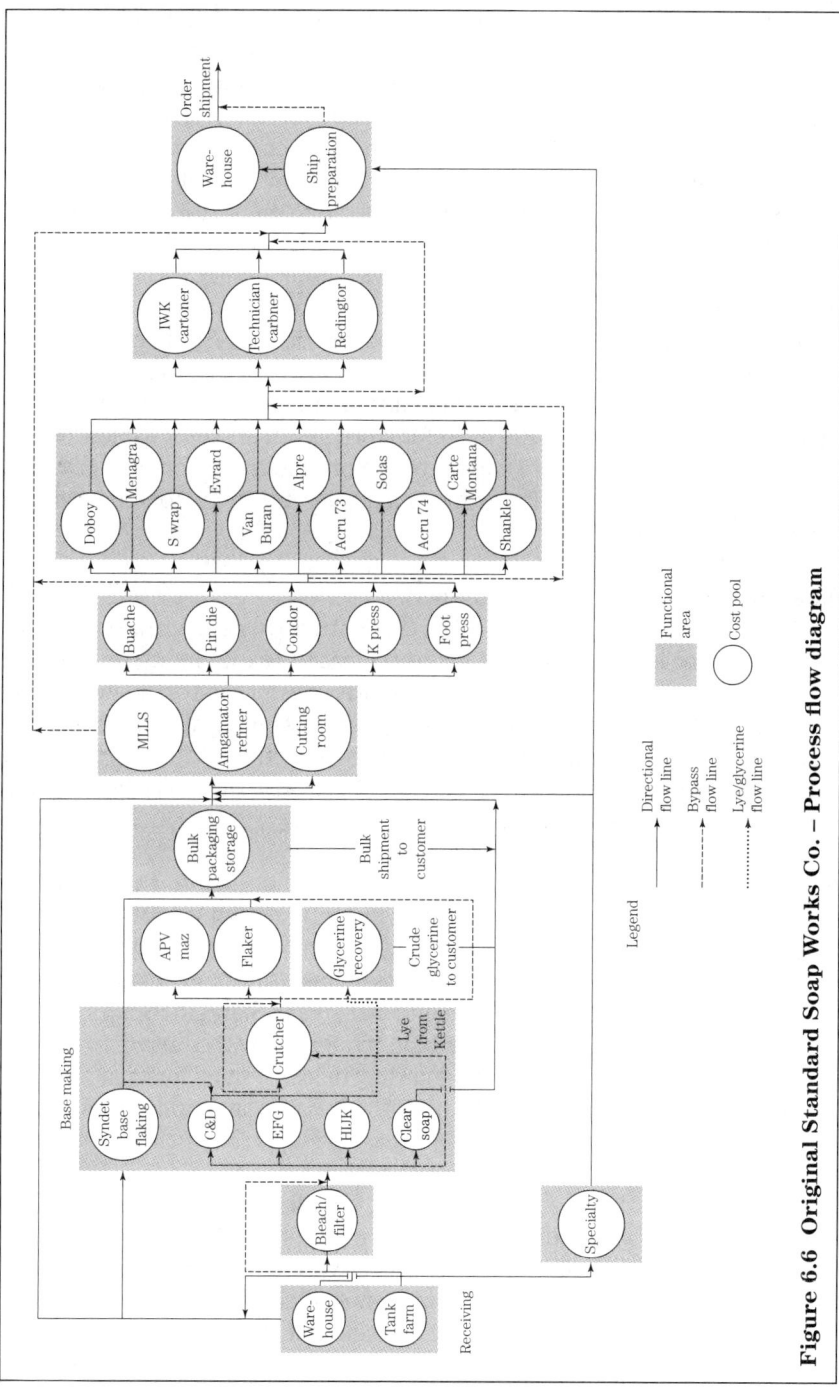

Figure 6.6 Original Standard Soap Works Co. – Process flow diagram

bars are allowed to pass on to the packaging machines attached to the end of the line where bars can be wrapped, boxed and packed in number of ways. Defective bars and scrap from the press are recycled, returning to the amalgamator for remixing and re-entry to the soap flow. The apparent simplicity of the process is misleading; there are, in fact, over 5,000 different paths a bar of soap can take through the production facility. Most of this complexity occurs during the packaging stage, where any combination of inner and outer wrappings is possible.

6.15.30 Spanning the entire value chain from base soap production to the completion of a speciality bar of pleat-wrapped soap, Standard Soap has been able to provide a higher level of service and variety to its customers than its competitors. But the complexity of the job shop environment at Standard Soap has created the need for more information to manage operations. In addition to the core variety of the products and services provided by Standard Soap, it has faced major changes in its customer base and product expectations.

New customers and new problems

6.15.31 Up through the late 1960s, Standard Soap concentrated its sales efforts on speciality chemicals for the UK-based textile industries. As the 1960s came to an end, though, so did the presence of the textile industry in the region. Faced with the loss of its key business line, Allen Janssen, MD and owner of the company, refocused the firm's activities into the fledgling private label bar soap industry. It was a strategic move that has paid off handsomely for the firm and the family.

6.15.32 This shift of focus has resulted in rising sales to the point that available line time has been booked to capacity. And Standard Soap's soap-making expertise was gaining it a strong reputation in the market place as the producer of choice for speciality soaps. In fact, the major growth area for the firm was the skin care and 'high end' bar soaps. Standard Soap's willingness to try to make any soap formulation requested by the customer, as well as its well-known concern for safe-guarding its customers' formulations and 'secret ingredients', had quickly moved the firm into the top position in this emerging industry.

6.15.33 As can be seen in Figure 6.7, Standard Soap's sales mix and volume have changed radically since the mid 1960s. Moving from a dominant position in speciality chemicals to private label bar soap, Standard Soap has expanded its customer base. New customers, though, come with new expectations for performance. Acceptable bar quality levels have racheted upward. For instance, high end cosmetic bars, retailing for

£15–20 each in department stores, have to be visually perfect. Even the slightest mar on a bar's surface can cause a customer to reject the finished good.

Type of product	Time:					
	Mid 60's	Early 70's	Late 70's	Early 80's	Late 80's	Early 90's
Industrial soap	50%	30%	17%	15%	13%	5%
Specialty chemicals	45%	40%	9%	4%	2%	2%
Commodity bar soap	5%	17%	23%	22%	6%	2%
Specialty bar soap	0%	13%	51%	58%	79%	91%

Figure 6.7 Standard Soap change in sales mix

6.15.34 The demand for the 'perfect' bar is a new force at Standard Soap. Prior customers, such as hotel bar and novelty soap wholesalers (sea shells, stars and so on), placed the highest priority on price. A nick on a bar was of little concern. Bulk packing was the norm, with little concern for any but the grossest defects (broken bars). Cosmetic line customers, though, sell hopes and dreams. Hopes and dreams have to be perfect.

6.15.35 While bar quality levels have escalated, total bars per order have dropped. Hotel bars are made in massive quantities resulting in price breaks for the customers and simple scheduling of lines at the plant. Cosmetic bars, on the other hand, are made in smaller quantities. That means, in total, the number of set-ups, inspections, handling operations, and support activities have escalated considerably over the past five years. These forces were coming together in late 1989, creating the 'loss of control' phenomenon Joe described.

Stepping into the future

6.15.36 To understand better the issues at the company, K.T. asked the Standard Soap managers if a student team could come into the firm and map the process flow and document the current types and amount of information available to managers across the firm. Agreement was reached on the boundaries of the project and its timing.

6.15.37 After three months of data dredging and scurrying through the catacombs of the Standard Soap plant, the student team was ready with their report. While many facts about current operations were revealed, the most overwhelming finding was that the firm was drowning in data but had no information. Facts and figures were collected on the plant floor on a daily

Activity accounting

basis, but these 'numbers' did not provide management with the facts necessary to make decisions and manage the plant. So, while it appeared that the company had a sound information system in place, the reality was that it collected a lot of data, but used almost none of it. In addition, the information system had a very short 'memory' – data was moved off the mainframe to tape back-up, or dumped, once a month. The result? Joe was really managing the plant on intuition and a few hastily calculated performance measures. This management approach even had a name at Standard Soap: gutfact.

6.15.38 Gutfact-based management was occurring everywhere in the organisation. Sometimes gutfact was right (managers were very experienced), but many other times it was wrong. The problem was that there was no alternative available, and no real way to separate good gutfact from bad. This was the real challenge facing Standard Soap – it had to design an information system that would support the complexity and uniqueness of its operations, that would be accessible and believed by its managers (it had to replace gutfact), and that could be implemented at minimal cost to the company.

Replacing gutfact with information

6.15.39 By early 1990, the implementation of the new information system was underway. The implementation time line, shown in Figure 6.8, reflects the major pressures that were hitting the firm during this period. The 'quick fix' database was one outgrowth of these pressures. Consisting of patched numbers and reconstructed data, the quick fix project focused on defining customer profitabilities (see Figure 6.9). The benefits that came from this pilot project are outlined below.

6.15.40 Definition of key data points needed to construct a long-term database:

- recognition that data could not be reconstructed with any level of accuracy;
- identification of key weaknesses in the existing general ledger package leading to the redesign of the general ledger;
- introduction of activity-based concepts and approaches to the organisation;
- highlighting of key errors in 'gutfact' based on a preliminary analysis of customer and product line profitabilities.

6.15.41 The pilot project laid the groundwork for the development of the current activity-based cost management system (ACMS). It also nudged

Gap between theory and practice

ACMS system timeline

Fall 1988	Opening contact with K.T.	
	Joe S., Bob N., Fran G.	Joe S. reassigned to H.R.
1989	Sequence of proposals	Interviews with management
Spring 1990	MBA Students' Project	
	K.T. – facilitator, Process Flow Diagram with cost pools & drivers	
Summer 1990	CAT. visit, Quick Fix	
Fall/Winter 1990	Realign G/L, restate 1990 G/L, Erin V. hired in 1st quarter 1991	
Spring 1991	First report, patched info	
	Training sessions with supervisors, crew leaders renew forms, data collection	
Spring/Summer 1991	Refine inputs	Politics, Open Kimono
	K.T.'s report on second round of interviews with management	
Winter 1991	Database development, reports	
	Understanding critical elements of price estimating	
	Strong, clear data	
	2nd half 1991, real clear data	
1992	Further development of reports, understanding of info in database	
	Info used on daily/weekly basis by production, planning managers	
	Info used by sales for pricing & negotiating	
	Acceptance of data as accurate	
	Estimates tied to G/L twice a year & adjustment slight	

Figure 6.8

along the cultural change needed to help Standard Soap jump the growth threshold by pinpointing areas where gutfact failures were leading to poor operational and financial performance.

6.15.42 The restatement of the general ledger accounts resulted in the structure summarised in Figure 6.10. As can be seen, the major change made was the recoding of accounts to reflect the underlying structure of the soap-making process. Indirect expense categories were broken apart and regrouped by activity; general plant overhead was reassigned to machine pools and activities. The general ledger grew by one-third as a result of these changes, but it now became possible physically to match the cost information in the general ledger to operations. The system was ready for a test; would the organisation really listen to the new information?

The politics of change
6.15.43 Picture a family-run business faced with competitive pressures, operational problems (the control loss issue) and the transfer of power from one generation to the next, and you have an organisation under stress.

Activity accounting

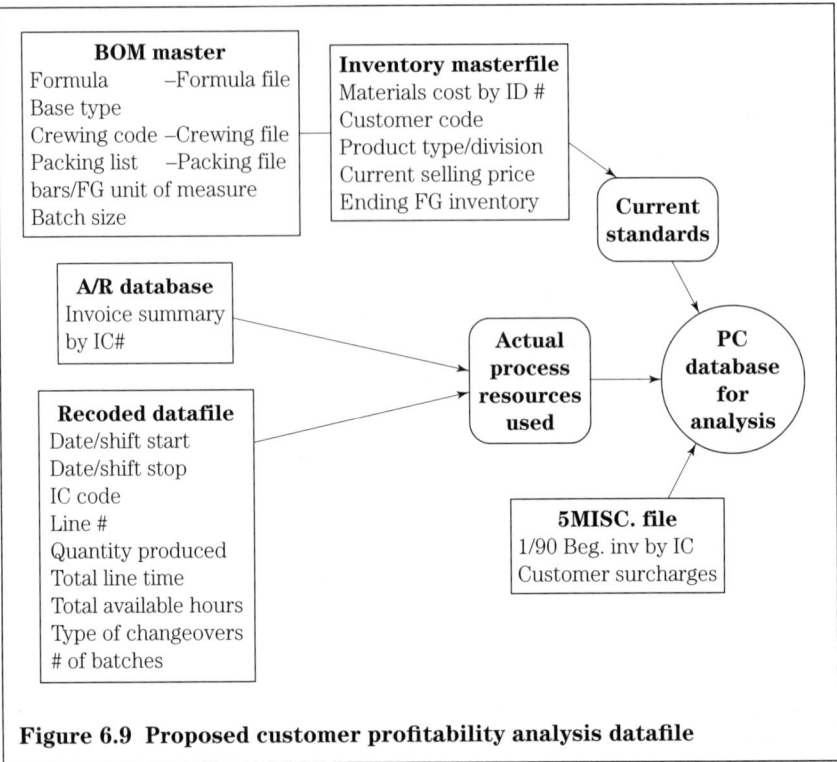

Figure 6.9 Proposed customer profitability analysis datafile

Standard Soap is just such an organisation. Two family members, Fran and her brother, John, are both actively involved in the firm. John serves as MD, Fran as Finance Director. The pressures in the business, Allen's gradual withdrawal from daily operations, sibling rivalry and the natural conflicts accompanying a 'changing of the guard' at any firm, combined forces to make the implementation of TQM and ACMS at Standard Soap a highly political process.

6.15.44 Logic serves little purpose when emotions and egos are on the line. The ACMS was built on a logic of activities, costs and business complexity. Organisations run on personal skills, emotions and history. While fact can often be used to guide management, it is unusual to see a company use facts to drive the change process. In essence, that is what Standard Soap did. Numbers generated by the ACMS were built from gutfact, enhanced by basic cost and engineering concepts, and moulded to fit the information needs of the company's managers. Until profits could be turned around, though, these facts would remain merely interesting tidbits to be used in the political process of managing the organisation.

Gap between theory and practice

Restatement of income statement G/L accounts

Description	Old method	New method
Schedule 2 (square footage)		
Insurance	Sq. footage	Sq. footage
Workers comp insurance	Sq. footage	Labor cost pool by # of employee's
Bldg. & land depreciation	Sq. footage & % of sales	Sq. footage
Allocation % changed		
Bar mfg.	49%	57%
Bulk mfg.	34%	37%
Central services	15%	
Adm.	2%	6%
Schedule 3	Allocated on use	Based on studies by Plant Engineer. A. Howland, F. Gammell
	Bar Bulk Cent'l srv. Adm	Bar Bulk Cent'l srv. Adm.
Electric	50% 42% 5% 3%	75% 25%
Heat – steam	50% 42% 5% 3%	75% 25%
Water	50% 42% 5% 3%	16% 84%
Sewer use fees	50% 42% 5% 3%	80% 20%
Depreciation – machinery	50% 42% 5% 3%	70% 30%
Storage	50% 42% 5% 3%	80% 20%
Schedule 4		
Direct mfg. expenses		
Dies, supplies	Direct to bar, bulk, centr'l service	Same as before
Shipping	Arbitrarily allocated by Finance	Pounds shipped
Lab.	Arbitrarily allocated by Finance	Employee time & function study to bulk as well as lbs shipped
Trash	Arbitrarily allocated by Finance	
Training	Arbitrarily allocated by Finance	Labor pools by # of employees
Machinery repairs	Direct to bar, bulk, centr'l service	to machine pool G/L #'s by type

Figure 6.10

Activity accounting

'But a bar isn't a bar . . .'

6.15.45 The information system at Standard Soap had been built on ongoing input and recommendations from first and second level managers at the company. It would seem that with all of this expert knowledge to draw from, the system should fit the organisation and be accepted by it. Based on this assumption, the ACMS project team began using the information coming out of the system to analyse ongoing business and identify areas for improvement.

6.15.46 While there were many ways the information could be used in the company, the job shop environment surrounding the business suggested that focusing on the bid price estimating system would be a logical place to focus the information system. The sales force was interviewed in an attempt to find out exactly how they thought about the business, what factors they used in developing a bid price for a customer and what type of information system interface would work best for them in the field. The results of these efforts was a bid price estimator programme that used the key cost estimates from the ACMS to bid jobs (see Figure 6.11).

6.15.47 To test the programme a sample of current jobs running in the plant was rebid using the ACMS estimates. The results of this analysis are presented in Figure 6.12. According to the data many jobs were severely under-costed while others were over-costed. This result was just what the ABC experts had said would happen (see Figure 6.13). So the results were no surprise to the ACMS project team. A meeting was set up with top management and the sales department to discuss the changes that would need to take place in the bid price procedures based on the new ACMS information.

6.15.48 The meeting was held on a Monday afternoon, the only day all of the salespeople were in the office. Preliminary analysis of the bid price accuracy versus estimated production costs were distributed in advance to everyone to give them time to digest the information and prepare comments. Comments are what the ACMS team got . . .

6.15.49 Steve, Marketing Manager: 'Where did you get these numbers from? Are you living in la-la land, or what? I've never seen anything so ridiculous! We won't get any business if we price the way you're suggesting!'

6.15.50 Fran: 'What's the problem, Steve? You're the one who told us how each of you prices a job. We simply used the information you gave us and put it into the system, used the cost estimates we all agreed upon and this is what we got. You may not like what you see, but it's reality.'

Gap between theory and practice

Standard Soap Works
Bid price estimator sheet

Customer name:
Job description:
Date:
Originator:
Pieces to run:
Bar size legal wt.:
  (enter oz. or grams)

Material costs:

Base	%	/bar	# req'd	$/lb

$ _____ Total materials

Packaging materials:

Description	Bars/unit	Units req'd	$/unit

_____ Total pckg mats

Machine set-up cost:

Number of pckg machines
Press setup
Total "setups"
× .5 (av. hr/setup)
Total setup hours   × $55.00/set up hr.   Set-up costs

Life time estimate:

Bars req'd
Est. run rate (bars/hr)
Press hours   × $60.00/press hr.   Line time cost

\# laborers/press hour
× press hours
  Total labor hours   × $25.00/lbr hr.   Labor cost

Lab/QC charge:

Press hours   × $55.00/QC test
× .25
Total QC tests   QC/QA cost

Line cleaning charge: $150.00   Clean cost

Total job cost $

Figure 6.11

309

Activity accounting

Company/Product	Cost per traditional system	Cost per revised system
Ace Soap Company:		

Yellow roses – 5,000 bars
    Run rate: 1,000/hr
    No pckg machines
    1 laborer/press hr.
    Materials ($400.00)
	$88.00	$1,065.00

Hope Novelty:		

Black horses – 1,000 bars
    Run rate: 500/hr
    2 pckg machines
    2 laborers/press hr.
    Materials ($250.00)
	$500.00	$727.00

International Cosmetics:		

Oatmeal Beauty Bar – 500 bars
    Run rate: 500/hr
    3 pckg machines
    1 laborer/press hr.
    Materials ($800.00)
	$1,600.00	$1,157.00

Strand Health & Beauty:		

Louffe Face Bar – 10,000 bars
    Run rate: 2,000/hr
    2 pckg machines
    1 laborer/press hr.
    Materials ($1,500.00)
	$3,000.00	$1,870.00

Norwood Guest Amenities:		

Hotel bars – 10,000 pieces
    Run rate: 2,500/hr
    1 pckg machine
    1 laborer/press hr.
    Materials ($500.00)
	$1,000.00	$1,095.00

Figure 6.12 Job cost comparisons

6.15.51 Steve: 'I tend to disagree, Fran. You and K.T. may think these numbers look good, but they aren't. The business just isn't this simple . . . a bar isn't a bar isn't a bar . . .'

6.15.52 K.T.: 'What do you mean, Steve? We've accounted for the weight of the bar, the raw materials, the number of packaging machines and set-up times, the pack rates and machine time. And we've used ABC charging rates

Gap between theory and practice

Summary of cost information by activity pool:

Raw material testing	$480,000/yr	12,000 hours
QC – Bar appearance	$600,000/yr	12,000 hours
Line cleaning	$960,000/yr	22,000 hours

* High QC bars take about 8 times as much effort as low QC bars. Low QC orders use about 1 hour of QC per 8 hours of production

Cleaning time

Color or additive	Time (hours)
White	0.5
Yellow	1.0
Red	2.0
Blue	4.0
Black	4.0
Sparkle	0.5
Oatmeal	3.0
Lanolin	1.0
Louffa	4.0

Raw material testing

Customer	# of raw tested	Average test time
Ace Soap Company	5	30 minutes
Hope Novelty	0	
International Cosmetics	1	15 minutes
Strand Health & Beauty	3	30 minutes
Norwood Guest Amenities	0	

Bar appearance level

Customer	
Ace Soap Company	High
Hope Novelty	Medium
International Cosmetics	High
Strand Health & Beauty	Medium
Norwood Guest Amenities	Low

Figure 6.13 Case data tables

Activity accounting

for inspection, quality control and cleaning. What else could you want? That's the business, isn't it?'

6.15.53   Ed, QA/QC/Development Manager: 'What? You treated everything we do in the lab as one big chunk of cost! You must be kidding! Some customers want a lot of testing, some just a little. And with the new cosmetic bars, the customers won't allow even a small nick in the bar – it has to be visually as well as chemically perfect. How can you compare these bars? They're not the same. We may do the same activities, but how often and how much differs a lot.'

6.15.54   Rick, Production Manager: 'The same goes for the cleaning operation, Fran. You know the business. When we get an order for a black soap, it takes us forever to clean up the machines before we can go back to pastels or white soap. Are you going to charge the same price for clean-ups, no matter what we really do out there? What good is that?'

6.15.55   Fran: 'If I'm hearing all of you correctly, it seems we've missed some things in the costing system that are very important to getting an accurate read on the cost of doing business at Standard Soap. I want to know what makes one bar different from another from each of you, then we'll sit down and find a way to get this information in the system. I don't know how, but between K.T. and me we'll figure something out. So, what are all of these "differences"?'

6.15.56   The meeting shifted gears and the next hour was spent identifying features of a bar or a job that made a big impact on the runnability of the soap or the complexity of the job. After the meeting, K.T. and Fran collected data on the key features of the orders run based on the facts unearthed at the meeting. Several of the summary tables for this information are presented in Figure 6.8.

6.15.57   The question that remained was, what to do about the lack of fit between the ACMS and the complex business processes that defined Standard Soap? It was possible to keep track of each and every order and the amount of time spent on the various types of tasks in the plant. This data could ultimately be used to create a new set of cost estimates that might be more realistic. But, would that do the trick? In talking about the problem, K.T. and Fran came to a basic conclusion: capturing the static complexity, or 'drivers', of cost at Standard Soap simply wasn't good enough. There were differences in orders, and in bars – some that mattered and some that didn't. What to do, though? Abandon the ACMS? Fran's frustration was evident:

Gap between theory and practice

'We know this system isn't perfect, but we can't go back to the way we used to do things. We need good information to run this business, or we won't be able to grow profitably. The fact that a bar isn't a bar, that's a problem, but I know we can find a way to include this in the system. But, it can't be by using a ton of detail to get the information – it has to be a quick, easy to understand proxy – we have to capture the dynamic elements of the system in a way we all can understand and agree with. If we don't, we still won't really know if we're doing the best we can do on an order, or where to focus our improvement efforts. No one talks about this problem in any of the articles out there . . . are we the only ones who don't fit the simple ABC model? I can't imagine that we are, but, the fact is, it's our problem now. It has to be solved, or no one will believe the system'.

6.15.58 The story underlying the changes at this company spans such issues as the transition from one generation to the next in a family-owned business, the inevitable sibling rivalries as this transition takes place, the implementation hurdles accompanying any new information system, the interaction between a company's strategy and its costing system and, finally, the need to keep market concepts and costing in their appropriate places in the decision-making process. All of this 'richness' lies behind the very real structural issue of how to build organisational complexity, and product mix differences, into an activity-based costing system.

6.15.59 The actual implementation process did proceed as described above. A study was done to identify the major drivers of cost, and develop the related cost pools. This information was developed from both operational and general ledger data, and was reworked until a 'balance' of old work and the related estimated costs were achieved. In other words, the estimates developed were used to go backwards, recost old business and assess whether the estimates would 'zero out' the general ledger manufacturing cost accounts. They did. In addition, the system remains self-balancing, with activity-based estimates being used for all decision analysis and management reporting. General ledger information is used as a 'check' on the estimates, to trigger analysis and potential adjustment of activity rates where necessary, and to verify that the information system is leading the company where it wants to go. The relational database structure that forms the architecture of the system allows for easy, instantaneous adjustments of any and all files with minimal levels of data entry or potential for error.

6.15.60 Finally, the system described is totally integrated. Specifically, all cost measures are driven by operational data and results. Costs are matched to the processes, flows, value chains and operational measures that comprise the business. Cost roll-ups can be done across any customer, market segment, specific order or production run, or product line on demand, based on actual run profiles and actual costs of production (versus estimated costs).

Activity accounting

Developing intensity factors

6.15.61 Within Standard, product-driven differences in activity costs were focused on their impact on run times and first pass yields per hour of run time. While many different mathematical adjustments could have been made, the focus on easy to understand, actionable and logical measurements led to the decision to create categories of 'complexity' for each major area where product characteristics or customer demand changed the 'cost' of an activity performed. For example:

Activity: quality assurance

Issue: 'Perfect' bars for the high end customer require much more inspection, have a higher reject rate and consume more time in the laboratory and on the line.

Decision: create four different QC/QA classes

Level 4: 'Perfect' bars; QC testing every hour.

Level 3: Minimal mars on surface; chemical content tightly monitored (QC testing every 2 hours).

Level 2: Minor mars accepted; QC testing every 4 hours.

Level 1: Minimal quality standards (QC testing every 8 hours of run time; only major flaws lead to rejection; bulk-pack novelties and hotel bars).

Costing implication

Level 4 received an '8X' weighting in the costing analysis, Level 3 a '4X' weighting, Level 2 a '2X' weighting, and Level 1 a '1X' weighting. Specifically, then, the denominator of the activity-based costing formula becomes:

$\{[8 \times (\text{Projected number of Level 4 runs})] + [4 \times (\text{Projected number of Level 3 runs})] + [2 \times (\text{Projected number of Level 2 runs})] + [1 \times (\text{Projected number of Level 1 runs})]\}$

= Mix adjusted 'capacity' for the activity

6.15.62 This new denominator, weighted by the intensity factors for the various product families run by Standard, is then used to create the activity cost estimate, as suggested by the following formula:

Gap between theory and practice

$$\text{Cost per activity equivalent} = \frac{\text{Total 'Quality Assurance' costs}}{\text{Mix adjusted capacity of activity pool}}$$

$$\text{Cost per activity equivalent} = \frac{\text{Total 'Quality Assurance' costs}}{\text{Mix adjusted capacity of activity pool}}$$

6.15.63 Charging out these activity charges, then, takes place as follows:

Level 4 job: 8 × (cost per activity equivalent) = Quality assurance costs to job

6.15.64 Consider the following example.

Assume that the costs traced to the quality assurance activity pool for 2000 total $2,500,000. In reviewing sales projections for the coming year, Fran determines that the mix of products that can be expected are:

Level 4:	1,000 orders
Level 3:	1,500 orders
Level 2:	500 orders
Level 1:	1,000 orders

6.15.65 To determine the estimated cost per activity equivalent for the coming year, as well as the activity cost assigned to each product type, calculate the following:

(1) Develop estimate of activity equivalents

8 (1,000) + 4 (1,500) + 2 (500) + 1 (1,000) = 16,000 activity equivalents

(2) Develop cost per activity equivalent

$$\frac{\$2,500,000}{16,000 \text{ A.E.s}} = \$156.25/\text{activity equivalent}$$

(3) Charging rates to different product types

    (a) Level 4 = 8 ($156.25) or $1,250.00 for quality assurance
    (b) Level 3 = 4 ($156.25) or $625.00 for quality assurance
    (c) Level 2 = 2 ($156.25) or $312.50 for quality assurance
    (d) Level 1 = 1 ($156.25) or $156.25 for quality assurance

6.15.66 Clearly, these are batch-driven charges and, as such, reduce on a per unit basis as the size of the run increases. It is clear that the new 'high end' products are made up of many smaller batches. The unitised impact of these activity-equivalent charges, then, is significant for this product line.

Activity accounting

6.15.67 The Standard Soap case represents an opportunity to consider the concept of 'fit' in the design and use of cost management systems. It also depicts the ways in which product mix and customer diversity impact the development of activity-based charges. While many different approaches could be used to generate the activity-equivalent charges, the benefit of the solution chosen by Standard is its practicality. These costs are used as estimates by the company, allowing it to track product line profitability and set continuous improvement goals. Being 'approximately right' in the creation of cost estimates means more than tracing costs to their causes – it means capturing the key drivers of changes in the way resources are consumed (e.g., costs are caused).

(Source: adapted from IMA 1997 with permission.)

6.16 Resistance to change

6.16.1 Player and Keys (1995c) identify issues concerning AA systems which go 'mainstream'. When change is effected, it is often met with resistance. Sometimes, individual resistance is due to fear. It is therefore essential that the strengths and weaknesses of activity accounting be made clear from the beginning.

6.16.2 AA systems tend to sidestep the functional structure of organisations in making assignments to activities and then to products or customers. While they may yield valuable information about activities, they tend not to focus on departmental information.

6.16.3 Player & Keys (1995c) consider that many activity accounting systems define activities across departmental lines, and while the use of interdepartmental teams and activities can be valuable, ignoring the functional organisation of a company can endanger the success of AA since departmental groups may view this as a threat. They may fear loss of power, prestige and importance in the company. Some managers may think that ABM information will be used to decrease the size of their departments or lead to outsourcing of the entire department. Consequently, department heads who perceive a potential loss of power or resources may try to subvert the activity accounting system.

6.16.4 Perhaps most importantly, there may be resistance to changing beliefs and value systems. Cultural or societal proclivities can form resistance points to implementation of an activity accounting system. Activity-based analyses may provide new and different views of an organisation and its performance. Using these new views may require a radical departure from the traditional perspective.

Resistance to change

6.16.5 Sometimes managers will not or cannot take action once they receive activity accounting information. Perhaps managers may not act to eliminate activities, marketing may refuse to change prices and the signals of cost drivers may be ignored.

6.16.6 Even if an ABM system generates insightful information, no benefit can be derived if managers do not or cannot act on that information.

6.16.7 Performance evaluation systems can hinder action based on ABM information. If ABM is implemented at a plant that is a cost centre, managers at the cost centre may fail to perceive the strategic benefits of ABM. These managers may normally be evaluated on how their actual costs compare to budgets, and thus not be concerned by ABM data.

6.16.8 Some companies that are profitable do not see the need to change. For them, ABM may represent a change from the status quo, but if the status quo is comfortable, then ABM will not be seen as a priority.

6.16.9 While the initial cost of an ABM system is an issue, the cost of maintaining an ABM system can be too. Mistakes are inevitably found in the implementation of ABM systems and must be corrected. Suggestions for improvements must be identified and acted upon. This adds to maintenance costs.

(Source: Player and Keys, 1995c. Reprinted with permission. For more information, visit www.wglcorpfinance@riag.com)

A case study: the effective design of an ABM system

6.16.10 Selto (1995) describes how a large consumer products company (EXCO) experimented with pilot projects to learn how to implement value chain analysis, ABC and, more broadly, activity-based management (ABM). He identifies factors that led to success of the implementation and shortcomings in design and consequences.

6.16.11 Selto (1995) believes that value chain analysis and ABM may guide organisations to reallocate resources in ways that will improve performance. The strategic organisational design concern should be to structure an organisation's value chain effectively and efficiently. This means reducing or removing activities that do not add value to services or products and enhancing those that do. An organisation with an improved value chain should be able to gain competitive advantage in both cost and quality so as to meet or exceed customers' expectations at the lowest cost possible.

Understanding cost incursion

6.16.12 ABM's focus is on the links between understanding cost incursion and recognising which organisational activities add value to the products. One critical question for companies that are contemplating implementing ABM is whether it will help streamline the organisation by minimising non-value added activities and whether ABM can enhance the ability to achieve business objectives by redeploying resources to value added activities. The likely effectiveness of ABM will rest not only on dealing with technical issues but also whether it is expanded to create an environment conducive to ABM and to make critical and sometimes unpopular decisions about resource allocation. Selto (1995) notes that activity accounting relies on employees' declarations of how they spend their time. Consequently, the following characteristics are relevant.

- Shared goals and objectives.
- Focus on activities throughout organisation.
- Use of group or team analysis.
- Reliable and accessible information.
- Empowerment of workers to access information and make critical decisions.
- Employment security.

Understanding the value chain

6.16.13 Selto (1995) discusses the Packaging Department of EXCO: Packaging is an example of a manufacturing operation with a relatively simple value chain – the product is packaged in various sized containers, cased, put on pallets and shipped to customers. The plant decision revolves around product and size mix, and some notion of the cost of five different sized containers that are packaged each period. This stage of manufacturing is similar to other EXCO operations across the world, except that the product itself may differ. Thus EXCO can gain insights from its packaging operations that would apply to its many manufacturing facilities.

Packaging ABM objectives

6.16.14 Corporate staff at EXCO presented the following objectives for the ABM effort to plant managers at a year-end meeting:

- to help manufacturing upstream and downstream internal customers get more relevant cost data;
- to get better product cost information;
- to use ABC's value added focus to help cost-improvement efforts.

Packaging ABM implementation

6.16.15 Under direction from a company-level manager, the assigned cost analyst (CA) tried to implement a two-stage ABC approach.

6.16.16 First, to identify and cost basic activities; and subsequently to allocate activity costs to products based on their consumption of the basic activities. The CA spent the first three months as an operator, making product, running a packing line and driving a forklift in the warehouse. After getting exposure to the operations of the plant, the CA worked with 'manufacturing peers' to identify basic activity drivers that drove the cost of different sizes; that consumed the most cost; and that could be controlled.

6.16.17 The CA identified 11 packaging activities that met these criteria. The costs of these activities were based on time devoted to each by either people or machines, determined by interviews, questionnaires and machine logs. The next step was to divide these activities into non-value added and value added activities which can at times call for considerable judgement.

6.16.18 The second stage of ABC entailed allocating the cost of each activity to each product size according to its estimated consumption of activity drivers, obtained from manufacturing personnel. For example:

Activity	Activity driver
Changeover (for different sizes)	Changeover hours
Packaging product	Number of cases packed
Scheduling	Number of pack codes

6.16.19 The intention was that, with this activity and cost information, the manufacturing plant managers would feel better able to make decisions on product size mix and assess the impact of redeploying efforts to value added activities. No distinction was made between fixed and variable costs in line with the implementation of ABC generally.

Packaging ABM evaluation

6.16.20 The CA identified insights gained from the ABC analysis of packaging the different sizes of product. The smaller sizes required half the changeover hours, so they were allocated half the total changeover costs. This was done even though these smaller sizes provide much less than half the total output volume in many cases. Likewise, larger package sizes accounted for more than 70 per cent of scheduling activity and were consequently allocated more than 70 per cent of the scheduling cost. Only about half of the total packaging cost was driven by the number of cases packed, i.e., the output volume activity.

Activity accounting

Acting on ABC information

6.16.21 As with the result of activity accounting implementations in many firms, the ABC analysis revealed that the smallest size was found to be much more costly than the company had previously thought because of its disproportionate consumption of certain activities. Several options were presented:

- drop the product;
- outsource the packaging;
- improve changeover times;
- change pricing.

6.16.22 Since improving changeover times would decrease non-value added set-up activity and should increase overall effectiveness, this option was explored regardless of package size. It turned out that very little of the cost allocated to the smallest size was avoidable. This observation, coupled with the excess capacity at the plant, indicated that the smallest size should not be dropped and that packaging should not be outsourced.

6.16.23 Though traditional 'relevant' costing (see Chapter **2**) would indicate that, in the short term, any price exceeding variable plus avoidable costs would be acceptable, EXCO was concerned with its pricing strategy. Since the smallest size consumes disproportionate shares of many activities, in the long run it must adequately cover the costs of those activities or else it would be dropped and the resources redeployed. What was previously considered a premium price came to be seen as a minimal price needed to cover the resource consumption of activities.

6.16.24 Selto (1995) notes that the greatest benefit of the ABM exercise was not the insights on product pricing, but that more than half the cost of packaging was from non-value added activities. Though not all of these activities could be eliminated, efforts to minimise non-value added activities could greatly reduce operating costs in the long run without dysfunctionally affecting operations. If such resources could be redeployed to value added activities, the effectiveness and performance of the packaging operation could potentially increase. Indeed, the CA later reported significant increases in plant reliability and reductions in manufacturing expense that accompanied significant decreases in non-value added activities and resource redeployment. The most-reduced non-value added activities were unplanned downtime, changeovers and start-up or shutdown time. Consequently the ABM implementation was effective in meeting its stated, short-term objectives.

6.16.25 EXCO subsequently extended the ABM philosophy to its manufacturing plant, warehousing capacity and administrative services. As discussed above, organisations often use this pilot-based approach: one part of their operations is converted to ABM and, based on the result, the approach is rolled out to other operations.

Activity accounting and manufacturing plant overhead
6.16.26 Manufacturing plant overhead (MO) contains many activities that drive overall costs. If many of these hidden activities are non-value added, eliminating them and refocusing on value added activities could result in increases in productivity.

The outcome
6.16.27 Often, the focus of pilot ABM studies is on achieving cost reductions, but at EXCO, some stress was placed on reconfiguring organisations' value chains. Many of these reconfigurations were ad hoc rather than resulting from planned reductions or eliminations of non-value added activities and redeployment of personnel to value added activities.

6.16.28 Selto (1995) reports that it did not appear that an objective of any of the ABM pilot studies was to develop a reliable and sustainable ABM system. More planning before the pilot studies perhaps could have led to a more uniform approach. Perhaps more effort should be devoted to system development to learn from the pilot study experiences.

6.16.29 In implementing ABM, measuring resources consumed by various activities is a crucial task. At EXCO the time estimates were generally made without explicit reference to work measurement. For machine-related activities, machine logs provided some validation, but validating labour time estimates proved more difficult. Naturally, the question will arise as to what incentive individuals have to declare truthfully how they spend their time, particularly if they sense that their primary function could be viewed as a non-value added activity. But by the same token, operational staff are best placed to know about the time requirements of their work and improvement options. This is a general problem with ABM techniques, and employment security can be a requisite for successful implementation of ABM. Broadly, for EXCO, the ABM studies led to cost savings at or near targeted levels.

6.17 Tangible costs versus intangible benefits

6.17.1 Reeve (1996) discusses problems and challenges encountered by companies implementing ABM. He suggests that the costs of any ABM implementation are tangible. They can include the immediate investment of time,

Activity accounting

money and management commitment. Conversely, the benefits of ABM are less tangible. The primary benefit of ABM may be the promise of improved decision making at some time. But tracing the benefits of improved decision making, if it is there, back to the original ABM implementation efforts is a near impossible exercise. Perhaps the pay-offs from a novel management philosophy ought to remain, at least in part, non-quantifiable. The question of whether a company achieves improved financial performance because of its information from ABM is likely to remain unanswered.

6.17.2 Reeve (1996) notes that an ABM implementation does not produce the visible reduction of stock and cycle times associated with implementing JIT. Companies that implement ABM must come to terms with developing a system that is difficult to design and capturing information that is difficult to acquire, all in aid of the promise of better decision making at some future stage. Often, organisations effect change not based on calculated pursuits of financial returns but because the pay-offs will likely exceed quantifiable benefits.

6.17.3 Reeve (1996) considers an ABM system to be essentially a relational database with data input from a variety of information sources. He gives an example from manufacturing. Many design decisions must be made to develop an ABM system. The first decision is whether to use standard activity information, actual activity costs or both in combination. The example begins by illustrating the design characteristics of an activity-based standard cost system. It then shows how an actual activity-based system can be used. The example illustrates how the implementation process is highly organisation-specific.

6.17.4 The first step is to develop activity standards by reconstructing the routing file in terms of a product bill of activities. This can be developed as a table to be used in a relational database. The table represents the standard amount of physical activity (e.g., number of glass seals) required for a particular product and reflects existing knowledge about how much of the activity is required to process a unit. Clearly, such knowledge requires the input of operational staff. As the standard for the frequency of an activity for a particular product changes (because of design changes or process improvements, for example), the table would have to be updated.

6.17.5 This table is multiplied by a demand forecast to develop a table of expected activity frequencies for a forecasted volume of mix of products. As Reeve (1996) notes, the planned production volume and mix are 'exploded' by the standard activity frequency per unit of product. An example of total planned activity frequency and rates is shown in Table 6.22.

Tangible costs versus intangible benefits

Table 6.22 Standard activity frequencies for planned volumes

Facility	Activity	Planned activity frequency	Activity rates
Fabrication	Wafer saw (WS)	150	$20.00
	Wafer break (WB)	7,900	0.90
	Sorting (S)	63,700	0.20
Assembly	Inspections	89,000	0.40
	Silver/Glass	1,110,000	0.16
	Glass seal	62,200	2.00
Test	Testing	417,000	0.25

6.17.6 Standard activity rates can be used for two major reports:

(a) a 'front to back' product cost report is a standard-cost bill of activities for a particular product. The information is of use to designers, process engineers and marketing personnel;

(b) production reports.

6.17.7 For production reports, standard activity cost can be compared with actual spending at the operational level at which actual spending is collected. Depending on the precision of the system, actual costs can be collected at three generic levels: cost-centre level, activity level, or activity by lot level. Reeve (1996) examines each generic level in more detail.

Cost-centre control

6.17.8 Figure 6.14 illustrates activity cost control when actual costs are captured at the cost-centre level. Cost centre 9010 provides three activities: wafer saw (WS) wafer breaking (WB) and sorting (S).

6.17.9 The activity-based production report is determined by multiplying actual activity frequencies by the standard rate. This feature distinguishes this company's system. The system updates cost information automatically by connecting the ABM system to data about the physical activity driver. The detail about the activity driver is collected automatically from prevailing systems and integrated into the ABM system. The ABM system is simple to maintain because the real-time data is collected only at the activity driver level, not at the activity cost level. Consequently, no additional reporting effort is imposed on employees for charging time and other resources to activities and the periodic updating becomes transparent to the employees.

6.17.10 Assume for instance that work centre 9010 (fab) actually produced products according to the plan in Table 6.22. Multiplying these frequencies by

Activity accounting

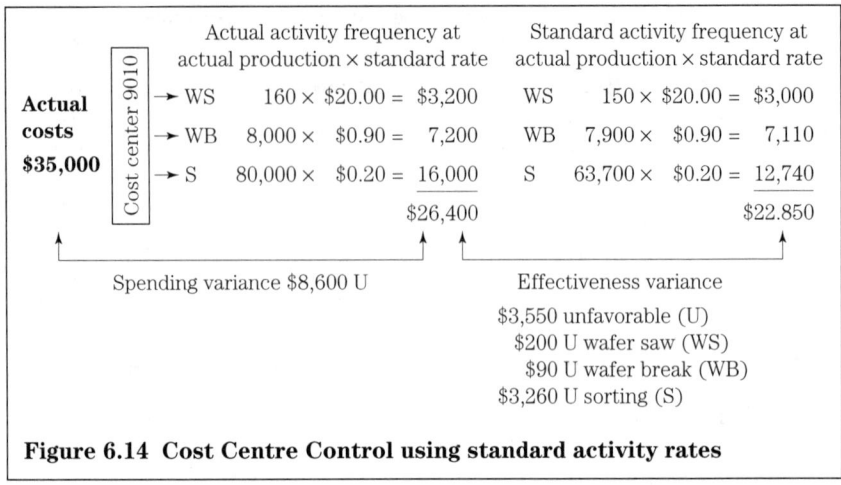

Figure 6.14 Cost Centre Control using standard activity rates

the activity rate provides the expected controllable costs to be incurred in the cost centre – in this case, $22,850.

6.17.11 Assume also that the actual frequency of activities differs from the plan. This was because many more sorts were required for this level of production than planned. Specifically (as shown in Figure 6.14) the plan called for 63,700 sorting operations, but 80,000 were actually incurred. The total standard cost charged to work centre 9010 is $26,400, which is $3,550 higher (unfavourable) than expected for this production volume. Individual variances at the activity level can be calculated to demonstrate that the actual activity frequency for sorting was much higher than planned. Such information can be used to investigate the sorting activity in work centre 9010 to determine why the actual frequency was so high during the period.

6.17.12 Note that the actual costs charged to the cost centre were $35,000. Since the centre was credited with only $26,400, an additional $8,600 spending variance is incurred. This variance may result from one of three major causes according to Reeve (1996).

(a) Excess capacity: the controllable capacity may be purchased in increments greater than the divisibility implied by the activity frequencies, i.e., actual spending will not vary or 'flex' exactly as the activity model suggests. People and other resources are purchased in 'lumps' which can cause excess capacity. Therefore, the spending variance could be excess indivisible capacity.

(b) Inefficiency: the spending variance could arise from performing activities inefficiently. For example, if each sort takes 33 per cent longer to

Tangible costs versus intangible benefits

perform than implied by the standard, additional resources may need to be purchased to meet the sorting demands. The loss in efficiency would be embedded in the unfavourable spending variance. This differs from the effectiveness variance, which measures the ability to meet the frequency standard, not necessarily the ability to perform each unit of activity efficiently.

(c) Measurement error: if the standards are updated infrequently, the spending variance may only represent measurement error, which is the classic problem with standards.

6.17.13 It is not possible to differentiate excess capacity from inefficiency. Moreover, since the actual cost information is collected at the cost-centre level, it is not possible to identify the activities that may be contributing to the capacity or efficiency problem. All that is known is that the spending variance is specific to a cost centre.

Activity-level control

6.17.14 In Figure 6.15, the same scenario is illustrated with actual costs captured at the activity level. This means that employees charge time and other resources to activities as well as to the cost centre. The information demands on employees are as a consequence higher.

Actuals	Cost center 9010	Actual activity frequency at actual production × standard rate	Standard activity frequency at actual production × standard rate	
Actual $3,300	Wafer saw	$3,200	$3,000	200 U
Actual $7,000	Wafer breaks	$7,200	$7,110	90 U
Actual $24,700	Sorting	$16,000	$12,740	3,260 U
		$26,400	$22,850	

$8,700 U sorting spending variance

Figure 6.15 Activity control using standard activity rates

6.17.15 Under this design, the effectiveness variances may be interpreted in the same way as before. However, the spending variance can be decomposed by activity. Now, the capacity/efficiency problems can be isolated to a specific activity in the cost centre.

325

Activity accounting

6.17.16 In Reeve's (1996) illustration, the sorting activity has effectiveness problems with excess frequency. In addition, more time is being charged to this activity than the amount that would be supported by the actual sorting frequency. This provides evidence that the sorting operation is inefficient (i.e., taking longer per sort than the standard) or that there is excess capacity (i.e., using the partial services of a whole full-time equivalent for this activity).

Lot-level control

6.17.17 The most precise (and most information-intensive) design is illustrated in Figure 6.16, by Reeve (1996) for the same scenario. In Figure 6.16 employees report their time and other resource consumption by activity for each lot of production. In practice, employees would have to record the time they spent on each of the three activities for every lot completed (lot-level tracking).

6.17.18 For example, after sorting a particular production lot, employees in the work centre or the cell would record in the labour tracking system the time spent to cut the wafers, score and break out the dies, and sort the dies. These times would be used to develop the actual cost of activities by work centre and by product identification (lot). Scrap information would also be recorded for the lot.

Lot-level tracking

6.17.19 Many companies do not have the ability to perform lot tracking for basic scrap and labour reporting, much less activity reporting at this level. Therefore, capturing actual activity information at the lot level might be over-ambitious in many settings. Not only would actual activity information be captured at the lot level, but so would activity frequency information. For example, the 160 wafer sawing operations from Figures 6.15 and 6.16 would be stratified by lot: 10 to FF-362; 120 to ZT-400; and 30 to MK-101. The actual frequencies of the other two activities would be stratified in the same way. Capturing the activity frequency information by lot is within existing data-capturing technologies using lot-level shop floor control.

6.17.20 Cost evaluations by activity and lot. The ABM reporting capabilities now make it possible to have cost evaluations stratified by activity and by lot. Low-level information now indicates that the sorting problems were specific to lot 3, the MK-101 device. Apparently, problems occurred in the processing of lot 3 so that more time was charged for sorting this lot than allowed by the standard frequency (the spending variance). There was also

Tangible costs versus intangible benefits

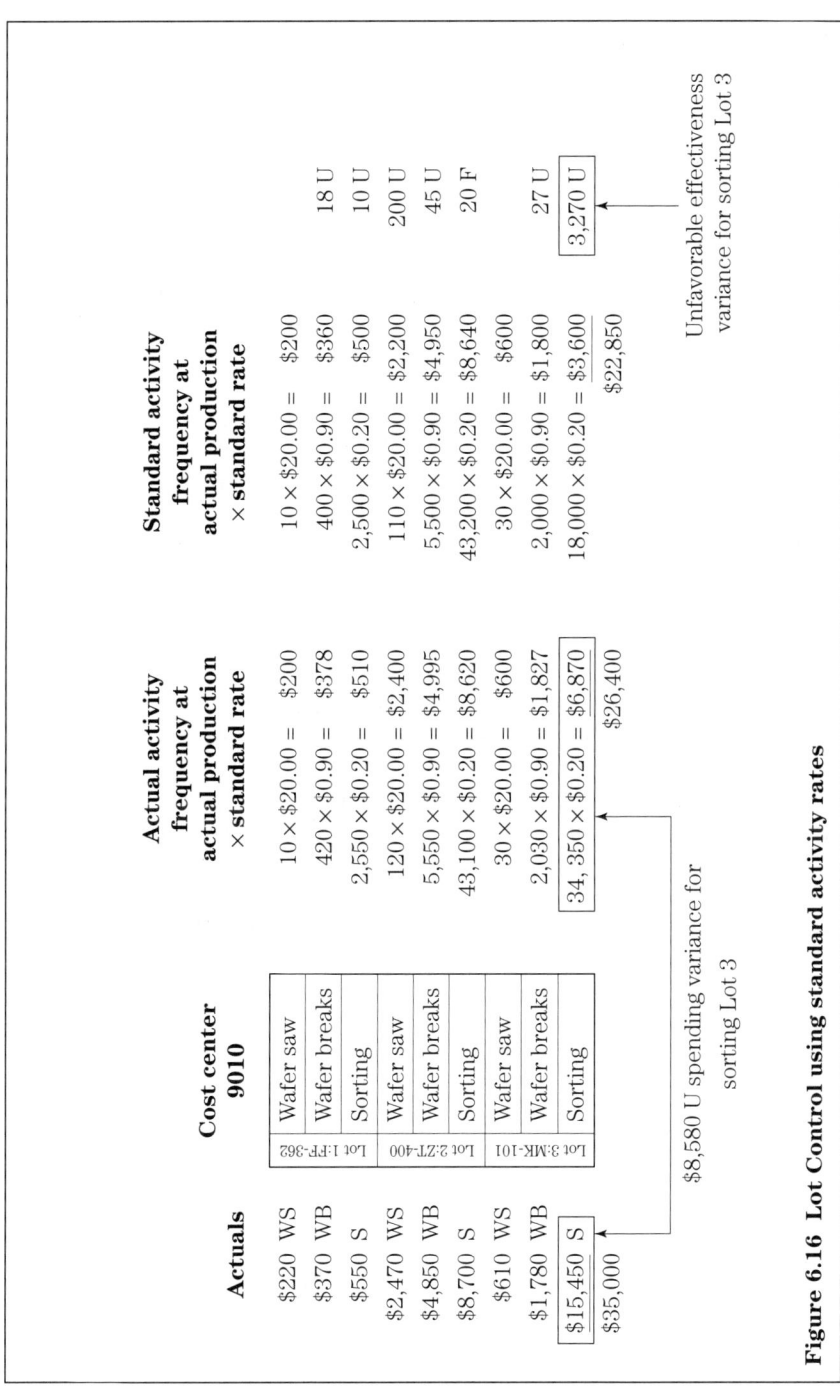

Figure 6.16 Lot Control using standard activity rates

Activity accounting

a higher frequency of sorting activity than was expected for this device (i.e., an effectiveness variance). Thus, lot-level control allows analysis to be stratified by product.

Design trade-offs

6.17.21 The above suggest that various design alternatives have trade-offs. Activity-based cost-centre control is the easiest to implement and provides good activity-based information (at standard) to support modest production control, while simultaneously supporting process improvement and product design decisions.

6.17.22 Additional information can be provided by capturing actual resource consumption by either activity or activity by lot. Capturing actual lot-level activity-based resource consumption may be superior to capturing just activity resource consumption for two reasons, according to Reeve (1996).

(a) Capturing only activity information leads to measurement errors because employees do not accurately recall the time spent during a week on the various activities.

(b) Without lot information, product-level actuals cannot be determined because the activity information is not stratified this way.

6.17.23 Therefore, without lot-levels actuals, product-level design and process flow decisions can only be supported from the standard bill of activity life, which is updated infrequently.

Activity-based management with actuals only

6.17.24 Some commentators have noted that a standard cost system should not be used for performance reporting and that period to period actuals are the appropriate method for improving costs. But it needs to be noted that the activity-level control and lot-level control designs discussed previously use actual activity-based costs for variance reporting. (The cost centre control design does not capture actual activity cost information, but relies on activity standards and actual activity frequencies to provide reporting.) This would relieve system administrators from maintaining a standard activity frequency file for each product and from developing standard activity rates (from planned or practical activity usage). Such a system is highly supportable in discretionary cost centre environments, where the concept of an activity standard has little validity. In such administrative and service settings, an actual activity-based costing system is viable according to Reeve (1996).

Tangible costs versus intangible benefits

6.17.25 An actual system tracks the actual activity cost and actual activity driver frequencies over time and by relevant stratifications (e.g., units, products, customers or projects). The design must match the activity resource consumption data with the frequency data. Thus, the stratifications of the two data sets must be the same to support performance reporting. Performance reports are determined by dividing actual activity cost by the actual cost driver frequency to develop the actual activity rate. This rate can be plotted over time for a particular activity or compared at a point in time across a stratification dimension.

6.17.26 Ultimately a user can query an ABM database to discover the actual cost per driver unit by various stratifications and determine profitability by the same stratifications.

6.17.27 Reeve (1996) illustrates this as follows: consider the actual activity information for sorting by lot (product) in Figure 6.16. The lot-level detail provides product stratification information for both activity costs and activity frequencies. The performance graph in Figure 6.17 could be produced by dividing the actual sorting costs by the actual sorting frequencies (from Figure 6.16). As the Figure indicates, the cost to sort MK-101 was almost twice as high as for either of the other two products. Therefore, the actual activity information provides nearly the same information as the standard activity cost system did – i.e., sorting for lot 3 is where the cost problem lies.

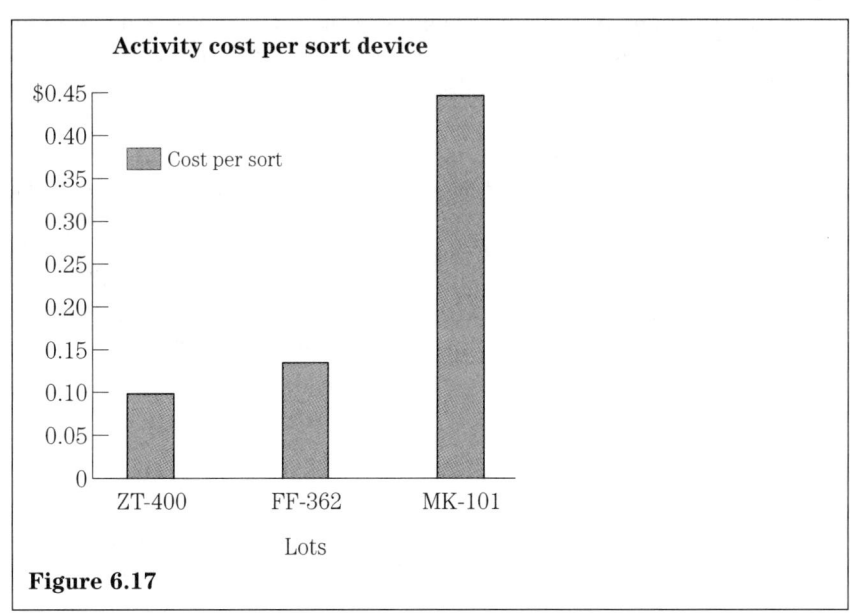

Figure 6.17

Activity accounting

Activity-based standards

6.17.28 There are two reasons for activity-based standards:

(a) activity-based standards can be used in the cost-centre control design without collecting actual activity resource consumption. Thus, an ABM system can be had without the burden of real-time effort and resource tracking;

(b) some information is lost by using only actual information.

6.17.29 Reeve (1996) illustrates the second point as follows: assume that actual activity cost is collected by lot and that the actual activity cost for sorting the dies in lot 3 was $7,000 rather than the $15,450 shown in Figure 6.16. If the actual cost is divided by the actual 34,350 sorts (from Figure 6.16), the cost per sort is a little over $0.20. The sorting activities for lot 3 now appear in line with the other lots.

6.17.30 However, as Reeve (1996) notes, the standard frequency information might reveal that more sorts were required for lot 3 than many expected. Dividing the actual activity costs by the actual frequencies will not reveal ineffective activity usage from using more physical activity than is needed. Since a standard system identifies the expected physical usage of an activity by product, the ineffectiveness (standard activity quantity to actual) can be revealed in the standard system. Given this, one would expect that the more uncertain the yield (i.e., standard output to actual), the more important the standard activity information is likely to be. Whether the additional precision of the information is worth the additional costs for maintaining the standards is open to debate.

6.17.31 Reeve (1996) believes that ABM systems will ultimately be able to provide timely activity cost per driver unit information that can be used to manage real time *kaizen* cost improvements in the organisation. What is important for ABM is immediate managerial access to the information which should be collected effortlessly through feeder subsystems. Ideally, the information should be integrated with the ongoing work of the business, and reveal profit patterns or opportunities for cost improvements.

(Source: Reeve, 1996.)

6.18 Outdated habits

6.18.1 Pryor (1997) identifies a number of outdated management accounting habits and attitudes which have been exposed by companies' ABM experiences.

Outdated habits

- The management of headcount and cost by function is irrelevant: what is relevant is managing the activities that consume the resources.

- The reporting and management of indirect versus direct headcount are irrelevant: what is relevant is managing the activities of an organisation, not the classification of the people who perform the activites.

- The reporting and management of fixed versus variable cost are irrelevant: what is relevant is managing used and unused activity and process capacity.

- Holding departmental managers responsible for budgets is irrelevant: what is relevant in recognising that the root causes of most departmental activities are not under the control of the people who perform the activities.

- Traditional budgets represent an irrelevant monthly benchmark for an organisation: a budget does not represent the best an organisation can be. People must recognise that all organisations contain significant non-value added cost.

- More detail, data, and decimal points do not make for a better accounting system: management of the 8–10 significant activities by cost centre and the 10–15 significant cross-functional business processes is more relevant.

- Closing the books in three days is irrelevant: the goal is not to account for costs after inclusion, but to prevent costs before they happen.

- Traditional accounting systems that encourage managers to control the vertical organisational chart are irrelevant: what is relevant is management of the lateral process company.

- The allocation of functional overhead cost to products after development is irrelevant: designing products that fit the existing functional activities and processes of the organisation is relevant.

- Limiting cost management to the organisational P&L is irrelevant: processes do not begin and end inside the company. Activities performed by suppliers and customers are also relevant.

6.18.2 Whilst these points are carefully thought through by many ABM systems implementors, they provide a sound checklist of dos and don'ts. Pryor (1997) also identifies management practices that are intended to bridge the gap between existing cost data and the knowledge about activities required to improve decision making.

Activity accounting

6.18.3 He advocates that enterprises eliminate functional based P&L statements given that many organisations are re-engineering themselves from a vertical, layered pyramid to flat, horizontal structures. The economic representation of the enterprise should strive to reflect its underlying structure.

6.18.4 Pryor (1997) notes that a P&L that lists functional spending is outdated and irrelevant. Management accounting systems should mirror the basis of the process-based organisation. Business processes, which are made up of activities, flow across functional boundaries on a daily basis. Processes represent the economic value chain of the organisation. As Figure 6.18 shows, a process-based P&L provides valuable information that is unavailable in a traditional functional P&L.

A case study: cost analysis versus business analysis

6.18.5 Chalice Wines operates from California's Sonoma Valley, home of many wine-making millionaires. Here is where they spend their millions, not where they make them.

6.18.6 The Chalice Wine Group's brochures describe its Cimarron winery in the following terms:

> 'A pair of red-tailed hawks hover in the thermal plume rising from the cliffs below the Feather Vine-yard. In winter, you hear the muted roar of three creeks cascading down the canyons from the ridges above. Fog nestles like ocean foam over the bay and valleys. The rocky outcrops and dense chaparral of madrone, oak, laurel and aromatic wild sage are the natural home of coyotes, rattlesnakes and mountain lions. The vineyards and winery of Cimarron are literally carved into the volcanic stone of the mountain – we are here for the long term. A great wine is not a commodity. It must artistically communicate its context, its place and time. We are dedicated to expressing the most beautiful and unique aspects of a place we love. We hope that you will share in our love of this place called Cimarron as we apply our skills each vintage to create for you a memorable sensory snapshot in a bottle of wine.'

6.18.7 The company is somewhat less effusive in describing its financial results in the 1993 Annual Report:

> 'Notwithstanding our strong fourth quarter, we had a net loss of $700,000 (after tax) for the year, but that is almost $50,000 less than we lost in 1992.'

6.18.8 In fact, things have been pretty much downhill, financially, for Chalice since 1990 as the following trend indicates.

From focus on functions
Traditional profit & loss statement

($000)	Actual	Budget	Variance
Sales	$40,000	$38,000	$+2,000
Cost of goods sold	20,000	17,000	+3,000
Gross margin	$20,000	$21,000	$−1,000
Operating expenses:			
Sales	4,000	4,100	−100
Marketing	3,000	2,900	+100
Finance	2,000	2,200	+200
R&D	4,000	4,500	−500
Personnel	2,000	2,000	—
	$15,000	$15,700	−700
Pretax profit	$ 5,000	$ 5,300	$ −300

Toward focus on processes
ABM profit & loss statement

($000)	Value	NVA	Total
Sales	$40,000	$	$40,000
Less:			
Raw materials	9,000	1,000	10,000
Less:			
Procurement process	2,000	700	2,700
Sales order process	2,000	1,500	$3,500
Manufacturing process	6,400	2,900	9,300
New product process	1,500	500	2,000
Line extension process	1,000	500	1,500
Budgeting process	200	400	600
Maintenance process	500	500	1,000
Marketing process	2,000	1,500	3,500
Administrator process	390	10	400
Facility process	450	50	500
Total costs	$16,440	$ 8,560	$25,000
	$25,440	$ 9,560	$35,000
Pretax profit	$14,560	$−9,560	$ 5,000

Figure 6.18

Activity accounting

Assets	Sales	Net Earnings	
1990	$49 million	$14.2 million	$650,000
1991	$68 million	$15.0 million	$58,000
1992	$70 million	$17.3 million	$(741,000)
1993	$74 million	$18.3 million	$(700,000)

The project

6.18.9 Bill Evanson, President and CEO of Chalice, was sharing a bottle of his wine with former colleague Sam Davis. Sam was describing how his just completed first year in the MBA program of a small eastern college had changed his perspective on the wine industry.

> 'Personally, if a business has no hope of profit then I'm just not interested. But it's not at all clear to me that small wineries are a hopeless cause. I'd hesitate to make that call without understanding what's happening along the entire value chain. Of the retail price somebody pays for a bottle of your wine, where does the money go? How much is profit versus cost for each of the players involved in making the product and delivering it to the consumer? Is there room for a winery to manoeuvre upstream or downstream in the value chain? And what causes the costs of each stage for each player? If you don't understand the whole picture, then you may misassess the options when you develop strategies to cope with changing business conditions, or even decide to abandon the effort. The value chain concept is a big deal at B-school these days, and I'm sold on it.'

6.18.10 Evanson looked intrigued. 'That's interesting Sam. I've been thinking along these same lines lately. What does it cost us to make wines the way we do? Many of our specific costs seem to get lost within our accounting system. I suspect we understate some and overstate others. Who is making money in this industry, and how do they do it? This would be great stuff to know. But this is a complex industry – practically every winery has a unique approach, and every wine is different. And Chalice is a particularly complicated company. Would a value chain analysis be meaningful, or even possible, for this company in this industry?'

6.18.11 Sam Davis grinned and raised his glass. 'Why don't we find out, Bill? We can certainly set up the value chain for a particular wine, and hopefully the process will reveal some generalisable insights. I've got the time if you've got the interest. We're drinking one of your wines now, aren't we? Why don't we track this one?'

6.18.12 Bill Evanson watched the sun reflect through the delicate flaxen colour of the 1991 Cimarron Meritage White in his glass. 'OK, hotshot, let's do it! Come to my office next week and I'll show you the numbers we've got.'

Outdated habits

The Chalice Wine Group (CWG)

6.18.13   Evanson had not exaggerated when he described Chalice as complicated. The group owns two vineyards (Chalice and Cimarron) and one-half of a third (Delta). It owns three wineries (Chalice, Cimarron and Alicia) and one-half of a fourth (Opera Valley) which it operates for a management fee on behalf of the joint venture owners. It has a cross-investment with a prominent French wine company for distribution in the US of its French and Chilean wines. CWG also owns a one-half interest in a vineyard in eastern Washington state with plans to build a winery at this site.

6.18.14   Of the four wineries, the flagship is Chalice, founded in 1969. The Opera Valley joint venture was established in 1980. Cimarron and Alicia were acquired in 1982 and 1986 respectively. Chalice went public in May of 1984. Until June 1993 with the initial public offering for Robert Mondavi winery, Chalice was the only publicly-held company in the United States whose principal business was the production and sale of premium wines. Among the serious patrons of the California wine industry, CWG enjoys a prestigious reputation for producing consistently elegant wines.

6.18.15   Each of its four California wineries is located in a different legally designated viticultural area. Each one is a separate profit centre with its own president, typically the winemaker. The company's wines are sold in speciality wine shops and grocery stores, and selected restaurants, hotels and private clubs across the country and in certain overseas markets. Virtually every distribution channel in the industry is used by CWG in one market or another. Its wines are distributed via direct mail in those states where it is legal and, in limited quantities, 'over the counter' at the wineries. Out of state, the company sells through the traditional three-tier system (maker, distributor, retailer). In northern California, a wine distributor is used as a broker. In southern California, CWG owns and operates its own distribution network.

6.18.16   Because of aging, sales in any one year do not match that year's production. Figure 6.19 contains selected industry sales and concentration data for 1991 and 1992. Total production and sales for the company for 1990, 1991 and 1992 are shown in Figure 6.20. Figure 6.21 shows the consolidated financial statements for the company for 1990, 1991 and 1992.

6.18.17   The big picture portrayed in these numbers was certainly not strong. Sam's task was to break the numbers down in order to understand the financial story of one particular wine from one of the particular wineries of the company. Was it losing money? If so, where? Was anyone making money on it? How much? How? The inquiry would require tracing the

Activity accounting

Figure 6.19 California winery shipments (Thousands of cases)[1]

	1992 cases	% total	1991 cases	% total	
All California Wineries	160,536	100%	157,734	100%	
E & J Gallo	64,219	40%	66,070	42%	
Heublein Wines	17,139	11%	15,712	10%	(Almaden, Inglenook)
The Wine Group	12,777	8%	9,981	6%	(Franzia, Summit, MD)
Vintners International	8,328	5%	8,549	5%	(Taylor, Paul Masson)
Top 4 Bulk Wineries	102,463	64%	100,312	63%	
Sebastiani	4,762	3%	4,749	3%	
Sutter Home	4,760	3%	4,163	3%	
Robert Mondavi	3,950	2%	3,261	2%	
Wine World	3,863	2%	3,285	2%	(Beringer, Napa Ridge)
Glen Ellen	3,778	2%	3,270	2%	
Top 5 Premium Wineries	21,113	12%	18,728	12%	
18 Wineries w/ Sales of 100K-250K Cases	2,570	1.60%	2,406	1.53%	
Chalice Wine Group	175	0.11%	138	0.09%	

[1] estimates from Gomberg, Fredrikson & Associates

path(s) followed by the 1991 Cimarron Meritage White, from the grape grower all the way through to the final consumer along the Meritage White value chain.

The Winery

6.18.18 'The vineyard would be the logical place to start, but we're here now, so let's start here. It's simple: I need revenues and costs, starting with cost of goods.'

6.18.19 Bill Evanson glanced down at his most recent Report to Stockholders. 'No problem. Revenues – $17.3 million; cost of goods sold – $11 million.'

6.18.20 'It's not that simple, Bill. How much per case of 1991 Cimarron Meritage White?'

6.18.21 'I was kidding. Of course we track all of our wines separately. We sell the Meritage White to our distributors for $76.00 per case. As of

Outdated habits

Figure 6.20 Wine production in case equivalents

By variety	1992 cases	% total	1991 cases	% total	1990 cases	% total
Chardonnay	141,200	68%	131,600	71%	117,900	71%
Sauvignon Blanc	4,000	2%	4,100	2%	10,100	6%
Pinot Blanc	6,700	3%	2,800	1%	3,100	2%
Other White	5,800	3%	5,600	3%	5,700	4%
Total White	157,700	76%	144,100	77%	136,800	83%
Pinot Noir	26,100	13%	23,100	13%	20,200	12%
Cabernet Sauvignon	16,900	8%	17,600	9%	6,600	4%
Other Red	5,500	3%	1,600	1%	1,600	1%
Total Red	48,500	24%	42,300	23%	28,400	17%
Total	206,200	100%	186,400	100%	165,200	100%
Wine sales in cases						
By Channel						
Independent Distributors						
US	61,100	35%	45,300	33%	42,000	31%
International	9,100	5%	5,600	4%	8,700	7%
	70,200	40%	50,900	37%	50,700	38%
Company direct						
California retail	90,200	51%	76,000	55%	71,800	53%
Mailing list	15,300	9%	11,600	8%	12,000	9%
	105,500	60%	87,600	63%	83,800	62%
Total sales	175,700	100%	138,500	100%	134,500	100%

31/12/92, the wine carried $52.73 in product costs. Here's the file showing where our numbers come from.' Evanson gave Sam a thick file folder from his desk.

6.18.22 The file was thick because of the complex production process. Wine isn't produced in a day or even a month. Some wines are effectively 'in production' for years, so the various pools of periodic production costs must be allocated among many different wines from different vintage years. CWG's method was as straightforward as possible, given the complexity of the situation. All of the Cimarron Winery's costs were considered product costs and wound up as Cost of Goods Sold for some particular wine. Grape costs were easy to assign directly to particular wines. Winemaking, bottling and bottle aging costs were collected into pools and allocated equally to specific wines according to the percentage of the total volume processed. Obviously, only wines that were bottled in a year absorbed bottling costs for that year. But all wines held in bulk inventory in a period absorbed their relative proportions of winemaking costs for that period (regardless of what actually happened to the wine) and all wines held in bottled inventory absorbed bottle aging costs. Figure 6.22 shows the yields and the product cost break-down for the 1991 Meritage White.

Figure 6.21 Consolidated balance sheets, The Chalice Wine Group, Ltd (Thousands)

	December 31,		
	1992	**1991**	**1990**
Assets			
Cash	$ 74	$ 78	$ 185
Accounts receivable	3,464	2,650	2,516
Inventories	26,091	24,298	19,601
Other current	1,007	1,154	89
Investment in French Wine Company	12,524	12,524	3,176
Property, plant & equipment (net)	22,454	22,290	19,582
Goodwill (net)	3,297	3,394	3,492
Other	1,503	1,541	509
Total	$70,414	$67,928	$49,150
Liabilities			
S/T notes & current maturities	$15,512	$12,593	$7,906
Accounts payable & accruals	3,522	2,236	2,352
Long-term debt	30,414	31,945	19,658
Other	3,935	4,073	3,643
	53,383	50,847	33,559
Shareholders' equity			
Common stock	16,633	15,942	15,215
Retained earnings	398	1,139	1,376
	17,031	17,081	16,591
Total	$70,414	$67,928	$49,150

The Chalice Group
Consolidated income statements

	1992	**1991**	**1990**
Wine sales	$17,319	$14,951	$14,182
Cost of sales	11,011	8,096	7,296
Selling, general & administrative expenses	4,610	4,119	3,760
Interest expense	2,757	2,334	1,679
Other expense (net)	7	239	293
Income tax	(323)	104	505
Net earnings	$ (741)	$ 58	$ 650
Net earnings per common share	(0.19)	0.02	0.18
Stock price, high	9.75	11.00	11.00
Low	7.00	8.50	7.75

Outdated habits

Figure 6.22 1991 Meritage White product costs

Tons crushed	89.17	
Gallons of juice fermented	14,713	
Gallons aged	13,984	
Gallons of wine produced	13,255	
Cases bottled	5,575	
Production cost	Total	Per Case
Grapes	$73,901	$13.26
Winemaking	117,486	21.07
Bottling	93,657	16.80
Bottle Aging	8,937	1.60
Total	$293,981	$52.73

6.18.23 Sam Davis knew that eventually each of the components of product cost would warrant further analysis. But, for the purpose of constructing the first level of the value chain profitability analysis, he decided to accept CWG's numbers. The task now was to derive a per case operating profit for this wine, and the per case Return on Assets (ROA). An estimate of per case SG&A expenses was derived by applying the percentage of CWG's sales revenue generated by Cimarron to the total corporate SG&A, then dividing by Cimarron's case sales for the year. A similar approach could be used to estimate the CWG assets employed specifically by Cimarron Meritage White. In 1992, the Cimarron winery sold 37,205 cases for total revenues of $2.7 million with a cost of sales of $2.1 million, and a depreciable asset base of $4.9 million set on three acres. Because its bottling line and crushing/pressing equipment were only in operation during a short period each year, overall utilisation of these assets was less than 10 per cent of annual capacity.

6.18.24 The profitability analysis for one case of 1991 Cimarron Meritage White demonstrated the contribution of that wine to the overall financial performance of the Chalice Group according to the cost accounting methods used by the winery. As he went about the task of collecting financial data from other links in the value chain, Sam couldn't help thinking about those product costs that were assigned 'equally' to the various wines. If no two wines are the same, then why should they absorb production costs at the same rate? How are they different, and is the difference relevant? He made a mental note to revisit this question once the first level value chain was complete.

The Vineyard
6.18.25 Cimarron Meritage White is a blend of Sauvignon Blanc and Semillon grapes, neither of which is grown at Cimarron Vineyard. All the

Activity accounting

grapes for this wine are purchased from Pinnacle Vineyards, CWG's partner in the Opera Valley Joint Venture. The price paid in 1991 for both varieties was $812.36/ton (62.42 tons of Sauvignon Blanc and 26.75 tons of Semillon). Total hauling costs from Opera Valley to the winery in Sonoma Valley amounted to $1,463. A review of price information published by The California Department of Agriculture revealed that the average price paid per ton for grapes grown in that district that year was $562.50 for Sauvignon Blanc, and $350 for Semillon. Had these prices been paid by CWG the total grape cost, including hauling, would have been only $45,937 instead of $73,901. The potential incremental $5 per case profit led Sam to ask, 'Bill, why are you spending so much money on grapes?'

> 'The simple answer, Sam, is you get what you pay for. We don't produce average wines, so we don't buy average grapes. We also consider our contract for these grapes in the context of our long-term relationship with Pinnacle and the Opera Valley Joint Venture which is very important to us. But we have to get our costs down, and you've raised a good point. Actually, we've been looking at a 30 acre vineyard in Sonoma County near Cimarron as a potential alternative source of supply. The price is right: $525,000. That's tempting just as a real estate investment. And the land is clearly capable of producing the quality of grapes we need. But since the vine-yard has phylloxera1, it would have to be cleared and replanted. So it's tough to say if it would represent a significant improvement on our $13.26/case grape cost.'

6.18.26 Sam began thinking out loud. 'I need accurate revenue, cost and asset information for a typical vineyard to complete that piece of the value chain, and you need to know if it makes sense for you to develop your own vineyard to provide grapes for the Meritage White. Let's kill two birds with one stone. I know that the University of California Extension Service and the Sonoma County Farm Advisor have done a lot of research on vineyard costs. Let's see what they can tell us.'

6.18.27 Figures 6.23 and 6.24 describe the costs and assets involved in the establishment and operation of a 30 acre vineyard in Sonoma County as of the end of 1992.

6.18.28 With these cost and asset numbers it was possible to complete a profitability analysis for the vineyard (in full production) in terms of each case of 1991 Meritage White sold. Sam assumed revenue for the vineyard would be $812.36/ton, the price paid by Cimarron to Pinnacle Vineyards. This, of course, assumed production of 'better than average' grapes.

6.18.29 It should be noted that vineyard profitability is extremely sensitive to fluctuations in grape prices. A ten-year history of the weighted

Outdated habits

Figure 6.23 Costs per acre to establish and operate a vineyard

	Years				
	1	2	3	4	5 & forward
Yield (tons/acre)			1.5	3.5	6
Total planting costs	5,138	2,440			
Total cultural costs	609	1,062	1,216	1,317	1,317
Total harvest costs @ $120/ton			180	420	720
Total overhead costs	622	622	642	698	718
Total cash costs	6,369	4,124	2,038	2,435	2,755
Depreciation (see Figure 6.24)				843	843
Total				3,278	$3,598[1]

[1] $3,598/Acre = $600/T = $9.59/case (62.5 cases per ton)

Figure 6.24 Assets required to establish and operate a 30 acre vineyard

Investment	Purchase price (new)	Useful life	Salvage value	Annual depreciation
Land (30 plantable acres)	525,000			
Vineyard establishment (A)	339,374	22	0%	15,426
Reservoir	30,000	30	0%	1,000
Buildings	15,750	30	10%	473
Drip irrigation system	52,400	25	10%	1,886
Frost protection system	40,300	25	10%	1,451
Shop tools	10,000	15	10%	600
Pruning equipment	1,200	10	10%	108
ATV, 4wd	6,500	5	10%	1,170
Tractor	29,900	15	10%	1,794
Duster	3,035	10	10%	273
Mower (B)	5,500	10	10%	495
Orchard sprayer	4,560	10	10%	410
Weed sprayer	2,000	10	10%	180
Pickup truck	16,500	7	10%	2,121
Total investment, with new equip.	1,082,019			27,388
* Allowance for used equipment	(24,598)			(2,110)
Total investment, 30 Acre Vineyard	$1,057,421			$25,278

(A) 'Vineyard establishment' is the accumulated cash costs for first three years, net of revenue earned in year 3 using the price paid by Cimarron in 1991 as a proxy value for each ton produced.

(B) Last six items can be purchased used @ an average of 60 per cent of new cost. Allowance is made above (*).

Activity accounting

average market price paid in California for five leading varieties is shown in Figure 6.25. The Sonoma County average prices are always higher than the state average. The 1992 Sonoma County premium is shown in parentheses for each variety.

Figure 6.25 History of California grape prices per ton

Variety[1]	1983	1984	1985	1986	1987
Chardonnay (18%)	$980	$998	$904	$856	$922
Cabernet (32%)	$467	$527	$533	$550	$631
Zinfandel (56%)	$269	$253	$269	$340	$480
Sauvignon Blanc (35%)	$487	$486	$441	$401	$414
Semillon (73%)	$215	$260	$210	$245	$254
Variety[1]	**1988**	**1989**	**1990**	**1991**	**1992**
Chardonnay (18%)	$1,122	$1,225	$1,128	$1,122	$1,038
Cabernet (32%)	$822	$1,032	$977	$918	$872
Zinfandel (56%)	$817	$546	$391	$363	$434
Sauvignon Blanc (35%)	$474	$571	$518	$541	$552
Semillon (73%)	$289	$311	$310	$328	$360

[1] The percentages in parentheses represent the premiums paid to Sonoma County growers over the state averages in 1992.

6.18.30 Although grape cost of $9.59 per case for this vineyard represented an improvement over the $12.99 ($13.26 – $.27 freight) the winery was paying now, was it a compelling argument for CWG to change its make/buy policy on grapes for this wine? Bill Evanson was pensive.

> 'How should we look at this? I suppose we could plant about half the vineyard to supply the Meritage White at cost, and the rest to another variety to sell elsewhere. That would lower our product costs at the winery, and possibly generate an interesting grape business on the side, provided we can predict what the market will want in future years. In light of our current financial situation, it would be a tricky proposition to present to the Board! The fact is that grape and wine production is a capital intensive proposition, and the returns just aren't overwhelming. What do the numbers look like downstream in the value chain?'

The distributor

6.18.31 Stellar Wines is a typical East Coast wine distributor. Stellar's financial statements for 1991 and 1992 are shown in Figure 6.26. In 1992, the company sold 225,000 cases of wine, roughly 50 per cent imported and 50 per cent domestic.

6.18.32 Stellar's product cost for Cimarron Meritage White includes $2.25/case to cover freight from California and state excise tax of $1.56/case.

Outdated habits

Figure 6.26 Stellar Wines financial statements (in thousands)

Balance sheets		
	\multicolumn{2}{c}{December 31,}	
	1992	1991
Assets		
Cash	$ 24	$ 9
Accounts receivable	2,273	1,806
Inventory	6,500	6,592
Equipment (net)	108	105
Other	333	312
Total	$9,238	$8,824
Liabilities		
Note payable, bank	$4,953	$4,794
Accounts payable & accruals	1,735	1,544
Stockholders' equity		
Common stock	10	9
Retained earnings	2,540	2,477
	2,550	2,486
Total	$9,238	$8,824
Income statements		
	Year ended December 31,	
	1992	1991
Sales	$17,078	$15,389
Cost of goods sold	12,771	11,313
Operating expenses	3,394	3,187
Interest expense	425	507
Net income before tax	$488	$381

On all premium wines, Stellar's planned gross margin percentage was 25 per cent. Operating expenses per case do not vary significantly among the various wines that Stellar sells. From this information and the financial statements, Sam determined the operating profit and ROA per case of Meritage White sold by the distributor.

6.18.33 A wine distributor sells wine to both 'on-premise' accounts (restaurants, bars, hotels) and 'off-premise' accounts (grocery stores, liquor stores, wine shops). The profitability of wine sales in on-premise businesses varies considerably with the type of business and the wine pricing philosophy. Some restaurants mark up a bottle of wine 50 cents, others mark it up 250 per cent. 'Typical profitability' is a more meaningful concept when

Activity accounting

applied to off-premise wine sales. Since most of CWG's off-premise wine sales occur in relatively small premium wine shops, it was decided that this type of business should provide the final piece of the value chain.

The retailer

6.18.34 Riverside Wine Company is one of Stellar's best customers. As grocery chains and discount clubs have gained market share, many small premium wine shops have been driven out of business. However, at the top end of the business there remains a demand for service and selection that is difficult to provide in a high volume setting. Figure 6.27 contains selected financial information for Riverside for 1992. As with the distributor, a case is a case. So one way of assigning operating expenses and assets among the cases sold is equal weight. Other approaches are, of course, possible. Sam computed the operating profit and ROA for the retailer as he had for the other players.

Figure 6.27 Riverside Wine Company, 1992

Total Sales	$1,889,916	
Cost of Goods Sold	$1,412,000	
Operating Costs	$438,134	
Profit (before tax)	$39,782	
Cases Sold	14,776	
Total Assets	$719,261	($235,333 of inventory)

Overall value chain

6.18.35 With this last piece of the value chain in place, Sam and Bill stepped back to consider what the numbers meant, and what the strategic implications were for Chalice. Remembering the original question, 'Can this be a good business?', Sam put the profitability figures for the four participants in this value chain together to determine the overall profit margin and the overall return on assets for the industry on every case of 1991 Cimarron Meritage White sold to consumers in retail wine shops.

6.18.36 'Oh well,' sighed Evanson, 'at least it is a beautiful way of life!'

6.18.37 'Yes, but these numbers don't necessarily prove that it can't be profitable. Obviously, some parts are more profitable than others. But this is only the story as told by your cost accounting methods. Are you confident that those methods provide accurate measures of your costs for individual wines? I have some doubts.'

6.18.38 'So do I. But the methods are fairly standard for the industry, and the auditors are satisfied. I told you at the outset, every wine is a complex

Outdated habits

product in the context of a complex product mix. Maybe it is too complex for truly accurate cost accounting.'

6.18.39 'Maybe, maybe not. But it's worth a try. The trick is to get your production costs out of the periods in which they happen and into the activities that cause them. Then the activity-based costs can be allocated according to the participation of particular wines in each activity. Under the periodic system, a year old wine that sleeps through the following harvest in a barrel still absorbs some of the new costs of crushing, pressing and fermenting. That can't be right. Let's take another look at the breakdown of the product costs for the Meritage White.'

Winery costs revisited

6.18.40 Sam knew the production cost of $52.73/case from Figure 6.22 was a very crude aggregate average cost. Upon careful reflection, he concluded that the winemaking process can be viewed as involving three distinct stages:

Stage 1 (crushing, pressing and fermenting)

Stage 2 (fining, filtering, bulk aging)

Stage 3 (preparation for bottling)

6.18.41 But at CWG, all wines shared equally in the allocation of all winemaking cost, based on processing volumes. The 1991 Meritage White was made (crushed, pressed and fermented) in the fourth quarter of 1991. It was bulk aged for nine months in 1992, and was prepared for bottling in the fourth quarter of 1992. Yet this wine's allocation of winemaking cost was a simple 7 per cent of the 1991 total and 6 per cent of the 1992 total, based on its share of total volume processed in each year. The allocation of $21.07 per case missed all the refinement which an ABC analysis could bring. After a careful review of all cost categories and a careful analysis of activities, Sam prepared Figure 6.28 showing a breakdown of winemaking cost, by stages, for 1991 and 1992, with usage data for the 1991 Meritage White.

Figure 6.28 Winemaking cost – ABC approach

	1991	1992
Stage 1	$285,000[1]	$268,000
Stage 2	571,000	559,000[2]
Stage 3	57,000	56,000
Total	$913,000	$883,000

[1] Including $12,700 of barrel depreciation, because some white wines are barrel fermented.
[2] Including $154,900 of barrel depreciation.

345

Activity accounting

The 1991 Meritage White vintage represented 18 per cent of the wine made in 1991, 15 per cent of stage 2 costs in 1992, and 28 per cent of the wine prepared for bottling in 1992.

6.18.42 Sam also discovered that the $16.80 per case for bottling was a very simple overall average allocation. He found, for example, that the cost of wooden shipping boxes was allocated across all wines bottled even though Meritage White was shipped in much cheaper corrugated cartons. Meritage White also used cheaper than average bottles and labels. Figure 6.29 shows a comparison of the average approach and the ABC approach to bottling cost.

Figure 6.29 Bottling cost – per case

Cost category	Average cost	ABC cost for Meritage White
Labour	1.16	0.75
Supplies	0.07	0.07
Bottles	6.43	5.00
Corks	2.39	2.39
Capsules	1.19	1.19
Labels	1.99	1.50
Wooden boxes	0.55	0
Taxes	3.02	3.02
Total	16.80	13.92

6.18.43 Third, Sam discovered that barrel depreciation was a very complex issue, involving French oak barrels that had risen in cost from $362 in 1988 to $650 in 1993. White wines are both fermented (three months) and aged in barrels whereas red wines are fermented in tanks. But, red wines are aged two years in the barrels versus only nine months for white whites. Yet all barrels at the Cimarron winery are just depreciated, straight-line, over four years with barrel depreciation as one line item in winemaking cost. Of the $21.07 winemaking cost for the 1991 Meritage White, $4.03 (19 per cent) was for barrel depreciation. Sam had no intuition about how a more accurate ABC assignment of barrel depreciation would affect the $4.03 number. Figure 6.30 was constructed to estimate actual consumption of barrel cost, using estimated market values and the actual barrel usage plan for the 1991 Meritage White.

6.18.44 As the cost of French oak barrels had risen 80 per cent in five years, Cimarron had decided they needed at least to experiment with American oak barrels which had stayed at about $250 throughout. But the winemakers felt sure that French oak imparted better taste to the wine. Sam prepared the following summary table comparing barrel depreciation cost for various costing options:

Outdated habits

Figure 6.30 Barrel depreciation

	French oak barrels						American oak barrels
Year purchased	**1988**	**1989**	**1990**	**1991**	**1992**	**1993**	**All years**
Cost new	$362	$418	$515	$539	$608	$650	$250
Declining value							
After 1 year	209	257	269	304	325	125	(50% of cost of new barrel)
After 2 years	129	135	152	163	?	63	(25% of cost of new barrel)
After 3 years	67	76	81	?	?	32	(12.5% of cost of new barrel)
After 4 years	40	40	40	40	40	20	($40 imported/ $20 domestic)

French oak

	Depreciation in 1991	**Depreciation in 1992**
1989 barrels	59 (135–76)	36 (76–40)
1990 barrels	117 (269–152)	71 (152–81)
1991 barrels	235 (539–304)	141 (304–163)

Fermentation and aging plan for 1991 Meritage White (all French Oak)

Ferment in 25 per cent new barrels, 25 per cent one year old, and 50 per cent two years old. Age in the newest barrels used for fermenting.

Ferment:	92 barrels from 1991	Aging:	92 barrels from 1991
(3 months)	92 barrels from 1990	(9 months)	92 barrels from 1990
	184 barrels from 1989		49 barrels from 1989
Total	368 barrels*		233 barrels*

14,713 gallons / 40 gals/bbl = 368 barrels   *13,984 gallons / 60 gals/bbl = 233 barrels

(The barrel is only 2/3 filled for fermentation)

Barrel depreciation (French oak) for the 1991 Meritage White

Ferment
92 × $235 × 1/4 year = $5405
92 × $117 × 1/4 year = $2691
184 × $59 × 1/4 year = $2714

Age
92 × $141 × 3/4 year = $9729
92 × $71 × 3/4 year = $4899
49 × $36 × 3/4 year = $1323
Total = $26,761 ($4.80 per case)

Activity accounting

Barrel depreciation cost per case (1991 Meritage White)	
Average costing	$4.03
ABC approach (3 stage costing)	?
'Declining value' depreciation with actual barrel usage:	
French oak barrels	$4.80
Domestic oak barrels	?
Replacement cost depreciation	?

6.18.45 Based on his revised calculations, Sam now estimated the product cost of the 1991 Meritage White, for strategic assessment purposes. He also adjusted the overall value chain accordingly.

Lyford Winery

6.18.46 As one example of a very different approach to the value chain, Sam was aware of Lyford Winery which had been founded in Sonoma County in 1981. It was constructed as a state-of-the-art winemaking showplace with no expense spared in either the production of the wines or in the effort to build the brand in the market place. After the untimely death of the founder, the company was sold to a consortium of several other winery properties which ultimately failed. The winery was sold out of bankruptcy to another California wine company. The brand name was sold to a French company. Wine for the brand was sourced from the bulk wine market. Processing services were purchased from custom suppliers under the direction of the original winemaker who was retained by the French company.

6.18.47 Figure 6.31 gives the per case cost structure for one of Lyford's more recent releases, a 1991 Meritage White. The wine was a blend of three different varieties, each purchased on the bulk market. The final blend was 85 per cent Sauvignon Blanc, 13 per cent Semillon and 2 per cent White Muscat.

Figure 6.31 1991 Lyford Meritage White

Product costs per case	
Bulk Wine Cost	$9.26
Bottling	2.28
Corks	2.37
Capsules	1.16
Labels	0.70
Bottles	4.60
Lyford overhead & supplies	2.02
Wine tax	3.02
Total	$25.41

Outdated habits

6.18.48 The product costs shown in this exhibit tell nearly the entire story of this wine. The 'winery' has virtually no capital assets beyond leased office and warehouse space and working capital (assume 30 per cent of sales). All of the services required to bring the product from the bulk wine market to distribution can be purchased either from wineries with surplus capacity or from custom winemaking operations. An allocation of marketing expenses added only about $1.09 to the per case cost of the wine. Leased space and equipment added about another $5 per case.

6.18.49 Lyford sold the wine to wholesale distributors for $45.00 per case, with a target retail price of $7.50 per bottle.*

*Lyford Winery – the value chain	
Sales	45
Costs	?
Margin	?
Assets	?
ROA	?
Price to distributor	45.00
+ Freight & taxes	+3.81
Delivered	= 48.81
Price to retailer (÷.75)	= 65.00
Price to consumer (÷.75)	= 86.67
	= ~7.22/Bottle (~$7.50 with sales tax)

6.18.50 Sam knew the Chalice winemakers would totally reject this 'bogus' approach to 'winemaking'. But somebody was buying the wines and apparently enjoying them. Sam had to admit that even he thought the 1991 Lyford Meritage White showed very well in tastings. Could Chalice learn anything from the Lyford story?

Overview

Value chain analysis

6.18.51 As with many organisations considering the implementation of an ABC system, the company is facing negative financial trends. Total sales are increasing, but cost of sales is increasing faster and average revenue per case has declined. In addition, CWG has experienced a significant increase in interest expense. Over two years, net income has deteriorated from plus 5 per cent to minus 4 per cent of sales. Figure 6.32 is a condensed summary of the comparative income statements.

6.18.52 The balance sheet has grown by $21 million (43 per cent) in the past two years. About half of the growth is due to the investment in the

Activity accounting

Figure 6.32 Condensed comparative income statements, The Chalice Wine Group

Year Ended December 31						
	1992 Dollars[1]	% Sales	1991 Dollars[1]	% Sales	1990 Dollars[1]	% Sales
Wine Sales	$17,319	100%	$14,951	100%	$14,182	100%
Gross Margin	$6,309	36%	$6,855	46%	$6,886	49%
Operating Income	$1,699	10%	$2,736	18%	$3,126	22%
Interest Expense	$2,757	16%	$2,334	16%	$1,679	12%
Net Earnings	($741)	−4%	$58	0%	$650	5%
Cases Sold	175,700		138,500		134,500	
Average Revenue Per Case	$98.57		$107.95		$105.45	

[1] (Dollar amounts in thousands except per case)

French wine company through which Chalice controls several foreign wine brands in the US. Most of the rest of the asset growth relates to several additional California brands it controls and the pending Washington State brand. This all becomes extremely relevant when the issue of alternative wine distribution is raised. Even so, CWG is a very small fish in a very large pond.

6.18.53 The value chain analysis in Figure 6.33 can be assembled from the above information. 'Winery' refers to Cimarron only, not CWG. Vineyard dollars and case sales volume come from the price paid to and yields obtained from Pinnacle Vineyards. It is assumed that the vineyard only produces grapes for the Meritage White.

6.18.54 Figure 6.34 reorganises the value in flow chart format. For all players, the *average* per-case operating cost number is used for the Meritage White. This is probably fair enough because, for the most part, one case of wine requires the same treatment as any other. An obvious exception is a new wine requiring an elaborate product launch or a distressed wine requiring an extraordinary sales effort. However, the Meritage White is an established product that moves well.

6.18.55 The number for assets per case was derived in the same way, but this is suspect. More expensive wines are certainly responsible for a greater

Outdated habits

Figure 6.33 Value chain profitability analysis

	Vineyard	Winery	Distributor	Retailer
Total sales	$146	$2,697	$17,078	$1,890
Cost of sales	n/a	$2,098	$12,771	$1,412
Operating costs	$108	$719[1]	$3,394	$438
Profit	$38	($120)	$913	$40
Total assets	$1,057	$9,500[2]	$9,238	$719
Cases per year	11,253	37,205	225,000	14,776
Asset turnover	0.14	0.28	1.85	2.63

[1] 2.7/17.3 · $4,610
[2] $4.9 + WC of 17 per cent · $2.7 = $4.6

Per Case 1991 Cimarron Meritage White

	Vineyard	Winery	Distributor	Retailer	Overall
Revenue	$12.99	$76.00	$106.41	$142.43	$142.43
Cost of sales	n/a	$52.73	$79.81	$106.41	
Gross margin	n/a	$23.27	$24.19	$36.02	
Gross margin per cent	n/a	30.62%	23.26%	25.3%	
Operating costs	$9.59	$19.29	$15.08	$29.65	
Operating profit	$3.40	$3.98	$11.52	$6.37	$25.27
Operating profit per cent	26.17%	5.23%	10.8%	4.5%	17.8%
Assets	$93.97	$255.00	$41.06	$48.68	$439.00
Pre tax ROA	3.7%	1.6%	28%	13%	5.7%

(Aggregate dollar amounts in thousands)

percentage of inventory than cheaper wines, so in reality the Meritage White may be even less profitable than it appears.

6.18.56 This profitability analysis assumes that the product cost used by the winery is correct. The winery is by far the most complex stage in the value chain, and really the only player with materially relevant cost allocation issues. The next major step in the case is to apply an activity-based allocation method to the winery's product costs. But let's first consider the vineyard stage.

6.18.57 Grapes: make or buy? CWG faces a make/buy decision for the Meritage White. It is fairly easy to see from Figure 6.23 that after four years, without financing costs, CWG can get its grape costs down to around $600/ton. It is currently paying $829/ton, including hauling. This amounts to a decrease in grape costs of $3.66/case, which helps, but not much. The proposed new vineyard could potentially supply twice the fruit required for the

Activity accounting

Figure 6.34 The value chain – 1991 Cimarron Meritage White (per case)

Vineyard			
Revenue	12.99		P/S = 26.2%
Operating costs	9.59		S/A = 0.14
Margin	3.40		ROA = 3.6%
Assets	93.97	+$.27 handling cost	
Winery			
Revenue Costs	76.00		
Grapes	13.26		
Winemaking	21.07		P/S = 5.2%
Bottling	16.80		S/A = 0.30
Bottle Aging	1.60		ROA = 1.6%
SG&A	19.29	+ $2.25 freight	
Margin	3.98	+ 1.56 tax	
Assets	255.00		
Distributor			
Revenue	106.41		P/S = 10.8%
Wine Cost	79.81		S/A = 2.59
Operating Cost	15.08		ROA = 28.0%
Margin	11.52		
Assets	41.06		
Retailer			
Revenue	142.43		
Wine Cost	106.41		P/S = 4.5%
Operating Costs	29.65		S/A = 2.93
Margin	6.37		ROA = 13.0%
Assets	48.68		
The overall value chain			
Revenue	$143.43	P/S =	17.8%
Profit	$25.27	S/A =	0.32%
Assets	$4.39	ROA =	5.7%

Meritage White. The extra grapes could be of any variety and be sold on the open market. Figure 6.25 is intended to show the volatility of the market for wine grapes. A grower must commit to a variety several years before any significant revenue is generated. In the meantime, it is the wine-buying public that ultimately determines the value of the crop. In the United States, this can be a crapshoot. Consider the price effect of the White Zinfandel phenomenon of the mid to late 1980s.

6.18.58 What Figure 6.25 does not show is the variability of vineyard yields relative to a completely uncontrollable element: the weather. No decision to plant an agricultural product can be made without regard to the associated risks, especially a product that requires as much money and time to generate a return. Finally, another look at CWG's financial statements indi-

Outdated habits

cates a heavily leveraged company with little cash and a relatively weak stock price. Realistically, the company is not in a position to undertake a speculative vineyard project at this time, even if the potential ROA were much greater.

6.18.59 ABC allocation of winemaking costs. The first step in assigning the periodic winemaking costs into the activities that cause them is to assign all the winery assets to production stages. Three discrete (realistically outsourceable) stages have been identified. Stage 1: crushing, pressing and fermenting. Technically, wine is 'produced' in this stage. Stage 2: fining, filtering and aging. In this stage, the wine is 'fine-tuned' in preparation for bottling. Stage 3: bottling. Using the 'clues' provided by the winemaker, the following cost assignment schedule can be derived.

1991 Meritage White ABC for winemaking						
Stage 1	$285,000	(1991)	∞	18%	=	$53,600
Stage 2	$559,000	(1992)	∞	15%	=	$85,600
Stage 3	$56,000	(1992)	∞	28%	=	$16,000
(Including barrel depreciation of $25,648 = 4.60/case)						
						$155,200
						5,575 cases
Per case					=	$27.84

The barrel depreciation issue

6.18.60 The ABC version of winemaking cost is flawed by failure explicitly to account for barrel depreciation. By using the ratio of stage 1 barrel depreciation to total depreciation for 1992, an estimate of stage 1 barrel depreciation for 1991 can be made, and a number for barrel costs for the 1991 Meritage White can be backed out of the ABC winemaking cost number.

Barrel costs per ABC analysis	
Per cent '91 MW in '91 Stage 1	18%
Barrel depreciation in '91 Stage 1	$12,700
Amount to '91 MW	$2,286
per cent '91 MW in '92 Stage 2	15%
Barrel depreciation in '92 Stage 2	$154,900
Amount to '91 MW	$23,235
Total barrel depreciation to '91 MW	$25,551
Barrel depreciation per case	$4.60

Activity accounting

6.18.61 A more realistic and wine-specific approach would consider the 'fair value' of barrel costs for the 1991 Meritage White. Two depreciation schemes may be explored which are equivalent if barrel prices are stable. However, French oak prices have certainly not been stable, largely because of exchange rate changes. Scheme 2 is the correct approach, and illustrates the effect of rising barrel prices on the depreciation and residual value of used barrels. But scheme 2 is also very complicated.

6.18.62 Depreciation scheme 1: 50 per cent of the cost of a new barrel is consumed in the first year. In the second year, 50 per cent of the remainder (another 25 per cent of the cost) is consumed. And so on through four years, after which the barrel is worth $40.

Barrel Depreciation (replacement cost – scheme 1)	
1991 = $539	
1992 = $608	
All barrels being used in 1991	
New	(539 ∞ 1/2) = 270
1 yr	(539 ∞ 1/4) = 135
2 yrs	(539 ∞ 1/8) = 67
All barrels used in 1992	
New	= 304
1 yr	= 152
2 yrs	= 76
Ferment	[92 ∞ $270 + 92 ∞ $135 + 184 ∞ $67]
	∞ 1/4 = $12,397
Aging	[92 ∞ $152 + 92 ∞ $ 76 + 49 ∞ $36]
	∞ 3/4 = $17,055
	$30,252 = $5.43/case

6.18.63 Depreciation scheme 2: A more sophisticated scheme takes into account that a one-year-old barrel is worth 50 per cent of the cost of a new barrel. That value, subtracted from its cost, is the depreciation for the first year. A two-year-old barrel is worth 25 per cent of the cost of a new barrel, so that value subtracted from its value after one year is the depreciation for the second year. And so on through four years, after which the barrel is worth $40.

6.18.64 A 60-gallon barrel can only hold 40 gallons when used for fermenting. Therefore 14,713 gallons of juice divided by 40 gives 368 as the number of barrels needed to ferment. After fermentation, 13,984 gallons remain, divided by 60 = 233 barrels. The 135 surplus barrels (368 minus 233) were two years old at the beginning of this fermentation. At the end they are valued as 2?-year-old barrels.

6.18.65 If American oak barrels were used, these two schemes merge since the cost of a barrel did not change from $250 over the years 1989–1992.

Depreciation scheme 2: French oak				
Barrel purchased in:	1992	1991	1990	1989
Exchange rate, 7/1:	$.19/ff	$.16/ff	$.18/ff	$.15/ff
Cost of new barrel:	$608	539.00	$515	$418
Value after 1 year:	?	304.00	$269	$258
Value after 2 years:	?	?	$152	$135
Value after 3 years:	?	?	?	$76
Value after 4 years:	$40	40.00	$40	$40

Barrel age:	New	1 year	2 years		Totals
Barrels used for:	stages 1 and 2			Stage 1	
per cent of total:	25%	25%	combined 50%		100%
No. of barrels:	92	92	49	135	368
Cost per barrel:	$235	$117	$59	$29	
Total cost:	$21,594	$10,797	$2,875	$3,961	$39,228
Cost per case:	$3.87	$1.94	$0.52	$0.71	$7.04
		Total = $7.04/case			

American oak barrels

	Depreciation
1st yr	$125
2nd yr	$60
3rd yr	$33
4th yr	$12

Same for 1991 & 1992 barrels

Ferment: (92 ∞ $125 + 92 ∞ $60 + 184 ∞ $33) ∞ 1/4 = $5,773
Aging: (92 ∞ $60 + 92 ∞ $33 + 49 ∞ $12) ∞ 3/4 = $6,858

                                    $12,631
÷ 5775   = $2.19/case

6.18.66 Is the right to say 'fermented and aged in French oak barrels' worth $4.85 per case ($7.04–$2.19)? In either case, the business problem for Cimarron and the Meritage White cannot be resolved by 'smarter' analysis of the costs at the winery stage alone.

6.18.67 A summary of several different approaches to revised winery cost is shown in Figure 6.35.

6.18.68 The Lyford Wines Value Chain. Figure 6.36 shows the economics for Lyford Wines in the value chain. Only the winery stage is different. Returns for Lyford are phenomenal. Returns for the distributor and retailer would be lower because with operating costs assigned on a per-case basis,

Activity accounting

Figure 6.35 Product cost (1991 Meritage White), several versions

	Per CWG	'ABC'	ABC & FV Bbls.	'Make' grapes	'Avg.' grapes & Am. oak bbls.
Grapes	13.26	13.26	13.26	9.59	8.26
Winemaking	21.07	27.84	30.28	30.28	25.43
Bottling	1.60	1.60	1.60	1.60	1.60
Bottle aging	16.80	13.92	13.92	13.92	13.92
	52.73	56.62	59.06	55.39	49.21
Depreciation Included	4.03	4.60	7.04	7.04	2.19

they do less well on lower-priced wines. Should CWG seriously consider the 'short cuts' which characterise Lyford's approach?

6.18.69 Obviously, CWG is not interested in making or selling a wine like this. Cimarron is a 'serious' winery. And, as a result, it earns a seriously low ROA. Lyford is a 'business venture' rather than a 'serious wine'. But it shows reasonably well in comparative tastings and very well in the financial report!

6.18.70 Business issues for CWG. The value chain calculations reveal that the big money is made down the chain in distribution. This results from the power wholesale distributors have in many regions because the repeal of prohibition granted these regions the power to separate manufacturing from distribution and retailing for alcoholic beverages – so called 'three-tier' laws. Retailers will make normal margins because of competition. Manufacturers of premium wines make very low returns – a 'hobby business'. Distributors have power in both directions and use it to extract a disproportionate share of the overall returns. (See Figure 6.36.)

6.18.71 If CWG really want to be 'profitable', they should consider ways to become part of wholesale distribution in the major states. Figure 6.37 illustrates the phenomenon of growing concentration in California among the wholesale wine distributors.

6.18.72 There is an interesting link here to strategy considerations relating to 'core competencies'. What happens when a company's core competencies do not make money in the value chain and the place where money is made is not its competency? This is precisely the situation faced by the Meritage White wine of Cimarron Winery. Figure 6.38 identifies key business concerns relating to value chain analysis in the context of ABC.

Outdated habits

Figure 6.36 Lyford Wines: a different approach

Vineyard				
Revenue			P/S =	
Operating costs			S/A =	?
Margin			ROA =	
Assets				
Winery				
Revenue costs				
Grapes			P/S =	30%
Winemaking			S/A =	Infinite
Bottling			ROA =	Very high!
Bottle aging				
SG&A		+$2.25 freight		
Margin	45.00	+1.56 tax		
Assets				
	9.26			
Distributor	14.13			
Revenue	0		P/S =	1.7%
Wine cost	8.11		S/A =	1.58
Operating cost	13.50		ROA =	2.7%
Margin	0			
Assets				
Retailer	65.00			
Revenue	48.81			
Wine cost	15.08			
Operating costs	1.11		P/S =	
Margin	41.06		S/A =	
Assets			ROA =	Negative

Lyford sells for $7.25/bottle and the winery earns $13.50/case with zero investment.
Cimarron sells for $11.95/bottle and the winery earns 1 per cent per cent ROA. The two wines compare well in comparative blind tastings!

Figure 6.37 The evolution of 'Buyer Power' in California. Winery proliferation/distributor consolidation

	1976	1986	1992	1993
California Wineries	240	580	686	700
Wine distributors in California	28	15	7	6
Wineries per distributor	9	39	98	117
Nationwide	1992 market share			
4 Largest wineries	64% and growing!			
5 Largest distributors	22% and growing!			

Activity accounting

Figure 6.38 Understanding the business issues for profit improvement

(1) Understand the value chain: Where is the money spent? Where are the assets invested? Where are the returns earned?
(2) For key steps in the chain: Benchmark competitive success Identify core competencies for success in 'best practices' companies Identify key cost drivers
(3) What is our strategy? Convert to key programs (multi-year) Convert programs to key projects & tactics (one year) Identify the relevant strategic performance measures (SPMs) Milestone reporting of SPMs – manage the right drivers well and financial results take care of themselves!

(Source: adapted with permission Carr 1997.)

6.19 The choice of software

6.19.1 Software issues are important to address in the implementation of ABM systems. Although independent consultants may be hired to help install ABM software packages, these packages generally come with documentation and tutorials. Support is also usually available for a fee from the producer of the software.

6.19.2 Presently most packages operate in a Windows environment, and multi-user formats and enhanced graphical capabilities are becoming increasingly common. Baxendale (1997) has noted that the emphasis appears to be in developing user-friendly packages that can be widely accessed and used by people on the shop floor as well as by managers in corporate offices. There is a trend toward providing a link between ABC/ABM software and ERP systems (see Chapter **5**). Additionally, many of the software companies are designing their software to make use of the global information sharing capabilities of the Internet. Ultimately, generic benchmarking data on pools, cost drivers and related activity accounting data may become available as the drive towards full e-business functionality takes hold in more companies. Value chain hubs and B2B market spaces may eventually provide access to ABC data benchmarks as one form of content.

6.20 Activity-based budgetary control

6.20.1 The main difference between an activity-based and a conventional budget according to Börjesson (1997) is that the latter considers only the consumption of resources without reference to activities.

Activity-based budgetary control

6.20.2 Caution is needed when interpreting the actual results. Evaluation of the results must consider that misjudgements may have occurred not only about the resource consumption of the activities but also about the estimated activity volume. There can be errors in estimates of the resources required to accomplish the planned activities. A shortfall in outputs compared with the plan may occur because of under-estimates of the resources necessary to accomplish the work required, or the budget evaluation may reveal an under-utilisation of a correctly estimated resource supply. These issues must be kept in mind when interpreting figures of resource usage, especially when the workload is lower than estimated.

6.20.3 As for correcting possible resource misallocations, the problem is smaller if more resources are required than expected because of a larger actual workload than forecasted. When increases in resource supply are required to achieve the objectives set by the department, the activity-based budget compares actual with forecasted results (i.e., comparisons are made for both workload and resources), thus providing relevant information for managers according to Börjesson (1997).

6.20.4 A problem can arise when the resource supply turns out to be excessive or when improvement efforts free up capacity. The activity-based budgetary information may in such circumstances reveal the under-utilisation of resources, which means that managers must take action to realise any benefits. The freed-up resources must either be eliminated or redeployed for other value-added activities. Otherwise, past inaccuracies will recur in future budgetary plans.

What activity-based budgeting can bring

6.20.5 According to Börjesson (1997), an activity-based budget has several advantages over a conventional budget. The comparisons of resource consumption and actual activity volume are the most important because they make it possible to evaluate efficiency.

6.20.6 Indirect activity costs may be controlled both because the budget makes it easier to question the resources needed to fulfil the department's objective and by its report of how well the activities are performed. An activity-based approach integrated into a company's budgetary system provides more detailed information about indirect costs and could reveal inaccuracies in spending for specific overhead resources. Such an approach provides the means for improving the usage of these resources without adversely impacting competitiveness.

6.20.7 Moreover, integrating activity cost and budgetary information helps to disseminate activity-based thinking throughout the organisation. As

Activity accounting

activity-based information gains prominence, it will be regarded as information useful outside just the accounting function. The following case illustrates this.

A case study: activity-based budgeting in action

6.20.8 To illustrate how activity-based budgeting can be implemented, consider the following case study documented by Börjesson (1997). In 1993, Hagglunds Drives AB, a large Swedish manufacturing firm, prepared prototype activity-based budgets in two departments. These served as a prototype for the company's ABC system; ultimately the whole company engaged in analysis by activity. The information is used for control, without having fully replaced information from the company's traditional budget.

6.20.9 Hagglunds develops and produces large, high-torque hydraulic motors and power transmission units. Some 95 per cent of the products are exported. The market is highly competitive; Hagglunds has a 5 per cent market share. Hagglunds' products are unique in that competitors can offer only substitute solutions. The Swedish unit employs over 200 people, almost half being white-collar employees.

6.20.10 Hagglunds is organised into five functions, of which the manufacturing function is the largest. The manufacturing process includes both machining and assembling and is characterised by long machining times, high value added and tight tolerances. The manufacturing function had previously been changed by a new flow-oriented shop-floor layout, decentralisation of responsibility and job enlargement, a project that led to considerable increases in productivity. But decreasing sales and falling prices forced Hagglunds to search for ways to become more cost efficient. Costs in the manufacturing function had already been cut; what remained was to improve cost control of the indirect functions. Therefore, an activity-based approach was initiated.

Product costing first
6.20.11 The activity-based approach started with a focus on product costing, which led to preliminary calculations of product costs. Hagglunds's competitive market situation made it impossible to change its product mix. To increase profitability, therefore, Hagglunds had to reduce costs and focus on activity control.

6.20.12 Activity analyses were undertaken to get a better understanding of both cost and organisational behaviour. The organisation was reluctant to adopt activity-based thinking; old practices felt safe and convenient. The company's managers finally determined that the only way to implement activity-based thinking was to integrate it with an existing process to which many people were committed – namely, the annual budgeting process. Therefore, a prototype activity-based budget for 1993 was implemented in the accounting department. The prototype and the year-to-date evaluation for the first five months of 1993 for the order receiving department are described below.

The order receiving department

6.20.13 The order receiving department has seven full-time employees. Their primary occupation is processing customer orders, distribution arrangements, and some inventory storage planning. The department's budget comprises roughly 2 per cent of Hagglunds' total annual costs.

6.20.14 Under the conventional budget, resource consumption was estimated based on past actuals. Thus, the previous year's result (i.e., resource consumption) plus or minus a few percentage points essentially determined the next year's resource consumption. Slack was – more or less intentionally – incorporated into the budget to make future budgets easier to attain.

6.20.15 The conventional budget included 18 cost accounts, of which two were salary accounts. These accounts were retained in the activity-based budget. Evaluations of the department's performance occurred quarterly and annually by checking spending in these 18 different cost accounts. The focus was thus on the resources consumed without reference to the actual workload.

6.20.16 The preliminary forecast for 1993 based on the conventional budget indicated that the annual costs for the order receiving department should end up at 3.8 million Swedish crowns (SEK), which was the same as in 1992. Yet management had decided that a 4 per cent cost reduction was necessary.

Preparation of the activity-based budget

6.20.17 The activity analysis in the order receiving department developed as follows. First, employees' tasks were mapped and their time estimated, which resulted in 11 defined activities. The next step was logically to link the cost accounts to these activities without considering costs – i.e., a general relationship between activities and cost accounts was developed. The costs in each cost account were then examined and assigned only to those activities that were logically related to the costs. The data came from the previous year's total in each cost account.

Activity accounting

6.20.18 The company's directive to reduce costs led to reductions for each cost assignment. No explicit resource drivers were defined; the allocations were made based on estimates that managers and employees made. This stepwise cost allocation (i.e., links were first established between activities and accounts, then the costs were allocated to the activities) led to budgeted activities and costs and to figures represented the forecasted resource consumption for 1993.

Questioning resource requirements
6.20.19 The employees responsible for preparing the budget started to doubt that the resource requirements indicated by the previous year's figures really were needed to fulfil the activity's objective. Consequently, the department managed to cut more than 4 per cent and even grant employees a salary increase.

6.20.20 Managers argue that the activity-based approach for preparing the budget at Hagglunds facilitated the detection of inaccuracies in estimates based on the previous year's resource consumption. The adjustments made for 1993 would not have been accepted without the interactive cost assignment with reference to the activities; the inaccuracies would never have come to light.

6.20.21 The activity-based budget considers only costs for resources supplied. A volume measure is necessary to form a basis for the upcoming evaluation of efficiency at Hagglunds. The third step for preparing the budget, therefore, was to determine activity triggers and outputs of the activities – i.e., to determine what caused the activities and to define physical volume-related output measures. (This was possible for all but two of the 11 activities; two of the activities were thus left without triggers and output measures.) The volume of activities for the budget period was also forecasted and expressed as the number of activity outputs. Based on this chart, a total cost per output of each activity (i.e., cost per unit of activity) could be determined.

6.20.22 The forecasted workload in the order receiving department expressed as the number of times the defined activities will be performed during the year. It also shows the total annual cost for the individual activities. Note especially the difference between the activity costs of activities 8 and 9: the order receiving cost for a non-standard product is twice that for a standard product.

Activity-based budgets as standards for performance evaluation
6.20.23 The simultaneous consideration of workload and resource

Activity-based budgetary control

requirements provides a way to measure a department's performance. Comparing the forecasted activity outputs with the annual outputs provides information about whether the workload is larger or smaller than estimated.

6.20.24 If the actual activity volume is lower than forecasted, then the estimated resource requirements are too large. If the estimate about resource requirements per output was correct, excess resources exist. If, instead, activity volume is higher than forecasted, the resources for accomplishing the work were either used more efficiently than expected or the estimate was too generous because a higher activity volume could be performed with fewer resources than estimated. Over-capacity – both hidden over-capacity and over-capacity caused by changed conditions – is thus revealed.

6.20.25 In cases of resource shortage, additional resources may be justified by an increased activity volume. Year-to-date evaluations about activity volume thus provide information so that resource supplies can be adjusted if needed. Excess resources can be redeployed for other activities or additional resources can be requested. The budgeting process thus shows where corrections need to be made for the next year.

6.20.26 The most important advantage of an activity-based budget over conventional budgets according to Börjesson (1997) is that it simplifies evaluations of efficiency. Lack of good white-collar performance measurements has long been a major obstacle for process improvement. Measurements such as those provided by an activity-based budget partially address this problem.

6.20.27 Implementing an activity-based budget provides an opportunity to start the continuous process of analysing and streamlining indirect work. It may not be the breakthrough for performance measurement of indirect work, but it is a tool that can be used in challenging the overhead dilemma which many enterprises face.

(Source: Börjesson, 1997.)

Chapter 7
Time and cost management

7.1 Product life-cycle costing

7.1.1 Life-cycle considerations are now important across a large number of industries as new products are developed and replaced increasingly rapidly. It is no longer the case that once developed, a product can maintain acceptability from the consumers' perspective over a long time period. Producers survey markets for potential improvements in exchange for potential profits and consumers screen products to identify state-of-the-art features in the right mix at the right price.

7.1.2 A product's life-cycle begins with the initial product specification and ends with the withdrawal of the product from the market place. The production-related stages include product conception and design, product process and development, and production and logistics. Figure 7.1 offers a graphical outline of the stages at which funds are committed for a particular product and the actual cash outflows entailed. A very large portion of the funds committed coincides with product conception and 80 per cent of the expenditure is often determined before the start of production.

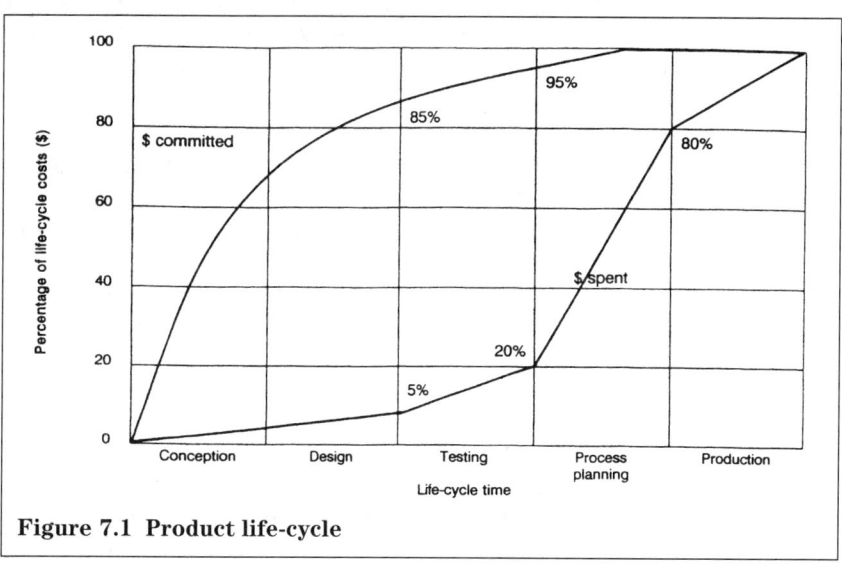

Figure 7.1 Product life-cycle

Time and cost management

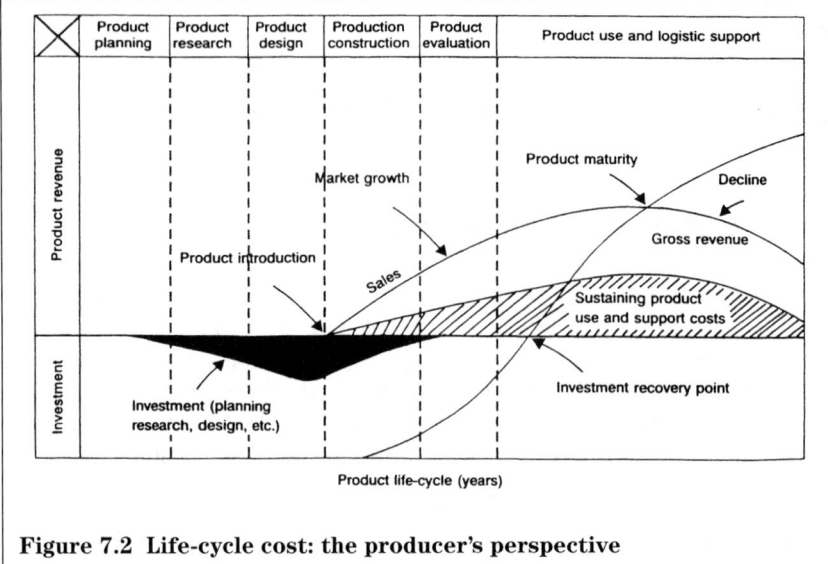

Figure 7.2 Life-cycle cost: the producer's perspective

7.1.3 Figure 7.2 provides a perspective from the producer's point of view. The curves depict the flow of cash throughout the life-cycle. Starting out in the negative, the curve that touches the bottom of the figure tracks cumulative cash flows. When it crosses the horizontal axis then positive cash flows accrue. Timing becomes crucial, and a costing system closely associated with that timing is important in order to make reasonable decisions about products, particularly those of the go/no-go kind. Figure 7.3 shows a sequence of decisions made throughout the life-cycle alongside the cost impact.

7.1.4 Suppose that an engineer begins by trying to find out the general configuration of an engine. Do we need a four cylinder, a six cylinder or an eight cylinder? Do we need a 90 degree angle if it is a V configuration? How many valves are we going to have? The manufacturing processes that are selected will have future impact in terms of materials management. Whatever manufacturing process is adopted, the structure of that process – the way plants are set up, what is fabrication, what is assembly, etc. – has a tremendous impact in terms of materials management. The early decisions are crucial to that whole process.

7.1.5 Each time decisions are made at a particular stage of the process, financial analyses are required. In fact, the outcomes of those decisions will become cost drivers throughout the later stages, just as the outcomes of

Product life-cycle costing

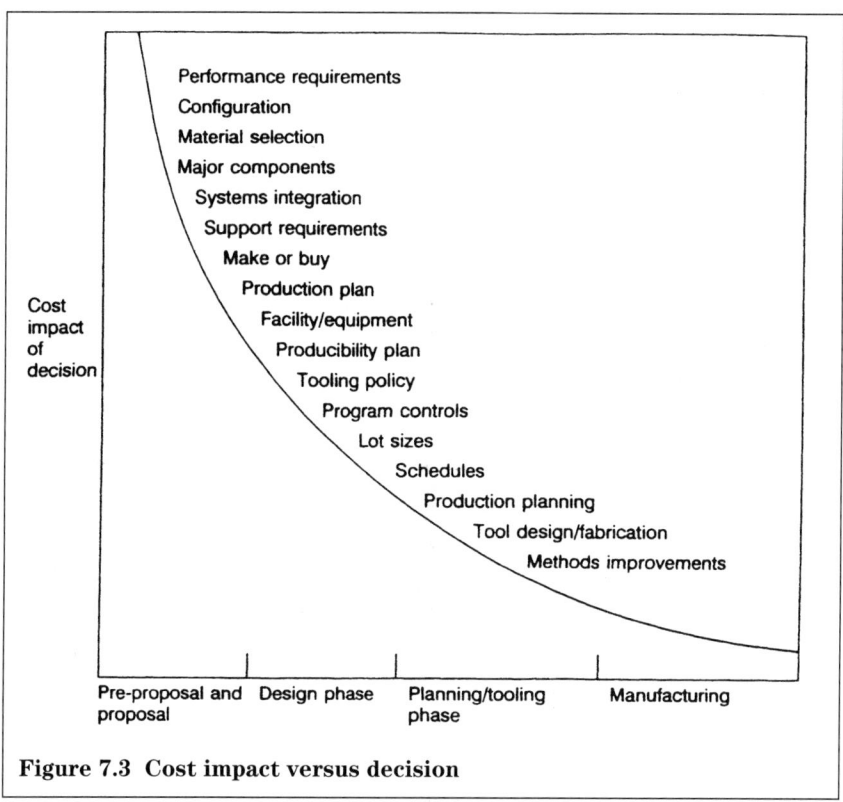

Figure 7.3 Cost impact versus decision

earlier decisions collectively become cost drivers of the present stage. Figure 7.4 shows the various stages with major activities in the life-cycle. Across the top are various characteristics. Designability is the research and development problem of the possibility of designing an engine to address a whole collection of market segments. Product features become important and difficult issues insofar as the designers are concerned.

7.1.6 Earlier decisions in terms of both materials and other technologies have a tremendous impact on the eventual producibility of the product. If we look at a whole series of decisions – the effect of R&D, the effect of decisions on design, the effects of decisions in manufacturing engineering – all are going to have an impact in terms of the product manageability up to the production stage. At each stage, executives make decisions. The decisions, in turn, become drivers of performance downstream in terms of the other activities in the life-cycle. The decisions made at that stage collectively determine the outcomes and cost at subsequent stages.

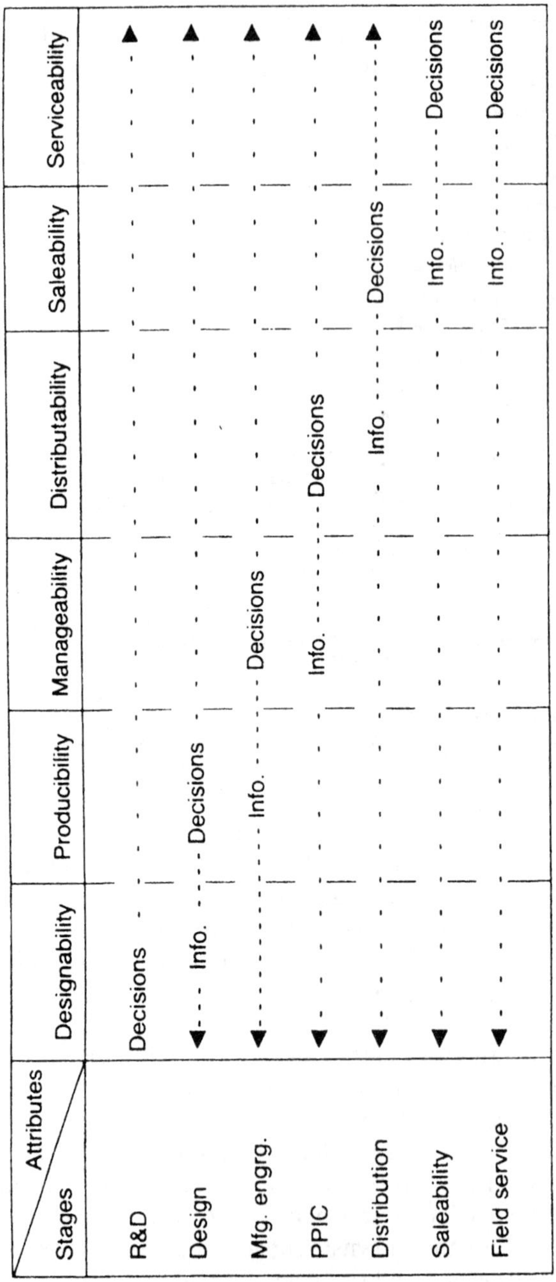

Time and cost management

Attributes Stages	Designability	Producibility	Manageability	Distributability	Saleability	Serviceability
R&D	Decisions ⇢ Info.	⇢ Decisions				⇡
Design	⇣	⇢ Decisions ⇢ Info.	⇢ Decisions			⇡
Mfg. engrg.	⇣	⇢ Info.	⇢ Decisions ⇢ Info.	⇢ Decisions		⇡
PPIC	⇣		⇢ Info.	⇢ Decisions ⇢ Info.	⇢ Decisions	⇡
Distribution	⇣			⇢ Info.	⇢ Decisions ⇢ Info.	⇢ Decisions
Saleability	⇣				⇢ Info.	⇢ Decisions
Field service	⇣					

Figure 7.4 LCC decision relationships

Time and product life-cycles

7.1.7 What is important to note is that although there is no established methodology for addressing life-cycle costs, it may be relevant to consider costs from a life-cycle viewpoint rather than simply in profit and loss terms. One relevant aspect is that product costs may be common to a number of products at the pre-production stages. Many such joint costs cannot be traced to a particular product, especially where one generation of products gives rise to another. Yet costs incurred often end up being attributed to the first product emerging from the pre-production stages and this possibly reduces the perceived profit potential of that product. One way of dealing with costs which are traditionally pooled as general overheads is to trace costs back to individual products by using activity-based costing and perhaps activity-based management (see Chapter **6**).

7.2 Time and product life-cycles

7.2.1 High-technology companies, which traditionally have extensive research and development (R&D) and product development functions, face an environment characterised by rapid technological change, shortened product life-cycles and global competition. In such an environment, the ability to develop products rapidly and bring them to market can become a primary source of competitive advantage.

7.2.2 Ray (1995) has noted that most production costs (an estimated 80 per cent as mentioned above) are believed to be committed *before* a product is ever produced. From 40–70 per cent of the life-cycle costs of high-technology products are determined by the end of the conceptual stage. As Figure 7.5 shows, the opportunities to realise savings in life-cycle costs diminish rapidly after the concept stage.

7.2.3 Modern cost management systems that can evaluate product costs before manufacturing begins can prove highly useful in the pursuit of competitiveness. To that end, companies have to reform their cost management efforts upstream from manufacturing to the product development process.

Trade-offs between cost and time

7.2.4 It is widely believed that time to market is a major source of competitive advantage. The primary advantage of accelerated product development is that a 'pioneer' can charge premium prices in the early years of a product's life cycle, then use process improvement initiatives to realise savings in later years. Late entrants may have to go to extraordinary lengths to succeed. Some Internet companies have witnessed a first mover advantage whereby 'eyeball' volume, site stickiness and brand names are established much faster

Time and cost management

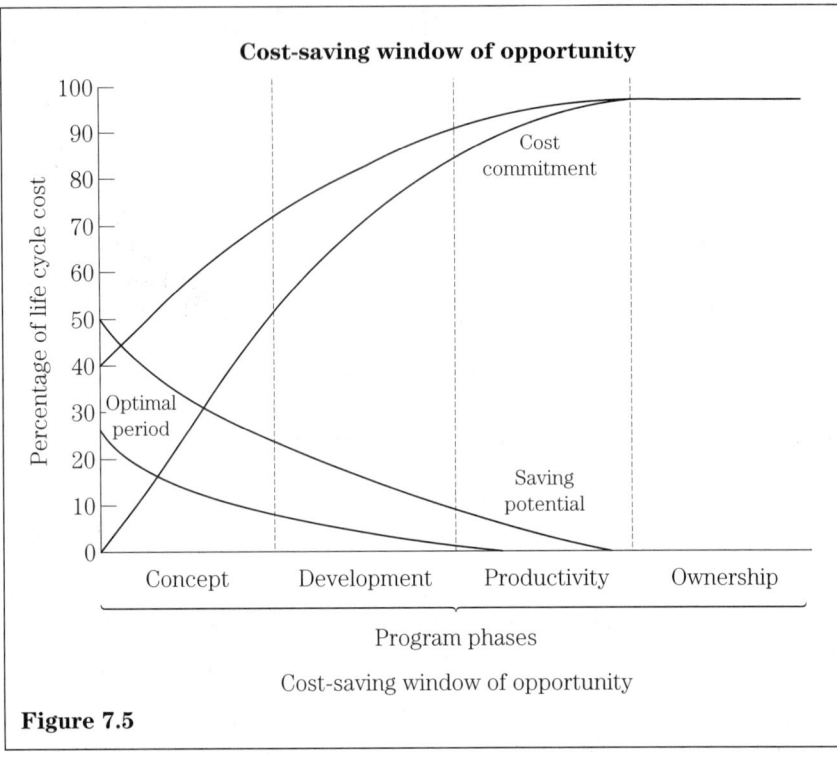

Figure 7.5

by the first entrants in different sectors, both in B2C and B2B contexts. The pioneer's advantage is illustrated in Figure 7.6.

7.2.5 According to Ray (1995), another benefit of accelerated product development is the cost savings as companies use resources more efficiently. Even when high-technology products are under budget, they can earn one-third less profit over a five-year period if they are six months late. By contrast, projects that are on time but 50 per cent over budget lose under 5 per cent in profits.

7.2.6 Studies show that there is a marked contrast between Japanese and US approaches to product development. Indeed, in order to accelerate new product development, the Japanese tend to deploy about twice the resources used by their US counterparts.

7.3 Life-cycle costs in selected industries

7.3.1 A survey on life-cycle cost data by industry classification reveals that a substantial portion of life-cycle costs can be incurred during the develop-

Role of ABM in new product development

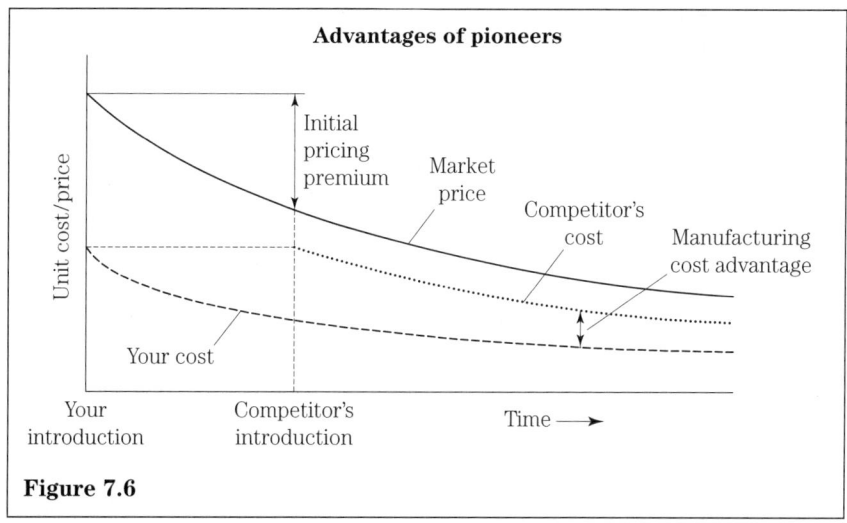

Figure 7.6

ment phase itself. Where figures are derived by subtracting percentage cost data (i.e., the first panel) from the time data (i.e., the second panel), a positive number indicates that the percentage duration of this stage was relatively greater than the percentage cost of this stage, while a negative number shows that the cost was greater. Thus, time is more often the dominant factor in exploratory research, prototype development, and prototype testing. Concept development and market development are more often cost-intensive. Manufacturing start-up, marketing start-up and technical services are often more time-intensive.

7.3.3 Therefore, effective management of product development should involve a recognition of where (i.e., at which stage) and how (i.e., with what resources and activities) time and costs are incurred. Every step toward accelerating development time should also recognise any accompanying cost trade-offs.

7.4 Role of ABM in new product development

7.4.1 ABM is one tool which can be useful to speed new product development (see Chapter **6**). The following are four suggested steps for using ABM.

- Determine for each development project the stage at which ABM should be applied.
- Identify and cost key activities within each stage to generate an awareness of costs. This requires identifying and costing activities that drive cost in each phase, then prioritising developmental activities that must be eliminated or reduced.

Time and cost management

- Participate in decisions about design and the change or addition of features. This step involves providing cost information about the impact of design choices. To be effective, the cost information has to be generated rapidly.

- Evaluate trade-offs between objectives. This step involves the use of activity-based information in two ways. First the ABM system can evaluate the effect of design on total life-cycle costs of the product (an extension of the step above). Second, ABM can be used to evaluate how decisions made or choices considered in each phase affect the development objectives of budget, cost specifications and time.

7.4.2 Experienced innovators usually allow informal, non-standardised procedures in the initial stages. Once the product proposition is finalised, formal controls are exercised to ensure a timely and successful launch.

7.4.3 There may not be any use for ABM in the early stages of the product development process. The stage at which ABM will be deployed should be determined based on the cost-time profile of various stages within a typical development effort. ABM can be employed within individual (or overlapping) stages to identify and cost typical activities. Activities such as engineering changes can be costed in terms of cost drivers and time drivers.

Cost and time drivers

7.4.4 Cost and time drivers can be analysed to evaluate their necessity for meeting overall developmental objectives. The costing of activities can lead to a general awareness about the consumption of both time and money. A development team that has gained this awareness is more likely to seek to do things right the first time and to link activities to enhance the efficient use of time and money, according to Ray (1995). ABM can also be used to provide input into decisions concerning the evaluation of alternative designs and features. An ABM system that rapidly provides manufacturing costs for each change in design can contribute toward making a development project more cost- and time-effective. In one company which used such a system to develop its new line of workstations, the cost accountants and engineers collaborated to develop a system to provide product cost estimates for each configuration of design and feature options. This approach enabled the company to meet its original product cost objectives and its development schedule.

7.4.5 ABM can be useful in evaluating trade-offs between objectives and to provide unobtrusive measures of project performance. The objectives of

Role of ABM in new product development

any product development effort can thus be expressed in terms of the following four project outcome factors:

- specified performance features;
- specified factory cost standards;
- development schedule;
- development project budget.

7.4.6 Every decision about a design, feature or development activity can lead to trade-offs among these objectives. Figure 7.7 depicts six potential trade-offs among objectives that must be examined and resolved. The challenge – and the most important application of ABM in this light according to Ray (1995) – is to provide accurate data to facilitate decisions involving these trade-offs. Because three of the six sources of conflict involve development time, a major challenge is to quantify the affect of delay.

Figure 7.7 Trade-offs among objectives

Objectives	Product cost	Development cost	Development time
Product Performance	X	X	X
Product Cost		X	X
Development Cost			X

7.4.7 A question which may be posed is, 'To what extent should development be accelerated at the cost of higher development costs?' Possibly the goal should be to reduce development time and cost simultaneously. Japanese automobile manufacturers, for example, have managed to develop a car at a cost of 30 per cent less and with 50 per cent fewer engineering hours than their Western counterparts. In the United States, Deere & Company has reduced development cycle time by 60 per cent and development costs by 30 per cent, while Xerox has reported 50 per cent reductions in both development cycle time and development cost.

7.4.8 Figure 7.8 illustrates a method that development teams can use to quantify the effects of a development delay; the resulting numbers can be used to evaluate time and cost trade-offs. Given the critical importance of new product development, the major emphasis of cost managers in the future will be to participate in ongoing product development activities and provide information to address the potential trade-offs.

7.4.9 Because Figure 7.8 deals with both cost and time, it is a good point of reference for cost management in that it provides a basis for developing

Time and cost management

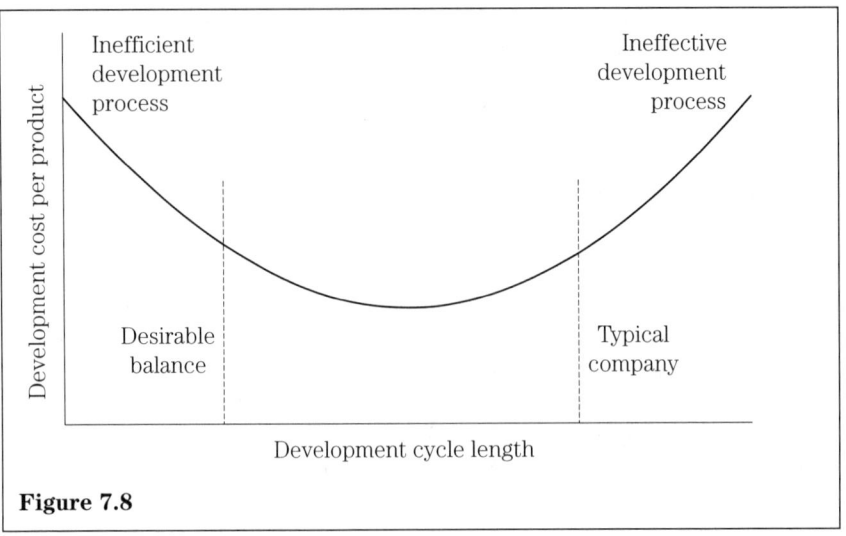

Figure 7.8

trade-off rules for resolving cost-time tensions within the product development function.

7.5 The role of TQM

7.5.1 Many of the issues discussed concerning ABM also apply to TQM (see Chapter **8**). TQM techniques have been used by a number of companies in their R&D functions. Reports from these companies deal primarily with the use of TQM to improve internal operations within R&D functions to maximise external and internal customer satisfaction.

7.5.2 It would be a mistake to consider TQM and ABM as mutually exclusive. Increasingly, companies are forming cross-functional quality improvement teams to understand better the organisation-wide impact of a particular function. A quality improvement team that includes a cost accountant can examine the trade-offs depicted in Figure 7.7 and arrive at options that speed up new product development while simultaneously generating cost savings, in which case ABM becomes part of the quality control frame of reference. Addressing cost issues within the structure of a quality initiative may prove to be useful in making managers think in terms of both time and cost.

7.5.3 In addition to addressing the trade-offs between cost and time in new product development, ABM can be used to enhance external customer satisfaction. Analysing the demands that specific customers make on a company's resources can lead to improvements in both processes and logistics. Ideally, better ways of doing business with specific customers can be devised and the cost savings shared. This perspective provides a means of linking the different factors of both the product life-cycle and individual organisational processes through to market concerns.

7.5.4 As with any quality project implementation, the quality improvement team and members of the organisation need to be given access to all aspects of operations and to make improvements. As suggested in Chapter **6**, the sharing of ABM information makes it possible for empowered employees to focus on non-value added activities that add the most cost.

7.6 The role of strategy

7.6.1 Strategy may be considered an overarching factor which can be taken to guide different organisational initiatives and determine which management approaches a company should use. With intense competition for global markets and decreasing product life-cycles, companies need to study carefully the competitive forces that affect each line of business. Using Porter's model (see Chapter **9**), the competitive forces in terms of threats include those posed by:

- competitors;
- new entrants;
- substitution;
- bargaining power of buyers;
- bargaining power of suppliers.

7.6.2 For high-technology companies, the threat from competitors and the threat of substitution can create tremendous pressures to develop new products and rapidly bring them to market. At the broadest level, companies examine competitive pressures for each line of business and formulate strategic responses for each line. These responses can include the following:

- development of new products;
- expansion of market niches;
- automation and investment in manufacturing systems;
- investment in information technology;
- enhancement of quality;
- enhancement of customer satisfaction.

Time and cost management

7.6.3 Companies can, on occasion, formulate strategic responses based on core competencies which can form the roots of competitive advantage. Often, companies invest in new technology or development to strengthen their core competencies. These can then be leveraged to develop new products in several different lines of business rapidly.

7.6.4 Once a strategic response has been formulated following the analysis of competitive forces and core competencies, tools such as TQM and ABM can be used to facilitate rapid implementation of strategy. According to Ray (1995), the type and mix of tools varies depending on the line of business and the chosen strategic response. Strategy may be seen to subsume such concepts as TQM and ABM.

7.6.5 Cost managers in high-technology companies with rapid product development strategies need to adapt quickly to an ever-changing environment. As companies leverage their key competencies and move toward core products, those that adopt ABM and TQM will face considerable challenges in tracing the cost of these core resources to a rapidly expanding line of core products with ever-diminishing life-cycles. Ultimately, managers will have to reorient their focus from cost to a cost-time orientation as dictated by strategic concerns. Managers ought to be involved in new product development and carefully orchestrate the use of different cost management approaches in addressing concerns of strategic relevance. Time constraints have become key to the management of both old and new economy companies. Time and cost issues are now intimately intertwined in the management of most modern enterprises.

7.7 Activities and continuous improvement

7.7.1 Pryor and Sahm (1995) posit two basic problems with traditionally organised companies. First, they tend to be organised into functional units or departments (e.g., a receiving department in a manufacturing firm). Second, traditional management accounting information is organised according to functions or departments (e.g., such as a receiving department). Managers should not focus solely on departmental costs, Pryor and Sahm (1995) argue, but on the activities that drive the costs. That is, managers must manage activities. To do this, managers must determine what activities are driving costs. Whilst this is the philosophy which underpins activity accounting (see Chapter **6**), continuous improvement introduces the element of time in the management of costs.

7.7.2 The authors define an activity as a verb + noun description of what an organisation does. Using verb + noun descriptions, activities in the receiv-

Activities and continuous improvement

ing department might include 'receive material', 'move material', 'expedite material', 'manage employees', and 'do administrative tasks'. Managers should therefore manage the activities 'receive material', 'move material', and so on. Further, managers should be able to manage costs better when accounting information is collected by activities instead of departments. Strictly speaking, it is impossible to manage costs; all that can really be managed is whatever drives the costs. This implies possible avenues for change in accounting control systems including a concern with time issues.

7.7.3 It is understood that activity-based management refers to the planning, improvement and control of an organisation's activities to meet customer and external requirements (see Chapter **6**). An ABM hierarchy of information provides a framework for an ABM information system. The ABM hierarchy can be described as a pyramid consisting of tasks at the base of the pyramid; moving up the pyramid toward the top are activities, business processes, departments/cost centres, and functions.

7.7.4 Tasks are the steps necessary to perform an activity; examples are 'count boxes' or 'match purchase order to receipt'. Activities are what an organisation does; examples are 'take order', 'do set-up', and 'issue report'. A business process is a collection of related activities operating under a set of procedures to accomplish a set of objectives, such as process a customer order, procure raw materials or design a new product. It is important to note that business processes may be viewed as transcending standard departmental boundaries. Staff performance in terms of their activities has a domino effect on employees in subsequent departments. A department or cost centre represents one portion of a function. A department often contains people or machines that share a common purpose or mission. Examples of departments are receiving, field sales or accounts payable. A function by contrast is a collection of people in one or more locations who share a common responsibility. Examples of functions include the sales function and the manufacturing function. Functions are typically shown at the top of an organisation chart.

7.7.5 Pryor and Sahm (1995) focus on two parts of the pyramid described above: activities and business processes. Activities are classified as either primary or secondary. Primary activities contribute directly to the central mission of the department or organisation. For the receiving department, primary activities include 'receive material' and 'move material'. Secondary activities support an organisation's primary activities.

7.7.6 Virtually every department has secondary activities. The authors state that at least 90 per cent of an organisation's resources should be spent

Time and cost management

on primary activities – hence, no more than ten per cent of the total should be spent on secondary activities.

7.7.7 Activities may also be classified as value added or non-value added. A value added activity is one required to meet customer or external requirements. For the receiving department, a value added activity is to receive material; a non-value added activity is to move material. The authors state that companies frequently spend as much as 35 per cent of their resources on non-value added activities. A manager's goal should be to drive the percentage to zero.

7.7.8 After understanding where activities fit into the overall ABM hierarchy, a company can follow a two-step process to create an ABM information system. Step 1 is activity analysis, which is the process of identifying what an organisation does. Activity analysis often involves activity analysis interviews with employees who perform the activities. The authors provide a sample list of useful interview questions.

7.7.9 Step 2 involves gathering activity accounting information, which involves tracing to each activity the departmental resources required to perform it. For example, to perform the activity 'receive material', the following resources may be required:

- supplies;
- equipment;
- people;
- floorspace;
- telephones.

7.7.10 ABM and the ABM information systems are practical tools that, when combined with time issues and targets, can bring about important management options. Activity information can become inputs to continuous improvement.

Steps to continuous improvement

7.7.11 The core of Pryor and Sahm's (1995) approach is a five-step process to continuous improvement. These are:

- identify improvement opportunities;
- identify root causes;

Activities and continuous improvement

- identify possible solutions;
- implement best solution;
- monitor the improvement.

7.7.12 A continuous improvement (CI) team can be established to carry out improvement initiatives. Before investing time and money in an improvement project, the CI team must have a clear direction for its efforts.

7.7.13 An ABM information system can facilitate the continuous improvement process by providing ideas for improvement opportunities.

7.7.14 For example, improving an activity could mean improving the primary/secondary ratio so that fewer resources are spent on secondary activities, or it could mean eliminating certain non-value adding activities, or reducing time to process where time is seen as a major cost driver.

7.7.15 A CI team could also focus on process improvements rather than improving activities. This might involve performing a process in a radically new way (process innovation) or slightly increasing the efficiency or effectiveness of a process (process improvement). Several steps can be taken to uncover ideas for improvement.

7.7.16 Identifying root causes of an activity, business process or problem is a relevant step to continuous improvement. Brainstorming or storyboarding can be useful in this light.

7.7.17 Brainstorming is one way to identify possible solutions and ideas related to the root causes that have been identified. This involves narrowing a long list of ideas to a shorter list. Storyboarding is a visualisation tool used to help generate a large number of ideas. It is similar to brainstorming except that it allows for anonymous contributions of ideas and it produces organised groupings of ideas. Storyboarding is especially useful when the CI team is addressing sensitive issues or problems.

7.7.18 Once possibilities which are deemed to be the best solutions have been identified, management can implement these with a continuous improvement plan. This involves identifying key criteria, such as ease of implementation, effectiveness of solution and probability of success. This entails understanding how important ease of implementation is compared with the effectiveness of the solution. Having identified the key criteria, the CI team then selects the best solution and develops a detailed implementation plan. The final step is implementation, which may involve a pilot test of the solution in a subsection of the company.

Time and cost management

7.7.19 The last step in the continuous improvement process is to monitor the improvement that results from the implementation of the best solution. Monitoring improvement means developing a set of simple, relevant performance measures that focus on activity output. Pryor and Sahm (1995) provide three guiding principles of ABM performance measurement. First, the measures must be simple and easy for everyone to understand. Second, the measures must be relevant to achieving the company's defined strategy. Third, the measures must be measures of activity output or process output. The last step of a continuous improvement process leads to a new cycle of improvement, which begins with identifying further improvement opportunities.

7.8 The theory of constraints

7.8.1 The theory of constraints (TOC) is a systems-management philosophy developed by Goldratt since the early 1980s in a series of non-fiction books, articles and novels. The fundamental thesis of TOC is that *constraints* determine the performance of any system and that any system contains only a few constraints.

7.8.2 A constraint is anything that limits a system's performance relative to its goal. For example, a production bottleneck that limits the overall profitability of a manufacturing company can be considered a constraint. TOC advocates emphasising the importance of constraints and suggests that managers should focus on these constraints rather than on product costs.

Managing constraints

7.8.3 According to Ruhl (1996), TOC was once considered simply a production scheduling technique. It now has broad applications in manufacturing organisations. TOC can be used, for example, to do the following:

- decrease production lead times;
- improve the quality of products;
- provide dramatic increases in profitability.

7.8.4 TOC also provides a multi-step process for managing constraints which can be used as part of an effort at continuous improvement. Further, TOC can be used with other management techniques such as total quality management (TQM), just-in-time (JIT) and activity-based management (ABM).

Controversies about TOC

7.8.5 Despite being consistent with these well-accepted management techniques, TOC has proved controversial. Goldratt describes TOC as diametrically opposed to traditional costing. In fact, he has called cost accounting the 'number one enemy of productivity' (see Noreen et al., 1995).

7.8.6 Goldratt (1990) argues that managers must break out of the 'cost world' and suggests that managers should drop the term 'product cost' from their vocabularies:

> 'Product cost . . . is a concept which must be eliminated, along with its creator, the decision process based on the "cost world".'

7.8.7 The term 'cost world' apparently refers to the emphasis managers place on cost reduction, especially the reduction of a product's cost per unit.

The goal is to make money – not reduce costs

7.8.8 According to Ruhl (1996), before implementing TOC, managers must first consider their fundamental assumptions about the goals of the owners of their companies. TOC assumes that the goal of owners of for-profit companies is not reducing costs or improving efficiencies, but to make money, both now and in the future. While lowering costs or increasing efficiencies may support the achievement of this goal, often they do not. In their efforts to reduce costs or increase efficiencies, managers often make decisions that make it difficult for the company to make more money.

7.8.9 Successful TOC implementations require a new set of measurements to move toward the goal. Companies cannot retain traditional accounting practices such as absorption costing and standard cost variance analysis and expect to implement TOC successfully. Measurements are critical because TOC recognises that performance measurement systems have a major influence on employees. The resulting type of accounting developed for TOC is called 'throughput accounting' (TA). TA provides a set of performance measurements that managers can use to implement TOC.

7.9 Throughput

7.9.1 Ruhl (1996) notes that TA measurements support the goal of making money and provide a way of making the ideas expressed in TOC operational. TA measurements answer the following questions:

Time and cost management

(1) How much money is the company generating?

(2) How much money does the company capture?

(3) How much money is spent to operate the company?

7.9.2 The three measurements used to answer these questions are, respectively:

(1) Throughput (T);

(2) Inventory (I); and

(3) Operating expense (OE).

7.9.3 Throughput is the rate at which a system generates money through sales. A company generates money through sales, not production. To generate money, the focus must be on producing products that can be sold; it makes no sense to manufacture products for stock.

7.9.4 Throughput is not the same as sales. To calculate throughput, subtract all money that has not been generated by the company. To illustrate, suppose that a company sells a product for $50. If the product contains parts or components that were purchased from vendors for $15, the throughput is $35 (i.e., $50 – $15). Throughput is $35 rather than the total sales price of $50 because only $35 was generated by the company.

7.9.5 The following should be deducted from sales to calculate throughput:

- subcontracting costs;
- commissions paid to salespeople;
- customs duties;
- transportation, if the company does not own the transportation channel.

7.9.6 In TOC, direct manufacturing labour costs are not deducted from sales in calculating throughput. This methodology is followed because labour today is often a fixed cost, especially in companies that use skilled workers who cannot easily be laid off in periods of low demand then rehired later when demand increases. Defining throughput in this way also reduces the confusion over which amounts to include in inventory and which amounts to consider period expenses.

Inventory (I)

7.9.7 Inventory is defined as all the money a system invests in purchasing things the system intends to sell, including buildings and machinery. Of course, buildings and machinery are not normally classified as inventory because managers usually do not intend to sell the company's buildings and machinery. The TOC position, however, is that *everything* in the system is for sale.

7.9.8 When a company's shareholders sell their shares, they are selling their interest in everything defined as inventory in TOC.

7.9.9 This category is called inventory rather than assets because management should consider inventories liabilities, not assets. Companies burdened with excess inventory are really burdened with a liability – i.e., something that frustrates the achievement of the goal.

7.9.10 In TOC, the value of inventory does not include the value added by the system itself – specifically, inventory value does not include the value of direct manufacturing labour and manufacturing overhead. Instead, inventory includes only amounts paid for components that are purchased from outside vendors and used in the manufacture of inventory. This is consistent with the TOC notion that it is not important to add value to the inventory; rather, managers must add value to the company.

Operating expense (OE)

7.9.11 The term operating expense refers to all the money a system spends in turning inventory into throughput, including the cost of the following:

- direct labour;
- sales personnel;
- supervisors;
- managers;
- secretaries.

7.9.12 These costs are considered operating expenses because the employees are all responsible for turning inventory into throughput. Note, moreover, that depreciation is also classified as an operating expense because it represents a cost of turning inventory into throughput.

Time and cost management

7.9.13 Performance measures can be prioritised in terms of their importance in achieving the goal. These priorities are as follows:

- throughput;
- inventory;
- operating expense.

7.9.14 Managers should thus place the most emphasis on increasing throughput, though they cannot ignore inventory levels and operating expenses. These priorities contrast with the usual management practice of trying to lower operating expenses and paying little or no attention to inventory levels.

7.9.15 Lower inventory levels make it easier for managers to achieve the goal for a number of reasons, which can be classified as indirect or intangible. The indirect benefits of carrying low levels of inventory are well-known. They include lower carrying costs because of reductions in operating expenses such as:

- interest charges;
- storage space;
- scrap;
- obsolescence;
- material handling;
- rework.

7.9.16 The intangible benefits of low inventory levels may be even more important than the indirect benefits. Intangible benefits relate to a company's ability to gain a competitive edge, which may be derived from:

- producing better products;
- selling at lower prices; or
- responding better to customers.

7.9.17 Low inventory levels may lead to the production of better products if a company manufactures in small batches. Companies that produce small batches can find and fix product defects faster and more easily than companies that produce large batches, so they tend to make higher-quality products.

7.9.18 Companies with low inventories can also usually undersell their competitors because they typically have lower investments in equipment and facilities than their high-inventory counterparts. As a result, they have lower costs and can charge lower prices. Low-inventory companies may also be more responsive to customers; a company's due-date performance often improves as its inventory levels shrink.

7.9.19 Reductions in inventories are essential to TOC. Specifically, managers who are serious about reducing inventory levels have to learn how to manage bottlenecks and constraints.

Bottlenecks and constraints

7.9.20 The concepts of bottlenecks and constraints are central to the theory of TOC. A bottleneck is simply a resource on which the load placed is greater than its available capacity. If demand exceeds capacity in a manufacturing plant, there must be at least one bottleneck in the production process. A company can have one or more bottlenecks, and over time the number and location of bottlenecks may change. A bottleneck that limits the throughput of an entire system is called the capacity-constrained resource (CCR), which is also known as the bottleneck constraint (or simply 'the constraint').

7.9.21 Using the analogy of a chain, a constraint is the weakest link in a chain; it limits the overall strength or performance of the chain. The constraint can be either internal or external. Insufficient orders for a product are an example of an external constraint. A machine that is the weakest or slowest link in a manufacturing production process is an example of an internal bottleneck constraint.

The analogy of soldiers in line
7.9.22 The concept of a constraint may be illustrated using the analogy of a group of soldiers marching in single file. The soldiers begin their march as a tightly packed column, one soldier immediately behind the next. Soon, however, gaps appear in the column because a slow or weak soldier cannot march as fast as the other soldiers. As a result, soldiers bunch up behind the weak soldiers. A gap appears in front of the weak soldier because the soldiers in front of him are marching faster than he is.

7.9.23 The soldiers marching single file are an analogy for production resources in a manufacturing setting, where each 'soldier' stands for a separate production resource (e.g., a machine) and the 'walk trail' is the product. Throughput occurs only when the last soldier comes to the end of the trail.

Time and cost management

As gaps in the line of soldiers appear, the line lengthens – i.e., more 'work-in-process' accumulates. The challenge is to close the gaps (i.e., limit the build-up of excess inventory) without slowing throughput. The important point is that the overall speed of the line of soldiers is determined by the weakest soldier – i.e., the CCR.

Dependent events and statistical fluctuations

7.9.24 Any gaps appearing in the line of marching soldiers can be explained by reference to two phenomena:

- dependent events;
- statistical fluctuations.

7.9.25 The term 'dependent events' refers to a situation where one operation must be completed before a second operation can begin. Thus, for example, Machine A might have to complete step one before Machine B can begin step two. To continue the soldier analogy, the progress of any one soldier depends on the progress of the soldier who is in line ahead of him; the weakest soldier must march the trail before the soldier behind him can march it.

7.9.26 The term 'statistical fluctuations' refers to outcomes that cannot be precisely predicted. In a manufacturing environment, statistical fluctuations can be illustrated by considering the time it takes a worker to complete a specific task. The time required to complete the task varies slightly every time the worker completes the task. One day the task may require five minutes, the next day six minutes, and the third day four-and-a-half minutes. In the soldier illustration, each of the soldiers walks at a non-constant rate, which may fluctuate around some average speed of, say, two miles per hour. The fluctuations of the various speeds do not average out. Rather, the fluctuations accumulate, and most of the fluctuation leads to reductions in the average speed.

Ways to prevent wasting constraint time

7.9.27 One way to prevent wasting constraint time is to put quality control in front of the CCR to prevent the CCR from working on units that are defective. Scrapping parts that have been processed by the CCR means scrapping CCR time that can never be recovered.

7.9.28 Another way to avoid wasting CCR time is to make sure that the CCR works only on parts that will immediately become throughput. The CCR's time should not be spent working on parts that will go into finished goods inventory, only to be sold months later.

7.10 Throughput accounting

7.10.1 As noted above throughput accounting (TA) is based on premises established by the theory of constraints (Goldratt and Cox, 1984). Three performance measures provide a focus for TA: throughput accounting (i.e., the amount of money generated by the company), inventory (the amount of money captured by the company) and operating expenses (the amount of money spent on operating the company). Fundamentally, throughput and contribution margin analysis are not completely independent concepts (Balderstone and Keef, 1999).

7.10.2 The starting point of throughput accounting is the development of concepts which enable managers to guide a manufacturing enterprise towards greater profitability by a process of arithmetical calculation. The technique, which does not enjoy the popularity of activity-based costing, stems from the concept that in the short to medium term, the entire cost of a factory is fixed except for material costs. It is, therefore, acceptable to spurn decision-making based on conventional costing procedures which produce, for instance, cost per machine hour or per direct labour hour data. It is simpler and more appropriate to consider 'total factory cost'. Moreover, treating inventory as comprising solely material value rather than adding value to material to account for labour and overhead costs enables a focus on profitability tied to manufacturing activities. This is because the incentive to produce in order to absorb costs is removed.

> 'For all businesses, profit is a function of the time taken for manufacturing to respond to the needs of the market. This in turn means that profitability is inversely proportional to the level of inventory in the system, since the response time is itself a function of all inventory.'

> (Source: Galloway and Waldron, 1998.)

7.10.3 Another precept of the throughput accounting school is that it is not absolute product profitability which matters for a multi-product firm but relative product profitability. Profitability must be a measure of how quickly monetary returns can be obtained from manufacturing operations, which in turn is dependent on the volume of products produced. Thus, what is of the essence is each product's contribution per production operation, where the object must be to maximise output of that product which returns the most based on the operation which has the least relative capacity.

> 'It is the rate at which a product contributes money that determines relative product profitability. And it is the rate at which a product contributes money

Time and cost management

compared to the rate at which the factory spends it that determines absolute profitability.'

(Source: Galloway and Waldron, 1988.)

7.10.4 The following example illustrates the throughput accounting rationale together with some relevant ratios.

An example

7.10.5 Consider two machined products, X and Y, with contribution margins (selling price less variable costs) of $8.25 and $8.82 respectively. Their production entails three operations whose relative timings (in minutes) are given in Table 7.1.

Table 7.1 Production of products X and Y

Operations	1	2	3
Product X	0.2	0.3	0.2
Product Y	0.2	0.15	0.25
Capacity (minutes)	6,000	5,000	6,000

7.10.6 Since at operation 2, which has the least relative capacity, 16,666 units of X (5,000/0.3) can be manufactured whereas 33,333 units of Y (5,000/0.15) can be produced, it is in fact more profitable to produce Y rather than X. What the manager needs to ascertain is that the rate at which product Y earns money exceeds the rate at which money is spent making it. In other words, the return per factory minute (defined as selling price − material cost/time on key resource) must exceed the cost per factory minute (defined as total factory cost/total time available on the key resource). Alternatively, the throughput accounting ratio (defined as return per factory minute/cost per factory minute) must exceed one before a product can be considered as making money. Although the level of detail in analysing manufacturing operations can become more involved, the basic rationale of throughput accounting is to determine a product mix which makes the best use of resources whilst maximising the company's profits per unit time. In applying throughput accounting, a number of performance indicators linked to enterprise performance and strategy may be developed to suit the requirements of an organisation.

A case study: redirecting managerial attention

7.10.7 Darlington *et al.* (1992) provide an excellent case study of a UK company within which throughput accounting was one factor helping the

Throughput accounting

enterprise double its profits from the same sales volume without any reduction in its number of employees. The case study concentrates on one plant of the Garrett Corporation – Garrett Automotive Ltd (GAL), with approximately 600 employees manufacturing turbochargers for the automotive industry. GAL is a subsidiary of an American parent company.

7.10.8 In 1988, Garrett's European operations were reorganised with the result that this factory changed to producing for a market segment requiring many more product lines and parts with much smaller batches than in the past. At the beginning of 1989, the factory was consolidating on one site from three and, at the same time, was introducing some new software to run its manufacturing operations, called optimised production technology (OPT). These changes, coupled with increased competition and a new top management team, led to a re-examination of GAL's existing accounting information system. In 1988 and early 1989, the accounting information was based on a standard costing system which generated periodic sets of very detailed variances.

7.10.9 GAL decided to begin its profit-improvement programme by examining its factory throughput. Throughput was defined as the rate at which raw materials were turned into sales. In other words, throughput was defined as sales less material costs per period of time. In conjunction with its new OPT scheduling system this led to an examination of the factory bottlenecks and constraints which were defined as follows:

- a bottleneck is an activity within the organisation where the demand for that resource outstrips its capacity to supply;
- a constraint is a situational factor which makes the achievement of throughput more difficult than it would otherwise be. Constraints may take several forms such as lack of skilled employees or the need to achieve a high level of quality in product output.

7.10.10 Using GAL's definitions, therefore, a bottleneck is always a constraint, but a constraint need not be a bottleneck. Managers in each department can usually identify their bottlenecks and constraints but these are not normally monitored as part of the formal reporting system. In this particular factory the major constraint was considered to be the customer due-date performance, i.e., meeting the delivery schedule for customer orders.

7.10.11 The bottlenecks became certain machines in the factory. Throughput was then related directly to the ability to cope with the constraint and manage the bottlenecks. This focus on throughput forced management to examine both the constraints and the bottlenecks in order to increase throughput.

Time and cost management

7.10.12 The throughput accounting approach is similar to maximising the contribution per unit of a scarce resource. One measurement difference is that throughput is defined as sales less material costs, in contrast to contribution, which equals sales less all variable costs (material, labour and variable overhead costs). The implicit assumption of throughput accounting is that all costs except materials can be assumed fixed in relation to changes in throughput in the short run.

7.10.13 However, the identification of bottlenecks, which is integral to throughput accounting, also stimulates managerial action to alleviate the problem. One bottleneck at GAL relating to machine capacity and the action taken is illustrated in Table 7.2. It shows that in this machining line the bottleneck was machine B, with a capacity of only 18 units per hour. The first improvement was to introduce machine D which was already operating in a non-bottleneck part of the factory and to remove one operation from machine B to be performed by machine D.

Table 7.2 Example of bottleneck improvements.

Existing				
Output machine A 30 units per hour	to	Machine B 18 units per hour	to	Machine C 80 units per hour
First improvement				
Output machine A 30 units per hour	to	Machines B and D 21 units per hour	to	Machine C 80 units per hour
Second improvement				
Output machine A 30 units per hour	to	Machines B, D and E 24 units per hour	to	Machine F 26 units per hour

7.10.14 This raised the capacity of the bottleneck from 18 to 21 units per hour at a cost of £2,000. The second improvement was to buy machine E (costing £6,000), which raised the capacity of the bottleneck from 21 to 24 units per hour. At the same time, when machine C had to be replaced it was replaced by a much smaller machine than previously, with an output of 26 units per hour. With a 125-hour week and 90 per cent utilisation this raised the weekly output from 2,025 to 2,700 units. This example emphasises an important assumption underlying throughput accounting and bottlenecks: it assumes that the extra output can be sold and this was the case at GAL.

7.10.15 Some observations can be made about the above example.
- GAL used to produce an 'efficiency' report which split the turbocharger into component groups and showed efficiency by measuring total

direct labour hours available compared with the standard hours of components produced. If the efficiency of a section fell below what was considered an acceptable level, then managers were pressurised to improve. If you consider this in relation to machine A, you realise the weakness of such an approach. If machine A works faster than machine B to increase its 'efficiency', it is making units which the company does not need. If you measure manufacturing on efficiency, unwanted units may be produced.

- If a manufacturing engineer told us that machine A is getting old and a new machine is needed which would double the output of machine A, our bottleneck analysis would show that such an investment would not improve throughput. An increase in production from machine A will not lead to better company performance at present. Many capital investment appraisals have been based on a reduction of the fully absorbed or marginal cost by producing more units without considering fully whether these extra units will result in more sales. This concentration on bottlenecks can influence capital investment decisions. One implication is to give priority to investment in your bottlenecks. However, it is frequently the case that when you solve one bottleneck problem, another will arise. Similarly, a major change in the product mix may change the bottlenecks. Bottlenecks are dynamic and managing the bottlenecks is a process of ongoing improvement.

- The changes can be considered in the context of their full impact on cost and not simply on throughput. The changes such as using another machine to perform one particular operation and reducing the capacity of other machines meant an increased number of material movements but this gave an increased throughput with an overall cost saving.

7.10.16 Although GAL used throughput accounting with optimised production technology (OPT), the ideas behind throughput accounting can be applied without using OPT which is not now favoured by companies. However, it would be misleading to suggest that throughput accounting can be introduced without any problems. GAL has identified three areas of difficulty. First, it can be difficult to identify correctly the constraints and the bottlenecks. Second, the reduction in stocks and work in procress stemming from the use of TA means a short-term profit problem in that fewer overheads are carried forward in the stocks and this gives a one-off profit reduction. Third, reduced inventories highlight problems which have been hidden previously. For example, suppliers may be unable to meet their delivery schedules and this can cause major problems in maintaining throughput which have to be solved either by working with existing suppliers or by finding better suppliers.

Time and cost management

7.10.17 GAL realised that when you reduce inventories, problems are revealed which are common to many manufacturing companies. Once your safety net of inventory has gone, you must solve problems such as unexpected holidays, physical stocktakes, machine breakdowns and absenteeism. TA emphasises the importance of the ability to manage bottlenecks in the factory. This generated considerable financial benefits for GAL in a quite short space of time. In addition, the concentration on throughput (sales less material costs) has highlighted three critical needs, namely to raise selling prices, to reduce material costs and to increase sales volume.

7.10.18 TA played a role in helping to maintain sales volume. For example, one customer in a specialised market segment bought its turbochargers from GAL and another supplier. However, with the help of TA, GAL was able to increase its throughput and to challenge the competitor's selling price. GAL subsequently became the sole supplier to this customer.

7.10.19 TA has demonstrated to everyone in the factory the critical need to adhere to the production schedule, which was previously regarded as relatively unimportant. For example, in one case, if each of three cells achieves 80 per cent schedule adherence, then the final customer orders will be only 51 per cent satisfied. GAL has found that the reasons for departures from the schedule can be complex but provide valuable insights into the operations of the business.

7.10.20 Schedule adherence has highlighted the importance of first-time capability ('do it right first-time') and also of everyone knowing exactly what is happening in other sections of the production process so that actions can be modified as necessary. Charts around the factory explain what has been achieved in relation to the schedule for each particular work cell.

7.10.21 Presentations on TA have been made to all employees within the factory. This has led to increased communication to all employees including reports on the overall performance of the factory every month. TA has also led to a reduction in the monthly management reporting package from a 40-page report to a five-page report consisting of:

- controller's commentary (pages 1 and 2);
- key operating and investment statistics (page 3);
- schedule adherence summary by cell (page 5).

7.10.22 This monthly package is also available to any employee who requests a copy.

Throughput accounting

7.10.23 The profit and loss account is now reported in a throughput format as follows:

- sales;
- material cost upper level throughput;
- royalties;
- sub-contract.

7.10.24 The monthly reporting package includes the following details about schedule adherence:

- percentage of schedule adherence;
- scheduled quantity;
- scheduled finished;
- percentage of mix adherence;
- quantity finished;
- percentage of unscheduled.

7.10.25 Such reporting highlights the importance of schedule adherence. Inventory is less than half of its level two years before while sales volume has basically remained the same. However, inventory has not been reduced everywhere. The critical importance of bottlenecks has meant that some buffer stock is held before the bottlenecks. Experience has shown that such buffer stock is useful in the shortrun to cope with unexpected problems. Its existence helps to guarantee that throughput does not cease due to temporary hold-ups further down the line.

7.10.26 Schedule adherence has highlighted the related factor of supplier adherence as critical to GAL's success. If suppliers do not meet their delivery dates, quantities and quality levels, then schedule adherence and throughput can be seriously affected. TA also emphasises the importance of teamwork and has enabled GAL to understand more clearly its own capacity.

7.10.27 Finally, although the most important quantifiable advantage of TA has been the new emphasis given to schedule adherence and the consequent success in inventory reduction, perhaps the most important overall advantage is the favourable reaction of the managers. Previously, managers did not understand, believe or use the outputs from the former standard costing system; they find it much easier to accept, understand and use the

Time and cost management

information generated by the TA system to improve their performance. The internal performance measures have changed to measures which identify one of the following:

- selling price opportunities;
- throughput opportunities;
- material cost opportunities;
- improvements to working capital;
- operating expense reductions.

7.10.28 Although TA is in essence a technique, the accountants and managers would claim that it affects how you perceive the running of the business and would see it as part of an approach to management rather than just a tool. It is an approach affecting many departments and involving plans for continuous involvement.

(Source: Darlington *et al.*, 1992.)

Calculating throughput time

7.10.29 Estrin and Kantor (1998) note that a computational technique for determining throughput time should involve some method of averaging based on various production starting times and various times for shipping finished goods inventory. This can be achieved by weighting the throughput times of each kind of component comprising the batch of finished goods. The most practical base to use for such weighting is the money value of the cost of each of the raw materials and components comprising the finished product. When a total of 'money times time' for each component is divided by the total cost of all components a throughput time number is derived for the batch.

$$\frac{\Sigma \text{ Component costs} \times \text{their throughput times}}{\text{Total cost of all components}} = \text{Weighted average throughput time}$$

7.10.30 This formula provides for a measure of throughput time. The dates and costs or prices when raw materials are delivered and when finished goods are shipped can be easily verified by referring to routine transaction documents. There will be an audit trail. In almost every case there will be paperwork or computer records with independent verification from suppliers of the dates when all materials were shipped as well as records of customer invoices and payments which will confirm shipping dates. Any partial or departmental computation of throughput time must ultimately reconcile with these boundary dates.

Throughput accounting

7.10.31 Estrin and Kantor (1998) note that the primary unit of analysis for throughput-time accounting is a batch of a specific product. A batch is defined as one or more units of a specific product which are sold together. There should be a calculation of throughput time for each different product or batch of products in each shipment. Depending on the productive process, throughput time per batch can be measured in minutes, hours, days or weeks. The most common unit will likely be days measured to three or more decimal places. Times can be aggregated to determine the total throughput time for each product, the time for all of one kind (SKU or stock-keeping unit) of product, or the aggregate time for all products of any type (SKU) shipped during a given month. For periodic, monthly or yearly accounting purposes, product throughput times can be recast so as to show throughput times for each and for all products for a given month or other period. It is also possible to calculate the throughput time of each specific material purchased.

7.10.32 When goods are shipped their constituent components are determined by a 'parts explosion' process and removed or 'backflushed' from inventory on a FIFO basis (see Chapter **5**).

7.10.33 For each shipment, the number of units of each purchased material which is shipped as part of finished goods, should be multiplied by its price per unit then multiplied by the number of days from its purchase date to the shipment date. The time that each purchased raw material has remained in process can be obtained by first determining the weighted average FIFO-based number of days elapsed between the dates the units of each material were purchased and the date on which they were shipped to the customer as part of finished goods. This elapsed time for each of the FIFO-determined purchases of a raw material is then multiplied by the units of the raw material.

7.10.34 The above procedure computes numbers that constitute the duration of time that each material was owned, weighted by the total purchase amount of the particular material. The number obtained can be called the number of 'pound days' used for the production of a batch of finished goods. The 'pound days' of each of the materials which constitute the batch of finished goods shipped should be totalled. This aggregate money-day figure for an entire batch shipment of a particular product can then be divided by the total cost of material involved in order to derive a time-only number for the throughput time required to manufacture the batch.

7.10.35 Estrin and Kantor (1998) give an example of a standard FIFO perpetual inventory printout which is used as the basis for calculating the

Time and cost management

weighted average cost of material and weighted average throughput time (presented in Figure 7.9). It depicts the inventory card showing some of the additions and deletions for hypothetical material number 614.

Figure 7.9 Inventory calculations for material number 614

	Time is Money Ltd				
	Inventory card for material number 614				
Date	Cost per unit (£)	Units bot. (into inv.)	Units shipped	Cumulative units	FIFO cost (£)
04/04/00	5.48	100		100	548.00
05/15/00			60	40	219.20
05/18/00	5.59	100		140	554.60
06/15/00			100	40	223.60

7.10.36 When product is shipped, the weighted average cost of materials and the weighted average throughput time for the materials in the shipment can be computed. Figure 7.10 outlines these calculations.

Figure 7.10 Throughput days per weighted average material £

TIME IS MONEY LTD				
Material number 614				
Computations of weighted average cost & throughput days for material number 614 which was part of products shipped June 15, 2000[1]				
Units	Purchase date	Days to 15 June 2000	Total cost	Pounds × days
60	4 April 2000	71	328.800	23,344.800
40	18 May 2000	71	219.200	15,563.200
60	18 May 2000	28	335.400	9,391.200
160	Totals		883.400	48,299.200
Weighted Averages				54.6742

Note: [1]100 units were used for product number W101 and 60 units for product E402.

7.10.37 In a similar manner, on the basis of a parts explosion, the total costs, weighted average cost and weighted average pound days of every relevant material of each shipment can be computed. These can be combined in order to compute the totals for each product shipped to a customer. Figure 7.11 shows the entries for a shipment of 100 units of product W101, made on 15 June 2000, to customer ABC.

Throughput accounting

Figure 7.11 Calculation of material cost and throughput time for a batch of product

	Time is Money Ltd			
	100 Units of product number 101 shipped 15 June 2000			
	Table showing the calculation of material cost and throughput time			
Name of material	Quantity of material in 100 units of W101	Cost of material shipped (FIFO)	Weighted average days from acquisition to shipment	Weighted average material – pound days
123	100	₤60.350	14.0000	844.900
415	400	52.000	33.0000	1,701.480
614	100	552.000[1]	54.6742	30,178.9440
799	48	38.000	89.000	3,374.880
Totals		₤702.350		36,100.204

Notes: Only the figures for material 614 (shaded) are derived in prior tables. Other figures are given for illustrative purposes to show how throughput time for a given batch of products is calculated. [1]$883.400/160 \times 100 = 552$

7.10.38 The weighted average throughput time for the shipment of 100 units of product number W101 which were shipped on 15 June was:

$$\frac{36,100.204}{₤704,950} = 51.39992 \text{ days}$$

7.10.39 That is to say that it takes an average pound's worth of purchased material 51.3992 days from the time it is purchased until the time it is shipped as part of product number W101.

7.10.40 Compilation of aggregate throughput time for all products for a month is illustrated in Figure 7.12. In addition to providing a pound day number to be used for overhead cost allocation, a throughput time measure to be used in determining how quickly money is generated for each product and for the entire plant can be computed. Dividing the total revenue billed for shipments of product during a month by the aggregate throughput time for that product yields a measure of how quickly money is being made with each product. This is key to throughput accounting. Dividing the grand total shipment revenues by the grand total throughput time gives an overall measure of how quickly revenues are being generated by the entire operation.

7.10.41 Using the procedure illustrated in Figure 7.12, Estrin and Kantor (1998) state that the throughput time for each batch of every product and

397

Time and cost management

Figure 7.12 Throughput time for all products shipped on a given date

			Time is Money Ltd		
		Computation of material cost revenue & throughput time for all output produced during the month of June 2000			
Product name (Number)	Units shipped	Total cost of materials	Revenue on goods shipped	Throughput time in Days	Revenue pounds generated per 100 T.T. Days
A591	10,000	£200,000	£350,000	10,000	£3,500.00
W101	200,000	540,000	1,950,000	174,000	1,120.69
C653	40,000	160,000	480,000	55,000	872.73
D229	100,000	50,000	135,000	7,000	1,928.57
E402	7,000	420,000	2,825,000	360,000	784.89
Totals (wtd average)		£1,370.00	£5,740,000	606,000	£8,206.880

Note: All figures in this table are given for purposes of illustrating the form by which monthly aggregated pound days for all products shipped during the month are calculated

for aggregate product shipped can be computed and reported by the day after shipment or aggregated in order to prepare a monthly report.

7.11 Integrating ABC, TOC and financial reporting

7.11.1 Activity-based costing (ABC) and the theory of constraints (TOC) (upon which TA is based) are two popular cost accounting and production theories. Both were developed as a result of automation and the adaptation of changing manufacturing technologies. Claims have been made that either ABC or TOC should offer a firm improved financial performance. Managerial accountants need to address whether ABC and TOC are competing or complementary theories. Moreover, can ABC and TOC be integrated with financial reporting? Coate and Frey (1999) have provided some useful insights to reconcile ABC and TOC.

7.11.2 Relative to traditional costing systems, ABC offers alternative product costing by using the cost of activities as the basis for assigning costs to products. ABC's emphasis is on identifying the activities that cause indirect costs to be incurred. A single activity, or cost driver, is associated with each cost pool. Costs are assigned to products based upon the products' con-

Integrating ABC, TOC and financial reporting

sumption of those activities. ABC attempts to provide an understanding of the balance between activity demanded with activity supplied.

7.11.3 However, TOC advocates claim that the product cost distortions that ABC was designed to eliminate are not the cause of firms' problems in decision-making. TOC focuses on bottlenecks (constraints) and their importance in production flow (and, hence, throughput). Every system has constraints, whether internal or external to the firm, which limit the firm's ability to generate profits. The TOC process suggests that a firm should identify the system's constraints, decide how to make the best use of them, and subordinate everything else to those decisions. If a constraint can be elevated, or even removed, then the TOC process begins anew.

7.11.4 TOC requires thinking in a throughput world rather than a cost world. Since throughput is the rate at which a system generates money through sales, throughput is not equal to accounting measures of income. This TOC perspective originally questioned the usefulness of cost allocations and labelled cost drivers and ABC as 'fruitless efforts'. TOC proponents initially made comments such as, 'Traditional cost mentality almost invariably leads to flawed decisions', and have questioned the use of standard cost systems by asking, 'Should TOC replace the standard cost system?'

7.11.5 While the early work in ABC and TOC treated the two theories as incompatible, recent work has begun to consider them as complementary to each other.

7.11.6 One argument which has been made is that ABC may be seen as a long-term approach while TOC is a short-term approach. TOC's assumption of fixed capacity and labour costs represents a short-term approach, while ABC takes the more long-term view that management can act to adjust spending on resources to reflect their usage. The difference between the long term and the short term is whether the firm's capacity can be changed.

7.11.7 Despite the professed benefits of ABC, TOC or a combination of the two, some firms have been reluctant to abandon the more traditional standard cost systems in favour of the new systems. A variety of factors contribute to this. Implementation cost is one factor, according to Coate and Frey (1999). Another is that no method has been developed to integrate these new theories and systems, particularly financial reporting.

7.11.8 The integration of ABC with periodic reporting can be achieved by calculating a variance which reflects the unused capacity and its associated costs. Thus a single activity is used to provide an example that integrates

Time and cost management

ABC with periodic financial reporting. To integrate TOC, one can add a second activity. A second activity illustrates both a resource at capacity and an inter-dependency between resources. Both are critical TOC concepts.

7.11.9 Suppose inspection is the activity – call it activity Y. Activity Y's total expense was budgeted at $280,000 ($200,000 Committed; $80,000 Flexible); actual expenses are $250,000. The activity levels are 5,000 capacity, 4,000 budget, and 3,500 actual (see Figure 7.13).

Activity Y: Operating expenses and activity levels

Operating expenses

Budgeted committed (supplying capacity)	$200,000
Budgeted flexible (varying with volume)	80,000
Budgeted total	$280,000
Actual realized	$250,000

Activity level   *Driver rates*
5,000 (capacity) $40 (= $200,000/5,000)
4,000 (budgeted) $20 (= $ 80,000/4,000)
3,500 (actual)

Variance computation

Activity Y expense charged to products	$210,000
3,500 @ ($40 + $20)	
Budgeted unused capacity cost	$40,000 U
(5,000 – 4,000) @ $40	
Capacity utilization variance	$20,000 U
(4,000 – 3,500) @ $40	
Spending variance: Actual – Budgeted expense	$20,000 F
$250,000 – $270,000	
Total actual expenses	$250,000

Note: Flexible budget for expenses = $200,000 + ($20 * 3,500)

Figure 7.13

7.11.10 Variances are computed to reconcile the amount charged to products with recorded expenses. These variances are computed using both committed ($40 = $200,000/5,000 capacity) and flexible ($20 = $80,000/4,000 budget) cost driver rates. Using the activity's capacity level, rather than its budget level, highlights unused activity – an advantage gained

Integrating ABC, TOC and financial reporting

by having an ABC perspective. Because product costs are unchanged by production levels in this type of analysis, ABC is integrated with financial reporting.

7.11.11   The second activity, activity X, may be thought of as a product processing activity. Activity X was budgeted at £240,000 (£120,000 Committed; £120,000 Flexible); actual expenses were £230,000. The activity levels are 4,000 capacity, 4,000 budget, and 3,500 actual. The method of computing variances, reconciling the amount charged to products with the amount recorded as expenses, is illustrated in Figure 7.14. Note that a unit of capacity for activity Y is meant to match a unit of capacity for activity X. Hence, the budget capacity for both activities is equal and set to 4,000. The actual activity level for both activities is also equal. This means that the activity levels have been 'balanced'.

Figure 7.14 Throughput time for all products shipped on a given date

Operating expenses		
Budgeted committed (supplying capacity)		£120,000
Budgeted flexible (varying with volume)		120,000
Budgeted total		£240,000
Actual realised		£230,000
Activity level	Driver rates	
4,000 (capacity)	£30 (= £120,000/4,000)	
4,000 (budgeted)	£30 (= £120,000/4,000)	
3,500 (actual)		
Variance computation		
Activity × expense charged to products		£210,000
3,500 @ (£30 + £30)		
Budgeted unused capacity cost		£0 U
(4,000 − 4,000) @ £30		
Capacity utilisation variance		£15,000 U
(4,000 − 3,500) @ £30		
Spending variance: actual − budgeted expense		£5,000 F
£230,000 − £225,000		
Total actual expenses		£230,000
Note Flexible budget for expenses = £120,000 + (£30 × 3,500)		

Constrained and non-constrained activities

7.11.12   ABC and TOC both recognise the importance of capacity. ABC's budgeted unused capacity (BUC) variance explicitly addresses capacity, and can be used to identify which activity is budgeted as a binding production constraint (a TOC concept).

Time and cost management

7.11.13 Consider the BUC variances of activities Y and X. In a strictly ABC context, the positive BUC variance of activity Y is a signal to management of an opportunity to reduce resource supply or search for additional activity for a resource. That is, management, with the objective of utilising each resource as fully as possible, may take action to adjust either the resource's capacity or its usage. Management may be satisfied that activity X, with its BUC of zero, is already fully utilised, and choose not to devote any time to it. In a TOC context, the positive BUC variance for activity Y identifies a non-binding constraint on production. Management, with the objective of utilising constrained resources as fully as possible, will choose not to focus on activity Y. Conversely, the zero BUC variance for activity X identifies a resource that is budgeted as a binding constraint on production. Thus, activity X will become management's target to exploit and to elevate.

7.11.14 Next, consider the role of the capacity utilisation (CU) variances for activity Y (with a positive BUC variance) and activity X (with a zero BUC variance). The unfavourable CU variance in both cases indicates an unexpectedly low utilisation level of each activity. However, interpretation of this variance differs depending on the BUC variance.

7.11.15 If the BUC variance is unfavourable (positive), then excess capacity is available for the activity. Thus, any production loss represented by an unfavourable CU variance in the current period can be recovered (or made up) in the following period. If the BUC variance is zero, however, capacity for that activity is a binding constraint in the production budget. In this case, TOC suggests that the variance is more critical. TOC demonstrates that, for a constrained activity, a unit of capacity lost (i.e., an unfavourable CU variance) or gained (i.e., a favourable CU variance) represents a capacity loss or gain for the entire plant.

Interdependencies among activities

7.11.16 TOC advocates not only the identification of binding constraints but also the exploitation of these constraints by subordinating everything else to them. TOC recognises the interdependencies among resources or activities. The relationship between a constrained activity (X) and a non-constrained activity (Y) can be expressed as one of the three possibilities:

- production flows from a constrained resource (x) to a non-constrained resource (y);
- production flows from a non-constrained resource (y) to a constrained resource (x);

- production flows into a non-constrained resource (z) from a constrained resource (x) and a non-constrained resource (y). (Note that actual demand may not equal budget demand; thus, the budget and actual constrained activities may not be the same. In this section we assume the budget remains the desired plan. In either case, budget or actual, the order of the constrained activities relative to non-constrained activities is important in the interpretation of variances.)

Bottleneck precedes

7.11.17 First consider the possibility that X leads to Y: i.e., the constrained activity, or bottleneck, precedes the unconstrained activity. A £15,000 unfavourable CU variance on activity X indicates a loss of production capacity. Without the completion of activity X, activity Y cannot occur. Thus, not only is capacity reduced for activity X, but utilised capacity is reduced for activity Y as well, causing an additional £20,000 unfavourable CU variance.

7.11.18 An alternative explanation consistent with the variances in the example is that activity Y is temporarily constrained and the level of activity X has been reduced to match activity Y. However, temporarily reducing the level of activity X would be a sub-optimal decision. Because activity X is the constrained activity, TOC says it should be maintained at its maximum pace. Although this will cause an inventory build-up, the level of activity Y can be increased in the following period, causing both a favourable CU variance in that period and a reduction of the inventory build-up.

Bottleneck follows

7.11.19 Next, consider the possibility that Y leads to X (i.e., the constrained activity follows the unconstrained activity). As before, the £15,000 unfavourable CU variance for activity X indicates a plant-wide loss of productive capacity. However, under this possibility the unfavourable CU variance on activity Y is not only expected, but planned. Because the BUC variance of activity X is zero, management takes action to match the activity Y level to that of activity X. Holding the activity level of Y at its budgeted rate would generate a zero CU variance, but inventory would build up in front of activity X. As activity X is a constrained resource already budgeted to operate at capacity, the only way to reduce the inventory build-up would be to decrease the production rate of activity Y in a future period. Reducing the inventory build-up would generate an unfavourable CU variance on activity Y at that time.

7.11.20 If, on the other hand, an unfavourable CU variance on activity Y is due to a temporary constraint (e.g., a machine breakdown), activity X should have no CU variance. An inventory buffer between activity Y and

Time and cost management

activity X, as prescribed by TOC, would prevent the loss of plant-wide capacity.

7.11.21 Inventory build-ups are one of the criticisms of standard cost systems and variance analysis. These examples show, according to Coates and Frey (1999), how variance analysis at the activity level, together with knowledge of constraints, can help identify wanted and unwanted inventory build-ups.

Bottleneck parallels
7.11.22 Finally, consider the possibility that X and Y lead to Z, that is, both activities X and Y must be completed before a third activity, Z, can be performed. In terms of variances, this possibility has elements of both Y leading to X and X leading to Y. Given an unfavourable CU variance for activity X, an unfavourable CU variance for activity Y is expected, and even encouraged, to preclude an inventory build-up. Conversely, a temporary unfavourable CU variance for activity Y should not trigger an unfavourable CU variance for activity X.

7.11.23 Regardless of the nature of the interdependencies, a few general issues are noteworthy. First, it is important to remember variances on the constrained activity are most critical. Second, temporary inventory build-ups may be 'good things'. A variance caused by an anomaly on a constrained activity dictates the size and direction of variances that should be realised on related activities. A variance caused by an anomaly on an unconstrained activity should not influence the variance on a constrained activity. Variances play a role in determining when inventory build-ups are necessary and when they are unnecessary.

7.11.24 In the examples above, the CU variances are all unfavourable. If these variances are favourable, similar analyses apply. A favourable CU variance for activity X should be accompanied by a favourable CU variance for activity Y. However, a favourable CU variance for activity Y without an increase in the capacity of activity X generates an unwanted inventory build-up.

Effects on financial reporting

7.11.25 In the section above, variance analysis in an ABC system was used to identify binding constraints (a TOC concept). Interdependencies among activities led to interdependencies among variances, as well as to inventory build-ups. These interdependencies among variances form the basis for an illustration of how the amount of a variance may or may not equal its net effect on profit. The ABC variance analysis accounts for differences between actual expenses and expenses applied to products, but it does not always measure the full impact on profit. Because of the interdependencies among activities, the amount of the variance computed under ABC methods may or may not represent the total change in profit resulting from the anomaly causing the variance. Activities, as TOC emphasises, are interrelated, and those activities that are constrained are critical. The TOC focus helps to interpret these variances and improve the overall control process.

7.11.26 Consider an unfavourable spending variance (i.e., the actual resource cost exceeds the budgeted costs) on an unconstrained activity. Generally, a spending variance is independent of other activities, and the amount of the variance represents a pound-for-pound impact on profit. An exception is when a spending variance is incurred to generate additional capacity on a constrained resource. In that case, the unfavourable spending variance generates, and is off-set by, favourable CU variances plant-wide.

7.11.27 Similarly, consider an increased efficiency in the use of a constrained activity, resulting in a favourable CU variance on the constrained activity. The amount of this variance understates the profit impact of the efficiency gain. Increasing utilisation of the constrained resource allows a plant-wide production level above budget, which in turn generates favourable variances on other activities as well as favourable sales margin variances.

7.11.28 Focusing on the key TOC issues of constraint identification and interdependencies among resources lays the foundation for integrating both ABC and TOC into the framework of a traditional cost accounting system. ABC and TOC principles are utilised in conjunction with product costing, management decisions and financial reporting. The resulting system combines variance analysis with three key elements of TOC: constraint identification, constraint exploitation and interdependencies of resources.

7.11.29 Considering system constraints in an ABC-based variance analysis offers an excellent way to co-ordinate cost systems, TOC and Financial Reporting. TOC tells managers that under-utilising constraints leads to lower production and less profit; variance analysis helps indicate the extent of the effect. In short, according to Coates and Frey (1999), ABC and TOC are both useful, complementary concepts and are not incompatible with Financial Reporting.

7.12 Activity mapping

7.12.1 One way to identify the location of bottlenecks is by walking through a factory and observing where work-in-process (WIP) inventory

Time and cost management

backs up in front of specific machines or processes. Usually, however, a better way to identify bottlenecks in the factory is through the use of activity maps. Salafatinos (1995) provides an excellent illustration of how TOC can be integrated with ABC.

7.12.2 Activity mapping can be described as an aid to business process improvement. It is essentially a flowchart of activities that displays the following:

- vertical relationships between activities in a department;
- horizontal connections between departments;
- cycle times necessary to perform each activity.

7.12.3 Activity maps can give decision makers the tools they need to identify and analyse bottlenecks and then apply TA.

7.12.4 In using activity mapping, the definition of the cost object can include the business process itself. A business process can be broadly defined as a value adding system. This includes all functions of the company that work together to add value to a product or service, including purchasing, accounting, marketing and production. By defining the cost object as the business process, activities can be mapped to determine the flow of a product through the entire organisation.

7.12.5 Activity maps as suggested by Salafatinos (1995) entail the following:

- both production and non-production activities are incorporated into the map structure;
- activities are mapped first by cycle time using a Gantt chart, activities are susequently placed inside a dependency grid to show activity interdependence.

7.12.6 A Gantt chart is a two-dimensional diagram relating time (on the horizontal axis) to activity (on the vertical axis). A dependency grid is also a two-dimensional diagram relating supplier processes (on the vertical axis) to customer processes (on the horizontal axis). The Gantt chart directs management's attention to potential problem activities, then the dependency grid is used to help managers determine the composition of the bottleneck.

Activity mapping

Dependency grids

7.12.7 A dependency grid helps to reveal the relationships between activities. There are 'customer' and 'supplier' relationships that exist between activities. Some activities supply output to other activities. The activity receiving output from another activity is thus a customer of the supplier activity. Dependency grids are used to plot the activities along a two-dimensional diagram reflecting this customer/supplier relationship. For example, consider the activity of delivering material to a fabricating workstation. This is an activity performed by a material-handling process that serves the fabricating process.

7.12.8 It is important to know which activities are supportive and dependent on each other to reduce potential bottlenecks effectively. All the activities plotted in a box at an intersection between the vertical axis and horizontal axis are dependent-related activities. If a potential bottleneck is discovered using the Gantt chart, the activity could be found on the dependency grid to reveal the other related activities that compose the bottleneck.

7.12.9 Understanding the intricate web of activities in the production process and in related processes is the key to improving throughput and applying the theory of constraints.

Using activity analyses to find bottlenecks

7.12.10 How would a factory manager begin to look for a bottleneck resource? One way would be to observe the factory floor for inventory backing up in front of a process. The problem with looking for bottlenecks by observation or through interviews is that these techniques work only when the bottleneck is created sequentially. In practice, finding bottlenecks can be considerably more complex.

7.12.11 The problem of how to identify bottlenecks stems in part from the definition used according to Salafatinos (1995). The normal definition of a bottleneck is a resource that is being pressed beyond its capacity. Thus, a bottleneck occurs when demand on a resource equals or is greater than the capacity of that resource. This relationship can be expressed as follows:

$$C(r) <= D(r)$$

where: $C(r)$ = (capacity resource R); and
$D(r)$ = (demand placed on resource R).

Time and cost management

An example

7.12.12 Suppose that a factory manager, while looking for bottlenecks, discovers that the packaging process (a resource) was not keeping up with the demand placed on it. The manager identifies the packaging process as a bottleneck by observing a large pile of WIP stacked in front of the packaging machines.

7.12.13 To deal with the problem Salafatinos (1995) notes that the manager assembles his management team and works on making the packaging process balance the flow of production with demand by either speeding up the packaging process or slowing down the preceding process. But, as it turns out, the manager's efforts may be misdirected because the bottleneck may not have been in the packaging process at all. The problem may have been that the purchasing department ordered boxes of the wrong size or ordered boxes at the wrong time; as a result, when the packaging machines begin to run, they have to wait for more boxes or adjust the machine to accommodate different size boxes. Or perhaps the shipping department was not able to prepare the skids on time for the packaged product to be delivered.

7.12.14 There can be any number of reasons for the pile-up in front of the packaging machines. The point is that a bottleneck may not be attributable to an individual resource or location or even to the relationship between two sequential resources. In fact, a bottleneck is more likely to occur because of a complex web of connecting activities that cross a company's functional areas.

7.12.15 Thus, although a pile of WIP clearly indicates that a production flow problem exists, this identification of a problem is not enough. Managers must know how to define the problem, locate its source, and address it effectively.

7.12.16 To define a bottleneck as existing inside a resource ignores the complexity of a business process; activities are needed to explain and understand the points between the gaps. This is a more flexible and instructive approach. It recognises the non-linear behaviour of the processes of a business. An improved definition of a bottleneck, therefore, can be expressed as the condition that exists when demand on a set of activities exceeds the capacity of that set of activities to support the demand, as follows:

$$C\{a,a...\} , 5 D\{a,a...\}$$

where: $C\{a,a...\}$ = (capacity of a set of activities); and
$D\{a,a...\}$ = (demand on the same set of activities)

Activity mapping and the theory of constraints

7.12.17 This definition according to Salafatinos (1995) recognises that a process is made up of activities and that throughput depends on the complex, non-linear co-ordination of activities in each process.

7.13 Activity mapping and the theory of constraints

7.13.1 By using this particular view of bottlenecks, it becomes clearer why activity mapping can facilitate the application of the theory of constraints. An understanding of how activities interconnect is essential for bottleneck analysis. Activity mapping provides a way to gain insight into the complex interconnections between activities. Having this insight can assist to increase throughput.

7.13.2 Activity maps are a graphical presentation of the interconnecting activities of business processes. Activity mapping for ABC applications has normally been applied to overhead activities such as quality control, set-up, material handling and purchasing. The mapping of these activities can provide the three-dimensional view of a company necessary to find bottlenecks, because the flow of production in an organisation depends on co-ordinating both overhead and direct production activities. By gaining an appreciation of how direct production activities are linked to other areas in the organisation, managers gain a more complete picture of the flow of production. Given the new definition of a bottleneck, management needs a way to identify those sets of activities that meet the condition specified in the definition. Activity mapping is designed to help highlight gaps that exist between activities. Once management knows the location of a bottleneck and has determined its cause, they can then focus their attention on correcting the capacity and co-ordination of activities that give rise to the problem.

7.13.3 Activity maps can be constructed in various ways depending on the size and type of the organisation but, to be applicable to the theory of constraints, activity maps must satisfy at least two requirements.

- They must illustrate gaps between activities for both overhead and production areas of the company.
- They must locate the set of activities that cause these gaps.

7.13.4 An effective way of activity mapping to achieve these aims is to employ a combination of Gantt charts and dependency grids. Three necessary steps are involved in the analysis. Salafatinos (1995) defines a process as a series of activities that are linked together to perform a specific objective. For example, the purchasing process is a group of integrated activities

Time and cost management

that together compose the purchasing function of the organisation. Activities are defined as a single unit of work performed in a process. Therefore, activities are components of a process. Preparing a purchase order and then sending the purchase order through the proper channels are examples of activities.

Three steps to using activity maps

7.13.5 There are three basics steps to using activity maps to locate and reduce the effects of bottlenecks.

- *Prepare an activity list.* The first step is to list all the activities in both production and non-production processes. Activities are usually identified and defined through interviews. Related activities are then grouped by process and numbered to make mapping easier.

- Activities for mapping purposes can be more detailed than is usual for the purposes of ABC, because not all activities are significant for costing purposes. In activity mapping (unlike in most ABC systems), it is common (and not prohibitively expensive) to identify and list hundreds of activities.

- *Prepare a Gantt chart.* The second step is to prepare a Gantt chart that lists the activities along the vertical axis and cycle times across the horizontal axis. Sequentially related activities should begin at the points where the previous activities end. Blank spaces should precede an activity if there is a waiting or 'do-nothing' period.

- *Prepare a dependency grid.* The third step is to list all processes along both the vertical and horizontal axis. The vertical axis represents the support dimension of activities. The horizontal axis represents the consumption dimension. Place activity numbers in the box that best characterises its relationship to other processes.

7.13.7 The mapping of activities through use of a Gantt chart provides a basis for locating the gaps between activities, while the dependency grid provides a way of identifying which sets of activities are involved in the bottleneck. Both of these help to complete the bottleneck equation $c\{a,a...\} <= D\{a,a...\}$.

7.13.8 An illustration of how to use activity maps is provided by Salafatinos (1995). The illustration involves the purchasing, material handling and other processes. The example uses activity mapping to identify the bottlenecks caused by the interrelationships between these processes and

Activity mapping and the theory of constraints

then to mitigate those bottlenecks. The five-step sequence for the analysis is given in the paragraphs that follow.

7.13.9 (1) *Examine the activity map Gantt chart and look for the longest graphed horizontal lines.* In the purchasing department, activity 1 (examine MRP report) and activity 4 (call vendor for delivery information) consume the most time. In the packaging process, activities 27 and 28 (sorting product by type and checking for bad product) have the longest cycle times.

(2) *Using the activity map again, examine the process, and look for the largest blank spaces between activities.* In the packaging process, large space may exist between activities. This represents a wait state between preparing a material requisition form and sorting products by type. Management should enquire why there is a long wait between these activities and investigate how this gap can be shortened. Throughput will be most affected by the activities with the longer cycle time and the longest blank space adjacent to them. The question then becomes 'which set of activities creates this problem?'

(3) *To identify the activities that cause the bottleneck, examine the dependency grid and look for the relevant activity numbers.*

(4) *Investigate long wait states and large cycle times.*

(5) *Consider new options and alternatives to redesign the process.* The final stage in the analysis is to consider new options to how resources are currently balanced. By using dependency grids and Gantt charts as described above, the linkages between activities become clear, which gives managers the information they need to make adjustments in the production flow.

7.13.10 Salafatinos (1995) believes that the theory of constraints and ABC are both valuable techniques in their own right. Together, however, they offer significant benefits. The theory of constraints has brought a new dimension to production philosophy and has stimulated an interesting challenge to the traditional ways of looking at a company's profitability. Specifically, a company is not a mere aggregation of separate investments that can be managed independently, but rather a complex system of resources that require co-ordination. The theory of constraints thus focuses on the flow of production through the system to increase throughput, which is accomplished by eliminating bottlenecks to reduce inventory and cut operating expenses.

Time and cost management

A case study: dealing with bottlenecks

7.13.11 'Balancing our lines to produce only bleached pulp has been a piece of cake, but, that's sure going to change when we start processing unbleached pulp for that new product line!' This was John Marshal's opening comment as he slid into the booth with his tray at the Homestyle BBQ restaurant. John is Plant Manager at Southern Pulp Company's (SPC) plant in South City, Georgia

7.13.12 The others already eating lunch at the table included Mary Wilson, the Plant Controller, and Judd McClinton, the Plant Engineer. It was the group's weekly meeting for 'lunch out' to get away from the plant. The decision by the home office to begin processing unbleached pulp at the plant made today's lunch an exception to the 'no business talk' rule.

7.13.13 'Yeah, and the plant's overall performance is really going to be affected by adding that new line,' said Judd. 'Marketing could have used some input on this one. Anyone with a production background would know in an instant that throughput drops and scrap goes up when product mix gets more varied.'

7.13.14 'I wonder if they really thought it all through to see how the cost of a unit of processed pulp is affected by changeovers,[1]' said Mary, 'and if the price on that new product is high enough to cover them. They needed an accountant at that meeting!' [1](Terms in bold print are defined in the terminology section at the end of the case.)

7.13.15 'All of this wouldn't be "guess-timating" if they just ran a couple of simple experiments on that simulation package of yours, Judd. What's it called, "XCELL+"?' asked Mary.

7.13.16 'Yeah,' said John, 'Let's run some basic examples to demonstrate our concerns; I'll add comments on them and send the whole thing to the home office. We'll start on it as soon as we get back to the plant after lunch! Please, pass the hot sauce.'

Company background

7.13.17 In 1979 the Southern Pulp Company (SPC) began production of bleached kraft market pulp at its facility in South City, Georgia. By 1999, a $400 million newsprint mill, a $700 million softwood pulp mill and a $36 million de-inking plant were added to the original manufacturing complex. The company is a major employer in the small southern Georgia community. Approximately 875 people are employed at the four-mill complex, with an annual payroll exceeding $58 million.

Activity mapping and the theory of constraints

7.13.18 SPC currently exports over 72 per cent of its pulp production to customers in 19 countries. During 1999, the pulp mills at South City delivered over 16,000 truckloads of pulp to docks for shipment to customers overseas. In addition, over 1,500 truckloads and 3,200 railcars of pulp were delivered to customers on the North American continent.

7.13.19 The mills at the South City site contain modern environmental and process technologies that far exceed the requirements and limitations set by federal and state environmental regulatory agencies. Emission control devices include scrubbers, stripping equipment, large low-odour recovery boilers that eliminate odour at source, and power boilers with electrostatic precipitators that control particulate emissions from the recovery and power boilers.

The manufacturing process

7.13.20 Private land owners and wood dealers provide SPC with raw materials (hardwood and softwood timber in the form of logs or wood chips) delivered to the mill by truck or rail. Workers in the woodyard use many forms of automation to unload and process logs. An example is woodyard dumpers that literally pick up and invert railcars loaded with wood chips.

7.13.21 The manufacturing process at SPC consists of two separate, yet interrelated systems: pulp production, described in steps 1 to 5 below; and chemical recovery, to reclaim used chemicals, described in steps 6 to 8 below. The digester is the common link between these two processes within the pulp mill.

7.13.22 *Step 1. Debarking and Chipping.* If raw materials are received in the form of timber, the first step in the process is debarking. Logs are placed into rotating debarking drums that measure 16 feet in diameter by 100 feet in length. The bark is removed by the tumbling action of the logs. After debarking, logs are processed through chippers that are driven by motors of up to 3,000 hp to cut them into nominal 1"×1"×5/8" chips, screened to ensure chip size homogeneity, and stored in the 'Chip Pile'. Chips larger than specifications are reprocessed, while those significantly smaller than specifications are burned (together with bark from the debarking process) as fuel in the mill's electric generating facility. The debarking drum and chipper can process approximately 6,000 tons of logs per day.

7.13.23 *Step 2. Digesting.* Wood chips proceed to the digesting facility where they are cooked at 325°F in continuous digesters (large pressure cookers up to 28 feet in diameter and 176 feet tall) containing water and 'white liquor' (from step 8 – active ingredients are sodium hydroxide/sodium

Time and cost management

sulphide) to break down and reuse the lignin (glue-like material bonding the wood fibres). As pulp moves down through the digester, washing is done using filtrate from the wash stage (step 3). Liquor (called 'black liquor') is extracted at the bottom of the digester and sent to a black liquor tank before going to the evaporator in the chemical recovery cycle (step 6). Washed pulp is blown from the digester to the blow tank which acts as a buffer between the digester and the washer and oxygen reactor phase (step 3) of the pulp production cycle.

7.13.24 *Step 3. Washer and oxygen reactor.* Following the blow tank, brown fibres are washed and screened and put through oxygen delignification, a process that allows further lignin removal by the action of oxygen on the fibres in the oxygen reactor. The oxygen delignification stage allows for 60 per cent reduction in bleach plant chemicals. After oxygen delignification, the pulp undergoes further stages of washing before being pumped to the unbleached pulp storage tank.

7.13.25 *Step 4. Bleaching.* The bleaching process converts brown pulp (used in manufacturing brown coffee filters and electrical dielectric papers, for example) into white pulp (for printing, writing and computer paper, for example). The process uses chlorine, chlorine dioxide, oxygen, caustic soda and sulphur dioxide, which are prepared in a chemical preparation plant on site. SPC operates two chlorine dioxide generating modules that use sodium chlorate and methanol to produce chlorine dioxide, a bleaching agent more environmentally friendly than chlorine. Scrap bleached and unbleached pulp is collected and either sold at lower market prices, discarded or recycled.

7.13.26 *Step 5. Drying.* Prior to drying, processed pulp from the bleaching plant is stored in a storage tank. As a final step, the processed pulp mixture is dried, cut into sheets and baled for shipment as either finished bleached pulp or finished unbleached pulp.

7.13.27 *Step 6. Evaporation.* As raw pulp exits the digester (step 2), a mixture of chemicals, water and lignin (black liquor) is stored in black liquor tank number 1 before proceeding to the evaporator in the chemical recovery cycle where water is extracted, leaving behind a mixture of lignin and chemicals.

7.13.28 *Step 7. Recovery.* From the evaporation process, concentrated black liquor is stored in black liquor tank number 2 before advancing to the recovery boiler. Black liquor is the fuel burned in the recovery boiler to produce heat that is used to generate steam for the pulping and drying processes and for the production of electricity. SPC generates enough electrical power to meet all of its energy requirements. Oxidation of the black liquor compounds during combustion changes the chemical properties of black liquor, converting it to a 'green liquor' that exits the recovery boiler as smelt and goes to the green liquor tank.

7.13.29 *Step 8. Recausticising.* Purification processes, such as slaking and recausticising take place in step 8, the final step in the chemical recovery cycle. Green liquor from the recovery boiler is transferred to the recausticising process where it is mixed with lime to cause chemical reactions converting it into 'white liquor' that is stored in the white liquor tank before being reintroduced into the system at the digester (step 2) to close the chemical recovery loop.

Southern Pulp Company's computer simulation models
7.13.30 Back at the plant, Judd turned on his desktop PC and said, 'John, you wanted to go back to your office to check phone messages. While you're gone, Mary can review the manuals and get some practice with XCELL+'s features, and I'll start laying out an 'all-bleach' processing model. When you come back, bring a clean copy of the printout of the plant's flow diagram from your office. It's a nice overview that lets home office see every part of our processes. I can't seem to get my hands on my copy of it.'

7.13.31 As John leaves, Judd hands the XCELL+ Reference Card to Mary and says, 'This is a good summary of XCELL+ that you can go over to get familiar with the model again. But, before you can bring XCELL+ up on my PC, you'll have to get out of that application on the screen, get back to the C: drive, and then do a change directory command to get into the subdirectory named "XCELL". After that you can invoke XCELL+, by typing "XLP" and hitting return.'

7.13.32 'OK,' Mary answered, 'And while I'm refreshing myself on XCELL+, you're going to lay out a basic model of our plant that will be processing only bleached pulp.' 'Right,' Judd said as he settled into his desk chair, 'but first, I'm calling my secretary to have her hold my calls. This could take a little time!'

Using XCELL+
7.13.33 After some time passed, Mary said, 'Judd, I think I'm OK with this model but I want to be sure to get this right. So let me talk through this process of bringing up XCELL+ and running a model with you. Why don't you correct me, if necessary, as we go along.' 'OK,' Judd said, as he rolled his chair closer to see the monitor screen.

Time and cost management

7.13.34 'I'm in the XCELL sub-directory, and to invoke XCELL+,' Mary started, 'I type **XLP** and the Main menu comes up. I know the function keys **F1** through **F8** are used to activate my menu choices, and the F8 key generally takes me back to the previous menu. To bring up a model, at the main menu I touch **F6**, which is labelled "file manager", and I get to the File Manager menu where I again touch F6 – but this time it's labelled "retrieve factory". I want to bring up a sample model provided with the software called SEMIAUTO, so I type "SEMIAUTO", and press enter. After the SEMIAUTO model appears, if I want to run it I touch F8 to leave the File Manager menu to get to the Main menu again, and touch **F7**, labelled "run", F7 again, but now it's labelled "begin run", and F7 one more time – now it's "auto run" – and voilà! "Things" are running through the sample model and the time bar is advancing – it runs!' 'So, what am I doing here?' asked Judd. 'Wait, don't leave!' says Mary, 'I haven't gotten through to the results yet – and I have to get out of this SEMIAUTO model too.'

7.13.35 Mary continued, 'I also found out that while the model is running, I can control execution speed by touching **F4** called "one step", **F5**, called "slower" or F6, called "faster", and I can even stop the run by touching the "pause" key, F8.' 'Very good!' Judd acknowledges.

7.13.36 'When the run finishes,' continued Mary, 'if I want to see the results, I can touch F6 called "results" to get to the Results menu, where several keys can be touched to get specific results generated by the simulation run, like: **F3** for "throughput", F4 for "WIP", F5 for "**Utilisation**", and F6 for "**flowtime**". Since I'm not interested in the SEMIAUTO model's results, I'll exit by touching F8 which is labelled "back to main", and in the Main menu I can touch "QUIT", the F8 key, and then F7 which asks "really quit?", and I'm back at the C:\XCELL prompt.' 'Looks like you have it,' said Judd.

7.13.37 At that point Judd suggests, 'I only have a sketchy outline of the model we're going to build, but I have to break off now and go to another meeting. Why don't you stay with this, enter this model and get it to run. Save it as PULP1, and in the morning let's look at the results you got.' 'Sure, sketch and run,' said Mary. 'I'll see what I can do, but you owe me for this one!'

7.13.38 John opened the meeting the next morning by saying, 'Let me review the situation. You created a model called PULP1 that replicates the pulp and chemical recovery processes at the South City plant, but it doesn't use the plant's specific operating characteristics, capacities or volumes of flow. It's really a "schematic" that's just like our processes, and we're using it to demonstrate the impact of changing our product mix – that is, adding a small volume of unbleached pulp to our output.' 'That's right!' Mary and Judd said simultaneously.

Analysis of the PULP1 model's results
7.13.39 'Let me explain what we have here,' said Mary. 'In the PULP1 model, only bleached pulp is processed and all **Work centres** produce at equal speeds so the lines are "in balance", and there are no process interruptions caused by such things as grade changes. A **time unit** is set at a constant of 1 in this model and I ran it for a single run of 500 timeunits.'

7.13.40 'Here are the results I got with one processed **unit** in ten tagged at **Receiving area** R2 so the unit can be observed flowing through the process and tracked for data gathering purposes,' Mary said as she distributed copies around the table. 'Note that 50 tagged units went through S23, which is the **Shipping area** finished bleached pulp,' she continued. 'There were 499 good units of bleached pulp produced and shipped through S2 and we had one unit of scrap bleached pulp at S3. But, more important, flowtime of a unit is 12.0 time units as seen in the Average Flow column. This is how long it takes for a unit to move through the process from its Receiving Area to its Shipping Area. Process time is the sum of the time a unit spends at Work Centres along its route through the process. The four Work Centres that process pulp each require one unit of time for each unit processed – and 4.0 can be seen in the Average Processing column. The wait time is the difference between flowtime and **processing-time**, and 8.0 appears in the average waiting column. Since the line is balanced there are no delays; however, each buffer contains some inventory so some waiting time is present.' 'Buffers each hold some units – see the Minimum and Maximum Period columns in the WIP section down below? In my run, the system had 27.00 units, on average, in work in process inventory. Finally, in the last section of the page, all Work Centres had 100 per cent machine utilisation rates, except work centre 10 which had 99.8 per cent, which is probably due to rounding. For all practical purposes we can treat that as 100 per cent.'

7.13.41 'Ah! The ideal factory! The line is balanced since all work centres have equal average processing-times and they're all running at capacity with 100 per cent utilisation,' said John. 'We only intended to represent the simplicity of a process producing a single, homogeneous product – like our bleached pulp,' Judd responded. 'But we know the process in PULP1 isn't practical since randomness occurs in processing times, some **bottlenecks** and **blocking** will occur, and Work Centres can become **idle**,' he continued. 'This negatively impacts the performance of the process. And we can evaluate that by doing a **flow analysis** of the XCELL+ model's results.'

Time and cost management

7.13.42 'But,' John interrupted, 'our supervisors are pretty good at co-operating to balance our lines "on the fly" by watching the rate of flow in each section.' 'Yeah,' said Mary, 'monitoring the "speedometer" in their section and communicating the readings up and down the line allows everyone to make adjustments that avoid bottlenecks. But, that's not going to do the job if we start producing unbleached pulp.'

7.13.43 'Changeovers require a purging of the system, causing more material to be scrapped, and **set-up-time** is needed to start the new process,' said Judd. 'We need another model to demonstrate this,' John suggested. 'I'll build it,' offered Judd, 'and I'll call it PULP2. Then we can compare its output with the PULP1 results to demonstrate the impact changing the product mix has on a plant.' 'Remember though,' Mary said, 'when we have two products we have to think in terms of batches even though we have a continuous manufacturing process, and the batch sizes of bleached and unbleached pulp differ – a batch of unbleached pulp is 10 units of product, while the batch size of bleached pulp is 50 product units.'

7.13.44 'Yes, but,' John said, 'even when you get PULP2 in balance, processing bleached and unbleached pulp can create other problems that impact the performance of the system. For example, unbleached pulp is harder to dewater, and it takes longer to dry it than bleached pulp. What effect will that have on our system?' 'I don't know,' replied Judd, 'let me alter PULP2 for that condition, and we'll see what we get. I'll call that model PULP3.'

7.13.45 'This is really interesting,' said Mary. 'As you both know, I've only worked here six months and my prior job was in a foundry – strictly a one-at-a-time production process. Working on this simulation model of a continuous-manufacturing process really is an eye opener on the differences between the two production methods.' 'Maybe you can scratch a note on that to run past the home office people,' suggested Judd. 'I'm sure some of them aren't aware of those differences.' 'Sketch and run, scratch and run, now you owe me two times!' quipped Mary.

Summing it up – restating what's required
7.13.46 John started to organise his papers to get ready to leave, and said, 'Before we break up, let me summarise where we are and be sure our assignments are clear. We're preparing a packet of materials to send to home office to brief them on our concerns over adding an unbleached product line at the South City plant. We're sending them three XCELL+ simulation models, and the results we got from running them. For members of the Board who don't have a background in continuous process manufacturing,

Mary will prepare a write-up comparing continuous and discrete-part manufacturing processes, and point out differences in their operational and cost management features.'

7.13.47 'Oh yes, I almost forgot,' said John, 'that new diagram of our processes hasn't come back from the printer yet. So you had better prepare your own flow chart of the processes to send along with the simulation models.' 'I'll do that,' said John. 'Good thing you didn't want a sketch of the system,' Mary mumbled.

7.13.48 'Judd will do a write-up on the basics of line balancing,' John continued, 'pointing out some things that throw a continuous process like ours out of balance, how to identify when that happens and what to do about it. He'll point out concepts like throughput and constraints, what are bottlenecks, how to find them, how they affect other phases of a process and how to remove them.

7.13.49 'I'm going to write up something describing how continuous process manufacturing systems are evaluated, and comment on some non-financial performance measures managers might consider in evaluating these systems.

7.13.50 'Using the first two simulation models we developed, PULP1 and PULP2, Mary will show the consequences of adding unbleached pulp into a plant that processes only bleached pulp with the objective of pointing out the effects it has on throughput, scrap levels and product costs.

7.13.51 'Judd will use the third model we developed, called PULP3, to demonstrate the effect a bottleneck has on the system we set up in the second model – the one that processed bleached and unbleached pulp, we called it PULP2.

7.13.52 'I need your write-ups tomorrow by 5pm if I'm to get this package to home office right away. Any questions?'

7.13.53 'John, we left one other operating condition out of all this,' said Judd. 'What's that?' asked John. 'Starving,' Judd responded. 'The effect an upstream bottleneck has on downstream processes, like if our digester has lower throughput than expected.' After some thought, John said, 'That would require us to build another simulation model, which we don't really have time to do if this package is to get to home office in the next three days. Why not pose that as an open question at the end of your write-up and they can use it as a discussion question.'

Time and cost management

7.13.54 'Yeah,' said Mary, 'kind of like a final exam to see if they really understand all of this.'

XCELL+ terminology

7.13.55 A glossary of XCELL+ terms follows.

- Blocking: state that occurs when a process cannot dispose of its output.
- Bottleneck: an element limiting the throughput capacity of a factory model.
- Changeover: switch of a work centre from one process to another.
- Flowtime: time for a unit to pass through the factory, from release from a receiving area to acceptance at a shipping area.
- Flow analysis: calculation of flows, utilisations, cycle-times, and minimum process batch-sizes.
- Idle: state of a work centre when no input material is available.
- Line balancing: shifting work between adjacent processes to equalise the unit processing-times.
- Process: an operation on a particular unit at a particular work centre. The activity of processing a particular unit at a particular work centre.
- Processes: The key elements of an XCELL+ model since these are the elements that actually do the work; work done at a work centre.
- Processing-time: Time required for a process to perform one cycle, that is to produce unit of its part; also, a total of all processing-times for a tagged unit.
- Receiving area: Where material is received from the outside world.
- Set-up-time: The time required to prepare a work centre to run one process when it previously has been running another process.
- Shipping area: Where finished material is shipped to the outside world.
- Time unit: an undimensioned measure of the time required to perform the process on each unit – it is the cycle time or operation time.
- Unit: the increment of material movement in the model.
- Utilisation: the fraction of available time a work centre performs useful work.
- Work centre: provides a physical host for processes; where processes are run to perform work; active element of a model; site where processes are performed.

Activity mapping and the theory of constraints

Introduction to XCELL+ and Southern Pulp's model

7.13.56 XCELL+ is a computer application package that enables one to build a 'logical model' of a manufacturing process. An XCELL+ model can simulate the operation of a factory so as to estimate its production capacity and study alternative ways to improve its performance.

7.13.57 In XCELL+, graphics are used to help construct the model. But XCELL+ uses symbolic graphics rather than realistic pictorial graphics. That is, no attempt is made to make the elements of an XCELL+ model look like their real counterparts. This reduces errors in model construction and makes 'debugging' much easier. Furthermore, running the model in a choice of three animation modes makes it easier to understand the operation of a complex factory.

7.13.58 The flow of material through a factory model is measured in material units (just called 'units') per time unit. Each unit can, in fact, represent a single piece, or it can represent a pallet, tote box, carton, barrel or whatever physical entities are moved through the factory. The time units are also general, undimensioned units, so you can let one time unit represent whatever amount of real time is appropriate. Units originate at a receiving area, and presumably finish their travels at a Shipping Area. In between, they travel along links, passing through work centres and buffers.

7.13.59 Following is a brief explanation of the elements within the PULP1 model in XCELL+.

- Receiving areas allow materials to enter the system and are designated with an 'R' in their icon. There are two receiving areas, one to provide chemicals for the chemical preparation process (R2), and the chip pile (R1).

- Work centres are where processes take place, and are designated with a 'W'. Each step in the process description has a corresponding work centre. Examples are the evaporator (W2), and the bleach plant (W9).

- Buffers are located between work centres and contain work-in-process (WIP) inventory. A yellow bar within the buffer rises and falls to indicate changing levels of WIP. Examples are the blow tank (B5) and the black liquor tanks (B1 and B2).

- Shipping areas have an 'S' in their icon and provide exits from the system in two forms: finished product and scrap. Bales of finished unbleached and finished bleached pulp flow through shipping points S1 and S2 respectively. Scrap bleached pulp flows through S3, and scrap unbleached pulp flows through S4.

Time and cost management

- Paths, indicated by yellow lines, represent avenues along which materials and work-in-process are transferred.

Exhibit 1 Southern Pulp Company, Summary of results – simulation run of PULP1 model

Time units = 500							
				Average flow time (F6)			
Throughput:				Number	Avg-flow	Avg-proc	Avg-wait
S1	0		S1	0	0.000	0.000	0.000
S2	499		S2	50	12.000	4.000	8.000
S3	1		S3	0	0.000	0.000	0.000
S4	0		S4	0	0.000	0.000	0.000
	500						
Average WIP: 27.00							

Results: throughput (F3)
Shipping area output at time: 500

	Output period	Output cum	Shortage period	Shortage cum
S1	0	0	0	0
S2	499	499	0	0
S3	1	1	0	0
S4	0	0	0	0
	500	500	0	0

Results: WIP (F4)
Status at time: 500

	Current	Minimum period	Minimum cum	Maximum period	Maximum cum	Average period	Average cum
B1	3	3	3	4	4	3.000	3.000
B2	4	4	4	5	5	4.000	4.000
B3	3	3	3	4	4	3.000	3.000
B4	9	8	8	9	9	9.000	9.000
B5	4	4	4	5	5	4.000	4.000
B6	4	4	4	5	5	4.000	4.000
B8	0	0	0	1	1	0.000	0.000
						27.000	27.000

Results: utilisation (F5)
At time: 500

	% busy Period	% busy Cum	% set-up Period	% set-up Cum	% maint Period	% maint Cum	% blocked Period	% blocked Cum
W1	100.000	100.000	0.000	0.000	0.000	0.000	0.000	0.000
W2	100.000	100.000	0.000	0.000	0.000	0.000	0.000	0.000
W3	100.000	100.000	0.000	0.000	0.000	0.000	0.000	0.000
W4	100.000	100.000	0.000	0.000	0.000	0.000	0.000	0.000
W5	100.000	100.000	0.000	0.000	0.000	0.000	0.000	0.000
W6	100.000	100.000	0.000	0.000	0.000	0.000	0.000	0.000
W8	100.000	100.000	0.000	0.000	0.000	0.000	0.000	0.000
W9	100.000	100.000	0.000	0.000	0.000	0.000	0.000	0.000
W10	99.800	99.800	0.000	0.000	0.000	0.000	0.000	0.000

Bottlenecks at SPC

7.13.60 The Southern Pulp Company (SPC) situation illustrates how a simulation model can be used to understand and evaluate the performance of continuous-manufacturing processes and to assess the financial and operational impact of bottlenecks in a process environment. The simulation models are based on the continuous-manufacturing processes at SPC consisting of two separate but interrelated continuous processes: one for pulp production (consisting of debarking and chipping, digesting, washing and oxygen delignification, bleaching and drying activities); and another for chemical recovery to reclaim used chemicals (consisting of evaporation, recovery and recausticising). It is important to note that changes in product mix can directly affect the performance of a continuous process which can subsequently affect the amount of scrap material generated and the costs of each item produced. If bottlenecks are identified, the impact(s) on throughput and work-in-process can be assessed.

7.13.61 The SPC situation is useful to:

- compare the operational characteristics of continuous-manufacturing systems with discrete-part manufacturing systems;

- integrate management accounting and operations management issues;

- identify the cost accounting and product cost implications of changes in production processes;

- see how manufacturing processes are evaluated and how non-financial performance measures can be used in that evaluation;

- see how a computer simulation model can be used to demonstrate how a system's performance is affected by changed operating conditions.

7.13.62 It is readily apparent that discrete-part manufacturing processes differ from continuous-process manufacturers. As the name indicates, in a discrete-part manufacturing process individual products (or batches of products) can be seen, handled and even separated from other products.

7.13.63 Discrete-part manufacturing environments are characterised as a convergent process, i.e., components are fabricated, finished, inspected and assembled in subassemblies. They are then assembled into a complete unit. Extensive co-ordination is required between many in-plant systems to ensure that materials and components of the right quantity and quality arrive at the right place at the right time. The overhead costs needed to support such systems can become quite large.

Time and cost management

7.13.64 Since divergent processes are material-intensive, capital-intensive and fast, cost systems for continuous processors focus on process variables like equipment utilisation, equipment support, and wasted materials. Equipment can be expensive, and time lost processing off-grade material results in lower utilisation of capacity, a critical operating variable.

7.13.65 A continuous-manufacturing process is an integrated system of interdependent processes, where performance can be measured at separate work centres or segments, but system or plant-wide performance is of greater concern. As a process becomes more automated – as in continuous process manufacturing – changes take place in how standard costs are used. Labour standards are less prominent since labour is in a supportive role to the equipment and it tends to be fixed and not a significant cost element. Materials become more important as they make up a more significant portion of manufacturing costs, and material waste can increase with product changeovers and system upsets. Also, instead of including an 'acceptable' level of scrap as part of material cost, scrap may be treated as a separate item that is viewed as a loss, even though it cannot be completely eliminated. In continuous-manufacturing processes, the emphasis shifts to non-financial measures at the plant level due to the integrated nature of the operation.

7.13.66 Important line balancing considerations are whether tasks in the process are deterministic (task times are essentially constant) or stochastic (task times have high variance), and if the line is paced (work flow is controlled) or unpaced (workers move at their own pace). The PULP1 model is an example of a deterministic paced line that is balanced – each time unit is set at a constant of 1 and all work centres produce at equal speed.

7.13.67 If a line cannot be balanced perfectly, then individual tasks become either a bottleneck – since the work performed approaches or exceeds the capacity of the task – or a non-bottleneck where the task's capacity is not fully utilised. A bottleneck constrains the amount of material processed – throughput – to the capacity of the bottleneck task. Bottlenecks can be identified by a high utilisation percentage or by the build up of inventory in front of it. When a bottleneck exists, system waiting time increases because parts 'sit' in an inventory that builds up in front of a bottleneck task. They cannot be processed as they arrive, or throughput 'tops out' since succeeding non-bottleneck tasks are dependent on the parts sent from bottlenecked tasks.

7.13.68 A bottleneck early in a process can cause a reduction in the flow of products to downstream tasks causing them to 'starve', while a bottleneck in a task late in the process can cause blocking which means units produced by upstream tasks have no place to go. When they 'pile up', they block the flow of units causing following tasks to be shut down.

7.13.69 The primary effect of a bottleneck is to limit (constrain) throughput. Bottlenecks can be 'relieved' by increasing the processing capacity of the bottleneck task with more equipment, increasing throughput with greater operating efficiency, reducing downtime by a careful plan of preventive maintenance, alternating routing, or by reducing the flow of units produced by tasks upstream from the bottleneck task.

7.13.70 Variability in completion time can cause bottlenecks to occur. As process time variability increases, inventory in the system increases and capacity of the line (throughput) decreases. This is demonstrated by the following series of simulations where a five station line requires an average of 300 seconds to process a part, 500 units are produced (requiring 150,000 seconds of production time), only one unit of work-in-process is permitted at each station, and 10 runs are made with the standard deviation of processing time set at 50, 100, 200 and 300.

Maximum queue	1	1	1	1
Process time deviation	50	100	200	300
Mean total time	156,324	168,935	202,261	237,949

7.13.71 The large increases in the mean total processing time can be overcome by increasing the maximum inventory in the queue, which has the effect of making a work centre independent of its upstream work centre. For example, increasing the maximum units in the queue to 20 units results in the following mean total times for the same series of simulations.

| Mean total time | 153,564 | 157,359 | 166,236 | 182,236 |

7.13.72 However, it is important to point out that 'flow, not capacity, should be balanced. We should not attempt to keep all the resources (workers, machines, etc.) busy, but should focus on maintaining a smooth flow of material.'

Throughput
7.13.73 In continuous-manufacturing processes, greater emphasis is placed on identifying and controlling bottleneck operations that hinder throughput. Equipment in a bottleneck operation should be kept at 100 per cent of its available capacity in order to attain maximum throughput. In a non-bottleneck operation, the goal is to use the equipment only as needed

Time and cost management

in order to avoid wasting resources and the needless build up of excess buffer inventories.

7.13.74 In manufacturing discrete-part products, set-up time is an important element relating to equipment utilisation. In continuous-manufacturing processes, system changeovers are analogous to set-ups, except they are made 'on the fly', causing wasted products as new materials 'flush out' some aspect of the prior process, i.e., colour changes, reducing throughput.

7.13.75 The production of pulp and paper products requires expensive and complex equipment that operates on a continuous basis. In pulp process manufacturing, liquids or solids continuously flow through pipelines or on conveyor belts and each piece of equipment is linked to both upstream and downstream processes, often with buffers for work-in-process inventory in large tanks or vats. The processing speed of the various machines must be co-ordinated to ensure a balanced and steady flow of products in process.

7.13.76 Although machines have similar processing capabilities, some products can have different manufacturing specifications and requirements. For example, SPC can manufacture either bleached or unbleached pulp, where bleached pulp comprises a majority of the tonnage produced at South City. Changing from bleached to unbleached processing (or vice versa) disrupts production in a manner similar to that of a machine set-up in a discrete-part environment where production is halted while a performance characteristic is changed, e.g., dies are replaced on punch press machines, or cutting widths are adjusted on metal shears.

7.13.77 But in continuous process environments, the production line does not stop during a grade change and several hours are required before unbleached (or bleached) pulp is 'flushed' from the system. During a changeover 'twilight' pulp, a mixture of both bleached and unbleached pulp, is manufactured. Twilight pulp must be discarded, recycled or sold at vastly reduced prices as customers who demand pure white pulp will not accept brown fibres appearing in a random pattern within the product. The problem of mixed fibres also occurs when switching from bleached to unbleached production; thus, all grade changes result in wasted pulp.

7.13.78 The implications of producing twilight pulp are: (1) throughput declines, thus utilisation of the equipment declines; (2) scrap increases so revenue from the number of 'good' units sold declines; and (3) unit costs increase since the cost of equipment and support processes must now be spread over fewer 'good' units.

Activity mapping and the theory of constraints

7.13.79 See Figure 7.15 for a flow chart of SPC's processes at their South city plant.

Line balancing, throughput, constraints and bottlenecks

7.13.80 Line balancing is concerned with assigning workers and equipment to perform tasks to assemble a product. The tasks usually have to be done in a specific sequence and dependencies (or precedence constraints) exist, e.g., a hole has to be drilled prior to inserting a bolt. Line balancing involves:

'(1) breaking down a complex product and process into its component pieces and tasks; and

(2) juggling the co-ordination of those pieces and tasks so that the process is smooth and no bottlenecks are built into it.'

7.13.81 The implications of having unbalanced production lines are:

(1) bottlenecks occur and throughput declines, thus the overall utilisation of the production process declines;

(2) added (but unnecessary) capital expenditures may be made for equipment to restore throughput to the level 'expected';

(3) additional costs are incurred to maintain larger work-in-process inventories; and

(4) unit costs increase because either: (a) fewer 'good' units absorb the cost of equipment and support processes at the reduced level of throughput; or (b) higher costs of equipment and support processes are spread over the original 'expected' level of throughput.

The simulations

7.13.82 In addition to understanding the elements of the simulation, one should be aware of signals the simulation sends as it runs. For example, a work centre is actively processing when its icon is yellow. But, a work centre icon may also change to a red or black colour because of blocking and starving, respectively. Blocking occurs when a work centre must stop processing because no space exists for its output. In other words, the downstream buffer for WIP is full. Alternatively, starving occurs when a work centre must stop processing because it has no raw material input – something has happened upstream to interrupt the flow of products to downstream work centres. Occasionally a box of a different colour will pass through the system. This box represents a tagged unit which is used to calculate summary statistics of the operation of the system.

Time and cost management

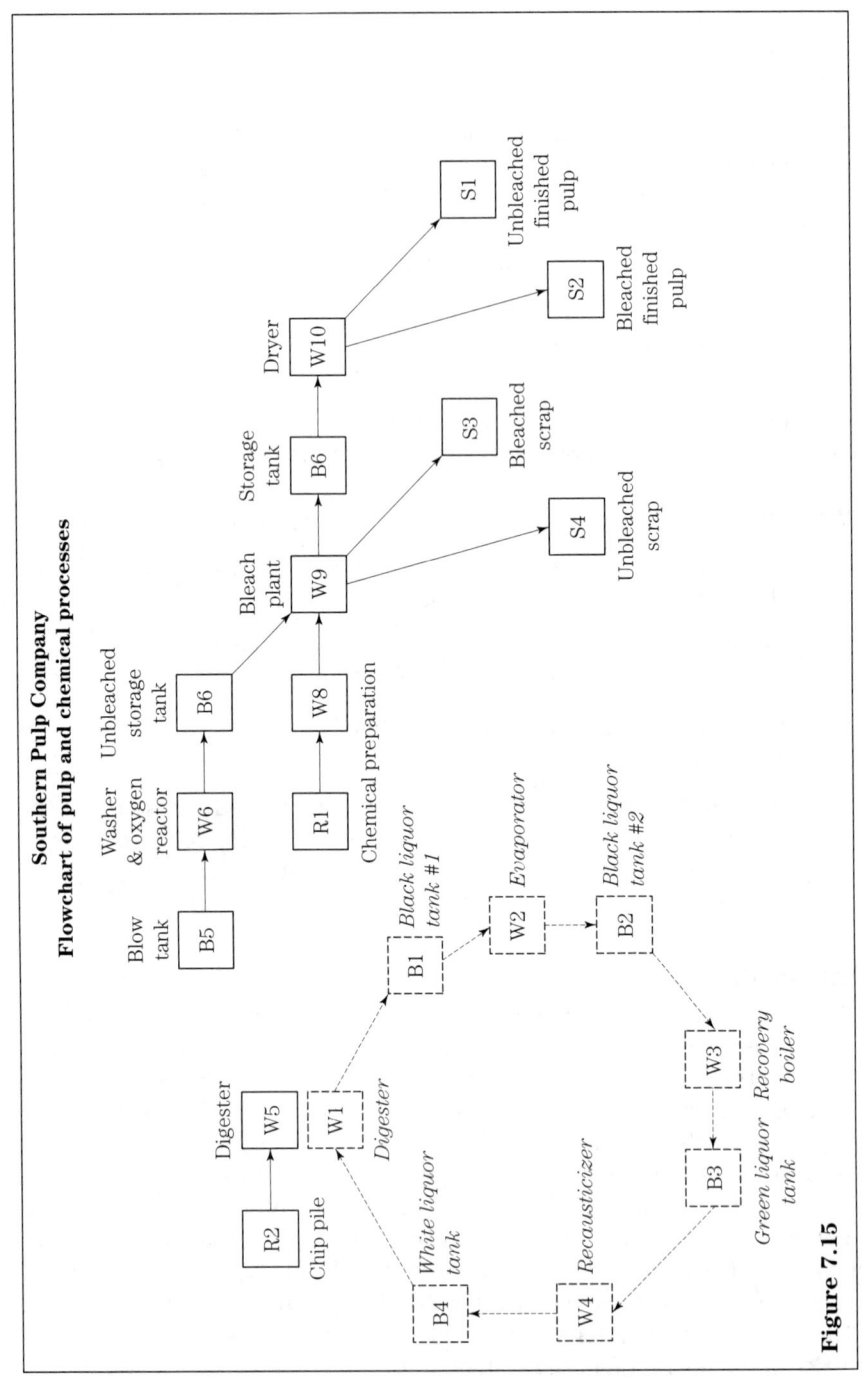

Figure 7.15

7.13.83 Since predictable amounts of scrap (twilight pulp) occur following a grade change, several interesting points can be discussed. First, the size of a batch of unbleached pulp processed is 10 units, while the size of a batch of bleached pulp is 50 units. Thus, if one unit is lost following a grade change, bleached pulp has a scrap rate of 2 per cent (1/50) while unbleached pulp has a scrap rate of 10 per cent (1/10). The simulations reflect similar total scrap losses per batch. (Note: The PULP simulations are based on a small amount of probability in the time unit to complete a process, so no two simulation runs will be exactly alike.) When the plant is dedicated to the production of only one product, scrap losses resulting from grade changes are non-existent. However, if the loss of one unit is spread over the output in PULP1, the scrap percentage is 0.2 per cent (1/500). The effects of these scrap rates on batch level cost per unit can be discussed at this point.

7.13.84 When PULP2 is executed, several performance measurement (as well as cost management) lessons can be taught. Recall that in PULP2 both bleached and unbleached pulp were processed, requiring changeovers which caused scrap material to increase. A review of Figure 7.16 shows the additional effects of producing bleached and unbleached pulp to be as follows.

- Throughput decreased from 500 to 491 units.
- Number of units scrapped increased from one to nine.
- Average WIP increased from 27.00 to 37.25, all of it occurring in B8.
- Average flow time through S2 increased from 12.0 to 22.7.
- Average wait time in S2 increased from 8.0 to 18.9.
- Utilisation of W8 dropped from 100 per cent to 82 per cent.

7.13.85 In summary, throughput decreased, WIP increased, flow time and wait time increased, and utilisation of one work centre decreased. The overall effect of these changes is fewer units produced, which causes the cost per unit of the good units produced to increase.

7.13.86 Model PULP3 illustrates the impact of a bottleneck located at the end of a process that produces both bleached and unbleached pulp. This was implemented by increasing the processing time of the dryer in PULP2 by approximately 25 per cent since it takes longer to de-water unbleached pulp. Thus, the dryer became a bottleneck and the entire pulp production process backed up (as evidenced by work centre icons that turned red because they could not dispose of output).

Time and cost management

Timeunits = 500

Average flow time (F6)

Throughput

			Number	Avg-flow	Avg-proc	Avg-wait
S1	75	S1	6	21.949	4.040	17.909
S2	407	S2	41	22.733	3.840	18.893
S3	4	S3	0	0.000	0.000	0.000
S4	5	S4	2	11.000	3.000	8.000
	491					

Average WIP: 37.25

Results: Throughput (F3)
Shipping area output at time: 500

	Output period	Output cum.	Shortage period	Shortage cum.
S1	75	75	0	0
S2	407	407	0	0
S3	4	4	0	0
S4	5	5	0	0
	491	491	0	0

Results: WIP (F4)
Status at time: 500

	Current	Minimum period	Minimum cum.	Maximum period	Maximum cum.	Average period	Average cum.
B1	3	3	3	4	4	3.000	3.000
B2	4	4	4	5	5	4.000	4.000
B3	3	3	3	4	4	3.000	3.000
B4	9	8	9	9	9	9.000	9.000
B5	4	4	4	5	5	4.000	4.000
B6	4	4	4	5	5	4.000	4.000
B8	15	5	6	15	15	10.249	10.249
						37.249	37.249

Results: Utilization (F5)
At time: 500

	% busy period	% busy cum.	% setup period	% setup cum.	% maint period	% maint cum.	% blocked period	% blocked cum.
W1	100.000	100.000	0.000	0.000	0.000	0.000	0.000	0.000
W2	100.000	100.000	0.000	0.000	0.000	0.000	0.000	0.000
W3	100.000	100.000	0.000	0.000	0.000	0.000	0.000	0.000
W4	100.000	100.000	0.000	0.000	0.000	0.000	0.000	0.000
W5	100.000	100.000	0.000	0.000	0.000	0.000	0.000	0.000
W6	100.000	100.000	0.000	0.000	0.000	0.000	0.000	0.000
W8	82.000	82.000	0.000	0.000	0.000	0.000	18.000	18.000
W9	100.000	100.000	0.000	0.000	0.000	0.000	0.000	0.000
W10	99.800	99.800	0.000	0.000	0.000	0.000	0.200	0.200

Figure 7.16 Southern Pulp Company – Summary of results – simulation run of PULP2 model

Non-financial performance measures

7.13.87 The incremental effects of introducing this change can be seen in Figure 7.17 (see page 432), as follows.

- Throughput decreased further, from 491 to 430 units.
- Number of units scrapped increased again, from nine to 30.
- Average WIP increased from 37.25 to 53.76, with changes in B5, B6 and B8.
- Average flow time increased significantly for S1, S2, S3 and S4.
- Average wait time increased significantly for S1, S2, S3 and S4.
- Utilisation of W8 dropped from 82% to 71.4% with decreases also in W5, W6 and W9.
- In summary, in comparison with PULP2 throughput decreased further, WIP increased more, flow time and wait time increased significantly for more work centres, and utilisation of four work centres decreased. Again, the overall effect is an increase in the cost of the good units produced since even fewer units are now produced and the use of facilities decreased.

(Source: adapted with permission from Carr, 1997.)

7.14 Non-financial performance measures

7.14.1 The performance of production processes is traditionally measured in terms of the production rate, work centre efficiency, inventory level and flow time.

7.14.2 Production rate is the amount of product a process completes in a specified time period. It is usually quantified as product per hour or product per shift, and is determined by simply counting the amount of completed product. However, this measure is dependent on the production mix and the quantity of each type of part produced in a specified period of time, which changes constantly; therefore, production rates are not effective measures of performance.

7.14.3 Work centre efficiency is a measure of the hours a work centre is available in a specified period of time. A work centre might be considered unavailable if it is being repaired, waiting for an operator, producing a reject part, waiting for tools or undergoing preventive maintenance. Although it can be identified with each work centre and is an easy-to-observe value, a system's performance is usually not determined by one work centre's efficiency. A bottleneck work centre might be used to establish a performance

Time and cost management

Timeunits = 500

Average flow time (F6)

Throughput			Number	Avg-flow	Avg-proc	Avg-wait
S1	69	S1	5	47.250	4.250	43.000
S2	331	S2	33	45.917	4.189	41.728
S3	12	S3	2	17.750	3.000	14.750
S4	18	S4	2	18.750	3.000	15.750
	430					

Average WIP: 53.76

Results: Throughput (F3)
Shipping area output at time: 500

	Output period	Output cum.	Shortage period	Shortage cum.
S1	69	69	0	0
S2	331	331	0	0
S3	12	12	0	0
S4	18	18	0	0
	430	430	0	0

Results: WIP (F4)
Status at time: 500

	Current	Minimum period	Minimum cum.	Maximum period	Maximum cum.	Average period	Average cum.
B1	3	3	3	4	4	3.000	3.000
B2	4	4	4	5	5	4.000	4.000
B3	3	3	3	4	4	3.000	3.000
B4	9	8	9	9	9	9.000	9.000
B5	10	4	4	10	10	8.109	8.109
B6	10	4	4	10	10	8.590	8.590
B8	20	4	5	20	20	18.058	18.058
						53.757	53.757

Results: Utilization (F5)
At time: 500

	% busy period	% busy cum.	% setup period	% setup cum.	% maint period	% maint cum.	% blocked period	% blocked cum.
W1	100.000	100.000	0.000	0.000	0.000	0.000	0.000	0.000
W2	100.000	100.000	0.000	0.000	0.000	0.000	0.000	0.000
W3	100.000	100.000	0.000	0.000	0.000	0.000	0.000	0.000
W4	100.000	100.000	0.000	0.000	0.000	0.000	0.000	0.000
W5	91.600	91.600	0.000	0.000	0.000	0.000	8.400	8.400
W6	90.400	90.400	0.000	0.000	0.000	0.000	9.600	9.600
W8	71.400	71.400	0.000	0.000	0.000	0.000	28.600	28.600
W9	89.200	89.200	0.000	0.000	0.000	0.000	10.800	10.800
W10	100.000	100.000	0.000	0.000	0.000	0.000	0.000	0.000

Figure 7.17 Southern Pulp Company – Summary of results – simulation run of PULP3 model

Non-financial performance measures

measure for the system, but it may be difficult to identify the bottleneck work centre and the bottleneck may move.

7.14.4 Inventory level is the number of parts waiting between a specified set of operations. But a difficulty in using inventory as a performance measure is that inventory level and performance may be negatively related – as buffer inventories increase, throughput can be declining or, at least, not increasing. Inventory level should probably be viewed more as a decision alternative and an input in setting up a schedule for the system, but not as an output performance measure.

7.14.5 Flow time is the elapsed time from when a part begins the first operation in a specified set until it completes the last operation in the specified set. This time will be the total of the actual process time, transportation time and waiting time. The waiting time can occur in a work centre, as in set-up time, or waiting in a buffer. Flow time is not as easy to observe and measure as other performance measures. This measurement requires that a time be recorded for each part when it starts its first operation, i.e., a part is 'time stamped'. Then, when the part completes its last operation in the specified set of operations, the time stamp is used to observe the flow time or elapsed time between the first and last operations.

7.14.6 Performance measurement may be considered management accounting's most important and most difficult task. It has been argued that an effective system of performance measurement should contain critical performance measures that:

- consider each activity and the organisation itself from the *customer's perspective*;
- evaluate each activity using *customer-validated* measures of performance;
- consider all facets of activity performance that affect customers and, therefore, are *comprehensive*;
- provide *feedback* to help organisation members identify problems and opportunities for improvement.

7.14.7 An organisation must identify critical features of its operations to monitor in order to determine whether the operation is functioning as intended. Performance evaluation is a critical part of operations control used to keep a process on track to achieve its objectives. Evaluating performance involves comparing actual results to some standard or target, which is developed in a variety of ways – past performance, industry or normative guidelines

Time and cost management

or potential performance. The latter incorporates a notion of continuous improvement to re-evaluate and improve ongoing activities based on competitive benchmarking.

7.14.8 Important measures of performance in continuous process systems are throughput, cycle time and throughput time. Whilst materials yield (ratio of materials output quantity to input quantity) is also an important measure for continuous process manufacturers.

7.14.9 Interest in cycle time is based on the notion that a product's service, quality and cost are all affected by time – service and quality decline as cycle time increases, and cost to produce good units increases as cycle time decreases. Cycle time is directly affected by the number of activities in a process and the amount of time spent on each one. Improvement in cycle time can be made by classifying activities as value added or non-value added, eliminating as many non-value added activities as possible, and reducing the time required for each activity that remains.

7.14.10 Cycle time refers to the total time it takes for a process to produce its product. It is calculated as a sum of the times spent on the activities of: (1) processing; (2) moving; (3) storing (or waiting); and (4) inspecting. Manufacturing cycle efficiency (MCE) is a measure for assessing process efficiency.

7.14.11 Conventional accounting reports on financial performance are akin to looking at a scoreboard at a sporting event – players know if they are winning or losing, but little is gained on what is being done right or wrong in 'playing the game'. Success is actually a function of how well players execute 'fundamentals'.

7.14.12 By using non-financial (operational) performance measures, an attempt is made to track progress on the actionable steps managers can take to be successful.

7.14.13 Kaplan and Norton (1992) support such a broadened perspective since single measures give neither a clear picture nor focus attention on the critical areas of a business, and what managers need is a balanced presentation of both financial and operational measures. In response to this need, they suggest a 'balanced scorecard' approach (see Chapter **11**) which provides measures giving managers a fast and comprehensive view of their business.

7.14.14 The balanced scorecard has financial measures that indicate the results of actions already taken. It complements the financial measures with operational measures on customer satisfaction, internal processes and the organisation's innovation and improvement activities, i.e., the operational measures that are the potential drivers of future financial performance.

7.14.15 The balanced scorecard aims to allow managers to 'link' performance measures and to look at their business from four important perspectives:

- How do customers see us? (Customer perspective);
- What must we excel at? (Internal perspective);
- Can we continue to improve and create value? (Innovation and learning perspective);
- How do we look to shareholders? (Financial perspective).

7.14.16 The basic concepts of using operational measures to assess performance can be found in the measures discussed above – production rate, work centre efficiency, inventory level and flow time as well as throughput, cycle time, and throughput time measures.

Chapter 8
Quality and cost management

8.1 Quality: how much is enough?

8.1.1 In competitive business environments, organisations need to ensure that high quality standards change with time.

8.1.2 Objectives for quality were formerly confined to product quality and therefore restricted to the shop floor where products were made. They must now attempt to embrace every function within the organisation, from purchasing through to marketing and finance. Morrow (1992) views quality in terms of the following.

- Accepting that the only factor that really matters is the customer: if the customer is not happy with the product or service received then, by definition, there is room for improvement.

- Recognising the all-pervasive nature of the customer/supplier relationship. Focusing on internal customers and satisfying their needs will also contribute to the final customer's satisfaction. In this way, the computer department supplies the design office engineers with design systems and may agree in advance a level of service which should ensure that these systems are always on-line when required.

- Moving from inspecting for conformance to a predefined level of quality to prevention of the cause of the defect in the first place.

- Instead of an operator making defects which are only recognised 'further down the line' after quality controllers have done their inspection, making each operator 'personally' responsible for defect-free production in their own domain.

- In production, moving from acceptable quality levels to defect levels measured in parts per million.

- Zero defect programmes, in which an obsessive drive to produce things right first time is enforced. This is equally applicable to activities as diverse as raising a purchase order or generating the monthly management accounts, as to manufacturing defect-free components in the plant.

Quality and cost management

- Quality certification programmes are based on third-party audits of the extent to which a company can demonstrate that it has complete procedural control over all processes which, if operating properly, will result in the customer receiving the goods on time and to specification.

- Emphasising the total cost of quality as a primary measure of all quality-related activities.

8.1.3 For any quality control endeavour, some notion of what constitutes quality is desirable.

8.2 What is quality?

8.2.1 The quality of a product or service may be viewed as the totality of features which determine its fitness for the use intended by the customer. It is ultimately a function and a measure of customer satisfaction. It is also a reference to conformance to the requirements. These and many other definitions in a similar vein have been given, and all of them are correct depending on the context. All relate to fulfilling the customer's needs, and these needs include affordability, delivery at the right time, safety, reliability and after-sales support. One may view quality costs as falling into one or other of two major categories. One category is that of the costs deliberately incurred in efforts to maintain or improve quality. This is called the 'cost of conformance'. It includes the costs of both prevention and appraisal activities. The other category is that of the costs suffered as a result of bad quality. This is referred to as the 'cost of non-conformance' and represents the failure costs. The former deals with what could go wrong, whilst the latter deals with what has gone wrong.

8.2.2 Musgrove and Fox (1991) note that quality-related costs comprise both the voluntary costs of achieving a desired level of quality, and also the involuntary costs of failing to achieve it, i.e., the costs of conformance, and non-conformance (sometimes referred to as 'cost of quality' and 'cost of unquality').

8.2.3 Each category of quality cost can be broken down into two further divisions.

8.2.4 *Cost of appraisal* refers to the cost of assessing the quality achieved. Appraisal costs can include the costs of inspecting, testing etc. carried out during and on completion of the product.

8.2.5 *Cost of prevention* refers to the cost of any action taken to investigate, prevent or reduce defects and failures. Prevention costs can include the cost of planning, setting-up and maintaining the quality system.

What is quality?

8.2.6 *Failure costs (internal)* are the costs arising from within the organisation of the failure to achieve the quality specified. The term can include the cost of scrap, rework and reinspection, as well as consequential losses within the organisation.

8.2.7 *Failure costs (external)* are the costs arising outside the organisation from the failure to achieve the quality specified. The term can include the costs of claims against warranty, replacement and consequential losses of custom and goodwill.

Conformance and non-conformance

8.2.8 Each cost category has several elements which can be identified distinctly.

8.2.9 *Prevention costs* are incurred to reduce failures and appraisal costs to a minimum. They may include the following:

- quality planning;
- design and development of quality measuring and test equipment;
- quality review and verification of design;
- calibration and maintenance of quality measurement and test equipment;
- calibration and maintenance of production equipment used to measure quality;
- supplier assurance;
- quality training;
- quality auditing;
- acquisition, analysis and reporting of quality data;
- quality improvement programmes.

8.2.10 *Appraisal costs* are incurred in initially ascertaining the conformance of the product to quality requirements. They do not include costs from rework or reinspection following failure. Appraisal costs may include:

- pre-production verification;
- receiving inspection;
- laboratory acceptance testing;

Quality and cost management

- inspection and testing;
- inspection and test equipment;
- materials consumed during inspection and testing;
- analysis and reporting of test and inspection results;
- field performance testing;
- approvals and endorsements;
- stock evaluation;
- record storage.

8.2.11 *Failure costs* are, as noted above, subdivided into internal and external failure costs. Internal costs arise from inadequate quality discovered before the transfer of ownership from supplier to purchaser and external costs arise from inadequate quality discovered after transfer of ownership from the supplier to the purchaser. Internal failure costs may include the following:

- scrap;
- replacement, rework or repair;
- troubleshooting or defect/failure analysis;
- reinspection and retesting;
- fault of subcontractor;
- modification permits and concessions;
- downgrading;
- downtime.

8.2.12 The external failure costs may include the following:

- complaints;
- warranty claims;
- products rejected and returned;
- concessions;
- loss of sales;
- recall;
- product liability.

8.2.13 The quality assurance department which takes the first steps towards producing an estimate of quality-related costs should aim to do the following.

(1) Involve the finance department in order to:
- demonstrate what the exercise is trying to achieve;
- discover where the difficulties in presenting data in the desired form lie;
- ensure the figures finally arrived at will be supported by the finance department;
- prepare them for future responsibility for collecting the figures on a routine basis.

(2) Produce figures which are valid within accepted limits of uncertainty:
- but without wasting effort establishing an unnecessary level of accuracy;
- with the objective of establishing the major areas of cost (which can then be re-examined if greater accuracy is needed).

(3) Present the findings to senior management in order to:
- give some measure of the cost of quality, and the savings potentially achievable;
- give a means of comparison between product and product, unit and unit, and possibly between the company and its competitors;
- give a base line against which future goals can be set and improvements measured;
- encourage the acceptance of quality cost data gathering as a routine finance activity;
- propose actions to control and limit quality-related expense.

8.2.14 Some commonly useful sources of information are:
- payroll analyses;
- manufacturing expense reports;
- scrap reports;
- rework or rectification authorisations or reports;
- travel expense claims;
- product cost information;
- field repair, replacement and warranty cost reports;
- inspection and test records;
- material review records.

Quality and cost management

8.2.15 Additional sources include:

- organisation charts;
- job descriptions;
- departmental budgets;
- standard costs at all stages of manufacture;
- standard or historic yields at all stages of manufacture.

8.2.16 Measured costs of external failure can be based on data from sources such as:

- customer service department records of returns and replacements;
- legal department records of warranty claims and liability costs;
- failure analysis laboratory records of investigations and sources of fault.

8.2.17 When comparing quality costs in different plants, or on different occasions, one should attempt to make comparisons on a like basis. The particular ratio used will depend on the factor to be highlighted, e.g., quality costs in relation to labour utilisation, sales value, production costs etc. Some such ratios are:

- labour-based: internal failure costs/direct labour costs;
- cost-based: total failure costs/manufacturing costs;
- sales-based: total quality costs/net sales;
- unit-based: total quality costs/units of production;
- added value-based: total quality costs/value added.

8.2.18 Organisations often find that if there is little or no investment in conformance costs, quality is likely to be poor, i.e., non-conformance costs will be high. Conversely, if more resources are invested in conformance activities, non-conformance costs will decrease and quality will improve. As quality improves, more difficulty will be encountered in producing further improvement.

8.2.19 Traditionally at a point where the conformance cost introduced is greater than the non-conformance cost it is intended to eliminate, improvement activity was seen to be uneconomic. Conceptually there exists a point at which the sum of conformance and non-conformance costs is at a minimum. This has traditionally been seen as the point of 'Economic Quality'. Producer and supplier at this point might accept the economic necessity for the incidence of defective items.

8.2.20 It must be noted however that quality must be defined broadly. One cannot assume that the loss from quality control should not exceed the intrinsic value of the rejected item. Suppose that a defective unit is installed in some medical instrumentation causing a heart pacemaker to have failed. Or that a failure caused the purchaser to find a different source of supply. In those cases the loss of customer goodwill and product liability costs need to be considered. The costs of bad quality can far exceed the cost of good quality.

8.2.21 The traditional model ignores the time element. Preventive actions have no immediate impact on non-conformance, but once they are in place they can reduce non-conformance costs throughout the market life-cycle of the product without further investment.

8.2.22 Para 8.2.19 also fails to differentiate between appraisal and prevention, or between internal and external failure costs. But clearly appraisal and prevention have quite different effects on non-conformance costs.

8.2.23 The traditional representation takes no account of changes occurring over the course of time. Consequently, it is preferable to plot the total cost of quality and its four components against time. Such a plot allows improvements and setbacks to be made more visible. One can then ask: are our external failure costs being eliminated, since these represent our quality as seen by the customer? Are our total failure (non-conformance) costs being reduced, since this represents our internal measure of quality? Are we reducing total quality-related costs by using prevention rather than appraisal?

Hidden costs and customers

8.2.24 The modern view is a representation of the total cost of quality that does include the 'hidden' costs of quality. These hidden costs are included to recognise that they are often substantially greater than the traditionally measured failure costs. Hidden costs ultimately relate to customer satisfaction.

8.2.25 Indeed, customer satisfaction is perhaps the most important quality criterion. Naylor (1999) identifies the findings of a study concerned with why customers stop doing business with companies.

8.3 The cost of not minding quality costs

8.3.1   In the UK, quality related costs have been reported to range from 5 to 25 per cent of company turnover (Plunkett, Dale and Tyrrell, 1985) and of this total 95 per cent may comprise the cost of appraisal and failure. The same is true of the US (Musgrove and Fox, 1991). TQM methodologies are often able to focus on the problem relating to the identification and solving of operational problems and enable quality costs to be categorised subsequently as relating to prevention, appraisal or failure.

8.3.2   The potential exists for TQM philosophies to blend into existing and emerging cost management practices and thereby to integrate quality costing within internal costing infrastructures (Bromwich and Bhimani 1994). In this respect, the Chartered Institute of Management Accountants define quality costs as:

> 'The expenditure incurred in defect prevention and appraisal activities and the losses due to internal and external failure of a product or service through failure to meet agreed specification.'

A case study: developing COQ information

8.3.3   Many companies, having successfully applied TQM principles in their plants, are beginning to realise its potential in other areas as well. Kalagnanam and Matsumura (1995) provide a useful illustration of the use of cost of quality (COQ) in a manufacturing company's domestic order entry department and the changes that resulted.

8.3.4   The illustration is that of a typical order entry department which receives customer orders, enters them in its system and forwards them to manufacturing or the stockroom for further processing. Simple as the process sounds, it may take much longer than necessary for the order to be processed further because of delays or complexities introduced into the system.

8.3.5   Precision Systems International (PSI) manufactures and sells high-technology measurement instruments. It has been in business for over 25 years, and has generally been profitable. Only a handful of standard products belong to each product line at PSI, but configuration changes and add-ons can be accommodated as long as they are not radically different from the standard systems.

8.3.6   Faced with rising competition and increasing customer demands for quality, PSI adopted TQM in 1989. Many employees received training and

The cost of not minding quality costs

several quality initiatives were launched. Like most businesses, PSI concentrated on improvements in the manufacturing function and achieved significant improvements. However, little was done in other departments.

8.3.7 PSI decided to extend TQM to its order entry department, which handles the critical functions of preparing quotes for potential customers and processing orders.

8.3.8 Order processing is the first process in the chain of operations after an order is received. High-quality output from the order entry department improves quality later in the process and allows PSI to deliver better (i.e., higher-quality) systems both faster and cheaper, thus meeting the goals of timely delivery and lower cost.

COQ study commissioned
8.3.9 As a first step, PSI commissioned a COQ study in its order entry department. The study had two objectives:

- to develop a system for identifying order entry errors;
- to determine how much an order entry error costs.

8.3.10 The main purpose of the study was to create an awareness, especially among top management, about the financial impact of poor-quality order entry. Information was collected through:

- discussion and interviews with employees both in and outside the order entry department;
- documentary evidence;
- a two-week sample data collection.

PSI's order entry department
8.3.11 PSI's domestic order entry department is responsible for preparing quotations for potential customers and taking actual sales orders. PSI's sales representatives forward requests for quotations to the order entry department though actual orders are received directly from customers. Service-related orders, however, are generally placed by service representatives.

8.3.12 When PSI undertook the COQ study, the order entry department consisted of nine employees and two supervisors who reported to the order entry manager. Three of the nine employees dealt exclusively with taking parts orders, while the six were responsible for system orders. Traditionally, the other six employees were split equally into two groups: one was responsible

445

Quality and cost management

for preparing quotations, and the other was responsible for taking orders. (The department has changed: now each of the six employees is responsible for both quotations and orders. A restructuring occurred to increase ownership of the quote and its corresponding order. Management hoped this restructuring would reduce the number of errors because one individual was now handling both the quote and the order.)

8.3.13 The final outputs (products) of the order entry department are:

- the quote;
- the order acknowledgement or the 'green sheet', which is used by the manufacturing department and the stockroom for further processing of the order.

8.3.14 The COQ study concentrated more on the order processing function than on quote preparation because it was difficult to obtain data about external failure for the quotes. However, the results of the study have implications for the quote process as well. The order entry department has several suppliers and customers.

Suppliers

8.3.15 The order entry department's major suppliers are:

- sales or service representatives;
- the final customers who provide them with the basic information to process further;
- the technical information and marketing departments, which provide configuration guides, price masters and similar documents (some in printed form and others on-line) as supplementary information.

Customers

8.3.16 The order entry department has several customers in addition to the final (i.e., external) customers. These (internal) customers are all the other departments in PSI that directly use information from the order entry department, including:

- manufacturing;
- service (repair);
- stockroom;
- invoicing;
- sales administration;

The cost of not minding quality costs

- the shipping, customer support, and collections departments, which indirectly use order entry information.

8.3.17 A good order acknowledgement (i.e., one with no errors of any kind) can greatly reduce errors downstream within the process and prevent later non-value added costs.

COQ

8.3.18 Quality costs arise because poor quality may – or does – exist. The PSI study focused on the costs that are incurred because of poor quality (i.e., internal and external failure costs). These are costs that would 'disappear if . . . products and processes were perfect'. Since PSI does not have a COQ system, the results reported here are estimates based on sample data collected during the COQ study along with information that was already available.

Internal failure

8.3.19 Internal failure costs are incurred when materials, components or products are identified as non-conforming before they are shipped to customers. For PSI's order entry department, the term 'non-conforming' refers to poor information for further processing of an order or quotation. Examples include:

- part number or price not available on the quote request;
- freight or payment terms missing on the customer's purchase order;
- credit approval not obtained (the order acknowledgement cannot be prepared in the absence of credit approval for new customers).

8.3.20 The costs involved here pertain to the time spent by order entry staff and concerned employees in other departments (providers of information such as sales or technical information) to rectify the errors.

8.3.21 A non-conforming product (e.g., an incorrect quote or order) may be identified by the order entry staff or supervisors when a document is inspected. Internal failure costs on non-conforming products pertain to any rework time required to rectify errors in the quote or order. A typical error would be an incomplete customer address on the quote or order acknowledgement.

8.3.22 Analysis of the sample data suggests that on average, it takes 2.3 hours (including waiting time) to rectify errors on quotes and 2.7 working days for orders. In determining costs, the COQ study accounted only for the time it actually takes to solve the problem (i.e., excluding waiting time).

Quality and cost management

Waiting time was excluded because employees use this time to do other activities or work on other orders.

8.3.23 The total internal failure costs, which include only salary and fringe benefits for the time it takes to correct errors, amount to over 4 per cent of the order entry department's annual budget. This cost figure includes salary and fringe benefits; the annual budget against which this number is compared also contains only salary and fringe benefits.

External failure

8.3.24 External failure costs are incurred when non-conforming materials are shipped to customers. For PSI's order entry department, the term 'non-conforming' refers to an incorrect order acknowledgement as specified by the department's internal customers. The impact of order entry errors on final customers is low because order acknowledgements are inspected in several departments, so most errors are corrected before the invoice (which contains some information available in the order acknowledgement) is sent to the final customer. This procedure does not mean that the customer receives a good quality system, but simply that the order entry department's errors do not affect the final customer. Mistakes that affect the final customer can be made by individuals in other departments (e.g., manufacturing or shipping).

8.3.25 Sample data collected from the order entry department's internal customers suggests that at least 22 types of errors can be found on the order acknowledgement. Commonly occurring examples included:

- more than one part number on the order acknowledgement when only one is required;
- incorrect or omitted delivery information;
- incorrect customer purchase order number on the order acknowledgement.

8.3.26 The cost of correcting these errors (salary and fringe benefits of an order entry person and a concerned person from an internal customer department) accounts for a little under 7 per cent of the order entry department's annual budget.

8.3.27 In addition to the time spent on correcting the errors, the order entry staff must prepare a change order for at least six of the 22 types of errors. Moreover, a change order is required for several other reasons that are not necessarily controllable by order entry. Examples include:

The cost of not minding quality costs

- change in the ship-to or bill-to address by customer or sales representatives;
- cancelled orders;
- changes in invoicing instructions.

8.3.28 Regardless of why a change order has to be prepared, the order entry department incurs some cost. Analysis of the sample data suggests that, for every 100 new orders, the order entry department prepares 71 change orders. This activity accounts for 2.6 per cent of the order entry department's annual budget.

8.3.29 Although order entry's errors do not significantly affect final customers, customers that do find errors on their invoices often use the errors as an excuse to delay payments. Correcting these errors involves the joint efforts of the order entry, collections and invoicing departments. These costs account for just under 0.15 per cent of order entry's annual budget: an amount that is immaterial in this example, though the problem could prove significant in other companies.

8.3.30 The order entry staff also spend considerable time in handling return authorisations when final customers send their shipments back to PSI. Interestingly, over 17 per cent of the time goods are returned because of defective shipments. Over 49 per cent of the time, the goods are returned for one of the following reasons:

- ordered in error;
- 30-day return rights.

8.3.31 An in-depth analysis of the latter categories suggests that a majority of these returns can be traced to sales or service errors. The order entry department incurs costs to process these return authorisations, which account for some 1.9 per cent of the annual budget.

Other costs
8.3.32 The costs shown in Figure 8.1 account for 15.7 per cent of the order entry department's annual budget. However, these costs do not include items such as telephone, computer time (data processing), supplies and opportunity costs that are not easily quantifiable (e.g., loss in collections, loss of sales and loss in goodwill). Inclusion of these costs could well raise the total failure costs to over 25 per cent of the order entry department's annual budget. The figures here are thus a lower bound on the cost of poor quality. (Some commentators have reported that the 'true' losses from poor quality can be up to six times the measured losses.)

Quality and cost management

Estimated annual failure costs
(as a percentage of order entry's annual salary and fringe benefits budget)

	Order entry	Other departments	Total costs
Internal failure costs			
Quotations	1.1%	0.4%	1.5%
Orders	0.9%	1.7%	2.6%
Total internal failure	**2.0%**	**2.1%**	**4.1%**
External failure costs			
Internal customers	2.6%	4.4%	7.0%
Change orders	2.6%	–	2.6%
External customers	0.02%	0.1%	0.1%
Return authorizations	1.9%	–	1.9%
Total external failure	**7.1%**	**4.5%**	**11.6%**
Total failure costs	**9.1%**	**6.6%**	**15.7%**

Figure 8.1

Changes in PSI's order entry department

8.3.33 Six months after the start of the initiative, preliminary results of the COQ study were presented to:

- the order entry manager;
- the manager of manufacturing;
- the manager of service and quality.

8.3.34 The results were also presented to the executive council (PSI's top decision-making body). PSI then began working toward obtaining the International Standards Organisation (ISO) 9002 registration for order entry and manufacturing practices which it received within nine months.

8.3.35 The effort to obtain the ISO 9002 registration suggests that PSI gave considerable importance to order entry and invested significant effort toward improving the order entry process. The manager of the order entry department indicated that the changes would not have been pursued if cost information had not been presented. However, the manager stated that information pertaining to the different types of errors was more useful in actually making changes to the process. Therefore, COQ information functioned as a catalyst to accelerate the improvement effort.

8.3.36 PSI has implemented several changes that have resulted in incremental improvement. In addition, PSI's management has initiated breakthrough improvement projects that are discussed below.

Incremental improvement efforts
8.3.37 Several minor but important changes have been made to PSI's order entry process. First, the preparation of quotes for 'engineering specials' and orders for demonstration systems have been altered so that key information is obtained up-front by the sales representative (for engineering specials) or by manufacturing (for demonstration systems). Before this change, the information was obtained by order entry employees from the sales representative or manufacturing. Even though order entry had no control over delays in obtaining this information, the delay was imputed to the order entry department.

8.3.38 Second, customers are now asked to include quotation numbers on their purchase orders. This change enables order entry staff to match the order with the appropriate quotation; this prevents duplication in manufacturing. Manufacturing actually produced systems (with standard configurations) in anticipation of customer orders. To complete this task, the department used sales estimates and quotations. Because of the lack of matching orders with quotations, duplication in manufacturing was not uncommon.

8.3.39 Third, PSI is providing tools to the order entry staff in the form of:
- procedure manuals;
- guidelines for sales discounting;
- printed configuration guides that contain information in the same format as order entry requires it.

8.3.40 The absence of these tools required order entry staff to call back and forth both within and outside PSI (e.g., to sales representatives in the field or to potential customers) to obtain information needed to prepare quotes or process orders accurately. These tools constitute a standardisation of procedures and help reduce the cycle time of preparing quotes or orders. Fourth and finally, a regular feedback system is in place to exchange information. Each internal customer department provides feedback once every three months, and improvement efforts are initiated based on the information exchanged. For invoicing – a key internal customer of order entry – the

Quality and cost management

order entry manager now heads the invoicing department. As a result of this change, that manager is aware of problems within invoicing that are a result of order entry's errors. Previously, these errors were corrected by the invoicing staff but never pointed out to order entry.

8.3.41 The most important improvement as a result of these changes is a reduction in the cycle time for preparing quotes (by 50 per cent) and orders (by 60 per cent). The breakthrough improvement efforts, discussed below, will probably reduce the cycle time even more. Although some errors still remain, most of them are beyond the direct control of PSI (e.g., customers that do not provide adequate information or credit bureaux that delay reports needed to grant credit to new customers).

Breakthrough improvement efforts
8.3.42 In addition to the incremental improvement efforts, PSI is pursuing three 'breakthrough' improvement projects initiated by its Managing Director.

On-line configurator
8.3.43 PSI is working with a vendor to develop an on-line configurator that will configure their standard systems. Thus, order entry staff will no longer key in part numbers. Instead, the staff will key in only the product name, then the configurator will generate the list of parts required for the standard system. The order entry staff will, however, be required to key in the part numbers for add-on parts requested by customers. Once developed, the configurator will provide two benefits:

- a large reduction in the number of errors caused by incorrect part numbers, duplicate part numbers, or omitted part numbers;
- a resulting decrease in cycle time for preparing a quote or an order.

8.3.44 For quotes, sales representatives and potential customers will be assured of accuracy, thereby eliminating delays caused by quotes that travel back and forth from the sales representative to the potential customer to PSI. For orders, increased accuracy will allow manufacturing (order entry's immediate internal customer) to manufacture the right system without further delays. Thus, manufacturing will be better able to meet the delivery schedules requested by customers.

New order entry system
8.3.45 PSI is also acquiring a new order entry system that is more integrated than the current one. The system can communicate with the configurator. Another key feature of the system will be that it will have the

capability to turn a quote into an order without the order entry or invoicing staff having to rekey any information. Finally, the system will be capable of generating invoices for these orders without the order entry staff having to rekey any information. This will eliminate errors caused by rekeying and accelerate the process of generating orders and invoices.

Giving sales representatives tools for quotes
8.3.46 Finally, PSI is working towards giving each sales representative a laptop computer with a built-in configurator so that they can prepare quotes in the field.

8.3.47 All these changes are geared towards cutting cycle time by reducing waste. Their common aims are to improve accuracy (quality) and speed (delivery) and to cut costs.

8.3.48 This case suggests that quality cost information can play an important role in opening the eyes of senior managers about a commitment to quality. However, cost information can only suggest that opportunities exist; it does not identify the problems or their sources.

8.3.49 Quality improvement requires information about the types of errors which can lead towards identifying the sources of the errors and taking corrective action. Thus, quality costs information should not be used in isolation but only in conjunction with other measures of quality and productivity.

8.3.50 Generating monthly cost of quality reports in isolation can be a useless exercise as far as quality improvement is concerned. Moreover, using COQ numbers to evaluate managerial performance may also be counter-productive if managers end up focusing more on how to manipulate the numbers each month than on actually making improvements in the process.

(Source: Kalagnanam, S and Matsumura, E *Cost of Quality in an Order Entry Department* Journal of Cost Management Fall 1995. Reprinted with permission. For more information visit www.wglcorpfinance@riag.com)

8.4 Making COQ work

8.4.1 This section explores the linkage between corporate financial reporting systems, the active involvement of accountants in total quality management (TQM) and the successful use of cost of quality (COQ). Managers seek to understand the cost-benefit trade-off and use of the economics of quality to assess the financial and strategic impact of a quality programme. Companies

Quality and cost management

like Pilkington Glass and Xerox provide excellent examples of the flexible use of cost definitions to show how reliable cost estimates of quality can make COQ a realistic gauge. These firms use COQ in their regular reporting scheme and link COQ to return on investment (ROI). They are examplars of how to evaluate key success factors that are critical for product or service differentiation.

8.4.2 As companies pursue improved quality, the costs associated with poor quality inevitably become an issue. Accountants, in partnership with quality specialists, can develop quality cost models to include cost of quality (COQ) in their measurement and reporting systems.

8.4.3 According to Carr (1995), COQ is simply a measurement tool that, when skilfully applied, can provide a valuable insight into a company's quality efforts. Unfortunately, there is little consensus today about the value of using COQ. Some companies use COQ calculations to arouse enthusiasm for a quality programme but quickly abandon the measure. Others place little value on COQ from the start. Many enterprises use COQ successfully as part of their total quality management (TQM) programme and regularly translate their quality efforts into monetary terms.

Successful use of COQ

8.4.4 There are two characteristics of successful and sustained use of cost of quality (COQ) according to Carr (1995).

- Financial managers become actively involved by helping to evaluate quality performance.
- COQ becomes part of the overall management reporting scheme, which contributes to the acceptance and use of cost of quality information.

8.4.5 Despite the fact that they regularly communicate using cost information, managers often find the cost definitions about quality inconsistent or vague. The economics of business are often seen to be based on a knowledge of costs: costs are regarded as guiding managers' actions and often as the means of measuring an activity. At times, managers find operational measures, including statistical process control (SPC), to be good predictors and measures of quality.

8.4.6 Many companies pursue product or service quality because they believe it will improve their competitive position and, ultimately, their financial results. Quality is a necessary attribute for business success. Some firms use quality as the prime competitive weapon for differentiating their prod-

Making COQ work

ucts or service. The importance of quality has led to the development of measurement systems to quantify the pursuit of quality. These measurements aid in the management and control of the quality programme by providing managers with an indication of the operation's success. To be meaningful, however, the measurement scheme must provide valued feedback and be a part of the management process of the organisation.

8.4.7 The most successful users of COQ link quality-related costs to overall performance, thus enhancing the value of the COQ measure. With the assistance of the accountant, managers can regularly make the connection between product, process or service quality on the one hand and successful financial results on the other. They can question the cost of maintaining a given quality level for products or services.

8.4.8 Managers tend to be trained to balance cost and benefits. They must choose investments given limited resources. Thus, managers often consider spending on advertising, production or communication equipment rather than on a quality programme that might yield more financial benefits.

8.4.9 Flexible use of cost definitions and realistic estimates make COQ an excellent surrogate performance measure of an organisation's overall quality. When product or service quality is a key success factor, operating managers find that COQ takes on meaning. It serves as an effective indicator of achievement, while also aiding in the selection of process improvement projects.

Returns on quality

8.4.10 It is widely believed that good quality is synonymous with good earnings and return on investment (ROI). Companies like Xerox, Ford, National Westminster Bank, British Gas and British Airways have embraced this idea. Their adoption of quality as a central competitive methodology is considered to have produced enhanced economic performance. Quality is also viewed as a recurring theme of many successful Japanese companies.

8.4.11 The profit impact of marketing strategy (PIMS) database, derived from a large scale investigation, provides empirical data to support the link between quality and economic performance (see Buzzell and Gale, 1987). The average ROI for companies in the top 20 per cent of quality was 30 per cent, while the firms in the bottom 20 per cent of quality had an average ROI of 13 per cent. Net profit as a percentage of sales also supports the value of quality. The bottom 20 per cent in quality had an average 6 per cent net

Quality and cost management

profit, while the top 20 per cent in quality had an average 14 per cent net profit.

8.4.12 When a COQ system provides credible and useful information, managers can relate the data to the overall business performance and the management process of the company. It has been pointed out that to measure and control quality spending properly, the cost of lost sales should be incorporated into calculations of failure costs. This modifies both the traditional and modern COQ model. It requires reliable estimates, but makes the static costs more dynamic. The COQ calculations are more believable for managers if they reflect the reality of the situation. This modification leads to better decision making and acceptance of the cost of quality metric. The modified definitions of the costs reflect the nature of the business and the reality of the competitive situation. These adjustments are necessary to link the pursuit of quality to the organisation's overall financial performance.

8.4.13 Xerox has a successful and sustained COQ programme which offers an excellent example of the value of linking quality measurements to the overall performance of the company. Xerox uses COQ extensively as part of its 'Leadership Through Quality' programme, which helps managers set priorities and choose quality initiatives.

8.4.14 Xerox did not need a COQ assessment to stimulate the adoption of a quality programme; a significant loss of market share and persistent customer complaints led Xerox to the drive for quality. Determining COQ was one of the main components of the programme. Management was concerned with the company's deteriorating financial performance and sought a connection between the 'Total Quality Leadership' programme and the company's financial results. COQ offered another method to confirm the positive economic effect of quality and, thus, to help managers choose quality projects.

8.4.15 Xerox published a COQ guide for use in quality training efforts. The guide outlined the company's way of defining COQ. Besides the traditional cost categories of prevention, appraisal, internal failure and external failure, Xerox added the cost of lost opportunity, which is defined as follows:

> 'the profit impacts of lost revenues that result from failure to meet customer requirements... Lost opportunities result when a customer: cancels a service contract, is not dealt with readily when he calls with an inquiry and he selects another vendor, returns a piece of equipment, or spreads the word to other potential customers of a bad experience with Xerox.'

8.4.16 This definition made COQ meaningful to line managers.

Making COQ work

8.4.17 Xerox stressed the connection between the factors of cost of quality and the overall financial performance of the company. A return on assets (ROA) calculation was used to demonstrate the effects of COQ on the financial results as follows: the cost of lost opportunity reduces sales revenues; non-conformance plus conformance costs increase the cost of doing business; and non-conformance costs require the asset to be used to a greater degree. Figure 8.2 presents a graphic display of the concept; the arrows indicate the pressures on this overall financial performance measure. Managers recognise that their decisions and actions relating to quality costs are associated with the key corporate financial measure of ROA.

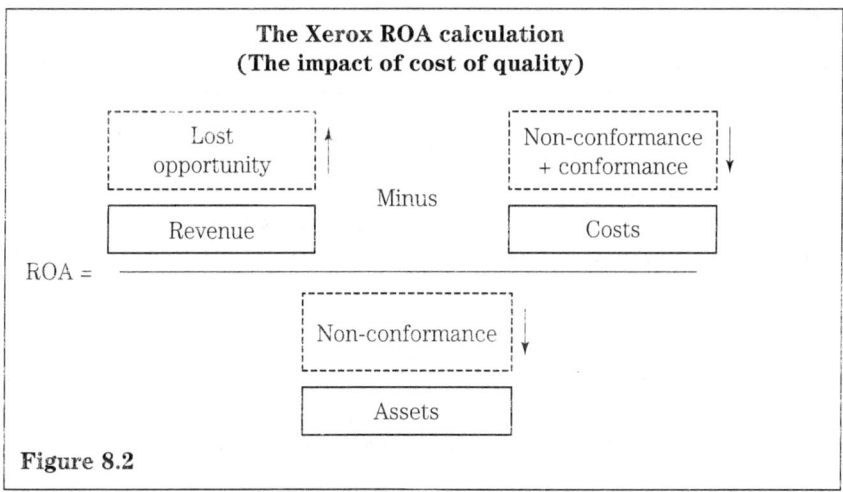

Figure 8.2

8.4.18 Xerox makes it clear that ROA can help managers do the following:

- reduce opportunity cost;
- reduce conformance and non-conformance costs;
- use assets more efficiently by reducing non-conformance costs.

8.4.19 The link between COQ and financial results thus becomes apparent and influences the behaviour of the managers. Xerox's quality training programme stresses this linkage, thus making it more relevant for managers. In this way, COQ was not limited to measuring the results of the quality effort, but became integral to the financial performance of the company.

8.4.20 COQ information consequences.

- Whilst cost of quality (COQ) is a measurement tool that can provide a valuable insight into a company's quality efforts, it also acts as a

Quality and cost management

potential indicator of process improvement and serves as a criterion for selecting projects to improve quality and return on assets (ROA).

- COQ can provide a link between economic performance and operational decisions.
- To use COQ successfully financial managers need to become actively involved by helping to evaluate quality performance, and use COQ as part of the overall management reporting scheme.
- Quality managers often realise that quality needs to be framed in the language management understands: money, costs and financial resources.

8.4.21 Companies that successfully use COQ develop reliable cost estimates. Appropriateness is more important than precision. Managers must consider the indirect cost consequences of poor quality, including lost opportunities and lost sales. They incorporate the timing differences of current spending and long-term investments to improve the process in their economic evaluation of quality. Given that COQ is consistent with other management reporting, it could be part of a firm's evaluation and measurement process.

8.4.22 With the expansion of information technology, managers are often inundated with data. Every management effort has its own possible set of associated metrics. COQ can serve as a useful management tool if managers can relate the format and data to the overall performance schemes of the company.

8.4.23 Quality is an attribute that can contribute to the economic performance of a corporation. COQ has meaning and purpose when it relates directly to financial results to ensure congruence between quality programmes and a company's goals. The cost-benefit trade-off is considered a basic business principle. COQ may thereby allow managers to generate excitement for quality projects and to link quality to the bottom line.

A case study: assessing quality and product line performance

8.4.24 'I'm not looking forward to breaking the news to Mrs W. She's going to take this pretty hard,' groaned Charlie Oliver, the finance director of Wellesley Paint Company. He and Don Smith, state liaison for the firm, were returning from a meeting with representatives of the Virginia General Services Administration (GSA), the agency that administers bidding on state contracts. Charlie and Don had expected to get the specifications to bid on the traffic paint contract, soon to be renewed. Instead of picking up the bid sheets and renewing old friendships at the GSA, however, they were stunned to learn that Wellesley's paint samples had performed poorly on the road test and the firm was not eligible to bid on the contract.

8.4.25 Charlie and Don were on their way to report to the president of the company, Victoria Wellesley. 'Mrs W,' as the employees fondly refer to her, is the 70-year-old widow of the company's founder and has served as president of the company since his death in 1987. 'Mrs W' is very proud of the quality of the firm's products and also of its close ties with the state of Virginia, where her family have been prominent citizens since before the Civil War. The label on cans of Wellesley's house paint features a picture of her antebellum home.

8.4.26 Wellesley's two main product lines are traffic paint, used for painting yellow and white lines on highways, and commercial paints, sold through local retail outlets. Because of the small size of the firm, all employees handle multiple tasks. For example, Don Smith's official job title is state liaison, and during contract negotiations he is the firm's main contact with state officials. When no negotiations are pending, however, he often drives a forklift in the warehouse or travels to road test sites where he operates the striping equipment that applies traffic paint to the highway.

Production process
8.4.27 The paint production process is fairly simple. Raw materials are kept in the storage area that occupies approximately half of the plant space. Large tanks that resemble silos are used to store the latex that is the main ingredient in their paint. These tanks are located on the loading dock just outside the plant so that when a shipment of latex arrives, it can be pumped directly from the tank truck into these storage tanks. Latex is extremely sensitive to cold. It cannot be stored outside or even shipped in the winter without heated trucks, which are prohibitively expensive for a small firm such as Wellesley.

8.4.28 Paint is mixed and packaged at six identical production stations. Each station has two 1,000-gallon mixing vats so that while the first batch of paint is being pumped into drums, another batch of paint can be mixed. An employee pours ingredients into a mixing vat according to a predetermined formula. When the mixing is complete, a sample is tested by the technical director for colour, thickness, texture and drying time. He issues directions for any additional ingredients or approves the batch. Workers then pump the paint into 55-gallon drums from a hose attached to the mixing vat. The

Quality and cost management

amount of paint that can be produced is limited by the available equipment and production space.

Traffic paint

8.4.29 Currently, Wellesley has the traffic paint contracts for the states of Pennsylvania, North Carolina, Delaware and Virginia. Of last year's total production of 380,000 gallons, 90 per cent was traffic paint. Of this amount, 88,000 gallons were for the Virginia contract. Each state has unique specifications for colour, thickness, texture, drying time and other characteristics of the paint. For example, paint sold to Pennsylvania must withstand heavy use of salt on roads during the winter. Paint for North Carolina highways must tolerate extended periods of intense heat during summer months.

8.4.30 The process of bidding on a traffic paint contract begins with a road test under the supervision of the National Association of Highway Paints (NAHP), an independent organisation supported by state funds. NAHP designates a certain stretch of highway to serve as the road test site. Any paint manufacturer may apply stripes of their paint at the test site. NAHP monitors the test site and reports the results to the state highway department. State personnel review the reports and invite the manufacturers of the best-performing paints to submit bids. The firm that submits the lowest bid wins the contract.

8.4.31 Contracts, which normally cover a five-year period, specify only the price per gallon and quality requirements such as drying time and road-life. The timing of deliveries is determined later based on state work schedules and weather constraints. Demand is highly seasonal, as states do most of their highway painting in June, July and August. The total amount of paint a state will order is not determined until spring, when the states know how much of their highway budget remains after winter snow removal costs have been paid.

8.4.32 After the paint is produced, the state must test the paint before approving it for shipment. A sample is sent to the state laboratory, which may take up to two months to perform the testing. In the meantime, Wellesley must store all the manufactured paint in its warehouse. At times, the warehouse has been filled to capacity and drums of paint are stored in the aisles, production areas and any available inch of space.

8.4.33 Due to the high cost of shipping paint, most paint producers can be competitive on price only in locations fairly close to their production facilities. Accordingly, Wellesley has enjoyed an advantage in bidding on contracts in the eastern states close to Virginia. However, one of their biggest competitors, Heron Paint Company of Houston, Texas, is building a new plant in

Making COQ work

North Carolina. With lower costs due to their efficient new facility and their proximity, Heron will become a major competitive threat.

Commercial paint

8.4.34 Wellesley's commercial paint line includes interior and exterior house paints in a wide range of colours formulated to approximate authentic colonial colours. Because of the historical association, the line has been well received in Virginia. Most of these paints are sold through paint and hardware stores as the stores' second or third line of paint. The large national firms such as Benjamin Moore or Sherwin Williams provide extensive services to paint retailers such as computerised colour matching equipment. Partly because they lack the resources to provide such amenities and partly because they have always considered the commercial paint a sideline, Wellesley has never tried to market their commercial line aggressively.

8.4.35 Mrs W is worried about the future of the company. The firm's strategic goal is to provide a quality product at the lowest possible cost and in a timely fashion. After absorbing the shock of losing the Virginia contract, Mrs W wondered whether the firm should consider increasing production of commercial paints to lessen the company's dependence on traffic paint contracts. Her son, who manages the day-to-day operation of the firm, believes they can double their sales of commercial paint if they undertake a promotional campaign estimated to cost $15,000. The average price of traffic paint sold last year was $9 per gallon. For commercial paint, the average price was $11.

Cost data

8.4.36 Charlie Oliver has assembled the following data to evaluate the financial performance of the two lines of paint. The primary raw material used in paint production is latex. The list price for latex is $13.50 per pound. If the firm uses more than 150,000 pounds annually they qualify for a 10 per cent discount; 450 pounds of latex are needed to produce 1,000 gallons of traffic paint. Commercial paint requires 325 pounds of latex per 1,000 gallons of paint. In addition to the cost of the latex, other variable costs are as shown below.

Raw materials cost per gallon of paint:	Traffic	Commercial
Camelcarb (limestone)	0.38	0.54
Silica	0.37	0.52
Pigment	0.12	0.38
Other ingredients	0.06	0.03
Direct labour cost per gallon	0.46	0.85
Freight cost per gallon	0.78	0.43

Quality and cost management

8.4.37 Last year, overhead costs attributable to the traffic paint totalled $85,000, including an estimated $25,000 of costs directly associated with the Virginia contract. Overhead costs attributable to the commercial paint are $13,000. Other manufacturing overhead costs total $110,000. Charlie estimates that $9,000 of this amount is inventory handling costs that will be avoided due to the loss of the Virginia contract. Both the remaining manufacturing overhead and the general and administrative costs of $140,000 are allocated equally to all gallons of paint produced.

8.4.38 Wellesley's strategy is 'to provide a quality product at the lowest possible cost and in a timely fashion'. Traditional thinking on strategy is that a firm can gain competitive advantage either by being the low-cost producer or by differentiating their product through superior quality (see Chapter **9**). The experience of Wellesley Paint demonstrates that in today's competitive environment a firm must be competitive on *both* quality and cost. In fact, all three strategic dimensions (quality, cost and time) are very much interrelated. For example, in the traffic paint market, while the low bid wins a contract, Wellesley has lost the contract due to quality failure.

8.4.39 The timeliness dimension of Wellesley's strategic objectives is problematic, particularly with regard to the traffic paint. The main reason they need substantial warehouse space in the plant is the delay in obtaining state approval of the paint after it is produced. Unfortunately, their ability to speed up this part of the process is probably quite limited. This is a good example of why some firms may have trouble adopting just-in-time inventory management.

8.4.40 An important lesson is that financial performance measures alone do not provide sufficient information for strategic decision-making. Non-financial and process information such as customer complaints, machine breakdowns and labour time distributions are important.

8.4.41 An important step for Wellesley is to determine exactly why their paint did not perform well on the road test for quality. It needs to investigate such issues as the following.

- Has there been a change in suppliers or type of raw material used in the production process? If either of these has changed, the material may not be of the same quality as formerly used, or possibly the formula needs to be altered to accommodate the change in raw material.

- Are the employees following the formula carefully? The employees may need additional training or guidance in mixing the paint.

Making COQ work

- Is the equipment working properly? The machinery may need to be tested and maintained to ensure it is performing as expected.
- Have quality standards in the industry risen? If so, why was the company's management not aware of it? Do they have a system for monitoring competitors' actions? Do they regularly get feedback from customers?

8.4.42 Figures 8.3, 8.4 and 8.5 present the profitability analysis for each of three scenarios. Figure 8.6 and 8.7 (see page 466) show supporting calculations.

8.4.43 One might initially expect that producing more commercial paint, with its higher contribution margin per unit, will improve the firm's profitability. The comparison of Scenarios A and B shows that without the Virginia contract they no longer qualify for the discount price on latex. This increases the direct materials cost for all paints produced. To some extent, the high profitability of the commercial paint is due to the quantity discounts available because of the large quantity of latex purchased for the traffic paint. The lesson here is that there is an inherent danger in evaluating the

	Traffic paint		*Commercial*	
Selling price per gallon		$9.00		$11.00
Direct materials costs:				
Latex	5.47		3.95	
Camelcarb	0.38		0.54	
Silica	0.37		0.52	
Pigment	0.12		0.38	
Other ingredients	0.06		0.03	
Total materials cost	6.40		5.42	
Direct labor cost	0.46		0.85	
Freight	0.78		0.43	
Total variable cost		7.64		6.70
Contribution margin		**1.36**		**4.30**
Attributable overhead		0.25		0.34
Gross margin		**$1.11**		**$3.96**
Allocated MOH		0.29		0.29
Allocated gen & admin		0.37		0.37
Net profit per gallon		**$0.46**		**$3.30**
Gallons produced and sold		342,000		38,000
Product line profit		**$155,975**		**$125,448**
Firm-wide profit				**$281,423**

Figure 8.3 Production line profitability – Scenario A: prior to losing the Virginia contract

Quality and cost management

	Traffic paint	Commercial
Selling price per gallon	$9.00	$11.00
Direct materials costs:		
Latex	6.08	4.39
Camelcarb	0.38	0.54
Silica	0.37	0.52
Pigment	0.12	0.38
Other ingredients	0.06	0.03
Total materials cost	7.01	5.86
Direct labor cost	0.46	0.85
Freight	0.78	0.43
Total variable cost	8.25	7.14
Contribution margin	**0.76**	**3.86**
Attributable overhead	0.24	0.34
Gross margin	**$0.52**	**$3.52**
Allocated MOH	0.35	0.35
Allocated gen & admin	0.48	0.58
Net profit per gallon	**$(0.31)**	**$2.70**
Gallons produced and sold	254,000	38,000
Product line profit	$(77,867)	$102,412
Firm-wide profit		**$24,545**

Figure 8.4 Production line profitability – Scenario B: without to losing the Virginia contract

financial performance of a single production line when two lines are closely related.

8.4.44 The comparison of Scenarios B and C shows the impact of changes in production volume on overhead cost per unit, because these costs, which are fixed, are now spread over fewer units. This comparison typically leads to a discussion of whether it is 'right' for the reported cost per gallon of commercial paint to go up because of a change in volume of the traffic paint. This is an opportune time to discuss issues related to allocation of overhead such as the desire to trace directly as many costs as possible, and how to determine the appropriate number of cost pools and allocation bases.

8.4.45 This demonstrates the 'death spiral' phenomenon (see Chapter **6**). In the recent emphasis on 'rationalising' product lines, some firms have discontinued less profitable products, only to find that the profitability of other products declines because fixed overhead costs must now be covered by the remaining products. To gain real financial benefit from narrowing the product line, management must take action to divest or redeploy assets and personnel associated with the dropped line. For example, if Wellesley per-

	Traffic paint	Commercial
Selling price per gallon	$9.00	$11.00
Direct materials costs:		
Latex	6.08	4.39
Camelcarb	0.38	0.54
Silica	0.37	0.52
Pigment	0.12	0.38
Other ingredients	0.06	0.03
Total materials cost	7.01	5.86
Direct labor cost	0.46	0.85
Freight	0.78	0.43
Total variable cost	8.25	7.14
Contribution margin	**0.76**	**3.86**
Attributable overhead	0.24	0.37
Gross margin	**$0.52**	**$3.49**
Allocated MOH	0.31	0.31
Allocated gen & admin	0.42	0.42
Net profit per gallon	**$(0.21)**	**$2.76**
Gallons produced and sold	254,000	76,000
Product line profit	$(53,727)	$210,047
Firm-wide profit		**$156,320**

Figure 8.5 Production line profitability – Scenario C: with double volume of commercial paint

manently discontinues significant segments of their traffic paint business, they will not need as much warehouse space. Ultimately, what is essential is to assess quality rather than simply focus on costs.

(Source: adapted with permission from Bremser and Dierks, 1998.)

A case study: achieving quality improvements

8.4.46 Recently, Mike MacFarlane, a cost analyst, transferred from The Boeing Company's corporate headquarters to Propulsion Systems Division (PSD). His prior responsibilities at headquarters did not completely satisfy him because most of his work there was too far removed from actual airplane production for his liking. Given his background in engineering and accounting, he felt that PSD would provide exciting career opportunities.

8.4.47 Because of his spirited attitude, ability to work as a team player, and knowledge of world-class accounting systems, he was assigned to a project team that examined the potential value of process and activity analysis (see

Quality and cost management

	Gallons of paint (a)	Lbs of latex (b)	Latex cost Total (c)	Per gallon
Scenario A				
Traffic paint	342,000	153,900[1]	$1,869,885[3]	**$5.47[4]**
Commercial paint	38,000	12,350[2]	150,053	**$3.95**
Total	380,000	166,250	$2,019,938	
Scenario B				
Traffic paint	254,000	114,300	$1,543,050[5]	**$6.08**
Commercial paint	38,000	12,350	166,725	**$4.39**
Total	292,000	126,650	$1,709,775	
Scenario C				
Traffic paint	254,000	114,300	1,543,050	**$6.08**
Commercial paint	76,000	24,700	333,450	**$4.39**
Total	330,000	139,000	$1,876,500	

[1] (a/1,000) × 450 pounds of latex per 1,000 gallons of traffic paint
[2] (a/1,000) × 325 pounds of latex per 1,000 gallons of commercial paint
[3] (b) × $12.15 price of a pound of latex, with volume discount
[4] (c)/(a)
[5] (b) × $13.15 price of a pound of latex, without volume discount

Figure 8.6 Latex cost per gallon of paint

	Traffic paint	Commercial paint
Scenario A		
Attributable overhead	$0.25[1]	$0.34[2]
Mfg OH	0.29[3]	0.29
Gen. & admin.	0.37[4]	0.37
Total	**$0.91**	**$1.00**
Scenario B		
Attributable overhead	$0.24[5]	$0.34
Mfg OH	0.35[6]	0.35
Gen. & admin.	0.48[7]	0.48
Total	**$1.07**	**$1.17**
Scenario C		
Attributable overhead	$0.24	$0.37[8]
Mfg OH	0.31[9]	0.31
Gen. & admin.	0.42[10]	0.42
Total	**$0.97**	**$1.10**

[1] $85,000/342,000 gallons
[2] $13,000/38,000
[3] $110,000/380,000
[4] $140,000/380,000
[5] ($85,000 − 25,000)/254,000
[6] ($110,000 − 9,000)/292,000
[7] $140,000/292,000
[8] ($13,000 + 15,000)/76,000
[9] ($110,000 − 25,000)/330,000

Figure 8.7 Assignment of overhead

Making COQ work

Chapter **6**). Mary Barclay, supervisor for programme cost targets and budgets, had been designated as the team leader of the process and activity analysis project team.

8.4.48 Joe Kelker, director of finance at PSD, explained to Mike the objective of the process and activity analysis project:

> 'As you know, a few years ago, Boeing launched several strategic initiatives to enhance our competitive standing. The central theme was to achieve continuous quality improvement in every aspect of the company's operation. Only by continuously improving The Boeing Company's competitive strengths will we prosper in an environment of rapid technological change, increasing competitive pressures and global markets.
>
> 'However, top management's commitment to continuous improvement can be realised only if we identify specific opportunities for improvement. Instead of just making statements about Boeing's competitiveness, we need to actually modify our manufacturing and service operations. I think that viewing cost data based on process and activity analysis is a key factor in enabling us to identify these opportunities.'

8.4.49 Joe further explained his ideas by quoting from one of Boeing's recent top management statements: 'Our objective is to realign the accounting system so that the cost information provided aligns with our understanding of the flow of resources in the processes at Boeing. Only then can we use with confidence our accounting data as an aid in targeting and measuring our CQI (continuous quality improvement) performance.'

8.4.50 After contemplating these notions for a while, Mike applied Joe's message to PSD:

> 'Currently we have a management accounting system that allows us to analyse cost variances interactively. However, the shortcoming of the cost visibility system is that it is structured largely along functional organisation lines (e.g., manufacturing, engineering, finance). If we want to identify opportunities for process improvement, we need to associate costs with processes and activities, not just functional organisations. Also, we need to be able to estimate the change in total cost given a change in the manufacturing process. Taking a process view of the data will enhance our ability to identify improvement opportunities. We must then be able to compare their relative importance and to judge what leverage we have in making modifications. This will allow us to prioritise improvement opportunities.
>
> 'Looking at the best manufacturing companies worldwide, we discovered that many of them employed activity-based cost management to achieve this. Propulsion Systems Division has been selected for a pilot project examining the value of this concept for Boeing. We hope the lessons learned will lead to a refined

Quality and cost management

methodology of analysis that can be used strategically throughout The Boeing Company.'

8.4.51 Joe continued by defining Mike's job: 'Your responsibility in this project will be to develop a database describing all the activities in our division. Mary and I decided it would be best to get you started in this project by having you perform a process and activity analysis for the engine build-up (EBU) shop. This way you will learn our methodology from the ground up.'

The Propulsion Systems Division
8.4.52 Boeing's Propulsion Systems Division provided the link between the engine manufacturer and the airplane. The division defined its responsibility as 'everything under the wing'.

8.4.53 Even though the engine itself was bought (according to airline customer specifications) from Pratt & Whitney, Rolls Royce or General Electric, there were several variations to accommodate. PSD's functions included the design, procurement, build-up and installation of all the hardware associated with the engine. The hardware PSD provided included the cowls, thrust reverser, strut, strut fairings and exhaust sleeve, as well as the engine build-up components.

8.4.54 PSD's assembly operations were fairly complex, since they included more than 20 possible different, basic engine-airplane combinations that were modified to customer specifications. This complexity was further increased by strict inspection requirements by Boeing's quality assurance organisation and the Federal Aviation Administration.

8.4.55 Mike's assignment involved the engine build-up (EBU) shop at PSD. The EBU line took the engine core and added the wire bundles, hoses, ducts, engine mounts, and components according to design specifications. Next the cowls, thrust reverser, plug and exhaust sleeve were added to meet functional and aerodynamic specifications. The engineering department listed the following considerations as the most important factors for the design of an engine: performance (i.e., thrust), reliability, maintainability and weight.

The process and activity analysis project
8.4.56 The division-wide process and activity analysis project grew out of a small pilot project considering only the engine build-up (EBU) within PSD. In Autumn 1990, this initial project was completed. Since the results were extremely promising, management decided to extend the project to the whole division.

Making COQ work

8.4.57 Carolyn Feller, the division general manager, summarised the outcome of the initial study: 'We gained a new appreciation of cost composition and activities in the EBU and of the gap between presently available cost data and the financial information that was needed for managing in an intensively competitive environment.'

8.4.58 One of the results of the pilot project included a definition of outputs for the division. The findings suggested there should be four process centres: engine build-up, strut, wire shop and new propulsion development.

8.4.59 Shop management contended that they had been doing activity analysis for years. They claimed that over time the company has placed a significant emphasis on improving detailed task efficiencies in the shop. While they recognised there were still opportunities for improvement in the shop, they believed there was additional benefit to be gained by analysing the support processes as well.

8.4.60 Propulsion Systems' senior management concurred, emphasising that once the entire business unit was analysed from a process perspective and value was assessed from the customer's point of view, PSD would have the information to identify high-leverage opportunities.

8.4.61 Since Carolyn believed that PSD could benefit significantly from this project, she wrote a memo to all supervisors at PSD, demonstrating commitment from top management and asking for consistent support throughout the division.

8.4.62 The methodology developed by the project team was referred to as *process and activity analysis*, rather than the popular industry term *activity-based costing*. While activity-based costing emphasised accounting, process and activity analysis emphasised Boeing's intention to apply the project's results to all business operations and not just to improve the cost management system. Process and activity analysis was like a comprehensive medical check-up, a labour-intensive diagnostic tool that pointed to the areas where high-leverage opportunities existed. Process and activity analysis did not provide the remeasurement capabilities of a costing system which the term activity-based costing implied.

8.4.63 In its statement of work, the project team agreed to five objectives for the process and activity analysis project:

- increase cost visibility;
- identify major cost drivers;

Quality and cost management

- trace overhead cost to processes where possible;
- identify non-value added activities;
- provide a process flowchart to help guide improvement measures.

8.4.64 First, Boeing's management felt that the current cost management system did not provide enough visibility. Specifically, when work crossed organisational boundaries, costs created by the underlying total production process remained largely hidden. Process and activity analysis would provide information that increased cost visibility.

8.4.65 Second, process and activity analysis would identify the major cost drivers so that Boeing could better identify items to be analysed and predict cost behaviour if a process were modified.

8.4.66 Third, the analysis would improve the traceability of overhead costs. A better understanding of the production process and its relation to total cost would improve management's ability to make each organisational unit responsible for the overhead resources it consumes.

8.4.67 Fourth, the project would support the continuous quality improvement initiative by identifying which activities add value to the end product and which activities are non-value added. Reducing or eliminating non-value added activities would ensure The Boeing Company's ability to maintain its competitive advantage.

Process and activity analysis

8.4.68 In the first step of process and activity analysis each work group developed a list of activities and tasks. In Boeing's terminology, a task was defined as a generic operation, whereas an activity represented a group of tasks. For manufacturing, the operations and inspection records (O&IRs) provided a guideline for the development of the activity and task list because they contained the assembly instructions as defined by the Manufacturing Production Planning department (see Figure 8.8). Bar charts showed the sequence and time allowed for each activity that a shop employee must perform each day to meet schedule requirements (see Figure 8.9).

8.4.69 Each task was characterised by its value, end product (or process), activity type, task time, flow time and task dollars. The value was either primary external (PE), primary internal (PI), support external (SE), or support internal (SI). Primary tasks were valueadded activities that changed the form, fit or function of the product, for which the customer was willing to pay. All other activities were support tasks (i.e., non-value added).

Making COQ work

Part #	Name	Quantity
314T3310-5	Sleeve	1
314T4320-13	Plug	1
333T4000-2	Bracket	2
69B97200	Pin	1
BACB30PN4-5	Bolt	66
BACB30PN4-6	Bolt	18
BACN10HR4C	Nut	67
NAS1587-4C	Washer	84

Reference drawings
301T4700 Sheet 1, 2, 4
333T4000 Plan, Sheet 1

Tool requirements
Ohme 314T3310 – Sleeve sling

Work to be performed

Operation	Description
010.00	Receive sleeve & plug and route packaging sheets to Q.C.
020.00	Record exhaust part number and serial number
030.00	Inspect – O.K. to install exhaust plug and sleeve
040.00	Install fasteners (16) places and torque per reference drawing
050.00	Inspect – witness/record torque on 10% of fasteners
060.00	Install index pin on outer flange
070.00	Install fasteners (66) places per drawing. Inspect – witness/record torque on 10% of fasteners
080.00	Remove Ohme sling
090.00	Note any fit or fair problems

Figure 8.8 Engine build-up

External tasks were done for anyone outside the work group, such as customers or other work groups, while internal tasks were performed to serve the same work group. Internal tasks were more easily modified than external tasks, since they were restricted to only one organisational unit. For tasks identified as internal, no party outside the organisation performing the task depended on its performance (see Figure 8.10).

8.4.70 The instruction manual for the interviewer contained the following examples for the different task types: typically, manufacturing operations

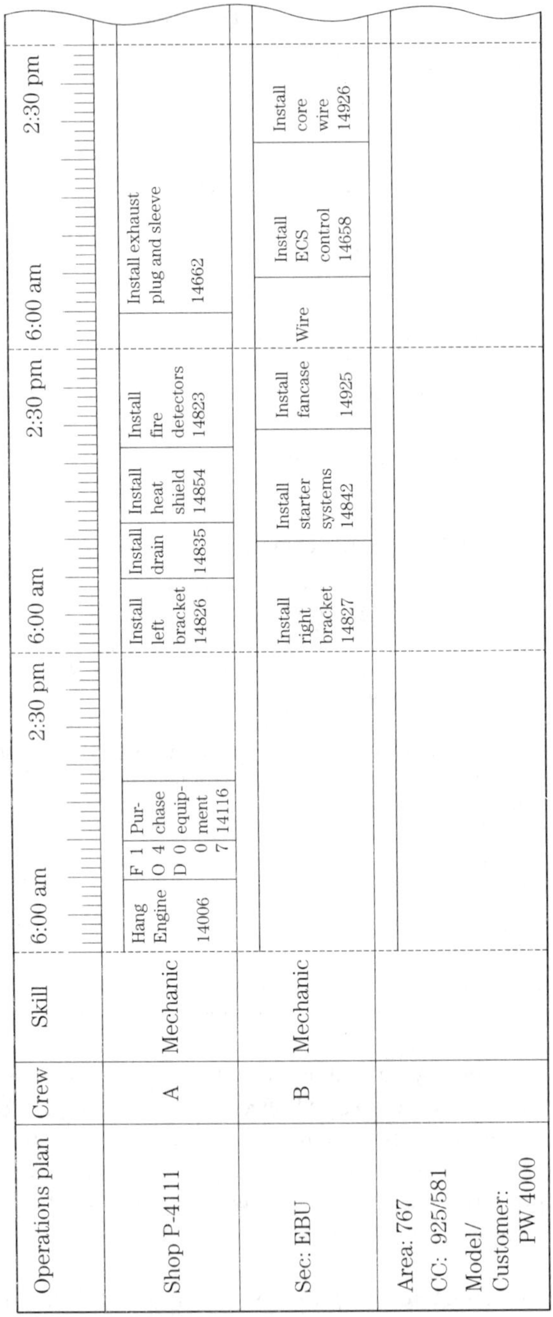

Quality and cost management

Operations plan	Crew	Skill	6:00 am	2:30 pm	6:00 am	2:30 pm	6:00 am	2:30 pm
Shop P-4111	A	Mechanic	Hang Engine 14006	F 1 Pur- O 4 chase D 0 equip- 0 ment 7 14116	Install left bracket 14826	Install drain 14835 / Install heat shield 14854	Install fire detectors 14823	Install exhaust plug and sleeve 14662
Sec: EBU	B	Mechanic			Install right bracket 14827	Install starter systems 14842	Install fancase 14925	Wire / Install ECS control 14658 / Install core wire 14926
Area: 767 CC: 925/581 Model/ Customer: PW 4000								

Figure 8.9 Engine build-up – shop bar chart

Making COQ work

Shop: **P-4111**   Model: **767**   Engine type: **P&W 4000**

O&IR# **14662**

O&IR (Activity) Title: Install exhaust plug & sleeve

Major activity: Inlet & exhaust

Operation	Task description	PE	PI	SE	SI Get drawings	SI Go to rotobin	SI Go to toolroom	SI Go to callsheet	SI Get test equip	SI Uncrate	Task total	Freq/yr
010.00	Receive plug/sleeve	.5			.2	.2				.5	1.6	200
020.00	Record pin # & serial #			.2							0.4	200
030.00	Inspect – o.k. to install plug and sleeve					.2					0.2	200
040.00	Install bolts & torque	.7									0.7	200
050.00	Inspect/witness/record torque on 10% of fasteners	.7									0.7	200
060.00	Install index pin	.2									0.2	200
070.00	Install fasteners (66) places/inspect/witness torque on 10% of fasteners	3.1					.2	.2			3.5	200
080.00	Remove sling				.5						0.5	200
090.00	Note any fit or fair problems				.2						0.2	200
	Analysis totals:	5.2		0.2	0.7	0.2	0.2	0.8	0.2	0.5	8.0	
		PE	PI	SE	SI	SI	SI	SI	SI	SI	Total	
								2.6				
								SI				

Figure 8.10 Engine build-up

Quality and cost management

were classified as primary external tasks, because they usually modified the form, fit or function of the product. Operations that prepared the product for the manufacturing process were typically primary internal tasks. So, for example, if hardware had to be removed to gain access to certain components, then its removal was considered primary internal.

8.4.71 Support tasks did not change the form, fit or function of the product. For instance, internal training or inspection procedures and quality control checks were typically support tasks in nature. If these tasks were performed for someone outside the work group, they were classified as external. Therefore, quality control was mostly support external. By default, all other tasks were support internal tasks. They included preparation of tools, preparation of internal flow control, training, group meetings and so on.

8.4.72 For each task, the work group estimated the task time, which was the number of hours spent on each task per product unit. The task time described the actual duration of the work performed. Task times were distinguished from flow times, which included task times as well as wait, transport and idle times. The hours spent per unit were then multiplied by the number of units produced to obtain estimated total hours. Since the estimates provided by the work groups often did not add up to the total hours worked, the estimated hours were adjusted.

8.4.73 Data collection was performed mainly through interviews. Before conducting the interviews, all interviewers went through a two-day training programme set up by the process and activity analysis project team. This training ensured reliable and consistent interviews. Crucial to the success of the project was consistent classification of tasks into primary and support, as well as external and internal.

8.4.74 In addition, the project team collected all directly assignable costs for each work group. These costs included direct labour, indirect labour, overtime, fringe benefits and non-labour costs such as supplies, training, furniture and fixtures, shipping material, etc. (see Figure 8.11). These costs were extracted from the current cost accounting system by the charge number, which uniquely identified each work group. That is, the only costs assignable to each work group were those that the group's supervisor could control.

8.4.75 Total labour hours were the base for measuring the cost of the activities (see Figure 8.11). The rate for each work group was calculated as:

Description	$ %	Dollars	Hours	Rate
Direct labor				
Quality assurance	0%	36	3	
Fabrication	0%	21	2	
Minor assembly	0%	180	16	
Major assembly	37%	185,652	15,650	
Rework	1%	7,361	568	
Developmental	0%	836	61	
Vendor rework	5%	27,578	2,174	
Total direct labor	44%	221,664	18,473	
Indirect labor	15%	74,791	4,829	
Overtime, fringe benefits and bonus	34%	173,436		
Total labour	93%	$469,891	23,302	
Non-labor				
Tool and shop equipment	3%	13,496		
Perishable tools and equipment	2%	9,549		
Shop supplies	1%	6,275		
Travel – general	0%	1,925		
Group administered training	0%	1,775		
Undergraduate & graduate study	0%	1,125		
Telephones	0%	925		
Support from Support Services	0%	675		
Office machines & equipment	0%	520		
Office furniture and fixtures	0%	450		
Misc expense	0%	200		
Office supplies	0%	75		
Data processing supplies	0%	20		
Conferences and seminars	0%	12		
Business meeting expense	0%	9		
Total non-labor $	7%	37,030		
Total	100%	$506,921 /	23,302 =	$21.75

Figure 8.11 Engine build-up – cost analysis

Rate = total $ ÷ total hours
    = [direct labour $ + indirect labour $ + non-labour $] ÷ [direct labour hours + indirect labour hours]

8.4.76 Multiplying the labour hours for each task by the rate gave a cost value for each activity (see Figure 8.12). These rates were often different for each first-line supervisor's work group because the workers in each group had different labour rates and consumed different overhead cost elements.

Quality and cost management

Operation	Task description	Value	Task time	*	Frequency/yr	*	Rate	=	Dollars
010.00	Receive plug and sleeve	PE	0.5		200		$21.75		$2,175
010.00	Get drawings	SI	0.2		200		$21.75		$870
010.00	Go to rotobin	SI	0.2		200		$21.75		$870
010.00	Go to callsheet	SI	0.2		200		$21.75		$870
010.00	Uncrate	SI	0.5		200		$21.75		$2,175
020.00	Record pin number and serial number	SE	0.2		200		$21.75		$870
020.00	Go to callsheet	SI	0.2		200		$21.75		$870
030.00	Inspect to install plug and sleeve								
030.00	Go to callsheet	SI	0.2		200		$21.75		$870
040.00	Install bolts and torque	PE	0.7		200		$21.75		$3,045
050.00	Inspect/witness torque – 10% fasteners	PE	0.7		200		$21.75		$3,045
060.00	Install pin index	PE	0.2		200		$21.75		$870
070.00	Install fasteners/witness torque	PE	3.1		200		$21.75		$13,485
070.00	Go to callsheet	SI	0.2		200		$21.75		$870
070.00	Get test equipment	SI	0.2		200		$21.75		$870
080.00	Remove sling	SI	0.5		200		$21.75		$2,175
090.00	Note problems	SI	0.2		200		$21.75		$870
Total	Install exhaust plug and sleeve		8.0		200		$21.75		$34,800

Figure 8.12 Engine build-up – Activity: install exhaust plug and sleeve – value analysis worksheet

Making COQ work

8.4.77 Given the activities and their dollar values, Pareto charts were prepared that indicated the importance of each task in terms of its cost (see Figures 8.13 and 8.14). In general, a Pareto chart is a bar chart that graphically represents the importance of a set of items. The length of the bar indicates the amount of resources expended on the associated item.

8.4.78 For the process and activity analysis project, Pareto charts provided an easily understood visual representation of the relative importance of activities. High-cost activities often provided the best opportunities for process improvements.

The 767 engine build-up group

8.4.79 Mike accompanied John Parker, a shop supervisor selected as one of the interviewers for the project, to meetings with the 767 engine build-up group. After several meetings, the operations group and the project team agreed on a list of activities performed by the operations group. The most difficult step was to find a good balance between specificity and generality of the activities identified. Too detailed activity lists were cumbersome to work with, whereas too general activity definitions did not describe the process accurately. The outcome of the meetings was a list (see below) that provided a framework within which to report the detailed task information collected through examining the operations and

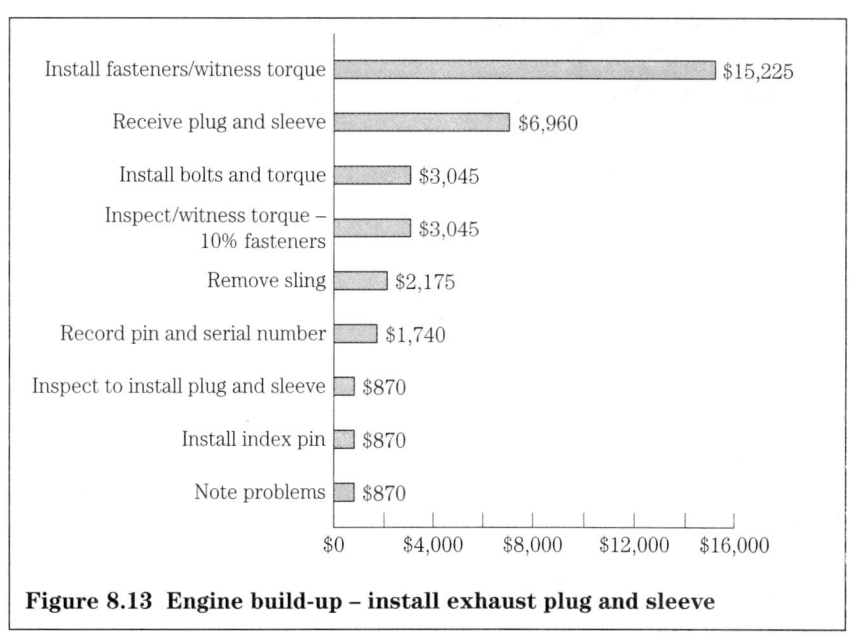

Figure 8.13 Engine build-up – install exhaust plug and sleeve

Quality and cost management

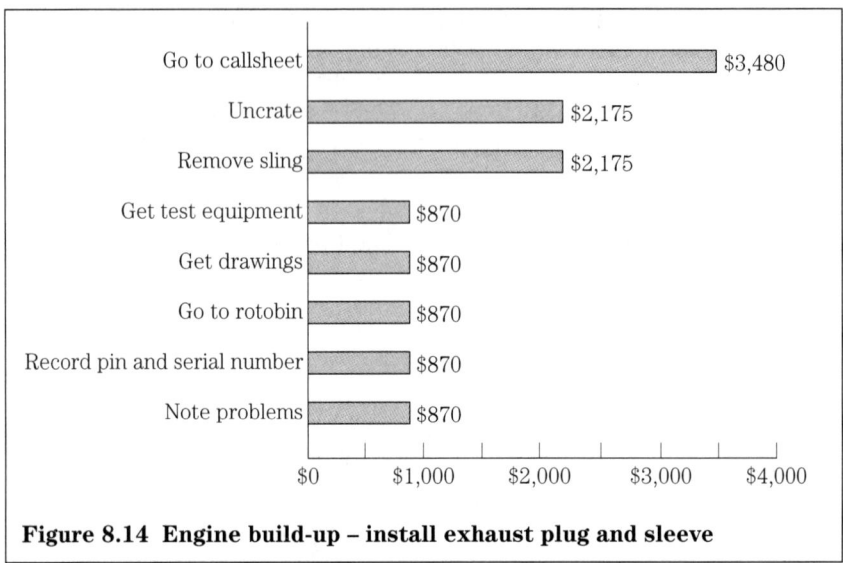

Figure 8.14 Engine build-up – install exhaust plug and sleeve

inspection records and shop bar charts. Figure 8.15 shows the task breakdown and analysis for activity no.6 from the list: 'Install exhaust plug and sleeve'.

767 engine build-up list of activities

1. Assist shop personnel	12. Install heat shields
2. Continuous quality improvement	13. Install left bracket
3. Install core wire	14. Meetings
4. Install electric wire	15. Miscellaneous supervision
5. Install engine drain	16. Rejection tags
6. Install exhaust plug and sleeve	17. Rework
7. Install fan case wire	18. Install right bracket
8. Install fire detector	19. Safety
9. Hang engine	20. Install starter systems
10. Install inlet	21. Vendor rework
11. Install ECS controller	22. Install wire

8.4.80 After combining data received from interviews, the shop bar charts and operations and inspection records (see Figures 8.10 and 8.11) with the cost analysis data included in Figure 8.14, the process and activity analysis project group prepared a Pareto chart for all the activities of the operations work group (see Figure 8.15). The Pareto chart showed that the activities 'Install fire detector' and 'Install wire' were the most significant in terms of resource consumption.

Making COQ work

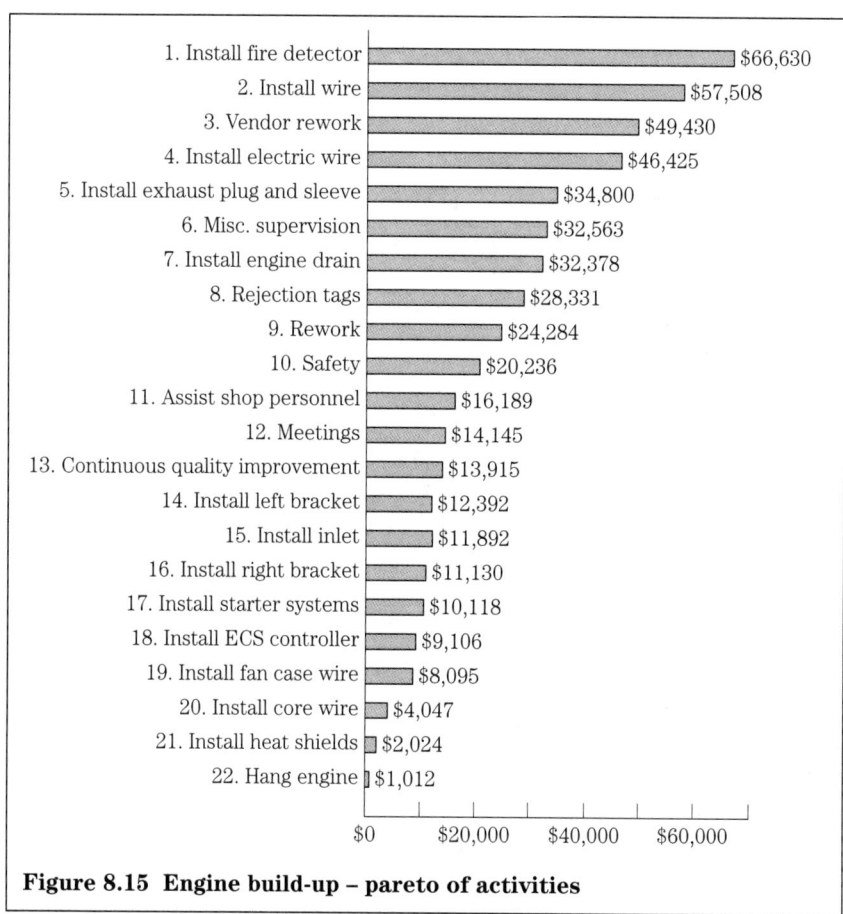

Figure 8.15 Engine build-up – pareto of activities

The 737 engine build-up group

8.4.81 After going through the process and activity analysis for the 767 engine build-up group, Mike understood the process well enough to lead the analysis effort in another operations group. Mike scheduled a meeting with Erik Olson and the 737 engine build-up group. Erik had been a supervisor on the EBU line for five years. He was recruited as an interviewer for the process and activity analysis project. His experience with the EBU process helped him to communicate with the workers and their supervisor. The meeting concentrated on the activity 'Install wire bundle'. As shown in Figure 8.16, this activity consumed the most resources within the 737 engine build-up work group.

8.4.82 Mike contacted Joanne Nguyen, a methods analyst in industrial engineering and a fellow team member on the process and activity analysis

Quality and cost management

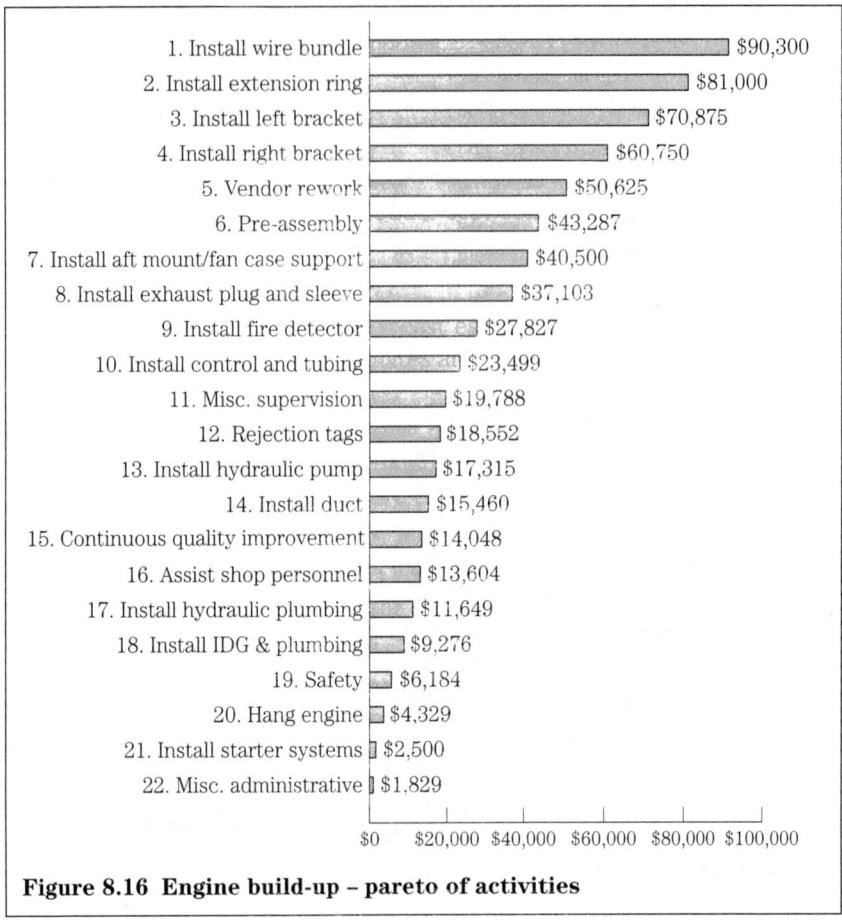

Figure 8.16 Engine build-up – pareto of activities

project, who supplied him with the relevant shop bar charts and operations and inspection records (see Figures 8.17 and 8.18).

8.4.83 Mike and Erik interviewed Tyrone Washington, the supervisor for the 737 engine build-up group, who described the work routine as follows:

> 'First, we check to see if we have the right wire bundles. To do this, we compare the wire cards with our call sheets. Removing the wire cards and checking the call sheets require 0.2 hour in total. Second, wire bundles W1504 and W1506 are routed over the oil return line and through the six o'clock position. The total task time here is 1.0 hour. Completing the wire bundle and hardware installation requires 8.0 hours. To perform this activity, the employee must go to the rotobin to pick up parts. This requires an additional 0.3 hour.

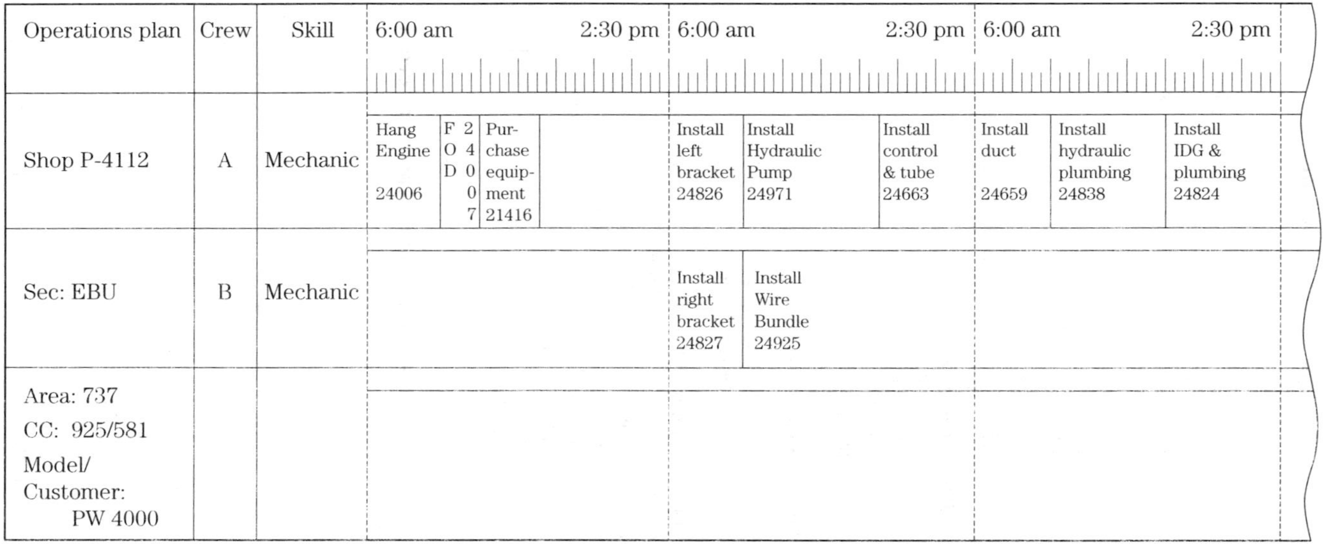

Making COQ work

Operations plan	Crew	Skill	6:00 am	2:30 pm	6:00 am	2:30 pm	6:00 am	2:30 pm
Shop P-4112	A	Mechanic	Hang Engine 24006	F O D 2 4 0 Pur- chase equip- ment 7 21416		Install left bracket 24826	Install Hydraulic Pump 24971	Install control & tube 24663	Install duct 24659	Install hydraulic plumbing 24838	Install IDG & plumbing 24824
Sec: EBU	B	Mechanic				Install right bracket 24827	Install Wire Bundle 24925			
Area: 737 CC: 925/581 Model/ Customer: PW 4000								

Figure 8.17 737 engine build-up – shop bar chart

481

Quality and cost management

Part #	Name	Quantity
W1504	Wire bundle	1
W1506	Wire bundle	1
W1508	Wire bundle	1
W1502	Wire bundle	1
W0200	Wire bundle	1
BACC10GU104	Clamp	19
BACC10GU106	Clamp	17
NAS1802-3-9	Screw	52
NAS1805-3	Nut	11
NAS43HT3-16	Spacer	2
MAS6703U2	Bolt	10

Reference drawings
330A8893
330A8894
330A8895
330A8896

Work to be performed:

Operation	Description
020.00	Verify wire bundle cards with wire bundle number list
030.00	Route wire bundle W1504 & W1506 over oil line & through 6 o'clock position & install bracket
040.00	Complete wire bundle and hardware installation
050.00	Install wire bundle W1502 & W0200 with brackets and fillers. Complete wire bundle installation
060.00	Install deflector assembly component & torque Install wire bundle W1508
070.00	Shop verify wire bundle installation

Figure 8.18 737 engine build-up – operations and inspection record: wire and bundle installation

'Next, wire bundles W1502 and W0200 are installed with the required brackets and fillers. The total time to complete this installation is 2.0 hours, with an additional 0.3 hour necessary to go to the rotobin to pick up parts. Then the mechanic installs the deflector assembly and installs wire bundle W1508, requiring 1.5 hours, with an additional 0.1 hour required to go to the rotobin, 0.2 hour to go to the tool room for parts, and 0.1 hour to go to the call sheet. Finally, the quality control inspector must verify that wire bundle installation is complete. This activity takes 0.3 hour.'

8.4.84 Tyrone went to the delivery schedule and determined that 150 ship sets (of two engines per ship set) were built up in one year's time. By multiplying the number of ship sets by the number of engines in each ship set, Mike determined that the tasks in this work group were performed 300 times per year.

8.4.85 After the meeting with the EBU work group, Mary provided Mike with cost information about the work group. Total direct labour hours in the 737 engine build-up shop last year were 22,808, which translated into $273,696. The breakout of the labour components and corresponding costs were as follows.

	Hours	Costs		Hours	Costs
Fabrication	6	$82	Minor assembly	21	$283
Major assembly	21,269	$254,502	Rework	443	$5,531
Developmental work	189	$2,238	Tooling	13	$186
Vendor rework	867	$10,874			

8.4.86 The indirect labour consumed was 4,192 hours, for a total of $73,616. Overtime, fringe benefits and bonus payment for the workers in the shop totalled $205,996. In addition, the following overhead costs were identified:

Perishable tools	$11,412
Tool and shop equipment	$6,734
Electrical, mechanical and miscellaneous shop supplies	$5,485
Resource support from support services	$1,291
Group-administered training	$1,176
Telephones	$410
General travel	$282
Business meeting expense	208
Undergraduate and graduate study	$64
Promotional items	$53
Entertainment	$24
Data processing supplies	$22
Office supplies	$21
Conferences and seminars	$10

8.4.87 After several meetings, the group agreed to the list of activities shown below that the 737 engine build-up group performed. With this information about the work group, Mike went to his office to complete the process and activity analysis.

Quality and cost management

737 engine build-up list of activities

1. Assist shop personnel	12. Install hydraulic plumbing
2. Install left bracket	13. Install hydraulic pump
3. Install right bracket	14. Install IDG & plumbing
4. Continuous quality improvement	15. Miscellaneous administrative
5. Install control and tubing	16. Miscellaneous supervision
6. Install duct	17. Pre-assembly
7. Install exhaust plug and sleeve	18. Rejection tags
8. Install extension ring	19. Safety
9. Install aft mount / fan case support	20. Install starter systems
10. Install fire detector	21. Vendor rework
11. Hang engine	22. Install wire bundle

Choice of cost drivers

8.4.88 Most companies adopting activity-based management will emphasise the need for multiple cost drivers in addition to or in preference to labour hours (see Chapter **6**). Yet at PSD the use of total labour hours is stressed as the exclusive cost driver used to cost activities.

8.4.89 The pilot team's choice was based on the recognition that the operation being analysed was labour intensive and that payroll costs accounted for 93 per cent of the controllable costs (see Figure 8.11). Labour appeared to provide the most leverage for achieving productivity gains and cost savings. Decisions regarding the choice of cost drivers as well as other aspects of the analysis would be subject to periodic review as the division gained experience with the PAA project.

8.4.90 It is useful to draw attention to cycle time, a critical variable influencing the division's productivity. Aircraft engines are extremely costly. Even modest gains in cycle time will translate into significant savings by reducing total carrying costs of engine inventory. Labour hours may not correlate with cycle time. Indeed, more labour hours on off-line processing may reduce cycle time significantly. A case can be made that the primary objective is to reduce cycle time, even at the expense of increased labour hours.

8.4.91 Both labour costs and cycle time costs are outcome costs in the sense that they offer no clue as to how to achieve savings in labour and cycle time. These outcome costs may influence behaviour in search of ways to reduce outcome costs. However, a more incisive analysis is necessary to determine the root causes that prevent shorter cycle times and also drive up line-item expenses in Figure 8.13. For example, reducing or eliminating vendor rework and overtime labour is possible only by developing a precise understanding of the causes that drive these factors. A comprehensive activity-based costing system would require that outcome costs be identified by individual (root-cause) cost drivers. It is debatable whether such comprehensive activity-based costing is essential for achieving process improvements. Indeed, many of the front-line process improvements are aided by monitoring groups of non-financial measures of performance that, in turn, are derived from relevant measures of customer satisfaction.

Vertical versus lateral perspectives

8.4.92 There are contrasts between traditional methods of budgetary reporting on the one hand and activity analysis on the other, insofar as they support CQI. One major difference is that the former provides delayed-outcome measures organised on hierarchical lines, whereas the latter provides reasonable real-time information that is useful in improving the process. Since a CQI culture directs everyone to stay focused on adding value to the customer, it is obvious that activity-based cost data segregated into value added and non-value added categories provide strong behavioural reinforcement. This process-based view has implications for organisational arrangements, as well as for informational arrangements.

8.4.93 Artificially breaking down an aggregate process into functional-organisation-based components may lead to sub-optimisation, as well as overlooked improvement potentials. Only a total process perspective will help identify all trade-off opportunities. However, there is wisdom in letting these further extensions evolve as the organisation gains experience in managing the change from a predominantly vertical to a predominantly lateral mode in selected pilot projects. Radical organisational design changes in a company that has been hugely successful operating under a traditional hierarchical structure pose major risks. A case can therefore be made for introducing lateral perspectives within broad hierarchical units before moving toward a complete process-based restructuring.

8.4.94 Key premises underlying CQI include:

- commitment to deliver continuously improving customer value;
- top-down direction based on a clear strategic vision;
- process ownership, self-direction, and lateral co-operation;
- targeting against world-class benchmarks;
- process-based performance measures – non-financial and financial;
- unending plan-do-check-act cycles;
- supporting values, leadership style, training, and rewards.

Quality and cost management

8.4.95 PAA generates data for each identified link in the value chain. Such information is extremely useful for target costing, value engineering, and strategic make-or-buy decisions. Process owners rely on PAA data for process improvements. More fundamentally, PAA provides the informational platform in organisations that are designed to be self-learning and self-directed, characteristics that have come to be recognised as central to maintaining a company's competitive edge.

The bases of Boeing's continuous quality improvement initiative
8.4.96 During the 1980s, Boeing's top management launched several strategic initiatives aimed at enhancing the company's competitive position. One of the strategic initiatives was to use continuous quality improvement (CQI) as the foundation for managing. The importance that management attached to the CQI initiative was expressed in Boeing's policy documents:

> 'The continuous improvement process is the cornerstone of our business strategy to be the world's leading aerospace company.
>
> 'We are committed to continuous quality improvement in our processes, products, and services to ensure overall customer, employee and community satisfaction.
>
> 'Each member of management is responsible for the creation and maintenance of an environment that encourages employees to make their maximum contribution toward the attainment of our goals.'

8.4.97 The CQI initiatives at PSD were designed to; (1) reduce total cost, (2) maintain a 'healthy' organisation, (3) simplify processes, (4) improve inventory management, and (5) reduce waste. For each initiative, specific measures were developed to track improvements (see Figure 8.19).

8.4.98 Within major segments, The Boeing Company is organised by business units, one of which is PSD. These business units are managed according to functional disciplines such as manufacturing, engineering and finance. A business process that crosses functional boundaries is subordinate to the functions. The concept of process ownership reverses this relationship. In this model, business units consist of specific processes. Functional structures exist only to support processes.

8.4.99 As a step toward changing the organisational culture, the company adopted the concept of process ownership. Figure 8.20 shows the nature of the planned transformation from the traditional, functional organisation structure to the process ownership structure.

Process improvement and process and activity analysis
8.4.100 Under the CQI initiative, PSD uses a four-step methodology to make process improvements:

Making COQ work

Division: Strategic initiatives	To measure our progress, we will track
1. Reduce total cost	– Division program cost targets – Controllable cost (labor and expenses)
2, Maintain a healthy organization	– Overtime – Greenlines (rework from earlier rejection tags) – Engineering drawing quality – Engineering schedule performance
3. Simplify processes	– Key Division processes identified – Key Division processes documented
4. Improve inventory management	– Division stores turn rate – Days of scheduled engine inventory
5. Reduce waste	– Cost of waste (specified waste items) – Identification of next five waste items – Reduction in next five waste items

Figure 8.19 Section of division's performance goals

- select a process for analysis;
- document the present process;
- establish detailed process measurements, benchmark and develop improvement options;
- improve and stabilise the process.

8.4.101 Once the process is stabilised, the same steps can be reapplied to achieve continuous improvement.

8.4.102 In the first step, a process is identified and selected. The process boundaries are defined and a work management team is organised to perform the analysis.

8.4.103 In the second step, the process is documented as is. This step involves defining the process objectives, listing the process inputs and outputs, and identifying the sources of the input and the customers of the output. The second step also involves process and activity analysis, which gives management an indication of where the current process is most deficient.

8.4.104 During the third step, the work management team determines process control points and collects and analyses detailed data about the process. In addition, customer requirements are verified so that the

Quality and cost management

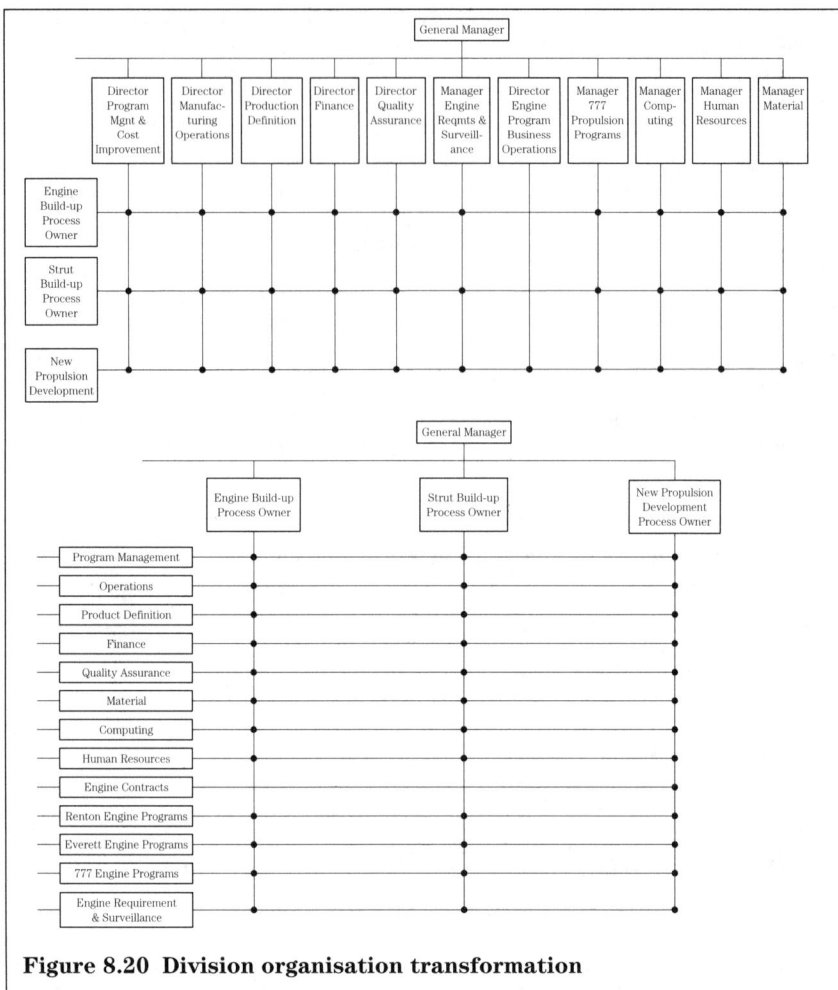

Figure 8.20 Division organisation transformation

effectiveness and efficiency of the process can be evaluated. Based on the analysis, the team develops improvement options.

8.4.105 In the fourth step, the team selects improvement projects. Once improvements are implemented, it is important to stabilise an improved process so that it can serve as a basis for further progress.

8.4.106 The key element of the process improvement methodology is the process and activity analysis in step two – a diagnostic tool that helps to identify improvement opportunities by providing information about product and activity costs, cycle time, and non-value added activities.

Making COQ work

8.4.107 PSD defines valueadded activities as actions that change the form, fit or function of its products or services. Non-value added activities are non-essential actions that do not change the form, fit, or function of its products or services.

8.4.108 When information about activities that are determined to be non-value added is combined with information about activity cost, the organisation can identify opportunities for improvement, process modifications and product enhancement. Steps can then be taken to improve the process in ways that eliminate the need for the non-value added activities.

8.4.109 The results of process and activity analysis include the following.
- Identification of major activities required to produce the process output, as well as the time and resources expended.
- Visibility of costs associated with the activities required to produce a product.
- Insight into the factors that cause cost to be incurred.
- Identification of value added and non-value added activities.
- A total process management view that improves the understanding of cross-organisational interdependencies.

8.4.110 Pareto charts are used to present the results of process and activity analysis in graphic form. Pareto charts are bar charts that depict the cost for a set of activities sorted by dollar consumption.

8.4.111 Figure 8.21 shows summary costs gathered through the process and activity analysis at PSD. Production at PSD consisted of four major product processes: the engine build-up (EBU), strut assembly, wire bundle fabrication and new propulsion development. The Pareto charts at the bottom of Figure 8.21 depict the recurring process costs broken down by major activity categories.

8.4.112 These process-based analyses required no change in the company's existing cost accounting system, which grouped costs under material, labour and overhead and allocated all overhead costs on the basis of direct labour dollars. Under the existing system, about $40 million of PSD's total costs of $57.8 million were considered non-controllable at the PSD level.

Engineering organisation

8.4.113 During May 1992, Wendy Holmstrom, director of Product Definition at PSD, reviewed proposed improvements to some of the processes in

Quality and cost management

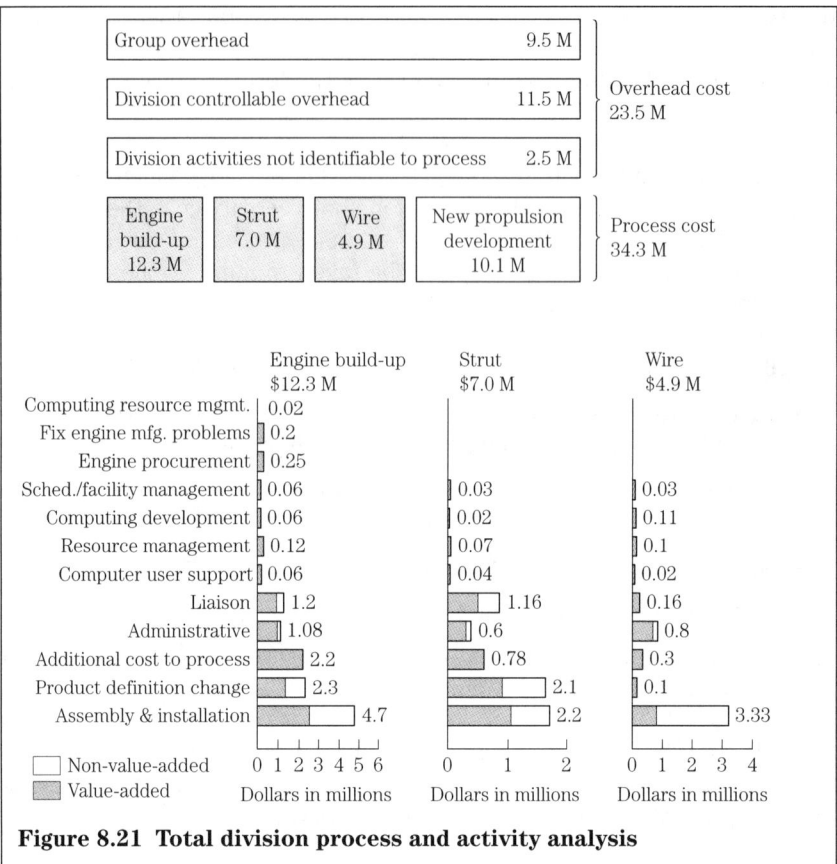

Figure 8.21 Total division process and activity analysis

her organisation. Wendy was determined to tackle the committed-change process, one of the processes that had caused substantial frustration throughout the division. The committed-change process controlled the incorporation of changes into an airplane. The process was plagued by a long flow time from the moment a request for change occurred to the actual release of updated drawings. Many managers at PSD had expressed their dissatisfaction with the committed-change process.

8.4.114 Even though Wendy was well aware of the poor performance of the committed-change process, she had little information on specific problems and their root causes. To a large extent, the committed-change process was managed by the Engineering Operations group, headed by Victor Klee (see Figure 8.22). Originally, Wendy had speculated that problems with the committed-change process might be due to an increased workload.

Making COQ work

However, an analysis of the monthly workload reports did not support this belief. Wendy concluded that currently reported data did not provide the process-oriented information she believed was needed to decide how to improve the committed-change process.

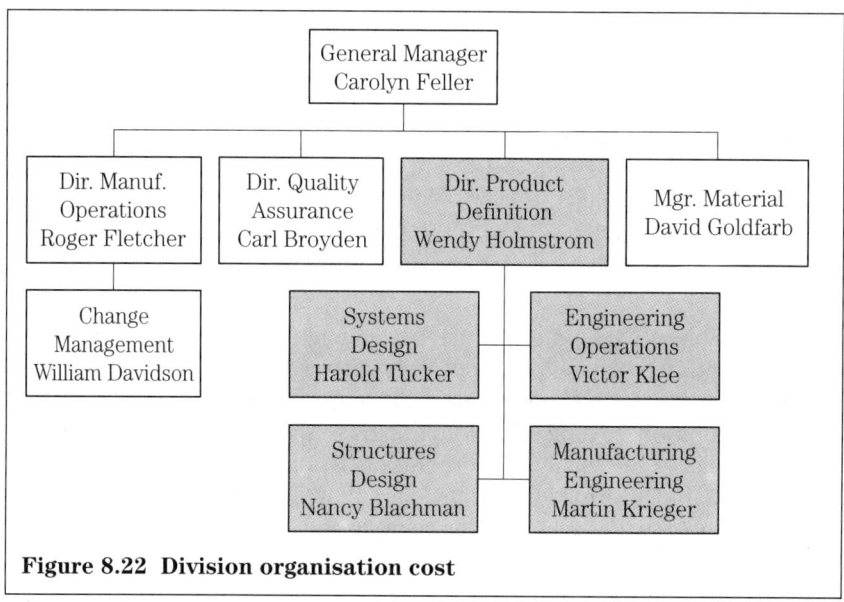

Figure 8.22 Division organisation cost

8.4.115 Figure 8.22 shows a simplified organisation chart for PSD focusing on the engineering functions. Three of Wendy's colleagues were Roger Fletcher, director of Manufacturing Operations, Carl Broyden, director of Quality Assurance, and David Goldfarb, director of Material.

8.4.116 The main responsibility of the Product Definition department was to provide all engineering design and support services related to the products produced at PSD. Under Product Definition's control were the Engineering Operations group, the Manufacturing Engineering group and several design groups. Engineering Operations was responsible for co-ordinating work within the Product Definition department.

8.4.117 Manufacturing Operations and Material were two functions that depended directly on the engineering specifications developed by Product Definition. Manufacturing Operations used the engineering drawings from Product Definition to define and control manufacturing and assembly operations at PSD. The Material department was responsible for purchasing required parts. The engineering drawings were Material's most important input for determining the appropriate parts to purchase.

Quality and cost management

8.4.118   At PSD, processes had not been studied in detail in terms of effectiveness and efficiency. Wendy felt that all of the functions at PSD could benefit greatly from process improvement. She was convinced that her department could be improved by using Boeing's new process improvement methodology.

Process identification

8.4.119   The PSD Pareto charts in Figure 8.21 show that the activity 'product definition change' consumed considerable resources and also contained a large portion of non-value added activity. Therefore, 'product definition change' might provide significant opportunity for process improvement. Figure 8.23 shows a breakdown of the activity 'product definition change' into more detailed activity categories.

8.4.120   The activity 'product definition change' was not equivalent to the engineering function called Product Definition. Even though a large part of the activities performed in 'product definition change' occurred within Product Definition, several other functions also were involved. For example, activities related to 'change incorporation management' were under the control of Manufacturing Operations, and 'new design' activities were performed by the new Product Development group.

8.4.121   One of the key activities within 'product definition change' was 'committed change'. Most of the managers in PSD Product Definition expressed their dissatisfaction with the committed-change process at some point in time. Victor Klee, manager of Engineering Operations, voiced his frustration with the high revision rates, due especially to incompleteness of the data required to design the change.

8.4.122   Frustration with the committed-change process was not limited to the engineering group. Carl Broyden, director of Quality Assurance, complained about the poor quality of the work coming out of the committed-change process which caused a lot of wasted effort downstream. David Goldfarb, director of Material, was dissatisfied as well. Material could not adapt to engineering changes when the committed-change process did not provide updated part requirements in a timely manner.

8.4.123   The importance of improving the committed-change process was also highlighted by the process and activity analysis. Figure 8.24 shows a Pareto chart of the non-value added activities that occurred in the Engineering Operations group. The chart shows that of the non-value added activities, committed-change activity was the most significant.

Making COQ work

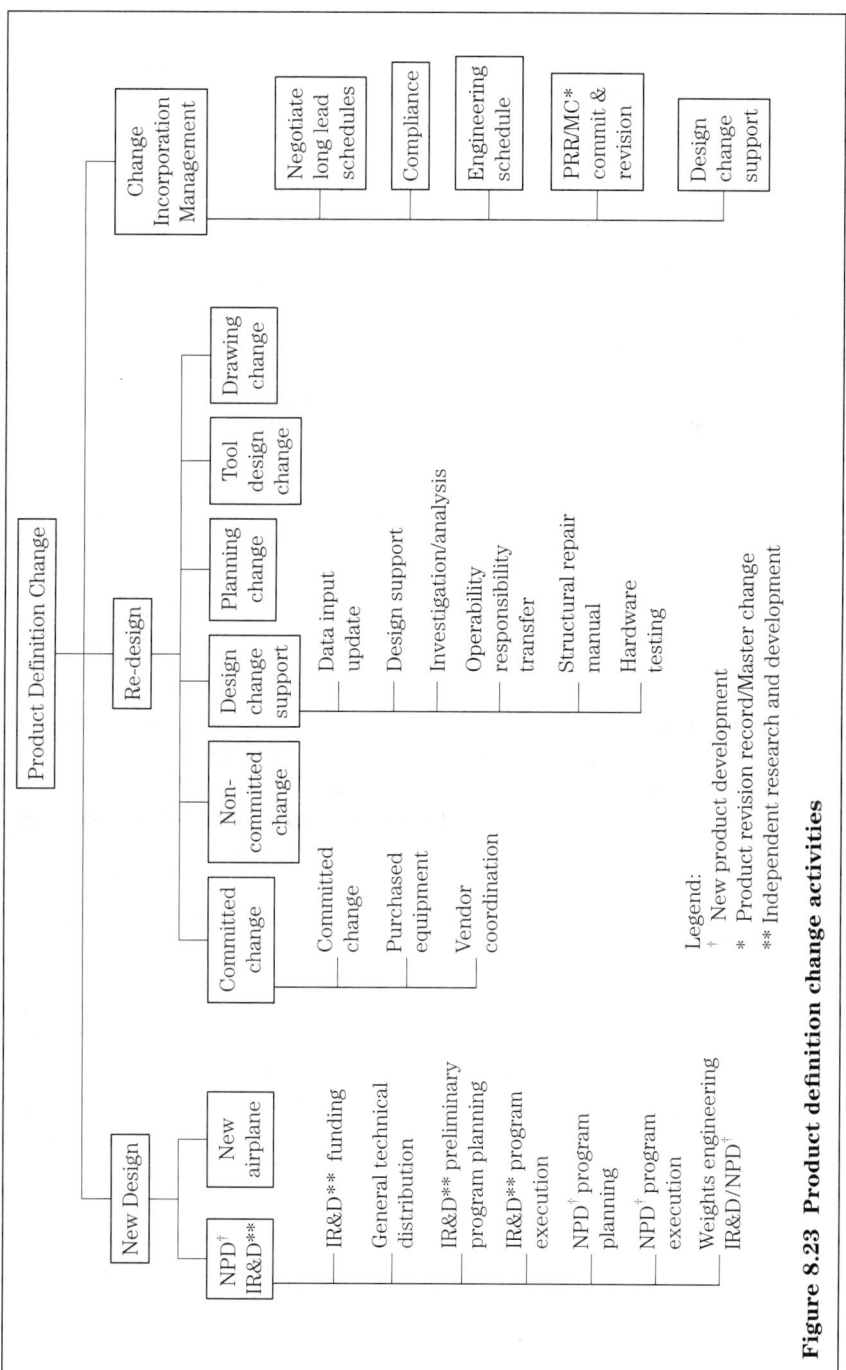

Figure 8.23 Product definition change activities

493

Quality and cost management

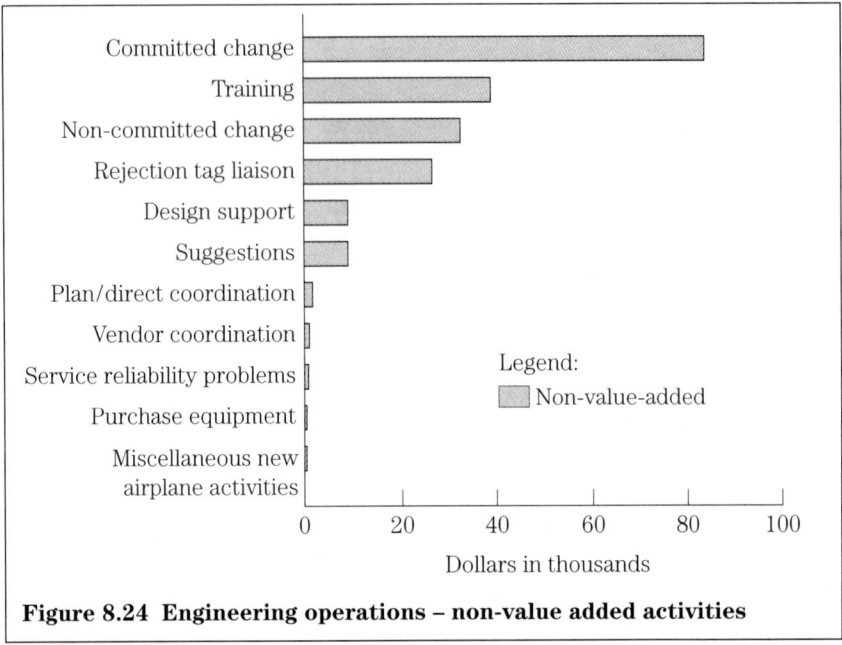

Figure 8.24 Engineering operations – non-value added activities

Process analysis

8.4.124 Each year, PSD received about 50 change requests. Requests for change came from several external and internal sources. For example, Customer Support received change requests from the airlines. These requests usually related to in-service problems. Another source of external requests came from suppliers. These requests were forwarded by the Material department. Changes could also be initiated internally. Generally, these changes were aimed at improving the manufacturability of airplane parts, correcting errors or introducing technical, cost or weight improvements.

8.4.125 Initially, change requests were handled by the Engineering Operations group. Their task was to sort the requests according to type, log and schedule actions, and route the request to the appropriate engineering group. The Engineering Operations group also had the responsibility of co-ordinating inputs and approvals and ensuring that processing was complete. The appropriate engineering groups then investigated each requested change and determined whether the request should be implemented or not. The criteria for accepting changes were safety, technical and manufacturing feasibility, weight maintainability and customer impact, schedule impact and cost. If Engineering decided not to make a change, the requester was informed that the change was denied.

8.4.126 If a change was approved, Engineering decided whether the request presented a minor or major change. Minor changes were incorporated into an airplane without a complicated review process because they required approval only from Engineering, Manufacturing Engineering and Material.

8.4.127 Each change request was evaluated by several criteria to assess whether or not it would be treated as a major or committed change. The list of criteria included cost, impact on the production schedule and complexity of contract negotiations with outside suppliers. The purpose of the committed-change process was to control the incorporation of committed changes into an airplane. For a graphical overview of the committed-change process, see Figure 8.25.

8.4.128 For committed changes, a work statement called a production revision record (PRR) was required. (See Figure 8.32 for excerpts from a PRR, describing the change of a firewall in a strut.) The purpose of the work statement was to ensure that all aspects of the change were known and had been addressed. The work statement included documentation of the changes to all affected parts as well as a priority for the actual incorporation of the change into production.

8.4.129 PRRs were developed and approved by Engineering. Each engineering discipline added input to the PRR. Because work on the PRR was, to a large degree, sequential, modifications suggested by engineering groups later in the chain were often inconsistent with changes made by earlier engineering groups. Generally, each PRR required multiple iterations in this loop before it was complete and consistent. Given approval from Engineering, the Finance organisation provided estimates for the cost of the change. These estimates triggered new revisions if the cost estimates were unacceptable.

8.4.130 The committed-change process became even more complicated when the change involved organisational units outside PSD (usually the prime airplane manufacturing divisions located in the nearby towns of Renton or Everett). In this case, management approval was required at every stage, from first-line supervisors to vice presidents of the affected outside division. A change could be rejected or reworked at any approval point.

8.4.131 Change requests that had completed the entire approval process were then issued and distributed by Engineering Operations. Another organisational unit called Change Board was responsible for incorporating the change at the most desirable point in the manufacturing process. The Change Board group obtained committed schedules from all affected Boeing organisations and suppliers.

Quality and cost management

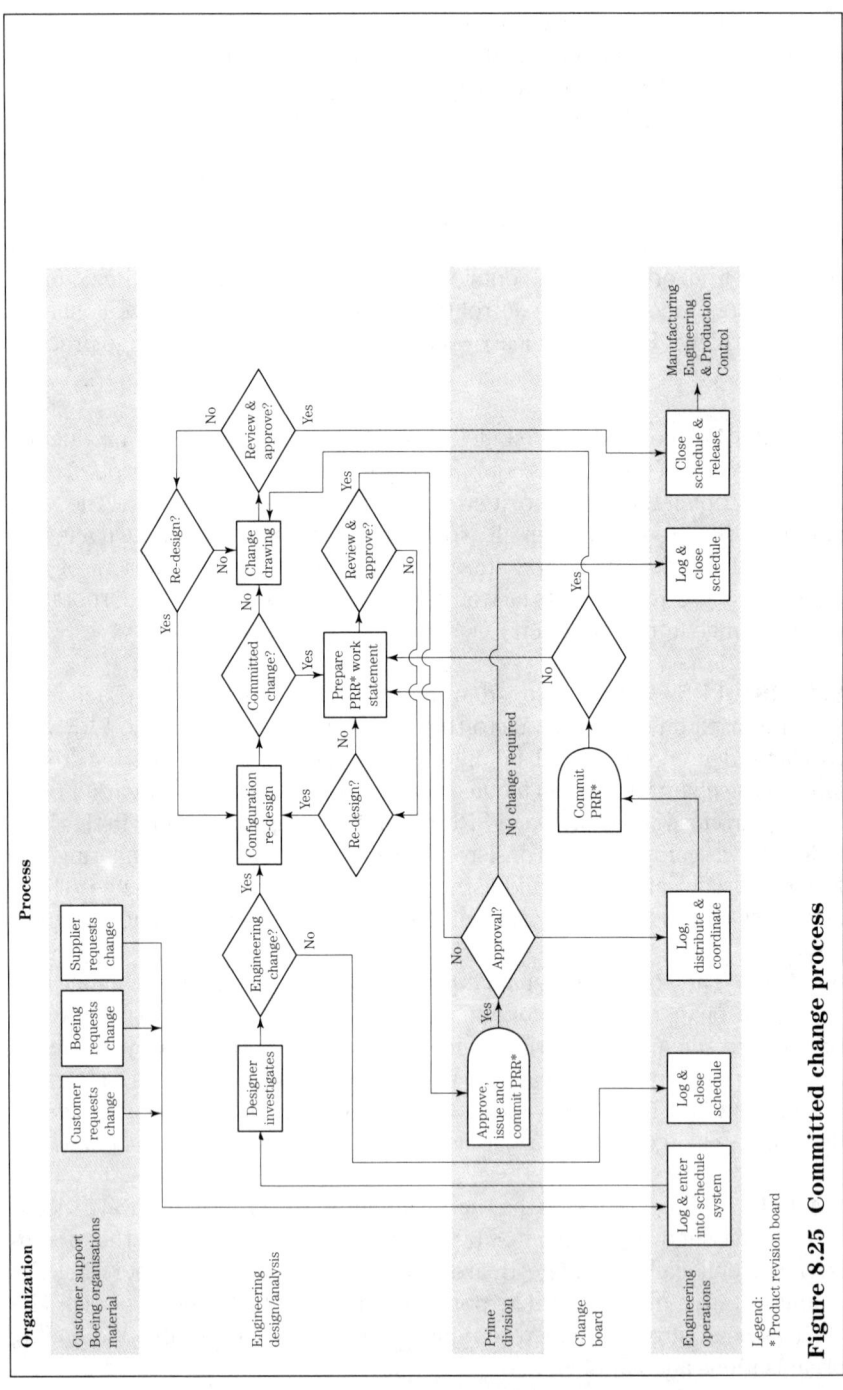

Figure 8.25 Committed change process

Making COQ work

8.4.132 To analyse the flow of the committed-change process, it was helpful to consider a value added timeline (Figure 8.26). The timeline depicted the time spent completing value added and non-value added activities during the process. The timeline showed that the cycle time from change request to change incorporation was a little more than one calendar year.

8.4.133 Engineering received the change request and routed it within two days. Based on the request, the Engineering Design group investigated the request, determined the new configuration, and developed a work statement, if appropriate. Developing an initial PRR for a committed-change request took 45 days. However, since several engineering groups were usually involved in a PRR, bin time, paper transport, logging and communication activities took up a large amount of time. This was indicated by the block of 50 days of non-value added activities shown in Figure 8.25. After the development of a consistent PRR, another 70 days were required to receive all the approvals within Engineering Design and to make the revisions requested by management. After approval by all engineering groups, a tip sheet was issued. The Finance organisation then made cost estimates based on the tip sheet. The Finance estimate took about 15 days.

8.4.134 Next, the prime division evaluated the work statement. Modifications initiated by the prime division plus management approvals required 50 days. After acceptance by the prime division, the PRR was issued and handed over to Engineering Operations and the Change Board for implementation. During the planning and co-ordination phase for manufacturing, errors in the work statement were often detected, requiring rework, bin time and re-approval from all prior parties. Rework time for this particular PRR took 115 days before it could finally be committed to production.

8.4.135 Even though much time had been spent on the work statement and several engineers had checked it, many errors in the PRR were not discovered until changes were actually incorporated into production. The chart in Figure 8.27 shows that the PRRs submitted to the Change Board for approval averaged five errors per month.

8.4.136 To analyse the reasons for the high error rate in the work statements, the Engineering group developed the fishbone diagram shown in Figure 8.28. Errors could be traced to four main causes: co-ordination problems, changes in the scope of the request, problems with the initial preparation of the PRR, and problems with the initial configuration definition.

Quality and cost management

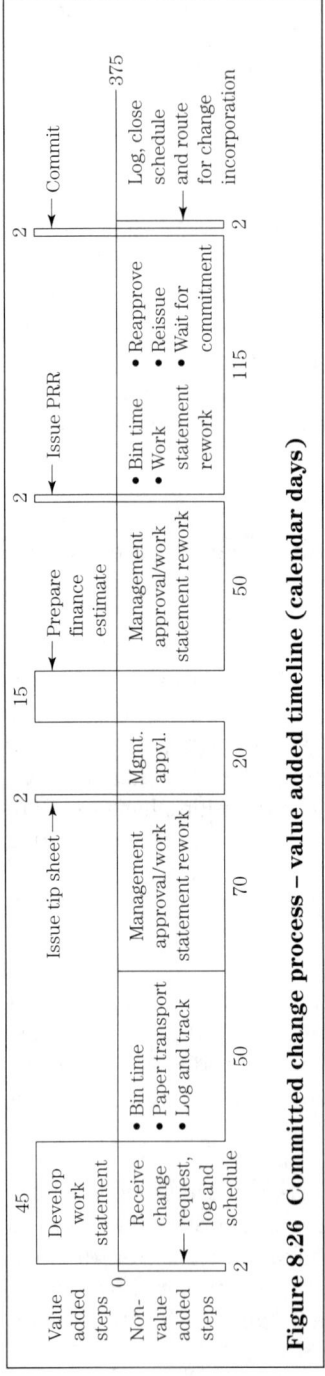

Figure 8.26 Committed change process – value added timeline (calendar days)

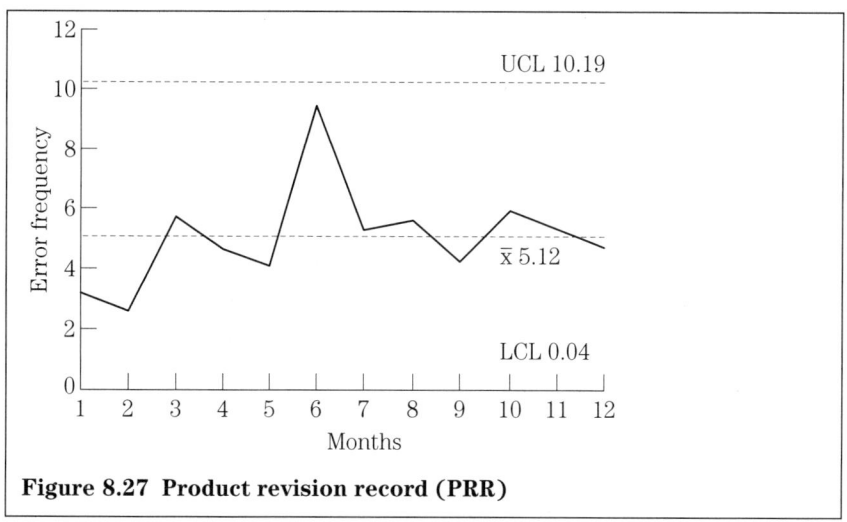

Figure 8.27 Product revision record (PRR)

Improvement alternatives

8.4.137 Wendy Holmstrom had received the latest staff report on the committed-change process. The report clearly documented two major problems: unacceptably long cycle time from the change request to the final drawing release and high error rate of released changes.

8.4.138 Determined to improve the committed-change process, Wendy asked two of her staff, Kurt Levenberg and Paul Wolfe, to develop improvement alternatives. Both had prior experience in analysing cross-functional engineering management problems. During a meeting, Kurt and Paul outlined their ideas.

8.4.139 According to Kurt, the two main reasons why problems occurred in the committed-change process were insufficient communication among the involved parties and the fact that most of the development work was done in sequence and not in parallel among the various engineering groups. Kurt's solution was to create a centralised database that contained work statements for each PRR. All parties involved in the change process, such as Engineering Operations, Design, Change Board and the prime division(s), would have simultaneous access to all documents related to the work statement. This way, inconsistency in the PRR could be detected early and the error rate would be reduced dramatically. In fact, Kurt estimated that the number of errors per PRR could be reduced to 0.2 and the cycle time could be halved.

8.4.140 Unfortunately, implementation of this suggestion would strain the department's resources. Kurt estimated the cost of the computer system,

Quality and cost management

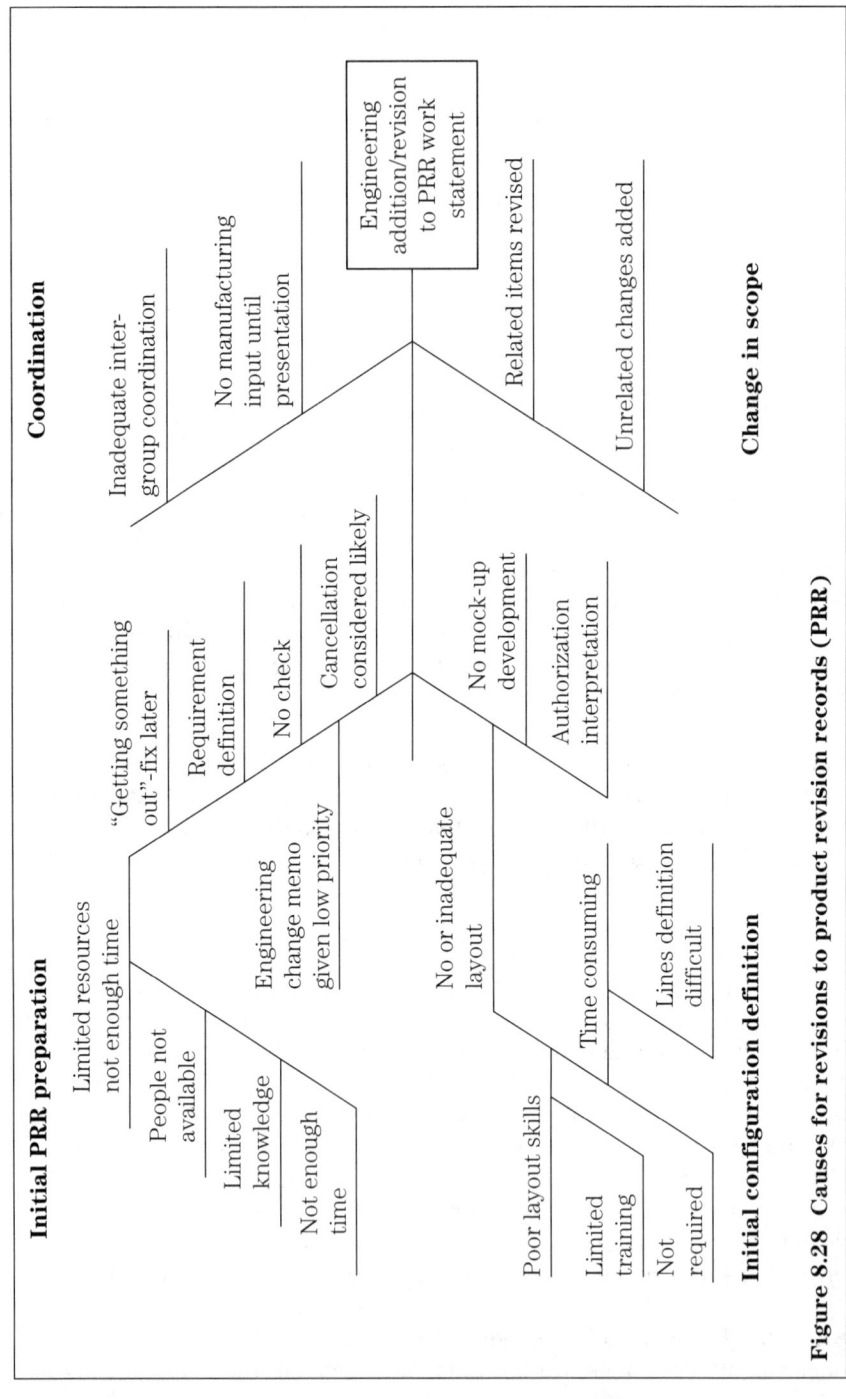

Figure 8.28 Causes for revisions to product revision records (PRR)

including hardware, software and installation labour, to be more than $800,000. Furthermore, it would require three software engineers dedicated to the project for two years.

8.4.141 Another difficulty with this solution was the resistance Kurt experienced when he mentioned this option to managers from the prime division. Some managers distrusted computer systems and electronic records. They considered a computer system a large waste of money, especially since they would have to develop an interface by themselves.

8.4.142 Paul Wolfe thought that problems with the committed-change process occurred because too many people had authority to reject the work statement. Therefore, Paul proposed a single process owner who would have the authority to approve a work statement. The main advantage of this solution would be to reduce the amount of non-value added time taken in revising and re-approving the PRR.

8.4.143 In the flow diagram shown in Figure 8.25, Paul would basically cut out all the decision loops. According to him, the estimated benefit from changing the responsibility and authority structure for the committed-change process would be a reduction in cycle time to less than 60 days and an error rate of less than 0.2 errors per PRR. Organisational resistance was expected to be the main obstacle to implementing this suggestion, because it would require most of the managers involved in the committed-change process to give up their power to make decisions. Before these managers would let go of their authority, they would need to develop trust in the quality of the committed-change process.

8.4.144 To support the process owner who co-ordinated the new committed-change process, one option Paul proposed was installing a computer support system that would cost $25,000. Alternatively, setting up a small work group with development procedures and guidelines for the manual system would cost $120,000. For each option, Paul estimated a development duration of two-and-a-half years.

8.4.145 Since Paul realised how difficult it would be to gain support for his radical suggestion, he also developed an intermediate improvement option. To increase trust in the committed-change process and decrease the error rate, Paul suggested a team-review process. Instead of having the engineering groups work independently, Paul recommended a team review for each PRR so that errors and inconsistencies could be detected more easily. This procedure would also increase communication among all the parties involved.

Quality and cost management

8.4.146 Paul estimated that the team review process could be set up in six months, with a project budget of $10,000. The team review would eliminate most of the errors in the PRRs. Paul's error prognosis was about 0.5 per work statement. Paul's suggestion would also reduce cycle time, perhaps by up to 50 per cent compared to the current situation. The only problem Paul could envision with the team-review suggestion was co-ordinating meetings for affected parties. It would be difficult to bring together representatives from eight to ten engineering groups on relatively short notice.

8.4.147 Wendy felt that all three of the proposed changes – computerisation, authority centralisation, and team review – had merit. She went back to her office to develop a completed plan.

The change process at Boeing
8.4.148 Two factors, one external and the other internal, can be highlighted as driving the change process in The Boeing Company during the 1980s.

8.4.149 The major external factor was the severe cost-price squeeze developing in the airplane manufacturing business as a result of air travel deregulation. The company responded by launching several strategic initiatives aimed at enhancing its competitive position. One of the strategic initiatives adopted was continuous quality improvement (CQI) as the foundation for managing. The CQI initiatives at PSD were designed to; (1) reduce total cost, (2) maintain a 'healthy' organisation, (3) simplify processes, (4) improve inventory management, and (5) reduce waste. For each initiative, specific measures were developed to track improvements (see Figure 8.19 on page 487).

8.4.150 The major internal factor was organisational re-engineering adopted to implement the new strategic initiatives. Within major segments, The Boeing Company is organised by business units, one of which is PSD. These business units are managed according to functional disciplines such as manufacturing, engineering and finance. A business process that crosses functional boundaries is subordinate to the functions. The concept of *process ownership* reverses this relationship. In this model, business units consist of specific *processes*. Functional structures exist only to support processes.

8.4.151 As a step toward changing the organisational culture, the company adopted the concept of process ownership. Figure 8.20 (see page 488) shows the nature of the planned transformation from the traditional,

Making COQ work

functional organisation structure to the process ownership structure in PSD. Simultaneously, process and activity analyses led to the development process-based performance indicators including costs. Changing Boeing's organisational culture was accompanied by changes in the cost management system.

8.4.152 The existing cost system reported costs by input categories (e.g., material, direct labour, utilities, etc.), by functional department and by products (e.g., 747 airplane). Process-based costs reported costs by process output also. This enabled management to analyse costs added at each process level and also how much of the cost addition represented value added.

8.4.153 The new method also helped identify more completely the costs controllable at the process levels and push responsibility for cost control to process owners. Traditionally, the company's cost accounting pooled overhead expenses of the division, along with its share of group and company overhead, all of which were charged to products, e.g., completed engines, based on labour hours. In the late 1980s, direct costs were 31 per cent ($17.8 million) and overhead costs were 69 per cent ($40 million) of total costs. Applying process-based costing principles, a large portion of the company-wide, group level and divisional overhead expenses were traced directly to the four key processes that made up the PSD operations. This resulted in identifying 60 per cent of total PSD costs as direct (controllable) costs, leaving only 40 per cent as pooled overhead expenses (see Figure 8.21 on page 490). While there can be debates about the specific process-based cost drivers and cost pools, the class generally concludes that the resulting cost measures are significantly more useful representations of resource flows in the division. Throughout there were continuing attempts to isolate more of the overhead costs as direct costs.

8.4.154 Based on Figures 8.21, 8.22 and 8.23 (see pages 490–493) the 'product definition change' process can be seen to account for $4.5 million in annual controllable costs, of which more than half were non-value added. One of the key activities under this process was committed change. With $85,000 of non-value added costs, it ranked as the most wasteful activity under the process 'product definition'.

8.4.155 It is clear that the cost-based Pareto charts are extremely helpful in prioritising division-wide process improvement efforts. Indeed, many proponents of activity-based costing emphasise that its major payoff is in revealing and prioritising improvement opportunities.

Quality and cost management

8.4.156 The key points to be noted from the above include the following.

- Requests for change came from several internal and external sources, and the changes affected several operating groups and end users. This made the co-ordination of the change process complex and time-consuming.

- The nature of the aerospace operations and the culture of the Boeing operations are such that it is normal to build-in multiple fail-safe procedures, even if it results in higher costs.

- The customers of the committed-change process seemed dissatisfied with the process; delay, errors, incomplete work, changes. Yet prior to the PAA, no information existed to diagnose these problems and their root causes.

- PAA revealed that committed-change activity included a large amount of waste ($85,000 per year in Figure 8.24). Figure 8.26 reports that it took a total of 375 calendar days to complete a typical committed-change activity, of which 309 (82 per cent) were non-value added.

8.4.157 It is to be noted that profit margin may serve as a financial measure of customer value, but this is an outcome measure. To facilitate process analysis and improvement, it is necessary to employ direct measures of performance. Boeing has established four broad criteria for monitoring customer value; (1) customer satisfaction, (2) cost, (3) quality, and (4) delivery. Judged against these criteria, the committed-change process has considerable room for improvement, as is evident from Figures 8.26 and 8.27 and from the reactions of various managers stated in the case. Rework and waiting in bin or waiting for approval accounts for the bulk of the non value added time. Also, Figure 8.25 reveals the activity loops listed against Engineering Design/Analysis group. These set the stage for considering how to minimise non-value added time and an evaluation of the three process improvement proposals.

8.4.158 It is clear that improved communication is the key to avoiding sequential handling of tasks and resulting waste in the committed-change process. It is possible to arrive at a ranking based on value created for customer, using the criteria of cost, quality, etc. Managers may not agree on the rankings, but will develop an appreciation for the fact that some solutions (e.g., proposal number 3 based on team review) are consistent with developing a process-based management culture whereas certain others (e.g., centralised database) do not challenge the existing vertical management culture.

Making COQ work

8.4.159 It is tempting to set ambitious goals for process improvement and then try to drive the initiative from above. However, it is more important to develop an organisational culture that stays focused on achieving modest but continuous improvements while providing overall direction in line with divisional mission. For this reason, proposals 2 and 3, based respectively on process ownership and team review, deserve particular consideration. These two proposals are consistent with the process ownership concept that the company has adopted. One view is that the division should adopt the team-review option because it has significantly lower start-up time and does not foreclose other options if it proves to be ineffective.

8.4.160 The company has adopted the process ownership concept. The resulting organisational design consequences are sketched in Figure 8.20. A pure vertical form can lead to functional sub-optimisation with detrimental effects on process management and customer satisfaction. A lateral design emphasises the supremacy of the process owner while the functional groups serve as support groups for the process owner. The functional managers, as custodians of expert resources, make these resources available to process owners on request. Functional costs will be charged out at negotiated or budgeted rates to users based on specific demands as opposed to treating them as pooled overheads to be spread on labour or other gross volume indicators. The case states that Boeing is committed to making the transition to a process-based management.

8.4.161 At the time the case was written, the division was exploring, but had not implemented, the concept of process-based management. Indeed, the problems associated with the committed-change process are representative of the difficulty in implementing the concept of process ownership. A complete transition to a lateral design could be viewed as a threat by vertical managers, especially those who cannot be reassigned as process owners. It is conceivable in such situations that the resistance would come from middle management while the front-line and the top management would see benefits in terms of job satisfaction, morale, productivity and organisational enhancement.

8.4.162 The present systems of performance measurement and incentives reinforce vertical behaviour and adherence to schedule and line item budget compliance. In such cases, quality and team spirit take a back seat, and skills associated with rework and with expediting out-of-sequence work receive premium rewards.

Quality and cost management

Proposals	1: Centralised Database	2: Single Process Owner	3: Team Review
Costs			
Computerisation	$800,000	$25,000	
Developing procedures	?	$120,000	$10,000
Recurring expenses	?	?	?
Start-up time	2 years	2.5 years	0.5 year
Benefits			
Cycle time reduction			
(Current cycle time = 375 days)	188 days	315 days	188 days
Error reduction			
(Current error rate = 5.12)	3.12/PRR	3.12/PRR	0.12/PRR
Realism of estimates	Conservative	Optimistic	Conservative
Organisational aspects			
Implementation risk	Low	High	Medium
Organisational resistance	Medium	High	Low
Potential for facilitating process-based reorganisation	Low	High	High

8.4.163 Ideally, under the process-ownership concept, several benefits are possible. Relevant process groups will interact laterally in a problem-solving mode, leading to gradual reduction and elimination of rework and out-of-sequence work. Employees will take pride in doing things right the first time, every time; and the primary incentives will be the opportunities for rapid professional advancement. Part of the savings from increased productivity will be shared among employees based on team achievements. This scenario assumes that it is possible to develop financial measures of the value added at each process level and that these measures will be part of the criteria in evaluating team contributions to overall productivity gains.

8.4.164 Boeing focused on delivering customised airplanes known for quality and safety and on earning a required overall return on investment. Individual divisions within the Commercial Airplane Group were not treated as profit centres. Historically, the emphasis at the operating unit levels was on meeting the schedule and delivering quality output. Divisional operating budgets reflected a large element of managerial discretion based on incremental reasoning. These factors helped to create stable vertical bureaucracies with a strong set of values that have contributed to the success of the company. To an extent the management believed that the traditional ways may not be relevant for preserving its competitive advantage in the future.

8.4.165 In this context, it is useful to recognise that the PSD was large enough to be a Fortune 500 company. Yet, the organisational design, information flow, performance measurement and incentives are not keyed toward inculcating a business view of PSD. All these might need to be reoriented in order to implement the process-based management successfully.

(Source: adapted with permission from Juras and Dierks, 1998.)

A case study: using cost of quality in environmental management

8.4.166 In 1989, the Union Pacific Corporation's Board of Directors relied on the expertise of USPCI Inc. (a wholly-owned subsidiary in the environmental management industry) to review environmental management issues at each of the Corporation's subsidiaries. This move was motivated by several factors. First, the costs of complying with various Federal, state and local environmental statutes was growing rapidly Further, the Corporation's directors were conscious of an increased societal awareness of and concern about environmental issues. The Board felt an obligation to the Corporation's shareholders, and its employees, and to society at large, to guarantee that Union Pacific was operating in an environmentally responsible manner.

8.4.167 After considering USPCI's review, the Board subsequently directed each of the subsidiaries to develop a comprehensive environmental management process. The Corporation's commitment to protect the environment is demonstrated by a growing investment in environmental spending. For example, capital expenditures for prevention and control activities increased from $4 million in 1990 to $16 million in 1993, while capital expenditures for remediation activities grew from $24 million to $42 million. During the same period, the Corporation substantially increased its staff of full-time environmental managers and expanded its employee training and communication programmes to include environmental issues.

8.4.168 The largest of the Corporation's subsidiaries is the Union Pacific Railroad Company (UPRR). UPRR owns over 19,000 miles of track; it owns or leases more than 3,000 locomotives and almost 70,000 freight cars. With headquarters in Omaha, Nebraska, the Railroad operates in 19 states and employs approximately 29,000 people. Financial highlights from 1993 for both the Corporation and the Railroad appear in Figure 8.30.

Quality and cost management

Figure 8.29 Primary Federal Environmental Acts

- *Resource Conservation and Recovery Act* (RCRA) – Enacted in 1976, RCRA regulates hazardous waste management from initial generation to ultimate disposal. It applies to generators and transporters of hazardous waste and to facilities that treat and dispose of hazardous waste.
- *Comprehensive Environmental Response Compensation and Liability Act* (CERCLA, also known as the Superfund Act) and *Superfund Amendment and Reauthorisation Act* (SARA) – CERCLA was enacted in 1980 and was amended by SARA in 1986. These Acts provide for the remediation of contaminated sites and impose liability for remediation on a broadly defined group of Potentially Responsible Parties (PRPs). PRPs include, for example, past and current site owners and operators, generators of the waste disposed at the site, and transporters of waste to the site.
- *Clean Air Act* (CAA) – Originally enacted in 1955 and amended in 1970, 1977, and 1990, CAA establishes air quality standards and emissions limits.
- *Clean Water Act* (CWA) – Enacted in 1972 and amended in 1987, CWA regulates the release of pollutants into US waterways.

Figure 8.30 1993 Financial highlights (in thousands)

	Union Pacific Corporation	Union Pacific Railroad
Operating revenues	$7,561	$4,987
Operating income	1,489	1,042
Income before accounting adjustments	766	669
Cash from operations	1,563	1,074
Assets (at year end)	15,001	10,014
Capital expenditures	1,520	805

Source: Union Pacific 1993 Annual Report.

UPRR's response to the corporate environmental directive

8.4.169 In response to the Board's directive, UPRR adopted an environmental policy, which states in part:

> 'Union Pacific Railroad is committed to protecting the environment for our customers, our employees, the communities in which we operate. Beyond compliance with laws and regulations, Union Pacific is committed to the development and use of new technologies to preserve the environment for future generations. Environmental protection is a primary management responsibility as well as the responsibility of every Union Pacific employee.'

8.4.170 Figure 8.31 presents the remainder of the Railroad's policy statement.

Figure 8.31 Union Pacific Railroad environmental policy

8.8.10 Union Pacific and its employees will:
- comply with applicable environmental laws and regulations;
- establish measurable business objectives for environmental performance with the goal of achieving continuous improvement;
- develop employee awareness of environmental responsibilities and encourage adherence to sound environmental practices on and off the job;
- use environmentally sound treatment and disposal services for company waste;
- use sound environmental practices to address contaminated real property assets, including leased sites and right-of-ways;
- respond promptly to community and governmental inquiries about environmental issues and, where appropriate, initiate communications with customers and communities which might be affected;
- support and participate in governmental processes which seek to develop effective and balanced environmental laws and regulations;
- promote the conservation of resources through waste minimisation and the recycling/reuse of materials;
- support community Emergency Response Planning groups by furnishing current information on potential community hazards associated with railroad operations and conduct joint planning and response activities;
- develop and implement a self-monitoring programme to assure company facilities and operations adhere to our environmental policy.

8.4.171 In October 1991, UPRR centralised most of the company's environmental personnel in a single department called the Environmental Management Group (EMG). The EMG is housed within the company's Risk Management function and is chartered to serve as 'an environmentally proactive influence in the Company, to co-ordinate implementation of the Environmental Policy and to assist UPRR employees in developing ways to perform their work in an environmentally sound manner'.

8.4.172 By 1994, the EMG had over 40 employees. The group's Environmental Site Remediation team is charged with evaluating and remediating sites contaminated as a result of past operating practices. EMG's Environmental Operations team co-ordinates and oversees compliance activities throughout various parts of the Railroad. The EMG is also responsible for educating all UPRR employees on both the general need to care for the environment and the specific actions they can take to reduce the possibility of damaging the environment and perhaps violating the law. EMG personnel must therefore keep abreast of various regulations regarding the education of employees who handle hazardous materials and must develop appropriate training programmes to satisfy or exceed these regulations.

Quality and cost management

Environmental management activities

8.4.173 UPRR actively pursues policies and practices that demonstrate its commitment to protecting the environment. The following paragraphs provide a brief overview of some of the EMG's recent activities.

Clean-up

8.4.174 Like many companies, UPRR has numerous, decades-old facilities and processes that are in need of clean-up. In March 1993, UPRR initiated a comprehensive clean-up of all facilities in its system. By year end, the Railroad had identified and recycled or disposed of a wide variety of hazardous and non-hazardous wastes, including over 1,200 drums of petroleum products, more than 2,500 drums of other materials (both hazardous and non-hazardous), over 500 pallets of used signal batteries and almost 3,600 other miscellaneous containers (e.g., small drums, buckets, and paint cans).

Waste reduction

8.4.175 An investment of $140,000 at one railway yard resulted in a 90 per cent reduction in waste water produced there. The Railroad is also making its painting operations more environmentally sound by switching to water-based paints at some of its paint shops. In Texas, the Railroad is testing the use of a special adaptor that allows rechargeable radio batteries to be used in railroad lanterns. If successful, UPRR will have fewer batteries to dispose of or recycle.

Conservation

8.4.176 UPRR's locomotives must be washed periodically in order to remove petroleum residues, mud and exhaust from the exterior surfaces. The Railroad has numerous facilities where locomotives are manually washed. A recent investment of $3 million replaced one manual facility with a fully automatic facility. The new facility uses 50 per cent less water and 33 per cent less soap to wash an average of 40 more locomotives per day. At another facility, locomotives are washed with a high pressure spray that mixes steam with cold water. This method uses 90 per cent less water and significantly less energy than the traditional method.

Emissions reduction

8.4.177 UPRR has reduced the number of its fuelling facilities by 40 per cent and is currently replacing stationary fuel storage tanks with mobile tankers. UPRR is also in the process of retrofitting all its locomotives with retention tanks designed to collect oil and fuel that may otherwise leak onto the soil. The estimated cost of this project is $6 million.

8.4.178 Equipment upgrading to reduce nitrogen and sulphur oxide emissions by locomotives is underway, and many methods aimed at reducing fuel

Making COQ work

consumption and, consequently, air emissions are being adopted. UPRR is currently experimenting with alternative fuels as a long-term approach to the reduction of those emissions.

UPRR's cost of quality system and the EMG

8.4.179 Since 1988, UPRR has relied on a formalised, comprehensive quality cost reporting system as an integral part of its Total Quality Management System. By 1991, when the EMG was formed, cost of quality had been identified as a major company-wide business objective and formally incorporated into the company's performance management system. As such, reporting units through the company were asked to identify COQ accounts for their areas, and managers were expected to develop formal action plans for quality cost improvement. The managerial responsibilities for COQ are described in the company's 'Quality System Procedure 1002, Cost of Quality Control Process'. Figure 8.32 contains excerpts from this procedure.

Figure 8.32 Excerpts from Quality System procedure 1002, cost of Quality Control process

Objective
To provide the management process for identifying, capturing, reporting, and controlling quality costs. This process will be used to reduce failure costs and improve the effectiveness of control activities.
Scope
Quality costs are divided into four categories • Internal failure • External failure • Prevention • Appraisal. Costs in each category are defined by a set of assignable, measurable and controllable accounts which reflect costs directly associated with business activities.
Definitions • Internal failure costs: costs incurred as a result of failure activities that are transparent to the customer. • External failure costs: costs incurred as a result of failure activities that are known by the customer. • Prevention costs: costs associated with the prevention of failure activities. • Appraisal costs: costs associated with measuring, evaluating or reviewing processes, services or products to assure conformance to quality standards.

8.4.180 The reaction of the newly-formed EMG to the task of identifying COQ accounts was to question the applicability of the system to the EMG. UPRR's COQ system focuses on measuring current failures that could have been controlled by appropriate managerial actions. Any failure account must

Quality and cost management

therefore have an associated action plan for reducing that failure; similarly, no control account (i.e., prevention or appraisal) can be added to the system unless it relates to an existing failure account.

8.4.181 At first glance, the EMG did not appear to have any significant, readily identifiable accounts meeting these criteria because so many of its initial activities were concentrated on the correction of *past* environmental failures (i.e., remediation activities). The group did not see that action plans could be established to eliminate past occurrences, nor could any related controls be currently established to prevent those past failures.

8.4.182 In its second year of existence, the head of Risk Management (to whom the EMG reported) urged the group to reconsider these views concerning the primary nature of its activities. He observed that the company's environmental management practices were not perfect and could therefore be improved. He also pointed to the environmentally-related fines that the company was being assessed for current failures. (These fines were already being accumulated in COQ accounts for other departments.) In his opinion, COQ could help the EMG become more proactive, so he assigned a team the responsibility of identifying COQ accounts.

8.4.183 The team members identified several areas for investigation in their search for potential COQ accounts. First, the team members ascertained that an assessment of customer requirements could prove worthwhile since failure to meet customer requirements could result in controllable failure costs. They also recognised that an identification of the group's largest expenditures could reveal opportunities for improvement in control activities. Additional COQ accounts might be revealed by a careful review of the figures routinely reported elsewhere for their applicability to the COQ reporting framework. Conceivably, some COQ-related measures were already in place but had simply not been defined as such. Finally, the team determined that an evaluation and review of EMG's goals might suggest some new COQ accounts since failure properly to specify and attain the goals could cause otherwise unnecessary expenses for the company. The following sections describe a few of the COQ accounts that were ultimately identified by the team.

COQ related to customer requirements

8.4.184 The EMG has both external and internal customers. The external customers include the various city, state and federal agencies overseeing environmental regulations. Internal customers include all the other company departments receiving EMG services.

External customers

8.4.185 External customers' requirements are specified in numerous (and regularly changing) regulations and laws applicable to the geographic area covered by the Union Pacific's system. If UPRR fails to meet the external customers' requirements, the customers' dissatisfaction is expressed in the form of citations or letter complaining about, or serving notice on, violations of the present standards. Improved performance by the EMG would materialise in the form of fewer citations and, ultimately, in fewer fines and penalties.

8.4.186 Applying COQ concepts, the team determined that failure costs for each current incident could be estimated based on past experience. A failure cost per incident was estimated by dividing the total number of incidents in a recent year into the total dollar amount paid out in fines and penalties in the same year.

8.4.187 In any given month, the current COQ is thus reported to be the current month's number of incidents multiplied by the historical rate per incident. The team recognises that the measure is flawed in that the actual pay-outs in any given year may typically relate to failures that occurred in prior years. However, the figure is taken as an acceptable, rough estimate; it can be refined over time to reflect what the net present value of the actual payment will be when the incident is eventually settled (normally, in two or three years).

Internal customers

8.4.188 The internal customers' primary requirement is to minimise their own environmental costs. To these customers, sound environmental management practices (dictated to them by the EMG) sometimes seem to fail the cost-benefit criterion. For example, maintaining proper documentation of all 55-gallon drums is a time-consuming task that might not appear to have any payback. However, if a container's record is lost or if the label is destroyed, the contents must be analysed to determine what was in the drum so that the contents can be disposed of properly.

8.4.189 For COQ reporting purposes, the team determined the cost of analysing the contents of a 55-gallon drum to be the simple average derived from bills received over a 12-month period. In any given reporting period, the COQ is estimated as the number of drums analysed times the historical average analysis cost per drum. Actual analysis costs cannot be used on a timely basis because the number of drums tested and the results of the tests are not linked in the accounting system.

Quality and cost management

COQ in the large expenditure categories

8.4.190 The EMG's largest expenditures are associated with the clean-up of old sites. As discussed earlier, these costs are being incurred to correct past failures and are, by definition, not appropriate for inclusion in UPRR's COQ system. In developing its COQ accounts, the EMG team took a proactive view, however, and asked whether the clean-ups were being done to 'world class' standards. For example, they questioned whether the costs incurred were appropriate given the amount of material handled. They also expressed concern that the clean-up activities should reflect the latest in technology and process control.

8.4.191 A resulting account that the team developed is one that measures the disposal of diesel fuel-contaminated soil (the largest category of soil disposal). Before developing the account, the team reviewed the literature and interviewed consultants and subcontractors to determine the most efficient operation, i.e., a 'world class' standard. The new COQ account would reflect any costs incurred above this standard. Initially, the cost of disposing of one ton of hydrocarbon contaminated soil was in excess of $50 a ton. The best operation was processing it at $23 a ton.

8.4.192 The difference between the two costs times the tonnage handled is now reported as a failure account in the COQ system. Essentially, the account represents EMG's failure to meet an operating efficiency standard for disposal of the contaminated sail. This account focuses management attention on a significant environmental cost. It serves as a constant reminder to EMG management that the group can process larger quantities of soil and clean up sites faster if it can reduce the efficiency gaps.

8.4.193 Another large cost incurred by the EMG is the cost of treating water coming from various UPRR shops and fuelling facilities. Because the Railroad consumes a million gallons of diesel fuel per day, even a slight spillage rate implies that many gallons of diesel fuel are deposited into waste water treatment facilities each day. In addition, the use of non-biodegradable soaps and cleaning solvents increases the need for treatment chemicals and lowers the probability that the water can flow directly into local sewage treatment facilities.

8.4.194 In defining a related COQ account, the EMG took an aggressive stance and viewed the cost of the company's waste water treatment as a total failure cost. The EMG's position was simple: if the discharge water coming from the various shops and facilities always met the local standards, UPRR would incur no treatment costs. The COQ account was thus defined as any actual costs incurred. This particular account motivates various groups

Making COQ work

within UPRR to work together to reduce spillage at the company's fuelling facilities, decrease the use of non-biodegradable solvents and soaps and ensure that waste engine oil is disposed of properly.

8.4.195 The EMG also focused on the large expenditures associated with retrofitting all locomotives with retention tanks, or 'catch' pans. As mentioned earlier, these pans minimise the amount of hydrocarbons dropped on the ground. Based on a survey of 'best' practices, the EMG determined that the average locomotive leaks one quart of oil products per day. The group used this rate to estimate the amount of soil an average locomotive contaminates while idling on a year or industry track and incorporated the measure into a COQ failure account. (The idle time is considered more important because the amount of oil products leaked by a moving locomotive is significantly less.)

8.4.196 The COQ is the estimated cost of removing and treating the soil that the leaking hydrocarbons would contaminate during normal operating conditions. The account helps management track improvements associated with the retrofitting project. It also encourages management to reduce future exposures by installing catch basins at all major yards where locomotives stand idling for extended time periods.

Other COQ-related measures available in the company's existing systems

8.4.197 Another COQ account resulting directly from a review of the group's existing reports is the cost of cleaning up reportable, environmental spills that occur in the 'normal' course of business. Such spills happen for a number of reasons, ranging from a customer's failure to secure a valve on a 30,000 gallon tank to a track maintenance crew dropping a five gallon can of cleaning solvent at a siding. The clean-up costs associated with these incidents vary widely depending on the nature of the spill; further, there is typically a time delay between the incident date and the receipt of the final bill for clean-up. For these reasons, each period's COQ is estimated using an average historical cost per incident. The account allows the EMG Group to assess the potential magnitude of the spillages on an ongoing basis. The managers use this account to detect the presence of patterns in the spills and to evaluate the effectiveness of the corrective action programmes at specific locations.

COQ accounts related to the EMG's goals

8.4.198 A major objective of the EMG is to prevent environmental contaminations. Recognising the potential for small diesel fuel spills during routine refuelling operations, the EMG established a COQ account to draw

515

Quality and cost management

attention to the cumulative effects of these spills. This account assigned a dollar value to the amount of diesel fuel contained in a sample of the waste oil recovery tank at major fueling facilities. The COQ was estimated as the difference between the price paid for a gallon of diesel fuel and the price per gallon received from the oil recovery company.

8.4.199 This account focuses attention on the cost of fuelling mishaps. The EMG is not responsible for fuelling the locomotives, but is responsible for running the waste water treatment facilities and for cleaning up any spills. EMG managers believe this account can help the Group improve its own operating practices regarding waste water treatment; they also believe that the account will motivate managers in other departments to focus on the elimination of these fuel spillages.

8.4.200 The examples presented in this case demonstrate how UPRR relies on COQ as a management tool in the environmental area. Given that the Railroad has a long-standing commitment to total quality management and has experienced tremendous success with its use of COQ in other departments, the application of COQ to the environmental area does not require much 'stepping out of the box' thinking. In this instance, all that was necessary was for the COQ team to consider some relatively simple questions such as:

- What do the customers require, and what costs are incurred when their requirements are not met?
- Where is most of the money being spent, and are related activities being performed to world class standards?
- What measurements are already in place that do not reflect a financial impact, and what is the associated cost of failure?
- What are the group's goals or objectives, and what is the cost of not achieving those goals or objectives?

8.4.201 Determining the cost of not meeting the standard or requirement in each of these four categories is actually a fairly straightforward cost accounting exercise.

8.4.202 The Railroad views COQ as a useful management tool for all of its reporting units. Once costs have been assigned to each failure, management attention is focused on the largest account. Reducing the failure rate on these accounts not only improves the process, but also leads management to focus on other failure activity reductions. In many cases, failure reductions result in significant, immediate cash savings that can be applied to employee recognition programmes as well as to the prevention of failures in other areas.

The cost of future clean-up

8.4.203 The cost methodology for the cost of future clean-up was based upon the current cost the company was experiencing in cleaning older spills. The amount of soil contaminated was determined from the EPA standards (one pint contaminates a cubic yard of soil). The costs were developed from a historical cost perspective.

8.4.204 Engineering and research studies may be required to confirm the average amount of soil contaminated by a pint of oil/diesel fuel/lubricating oil before including these costs in the analysis. The mixture that is currently captured by the drip pans should be used in the studies to confirm the amount of soil contaminated over a given period. How fast does it leach out of the surrounding soil and drop below EPA standards?

8.4.205 In addition, the company should perform engineering studies to verify the amount of material leaking from the locomotive. Does the drip pan really collect all of the material dripping off the locomotive, or is there still some portion that is not captured and therefore should be excluded from the cost analysis?

8.4.206 In the classical definition, failure costs are those costs incurred when customers' requirements are not met. In this case, the customer is the Environmental Protection Agency, which has very technical specifications.

8.4.207 The cost of the waste water treatment plant is a failure cost if criteria allows for inefficiency costs. This means any inefficiencies contained within the operations are classified as failure costs. If there is a process that meets the EPA's requirements at a cost of $25 per 1,000 gallons treated and the industry average is $10 per 1,000 gallons treated, the customer is going to buy the most economic service. If your costs are 2.5 times the industry average in this area, how long will customers buy at this price? This is the reason for using the difference between the actual cost and the world class cost as the failure cost. One could include only the total cost of the plant if the cost of biodegradable soaps and spill-free fuelling stations were equal to the current costs.

8.4.208 The argument for labelling the cost of the waste water treatment plant as a prevention cost is that the customer (the EPA) requires a treatment facility and will levy fines if the requirement is not met. The fines are the failure cost and the expense of the waste water treatment plant is the prevention cost.

Quality and cost management

8.4.209 The best argument for treating the waste water treatment plant as a failure cost is that there are technological alternatives that would stop the pollutants from entering the water in the first place. These more costly (to the department using the solvents and soaps) alternatives would be justified by reductions in the operating costs of the waste water treatment plan. The major argument against using the operating costs of the waste water treatment plant to justify other technologies is that the waste water plant would have to remain in case these new techniques did not work.

8.4.210 The current method used to improve the water quality is to trace the pollutant back to its source and make the 'responsible party' bear the cost of improving water quality. This includes the costs of additional chemicals, expansion of the facility, and/or other operating costs. These are the costs one is trying to avoid. The mechanism for tracing and billing the source companies is improving. In addition, the capital costs have already been incurred and cannot be recovered. The only costs that can be eliminated are the operating costs. So the best course would be to shut down the facilities but not destroy them.

8.4.211 The major cost of a water treatment plant is the capital cost of installing the holding ponds, pumps and mixing chambers. These facilities will normally last 25 to 50 years and would cost additional money to tear out. They can always be reactivated on fairly short notice if the standards change. Unless they present a safety hazard, they can be left in place at no additional expense.

8.4.212 It is realistic to hold an operating unit responsible to a world class, competitive standard. If the organisation cannot meet its competitors' costing structures how long will the organisation survive? The use of outside standards could be mandated to produce lower costs as quickly as possible.

8.4.213 The things that one may want to see before agreeing to link salary increase to meeting a target are:

- engineering studies;
- the capital budget to support the improved operation;
- source of comparison data;
- historical trends and rate of improvement at the world class organisation.

(Source: adapted with permission from Carr, 1997.)

Chapter 9
Strategy and cost management

9.1 Business planning

9.1.1 Planning is considered fundamental to the effective management of an enterprise. Although countless definitions of the term exist, it broadly encompasses choosing objectives, identifying various ways of achieving goals and deciding on a set of actions which may then be monitored and controlled. An early definition of strategic planning is:

> 'the process of deciding on objectives for the organisation, on changes in these objectives, on the resources used to attain these objectives, and on the policies that are to govern the acquisition, use, and disposition of these resources.'
> (Source: Anthony, 1965)

9.1.2 With some qualifications, this definition is still generally accepted today. Planning is not to be equated with forecasting, which identifies what could happen to things not under an organisation's control. Nor is planning a 'box of tricks or a bundle of techniques' (Drucker, 1977) which acts as a substitute for cogitation. A number of management accounting techniques have been developed to assist management in the planning process.

9.1.3 Business planning if underpinned by concerns over what action is appropriate when confronted with action choices, each with differing possible effects. It therefore needs to be a controlled exercise. The corollary of planning is therefore control. Management control attempts to ensure that resources are obtained and used effectively and efficiently to realise organisational objectives indicated by the strategic plan. Investment appraisal (see Chapter **4**) and budgetary control are important facets of management control systems which provide information for partial feedback into the planning process.

9.2 Linking plans to strategy

9.2.1 Whilst efficiency is important, many industries have become more efficient without individual companies becoming more profitable. Porter (1999) offers an important insight:

Strategy and cost management

> 'Operational efficiency means you're running the same race faster, but strategy is choosing to run a different race because it's the one you've set yourself up to win.'

9.2.2 This logic leads us away from the search simply for internal efficiencies in the company, or even the supply chain, to focus on the general management responsibility for strategic positioning – defining the value provided to customers, compared to competitors, as the basis of competitive advantage and superior performance.

9.2.3 Strategising is about building the company's strategic direction for the future and designing the business model that will deliver superior performance. It is not regarded as equivalent to planning. Hamel (1996) makes this point clear – planning is scheduling, strategy is revolution. For example, he has described several routes to industry 'revolution' as the basis for strategising.

- Reconceiving the product or service: radically improve the value equation.
- Redefining market space: push the bounds of universatility.
- Redrawing industry boundaries: rescale industries – take a local business national or make a larger business local. Compress the supply chain. Drive convergence.

9.2.4 One way of capturing what is signified by strategy is to note that writings on the subject view it as constituting a logic underlying an organisation's interaction with its environment, which in turn influences its deployment of resources.

9.2.5 Hamel and Prahalad (1994) offer a way of testing whether the management team in an organisation is facing up to the challenges of becoming strategic instead of just planning and budgeting (see Worksheet 1)

(Source: Hamel, G and Prahalad, CK *Competing for the future*, 1994.)

9.2.6 Piercy (1999) outlines how management thinking about strategy has gone through a number of phases or eras. Some of the changes in the dominant emphasis of management theory and practice in different times are summarised in Figure 9.1 as a number of phases in which different approaches to the strategy issue have preoccupied top management.

9.2.7 The 'golden era' of the 1950s and 1960s, when demand outstripped supply in many industries and the global economy was recovering from World

Linking plans to strategy

How well does management in this company perform in the following areas:					
	Conventional and reactive			Distinctive and far-sighted	
Senior management's view of the future compared to that of our competitors?	1	2	3	4	5
	Re-engineering core processes			Regenerating core strategies	
What absorbs more senior management time?	1	2	3	4	5
	Mostly as a rule follower			Mostly as a rule maker	
How do competitors view our company?	1	2	3	4	5
	Operational efficiency			Innovation and growth	
What is our greatest strength?	1	2	3	4	5
	Mostly catching up			Mostly getting out in front	
What is the focus of our company's attempts to build competitive advantage?	1	2	3	4	5
	Our competitors			Our foresight	
What has mainly set our company's agenda for change?	1	2	3	4	5
	Mostly as an engineer			Mostly as an architect	
Do we spend most of our time monitoring the status quo (the maintenance engineer) or designing the future (the strategic architect)?	1	2	3	4	5

Source: Adapted from Hamel and Prahalad (1994).

Worksheet 9.1

War II, has long since ended for most organisations. In the late 1960s and 1970s the issue was strategic planning – business had become tougher and the environment less predictable. Better strategic plans were seen as the answer, and complex systems, techniques and models for planning were developed.

Competitive differentiation

9.2.8 Effective strategy is seen as relying on clear competitive differentiation exploiting the core competencies of a business – creating value by being the best at the key activities that competitors cannot equal.

521

Strategy and cost management

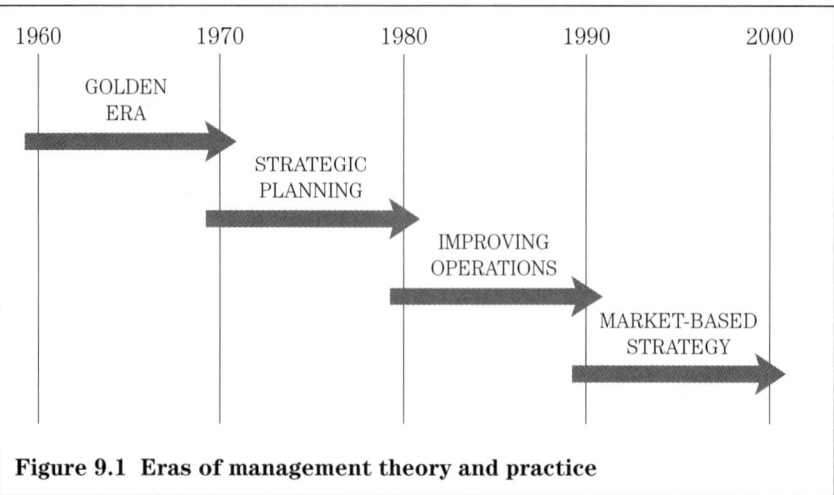

Figure 9.1 Eras of management theory and practice

9.2.9 The best-known approach to considering competitive differentiation is that provided by Michael Porter. Porter (1985) believes that in spite of the apparent complexity of competitive strategy there are two sources of competitive advantage: low cost and differentiation. This leads to the identification of three generic strategies, as illustrated in Figure 9.2.

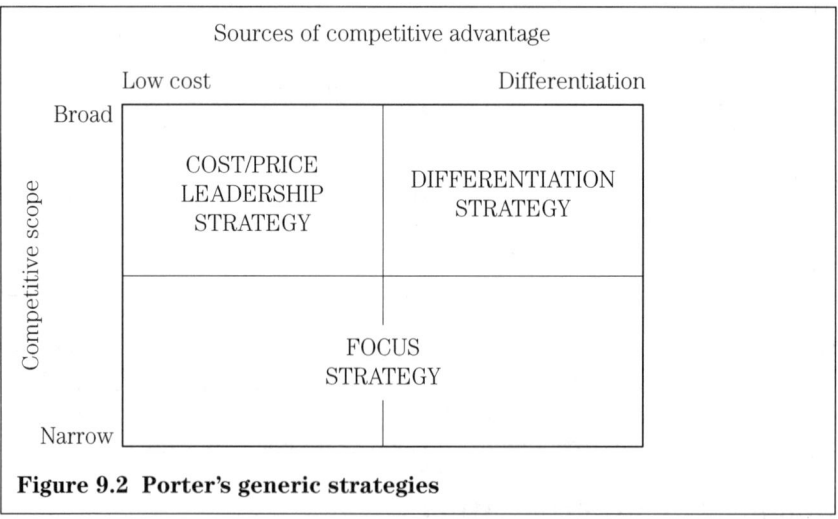

Figure 9.2 Porter's generic strategies

9.2.10 Porter's view of an enterprise's competitive choice is that it can compete on a broad or narrow scope, being either a *price leader* or a *differentiator*.

9.2.11 Two relevant points from Porter's work are: (1) one should think in terms of an organisation's particular competitive strategy type (to avoid the danger of becoming a 'stuck in the middle' firm which is weak and vulnerable as it is neither a differentiator nor a price leader); and (2) one can use the structure to see how groups of competitors are positioned in terms of their strategies – i.e., what are the 'strategic groups' and how well those groups perform. For instance, one might be able to categorise the complex market for personal writing instruments into:

- broad scope/price leadership: – throw-away ball-point pens, generics;
- broad scope/differentiators: – mass-market brands, Parker, Schaeffer, etc. which are differentiated by branding, design, packaging, and so on;
- narrow scope/price leadership: – own-label pens, badged hotel pens, etc.;
- narrow scope/differentiators: – exclusive brands like Cross, Mont Blanc, etc.

9.2.12 Naturally, what value means to different customers depends on the context. This renders problematic Porter's simple way of reducing a complex competitive market to a few basic groups. However, the question of *how* differentiation can be achieved remains relevant.

9.2.13 Porter considers that differentiation must be tied to operational efficiency if an organisation is to perform well:

> 'A company can outperform rivals only if it can establish a difference that it can preserve. It must deliver greater value to customers or create comparable value at a lower cost, or do both. The arithmetic of superior profitability then follows: delivering greater value allows a company to charge higher unit prices; greater efficiency results in lower average unit costs.'

(Source: Porter, 1995.)

9.2.14 This view raises three significant questions in building a strategy.

- What differences can an organisation establish or exploit in the market?
- In what ways do these differences represent superior value to all or some customers in the market?
- Can this form of differentiation be sustained and defend against 'me-too' imitations by existing or new competitors?

Strategy and cost management

9.2.15 Increasingly, the sustainability of competitive advantage in the New Economy is proving difficult to achieve. Both the speed of change in the market and the ability of competitors to identify and meet customer demands are creating entirely new challenges for market players.

Core competencies

9.2.16 At the broadest levels, Prahalad and Hamel (1990) provide an interesting view of the 'core competence of the corporation', which can be combined with the model of competitive differentiation and positioning. At stake is how an organisation can differentiate effectively if it does not understand its capabilities. The focus ought then to be on how an organisation addresses the issue of value to the customer, and the marketing assets the firm has at its disposal to create the value which underpins competitive positioning.

9.2.17 Prahalad and Hamel (1990) have examined the characteristics of companies that have succeeded in investing in new markets, quickly entering new markets and dramatically shifting patterns of customer choices in established markets. They conclude that the common characteristic is that these companies understand, exploit, invest to create, and sustain core competencies. Examples include:

- Sony: the capacity to miniaturise;
- Philips: optical-media expertise;
- Citicorp: competence in systems;
- 3M: competence with sticky tape;
- Black and Decker: expertise with small electrical motors;
- Canon: skills in optics, imaging and microprocessors;
- Casio: competence in display systems.

9.2.18 These are viewed as the most basic corporate resources, which lead to success in apparently diverse markets and products, and suggest that even the largest of companies are unlikely to have more than five or six core competences.

9.2.19 For example, the transformation of Rentokil in the UK from a pest control business into a diversified services company has been achieved through a radical focus on the company's core competence: 'the ability to carry out high-quality services (from pest control through healthcare to manned guarding) on other people's premises through well-recruited, well-trained and well-motivated people.'

9.2.20 Piercy (1999) suggests that companies need to think very hard about which of their core capabilities are valuable to them in particular markets.

- Does this capability create value for the customer in this market? If not, it is of no use in developing a strategy for this market.
- Will competitors find it hard to copy this capability? If every company can replicate this, there is no competitive advantage.
- What is the probable duration of the uniqueness? How long does the company have before the competition can catch up?
- Who is the primary beneficiary of the capability? Does it relate to particular segments of the market on which the company should focus?
- Does another capability satisfy the same market need? Does the organisation face competition from substitution?
- Is the firm's core capability really superior to the competition?

9.2.21 Ultimately strategic strength may be seen to come from competitive differentiation – doing the things that matter in the market differently to competitors, or doing different things – which exploits a company's core competencies. The idea of *differentiating capabilities* combines these two approaches – the issue is what activities an organisation does better than the rest, and which create superior value for customers.

9.3 SWOT analysis

9.3.1 An established approach to identifying a business's capabilities (and corresponding weaknesses) and relating these to opportunities and threats in the outside world is SWOT analysis (*s*trengths, *w*eaknesses, *o*pportunities and *t*hreats).

9.3.2 SWOT analysis provides a simple, but structured, approach to evaluating a company's strategic position. As Piercy (1999) notes, a major attraction of SWOT analysis is that it is familiar and easily understandable by users, and it provides a good structuring device for sorting out ideas about the future and a company's ability to exploit that future.

9.3.3 Experience with a wide variety of companies and managers suggest that SWOT analysis *can* be made to work, and real strategic insights *can* be generated and used.

Strategy and cost management

9.3.4 Following the 'rules' for using SWOT to produce dynamic results Piercy (1999) identified:

- focused SWOTs;
- shared vision;
- customer orientation;
- environmental analysis;
- structured strategy generation.

9.3.5 The more carefully one defines the area to be evaluated with a SWOT analysis, the more productive the analysis is likely to be. By focusing on a particular issue, and excluding non-relevant material, one can overcome the bland, meaningless generalisations that executives may produce if asked to take a global view of their business's strengths and weaknesses.

9.3.6 Because of its apparent simplicity and ease of communication, SWOT analysis is an excellent vehicle in working with planning teams or groups of executives. There is little or no barrier created through executives having to learn complex analytical techniques.

9.3.7 The way to use the SWOT technique in a particularly powerful form is summarised in Figure 9.3.

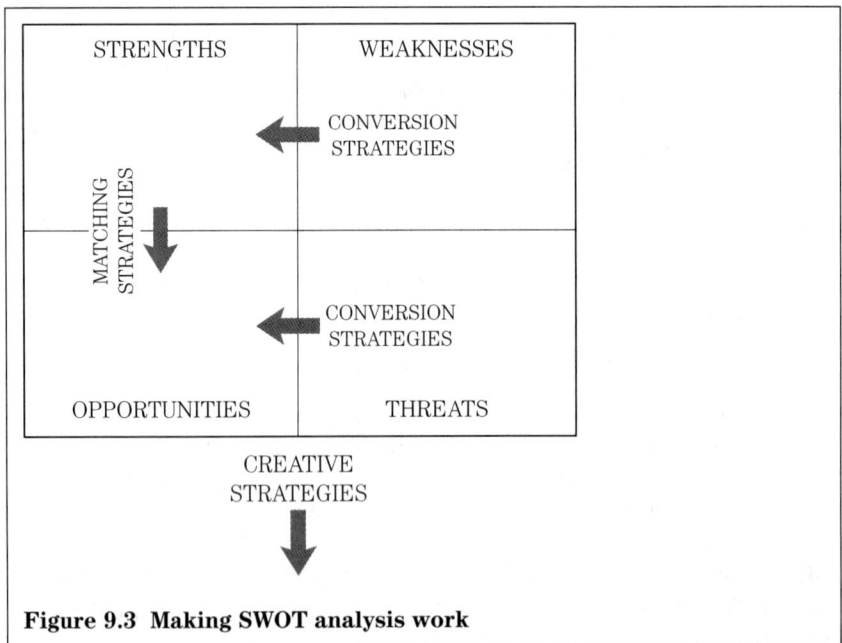

Figure 9.3 Making SWOT analysis work

SWOT analysis

9.3.8 The first requirement is that in evaluating a company's strengths and weaknesses, *only* those resources or capabilities which would be recognised and valued by the *customer* should be included. This helps to get to the 'motherhood' statements often produced as a list of strengths.

Environmental analysis

9.3.9 The same discipline is required to view the opportunities and threats in the environment – the specific market, customer, issue, etc. This turns the company's attention to the lower half of the model in Figure 9.3.

9.3.10 The goal is to list those aspects in the relevant environment which make it attractive or unattractive to the organisation whereby the search for ideas should be as thorough and widely-informed as possible. The major difficulty is that executives often jump the gun and put their strategies and tactics down as opportunities.

9.3.11 There must be insistence that opportunities and threats exist *only* in the outside world – the things one might propose to do about them are the *strategies*. For example, it may be suggested that price-cutting is an opportunity. This is *not* an opportunity in a SWOT analysis – it is a price tactic which one might adopt. One would *only* accept the desirability of price-cutting if, for example, the company's size gave it greater cost economies than its competitors, and that there was an identified, external market opportunity in terms of there being a price-sensitive segment of the market, or the need to meet a competitor's threatened entry to the market with low prices. The rule is that opportunities exist independently of policies and actions.

Structured strategy generation

9.3.12 When all four cells of the SWOT matrix are completed, and each item in each category is ranked in terms of importance, then the matrix acts automatically as a generator and tester of strategies, as shown in Figure 9.3.

- Matching strategies: the central focus is on matching strengths to opportunities in the outside world. The logic is that strengths which do not match any known opportunity are of little immediate value, while highly ranked opportunities for which the company has no strengths should be carefully considered.

- Conversion strategies: the design of appropriate responses to highly ranked weaknesses and threats is difficult. Ideally the goal is to convert these factors into strengths and opportunities. In some cases this may

Strategy and cost management

be relatively straightforward – a weakness in sales coverage may mean adding to the salesforce, a threat from a competitor may be bought off by collaboration or merger or neutralised by an advertising campaign, but in other cases one may be unable to think sensibly about converting or neutralising these factors. In the latter case, these factors remain the limiting problems in this business and determine how attractive it is

- Creative strategies: one has to recognise that going through this analytical process often simply generates new, creative ideas for how to develop the business. Good ideas should not be discarded simply because they are unusual. There should not be a box especially for creative ideas that may not fit elsewhere in the model.

9.3.13 The guidelines outlined above are simple to apply, but the discipline imposed can be very harsh. The approach can be effective and the SWOT technique can be a dynamic and productive tool for strategic audits and strategy generation.

9.3.14 In this light SWOT analysis can provide a mechanism for putting ideas about value proposition and key relationships into tangible form and testing them. It is also a good source of new ideas which can enrich the strategy. Worksheets 2, 3 and 4 enable SWOT analysis as described above to be carried out.

9.4 The mission

9.4.1 Whilst SWOT analysis can be a useful tool for contributing to the strategy development process, the actual development of a mission is seen by some organisations as essential to underpinning strategy.

9.4.2 One recurring observation of successful organisations is that of radical innovation and revolutionary change whenever a business is reinvented. There is always someone driving that change – whether it is Jeff Bezos at Amazon.com, Michael Dell at Dell Computers, Anita Roddick at the Body Shop, Lord Blyth at Boots or Bill Gates at Microsoft. There is always someone with a sense of purpose, who makes the unconventional happen and who shares that vision across an organisation.

9.4.3 But as Piercy (1999) notes, that visionary strategic architect is not always the CEO. Visionaries may not always be solely those at the top of the organisation. The trouble is that traditional organisations seem to do their best to stifle the visionaries. Handy (1998) has noted that:

The mission

SWOT worksheet 2 – Opportunities and threats	
Opportunities	Rank
Threats	Rank

Worksheet 9.2

'Companies need people with passion and integrity who can inspire trust in those working for the organisation. At present such characters find it difficult to flourish.'

9.4.4 The emergence of Sony's playstation products and its focus on digital as opposed to analogue technology emerged from the convictions of an employee running a renegade operation until he found top management support for the strategy.

9.4.5 Effectively managing talent, not hierarchy, is the first step in building the capability to survive in the revolutionary market place. One test of failing in this area is the number of a company's key personnel who leave to become competitors.

Strategy and cost management

SWOT worksheet 3 – Opportunities and threats

Opportunities	Rank

Threats	Rank

Worksheet 9.3

9.4.6 The challenge to management is to build a vision or sense of mission that underpins the organisation's strategy.

Building a sense of mission

9.4.7 Management vision and mission drive strategy in the way suggested in Figure 9.4.

9.4.8 The results of mission analysis tend to be statements of varying length that state what a firm wants its business to be.

The mission

SWOT worksheet 4 – Strategy generation

Market/
Segment/
Issue

Matching strategies

Strength	Matching opportunity	Strategy required

Conversion strategies

Weaknesses/ threat	Conversion strategy	Strength/opportunity created or weakness/ threat neutralised

Creative strategy ideas

Worksheet 9.4

9.4.9 If mission analysis is to contribute positively, then it should:

- reflect core competencies and how it is intended to apply them and sustain them;
- be closely tied to the critical success factors in the market place – the things one has to be good at to survive;

Strategy and cost management

Figure 9.4 Mission and strategy

- tell employees, managers, suppliers and partners what contribution is required from them to deliver the promise of value to the customer.

9.4.10 In some organisations, mission analysis has provided the broad logic for divisionalising and developing strategies for complex businesses in very simple terms.

9.4.11 One well-known example was a UK brewery which undertook mission analysis at the corporate level with the results described in Figure 9.5.

9.4.12 In this instance, mission analysis provided an enduring structure (now more than 20 years old) for developing organisational planning and identifying strategies, on the basis of capabilities in the different customer or user markets in which they planned to compete.

9.4.13 The sorts of benefits that this kind of market-based mission analysis can give are as follows.

- Defining the market from the customer's perspective, i.e., the need or problem to be solved, so as to get better insight into what matters to the customer.

- Mapping out the different types of customer market in which one needs to develop different types of market strategies and programmes to be a serious player.

- Helping to see where the real competition is coming from and where it is going to emerge.

- Finding new areas into which to develop, where the link to current business is the customer base and organisational capabilities.

The mission

Figure 9.5 UK brewery's mission analysis

The brewery's missions	Organisational and market characteristics	Strategies developed
Drink	A static market leading to a traditional bureaucratic organisation driven by the pressure of production efficiency and economies of scale.	Compete for market share against competitors by large advertising spends and new brands. Acquire new outlets where possible.
Catering	At the time a by-product of being in the business of running public houses.	Compete for customer spend by greater variety of food in pubs. Acquire restaurant groups. Acquire hotel groups.
Entertainment	Pubs are leisure centres. We have expertise in fulfilling people's social needs.	Acquisitions: gaming clubs, gambling machine manufacturers, holiday camps, holiday tour operators, private sports clubs.
Chemicals	The unavoidable by-product of brewing.	Strategy of R&D-based collaborations with third parties to exploit the biochemical material for new markets as diverse as blood replacement, fish food and genetic engineering.

Mission statements

9.4.14 Some organisations adopt a structured approach to building and evaluating a mission statement.

Structuring mission content

9.4.15 Views about the desirable content of mission statements are many and varied. One can distinguish four major areas of development:

- statements relating to *organisational philosophy*;
- the specification of the *product-market domain* or scope for the organisation;
- definition of *organisational key values* for participants;
- the identification of *critical success factors* in the market place or industry faced.

9.4.16 These issues vary in *focus* – internal or external – and *scope* – broad and narrow, as shown in Figure 9.6.

533

Strategy and cost management

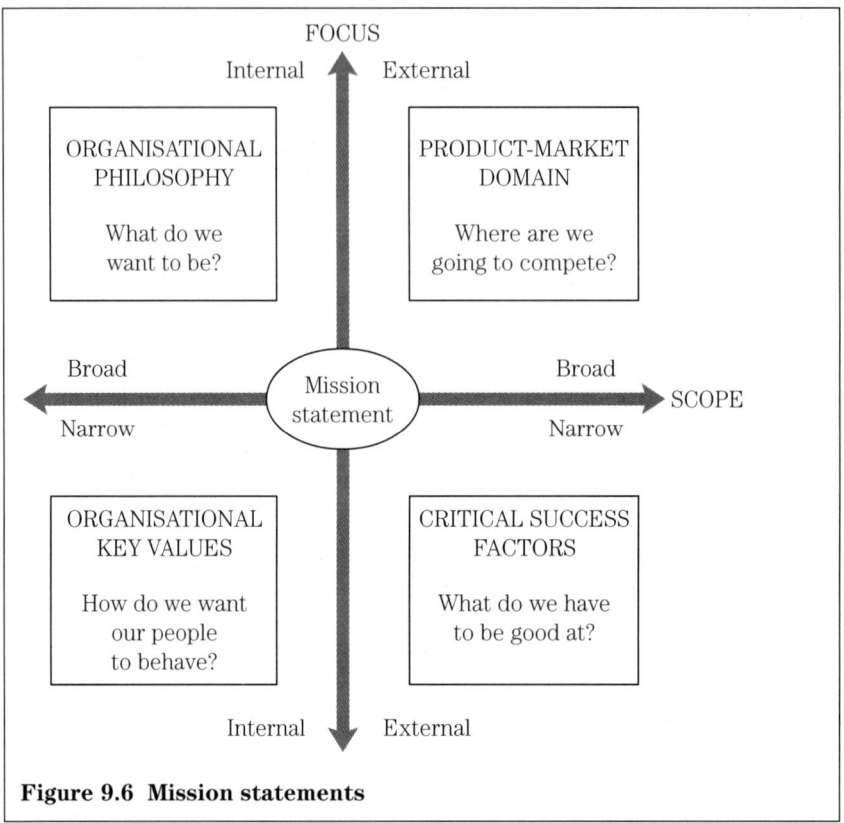

Figure 9.6 Mission statements

Organisational philosophy

9.4.17 At the centre of mission lies the definition of the central purpose or philosophy of the organisation, or even creating a form of 'corporate constitution'. Some see this as encompassing the broad issues: the grand design, quality orientation and atmosphere of the enterprise, and the firm's role in society, or the combination of managerial culture and ethos with social responsibility and public image. More focused perspectives emphasise specific service to internal and external stakeholders, and the identification of values, beliefs, guidelines, aspirations and thus the creation of a unifying force in the organisation. In the simplest terms, the underlying question here is: 'What do we want this organisation to *be* and to *stand for?*'

Product-market domain

9.4.18 Others look to the mission to define where the organisation is to operate, which is shifting from a focus on internal to external issues: the definition of the customer base, the product/service offering, location or geo-

geographic coverage and the core technologies or capability to be exploited. In the simplest terms, the central question to be addressed here is: '*Where* are we going to compete?', or 'What is our *field of operation* and what are our core *capabilities*?'

Organisational key values

9.4.19 This relates to ideas about defining the core values or principles which provide guides to action for members of the organisation, or the 'policies and behaviour that underpin the distinctive competence and value system'. Some see this area as building corporate culture and 'selling' corporate beliefs to employees, or motivating employees to achieve the organisation's objectives, and even providing the basis for appraisal and reward. In the simplest terms, the central question here is: 'What do we want people in this organisation to be *good* at, and how do we want them to *behave*?'

Critical success factors

9.4.20 As Piercy (1999) notes, less easily identified in the traditional approach are suggestions about the external impact of the mission. These are taken as the identification of critical success factors in the market or industry faced. In the simplest terms, the central issue is: 'What do we have to be *good* at to *succeed* in this market or industry?'

Evaluating mission statements

9.4.21 One can use this structure as a diagnostic tool to confront the mission issue in organisations, either in building a mission statement for the first time, or in evaluating an existing statement. The procedure is as follows.

- Summarise the key points of the existing or proposed new mission statement. For a new mission statement this may mean brainstorming and information gathering, while for the testing of an existing mission statement it may be more a process of extracting the key points from the available documentation.

- From those key points, identify the following dimensions of mission:
  (i) Organisational philosophy: what do we see as the enduring purpose of our organisation, its unique characteristics and what it wants to achieve?
  (ii) *Product-market domain*: where do we intend to operate and compete, what are our products, what needs do they meet, who are our customers, what technologies will we apply, what are the boundaries of our markets, what are our core capabilities?
  (iii) *Organisational key values*: what values, norms, guidelines do we think are important in our organisation, what things do we

Strategy and cost management

want people to have in their minds when they make decisions and carry things out for us?

(iv) *Critical success factors*: what things do we have to be good at to survive and prosper in our market place?

- Using the structure in Figure 9.6, one might look at the consistency between the different parts of mission: do the critical success factors derived from the mission actually make any sense in terms of the product markets the organisation has chosen, or is the company trying to be good at things that do not matter? Does the organisation's 'philosophy' relate to the key values to be transmitted to people who make decisions in the organisation, or are there inherent conflicts because these things need more thinking through? Do these key values (services, quality, social responsibilities or whatever) relate directly to the critical success factors in these product markets, or do internal values have nothing to do with what matters in the market place? Has the organisation chosen product markets where its philosophy and purpose make sense? If it works through this process, what conclusions can be reached about: the adequacy of the mission statement; the consistency between internal issues of philosophy and key values and external issues of product market domain and critical success factors?

- The conclusions may lead one to revise what is reflected in the mission statement or to revise the draft mission statement. The critical requirement is to move backwards and forwards between these stages – discussion, revising, testing, re-thinking – until one can move from the draft mission statement to the final version.

- Finally, one can test the mission statement in the way suggested in Worksheet 5, with managers, employees, shareholders, customers and suppliers.

9.4.22 If nothing else, a systematic structural analysis of the mission issue takes us forward from the vague, open-ended rhetoric of some executives. Experience in testing this approach in-company suggests it can be a good way to build strategy, and to highlight the process of matching core capabilities with internal values and with the critical success factors. According to Piercy, this is one route to clarifying and sharing management vision and a sense of mission to create and implement strategy effectively.

9.5 Why do strategies fail?

9.5.1 Corboy and O'Corrbui (1999) have described the main pitfalls of successful strategy implementation. They state that up to 70 per cent of

Why do strategies fail?

Worksheet 5

Testing mission statements
Give a score to the mission statement for each of the following questions
Score *0 = very poor* *5 = medium* *10 = excellent*
1 Does the mission statement make it clear what the organisation stands for and why it exists?
2 Does the mission statement make it clear where we have to compete and who our customers are?
3 Does the mission statement tell us the values we should adhere to in working for this organisation?
4 Does the mission statement make it clear what we have to be good at to survive and prosper?
5 Do the different parts of the mission statement hang together – does it make sense?
6 Is the mission statement short enough so that people can understand it?
7 Is the mission statement well written enough so that people will remember it?
8 Is the mission statement believable as a view of what this organisation is all about?
9 Is the mission statement challenging and exciting – will it motivate us?
10 Does the mission statement tell us what we should be doing and what we should not be doing?
TOTAL
Conclusions/Implications

business strategies fail to get implemented and yet strategy is of limited value unless it is acted upon. Strategy implementation nevertheless has a poor track record. Corboy and O'Corrbui (1999) note that this is often the result of an organisation committing one or more of 'the seven deadly sins of strategy implementation'. They describe these as follows.

1. The strategy is not worth implementing

9.5.2   This occurs where business strategy is deficient in analytical rigour, creative insight, ambition or practicality. The strategy represents just more of what has happened previously with no enhanced sense of vision or challenge for the organisation.

Strategy and cost management

2. People are not clear how the strategy will be implemented

9.5.3 When the strategy has been developed and evaluated, a plan may be considered necessary to prepare the organisation for its implementation. But there may be a number of issues which need to be addressed first, including:

- Priorities: what are your priorities? Which parts of the strategy should be implemented first? Have these priorities been made clear?
- Timescale: how quickly do you want to implement the strategy? Is it feasible to do it in that timeframe?
- Lessons learnt: what can you learn from your previous experiences of strategy implementation?
- Impact: what impact or implications will the strategy have on your customers, your people and on how you do things now?
- Participation: who needs to be involved and when? Have they got what it takes to make it work?
- Risks: what are the risks which might prevent you from implementing the strategy and can you manage or reduce those risks?

3. Customers and staff do not fully understand the strategy

9.5.4 Clearly this is a problem which may hinder other aspects of organisational functioning.

4. Individual responsibilities for implementing the change are not clear

9.5.5 Developing a very insightful and relevant strategy in the hope that the logic behind the strategy will be enough to make it a reality. Often, individuals should be given clear and specific responsibilities for making the strategy work.

5. Chief executives and senior managers step out of the picture once implementation begins

9.5.6 As is the case with any organisational activity which affects a large segment of individuals or resources, top management support and involvement is essential.

6. The 'brick walls' are not recognised

9.5.7 Unforeseen events or difficulties tend to arise during implementation. It is important that obstacles are acknowledged and addressed.

7. Forgetting to 'mind the shop'

9.5.8 At times, the process of developing and implementing strategy can become the all consuming concern of senior management. The operational priority is to run the organisation and meet targets to provide services and serve customers.

9.5.9 Whilst these seven 'deadly sins' are apparent, they are not always dealt with. Of equal significance is to assume that strategy development is a deliberate and purposive activity. In many, organisations it is described as an emergent rather than deliberate process. As such, imposing excessive functional structure and defined rationality to a process which defies such characterisation can prove inappropriate.

9.6 Strategic management accounting

9.6.1 Drtina and Monetti (1995) have remarked that control systems are sometimes expected to accomplish the impossible: plan for uncertain conditions and monitor outcomes under complex operating conditions. Control systems may be deemed successful when they assist an organisation to accomplish its strategic pursuits. An adequate fit between the methods used to control daily operations and the overall strategic direction of the company needs to be achieved whilst remaining attuned to changing customer needs and emerging product developments.

9.6.2 Strategic management accounting (SMA) is becoming firmly established at the conceptual level as a priority function for any senior accounting executive. SMA entails the preparation and presentation of information for decision-making, placing especial emphasis on external factors. The focus is on business strategy as affected by levels and trends in real costs and prices, volume, market share, cash flow and the demands made on a firm's total resources. The basis of such a view is that information affects strategy and conceptions of strategy must, in turn, affect the way in which information is constructed, presented and used. It follows that since individual organisations develop their own individual strategies, they must determine their own particular approach to determining the structure of SMA information. Only recently have guidelines emerged to provide a general approach for doing so.

SMA criteria

9.6.3 Various steps are involved in taking a strategic approach to producing management accounting information. The following form a potential sequence identified by Simmonds (1989; 1998; see also Simmonds *et al*, 1997).

(1) Develop a dynamic view of strategic business units

9.6.4 The idea of a strategic business unit (SBU) cannot be fixed and permanent, it must be identified at a particular time. The management accounting system can be redesigned so as to de-emphasise traditionally determined responsibility centres and to stimulate management to consider what might be appropriate units for strategic action. For this to take place there must be an acceptance of strategic competitive position as the determinant for identifying units. At the SBU level, there must be a concern for areas of the external environment which are critical to the achievement of its goals and objectives. Planning resources should be concentrated on these critical success factors and business strategies should be selected accordingly.

9.6.5 One approach is to consider Porter's 'value chain' as noted above. The value chain looks at the total value added by the industry and by the particular organisation within that industry. The contribution of each primary and support activity carried out by the organisation can then be separated. The activities which are identified to add most significantly to the total value added are focused upon. Certainly, this is of fundamental importance in cost management terms, but it also enables strategies to be developed to improve or defend the existing share of the value added from which the enterprise benefits. Figure 9.7 depicts Porter's value chain.

(2) Strategic achievement comes from relative performance

9.6.6 Profit comes from competing effectively, and the strategy is how to achieve this. Strategic success is about relative performance. On its own, internal cost efficiency is not enough for success, nor are volume, market share or accumulated experience. If the strategy produces relative success and profits, further expansion will follow profitability and bring with it an increase in relative volume, relative market share or relative accumulated experience. To provide management with strategy guidance, all indicators must thus be measured in terms of relative position against specified competitors. The orientation of management accounting information must as a consequence be turned outwards. According to Simmonds (1998), the relative cost graph can show the relative impact of strategies adopted by firms competing in the same business field over a number of years.

Strategic management accounting

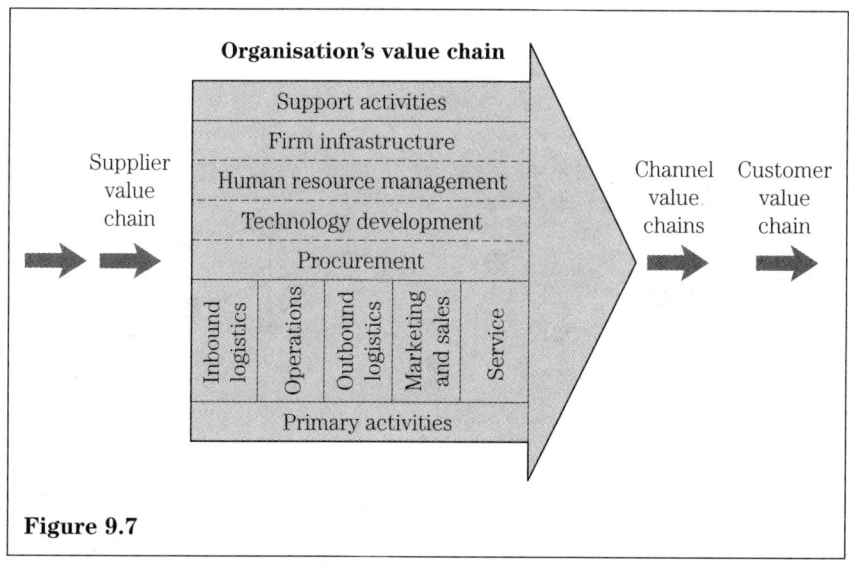

Figure 9.7

9.6.7 Traditionally, cost and experience curves have been used to plot a single firm's movements in real unit cost against volume over time. The volume measure makes it possible to gauge whether costs have been controlled relative to the firm's volume variation from capacity. Greater insight from cost information is, however, obtainable when the relative cost graph is produced by graphing the estimated unit costs of several relevant competitors alongside the firm's own costs.

9.6.8 In Figure 9.8, for example, firm A and firm B were both hit by dramatic market volume reductions in years 1 to 4. In year one, firm B was nearly three times as large as A and had a substantially lower cost. From years 1 to 3, firm B's costs increased less than A's and its volume fell off proportionately less. In year 4, B lost 35 per cent of its year 3 volume, and costs again increased. Firm A fared even worse, losing 50 per cent, but it held its unit cost. Then in year 5, A continued to reduce its cost dramatically, bringing its level down to that of B. Whatever A did in the market in year 6, possibly lowering price or improving distribution, proved the competitive turning point now that A was operating from an equal cost base. Its actions led to major sales gains and further unit cost reduction. At the same time, B lost control of its costs, possibly by forecasting higher sales and failing to achieve them.

9.6.9 By year 7, A had moved into leadership with higher volumes than the year 1 level. B still had more sales but struggled with a lower volume relative

Strategy and cost management

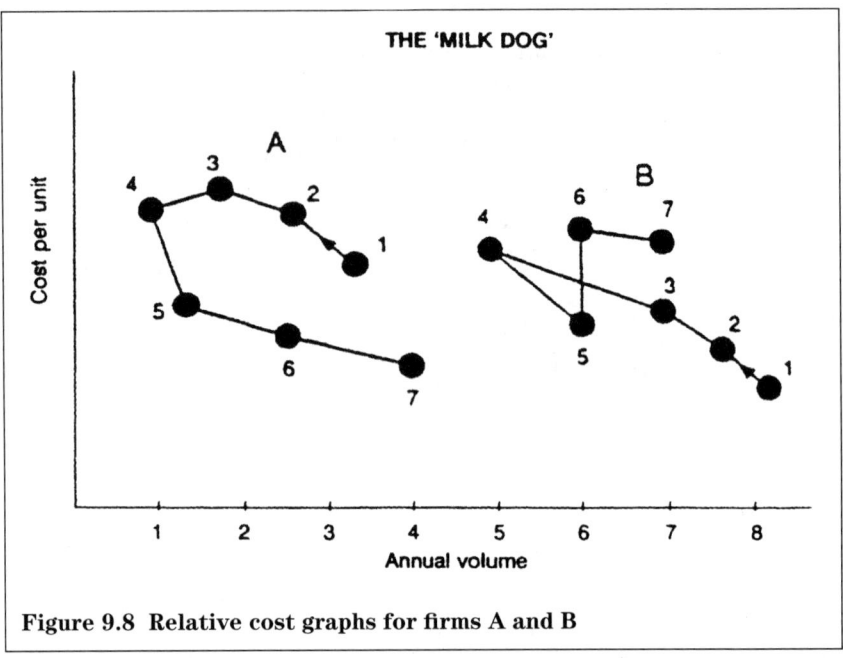

Figure 9.8 Relative cost graphs for firms A and B

to its initial capacity, and higher unit costs. The graph depicts B as a 'cash cow' whose milk has dried up and A as a 'dog' that now produces cream.

9.6.10 On a similar note, beyond the need for good internal information is the need to understand the competitive situation better. Accountants need to provide their companies with competitor cost and strategic information in addition to the information provided on internal operations. Jones (1992) discusses how 'competitor cost analysis' has been implemented at Caterpillar Inc. in the USA whose continuing objective is to be the lowest-cost, highest-value producer in the industry. Before undertaking factory modernisation, the competitive situation was analysed from perspectives of price, cost, industry capacity and competitor strategies. This effort resulted in the establishment of a total company-wide structural cost reduction target and individual product-by-product targets. These targets provide the impetus for strategies for modernising manufacturing operations and reducing costs, and provide the benchmarks against which the unfolding improvements are monitored.

9.6.11 There is a key aspect of competitor analysis that must be understood: there is a point at which a competitor's cost advantage is large enough that it cannot be eliminated through evolutionary or 'business as usual' cost

Strategic management accounting

reduction efforts. When a manufacturer's cost problems are beyond that point, revolutionary change is required.

9.6.12 The simplest form of analysis would be to divide a competitor's costs from the published financial statements by the units produced and determine an average product cost. This, however, would not yield very useful information for trying to analyse the cost of complex, multi-product manufacturers. At the other end of the spectrum would be the ideal: the development of very specific product cost estimates based on detailed information about the competitor's cost structure, products and the product's costs in the production process. This information is, understandably, not available. Therefore, available published information is used as the basis for analyses which, of course, have significant limitations.

9.6.13 Obtaining reliable internal product costs is a prerequisite for competitor cost analysis (see below). If a company's own product cost system cannot meet this test then competitor evaluation will be of little value. For the company with a good product costing system, however, competitor analysis is a powerful tool for maintaining or gaining competitive advantage.

9.6.14 The first step in a competitive study is to establish overall objectives, such as:

- providing specific estimates of the costs of competitors' products;
- gaining insight into competitor strategies, practices and plans.

9.6.15 This requires an intensive information-gathering approach using multi-functional teams. A macro plan might look something like this.

- Gather published information that would include: history, financial, products, sales/volumes, marketing/distribution/service, manufacturing facilities and processes, governmental relationships, strategies, value engineering, cost reduction, quality control, labour relations and people levels, technology/product design, organisation, and suppliers/purchased material.
- Use public information sources such as: annual reports, product and plant brochures, financial analysts' reports, seminars and symposia, industry sales/volumes reports, trade journals and published articles, governmental agencies and industry statistical publications.
- Gather information through techniques including multi-functional teams to study manufacturing and sourcing methods of operations; analysis of competitor's products from design, quality, processing and material sourcing perspectives.

Strategy and cost management

- Assess the information. Lift from it the portions which will provide the means of establishing cost models.

- Formulate product cost estimates using several approaches as a means of cross-checking and testing the answers which will ultimately be used.

- Test the aggregated final product cost estimates against the adjusted 'cost of goods sold' from the annual report to see if the answers are acceptably close.

- Compare competitor product cost estimates with individual in-house product costs once the estimates are judged to be acceptable.

- Arrive at an aggregated product cost difference by extending the competitor cost estimates by in-house volumes and product mix and compare with in-house aggregated costs calculated the same way.

- Analyse and quantify future competitor cost reduction programmes.

- Add to the individual product cost and aggregated cost differences any estimates of future competitor cost reductions.

- Include the cost effects of freight and duty or any other non-product-related costs if applicable.

- Adjust for value differences to complete the study. Business strategies such as distribution systems, product and parts support, product quality, product differentiation and product capabilities to be analysed as to benefit provided. A comparison to be made with the competing company's benefit yield from its various business strategies and a value advantage/disadvantage to be determined thereby. An aggregated cost profile may take the following form:

Our product costs	100
Competitor product costs	80
Gross product cost difference	20
Future competitor cost reduction	5
	25
Our freight and duty advantage	(8)
Our value advantage	(5)
Net total cost disadvantage	12

- Establish company-wide strategies to reduce costs to targeted levels.

Strategic management accounting

9.6.16 This demonstration illustrates some possible steps related to competitor cost and strategic analysis. The difficulty of the task, analysis methods and approaches, and quality of results will vary by company. The task of analysis becomes more difficult if the competitor:

- is in other, unrelated businesses;
- has abnormal and non-recurring costs buried in its cost structure;
- has different organisational structures;
- has factories located in other countries;
- has different levels of vertical integration;
- segregates costs differently for public reports;
- produces other products (not directly competitive);
- produces product, service parts, modified products and other non-standard products which are all lumped together in the cost structure;
- produces different volumes and mix of products.

9.6.17 Value differences should be assessed and included in the costing work. This is because one company could have a product cost advantage over another but could lose that advantage if the costs of merchandising and supporting its products were considerably higher, or if the quality or capabilities of its products were inferior.

9.6.18 Thus, comparative value or productivity judgements, although obviously more subjective than product cost comparisons, are nonetheless a vital and necessary element in assessing the overall cost differences between two competing companies. These elements can be referred to as a cost advantage or disadvantage. That is, a competitor may not be able to overcome these advantages with lower product costs. If the competitor wanted to negate these advantages it would have to increase its own costs in order to do so. Consequently, competitor analysis considers any possible value differences and includes an estimate of the cost implications. Once this adjustment is made, along with other adjustments for freight, duty and future cost reduction estimates – comparisons can be made to in-house costs as shown in Table 9.1.

9.6.19 Determining the total estimated cost structure difference (for the products being compared) requires that competitor unit costs be extended by in-house volumes and product mix, and compared with total in-house costs calculated the same way. This aggregated cost calculation generates

Strategy and cost management

Table 9.1 Product cost structure comparisons

Product	Our cost £	Their cost £	Cost reduction targets £	Percentage reduction needed
A	12,500	10,000	2,500	20
B	13,000	12,000	1,000	8
C	17,000	15,000	2,000	12
D	22,500	20,000	2,500	11
E	10,000	8,000	2,000	20
F	28,500	25,000	3,500	12
G	14,500	13,000	1,500	10
H	10,000	9,000	1,000	10

the total structural cost differences. This calculation completes the costing exercise. Thus, the product-by-product differences can be shown and a total cost difference provided.

9.6.20 The costing results should be augmented with detailed information as to which operational differences and elements of costs are causing the major differences and why. The strategic information should provide a clear understanding of competition from all key perspectives, including an assessment of future strategies.

(3) Present value of the business is the overriding objective
9.6.21 The overriding objective is the present value of the business: strategic performance is measured by change in the present value of the net cash flow that can be extracted from a business. When this change is added to or subtracted from the accounting profit for a period, it provides an estimate of real economic performance over the period. As an objective for business, maximisation of present value ties current performance and the future value of competitive position together. If adequate recognition is not given to change in the present value of competitive position, there may be a tendency to impair competitive position to gain current accounting profits. This is clearly not acceptable if it decreases the overall present value. With SMA the emphasis must be moved from performance measurement based on period accounting profit on its own, to performance measurement using at least some indicators of competitive position.

(4) Short-run cost variation is paramount
9.6.22 When strategic reversals happen, they happen in the present. Firms seldom meet their current capacity exactly, and the short-term cost implications of variation from optimal are usually quite major. In many mature industries such as motor vehicles, television manufacturing and bicy-

cles, competitors have come from smaller volume bases to overtake firms with huge accumulated experience. The experienced company will have been forced up a short-term cost curve that is much steeper than the long-term volume or experience curves.

> 'Once begun, retrenchment is difficult to reverse. Retrenchment becomes retreat ... as the short-term cost curve gets steeper and steeper and financial resources are drained.'
>
> (Source: Simmonds. 1989.)

9.6.23 However, competitors also have short-term cost curves. It is very likely that an attack on a leader could be dealt with early by a strong counterattack which would penalise the original attacker even more.

(5) Financial practices are changed radically

9.6.24 If each business in a firm adopts a strategy so as to maximise its present value, the firm's total present value can only be increased by some broad strategy that increases its value more than that of a competitor. The overall present value is not increased by taking more cash from one business unit to decrease its present value and giving it to another business unit. Portfolio adjustment solely as an internal cash-balancing process based on differential returns on investment would be a zero-sum game.

9.6.25 Under SMA, investment in each business is justified solely in terms of the strategy that maximises present value. Investment in the total firm is the sum of the investment in the individual businesses. The financial policy of the firm is thus derived from the business strategies rather than vice versa.

9.6.26 This approach runs contrary to a common financial approach of budgeting cash flow plus overall debt increase and then allocating this sum to businesses on the basis of return on investment. Such an approach also negates the commonly held view that return comes from the physical manifestations of capital such as plant, buildings, stock, etc. Physical assets become only the means to building competitive strength. Having a plant does not in itself produce profits if the competitive position it supports does not put the firm in a profit-earning position.

Implementing SMA

9.6.27 The ideas underlying strategic management accounting are not really new to finance departments. The information required is often utilised when defending the enterprise against a hostile bid or considering a takeover bid where, for example, using whatever information can be

Strategy and cost management

obtained, the buying firm seeks to evaluate the promise of the attributes possessed by the candidate firm's products and to determine any cost advantages this firm possesses or could possess in providing these attributes. Bromwich (1996) gives the example of Goldstar Electronics, a major Korean electronics firm which adopts such a procedure when planning for those projects fundamental to the company's success but about which the company lacks detailed information. Goldstar's first step in appraising such projects is to determine what are called environmental factors in the company's planning process. This involves answering detailed questions including:

- What are the uses of the product by consumers?
- What are the characteristics of the users?
- What technology is required?
- What is the current/future competition and what are their products?
- Who is the market leader?
- How did competitors start?
- What markets are they in and what are their plans?

9.6.28 Without the adoption of strategic management accounting, the control and monitoring of strategic objectives may have to take place outside the financial management system using disaggregated measures, thereby losing the ability to consider easily the overall impact of the enterprise's achievements in these areas.

9.6.29 Goldstar Electronics provides an example of these difficulties. It sets its strategic objectives in terms of ability to provide what customers may want – good after-sales service, product development and innovative production management – but does not appraise the achievement of these goals directly using its management accounting system. Rather, the company relies on a number of familiar indices such as indices of sales growth and of new market development, per capita sales ratios and product mix ratios. These measures, which are not all fully reflective of the chosen goals, may give conflicting signals, do not fully reflect cost factors and cannot be aggregated in a meaningful way.

9.6.30 The use of these and of other non-financial measures related directly to key success factors is increasing and is thought to contribute positively to business activities, not least at the level of the workplace. Strategic management accounting supplements this by sharing its concentration on key success factors but reporting on these in a way that is more meaningful and somewhat more familiar at the higher levels of decision-making.

9.6.31 Adopting a strategic perspective emphasises that each of the firm's strategies for products and markets should yield the customer some benefit. There are two usual strategies: diversification and product enhancement. Each component element of these strategies yields customers possible benefits. For example, an expanded product portfolio provides the consumer with more choice, and the enhancement of an existing product to improve its quality yields the customer clear benefit if this improvement of product quality is relative to competing firms.

9.6.32 One key perspective that allows strategic management accounting to be adopted is to see each product not as a whole or as a unit but to perceive it as comprising a number of separate characteristics offered to the customer. It is these attributes which actually constitute commodities and which appeal to consumers. Demands for goods are derived from the demands for their underlying characteristics. These attributes might include a variety of quality elements, such as operating performance variables, reliability and warranty arrangements; physical features and service factors, like the assurance of supply and of after-sales service. It is these elements which differentiate products and appeal to consumers. A firm's market share depends on the match between the attributes provided by its products and consumers' tastes and on the supply of these attributes by competitors.

9.6.33 Roslender *et al.* (1998) note that the amount of strategic management accounting activity being pursued is growing. In most cases this involves both management accounting and marketing practitioners working together in ways consistent with the interdisciplinary nature of the strategic management accounting concept.

9.7 Who needs SMA?

9.7.1 Bhimani and Keshtvarz (1999) note that the applied literature suggests that strategic management accounting (SMA) incorporates strategic product costing and performance measurement, analyses of the firm's product markets and competitive market forces, and the assessment of organisational strategies over extended periods of time. However, few examples of strategic management accounting in action have been documented.

9.7.2 Certain key differences between conventional management accounting and strategic management accounting have been posited in the literature (see Figure 9.9). While conventional management accounting adopts a historical

Strategy and cost management

orientation coupled with a focus on single decisions, single periods and single entities, strategic management accounting is oriented towards the future. Emphasis in SMA is also placed on an enterprise's position relative to its competitors in the context of sequences of decision over multiple time periods.

Figure 9.9 Conventional versus stragetic management accounting

Conventional Characteristics	Strategic Characteristics
Historical	Prospective
Single entity	Relative
Single period	Multiple
Single decision	Sequences, patterns
Subjective	Outward looking
Manufacturing focus	Competitive focus
Existing activities	Possibilities
Reactive	Proactive
Programmed	Unprogrammed
Overlooks linkages	Embraces linkages
Data orientation	Information orientation
Based on existing systems	Unconstrained by existing systems
Built on convention	Ignores conventions

(*Source:* Wilson, R.M.S. and Chua, W.F., *Managerial Accounting: Method and Meaning* 1993.)

9.7.3 A key question is how active a role management accountants play in strategic planning activities. In this light, it has been argued that the training of British management accountants emphasises a manufacturing focus that conditions management accountants to look at internal operational issues rather than outward competitive and market-based factors.

9.7.4 There is presently only a very small body of literature that directly addresses the relationship between management accounting and corporate strategy; no agreed comprehensive conceptual framework for strategic management accounting currently exists according to Roslender *et al* (1998). An increasing number of pedagogical texts have been written in the area, though the focus remains on prescriptiveness. Some scholarly efforts in SMA research are, however, in evidence, such as the work by Shank and Govindarajan (1996) and Bromwich (1990).

9.7.5 Shank and Govindarajan place considerable weight on Porter's notion of strategic positioning. To them, a value chain perspective on strategic cost management requires that firms recognise their product in the total value-creating chain of activities, and that they endeavour to develop accounting information that enables improvement of internal cost management performance. The emphasis, then, is not simply on competition, but

Who needs SMA?

also on the interaction that firms have with their suppliers. A management accounting case study of strategic value chain analysis that relies significantly on Shank and Govindarajan's perspective appears belows.

9.7.6 Bromwich (1990) sees strategic management accounting as going beyond collecting data on businesses and their competitors, to considering the benefits that products offer to customers, and how these benefits contribute to building and sustaining competitive advantage. He views the benefits provided by the product as the ultimate cost drivers. He posits that simply attributing cost to products rather than to benefits overlooks the notions that it is in the market that competitive advantage is achieved, and that commercial success depends upon having a product in demand. Bromwich suggests that the only products that will survive in the market are those that yield the maximum amount of a specific bundle of characteristics for the amount of money the customer wishes to spend. Deciding to provide a product with a particular configuration also requires achieving this at a competitive cost level, which links in with the idea of managing the value added process in producing any product. An objective of strategic management accounting, therefore, is to determine the cost of providing product characteristics to consumers given existing operating condition.

9.7.7 The strategic evaluation of organisational issues entails the analysis of a range of diverse factors. Many factors may be relevant in the provision of strategically-oriented management accounting information. These include financial and non-financial information, competitor activities, product characteristics, market share data and other value chain-related information. Bhimani and Keshtvarz's (1999) survey addresses, in part, the extent to which these information types are relevant to strategic decision-making, according to the group of management accountants surveyed.

9.7.8 The investigation was concerned with whether the most senior executives in charge of management accounting activities in large British companies see themselves as actively engaging in strategic planning activities and whether they desire such involvement. The investigation also assessed what information is deemed important for strategy formulation and in strategic decision-making, as well as the reasons underlying the perceived need, if felt, for more strategically-oriented management accounting information. Additionally, the study explored whether the 33 organisations surveyed actually practised SMA.

9.7.9 The survey results (see Figure 9.10) suggest great involvement on the part of responding management accountants in strategic planning activities,

Strategy and cost management

especially in terms of providing data or with the analysis of different elements of strategic planning. Involvement in choosing between alternatives was not as extensive.

Figure 9.10 Management accountants' involvement in strategic planning activities

Planning activity	% Participating	% Not participating	Informal advice	Data or analysis	Choose alternatives	All phases
Develop mission	87%	13%	42%	21%	9%	15%
Establish objectives	87	13	15	33	15	24
Co-ordinate planning	90	10	9	24	12	45
Make assumptions	90	10	18	21	30	21
Evaluate environment	87	13	24	30	24	9
Formulate strategy	84	16	27	30	15	12
Select best strategies	87	13	33	24	21	9
Translate strategies into operational plan	90	10	12	33	18	27
Translate strategies into budgets	94	6	3	18	15	58
Monitor past plans	94	6	0	33	6	55

9.7.10 The respondents tended to desire much greater involvement in choosing between alternatives, rather than simply engaging in providing informal advice or in preparing data and analysing this data (see Figure 9.11).

9.7.11 The strategic management accounting literature suggests that SMA can be useful in providing different types of information to assist decision-makers in dealing with a variety of strategic issues. The five most important factors identified by respondents as necessitating more strategically-oriented management accounting information were:

- competitive pressure;
- cost reduction;
- productivity improvement;
- to effect volume/market share changes;
- quality improvement.

Figure 9.11 Desired involvement in SMA

Planning Activity	% Participating	% Not participating	Informal advice	Data or analysis	Choose alternatives	All phases
Develop mission	87%	13%	21%	18%	18%	15%
Establish objectives	84	16	3	24	12	24
Co-ordinate planning	91	9	6	12	21	45
Make assumptions	90	10	3	12	30	21
Evaluate environment	87	13	3	21	33	9
Formulate strategy	84	16	6	15	21	12
Select Best strategies	87	6	12	6	36	33
Translate strategies into operational plan	94	6	6	9	21	58
Translate strategies into budgets	94	6	3	6	9	76
Monitor past plans	94	6	0	21	15	58

9.7.12 The questionnaire prompted respondents to identify information items used in strategy formulation. The results are presented in Figure 9.12 which indicates market environment, competitors' activities, and customer satisfaction cited most often as useful factors in strategy formulation.

9.7.13 Respondents were required to identify the types of information they thought were useful in strategic decision-making. The results presented in Figure 9.13 suggest that competitor activities, market share/market analysis, and financial/non-financial information are most widely used. The information is in part encompassed in the Balanced Scorecard approach (see Chapter **11**), although no mention of the term was made by respondents.

9.7.14 About 25 per cent of the respondents stated that they practised SMA. These respondents were invited to define what they understood by the term. Figure 9.14 provides the companies' responses, suggesting a wide range of definitions when the term SMA is used.

9.8 Linking customer value to product costs

9.8.1 The aim of strategic cost analysis might be seen as seeking to determine as well as possible the costs of providing product characteristics to the consumer, given existing knowledge in cost determination. Many firms, when faced with competitive challenges, undertake comparative investigations of

Strategy and cost management

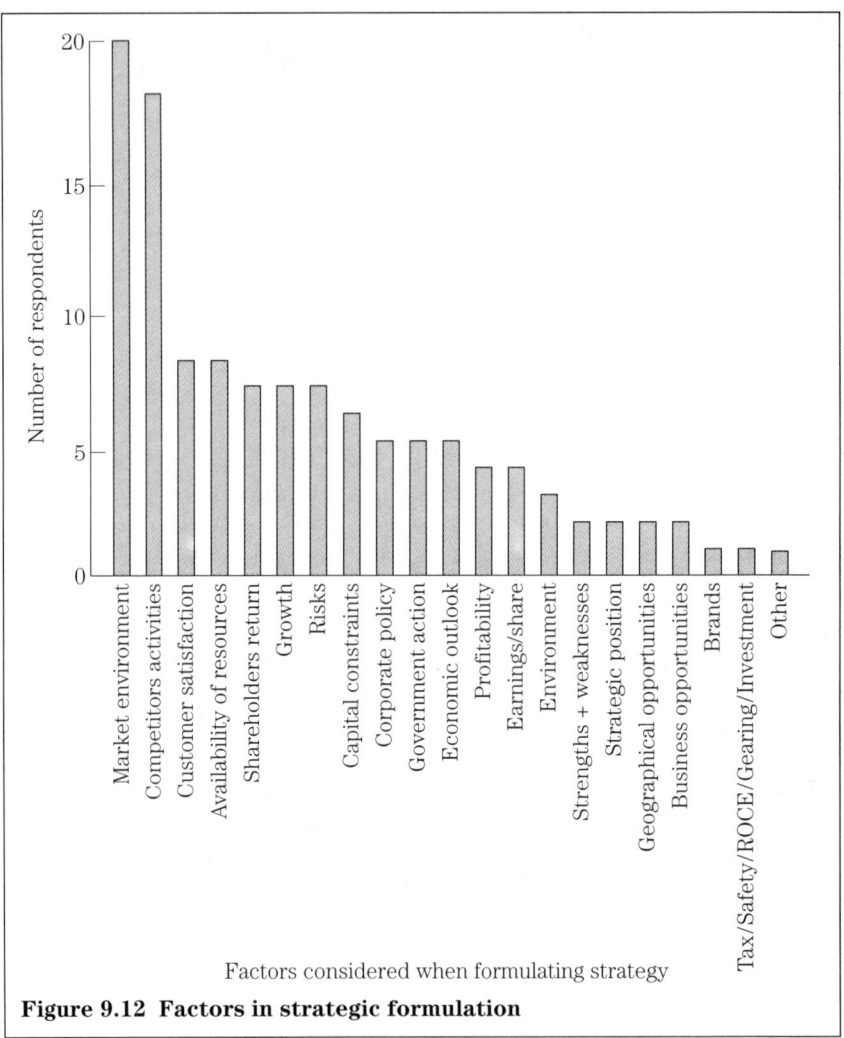

Figure 9.12 Factors in strategic formulation

product benefits offered by themselves and their competitors. Often the costs of providing such benefits are not considered in this process and these costs are subjected to the same general cuts as all other costs even though increasing them may be required to meet the competitive challenge. Similarly, in automotive firms, product planners developing a new model are often provided with figures based on product characteristics. Such reports can be provided regularly both for planned and existing products. Many of the cost figures needed can be obtained from a re-analysis of existing databases and more detailed analyses of existing figures. Typically, this does not require the

Linking customer value to product costs

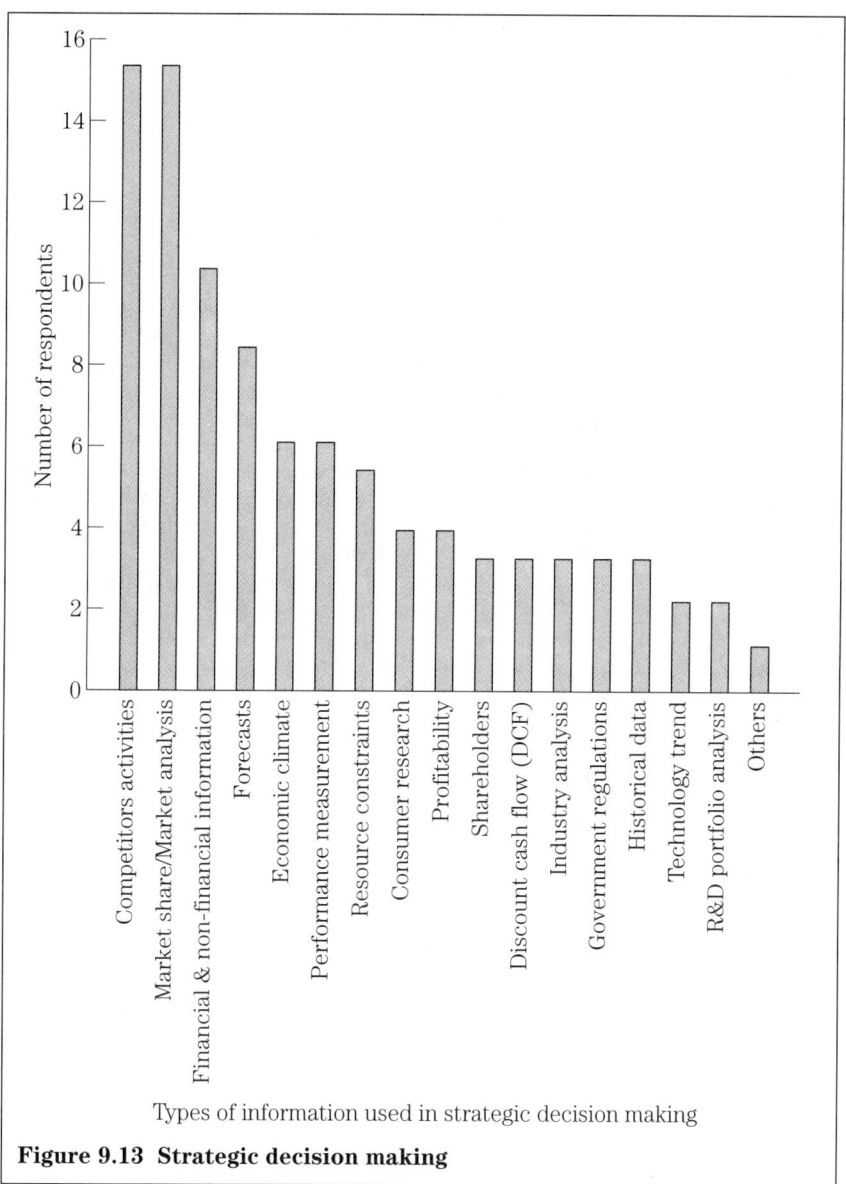

Figure 9.13 Strategic decision making

existing method of reporting the cost structure of the enterprise to be abandoned. The aim of this type of strategic cost analysis is to attribute some of those costs which are normally treated as product costs to the benefits they provide to the consumer, where these benefits are believed to be of strategic importance. Not all costs can necessarily be attributed to consumer benefits,

Strategy and cost management

Figure 9.14 SMA definitions by those who practise SMA

(1) 'Review the long term performance expected for the business in SUA terms, but also allow for a balanced scorecard of non-financial measures of market share, consumer "score", etc.'

(2) 'Competitor analysis. Measurements of profitability of business units against group objectives, and competitors.'

(3) 'Formulate a plan for the next five years – detailing volumes/market share anticipating movement in product cost and selling price. Impact on earnings/balance sheet and therefore return on capital rates. Monitor our past results against these plans.'

(4) 'Accounting in proactive rather than reactive manner. Accounting is by definition measuring historical performance strategic accounting forecasts.'

(5) 'Within our company there have recently been two examples in strategic management accounting which help to explain our understanding of this term – the year 2000 vision and country strategy year 2000. In both cases a vision has been established in terms of where we want the organisation to be in the market place and what our goals and aims are. We have then used the tools available within the term management accounting to weigh out the financial plans/target that will enable us to achieve these visions.'

(6) 'We operate a strategic planning process and have a separate business development function. My understanding of the term is evaluating future plans to meet the shareholders' value expectation of the business and to insure its future attainment.'

(7) 'Use of external and internal information (financial or otherwise) in the formation of strategic plans.'

(8) 'We use management accounting techniques which attempt to look at and evaluate long-term value creation, to manage the business strategically. The nature of the industry is such that such strategic approaches are essential where the gestation process for new power generation projects can be less than four years.'

(9) 'Accounting which supports a full value based management approach to running the business.'

and for some costs and benefits such an attribution may not be worth the cost of undertaking such an exercise. The first step in a strategic cost analysis of this type is to list separately the product benefits offered to consumers. These benefits will differ fundamentally depending on whether the customer is in the final goods market or is an intermediate firm in the chain leading to the final customer. With the latter type, strategic cost analysis facilitates analysis by customer rather than product.

9.8.2 Bromwich (1991) provides extracts from an exercise which attempts to model a fast-food supplier which supplies prepared and partly processed products to its network of selling outlets (see Figure 9.15). An illustrative set of consumer benefits are shown on the left axis of the figure.

Linking customer value to product costs

To simplify the presentation, it is assumed that all the firm's products provided similar consumer benefits. These benefits can be categorised in a number of ways. In the figure, those items directly related to a unit of product (items 1–7) are shown separately from those relating to sales outlets (items 8–11). Product advertising provides an example of other benefits not related directly to the other two categories but which can be attributed to the product. The total of costs which can be treated in this way are shown in the row labelled 'total costs attributable to consumer benefits'. The penultimate row is for those product costs that cannot be attributed to consumer benefits. It is included so that the analysis can be reconciled with product costs prepared in the conventional way.

9.8.3 The number of consumer benefits to which it is sought to assign a cost will depend on the strategy adopted by the enterprise. Thus a firm which concentrates on giving high benefits for only a few characteristics will report only the costs associated with these characteristics.

9.8.4 The second step in strategic cost analysis is to decide on a set of cost categories for the product. A variant of the firm's usual cost classification will often be best as this will encompass the matters of concern to that firm and thus reflect its economic environment. In Figure 9.15 the overall cost categories chosen are variable product costs, activity-related costs, capacity-related costs and decision-related costs. These costs can be further subdivided into such categories as those given in the note to the figure.

9.8.5 The first cost category shown in Figure 9.15 is variable product cost, which shows the normal direct cost of production. The second category is that of the activity- or transaction-related costs attributable to the product. The inclusion of such activity-related costs indicates that the approach is sufficiently flexible to incorporate the results of a variety of ways of collecting costs. Common cost problems arise with strategic cost analysis because costs such as materials, labour and variable overheads may contribute simultaneously to a number of consumer benefits and it may be impossible to attribute part of these costs to each of the consumer benefits to which they contribute. Bromwich (1991) gives the example of a confectionery business where an operation which blends two or more raw materials together may contribute to a number of consumer benefits, such as appearance, taste and texture. Any assignment of the costs of the operation to these consumer benefits would be arbitrary.

9.8.6 One approach to this problem is to bundle these benefits together for this cost category. For example, a fast-food supplier which sought to be seen as a lower-cost provider of its products using minimally sized and

Strategy and cost management

Illustrative costs	Product-volume related costs[1]	Activity-related costs[1]	Capacity-related costs[1]	Decision-related costs[1]	Total costs
Product benefits					
1. Texture					
2. Nutritional value					
3. Appearance					
4. Taste					
5. Consistency of above, over outlets and time					
6. Quality					
7. Low cost relative to competitors					
Outlet benefits					
8. Service					
9. Cleanliness					
10. Outlet facilities					
11. Location and geographical coverage					
Other benefits					
12. Product advertising					
Total costs attributable to consumer benefits					
Product costs not attributable to consumer benefits					
Total product cost					

[1]. Product-volume related costs include material, labour and variable overheads, each of which may be reported separately. Activity-related costs include material handling and transport, quality control, monitoring quality and service and site and facilities maintenance, each of which may be reported separately. Capacity-related costs include land and building occupancy costs and depreciation and leasing charges, each of which may be separately reported. Decision-related costs include product and site design, product and site engineering, quality improvement, marketing, including product advertising and personnel and administration, again each of these costs may be reported separately.

Figure 9.15 Strategic cost analysis: example for a fast-food supplier

equipped outlets might well only cost the relative value of its products and the costs of providing a good geographical coverage in convenient locations. A more up-market supplier would report on more product and outlet benefits.

9.8.7 The next major category of costs is capacity-related costs, which includes depreciation and land and building occupancy costs. These two cost categories – capacity and activity – illustrate both advantages and disadvantages of the approach. Their use associates these costs directly with products or groups of products, whereas normally they are aggregated into overheads and allocated on some arbitrary basis. With regard to depreciation and with occupancy costs, as a specific product or class of products is involved, it will be possible in some instances to determine what assets and capacity are attributable to the product or class of product. Strategic cost analysis seeks to report sensibly on the costs of resources that may be important in attracting customers. However, if these costs are just taken from the financial accounting reports, any numbers entered here may have little economic meaning. For many businesses, substituting leasing charges for depreciation charges may be feasible, as may charging a market-based rental for space, especially if these approaches are used in the company's conventional management accounts as they are, for example, by many well-known store and hotel chains.

9.8.8 Generally, an analysis of this type will be undertaken separately for each group of similar products. There will also be a need for additional statements at the level of the SBU or the enterprise to encompass any number of benefits following from diversification of the enterprise's product portfolio and other benefits generated at this level in the firm, such as non-product-related advertising and providing, say, a high-tech image for all the firm's products.

9.8.9 The final category of costs shown in the diagram, decision-related costs, are those whose level depends not on operational activity but on managerial decisions concerning the level of resources to be provided for certain functions. The costs associated with these decisions will generally not be affected by the actual level of activity in the enterprise at any given time. They are, however, the costs which are often especially geared to providing consumer benefits. Seeking to attribute them to the benefits they are meant to generate represents a major step forward in providing strategically oriented management accounting information because these costs are not rendered visible with conventional management accounting where, as noted, they are subsumed into fixed costs. The approach suggested here focuses directly on these costs which are often of strategic importance to the enterprise.

Strategy and cost management

9.8.10 Bromwich (1991) gives the example of a UK company selling a number of home cleansing products mainly through large stores which practised some of the approaches suggested here. The company sought to evaluate the attributes yielded by its products and those of its rivals by market research, by contracts with wholesalers and by analysing marketing literature. A clear thrust towards strategic management accounting was illustrated by the involvement of accountants in these tasks. The benefits of one product were established to be twofold. A minor benefit was in terms of the ease of use of the product relative to competing products. The overwhelming advantage of the product to its firm was its distinctive high quality package of a different size from that offered by competitors which disguised a price some 16 per cent higher than the competition. This analysis helped the firm when a rival firm was aiming to bring out a direct competitor to this product. The firm analysed in a general way the performance of its rivals but did not seek to collect competitors' costs or attempt to attach a cost to the major attributes of its own products, although it attempted to minimise the use of arbitrary allocations. The threat to its product required the company to undertake these exercises which represent important elements of strategic management accounting.

9.8.11 The firm's revised strategy of reducing the price of the product under threat and undertaking a modest advertising campaign was successful despite a direct cost advantage accruing to the rival firm discovered in the study leading up to the new strategy. Its rival is returning to the attack using its cost advantage and is attempting to out-perform in terms of the product ease of use.

9.8.12 As a first approach, the costs to be used in the analysis outlined by Bromwich (1991) can be taken from the enterprise's existing management accounting information. The mere attempt to assign these costs to the customer benefits they provide should yield additional insights on the importance and economic worth of the items in the enterprise's cost structure. Especially important will be the information gained about the consumer benefits which are provided by that category of conventional fixed overheads which have been referred to as decision-related costs. The approach suggested is to identify these costs and to link them with the consumer benefits which drive them. Cost drivers become visible in strategic cost analysis and sufficient information is available to allow a cost/benefit analysis of their value.

9.8.13 The above approach would attribute to each strategic consumer benefit that management thought it worthwhile to identify, the total account-

Linking customer value to product costs

ing cost in each cost category of providing the benefit. The aim is to try to determine the additional costs incurred because the benefit is provided. For decision-making concerning the level of consumer benefits to be provided, there would be advantages in seeking to determine the incremental cost of providing an extra 'unit' of each consumer benefit using economic rather than accounting costs. Another possible refinement of strategic cost analysis might be to seek to determine the cost of providing benefits which are additional to those provided by competitors.

9.8.14 The timespan encompassed in any strategic cost analysis will depend on the types of business in which the enterprise is involved, the importance of providing customer benefits in these businesses and the stability of the economic and competitive environment of these businesses. For many businesses, the costs reported should be those for the entire product life-cycle as many decision-driven costs will be dependent on stages in the product life-cycle. With this approach, the costs included in the strategic cost analysis will be both actual and planned costs. The frequency of the reporting of strategic cost analyses will again depend on the type of business and especially the turbulence of the economic and competitive environments faced by the business. The reporting cycle will be shortest for those enterprises facing highly uncertain markets.

9.8.15 Product-volume related costs include material, labour and variable overheads, each of which may be reported separately. Activity-related costs include material handling and transport, quality control, monitoring quality and service and site and facilities maintenance, each of which may be reported separately. Capacity-related costs include land and building occupancy costs and depreciation and leasing charges, each of which may be separately reported. Decision-related costs include product and site design, product and site engineering, quality improvement, marketing, including product advertising and personnel and administration, again each of these costs may be reported separately.

A case study: achievinging strategic cost analysis

9.8.16 In June 1999, Mr R. Kurtz, the managing director of the Grinding Machines Division (GMD) of the German company Reichard Maschinen GmbH, was considering how to handle an upcoming meeting with his sales manager, accountant and product engineering manager. The purpose of the meeting was to discuss a new competitive challenge: a Belgian competitor (Bruggeman Grinders SA) had introduced plastic rings to replace the steel rings that were a standard component in many grinding machines, including many machines that GMD made and sold.

Strategy and cost management

Competitive environment
9.8.17 Bruggeman had introduced the new plastic in April. The plastic rings had a longer useful life than the steel rings and were also far less expensive to manufacture. Responding to the introduction of the new plastic ring was complicated by the fact that GMD had 25,000 steel rings in inventory and 26 tons of special-alloy steel that GMD had recently purchased to make even more rings. To induce a steel mill to make the special-alloy steel, GMD had been required to buy a full year's supply. The raw steel in inventory could not even be sold as scrap because of the special alloys. Thus, as Figure 9.16 shows, GMD held about $93,000 (in DM equivalent) worth of inventory related to steel rings. Reichard Maschinen (RM) had manufactured industrial machines for over 100 years. The machines were sold throughout Europe and North America. RM enjoyed a reputation for high quality, technology leadership, and excellent customer service. Dozens of companies of all sizes competed in one way or another in the market for industrial machines in Europe, though RM was a leader in several segments. Each of RM's divisions operated as a fairly autonomous profit centre. Corporate management in Frankfurt operated mainly as a holding company.

Figure 9.16 Memorandum, Reichard Maschinen GmbH, Grinding Machines Division

To:	R. Kurtz, Managing Director		
From:	H. Politzer, Controller		
Re:	Steel inventory for rings		
	Units	$	
Finished rings in inventory	25,450	$67,149	(= 254.5 × $263.85 per 100)
Raw steel in inventory	34,500	26,400	
	59,950	$93,549	

(1) If we convert the raw steel to rings, the total of 59,950 rings would last about 87 weeks at our current sales rate of about 690 rings per week.
(2) If we do not produce any more steel rings, we will have about 15,000 rings in inventory in September, which is when we would be ready to begin producing and selling plastic rings.
(3) We have exhausted all possible sources for selling this raw steel in bulk. Because of its special chemistry, it has no value to anyone else.
(4) During our normal summer slowdown in July and August, the factory could convert all the raw steel to finished rings, if you wish.

Market shares
9.8.18 GMD had about a 10 per cent market share in its segments in Europe, which was its principal market. GMD's one plant in Cologne employed 400 production workers. The different machines GMD made were priced from $4,500 to $7,000, with an average of about $6,000. The machines

Linking customer value to product costs

were used by metal-working plants in many industries. Their useful life was about ten years with normal maintenance.

Replacement parts

9.8.19 Replacement parts accounted for more than half of GMD's annual sales. As is common for industrial machinery, margins on machine sales were often reduced in anticipation of higher margins on replacement parts over the life of the machine. However, this strategy creates the opportunity for price discounting by suppliers of replacement parts that are interchangeable across models and across manufacturers. The steel rings GMD made were one of the standard interchangeable items.

9.8.20 In recent years, Japanese manufacturers had entered GMD's markets with lower-priced spare parts. Other companies had also entered the market with lower-priced machines and parts of lower quality. Mr Kurtz felt sure that competition would continue to grow, but he was fully committed to GMD's strategy of high quality, innovation, and excellent service at a fair price.

Steel vs plastic rings

9.8.21 The steel rings GMD manufactured had a useful life of about two months given normal machine use. Usually, rings were replaced one at a time as they wore out. A worn-out ring could be replaced in minutes. Different machine models required from two to six rings, but the average was four rings per machine. Usually the rings were replaced one at a time as they wore out.

9.8.22 The sales manager, Mr Goerner, had heard about the new plastic rings almost immediately after they were introduced. He wanted to know when GMD would be able to supply them, particularly to customers in Belgium where Bruggeman was the strongest competitor.

9.8.23 In mid-May, the manufacturing manager, Mr Hainz, estimated that the factory could begin producing plastic rings by mid-September; GMD's plant in Cologne already had a small plastics injection molding department. The additional molds and tooling necessary could be produced for about £10,000, but the molds would have to be specially designed, which would take a few months.

9.8.24 Mr Hainz raised the issue of GMD's inventory of steel rings, which would not be used up by the end of September. Mr Goerner said that if the new plastic rings could be produced at a substantially lower cost than the steel rings, the inventory problem was irrelevant: the steel inventory should

Strategy and cost management

be sold for whatever could be obtained – or even thrown away if it could not be sold.

Pricing

9.8.25 Mr Goerner reported that Bruggeman was selling the plastic rings for about $340 per 100. This was $15 per 100 higher than the price GMD charged for its steel rings, even though the manufacturing cost of the plastic rings was much lower. Mr Goerner wanted GMD to start making the new plastic rings as soon as possible. Mr Hainz suggested that until the inventory of steel rings was exhausted, GMD could continue to sell the steel rings in markets where the plastic rings were not being sold. No one expected the new plastic rings to be produced by any companies other than Bruggeman for some time. This meant that no more than 10 per cent of GMD's markets would be affected.

A visit from corporate headquarters

9.8.26 In late May, Mr Mets from RM's corporate offices in Frankfurt visited Cologne. In a review of GMD's problems, the issue of the plastic rings was discussed. Although the rings were only a small part of the finished machines, Mr Metz was interested in the problem because top management wanted all of RM's divisions to establish comparable policies for the production and pricing of replacement parts. Mr Metz pointed out to Mr Kurtz that the pricing and availability of replacement parts was a critical component of RM's business strategy.

9.8.27 Mr Metz saw no problem with GMD's preparing to produce plastic rings, but he was sceptical about market acceptance of the plastic rings. He also told Mr Kurtz that he expected GMD to recover its investment in its steel inventory. Mr Kurtz understood from this discussion that he would need a very good story if he decided to scrap any of the steel rings or the supply of raw steel on hand.

The analysis

9.8.28 A few days after Mr Metz's visit, both Mr Hainz and Mr Goerner came to Mr Kurtz's office. Mr Hainz (the manufacturing manager) came because he believed that the plastic rings would destroy demand for the steel rings. New tests had shown that the plastic rings lasted at least four times longer than steel rings. But since the price of the plastic rings was high, Mr Hainz felt that the decision to sell the plastic rings only in Bruggeman's market area was a good one: 'In this way, we can probably continue to supply the steel ring until stocks – at least of the processed parts – are used up.'

9.8.29 Mr Goerner (the sales manager), however, remained strongly opposed to selling any steel rings after the new plastic rings became avail-

Linking customer value to product costs

able. Even if the higher-quality plastic rings were sold only in certain areas, customers would soon find out. This would affect the sales of machines, whose selling prices were many times that of the rings. Mr Goerner produced the report below to show that if the selling price of both rings was set at $325 per 100, the additional profit from the plastic rings – which would cost only $66.60 per 100 to make, compared with $263.85 per 100 for the steel rings – would more than cover the investment in the steel inventory in little more than a year at present sales volumes.

	Steel	Plastic
Selling price	$325	$325
Manufacturing cost	$264	$67
Profit (per 100)	$61	$258
Plastic > Steel	$197 per 100	
× Annual volume	36,000	
Annual profit improvement =		~$71,000
Current inventory of steel =		~$93,000
$93,000/$71,000 = 1.3 years to recover the investment		

Cost information

9.8.30 Mr Kurtz did not commit himself to a decision but agreed to meet again in a week. To prepare for the meeting, Mr Kurtz obtained the following cost information comparing plastic and steel rings from the accountant.

Per 100 rings	Plastic	Steel
Material	$4.20	$76.65
Direct labour	$15.60	$46.80
Overhead*		
Manufacturing	$31.20	$93.60
selling & admin.	$15.60	$46.80
Total	$66.60	$263.85

9.8.31 Note that overhead was allocated to products based on direct labour costs. Manufacturing overhead was allocated at 200 per cent of direct labour; selling and administration overhead was allocated at 100 per cent. The accountant estimated that the only variable overhead costs for ring production would be the payroll taxes and benefits related to direct labour (approximately 80 per cent of labour cost).

565

Strategy and cost management

Production during the summer

9.8.32 Mr Kurtz knew that during the next two or three months the plant would not be operating at capacity. Rather than laying off workers, GMD had a policy of employing its excess labour during slack periods at about 70 per cent of regular wages on various make-work projects. He wondered if it would be worthwhile to convert the inventory of raw steel into steel rings during this period to utilise the excess labour. If this were done, the workers would be paid their full wage rates.

Economics versus marketing

9.8.33 At a general level, the case deals with cost analysis to assess the economic impact of a product-replacement decision, but it also involves a broader spectrum of business issues. The economics of the situation need to be brought into focus. Fixed costs, marginal costs, and sunk costs need to be separated and evaluated for their relevance to the decision. But the marketing issues must also be considered. Financial signals say that steel rings are more profitable, but marketing signals say that the future belongs to plastic rings. The main dilemma is how long GMD can keep making and selling the much more profitable – but technologically obsolete – steel rings while still holding to its strategy of being a top-quality producer at a fair price. Of relevance is the differential cost to produce plastic rings.

9.8.34 Figure 9.17 shows the relevant cost calculations. The variable or incremental cost of producing 100 plastic rings is £32.28. This is the incremental cost of producing the second 100 rings, because GMD must first invest £10,000 in tooling and also pay any other expense associated with adding plastic rings to the product line of the plastics department. Once these modest start-up costs are sunk, the differential or incremental cost to produce 100 plastic rings is £32.28.

9.8.35 One might consider the incremental cost to produce the next 34,500 steel rings – i.e., the rings that can be made from the inventory of raw steel that GMD has on hand. This special steel has already been purchased and has no alternative market. Since the scrap value of the steel used to make the rings is zero, the opportunity cost of the raw material is also zero. Thus, there is zero further raw material cost, explicit or implicit, involved in the use of the raw steel to produce rings.

9.8.36 The labour cost for manufacturing steel rings in July and August also involves some analysis. It can be argued that the incremental cost of direct labour is only 30 per cent of the normal labour rate, given GMD's labour policy of keeping employees working through slack production periods by paying them 70 per cent of their normal wages to do make-work

Figure 9.17 Relevant costs per 100 rings

Steel rings	The 25,450 rings in stock	Summer production[1] (the next 34,500 rings)	Future rings Full cost	Future rings Variable cost
Raw materials	£0.00	£0.00	£76.65	£76.65
Direct labour	0.00	14.04	46.80	46.80
Variable OH**	0.00	11.23	37.44	37.44
Fixed OH	0.00	0.00	102.96	0.00
Total	£0.00	£25.27	£263.85	£160.89

Plastic rings	Full cost	Variable cost
Raw materials	£4.20	£4.20
Direct labour	15.60	15.60
Variable OH[2]	12.48	12.48
Fixed OH	34.32	0.00
Total	£66.60	£32.28

Notes:
[1] The make work projects have a zero real value to the company.
[2] The variable overhead is 40% of the departmental overhead or 0.8×direct labour.

projects. The numbers in Figure 9.17 assume that these projects have no real value to the company. The incremental cost of shifting workers to production of steel rings would thus be only the 30 per cent increment GMD would pay to bring the workers up to their full wage rates. The variable overhead (due largely to fringe benefits related to direct labour) amounts to about 80 per cent of labour cost and the incremental variable overhead cost will be 30 per cent of normal costs.

9.8.37 Consequently, as Figure 9.17 shows, the incremental cost per 100 rings to produce the next 34,500 steel rings over the summer is £25.27.

9.8.38 Of relevance is the differential cost of the 25,450 steel rings already in inventory at the end of May. The idea here is that the 25,450 finished steel rings in inventory have zero differential cost. No additional work needs to be done on these rings. Even though they carry a value of £263.85 per 100 rings in inventory, no additional expenditure is required to sell the rings.

Strategy and cost management

9.8.39 Ultimately, of issue is which ring is more profitable – steel or plastic. A layer of complexity is added here because of the unequal lives of the steel and plastic rings. If a plastic ring has about four times the life of a steel ring, the market demand (in units) for the plastic rings is likely to be significantly less than the current demand for steel rings. If GMD switches to plastic rings but does not increase its market share, it can expect to sell only about 25 per cent as many rings as it does now.

Relevant costs and profits

9.8.40 The relevant cost and profit calculations for the steel and plastic rings are shown in Figure 9.18 which assumes the same current selling prices for steel rings and plastic rings. (The implications of altering this are discussed later.) The profitability of plastic and steel rings can be compared assuming the following four scenarios:

- plastic rings vs the 25,450 steel rings already in stock;
- plastic rings vs the next 34,500 steel rings that can be produced over the summer;
- plastic rings vs future steel rings using contribution analysis;
- plastic rings vs future steel rings using full cost analysis.

Scenario 1

9.8.41 Plastic rings vs the 25,450 steel rings already in stock.

9.8.42 When plastic rings are compared with the 25,450 steel rings now in inventory, the steel rings are far more profitable because their marginal cost is zero. Any revenue gained from their sale is incremental profit contribution at this point. Assuming the current sale prices of $325 per 100 for steel rings and $340 per 100 for plastic rings, the profit contribution from the existing steel rings would be about $82,700 ($325×254.5) compared with about $19,600 from the plastic rings ($308×63.63). It is clearly much more profitable to sell the existing steel rings than to manufacture and sell plastic rings.

Scenario 2

9.8.43 Plastic rings vs the next 34,500 steel rings that could be produced over the summer.

9.8.44 The 34,500 steel rings that could be produced this summer from the raw material on hand will yield a profit contribution of $103,500 ($300×345). The corresponding number of plastic rings that would fill the same customer demand is 8,625. Their total profit contribution would be $26,600

Linking customer value to product costs

Figure 9.18 Comparison of incremental profitability per 100 rings

Steel rings	The 25,450 rings in stock	The next 34,500 rings	Future rings Contribution basis	Future rings Full Cost basis
Revenue	£325.00	£325.00	£325.00	£325.00
Cost:				
Raw materials	0.00	0.00	76.65	76.65
Direct labour	0.00	14.04	46.80	46.80
OH: Dept.	0.00	11.23	37.44	93.60
Admin.	0.00	0.00	0.00	46.80
Total cost	£0.00	£25.27	£160.89	£263.85
Incremental profit	£325.00	£299.73	£164.11	£61.15
	*4	*4	*4	*4
Per equivalent unit	£1,300.00	£1,199.00	£656.00	£245.00

Plastic rings	Contribution basis	Full cost basis
Revenue	£340.00	£340.00
Cost:		
Raw materials	4.20	4.20
Direct labour	15.60	15.60
OH: Dept.	12.48	31.20
Admin.	00.00	15.60
Total cost	£32.28	£66.60
Incremental profit	£307.72	£273.40

(£308×86.25) if the rings were sold for £340 per 100. Again, therefore, the steel rings that could be produced over summer are far more profitable than plastic rings.

Scenario 3
9.8.45 Plastic rings vs future steel rings using contribution analysis.

9.8.46 On a marginal cost basis, the steel rings bring a marginal contribution of £164 per 100. With a yearly volume of 36,000 (690 per week×52 weeks), rings contribute £59,000. Correspondingly, with a yearly volume of 9,000, the plastic rings contribute £28,000 (£308×89.7). Marginal contribution analysis suggests that the steel rings are more profitable, even in the longer run, but this analysis loses its usefulness when considering the long term.

Strategy and cost management

Scenario 4
9.8.47 Plastic rings vs future steel rings using full cost analysis.

9.8.48 On a full cost basis, steel rings have a profit of £61.15 per 100 when sold for £325. A yearly volume of 36,000 produces a profit of £22,000. Plastic rings, with a profit of £273.40 per 100 and a yearly volume of 9,000, would yield a profit of £25,000. Thus, on a full cost basis, the plastic ring is more profitable with current pricing.

What if prices change?
9.8.49 The assumption has been made that market prices remain unchanged, What price relationship is likely to prevail between the steel rings and the plastic rings once plastic become widespread? As Shank (1996) notes, the price relationship that will evolve between plastic rings and steel rings is a critical variable on which the final decision might hinge. This and other business issues are considered explicitly below.

Fixed overhead
9.8.50 At some stage in the discussion of the comparative profitability of the two types of rings, one must consider how much fixed overhead each ring absorbs. With a current yearly production volume of 36,000 units, the steel rings absorb about £37,000 of fixed overhead costs per year (£1.03 per unit). With a production volume of 9,000 units, the plastic rings will only absorb about £3,000 of fixed overhead costs per year (£0.35 per unit).

9.8.51 It is unlikely that the unabsorbed fixed overhead expense will go away. Rather, it will probably be transferred to other products, at least in the short run. In the same sense, plastic ring production will require only about 10 per cent of the direct labour required to make steel rings. Can the excess labour be used to manufacture some other product? Since steel rings only use about the equivalent of two workers a year now ($360 \times 46.80 = \sim£17,000$ = about 2 persons), the ability of the plant to absorb the displaced labour is not in much doubt.

9.8.52 Suppose GMD stays with steel only (i.e., business as usual). GMD could tell its customers right away that an 'experimental' plastic ring is being made available in some markets: although GMD does not see the merits of plastic replacement parts, some people do. If customers want to risk damaging their machines with plastic components, that is certainly their option. (But, of course, the warranties of the machines would not apply in that case!)

9.8.53 Alternatively: get ready to make plastic rings as soon as possible. Move to plastic in the timeframes shown below.

Linking customer value to product costs

- Immediately: throw away the existing inventory of raw material. Sell from the existing inventory of finished rings only until plastic rings can be supplied, then throw away the remaining steel rings.

- Gradually: convert the existing raw materials to steel rings in July and August. Do not buy any more raw steel. Sell both steel and plastic over the next one to two years until the supply of steel rings is exhausted. Then make and sell plastic only. (Comparative pricing of steel and plastic is a major issue for this alternative.)

- Later: introduce plastic only after the full inventory of steel is exhausted.

9.8.54 Offer both plastic and steel as a long-run option for customers. Manufacture and sell both plastic and steel for the foreseeable future.

9.8.55 Get out of the business of supplying replacement rings.

9.8.56 The purpose of the financial analysis is to help decide which of these alternatives seems best for the firm.

9.8.57 The financial analysis in Figure 9.18 yields the following conclusions.

- For the 25,450 rings in inventory, steel rings are much more profitable than plastic rings.

- For the next 34,500 rings that could be made from the raw steel in inventory, steel rings are still much more profitable than plastic rings.

- For all rings beyond these 59,950 units, steel rings are more profitable than plastic on a marginal contribution basis, but plastic rings are more profitable than steel rings on a full cost basis.

Strategic considerations
9.8.58 These conclusions which are based on incremental financial analysis (see Chapter **2**) need to be considered in light of marketing and strategic considerations before a final decision is made according to Shank (1995). Some of the considerations are as follows.

- Will the price of steel rings hold at $325 once plastic rings are introduced widely into the market?

- Will the price of steel rings fall to one-fourth of the price of plastic rings (since the plastic rings last four times longer than the steel rings), or will the price of the plastic rings rise?

Strategy and cost management

- What effects will the decision about the plastic rings have on the sale of machines?

- Can the plastic rings be sold in Belgium without affecting the other markets? Given the free flow of goods and information within the European Community, how can GMD sell plastic rings in only one country without affecting other EC markets?

- Should GMD exert its leadership in markets other than Belgium by being the first to introduce plastic rings? What is the strategic value of being first in other markets?

- How long is it prudent to sell a short-lived, highly profitable replacement part (i.e., the steel rings) without jeopardising the company's reputation and image as a leader in its field?

9.8.59 Consideration of these issues focuses on two key topics.

- The uncertainties surrounding the relative price of plastic and steel rings.

- The timeframe over which customers are likely to switch from steel to plastic.

9.8.60 Each of these issues is discussed in more detail below.

Uncertainties regarding steel and plastic ring prices

9.8.61 The financial analysis shown in Figure 9.18 assumes that the steel and plastic rings continue to be sold at the current prices (i.e., $325 and $340, respectively). Yet there are several other possible scenarios for future prices of the rings.

- Price of $1,300 for plastic rings. Given that plastic has four times the wearing properties of steel, it might be argued that the value price for plastic rings should be $1,300 ($325×4). But this scenario is highly unlikely for several reasons:

    (1) the full cost of producing plastic rings is only $67;
    (2) the barriers to entry into the plastic ring market are low for companies already in the plastics business; and
    (3) competition in the market is already fairly strong, with Japanese manufacturers entering the field and offering lower-priced spare parts.

- Price of $81 for plastic rings. The factors listed above suggest that, in the long run, the market price for plastic rings will probably fall to the cost of production plus some normal mark-up. One estimate for the

Linking customer value to product costs

long-run price for the plastic rings under this scenario would be about £81, based on a full cost of £67. This would give manufacturers a profit margin of about 17.3 per cent (£14/£81) – i.e., close to the same profit margin earned on the steel rings (£61/£325 = 18.8). Of course, the manufacturing cost for plastic rings in a plastics company with lower labour costs and overhead than GMD's plant in Germany could well be much lower than £67.

- Price of £20 for steel rings. Once customers are convinced that the plastic rings actually do last four times longer than the steel rings, will they pay more than one-fourth as much for steel rings? Thus, if plastic rings were to sell for £81 or less, does this suggest that the price for steel rings will drop to about £20?

Extending the analysis

9.8.62 GMD has an incentive to forestall the market's move toward plastic rings and might be able to do so, but at what cost? For example, GMD might have to lower the price of its steel rings to avoid losing market share. Marketing thinking argues for an immediate switch to plastic rings to keep the trust and loyalty of the customers. (Note that it is the sales manager, Mr Goerner, who is the most enthusiastic proponent for an immediate switch to plastic rings.) The sales manager's attitude is probably motivated by a simple desire to offer the best value to his customers, although he offers some spurious profitability arguments to support his position. His financial analysis is confused and faulty, because steel is more profitable, but plastic is the marketing choice. Speed of transition is really the only choice. A more explicit consideration of basic strategic issues and an even broader business perspective can take the analysis further.

How soon will the market switch to plastic rings?

9.8.63 One factor that mitigates against a quick changeover is the strategic concept of barriers to switching. Some businesses have high entry barriers and low switching costs (e.g., light bulbs). In other businesses the entry barriers are low but switching costs for the customers are high (e.g., machinery parts). The barriers to entry in the light bulb business are high because of the technology required to make light bulbs, the large capital investment and the substantial start-up time. However, the switching costs between different brands of light bulbs are low for most consumers because light bulbs are basically all the same. Further, the chances of damaging a lamp are minimal in switching from one brand of light bulb to another.

9.8.64 As noted previously, the barriers to entry in the plastic ring market are probably low, but the barriers to switching are high. There is an apparent

Strategy and cost management

difference between steel rings and plastic rings. If plastic rings are used and equipment problems occur, the company stands to lose far more than what it saves on rings. With 24 steel rings per year, the steel ring cost is only $6 per month on a $6,000 machine. In other words, the potential for damage to machines by using plastic rings may not be worth the saving.

9.8.65 Many machine owners will hesitate to convert to plastic rings until they are certain that their machines will not be damaged. The savings are just too small to be a big deal. This means that GMD can have some influence over the rate of switching from steel to plastic. Thus, GMD can slow the movement toward plastic rings by offering both types of rings while emphasising the 'experimental' nature of plastic. This approach might allow GMD to sell all its existing steel rings plus the additional ones produced over the summer during the transition period. As the analysis in Figure 9.18 shows, this would be financially attractive.

9.8.66 Ultimately, however, plastic rings seem destined to capture the market because of their lower cost and longer life. This being true, the question of which product is more profitable in the long run is easy – only plastic has a long run!

The good old days of steel

9.8.67 But GMD was much better off selling steel rings in the past than it will be in the future selling plastic rings. If we assume that market forces will drive the profit margin of plastic rings to the current profit margin of steel rings (about 18 per cent), then GMD will clearly be worse off, because the market for replacement rings will shrink by 75 per cent. Because of this technological improvement, replacement rings will become a less attractive market in the future for all manufacturers. As Figure 9.19 shows, steel rings generate a much higher annual contribution to profit than plastic rings will. Plastic rings are not nearly as attractive financially.

Figure 9.19 Annual contribution of plastic and steel rings

	Plastic rings in the future	Steel rings now
Sales price	~$80.00	~$325.00
Variable costs:		
Material	4.20	76.65
Direct labour	15.60	46.80
Overhead (40%)	12.48	37.44
	$32.28	$160.89
Contribution	~$48	~$164
Unit sales	9,000	36,000
Annual contribution	~$4,300	$59,000

Linking customer value to product costs

The consensus solution
9.8.68 So what should Mr Kurtz do? The following five steps represent a consensus solution reached over the years.

- Sell the 25,450 steel rings that are currently in stock. If the firm can sell them for at least £79 per 100 (and hopefully much more), the incremental contribution is more than the contribution on 6,340 equivalent plastic rings.

- Convert the raw steel inventory into rings during the summer using the excess labour. If the firm can sell the steel rings for at least £102, the contribution would be £77, which equals the contribution from plastic rings.

- Do not buy any more steel. As an aside, much of the problem GMD faces stems from the high inventory of steel and steel rings, which was probably motivated by quantity discounts in purchasing and cost efficiency form long production runs. GMD's reduced flexibility to respond to market changes has a high and very real cost here, though the cost never shows up directly in accounting reports. The value of manufacturing flexibility is real; it is a value that often deserves as much attention as the value of efficiency.

- Tell customers immediately about the new 'experimental' plastic rings available in some markets.

- Gear up immediately for plastic. This fifth consensus step was never really questioned. But whether the firm should gear up to produce plastic rings is highly debatable from a perspective that considers core competencies and manufacturing strategy as well as marketing.

Core competencies and manufacturing strategy
9.8.69 Figure 9.20 makes the case for abandoning the replacement-rings business versus switching to plastic. Note that GMD would find it far easier to hold the price on steel if it were not simultaneously selling plastic. GMD could simply tell customers that they are free to try plastic . . . if they want to take the risk.

9.8.70 Assuming GMD converts its raw steel into rings, the problem will be to manage the market transition from steel to plastic. The problem must consider the following issues:

- protecting market share;
- maintaining GMD's image as a high-quality, innovative company;
- also maximising short-run profits from the sale of steel rings.

Strategy and cost management

Figure 9.20 Exit the replacement rings business

GMD sells about 36,000 rings/year
The case says GMD has ~10% market share
World market = 360,000 steel rings
With plastic = 90,000 (÷4) plastic rings
Plastic price (within one year) $80 (or less)
The cost leader is now likely to be a plastics company and cost will be key to price
World market will be 90,000 × $80/100 = $72,000 = Tiny! (GMD sells $112,000 in rings now)
Leave this business to the plastics companies (small firms). GMD machine customers can buy easily from third party sources.

Relying on switching barriers

9.8.71 The really tough management issue is whether it is worth GMD trying to extend the transition period by relying on the high switching barriers for customers.

9.8.72 Leave this business to the plastics companies (small firms). Machine customers can buy easily from third party sources.

Are plastic rings a good addition to GMD's product line?

9.8.73 What if one argues that plastic rings make a poor addition to GMD's product line? Based on the analysis in Figure 9.18, plastic rings yield little profit. Strategically, moreover, selling low-profit replacement parts is not very attractive. Although GMD has a small plastic injection department, that department is not part of the core competency of the firm which is high-tech German precision manufacturing and customer engineering. The new product does not fit the manufacturing strategy.

9.8.74 Figure 9.21 shows one plausible exit strategy for the steel rings if GMD converts the raw steel during the summer, does not enter the plastic ring market, and then faces difficulty in moving the steel rings.

9.8.75 In recent years, this approach has often been advanced as a better response than entering the plastic ring market. Seeing the attractiveness of avoiding the plastic rings altogether requires a perspective that goes beyond financial and marketing issues to include considerations relating to manufacturing strategy and core competency.

Figure 9.21 Possible exit strategy

What if GMD manufactures the additional 34,500 steel rings this summer but later finds it difficult to sell them (versus plastic) in the replacement parts market at prices above £100? What could GMD do with the steel rings?

(1) GMD sells 36,000 rings per year now @ ~24/machine → ~1,500 machines in use
(2) @ 10 year 'normal life' → ~150 replacement machines sold per year
(3) With 10% market share, there are 15,000 machines in use
(4) 3–4% annual growth → new annual sales = 450 to 600 machines
(5) GMD's share = 45 to 60 machines per year
(6) Combining points 2 and 5, GMD sells about 200 machines/year (~150 + ~50)

Offer, as an introductory special, '100 steel rings for £100 with a new machine. Use steel replacement rings at least once to break-in the machine'. GMD would consume 40,000 steel rings in two years.

Conclusion

9.8.76 According to Shank (1996) this case provides an excellent example of how modern cost analysis blends financial considerations with broadly based business considerations to facilitate effective decision-making. The analysis takes explicit account of the full business context of the problem and of the full set of tools for strategic assessment. The resulting insights suggest a far different management response from that suggested by the narrower, more conventional analysis that was the best we could muster until recent years.

(Source: adapted with permission from Shank, 1996.)

A case study: strategy and financial reporting

9.8.77 When managers select a strategic plan, they must take into account the financial reporting implications of the strategic plan. The Start-up, Now case illustrates a situation in which the selection of a strategic plan will impact current financial results, which, in turn, may affect Start-up, Now's relationship with a lending institution.

9.8.78 Terry Merton, a chartered accountant, hardly noticed the bright sunshine as she drove down the motorway in late October 2000 on her way to her job as accountant for a small manufacturing company in Southampton. She was contemplating the prospect of starting one of two types of businesses, either her own tax consulting practice, or tax consulting and

Strategy and cost management

accounting practice. Although quite satisfied with her present employment, she was very excited about the possibility of owning her own business. Prior to assuming the post, Terry had worked for four years in the small business division at PWC's Southampton office and had dreamed of opening her own practice. Terry has decided that 2001 is the year her dream will become a reality.

9.8.79 Arriving at her office early, Terry began to think about the possible market segments she might serve and the types of tax and accounting problems these potential clients might have. For instance, Terry might simply establish a tax consulting practice which would focus on serving individuals who typically require only simple return preparation. Serving this target market segment would mean preparing simple tax returns.

9.8.80 On the other hand, Terry could establish both a tax consulting and accounting practice. This would mean she would serve both individuals and small businesses, although her primary target market would be small businesses. Pursuing this alternative would mean that she would render tax services for individuals and small businesses. Further, she would provide compilation, review and audit services for small businesses, as well as advice on designing accounting information systems. Terry knew that her first step would be to identify the market segment she wished to serve. To be successful, she would have to serve the selected target market very well.

9.8.81 Once she identified her target market segment, Terry could then make a decision about the three competitive strategies she might implement. These strategies are:

- cost leadership;
- differentiation;
- focus.

9.8.82 Terry decided to pursue a focus strategy, which meant that she would focus on a particular buyer group, segment of the product line or geographic market. Regardless of the target market served, Terry would serve only the geographic area surrounding Southampton; thus, she was sure she would implement a focus strategy. Therefore, the decisions which remained related to:

- the target market to be served;
- whether to implement a cost leadership or differentiation strategy.

Linking customer value to product costs

9.8.83 Terry's decision matrix is shown in Figure 9.22, which shows the combinations of market segments and strategies available to Terry.

Figure 9.22 Competitive strategy considerations

		Strategy	
		Cost Leadership	Differentiation
Target Market Segment	Individuals		▓▓▓
	Small businesses	▓▓▓	

The figure shows the possible strategies that Terry Merton might pursue as well as the target market segments she could serve. She could implement a cost leadership strategy focusing on individuals requiring help with simple tax return preparation. Terry's other alternative is to serve small businesses by providing a differentiated product consisting of a variety of tax return and accounting services. Note that the darkened cells represent strategy-target market segment combinations that Terry will not consider, since competitors are already serving these segments employing the indicated strategies.

9.8.84 Pursuing a cost leadership strategy meant that she would attract clients by keeping her prices (and her costs) low. At the same time, Terry would still be attentive to providing quality service on a timely basis. She would compete on the basis of price and monitor costs to be sure they were kept low.

9.8.85 Pursuing the differentiation strategy meant providing services which are considered to be unique. Differentiating her product probably meant that Terry would provide above-average service and develop a more personal relationship with clients. With the differentiation strategy, Terry would be able to charge above-average prices for the services provided to clients and would not have to be as attentive to cost control as she would under the cost leadership strategy.

9.8.86 Terry looked at the sketch she had drawn (Figure 9.22). She noted that theoretically she would be able to implement either the cost leadership or differentiation strategy with either of the two market segments. Thus, she had a total of four alternatives available. However, she immediately eliminated two of the four alternatives: cost leadership-small business and differentiation-individual since there were already other competitors in the Southampton area pursuing these alternatives. Therefore, from a practical standpoint, Terry was left with either selecting the cost leadership-individual tax return combination (hereafter referred to as cost leadership) or the differentiation-small business combination (hereafter referred to as differentiation).

Strategy and cost management

9.8.87 In considering which strategy to pursue, Terry thought about a nationally-known provider of tax preparation services which had offices located throughout the UK. This national firm used television, radio and billboard advertising to present reasons why taxpayers should do business with their firm. Terry was certain that the national firm had a costly centralised administrative structure. The firm's tax preparers were typically not chartered accountants, but underwent a training programme conducted by the firm as accounting technicians. Terry felt that this nationally-known firm was pursuing a differentiation-individual tax-return strategy, since it emphasised an array of reasons for using the services but did not emphasise low price.

9.8.88 If Terry selected the cost leadership strategy, the limited tax expertise required would allow her to remain with her present employers. She would hire Jim Wallace, an experienced semi-retired preparer of non-complicated tax returns. Terry would locate her tax practice in a storefront in the downtown shopping centre. Rent was very low there, and there was a high volume of pedestrian traffic past the location. Given this heavy pedestrian traffic, Terry reasoned that she would incur little advertising cost. Terry expected that her costs could be kept low compared with the nationally-known firm for two reasons:

- she would provide minimal training for Jim;
- she would have minimal administrative and advertising costs.

9.8.89 If she pursued a differentiation strategy, her target market would be small businesses. With the differentiation strategy, the services she would provide would be significantly different from the services provided by competitors. Terry would differentiate herself along a number of dimensions, many of which related to her extensive experience with the local business community. First, from her experience working in PWC's small business division, Terry is acquainted with all the bankers in town. She knows how to prepare financial presentations for clients seeking loans in such a way that the loan applications are almost always approved. She is also familiar with virtually all the small business rental property in town, and can direct clients to the most reasonably priced locations. Finally, she is thoroughly familiar with the operation of a small business and can provide extremely useful insights to small business owners. Therefore, like the nationally-known firm, Terry would provide small businesses with many reasons to patronise her new firm. If the differentiation-small businesses strategy is pursued, Terry will leave her £40,000 per year accountant position to become the principal employee of Start-up, Now.

9.8.90 Terry would like to finance her new business start-up costs entirely from her personal savings. This is not possible, however, since she recently purchased a new car for cash, which left her with a savings account balance of only £2,400. She will need a business loan to cover start-up costs including the purchase of a computer and software. Prior to contacting Bill Anderson, the loan officer at a nearby bank, Terry prepares some preliminary profit estimates. Terry's estimates of the revenues and costs associated with each strategy for the first year of operation, 2001, are presented in Figure 9.23. The projected balance sheet of Start-up, Now prior to any bank loans is presented in Figure 9.24.

Figure 9.23 Projected income statements under two competitive strategies for the 12 months ended 31 December 2001

	Strategies for practice	
	Cost leadership	Differentiation
Revenues (450 clients at £150)	£67,500	
(203 clients at £450)		£91,350
Variable expenses:		
Supplies (£10 per client)	4,500	2,030
Contribution margin	63,000	89,320
Fixed expenses:		
Depreciation-computer	1,600	1,600
software	500	4,000
Liability insurance	2,400	11,680
Rental-furniture	5,660	5,660
Club membership and entertainment		1,200
Preparer salary	26,000	31,200
Secretarial salary	16,000	16,000
Advertising	200	1,180
Rent-office	8,400	
Training		8,000
Total fixed expenses	60,760	80,520
Operating income	£2,240	£8,800

Figure 9.24 Balance sheet as at October 31, 2000

Cash	£2,400
Total assets	£2,400
Common stock, £1 par	£1,000
Additional paid-in capital	1,400
Total liabilities and shareholders' equity	£2,400

Strategy and cost management

9.8.91 Terry projects revenues of £67,500 (450 clients at £150/client) and £91,350 (203 clients at £450/client) under the cost leadership and differentiation strategies respectively (see Figure 9.23). Supplies average £10 per client and constitute the only variable costs for Start-up, Now. The fixed expenses vary between the strategies in several respects.

- If she pursues the differentiation strategy, Terry will incur significantly higher liability insurance costs each year than she would under the cost leadership strategy. This is due to the fact that she has much more liability exposure since she will be doing reviews and audits.

- Annual computer software costs will be greater under the differentiation strategy. This is because each year Terry will purchase specialised CD-ROM tax preparation disks needed properly to prepare the returns. Additional software is also needed if she wishes to advise clients with regard to pensions and investments.

- If she pursues the differentiation strategy, Terry will incur additional expense for club membership dues and entertainment expenses compared with the cost leadership strategy. This is due to the fact that Terry knows that she can develop the estate and trust work through social contacts with bankers and solicitors.

- Under the cost leadership provider strategy, Terry will continue in her present employment position. She will hire Jim Wallace for £500 per week. Although not a chartered accountant, Jim is approaching retirement at the firm where Terry works. Jim would be happy to work part-time at Start-up, Now; Terry is impressed with Jim's qualifications and is confident he could prepare uncomplicated tax returns. The differentiation strategy, however, will entail more complicated tax return preparations, which are beyond Jim's capabilities. Under the differentiation strategy, Terry would resign from her accountant position and work full-time for Start-up, Now, drawing a salary of £600 per week.

- Terry's home has a very large attached flat which she presently leases to two university students at a rent of £500 per month. The students' rent contracts expire on 31December 1999. Under the differentiation strategy, she will not renew the contracts. Instead, she will set up the offices of Start-up, Now in the flat. Under the cost leadership provider strategy, the students would continue to occupy the flat since space in a nearby shopping centre will be leased for Start-up's offices. The centre would provide needed pedestrian traffic and high visibility for Start-up, Now and avoid traffic congestion in Terry's residential neighbourhood.

Linking customer value to product costs

- Anticipating the complexity of clients under the differentiation strategy and considering the fact that she has been out of public accounting for three years, Terry estimates $8,000 in annual training costs. Minimal training costs are projected with the cost leadership preparer strategy since Jim Wallace already possesses the necessary experience, and the level of tax expertise required is minimal.

Obtaining a business loan

9.8.92 Terry faxed the financial projections in Figures 9.23 and 9.24 to Bill Andersen in early November 2000. As a loan officer, Bill must follow a set of specific guidelines in making his loan approval decisions. If Bill approves too many loans which are ultimately 'bad', he will lose his job. For all loan applications, he must be able to justify his decision after-the-fact to the branch senior manager, based largely on the loan applicant's financial statements. In assessing the creditworthiness of Terry's loan application, Bill plans to use operating income before depreciation and working capital as surrogates for cash-paying ability. Terry will offer her nearly new automobile as security for the loan. The bank's policy is to approve loans only if the annual payments are less than the beginning working capital balance and the projected before depreciation operating income for the next 12 months. The bank has also instituted a policy to have all loans due and payable on demand at the end of any calendar year if the payee is not in compliance with the original loan requirements.

9.8.93 Bill's bank has a maximum loan period for start-up companies of five years. At an interest rate of 10 per cent per annum, Start-up, Now qualifies for an $8,000 maximum loan requiring a $2,110 annual payment. Consequently, Start-up's 31 December working capital balance and annual operating income (before depreciation expense) must not fall below $2,110, or the bank loan becomes due and payable.

Start-up, Now – November 2001

9.8.94 By November 2001, Start-up had completed its first 11 months of operation, and had paid its first annual bank loan payment of $2,110. Start-up did not perform up to expectations in 2001. Operating income and depreciation expense for the year ended 31 December 2001 are estimated at $1,000 and $1,600 respectively. The average billings and variable costs per return for 2001 equalled the expected amounts, but client volume was down exactly 2 per cent from the projected volume levels. The pro forma balance sheet at 31 December 2001 is presented in Figure 9.25. Although somewhat disappointed with the level of operating profit, Terry is grateful that Start-up's projected 31 December 2001 working capital balance and operating income before depreciation exceed the $2,110 minimum loan requirements.

Strategy and cost management

9.8.95 Terry is thinking about how to make Start-up more successful in the future. She is contemplating pursuing one of three options to increase the volume of tax preparations. Terry believes that she must select one of these three options by 31 December 2001. After that date, potential clients may already have scheduled appointments with their present accountant. Increased volume of preparations seems appropriate to Terry since, as Figure 9.23 indicates, most of Start-up's costs are fixed.

Figure 9.25 Pro forma balance sheet as at 31 December 2001

Assets			
Current assets:			
Cash		$3,390	
Debitors		400	
Supplies		100	
Total current assets			$3,890
Property, plant and equipment:			
Computer		8,000	
Less: depreciation		(1,600)	
			6,400
Total assets			$10,290
Liabilities and shareholders' equity			
Current liabilities:			
creditors		$200	
Bank loan-current portion		1,441	
Total current liabilities			$1,641
Long-term liabilities:			
Bank loan (8,000-1,310)		6,690	
Less: current portion		(1,441)	
			5,249
Total liabilities			6,890
Shareholders' equity:			
Common stock, $1 par		1,000	
Additional paid-in-capital		1,400	
Earnings		1,000	
Total shareholders' equity			3,400
Total liabilities and shareholders' equity			$10,290

9.8.96 Terry believes that the average revenues and costs per client in 2002 will be the same as experienced in 2001. That is, the billings and costs of supplies per client in 2002 is expected to be the same as predicted for and experienced in 2001. A breakdown of the fees charged to clients in 2001 is

Linking customer value to product costs

presented in Figure 9.26. Fifty per cent of clients were charged the average billing fee, while 30 per cent were charged less than and 20 per cent more than the projected average billing fee per return.

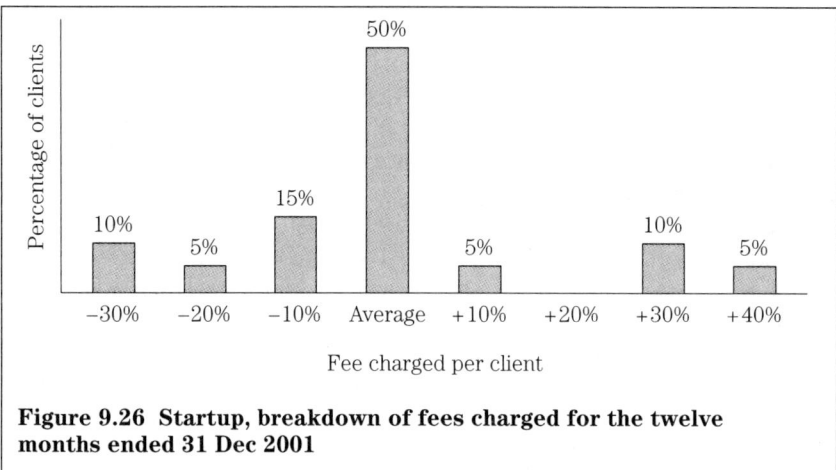

Figure 9.26 Startup, breakdown of fees charged for the twelve months ended 31 Dec 2001

9.8.97 Terry would like to pursue one of the following growth options.

Option 1
9.8.98 As part of the marketing strategy, Terry would give a coupon to each of the 54 people who had just moved to Southampton. Each coupon would entitle the holder to a free tax return preparation. Any additional tax schedules required will be billed at the standard billing rate of £75 per hour. The coupons would expire on 15 April 2002.

Option 2
9.8.99 In Option 2, Terry would present a coupon to a select group of 40 clients for whom Terry provided services in 2001. The coupons would entitle the holder to a 60 per cent discount off the normal billing rate on services provided during 2002. The coupons will expire on 31 December 2002. The only stipulation is that the user of the coupon must be a new client. That is, 40 individuals who were existing clients of Start-up must present the coupons to another 40 individuals. Since Terry believes these 40 first-year clients were pleased with the services provided by Start-up, and the coupons would make great stocking stuffers, she fully expected that all 40 coupons will be used by new clients.

Option 3
9.8.100 If Terry pursued Option 3, she would present all clients with the option to pay the average 2001 billing charge per client to purchase a coupon

Strategy and cost management

entitling them to the level of service with which they were provided in 2001. That is, if Start-up provides a client with the same level of service in 2002 as in 2001, the client would not be billed for the 2002 services since they have already paid the 2001 average billing per client, which was $150 under the cost leadership strategy and $450 with the differentiation strategy. Clients would only be billed for additional services provided by Start-up. The coupons would expire on 31 December 2002.

The strategic plan and financial reporting

9.8.101 Terry realises that, depending on which option she pursues, a liability and perhaps an expense or an asset will have to be recorded in Start-up's accounting records for the year ended 31 December 2001. Terry especially does not want to implement an option that would adversely affect the projected 2001 income of $1,000 and 31 December 2001 working capital balance of $2,249. If anything, Terry would like to shift income into 2001, since the projected 2001 operating income was below expectations. Terry is very concerned about how each option would be reflected in her financial statements for the calendar year ended 31 December 2001. She is worried because she realises that those financial reports will be monitored by banker Bill Anderson to determine whether she is complying with the loan agreement terms. Consequently, Terry and Bill are concerned about how the selected option is reflected in the financial reports. Above all, Terry knows that Bill wants her to use fair and honest accounting. The option selected must not interfere with the loan continuation approval, for without the continuing loan, Terry will not realise her dreams for Start-up. Therefore, she must carefully consider the financial reporting implications of each of the three potential growth options. That is, how each option will affect the projected 2001 operating income and working capital balance on 31 December 2001

9.8.102 How far can Terry go?

9.8.103 Terry made calculations incorporating a safety margin as follows.

Cost leadership:	
Break-even point	= Fixed costs/contribution margin per client
	= $60,760/$140 = 434 returns or $65,100 (434 @ $150)
Margin of safety	= Projected sales – break-even sales
	= $67,500 – $65,100
	= $2,400 or 3.6 per cent
Differentiation:	
Break-even point	= $80,520/$440 = 183 returns or $82,350 (183 @ $450)
Margin of safety	= $91,350 – $82,350
	= $9,000 or 9.9 per cent

Linking customer value to product costs

9.8.104 These calculation provide Terry with a different angle on the situation.

9.8.105 Bill Andersen is concerned with the ability of Start-up, Now to make timely loan payments. Another concern is Start-up's ability to stay in compliance with the loan agreement. According to the loan agreement, Start-up must maintain sufficient before depreciation operating incomes and working capital balances. Therefore, Bill would favour the alternative that is associated with the greatest possibility for meeting the loan requirements.

9.8.106 The differentiation strategy appears to be the 'safest' from Bill's perspective. Its projected operating income before depreciation for 2001 of $10,400 ($8,800 + $1,600) exceeds by 270.8 per cent the corresponding $3,840 ($2,240 + $1,600) amount for the cost leadership strategy. Moreover, the differentiation strategy's margin of safety is better (9.9 per cent compared to 3.6 per cent). Finally, Terry would become a full-time employee with the differentiation strategy. That level of commitment and involvement may be perceived favourably by Bill, especially compared to the absentee ownership arrangement of the cost leadership strategy.

9.8.107 From a managerial and strategic planning perspective, the cost leadership strategy is preferable for several reasons. The most important reason is financial. Although the operating income in Figure 9.23 is greater with differentiation, the cost leadership strategy is preferred when opportunity costs are considered. To determine the opportunity costs, one must know the opportunity set: cost leadership or differentiation. The profit figures for differentiation fail to indicate the $14,800 opportunity costs, namely the foregone $8,800 salary ($40,000 − $31,200) and $6,000 rental income. When opportunity costs are considered the projected operating income for differentiation becomes a negative $6,000 ($8,800 operating income less $14,800 in opportunity costs). Consequently, the cost leadership strategy is more profitable by $8,240 ($2,240 compared to a negative $6,000).

9.8.108 If Terry desires to become a full-time employee of Start-up, Now some 'psychic' income will be lost. However, Terry would have to receive $8,240 of annual 'psychic' income from pursuing differentiation as opposed to becoming a cost leadership tax return provider.

9.8.109 Finally, the question of absentee ownership could be addressed. Is the likelihood of substantial growth in sales and profits as great with absentee ownership (the cost leadership strategy) as it is with full-time involvement by the owner (with differentiation)? One thing is certain: Terry must be continually involved with Start-up, Now regardless of the strategy chosen.

Strategy and cost management

Calculating costs

9.8.110 Consider the cost leadership strategy.

9.8.111 An operating income of £1,000 for 2001 for cost leadership can be computed as follows:

Revenues [441 clients (450×98%) at £150]	£66,150
Variable costs [441 clients at £10]	4,410
Contribution margin	61,740
Fixed costs (derived)	60,740
Operating income	£1,000

9.8.112 The full cost per client is computed by dividing the £65,150 full cost by 441 clients for £147.73 per client.

9.8.113 Now consider the differentiation strategy.

9.8.114 Fixed costs under the differentiation strategy are £86,560, computed as follows.

Revenues [199 clients (203×98%) at £450]	£89,550
Variable costs [199 clients at £10]	1,990
Contribution margin	87,560
Fixed costs (derived)	86,560
Operating income	£1,000

9.8.115 The full cost per client is £444.97 (£88,550/199 returns) for the differentiation strategy. When one considers the £14,800 opportunity costs, however, the full cost per client equals £519.35 [(£88,550+£14,800)/199 clients].

9.8.116 Under both practice strategies, the incremental cost of serving a single client is £10, the cost of supplies. This incremental cost is constant at all levels of activity.

9.8.117 It is reasonable to assume that whether Terry pursues either cost leadership or differentiation, she will still incur the fixed costs in 2002. This being the case, then the fixed costs of £60,740 with cost leadership and

£86,560 for differentiation are not relevant to the strategic planning decision to choose among growth options. In the short run at least the relevant costs are those that will change, which amounts to £10 per client.

9.8.118 Suppose, under Option 1, Terry obtained responses from 35 new residents who indicated positively that they would have a free tax return prepared. It might be argued that a liability should be recognised in the amount of £5,250 (35×£150 average billing) for the cost leadership strategy and £15,750 (35×£450 average billing) for the differentiation strategy. That would measure the opportunity cost of the free tax return if Start-up, Now had to forgo revenue from other clients. However, since Start-up has not attained its projected volume at this point, the possibility of it turning away clients due to time constraints appears remote. Therefore, the £5,250 and £15,750 amounts really are not appropriate.

9.8.119 Given that a liability is the probable future economic sacrifice of economic benefits, the amount of the liability should be measured as the incremental cost of preparing the 35 tax returns for the new residents of Southampton. The only incremental costs Start-up, Now would incur would be £10 per return. It appears then that Start-up has a probable liability for free tax return coupons outstanding in the amount of £350 (35 returns at £10 per return).

9.8.120 The impact on 2001 operating income must also be determined. That is, should the proposed £350 tax return preparation cost be expensed in 2001 or 2002? It might be argued that 2002 would result in better matching since the return will be prepared in that time period. However, the cost really does not result in a cause-and-effect relationship with revenues. In fact, no revenues are associated with these returns except for additional charges for required tax schedules. The tax return preparation cost perhaps more closely resembles an advertising cost and fits the immediate write-off approach to matching. The £350 cost would then be expensed in 2001. Terry certainly would not favour this matching approach, however, because her operating income would be reduced from £1,000 to £650, a 35 per cent decline. Moreover, her working capital would be reduced from £2,249 to £1,899, which is below the minimum amount required.

9.8.121 Under Option 2 the possibility of Start-up, Now providing 40 discounted accounting services for the relatives and friends of this year's clients appears likely. It appears probable that most of the coupons will be redeemed for discounted accounting services. Therefore, one could assume that a probable obligation has been established. One could again assume that

Strategy and cost management

the likelihood of having any revenue foregone due to these discounted services appears remote.

9.8.122 Unlike Option 1 which limited the returns to tax return, these coupons entitle the holder to a discounted accounting services, regardless of the level of complication involved. To be consistent, if one advocated recognising a liability of $5,250 (low cost) or $15,750 (product differentiation) above one may now advocate recognising a liability of $3,600 [40 at ($150×60% discount)] for cost leadership and $10,800 [40 at ($150×60% discount)] for differentiation.

9.8.123 Alternatively, it is possible that the amount of the obligation cannot be reasonably estimated because of the unknown service difficulty and corresponding standard billing rate, so no obligation can be recognised currently. However, there appears to be a range of possible discounts for each practice strategy.

9.8.124 The cost leadership strategy, using the information in Figure 9.27, has billings ranging from $105 ($150×0.70) to $210 ($150×1.40) in 2001. Consequently, the discounts granted these 40 individuals could range from $2,520 [(40) ($105×0.60)] up to $5,040 [(40) ($210×0.60)]. From a conservative standpoint, an estimate of the probable discounts to be granted would be at least $2,520. So then should a liability and an expense be established for $2,520 as of 31 December 2001? The answer is no, since these discounts do not represent a potential cash outflow. They represent an opportunity cost (a benefit foregone).

9.8.125 No liability should be established since the cash required to satisfy these 40 discounted tax returns should approximate $400 (40 at $10 supply cost per return). The minimum expected revenues from these returns, $1,680 [(40 returns) ($105×0.40)], exceeds the cash required, so no liability recognition is warranted.

9.8.126 The analysis for the differentiation strategy is similar. Billings per client in 2001 ranged from a low of $315 ($450×0.70) to a high of $630 ($450×1.40). The discount allowed could possibly then range from $189 ($315×0.60) up to $378 ($630×0.60). However, Start-up, Now at the minimum, should receive cash of at least $126 ($315×0.40) per client served, which would more than cover the $10 supply cost.

9.8.127 Unlike Option 1, the discount fee coupons do not create a liability nor cause Start-up to recognise an expense. Consequently, the 2001 operating income and 31 December 2001 working capital balance amounts would

Linking customer value to product costs

Figure 9.27 Breakdown of fees charged for the 12 months ended 31 December 2001

	Fee	Number of clients	Total revenue
Cost leadership:			
	$105 (150×0.70)	44 (441×0.10)	$4,620
	120 (150×0.80)	22 (441×0.05)	2,640
	135 (150×0.90)	66 (441×0.15)	8,910
	150 (150)	221 (441×0.50)	33,150
	165 (150×1.10)	22 (441×0.05)	3,630
	195 (150×1.30)	44 (441×0.10)	8,580
	210 (150×1.40)	22 (441×0.05)	4,620
Totals		441 (450×0.98)	$66,150
Differentiation:			
	$315 (450×0.70)	20 (199×0.10)	$6,300
	360 (450×0.80)	10 (199×0.05)	3,600
	405 (450×0.90)	30 (199×0.15)	12,150
	450 (450)	99 (199×0.50)	44,550
	495 (450×1.10)	10 (199×0.05)	4,950
	585 (450×1.30)	20 (199×0.10)	11,700
	630 (450×1.40)	10 (199×0.05)	6.300
Totals		199 (203×0.98)	$89,550

be unaffected. This option appears to be viable, since the marginal revenue provided by these discounted coupons should exceed the associated incremental costs.

9.8.128 If Terry pursues Option 3, the revenue recognition concept may be more appropriate. That is, should Start-up, Now be able to currently recognise the $9,000 received in advance for the 2002 accounting services? If no revenue is recognised currently, how do we treat the $9,000 advanced payments? From a revenue recognition perspective, one should establish a liability in the amount of $9,000. The liability perspective advocated in Option 1 would not recognise a liability for the $9,000, but for the incremental costs associated with those future 2002 returns, of $600 for cost leadership and $200 for differentiation. Cost leadership: $9,000/$150 average billing per return = 60 taxpayers who purchased discount coupon at a $10 incremental cost per return = $600. Differentiation: $9,000/$450 per return = 20 taxpayers at a $10 cost = $200.

9.8.129 It is fairly clear that Option 3 may not be economically sound. By offering the coupons, Start-up, Now is actually reducing the amount of cash

591

Strategy and cost management

that would otherwise be available to pay the bank loan. If Startup offers all clients the opportunity to prepay their 2002 accounting services at the 2001 average billing amount per client, probably only those clients who had paid more than the average billing amount in 2001 will purchase the coupons, assuming that the complexity of their 2002 services is similar to that of their 2001 services.

9.8.130 Figure 9.27 was created using the information provided in Figure 9.26. One can see that 88 clients with the cost leadership strategy and 40 clients with the product differentiation strategy paid more than the average billing amount per client. A conservative estimate of the opportunity cost of Option 3 can be calculated by assuming the 60 cost leadership clients and the 20 product differentiation clients who prepaid their 2002 accounting services paid an amount slightly above the 2001 average billing per client. Figure 9.28 shows a conservative calculation of the opportunity cost of lost fees associated with Option 3 to be £2,040 for low cost leadership and £1,800 for product differentiation.

Figure 9.28 Calculation of opportunity cost associated with growth Option 3

Fee	Opportunity cost per client	Number of clients	Total opportunity cost
Cost leadership:			
£165	£165 − £150 = £15	22	£300
£195	£195 − £150 = £45	38	1,710
		60	£2,040
Differentiation:			
£495	£495 − £450 = £45	10	£450
£585	£165 − £150 = £135	10	1,350
		20	£1,800

9.8.131 Opportunity costs generally are not entered in the accounting records, therefore, Terry may be willing to pursue Option 3 because this option, like Option 2, does not reduce either 2001 operating income or the 31 December 2001 working capital balance. However, Option 2 will increase cash flows from new clients, while Option 3 can only reduce total cash flows to Start-up, Now.

(Source: adapted with permission from Ruhl and Kreuze, 1997.)

9.9 Customer profitability analysis

9.9.1 It is now widely recognised that different sources of revenues do not contribute equally to net income. Customer profitability analysis is an approach to addressing this issue. Foster *et al.* (1996) note that most management accounting systems focus not on the customer but on products, departments or geographic regions. Only rarely can a management accounting system produce customer profitability figures. Whilst customer accounting profitability (CAP) analysis can vary according to the context, it provides at the lowest level, profitability information on individual customers. At a more aggregate level, it can focus on groupings of customers (e.g., groupings by revenues, size of average transaction, number of transactions or time since the business association began). CAP can also provide information on the profitability of different distribution channels. Within a computer or food company, for example, a CAP analysis might consider major computer chain customers, large retail stores, independent retail stores, corporate accounts and direct-mail accounts. The focus differs however for an industrial parts manufacturer. Such an analysis would reveal potential disparities in the profitability of revenues stemming from different sources.

9.9.2 Revenue differences across customers of a company can arise from many sources, including:

- differences in the prices charged per unit to different customers;
- differences in the selling volume levels across customers;
- differences in the products or services delivered to different customers;
- differences in the items provided without charge to different customers.

9.9.3 Differences in cost across the spectrum of a company's customers arise from differences in the way different customers use the company's resources.

A case study: developing customer profitability information

9.9.4 Different distribution channels and levels of customer service influence resource usage. Foster *et al.* (1996) provide an excellent illustration of customer profitability analysis from a case originally documented by Juras and Dierks (1993). The Blue Ridge Company manufactures and sells sport towels, which differ in size, colour, logos, embroidery and dying. Individual customers of Blue Ridge vary in size as follows:

Strategy and cost management

- large customers: national retail chains;
- midsize customers: smaller retail chains and licensing agents for sport teams;
- small customers: customers who purchase towels in response to advertisements, mail-order campaigns, and other forms of marketing.

9.9.5 Figure 9.29 presents summary data about these three customer groupings. Panel A shows actual data, while Panel B presents the same data in percentage form. Note the heterogeneity among the three customer groupings, especially the following.

- Average number of units sold per order: large = 100,250/133 = 754; midsize = 58,544/845 = 69; small = 117,406/5,130 = 23.
- Percentage of units sold that are embroidered: large = 5,959/100,250 = 5.9 per cent; midsize = 6,490/58,544 = 11.0 per cent; and small = 29,394/117,406 = 25.0 per cent.
- Percentage of units sold that are dyed: large = 20,536/100,250 = 20.5 per cent; midsize = 9,935/58,544 = 17.0 per cent; small = 12,328/117,406 = 10.5 per cent.
- Average selling price per unit sold: large = £308,762/100,250 = £3.08; midsize = £183,744/58,544 = £3.14; small = £318,024/117,406 = £2.71.

Figure 9.29 Profile of customer groupings of Blue Ridge

Panel A	Large	Midsize	Small
Number of customers	8	154	824
Unit sold	100,250	58,544	117,406
Sales volume £	£308,762	£183,744	£318,024
Number of order received	133	845	5,130
Number of shipments	147	923	5,431
Number of units embroidered	5,959	6,490	29,394
Number of units dyed	20,536	9,935	12,328
Panel B	Large	Midsize	Small
Number of customers	0.8%	15.6%	83.6%
Unit sold	36.3	21.2	42.5
Sales volume £	38.1	22.7	39.2
Number of order received	2.2	13.8	84.0
Number of shipments	2.3	14.2	83.5
Number of units embroidered	14.2	15.5	70.3
Number of units dyed	48.0	23.2	28.8

(Source: Foster et al., 1996. Reprinted with permission. For more information, visit www.wglcorpfinance@riag.com)

Customer profitability analysis

9.9.6 Blue Ridge faced intense pressure from several large retail chains for price reductions beyond those already provided. To facilitate responding to price reduction requests, Blue Ridge initiated a customer profitability study.

9.9.7 An activity-based costing (see Chapter **6**) (ABC) approach was applied to Blue Ridge's marketing, distribution and customer service areas better to document how each customer used resources differentially. As Foster et al. (1996) explain, the initial focus of the study was on the three customer groupings rather than on the profitability of individual accounts within those groupings. For each customer, Blue Ridge traced direct costs such as discounts, commissions and licensing fees for logos. The activity-based cost pools and the related activity drivers were as follows.

Cost pool	Cost driver
Purchase orders	Number of orders
Shipping activities	Number of shipments
Invoices	Number of invoices
Product samples and catalogues	Sales dollars
Marketing by customer type	Sales dollars

9.9.8 The key conclusion of the ABC analysis was that the large customer group contributed by far the most toward Blue Ridge's total operating income, as the following table reveals.

	Percentage of revenues	Percentage of operating income
Large customers	38.1%	67.3%
Midsize customers	22.7%	32.8%
Small customers	39.2%	−0.1%

9.9.9 Given the importance of the large customer group, Blue Ridge realised that the large customers were potentially at risk. Competitors were likely to recognise how profitable the larger customers were and might therefore bid aggressively for these accounts. To understand large customer profitability, an individual customer study was conducted at Blue Ridge. Figure 9.30 shows individual customer profitability figures for the eight large customers. Panel A ranks the customers based on revenue, while Panel B ranks the customers based on operating income.

9.9.10 As Panel B of Figure 9.30 shows, three of the eight large customers (B, D and A) provide 80 per cent of the total operating income for large customers. Two of the eight large customers (E and G) cause operating losses.

Strategy and cost management

Figure 9.30 Customer profitability analysis of large customers of Blue Ridge

Panel A: Ranked on revenues

Customer	Revenues	Operating income	Cumulative revenues	Cumulative revenue/Total revenues of large customers
A	£71,632	£21,662	£71,632	23.2%
B	64,531	37,616	136,163	44.1
C	44,153	15,707	180,316	58.4
D	39,521	23,407	219,837	71.2
E	30,915	−4,209	250,752	81.2
F	25,627	13,654	276,379	89.5
G	18,279	−10,874	294,658	95.4
H	14,104	5,699	308,762	100.0

Panel B: Ranked on operating income

Customer	Operating income	Cumulative income	Cumulative % Operating income of large customers
B	£37,616	£37,616	36.6%
D	23,407	61,023	59.4
A	21,662	82,685	80.5
C	15,707	98,392	95.8
D	13,654	112,046	109.1
H	5,699	117,745	114.7
E	−4,209	113,536	110.6
G	−10,874	102,662	100.0

Options

9.9.11 Blue Ridge has the following options according to Foster *et al.* (1996) when attempting to improve its profitability.

- Reduce set-up times: reduce embroidery or dying costs by reducing set-up times.

- Change order interface: change the order interface with customers to reduce costs and speed the process (e.g., through use of faxes or electronic data exchange).

- Change customer options: change options available to customers (e.g., trim the embroidery options).

- Charge for all extras: fully price out all options so that customers are given economic signals to change their behaviour.

- Be consistent with revenue offsets: maintain consistency when making price discounts and other price offsets. For example, several CAP studies have found little economic rationale to the discounts provided to customers. There are instances in companies of unprofitable customers that show no growth prospect receiving the largest price discount. In part this may be due to short-run sales incentive schemes that reinforce revenue increases regardless of profitability levels.
- Identify preferred customers: identify the key characteristics of a preferred customer and use the resulting profile to guide sales strategy.
- Motivate salespeople appropriately: reward Blue Ridge salespeople on the basis of customer profitability as computed by an ABC system.
- Motivate customers appropriately: change the behaviour of Blue Ridge customers (e.g., by encouraging them to batch small orders into larger orders).
- Outsource distribution for some customers: outsource the selling and distribution for very small customers to independent distributors.

9.10 Key features of analyses of customer profitability

9.10.1 Several features of CAP analysis make it distinctive according to Foster *et al.* (1996).

- Entire value chain: CAP analysis cuts across costs from potentially all parts of the value chain.
- Multiple transactions: CAP analysis focuses on multiple transactions of a customer rather than any single transaction.
- Multiple products: CAP analysis focuses on multiple products bought by a single customer rather than a single product bought by multiple customers.
- Customer-specific costs: CAP analysis captures costs that are related to a customer but are not specific to a product, service, department or geographic area.
- Aggregate or narrow focus: CAP analysis can be kept at a highly aggregate level (e.g., different distribution outlets) or brought to the very granular level of individual customers.

9.10.2 These features require major changes in the way most management accounting systems are designed and operated.

Strategy and cost management

9.10.3 Epstein (2000) also notes in a *Management Accounting Guideline* published by the Society of Management Accountants of Canada that costs can vary depending on how customers draw upon a company's resources such as marketing, distribution and customer service. If a comprehensive analysis of the benefits and costs of customer relationships is not undertaken, companies can unknowingly continue to service unprofitable customers. It is therefore important to carry out thorough analysis of the costs and benefits of customers before deciding which customers to service and how to price strategically the firm's products and services.

9.10.4 As Epstein (2000) notes, many costs are often hidden within the production, support, marketing and general administrative areas. Hidden customer costs may include items such as the following.

- Inventory carrying costs.
- Stocking and handling costs.
- Quality control and inspection costs.
- Customer order processing.
- Order picking and order fulfilment.
- Billing, collection and payment processing costs.
- Accounts receivable and carrying costs.
- Customer service costs.
- Wholesale service and quality assurance costs.
- Selling and marketing costs.

9.10.5 As demonstrated in the Blue Ridge example above, different sources of revenue have different profitability implications. This applies to all customers, new and established. Customer profitability measures can reveal that some newly-acquired customers are unprofitable as a result of high customer acquisition costs. In early periods, this cost may not be covered by the margins earned through selling products and services to the customers. In these cases, lifetime profitability analysis (and product life-cycle costing – see Chapter **7**) can help in assessing the basis for retaining these customers. In many instances, customers that are unprofitable in the short run may become very profitable as their purchases increase and their cost to service decreases. Likewise, customers that are unprofitable in the long term may require immediate action to turn them towards profitability. According to Epstein (2000), this may include promoting more cross-selling opportunities to enhance the product range of customer purchases.

Moreover, other customers may be prestigious to retain, even when they are unprofitable on their own account; as long as they contribute to the perception of reputation and credibility of the company, and improve the ability to sell to others, they may add to the company's bottom line.

Implementing customer profitability analysis

9.10.6 Customer profitability analysis can draw significantly on an organisation in terms of the resources it entails. According to Epstein (2000), barriers to implementation can include:

- convincing management that potential organisational improvements justify the resource allocation;
- obtaining the significant required resources that include information technology, equipment, and staff for analysis and preparation;
- changing the sales incentive system to reward customer profitability rather than sales volume;
- obtaining buy-in from employees within the company who are often reluctant to change;
- training employees in the use of customer profitability analysis and its measurement and rewards.

Strategy and customer profitability analysis

9.10.7 Develin and Bellis-Jones (1999) note that because most organisations have a fairly wide range of products and customers, knowing the profit contribution of each one, while important in itself, is insufficient in helping to frame or modify commercial policies or strategy. To achieve this, and to focus management attention on action, it is important to be able to analyse such data. They suggest that cumulative customer contribution analysis can be helpful, whether applied to product or customer profitability analysis, by making patterns visible in the way that numbers alone do not.

9.10.8 According to these authors, cumulative customer contribution analysis (CCCA) highlights how major resources (and assets) frequently stand behind those customers that generate only marginal or negative contributions. It attempts to illustrate graphically the extent of profit erosion by customers with servicing costs that exceed the margins which they generate. Figure 9.31 shows a typical result of such analysis.

9.10.9 Such graphs often reveal examples of profit erosion to the extent of 20 to 60 per cent of the profit which has already been generated.

Strategy and cost management

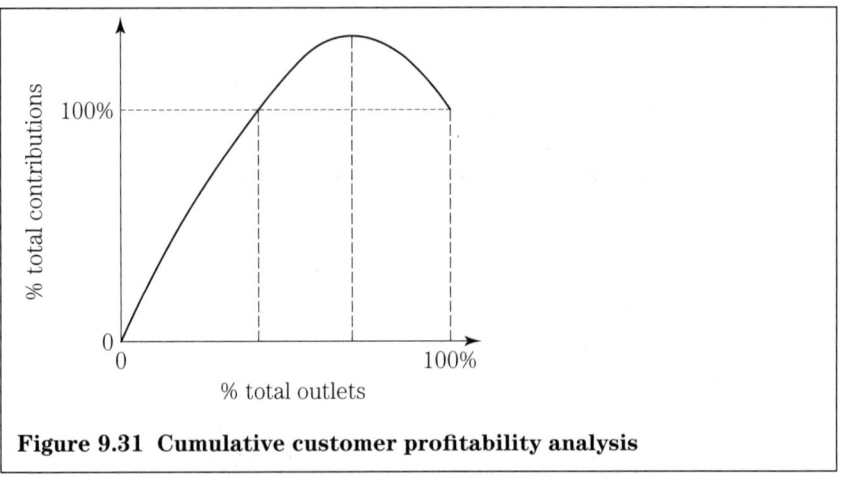

Figure 9.31 Cumulative customer profitability analysis

9.10.10 Develin and Bellis-Jones (1999) also suggest that a decision grid analysis (DGA) can be useful in providing a perspective on customers vis-à-vis strategy. The DGA plots each customer account on a graph of profitability against volumes of business, as illustrated in Figure 9.32.

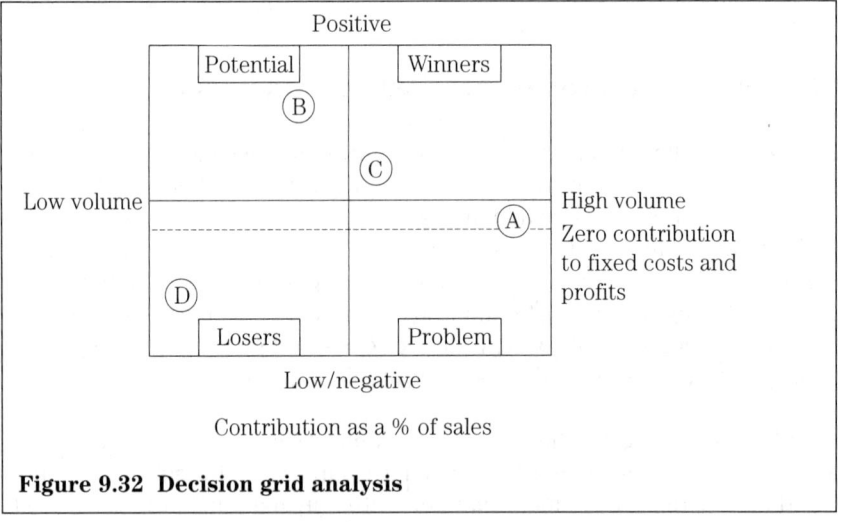

Figure 9.32 Decision grid analysis

9.10.11 Figure 9.32 highlights all customer accounts against one of four categories, each of which may require a different commercial response. It is also the first step in defining the characteristics of a profitable or unprofitable customer, so providing the company with a greater ability to identify, and then focus resources on developing and defending genuinely attractive accounts.

Key features of analyses of customer profitability

9.10.12 The thinking which underpins decision grid analysis can also be used to develop a powerful understanding of how the mix of product purchased by a particular customer contributes to their overall profitability, according to Develin and Bellis-Jones (1999). In particular, this form of analysis frequently highlights anomalies in pricing and discount structures. They cite the example of a manufacturer of commercial film which recognised that its largest customer in the UK was only just generating a positive contribution, and wished to understand the reasons why. They analysed the customer's contribution by product, with the result shown in Figure 9.33.

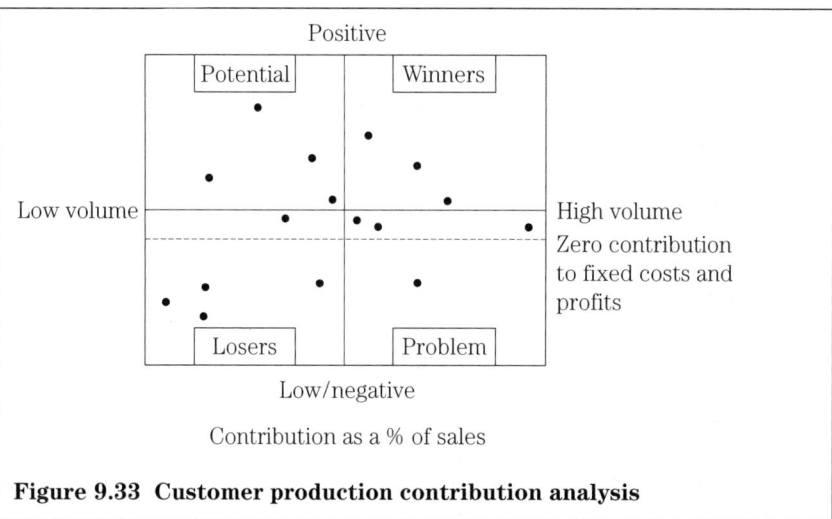

Figure 9.33 Customer production contribution analysis

9.10.13 The analysis revealed that while many products made an attractive return there were many more which were either low volume and/or negative contributors. With this information available it was then possible for the company to initiate a constructive discussion with the customer about the nature of the trading relationship between them, based on the costs driven by that relationship.

Challenges in developing customer profitability information
9.10.14 There are at least four challenges that must be overcome to analyse customer account profitability.

- How to develop reliable customer revenue and customer cost figures.
- How to recognise future downstream costs of customers.
- How to incorporate a multi-period horizon into the analysis.
- How to recognise different drivers of customer costs.

601

Strategy and cost management

New directions in analysing customer profitability

9.10.15 The emphasis on adopting a 'customer focus' has become pervasive across many areas of management. As a result, customer profitability has become central to advances in several high-profile areas of management thinking, including:

- supporting strategic decisions;
- valuing intangible assets;
- analysing customer retention rates.

9.10.16 Supporting strategic decisions: customer profitability systems typically assume that the existing business infrastructure will stay relatively constant in the face of various management decisions. Foster *et al.* (1996) consider however that this assumption becomes tenuous when significant re-engineering occurs.

9.10.17 Consider the Blue Ridge example above. One of Blue Ridge's strategic options for its small customers would be to use a third-party distributor. Costing out this approach, however, is likely to require adding extra cost pools and cost drivers to the company's ABC system.

9.10.18 Consider also the order interface between suppliers, manufacturers, and customers. By necessity, an ABC system reflects existing activities. If major changes in the company dramatically revamp those activities, supplementary costing analysis will be required. For example, an extensive use of electronic data exchange might make it possible to eliminate many activities modelled in an ABC system.

9.10.19 The more dramatic the re-engineering options considered, the less valuable an accounting system based solely on existing activities becomes. The next generation of customer profitability reports according to Foster *et al.* (1996), may therefore include cost pools and cost drivers for activities that alternative scenarios would require. This format would increase the usefulness of reports for strategic decision-making.

9.10.20 Valuing intangible assets: most management accounting systems restrict their attention to the valuation of tangible assets (e.g., property, plant, and equipment; computers; and motor vehicles). In many businesses, however, intangible assets (such as brands the company owns) are a significant component of the company's total value. Brand names are pivotal to valuations of consumer products for companies such as Cadbury's and Philip Morris. Similarly, a company's customer base is often a valuable intangible

Key features of analyses of customer profitability

asset. Examples include a doctor's patient base as well as Amazon.com or Cellnet's subscriber base. Consequently, valuations of service companies for acquisition decisions often recognise customer bases as the single most important asset. Given the importance of customer bases, assessments of management performance should track how the value of customer bases change periodically.

9.10.21 Management decisions can dramatically increase or decrease the value of these intangible assets. For example, consider the effect of implementing a total quality management (TQM) programme (see Chapter **8**) for a consumer product that has had a low quality ranking for years. If the TQM programme causes the company's product to be ranked first in quality, this improvement is likely to have both short-run and long-run effects, yet most accounting systems recognise only the short-run effect (i.e., an increase in income).

9.10.22 By periodically estimating the value of a customer base, the multi-period effect of increases in customer loyalty can be analysed systematically. Clearly, the estimates required involve uncertainty, but all management accounting systems involve uncertainty – e.g., in the form of the estimated service life of assets, allowances for bad debt and estimated warranty costs.

9.10.23 One reason for tracking changes in the value of customer bases is to highlight management actions that focus myopically on the short run. For example, price cuts may well boost short-run profitability for certain key customers, but they may also decrease long-term profitability because customers may begin to expect continued price reductions in the future. The argument for monitoring changes in customer bases is, according to Foster et al. (1996), analogous to the argument for monitoring changes in brand values.

9.10.24 Models of customer value are in their infancy. Some models take a certainty-based net present value approach. More refined models would recognise uncertainty in the form of likely competitor responses, differences in customer renewal profiles and alternative ways to compute customer profitability. A separate financial statement focused only on intangible assets may increase their visibility.

9.10.25 Analysing customer retention rates: the importance of retaining profitable customers is widely recognised. Various rules of thumb have been proposed for retaining customers – e.g., that it costs five times more to acquire a new customer than it does to keep an existing customer. Such rules of thumb are rarely based on systematic analysis.

Strategy and cost management

9.10.26 Customer profitability databases could facilitate development of more informed decision-making tools in the following ways:

- by tracking the resources required to attract new customers and retain existing customers;
- by providing more reliable estimates of the operating income derived from new and existing customers.

9.10.27 Alternative approaches to customer retention (e.g., lower prices or better customer service) may yield different customer retention rates. Refinements in tracking customer profitability will permit more extensive testing of the economics of these alternative approaches.

9.10.28 Foster *et al.* (1996) cite one study which reports the following increase in customer life-time profits from an annual 5 per cent reduction in customer defection rates.

Branch deposits	85 per cent
Credit card	75 per cent
Insurance brokerage	50 per cent
Software	35 per cent

9.10.29 A key input for this study is estimates of customer profitability. Refinements in these estimates can help managers make more informed decisions about alternative investments to improve customer-retention rates.

9.10.30 In the context of the Internet economy, customer relationship management is fast evolving given the costs and significance of branding and its implications for managing 'eye balls' once their gaze is captured. In such contexts, understanding customer profits becomes challenging but crucial to operational management and strategic decision-making.

Chapter 10
Target cost management

10.1 Target versus kaizen costing

10.1.1 Target costing is a cost management approach aimed at supporting the cost reduction process at the development and design stages of a new product or for a model modification. This contrasts with 'kaizen costing' which attempts to support cost reduction in the manufacturing phase of an existing model of product. Kaizen refers to the continuous accumulation of small improvements rather than innovative product enhancement. Target costing comprises two processes classified as; (1) the process of planning a specific product that satisfies customers' needs and of establishing the target cost from the target profit and targeted sales price of the new product, and (2) the process of realising the target cost by using value engineering (VE) and a comparison of target costs with achieved costs. The basic idea of VE is that products and services have functions to perform and the amount of their value is measured by the ratio of these functions to their costs. By this process, the decision as to whether the product is to be produced is made. For this purpose, it is necessary that the functions of each product, part and service are clarified and that all functions are subject to quantification of a type which enables their significance, cost effectiveness and customer perception to be approximated.

10.1.2 In general, target costing has the following properties.

- Target costing is applied in the developing and designing stage and it is different from 'kaizen' cost control which is applied in the production stage.

- Costing is not a management method for cost control in a traditional sense, but it is one which attempts to reduce costs among other aims.

- The target costing process, company-based management know-how and production engineering methods can in combination be useful.

- Co-operation of many departments and their interaction is essential to the execution of target costing.

- Target costing is more suitable in the multi-product, small production run firm than in the few-products, large production run firm.

10.2 The basis for target costing

10.2.1 Five basic issues of target costing have been identified as follows.

Corporate planning

10.2.2 In this step, the long- and medium-term profit plans for the whole company are established and the overall target profit for each period is determined for each product. In the three-year profit plan, marginal income (= sales price − variable costs), contribution margin (= marginal income − traceable fixed costs) and operating profit (contribution margin − allocated fixed costs) are computed as average figures for a series of developing models. Further, based on this average figure, each of these three kinds of profit is planned for several representative types of each model. In computing operating profits, depreciation costs of facilities, development costs and prototype manufacturing costs are allocated to each model. The ratio of return on sales is often used as the indicator of the profit ratio for establishing target profit because this ratio is easily computed for each product.

Developing the new project

10.2.3 In order to give shape to the general new product plan, details of the type of new product to be developed and the content of the model changes based on market research are determined.

Determining the basic plan for a specific new product

10.2.4 In this step, the major cost factors such as design and structure are determined and target costs are established. Each department needs to review material requirements and the manufacturing process, and to estimate costs. According to the reports of the departments, the total 'estimated cost' is computed.

10.2.5 At the same time, target price figures are gathered from company sources. From these prices and target profit, an 'allowable cost' is computed. The computation is: target sales price − target profit = allowable cost. Allowable cost is the cost desired to be attained, but it is necessary to establish a 'target cost' that is attainable and motivates employees to make efforts to ultimately achieve the 'allowable cost'.

10.2.6 The establishment of the target cost needs to be reviewed on various dimensions regarding the size of the gap between allowable cost and estimated cost. After the target cost is determined, the departments co-

The basis for target costing

operate in implementing VE activities regarding the design method in order to identify cost-effective products that will fulfil customers' demands.

10.2.7 The target cost is decomposed into cost element and functional element. Cost elements are typically material costs, purchased parts costs, direct labour costs, depreciation costs and so on. For a motor car, for instance, functional elements include engine, transmission system and chassis. Important points are clarified by these detailed classifications. An example of a form for classification is shown in Figure 10.1.

Cost elements / Functions	Material cost £	Purchases parts cost £	Direct labour costs £	.....	Total £
Engine					
Transmission system					
Chassis					
⋮					
Total					

Figure 10.1 Form for classification of target costs (motor car)

10.2.8 Functional analysis is carried out to learn more about the cost of providing functions vis-à-vis their volume. The technique mainly involves the following nine basic VE steps with functional analysis concentrating on (3)–(6) but also including all nine steps.

(1) Choose the object of analysis, such as product, service or overhead area.
(2) Select members of a team.
(3) Gather information.
(4) Define the functions of the object.
(5) Draw a functional tree.
(6) Evaluate the functions.
(7) Suggest alternatives and compare these with the target cost.
(8) Choose the alternatives for manufacturing.
(9) Review the actual results.

Target cost management

10.2.9 Target costs can be decomposed into parts as represented by Worksheet 1.

Product design

10.2.10 A trial blueprint is drafted according to the target cost set for every part. Information from each department is needed. If there is a gap between the target cost and the estimated cost, the departments undertake VE analysis and the trial blueprint is adjusted accordingly. After repeating this process several times, a final blueprint is established.

Production transfer plan

10.2.11 In this step, the necessary production equipment is obtained to match costs according to the final blueprint. Standard values of material consumption, labour hours and so on are established. Once the target cost is set, production begins. Performance evaluation of target costing is then implemented after about three months (since abnormal values can arise during the early stages).

10.2.12 The performance evaluation of target costing is implemented to examine the degree to which the target cost is achieved. If the target cost is not achieved, investigations are made to clarify where the responsibility lies and where the gap arises. These investigations also evaluate the effectiveness of the target costing activities. Once production is under way, kaizen costing can begin. Kaizen costing activities include cost reduction activities which require changes in the way the company manufactures existing products.

10.2.13 Roughly classified, kaizen costing activities are of two kinds. One consists of activities implemented to enhance actual performance when the difference between actual cost and target cost is large after new products have been in production for, say, three months. This entails implementing activities periodically to reduce any differences between target and estimated profit and to achieve 'allowable cost'.

10.2.14 The second category of kaizen costing aids in reaching cost reduction targets established for every department as a result of the short-term profit plan. Thus, for example, the variable costs such as direct materials, energy and direct labour costs are managed by setting the amount of kaizen cost per unit of each product type. Fixed costs are subjected to 'management by objectives' based on the overall amount of kaizen cost instead of the amount of kaizen cost per unit.

The basis for target costing

Function	Assembly number			Model					Name			
	Part number	Part name	Quantity	Process	A	B	C	Material cost	Purchased part cost $	Direct labour cost		
										Dept. $	Worker hours (min.)	Amount $

Worksheet 10.1

609

Target cost management

10.3 Target costing principles

10.3.1 Target costing as mentioned above entails the analysis of a product and/or process design by estimating a target cost. The actual design of the product and/or process to meet that cost is then undertaken. According to Dutton and Ferguson (1996), who explored the approach at Texas Instruments, certain principles can guide the target costing exercise. These include the following.

- Customers and competition in the market place determine market-based prices.
- Value for the customer is a function of the relationship between features, function, price and quality.
- Product decisions are based on the target costing formula 'expected sales price − target profit = target cost'.
- Profit planning is done over the product life-cycle.
- Accountability for product profit, cost and customer satisfaction are assigned to the same individual (i.e., strong product management).
- Cost-estimating skills are dispersed into the organisations where the skills are required (i.e., people in the design group have cost-estimating skills).
- Capital investment planning is linked to profitability and the costs associated with product development and delivery.
- Product development is linked with customer desires and to achieving a sustainable competitive advantage.
- Cost awareness, commitment, and accountability are generally pervasive in the organisation.
- Key members of the value chain become involved early in the planning and design process.

Design efforts focus on market-driven variables for quality and on reducing total cost of ownership.

A case study: implementing target costing

10.3.2 Dutton and Ferguson (1996) discuss target costing at the Digital Imaging Business Group at Texas Instrument. They note that Digital Imaging has applied target costing successfully in a potentially revolutionary technology called 'developed digital light processing' (DLP™), which is

Target costing principles

an all-digital solution for creating images using breakthrough reflective technology. DLP™ creates a new standard for image quality in projection displays, on-demand printing, and other applications. The DLP™ technology accurately controls and applies light to create images using a digital light switch (a digital micromirror device, or DMD™). DLP™ is the only all-digital imaging solution that precisely controls light in space and amplitude.

10.3.3 A DMD™ is a digital light switch with more than a half-million microscopic mirrors mounted on a complementary metal oxide semiconductor (CMOS) memory microchip. These highly reflective aluminium mirrors allow TI's customers to handle digital output from an all-digital source to create a front- or rear-projection display, make a high-quality printed image, or achieve other optically processed digital output. These mirrors allow incident light to be turned 'on' or 'off' pixel by pixel to position light on a target accurately. By varying the time the mirrors remain on or off, grey-scale images are created. The mirrors are turned on or off according to digital information stored in the memory cells beneath the mirrors.

The voice of the customer
10.3.4 Particular design decisions and planned offerings of the DLP-based subsystems have been influenced by the voice of the customer. Examples of these major decisions include:

- better definition of large-screen requirements for video graphics and text displays;
- understanding and influencing the emerging multimedia and high-definition television (HDTV) standards and requirements.

10.3.5 Since 1992, TI has been developing DLP subsystem solutions through prototype display systems. TI has moved beyond the prototype stages to its present-day interaction with leading projection-display, television, and computer manufacturers. To be successful, TI must fundamentally change the current video market, in which cathode ray tubes (CRTs) and liquid crystal displays (LCDs) have worked well and have been cost effective for a wide range of display applications.

10.3.6 CRTs dominate the rear-projection television market now because of their superior image and lower cost compared with LCD alternatives. LCD displays, on the other hand, have been used successfully in the portable professional projector market. TI's DLP technology will provide higher-quality, lower-cost solutions.

Target cost management

10.3.7 By focusing on high-end niches (e.g., professional class video projectors, front- and rear-projection home video systems, and portable business projectors), TI is preparing for broad acceptance and ultimate penetration into a number of consumer channels with DLP-based systems. In the future, TI sees many potential applications for front-and rear-screen projectors, including an all-digital personal computer display with a much cleaner signal, purer colours, and far more accuracy than traditional CRT screens which use scan lines rather than digital technology. TI is also developing subsystems to address the on-demand colour print market (which differ significantly from the printers now used because of their much higher volumes).

10.3.8 TI's strategy is to market these systems through original equipment manufacturers (OEMs) and to provide major subsystems. This process of designing and providing completed subsystems for customer integration is a departure from TI's heritage of supplying semiconductors and components, but it is strongly tied to TI's emerging strength in anticipating the need for digital solutions versus non-differentiated commodity microchips. Meeting costing targets will enable TI to demonstrate significant price and performance advantages to penetrate these highly competitive high-tech markets.

10.3.9 It became apparent from the outset of TI's strategic venture into DLP imaging systems that history and experience were poor predictors of the future. The technology was so radically different from anything else on the market that few relevant historical data points were available for planning purposes. Although risk and uncertainty were high, TI is striving to reduce both risk and uncertainty by replanning product mix, profits and costs regarding particular market opportunities and supply-chain alliances.

10.3.10 Target costing, therefore, is more than just a cost reduction technique; it is part of a comprehensive strategic profit management system.

10.3.11 TI is applying target costing to execute a forward-integration strategy to enter competitive markets that already have large, well-entrenched competitors and technologies. Competition in high technology industries is fierce and fast, so time-to-market is critical. Early entrants often fill market niches and enjoy significant cost advantages unavailable to followers for several years. Through extensive production preparation techniques, TI is gradually moving down the cost curve to achieve target cost goals before full-scale production begins.

A strategic decision: the product feature set
10.3.12 In high-technology industries, marketers and competitors listen to the voice of the customer when defining the product and feature set.

Target costing principles

Customers generally want a plethora of features at a bargain price, and marketers frequently assume the role of the representatives of the customer. Engineering is then faced with the daunting task of trying to accommodate these customer demands. Often intense negotiations occur between marketing and engineering about product specifications because engineers tend to think and describe products in technical terms, while marketers tend to think and describe products in the language consumers use. Target costing provides tools to evaluate the many trade-offs and compromises that must inevitably be made to meet target costs yet still support the product concept.

Setting the market price
10.3.13 Target costing uses a product's feature set to identify a target market price. Projected price-performance characteristics are judged against market proxies to estimate market penetration rates and volume. Projected prices for DLP products are compared against projected future prices for competing products and technologies.

10.3.14 For imaging applications, measures of customer value can be either qualitative (e.g., 'better than Brand X') or quantitative (e.g., 'number of pixels' or 'brightness'). In the hardcopy markets, speed (e.g., pages per minute) is a key differentiator. These projections may also be associated with competitors' brand names when such elements are relevant in the analysis (for example, marketing may project that Competitor Z will introduce new product Y in the spring of 2002 at a specific price point and with certain specific features).

Cost tables: the key to cost estimation
10.3.15 According to Dutton and Ferguson (1996) cost estimation depends in large part on reliable historical cost data. Cost tables at TI contain information regarding current and prospective costs from current and potential suppliers; they also show internal costs associated with the transformation of materials or the assembly of components. The information contained in cost tables is used at different levels of aggregation, such as total product cost, function-level costs, subassembly costs, and part-level costs (see Figure 10.2). TI applies the cost table information to an exploded bill of materials with target cost goals and the latest revised estimates by part and major subassembly.

Closing the gap
10.3.16 Engineers at TI use design-to-cost and value engineering approaches to set target costs, then evaluate designs in terms of their ability to satisfy customer requirements and achieve target-cost goals. This process is called 'closing the gap' between the cost estimate and the target cost for

Target cost management

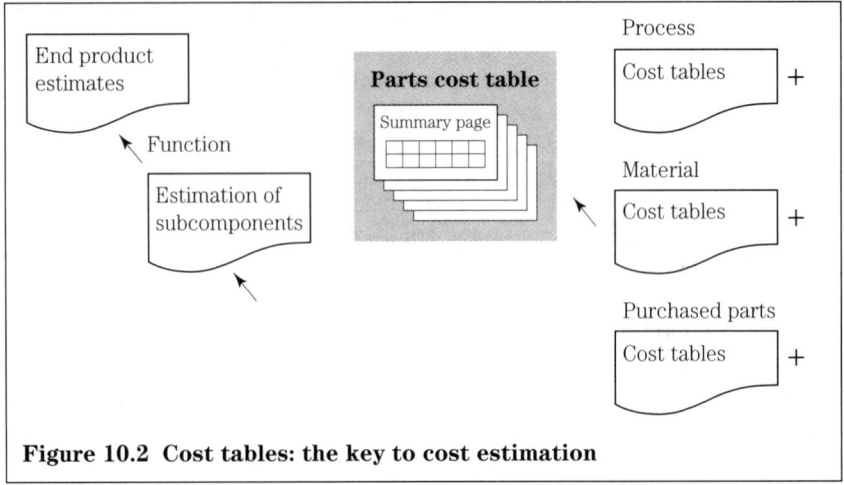

Figure 10.2 Cost tables: the key to cost estimation

potential designs (see Figure 10.3 on page 615). In new product development, TI establishes alliances with suppliers and original equipment manufacturers (OEMs). By planning the allowable costs throughout the value chain, target costing yields a valuable strategic and competitive advantage for all participants. Effective target costing thus requires co-operative, non-adversarial relationships with both suppliers and customers.

Exhibit 1 An overview of target costing

Source: Consortium for Advanced Manufacturing-International (CAM-I)

Exhibit 2 Cost reductions in the electronics industry

Customers expect continuous cost reductions and technical improvements. Competitors aggressively seek price advantage in the market place. Innovation in process and products moves products to new cost curves.

Source: Consortium for Advanced Manufacturing-International (CAM-I).

10.4 Target costing as an integrative management process

10.4.1 Kato, Böer and Chow (1995) consider target costing to be much more than a simple technique of setting cost targets. They see it as an integrative mechanism to link the various functional areas of a business into a coherent system. In companies that have used target costing successfully,

Target costing as an integrative management process

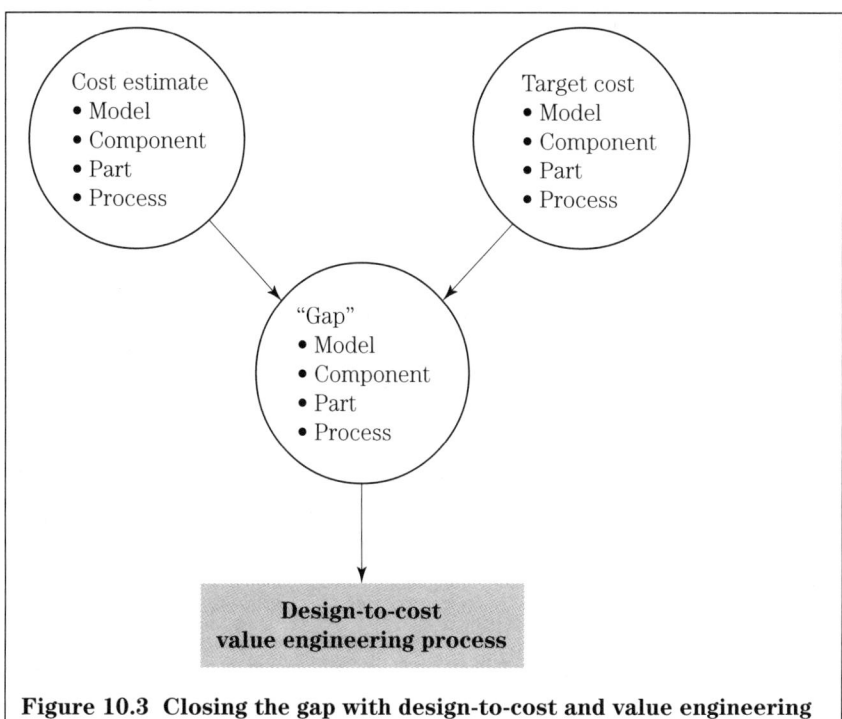

Figure 10.3 Closing the gap with design-to-cost and value engineering

information flows smoothly among marketing researchers, product designers, manufacturing personnel, and cost analysts. The target costing process is closely tied to the strategic planning process because target costing encompasses a broad range of both upstream and downstream costs from manufacturing. At the implementation level, target cost systems are linked to nearer-term operations by drawing on the medium-term profit plan for the profit targets used in the target cost computation:

$$[\text{Sales price} - \text{Target profit} = \text{Target cost}]$$

10.4.2 Target costing requires managers and engineers to estimate constantly the production cost of a product as it moves through the design process. They need to draw on information from all parts of the organisation. Instead of being a passive and isolated element of the management process, target costing is an active component that transcends the narrow boundaries of particular enterprise functional areas.

10.4.3 Target costing is a tool that seems to hold significant promise because it:

Target cost management

- is future oriented;
- focuses designers' attention on the cost implications of design decisions;
- helps managers to evaluate the profitability of a product before it is produced.

10.4.4 Like many other management techniques, target costing has some pitfalls. Kato, Böer and Chow (1995) report on case studies of Japanese firms which have implemented target costing. They discuss some of the problems that target costing can create. They view target costing as part of a comprehensive strategic profit management system that focuses on reducing the life-cycle costs of new products while also improving their quality and reliability. Managers accomplish this feat by examining and pursuing cost-reduction opportunities upstream of production (i.e., in research and development, product concept development, and product design) as well as in the early phases of production.

10.4.5 In one example, the authors discuss the phases of target costing at Daihatsu Motors as follows. Daihatsu Motors is a leading manufacturer of high-quality mini-vehicles such as small passenger cars, trucks and utility vehicles. It is one of the few auto manufacturers to have actually developed a working electric automobile. The company achieved wide recognition in the 1950s with its 'Midget' series of vehicles, which were popular in Japan as well as in the US.

10.4.6 At Daihatsu Motors, the target costing process passes through three phases:

(1) Phase 1, the period prior to the development of target costing;
(2) Phase 2, the development of target costing;
(3) Phase 3, the integration of target costing and the profit management system.

10.4.7 The activities characterising each phase are identified below by Kato, Böer and Chow (1995).

Phase 1

10.4.8 Phase 1 was the period preceding development of target costing. In 1960, Daihatsu Motors began a concerted effort to co-ordinate cost-reduction activities throughout the business. It was one of the first and most active com-

Target costing as an integrative management process

panies in the use of value analysis, especially for purchased parts, which make up about 70 per cent of the company's manufacturing cost.

10.4.9 The production engineering department at headquarters took charge of evaluating purchased parts but was unsatisfied with the process used for evaluating suppliers. Specifically, engineers were uncomfortable with choosing suppliers based solely on quoted prices. They wanted some more rational method for developing estimated cost of components for use in evaluating supplier prices.

10.4.10 Therefore, Daihatsu established a new cost-control section within the production engineering department. This group of ten engineers who had received special training in value analysis began their work by:

- developing the concept of cost tables to provide a sound basis for estimating the costs of purchased components;
- expanding their work to include examinations of product drawings to find possible cost reductions.

10.4.11 Through intensive application of value analysis and value engineering, this group made significant progress in reducing the cost of purchased parts. The group later expanded its activities to include other cost categories, such as supplies and materials. In 1966, the group moved out of the production engineering department and became a separate cost-control department. Its activities shifted away from value analysis (which emphasises cost reduction of current products that have existing designs) to value engineering (which emphasises cost reduction involving changes in product designs). Nonetheless, the engineers still focused on reducing the costs of current models (instead of new models) on a part-by-part basis rather than on the vehicle as a whole.

Phase 2

10.4.12 Phase 2 at Daihatsu covered the development of target costing. Daihatsu continued to improve the quality of the cost data in the cost tables used for assessing supplier quotes. These tables enabled Daihatsu engineers to:

- provide advice to suppliers on supplier cost improvement;
- critically evaluate supplier price quotes;
- learn more about the cost structures of its suppliers.

10.4.13 Daihatsu engineers wanted to know more than just the price a supplier could provide. They also wanted to understand the cost structure

617

Target cost management

of their suppliers. Cost tables contributed to this understanding. As their knowledge of supplier cost structures grew, the engineers at Daihatsu performed value analyses for suppliers and thus became more like consultants to the suppliers than business adversaries.

10.4.14 In 1969, the cost-control department at Daihatsu was dissolved. Most of its functions were absorbed by the purchasing department; the remainder were spread among the production engineering and accounting departments. This change was made because Daihatsu's manufacturing expenditures were concentrated in purchased parts, so it seemed logical to focus value analysis and value engineering efforts on the largest expenditures. Concurrent with this move, Daihatsu made its first trial application of value analysis and value engineering to the total vehicle (i.e., rather than to components of the vehicle). A contributing factor to this expanded scope was the ability of the accounting department to forecast profit for a vehicle while it was still being developed. In 1970, the accounting department prepared 'The Target Costing Implementation Manual' to define the target costing roles and responsibilities of each business unit in the organisation. Organisational changes occurred at the same time that the Manual was released. The technology management department established a cost section staffed by experienced target costing personnel whose responsibility was to:

- answer cost-related questions from other business units;
- communicate target cost information to and from the design department.

10.4.15 This organisational change signalled a significant shift in target costing activities away from the purchasing of parts toward the design of new products. Daihatsu managers decided to take the experience they had accumulated in working with suppliers to reduce costs and apply this experience to upstream processes – namely, product design. This change also reflected management's realisation that the key to cost reduction lies not in making manufacturing more efficient but, rather, in making design more effective.

10.4.16 Although Daihatsu made progress with target costing, top managers were still not completely satisfied with the results. Cost specialists were scattered throughout the company in technology management, production engineering, product design, purchasing and accounting. Each group used target costing to further its own objectives. The accounting department's attempts to act as mediator were never entirely successful. Moreover, with the target costing personnel scattered throughout the organisation, little formal or informal communication took place among them.

Target costing as an integrative management process

Nevertheless, the spread of target costing ideas throughout Daihatsu did increase management's awareness of the technique, and it laid the foundation for the next – and final – stage in its development.

Phase 3

10.4.17 Phase 3 of target costing at Daihatsu involved the integration of target costing and the profit management system. The oil crisis in the mid-1970s caused Daihatsu's managers to scrutinise the organisation to find places where costs could be cut and output increased. Target costing, which was scattered throughout the company, was one function that received special scrutiny. Ultimately, management decided to consolidate target costing activities into a new group called the cost management department with three sections:

(1) cost management;
(2) target costing;
(3) cost improvement

10.4.18 This organisational arrangement prevailed at Daihatsu until 1984, when the decision was made to absorb target costing into the advanced technology office, a unit whose responsibility was to promote and forecast future technology developments. This change was made in part because of the second oil crisis, which made Daihatsu managers realise that they had to move even further upstream with their cost-planning activities if they were to survive in the increasingly global economy. That is, managers realised that the greatest potential for cost reduction would come from new developments in technology that could produce products with high quality and low price. They hoped that this organisational location for the target cost group would enable the business to develop target costs for products that were still in the conceptual stage of development.

Management planning systems

10.4.19 The further upstream the target costing process moved, the more it resembled the management planning system the business used. In 1985, Daihatsu managers formally recognised this growing association and made target costing an integral part of their profit management system. Management no longer looked on target costing as a cost-reduction tool. Instead, target costing was considered a comprehensive profit management tool that applied to the entire organisation. Daihatsu centralised the cost management functions at company headquarters in part to promote cost consciousness throughout the business. Managers focused their attention on:

Target cost management

- understanding the business's basic cost structure; and
- identifying non-value added cost drivers.

10.4.20 Central managers wanted to locate and eliminate structural problems instead of engaging in temporary layoffs and plant closing. Target costing, with its focus on total cost reduction at the global level, provided a useful perspective for identifying and eliminating structural factors that add no value to the business or its products.

10.4.21 Daihatsu made further major organisational changes in an attempt to flatten its organisation and to speed decision-making whereby target costing was affected.

Procedural aspects of target costing

10.4.22 Daihatsu followed a number of procedures when it developed the various data used in its target costing process. Two especially important procedures were:

- developing target profit computations; and
- setting target costs.

10.4.23 When developing target profit computations, Daihatsu began by analysing its profit plan. Its medium-term (approximately three-year) profit plan provides the profit targets Daihatsu used to compute the product margins (revenue – variable costs), product contribution (product margin – product-specific fixed costs), and operating profit. As the business developed its profit plan, it did no target costing for specific products; instead, average costs of product families were used. Similarly, Daihatsu's estimated sales prices were developed by the product planning office based on market research techniques and procedures that focus on pricing by function.

10.4.24 As Kato, Böer and Chow (1995) note throughout this process, Daihatsu's managers stressed the importance of achieving profit targets. Target costs were a means to profitability, so meeting the target cost and missing the profit target was unacceptable. Although Daihatsu considered target costing a company-wide activity, cost-reduction activities occurred at the product level. Each product manager worked to reduce the costs of his product; communication among these managers was important to the attainment of the business's profit target. Consequently, Daihatsu organised its target costing activities into three major sections, each of which had a sub-section that considered related activities (see Figure 10.4). The sales section illustrated in Figure 10.4 was the most recent addition to the co-ordination

Target costing as an integrative management process

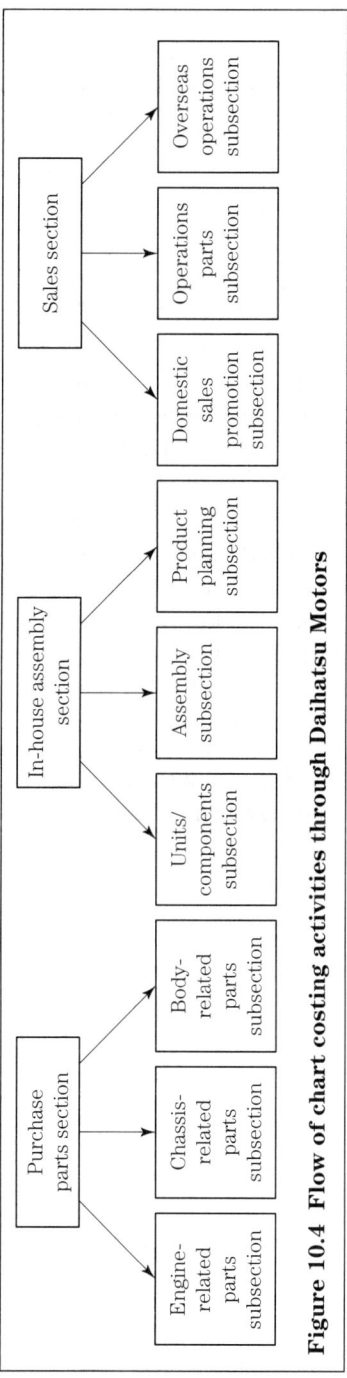

Figure 10.4 Flow of chart costing activities through Daihatsu Motors

Target cost management

sections. It was established to recognise the importance of sales-related information to target costing activities. This section also ensured that product managers focused on attaining target profits, which is the ultimate goal of target costing. The sales section also directly linked target costs to such market considerations as product features, product functions and product specifications.

Consumer perspective

10.4.25 The consumer's perspective was taken into account by the sales section. Example are as follows.

- An attempt was made to reduce claims-processing costs by reducing the number of claims rather than reducing the processing cost per claim. That is, the business tried to reduce costs over the total life-cycle of the product rather than merely reducing the manufacturing costs of the product.

- Daihatsu vehicles were wired for sophisticated audio systems, even though some vehicles included only ordinary radios. Although this wiring increased the cost of the individual vehicle, market research indicated that customers liked this feature because it allowed them to customise their audio system without having to pay for extra wiring.

10.4.26 In setting target costs, Daihatsu deducted its desired profit from estimated selling price. However, the development of specific target costs for components was delegated to departments and managers. Business units considered such factors as:

- monthly production volume;
- product life-cycle;
- depreciation conditions;
- production location;
- make-or-buy criteria for parts and components;
- foreign exchange rates.

10.4.27 If a competitor's introduction of a product while Daihatsu was designing a new one forced product designers to change their own design (thus increasing costs), the mid-range profit target was not reduced. Instead, managers looked for ways to:

- increase sales volume or sales price;
- decrease other costs to keep the profit target attainable.

Critical activities

10.4.28 In Daihatsu's target costing process, the critical activities took place during concept development. Daihatsu managers knew that carefully prepared cost-reduction programmes at the product concept development stage significantly reduced the actual production cost of the finished unit. This stage requires Daihatsu employees to do the following.

- Collect information.
- Tear down and evaluate competitors' products.
- Learn from experience with current production.
- Balance quality and costs.
- Conduct value engineering studies.

10.4.29 Each of these critical activities is described below.

Collecting information

10.4.30 Daihatsu managers evaluate new technologies for possible use in new vehicles in terms of potential applications, reliability, stability and cost. Although the focus is on cost-reduction ideas, managers also want to add value to products. That is, they look for ways to increase profitability rather than simply reduce costs.

Tear down and evaluate competitors' products

10.4.31 Daihatsu engineers tear down and evaluate competitors' products, the objectives being as follows.

- To gather information on technologies used.
- To identify other cost-reduction possibilities.

10.4.32 Daihatsu employees have become so skilled at teardowns that they can estimate competitors' production costs from the information derived.

Learn from experience with current production

10.4.33 When products enter the production process, problems inevitably arise that the designers did not anticipate. At Daihatsu, these problems were carefully investigated. Results from value engineering and hands-on knowledge about how to solve these problems were entered into a database for use on future product design projects. Value analysis and value engineering databases play an important role in product design and help designers to avoid many problems.

Target cost management

Balance quality and costs

10.4.34 Quality costing at Daihatsu focuses mainly on the elimination or reduction of quality costs at the design phase rather than after products enter production. Managers constantly discuss the appropriate level of quality for a product, because they know that, beyond some level, quality has no impact on sales yet may still increase costs. Consequently, managers attempt to balance quality considerations that increase sales against the incremental cost of producing those sales. These discussions do not focus on production costs; instead, their focus is on the life-cycle costs of the vehicle. That is, managers attempt to create the maximum profit by gaining the optimal difference between a vehicle's life-cycle costs and its selling price.

Conduct value engineering

10.4.35 Engineers perform numerous value engineering studies on parts, production processes, facilities, materials and spoilage levels to search for ways to bring estimated production cost within the range of the target cost. As part of this analysis, engineers look for ways to use common dies and moulds for parts because of the high cost of producing new dies or moulds. This is an iterative process. Value engineering analyses generate suggested improvements that are fed into the cost-estimating system. These analyses, together with estimates from purchasing and production technology, are used to create a new estimated production cost. If that cost exceeds the target cost, the value engineering process starts again for both purchased parts and parts made in-house.

10.4.36 Once project managers derive an estimated cost consistent with the target cost, they present it as a final proposal at a meeting of the cost committee, which consists of Daihatsu's chairman, president, vice-presidents and other executives. At the end of this meeting, the final target cost is agreed on and becomes the formal goal of the organisation. Periodic cost committee meetings are held throughout the remainder of the design process to ensure that the target cost will be met when the product goes into production.

Reducing cost at the detail design stage

10.4.37 Once a product concept is approved for further development, designers move into the next stage of product design; the detailed drawing stage. Drawings of all parts and components of the product are prepared with precise specifications of all dimensions, materials and components. Design of the manufacturing process required for the product occurs while engineers are developing detailed product drawings.

10.4.38 Daihatsu engineers prepare trial drawings that serve as the basis for building trial vehicles. Making the trial vehicles brings technical problems to light that engineers must solve before making a design final. Cost estimates are then developed based on the trial vehicles to assess conformance to target costs.

Reducing cost at the mass production stage

10.4.39 Because of all the cost-reduction activities carried out before production begins, Daihatsu presented a challenging cost standard for production. As Kato, Böer and Chow (1995) note, at the production stage Daihatsu calls its cost-control activities 'cost maintenance'. The major focus in production is to prevent costs from moving upward rather than to reduce costs to a lower level.

10.4.40 Daihatsu set its cost standards three months after production began by using the following process.

- The first three months of production were used to work out any remaining minor problems.
- The actual cost for the stabilised production at the end of the three months was used as the standard cost for future operations (provided that the actual cost of stabilised operations met the target cost). The target cost was used as the standard cost if the cost of stabilised operations exceeded the target cost.

10.4.41 Thus, if design could not meet the target cost, production had to develop ways to reduce costs. As one might imagine, this process causes some friction between production and design, but Daihatsu attempts to manage this discord by rewarding production managers for continuously improving their processes.

10.4.42 An important element of target costing at Daihatsu was the creation of a cost-improvement committee to co-ordinate the cost-maintenance activities. This committee included:

- the product manager;
- the vice-president of cost management;
- the plant manager;
- the engineering works manager.

10.4.43 The group discussed possible cost reductions and formed task forces to work on specific cost-reduction projects.

Target cost management

10.4.44 According to Kato, Böer and Chow (1995), some key observations from their investigations are as follows.

- Short- or medium-term profit plans were closely linked to target costing and provide critical input.

- Target costing was used to pull together employees from diverse functions.

- Continuous updating of projected production costs for the products under development was stressed. Each business followed a formal sequential process in which product costs were estimated at certain critical phases in the process. Daihatsu estimated its production costs upstream and also estimated quality costs on an ex ante basis as it considered trade-offs between product features.

- A constant emphasis was placed on profit attainment. Daihatsu managers emphasised that profit attainment was more important than meeting target cost goals.

- Target costing was used as a holistic management system that integrated all the diverse functions of the businesses. Marketing, production, accounting, product design and customer service all worked together to make the target costing system function smoothly.

10.4.45 Ultimately, businesses adopt their own style of target costing (Daihatsu followed a relatively structured approach to target costing). The contrasts in the products the businesses make probably had an impact though each company evidences corporate specificities which are product independent.

10.4.46 The studies carried out by Kato, Böer and Chow (1995) make it clear that target costing is much more than an accounting technique given that it:

- integrates diverse functions in the business;

- permeates the planning process;

- stimulates communication among important functions in the business.

10.4.47 Target costing is an ongoing process that involves all aspects of the business, from product design to material handling, from customer service to inventory management, and from financial management to product assembly. It cannot be implemented by accounting alone.

10.5 Implementation issues

10.5.1 Two major changes in operating environments have led managers to recognise that cost considerations should be addressed earlier in the product life-cycle, according to Fisher (1995). First, automation has changed the cost structure of many companies, so more costs are fixed in the short run. This change in cost mix has caused less emphasis on typical management accounting tools such as cost-volume-profit analysis and break-even analysis. Given a high level of automation, most production costs are determined in the product planning and design stages, so reducing product costs dramatically in the production stage is difficult, if not impossible. Most of the life-cycle of a product is determined by the time the design stage is completed.

10.5.2 Second, shortening of the product life-cycle has increased the importance of delivering a competitive product to the market quickly. Any errors in product cost or product quality are difficult to correct quickly because product life-cycles are so short.

10.5.3 Historically, most cost reduction and cost control efforts have focused on the production stage of the product life-cycle. Budgeting and standard cost systems are prime examples of this type of cost control. The chief concern at the product planning and design stages has been product performance and product scheduling, with little attention to product cost. Unfortunately, almost all production capabilities and costs are set during production planning and design; they are fixed once production begins.

10.5.4 The lack of concern about product cost in the product planning and design stages may cause reduced profitability. Because of changes in the business environment, many companies now recognise the importance of cost reduction efforts early in the product life-cycle. There is far more opportunity for cost reduction early in the product life-cycle (i.e., during the planning and design stages) than there is later in the life-cycle (production). Target costing in this light may be considered to be a systematic process for reducing product costs that begins in the product planning stage.

10.5.5 Following a comparison of target costing at Matsushita and Toyota, Fisher (1995) reports that both companies find target costing to be a valuable – if not the most important – tool in reducing product cost. However, managers at both companies note several difficulties in implementing it.

10.5.6 Difficulty in estimating product costs, prices and volumes leads to a less effective target costing system. As uncertainty increases, variables are

Target cost management

estimated with less precision, and the technique becomes less powerful. For example, high environmental uncertainty may cause difficulty in determining target price and target volume. Without good estimates of price and volume, target profit is difficult to determine, which means that a target cost also becomes problematical. High production uncertainty may cause difficulty in estimating cost, which can make the difference between estimated and target cost difficult to determine. Because of the importance of variable estimates, target costing has been used most effectively by companies that make incremental changes (i.e., model changes) rather than revolutionary products.

Target costing should directly address costs at the product planning and design stages
10.5.7 The focus of cost management can at time sway toward manufacturing costs but as product planning and design increase in importance, companies may need to apply target costing to these functions as well.

A case study: market strategy and target costing

10.5.8 Accounting and marketing policies interact when managers make decisions relating to costing, pricing, products differentiation and distribution issues. The Batdorf and Bronson case highlights the difficulties which such interaction raises.

Introduction
10.5.9 'Good morning, Batdorf and Bronson! How may we help you?' And so starts another day at Batdorf and Bronson (B&B), one of the country's premier coffee roasters. The employees of B&B share three common characteristics; (1) a passion for coffee, (2) an above average intellect, and (3) an interest in a variety of outside activities. In fact, B&B so values these characteristics that they represent the qualifications considered for anyone offered employment with the company. Although B&B employees recognise and value these commonalities, they also share one unexpected characteristic: a general lack of familiarity with accounting and other financial information. Today, those working at B&B have been forced to acknowledge that accounting/operating information is playing a bigger role in their decision-making processes. As a result, B&B's employees have been working hard recently to develop their understanding of the roles marketing and accounting play in operating their growing business.

10.5.10 Almost 85 per cent of B&B's total 1995 sales were to wholesale customers (e.g., cafes, carts, kiosks and restaurants). Retail locations and the mail order catalogue generated the remaining sales. Over the past 10

Implementation issues

years, the company's loyal customer base and word-of-mouth marketing have resulted in rapid and continuous growth in wholesale operations (see Figure 10.5). However, B&B anticipates sustaining growth by opening production facilities in new geographic markets (the Minneapolis roastery opened in 1994) and using new distribution channels (mail order sales). These strategic initiatives pressure B&B's management/staff to better understand both their potential markets and the costs associated with serving those markets.

	1991	1992	1993	1994	1995
Wholesale: Olympia	$598,725	$758,089	$996,855	$1,302,004	$1,744,140
Minneapolis	0	0	0	653,103	1,601,560
Retail stores	400,335	420,387	447,390	474,354	568,300
Mail order	0	11,374	16,585	20,789	33,750
Total sales	$999,060	$1,189,850	$1,460,830	$2,450,250	$3,947,750

Figure 10.5 Summary of sales by distribution channel

10.5.11 B&B's management has identified three aspects of current operations that could affect the feasibility of entering new coffee markets.

- *The highly competitive coffee market.* The coffee market, once dominated solely by supermarket coffee suppliers (Folgers and Maxwell House), has accommodated sales of specialty coffees (premium price/high quality coffees) as a new market segment. Consumers of specialty coffees represent approximately 12 per cent of the total coffee market and include individuals, cafes and restaurants. B&B tries to appeal to the top 25 per cent of the individual customers in the specialty coffee market segment and the top 33 per cent of cafe/restaurant customers. This market segment has become very attractive to coffee suppliers because of its sales growth and income potential.

- *B&B's current marketing strategy.* In positioning B&B in the specialty coffee market, company management considered four dimensions: price, quality, flexibility, and deliverability. These competitive dimensions represent a consistent force affecting B&B's decision making.

- *B&B's current cost structure.* As B&B's president has said, 'Batdorf & Bronson's profits are a result of providing the best product and service we can. If we focus on roasting coffee and serving our customers, the financial aspects will take care of themselves.' B&B views coffee roasting as an art, and their success has depended on their artistic skills. This commitment to roasting excellence has resulted in financial/cost structure issues taking a secondary role within the company. In fact, the company's current financial information system provides reports to facilitate tax return preparation rather than financial reporting or cost management.

The competitive coffee market

10.5.12 Three elements of the coffee market are analysed in this section; (1) industry history, (2) B&B's company history within the industry, and (3) trade associations within the industry.

Industry history

10.5.13 The US coffee market historically has focused on supplying customers with low-quality, high-caffeine products, using grocery store-based distribution channels. Companies such as Folgers, Maxwell House, and Hills Brothers have dominated this segment of the coffee industry. In 1962, American coffee consumption peaked on a per capita basis at about 3.1 cups per day. From 1963 through 1988, coffee consumption continued to decline overall. Today, coffee consumption is 1.8 cups per person per day.

10.5.14 In the late 1980s, however, specialty coffees began demonstrating significant growth. Using high-quality beans (known as varietals), coffee roasters around the country began producing coffees to serve the expanding specialty coffee market. In addition, many of these roasters began offering coffee drinks such as espresso, cappuccino or variations of them.

10.5.15 The industry leader in specialty coffee is Starbucks Inc. Starbucks emphasises the importance of varietal quality in the roasting process. They also recognise the potential for retail sales in coffee-house/restaurant settings. Initially operating exclusively in Seattle, Starbucks focused on mail order sales and word-of-mouth marketing to increase sales. Although sales grew by pursuing that strategy, Starbucks' management believed that more significant sales and profit growth was possible through retail locations. As Ted Tingle of the Specialty Coffee Association of America observed, 'For a long time, the focus was on coffee bean retailing; then Starbucks figured out the real money is in beverage retailing'. Having gone public in 1992, Starbucks now operates more than 600 company-owned retail locations and an additional 50 kiosk sites located in high-traffic areas such as malls and airports. Historically, Starbucks identified locations for future stores by targeting areas that have exhibited a strong mail order demand for the company's products.

Company history

10.5.16   B&B began roasting coffee in Olympia, Washington, in 1986, and sales of coffee have grown rapidly since that time. The company is committed to offering the highest quality coffee (in terms of bean quality and final product freshness) and providing exceptional customer service. As a result, the company has maintained a 'roast-to-order' approach to the roasting process. The roast-to-order philosophy has implications for both marketing and accounting.

- Coffee is shipped within 24 hours of roasting to ensure freshness.
- Customers get the coffee they want, when they want it, in the right quantity.
- B&B maintains virtually no work-in-process inventory.
- Roast-to-order production costs per pound are higher.

B&B's current marketing strategy

10.5.17   B&B sells moderately priced coffees to wholesale and retail customers by delivery via United Parcel Service (UPS). Management has established a market niche for B&B's products through three strategies: product differentiation, alternative distribution channel utilisation, and moderate pricing as opposed to premium pricing.

Product differentiation

10.5.18   As one employee stated, 'We will try and do whatever it takes to please the customer'. B&B has attempted to differentiate their products along three dimensions;

- *Quality*, commitment to both product and customer service excellence;
- *Deliverability*, shipping to customers within 24 hours of roasting; and
- *Flexibility*, adherence to the roast-to-order philosophy.

Distribution channels

10.5.19   B&B operates one retail store and has recently begun offering mail order/catalogue sales. However, B&B's main focus is on wholesale accounts. At this time, B&B has decided to increase sales through wholesale and mail order distribution channels rather than to expand their retail store operations through additional company-owned locations or franchises. The company has also avoided offering brewing equipment such as espresso machines because of the difficulty of maintaining the equipment.

Target cost management

10.5.20 As part of B&B's pursuit of new distribution channels, the company opened their new Minneapolis roastery in 1994. The decision to operate a roastery outside the Olympia area reflects the company's commitment to deliver coffee within 24 hours of roasting to any customer. The new Midwest location allows for quicker deliveries to customers on the East Coast and throughout the Midwest.

10.5.21 B&B's pursuit of additional sales through alternative distribution channels has caused company management to rethink their current product packaging, pricing policies and costing system. For example, sales to wholesale customers from either Olympia or Minneapolis follow B&B's 'rule of thumb' pricing model (see below). Wholesale customers receive their product in standard 5 lb plastic bags. Retail and mail order customers, however, buy B&B's products in 1 lb or 0.5 lb bags. Retail/mail order packaging also is more decorative and, accordingly, more expensive. The labour required to prepare five individual 1 lb bags is substantially more than the labour associated with preparing a single 5 lb bag. Therefore, B&B charges higher prices for their retail and mail orders, but they are somewhat inconsistent in establishing their various retail price points.

B&B's 'rule of thumb' pricing model

10.5.22 Since B&B began operations in 1986, the company has followed this 'rule of thumb' approach for establishing wholesale prices. The model consists of four parts.

(1) *Green bean cost per pound* (Figure 10.6, column 1). The 'green' cost is established by coffee brokers and represents the delivered cost of the green coffee beans. As expected, the market cost of green beans varies across varietals. For example, Columbian beans used for the 'Italian roast' cost $2.14 per lb, whereas Costa Rican 'La Minita' beans cost $3.66 per lb. Because a commodity market exists that prices raw materials on a per pound basis, B&B has always used the 'green' market per pound price as the first cost component for their pricing model.

(2) *Roasting allowance* (Figure 10.6, column 2). Once in the roaster, green beans lose approximately 20 per cent of their weight due to water evaporation. This 'up the stack' loss is accounted for by increasing the green bean cost by 25 per cent. The 25 per cent cost allowance represents the weight lost compared to the net roasting weight. For example, if 100 lb of greens were roasted, the process would yield only 80 lb of roasted beans. The 20 lb lost compared to the 80 lb remaining of roasted coffee result in a 25 per cent (20 lb / 80 lb) cost allowance being added to the initial green cost per pound.

Implementation issues

Varietal/Product type	Green bean cost/lb. (1)	Roasting allowance (2) = #1 × .25	Markup for profit & overhead (3)	Market adjustment (4)	Wholesale price (5) = sum of #1 to #4	Retail or Mail Order price (6)	Price difference (7) = #6 − #5	% price difference (8) = #7 ÷ #5
Columbia Decaffeinated	$2.58	$0.64	$3.00	$0.43	$6.65	$9.80	$3.15	47.37
Columbia "French Roast"	2.27	0.57	3.00	0.31	6.15	9.20	3.05	45.59
Columbia "Italian Roast"	2.14	0.53	3.00	0.63	6.30	9.40	3.10	49.21
Costa Rica SHB	2.18	0.54	3.00	0.33	6.05	8.90	2.85	47.11
Costa Rica "La Minita"	3.66	0.92	3.00	0.72	8.30	11.00	2.70	32.53
Estate Java	2.48	0.62	3.00	0.30	6.40	9.60	3.20	50.00
Ethiopia Harrar	2.58	0.64	3.00	0.43	6.65	10.30	3.65	54.89
Guatemala Antigua	2.48	0.62	3.00	0.35	6.45	9.10	2.65	41.09
Kenya AA	2.89	0.72	3.00	0.44	7.05	9.75	2.70	38.30
Kenya AA Decaffeinated	2.96	0.74	3.00	0.45	7.15	10.40	3.25	45.45
Mexico Altura Pluma	2.28	0.57	3.00	0.25	6.10	9.65	3.55	58.20
Sumatra Mandheling	2.38	0.59	3.00	0.38	6.35	9.55	3.20	50.39
Sumatra Decaffeinated	2.82	0.72	3.00	0.46	7.00	10.85	3.85	55.00
Tanzania Peaberry	2.07	0.52	3.00	0.36	5.95	9.10	3.15	52.94
Yemen Mocha Sarani	3.36	0.84	3.00	0.65	7.85	10.45	2.60	33.12

Figure 10.6 B&B's product line price list based on the 'rule of thumb' pricing mode

Target cost management

(3) *Mark-up for profit and overhead* (Figure 10.6, column 3). Historically, B&B has added a flat $3.00 to the per pound bean cost to 'cover' all other expenses and profit. No changes have been made in this rate since the company's inception 10 years ago.

(4) *Market adjustment* (Figure 10.6, column 4). B&B managers also attempt to keep a reserve 30 to 50 per centfor adjustment of their final wholesale price to position their products appropriately in the market. Their goal is to price B&B's products in the middle (moderate pricing strategy) of comparable coffees offered by competitors.

10.5.23 Although this pricing model has remained unchanged for the past 10 years, both the company's operations and costs have changed radically. Accordingly, B&B is considering revising their pricing model given their rapid sales growth, changing costs and pursuit of sales in alternative markets.

B&B's current cost structure

10.5.24 Three elements of B&B's competitive strategy determine the company's current cost structure.

(1) The roasting process dictates product quality. Therefore, costs associated with the roasting process are viewed as essential and 'worth every penny' because B&B's customers expect high-quality products.

(2) Management's decision to pursue new customers through alternative distribution channels requires a commitment of expenditure for product promotion, new customer identification and continuous customer service. Management considers the costs incurred in these areas essential for B&B's future growth and financial success.

(3) Additional administrative/management staff have been required to keep up with the volume of activity generated by rapidly increasing sales (see B&B's income statement, Figure 10.7).

Roasting process

10.5.25 The four steps in the roasting process include; (1) green coffee bean acquisition, (2) green bean storage, (3) roasting the beans, and (4) packing the roasted beans.

(1) *Green coffee bean acquisition*. The roasting process starts with the acquisition of the 'greens', green coffee beans. At B&B, the master roaster purchases the finest arabica beans on the coffee market. To accomplish this task, she deals with brokers in San Francisco and New

Implementation issues

Sales (see Table 2-4)		$3,947,750
Cost of sales (see Tables 2-5 and 2-6)		
Direct material (beans, scrap and spoilage, and packing/shipping)	2,205,775	
Direct labour	437,559	
Manufacturing overhead	281,874	
Total cost of goods sold		2,925,208
Gross margin		1,022,542
Selling expenses		349,118
Administrative expenses		387,662
Operating income		285,762
Interest expense		35,000
Tax expense		75,650
Net income		$175,112

Figure 10.7 Current Batdorf & Bronson income statement

York City, who in turn deal with importers. These brokers send samples to B&B, which are then roasted and taste tested for quality. Upon approval, B&B purchases a container of beans (250 bags).

(2) *Green coffee bean storage.* Once the beans have been purchased, they are stored by the brokers and later shipped by truck to the two production sites, Olympia and Minneapolis. B&B is charged a storage fee and invoice fee per order. At the production sites, B&B has on hand an average of two to three weeks of inventory. During storage, the greens must be protected from contamination. They need to be kept dry and away from heat since heat accelerates the moisture loss in coffee. In fact, coffee is similar to baking soda in that it absorbs flavours and odours easily. Therefore, extra precautions need to be taken to preserve quality.

(3) *Bean roasting.* B&B buys the beans green and sells them roasted. The beans are roasted to order, a unique characteristic of specialty coffees. Bean roasting is an art, not a science. Each lot of beans reacts differently during the actual roasting process, requiring roasters to rely on their eyes, ears and nose to prepare a perfect batch. It takes three months of training to become a full-fledged roaster. Due to the mental and physical demands placed on these artists, roasters roast only 20 hours per week. At B&B, each 'batch' to be roasted typically begins with 100 lb of green coffee beans being loaded into a hopper, which elevates the beans into the roaster. During the roasting process, the beans

Target cost management

undergo two chemical reactions. The first reaction occurs eight minutes into the roast and is known as the first cracking. At this time, the water in the beans boils and puffs up, causing the bean to increase in volume by two-thirds. The second reaction occurs 11 minutes into the roast, when the interior water of the bean expands, thereby forcing the bean oils to the surface. These oils are important because they are later extracted in water to provide the coffee with its flavour. Upon reaching a temperature of 500°F, the beans are discharged from the roaster into a cooling tray. The beans are cooled quickly to prevent them from roasting further or 'over-cooking'. The cooling tray is equipped with an arm that stirs the beans over the fans to help them cool. Once cooled, the beans are directed through a device known as a de-stoner, which uses a vacuum system to pull the beans up through a pipe and empty them into large containers. Any objects denser than the beans will fall to the ground, so rocks and other foreign objects are eliminated from the coffee.

(4) *Packing the roasted beans*. The final stage in the roasting process is blending or packing. For the orders that request blends of coffee, varietals are blended together in the cooling tray according to a bill of materials that specifies each blend's 'recipe' (mixture of beans). The beans are packed either in 5 lb state-of-the-art gas-barrier valve bags (wholesale) or smaller paper bags for more immediate use (retail/mail order). At this stage, the roasting process is complete and the coffee is ready for distribution.

Product promotion and customer service

10.5.26 B&B has established both a product promotion (new customer support) department and a customer service department to meet the growing customer needs associated with the pursuit of sales through additional distribution channels (see Figure 10.8). The product promotion department, staffed by three people, focuses on; (1) promotional materials (primarily emphasising B&B's national recognition), (2) mail order catalogue support, (3) new customer identification and training, and (4) on-going training for existing customers.

10.5.27 The customer service department, staffed by four people, handles existing customer requests involving; (1) standard orders, (2) special orders, including revisions to standard orders, and (3) customer order follow-up, including concerns and complaints. Customer service representatives require nearly a year of training to become sufficiently knowledgeable about the industry and coffee preparation to respond effectively to customers' questions over the phone.

Implementation issues

Varietal/Product type	Wholesale			Retail/Mail Order			Total sales (7) = #3 + #6
	Price (1)	Pounds sold (2)	Total sales (3) = #1 × #2	Price (4)	Pounds sold (5)	Total sales (6) = #4 × #5	
Columbia Decaffeinated	$6.65	26,824	$178,391	$9.80	2,298	$22,523	$200,914
Columbia "French Roast"	6.15	91,603	563,371	9.20	12,468	114,704	678,075
Columbia "Italian Roast"	6.30	26,551	167,287	9.40	1,781	16,739	184,026
Costa Rica SHB	6.05	100,798	609,840	8.90	17,066	151,883	761,723
Costa Rica "La Minita"	8.30	8,316	69,033	11.00	634	6,971	76,044
Estate Java	6.40	23,032	147,421	9.60	2,655	25,485	172,906
Ethiopia Harrar	6.65	20,657	137,382	10.30	1,969	20,281	157,663
Guatemala Antigua	6.45	10,268	66,240	9.10	416	3,790	70,030
Kenya AA	7.05	28,811	203,134	9.75	1,673	16,310	219,444
Kenya AA Decaffeinated	7.15	18,041	129,009	10.40	1,211	12,587	141,596
Mexico Altura Pluma	6.10	20,170	123,054	9.65	994	9,585	132,639
Sumatra Mandheling	6.35	75,746	480,998	9.55	14,605	139,480	620,478
Sumatra Decaffeinated	7.00	25,041	175,298	10.85	1,679	18,217	193,515
Tanzania Peaberry	5.95	40,373	240,235	9.10	4,653	42,343	282,578
Yemen Mocha Sanani	7.85	7,005	55,007	10.45	110	1,152	56,159
Total sales: pounds and dollars		523,236	$3,345,700		64,212	$602,050	$3,947,750

Figure 10.8 Sales by product and distribution channel

Target cost management

10.5.28   Interviews with the members and managers of each service department revealed their dissatisfaction with the current information system. The typical complaint was that the existing information system was designed for financial information (in reality, the information system focused on tax reporting) rather than customer service information. For example, the customer service manager would like a system which identifies customers who had not ordered from B&B in more than three weeks. A list of this type would provide an excellent source for new sales information and information concerning lost sales. Unfortunately, information of this type is not readily available under the current information system.

Administrative/management staff requirements
10.5.29   B&B's administrative staff consists mainly of persons responsible for accounting functions: chief bookkeeper, accounts receivable clerk and accounts payable clerk. These employees maintain B&B's accounting systems on a day-to-day basis. They also complete monthly financial statements, file payroll reports, and provide an outside accountant with the information necessary to complete quarterly and annual income tax filings. The accounting staff has grown in the last four years from one part-time bookkeeper to three full-time employees. Company management consists of three managers involved with day-to-day operations and two board members/investors who participate in weekly operations committee meetings. The only addition to the group has been Jeanne Pupke, who serves as the chief operating officer for B&B. Recently, these managers have become much more involved in the marketing and accounting of B&B because of the company's growth over the past several years.

B&B's financial performance expectations
10.5.30   This section includes two alternative income statement presentations. The first represents B&B's current income statement, prepared from the existing accounting information system. The alternative provides insight into B&B's cost structure based on a preliminary activity-based costing (ABC) analysis.

Current financial information
10.5.31   As shown in Figure 10.5, B&B's current financial results reflect an operating profit of $285,762 (7.24 per cent of sales). These results compare favourably with the industry leader, Starbucks, whose operating profit margin was 8.62 per cent in 1995. The cost of goods sold includes direct material (bean costs, see Figure 10.9; packaging/shipping supplies costs, see Figure 10.10; and shipping); direct labour (hourly and supervisory wages and benefits); and manufacturing overhead. B&B assumes that these product costs generally are variable with sales (although facility rent and

Implementation issues

Varietal/Product type	Green bean cost/lb (1)	Roasting allowance (2) = #1 × .25	Bean cost per roasted pound (3) #1 + #4	Roasted pounds sold (4)	Cost of beans sold (5) = #3 × #4
Columbia Decaffeinated	$2.58	$0.64	$3.22	29,122	$93,853
Columbia "French Roast"	2.27	0.57	2.84	104,071	295,778
Columbia "Italian Roast"	2.14	0.53	2.67	28,332	75,683
Costa Rica SHB	2.18	0.54	2.72	117,864	319,983
Costa Rica "La Minita"	3.66	0.92	4.58	8,950	40,968
Estate Java	2.48	0.62	3.10	25,687	79,513
Ethiopia Harrar	2.58	0.64	3.22	22,626	72,918
Guatemala Antigua	2.48	0.62	3.10	10,684	33,043
Kenya AA	2.89	0.72	3.61	30,484	109,888
Kenya AA Decaffeinated	2.96	0.74	3.70	19,252	71,018
Mexico Altura Pluma	2.28	0.57	2.85	21,164	60,113
Sumatra Mandheling	2.38	0.59	2.97	90,351	268,273
Sumatra Decaffeinated	2.82	0.72	3.53	26,720	94,053
Tanzania Peaberry	2.07	0.52	2.59	45,062	116,483
Yemen Mocha Sanani	3.36	0.84	4.20	7,115	29,833
Total pounds sold and bean costs				587,448	$1,761400

Figure 10.9 Cost of beans sold

Target cost management

Varietal/Product type	Pounds sold Wholesale (1)	Pounds sold Retail/Mail Order (2)	5-pound Wholesale bags (3)	1-pound Retail/Mail Order bags (4)	½-pound Retail/Mail Order bags (5)
Columbia Decaffeinated	26,824	2,298	5,365	1,532	766
Columbia "French Roast"	91,603	12,468	18,321	9,974	2,494
Columbia "Italian Roast"	26,551	1,781	5,310	1,272	509
Costa Rica SHB	100,798	17,066	20,160	14,840	2,226
Costa Rica "La Minita"	8,316	634	1,663	352	282
Estate Java	23,032	2,655	4,606	1,831	824
Ethiopia Harrar	20,657	1,969	4,131	1,270	698
Guatemala Antigua	10,268	416	2,054	245	171
Kenya AA	28,811	1,673	5,762	1,338	335
Kenya AA Decaffeinated	18,041	1,211	3,608	897	314
Mexico Altura Pluma	20,170	994	4,034	765	229
Sumatra Mandheling	75,746	14,605	15,149	12,171	2,434
Sumatra Decaffeinated	25,041	1,679	5,008	959	720
Tanzania Peaberry	40,373	4,653	8,075	3,325	1,329
Yemen Mocha Sanani	7,005	110	1,401	59	50
Bags required for product sold	523,236	64,212	104,647	50,830	13,381
Less: Allowance for bags wasted: 5 pound (6%) 1 pound (10%) ½ pound (12%)			6,683	5,650	1,824
Total bags consumed in production			111,330	56,480	15,205
Cost per bag			$0.45	$0.80	$0.75
Total packaging costs			$50,100	$45,184	$11,404

Figure 10.10 Cost of packaging/shipping supplies

some other costs remain fixed with volume). Currently, no cost accounting system exists to apply overhead at the product level because B&B has been comfortable with the 'rule of thumb' pricing model used in the past.

10.5.32 The cost categories demonstrating the greatest increases are selling and administrative expenses. With the added volume of sales activity and the additional personnel, costs in these two areas have increased rapidly. The resulting 1995 costs, in fact, show very little resemblance to the selling and administrative costs for 1994. These cost increases reflect management's position that customer service is critical for current and future success.

'Rule of thumb' product pricing model

10.5.33 B&B's current pricing model emphasises simplicity. The model relies on the green bean costs, readily available through the coffee markets, as the basis for establishing product prices. The green bean cost is then adjusted for 'up the stack loss', a standard dollar mark-up and a market adjustment to arrive at a product's price per pound.

Implementation issues

The pricing formula can be defined as follows:		
Product price	=	cost per roasted pound
	+	standard $3.00 mark-up
	+	market adjustment
where		
cost per roasted pound	=	green bean cost per pound × 1.25, the 'up the stack' loss adjustment
standard $3.00 mark-up	=	the adjustment, used since 1986, to approximates of the company's 'other' non-bean costs (or excluded costs) per pound
market adjustment	=	B&B management will attempt to adjust a product's market price within a range of 30 to 50 per cent to position the product as moderately priced compared to competitors

Mark-up pricing model

10.5.34 Traditional mark-up pricing or cost-based pricing was developed as a relatively straightforward approach to product pricing. The assumption is that each product's price must; (1) cover all the costs traceable to the product, (2) assist in covering the organisation's common expenses, and (3) contribute to the organisation's expected level of income. Under this method, a 'product cost' is determined and a product's price is established by 'marking up' the product cost. The pricing equation for this cost-based approach is:

Target price = product cost + [product cost × mark-up percentage]

$$\frac{(\text{Excluded expenses} + \text{income required})}{(\text{Product cost per unit} - \text{sales volume})}$$

where determination of the mark-up percentage is as follows:

excluded expenses	=	expenses not considered in determining product cost per unit.
income required	=	required rate of return × investment (or operating assets)
product cost per unit	=	costs identified with producing a product
sales volume	=	volume of sales expected for the company's products

Target costing

10.5.35 Target costing as noted earlier is a market-based approach that works backwards from a market price to determine an acceptable cost of producing a product or service. In contrast, target pricing represents a cost-based approach for determining the appropriate sales price of products or services. The two techniques are both opposite and complementary.

Target cost management

A computational model for target costing is as follows:

Target cost = sales − excluded expenses − income required

where
sales	=	Σ (sales price per unit × expected sales volume), for all products
excluded expenses	=	all expenses excluded from target cost
income required	=	required rate of return × investment (or operating assets)

10.5.36 The resulting target cost can then be compared to existing product cost estimates to indicate opportunities for cost reduction. For example, if the current product cost exceeds computed target cost, managers have three options; (1) reduce current product costs, (2) eliminate the product based on their company's inability to produce the product at the target cost, or (3) continue offering the unprofitable product because it provides benefits other than those measured by profit (e.g., a large customer demands the product).

10.5.37 Ordinarily, target costing presupposes a focus on the initial product design process. Target costing, however, can also direct managers toward existing products that may be losing their competitive position because of changing costs associated with the product. This is often independently referred to as kaizen costing as explained above.

10.5.38 B&B has always added $3.00 per pound. What cost and profit levels are implicitly included in this standard $3.00 per pound? The following calculation illustrates this.

Total 1995 costs (sales − beans − operating income)	$1,456,213
+ Interest	35,000
+ Return on investment ($1,500,000 × 21.0%)	315,000
Total amount inherent in $3.00 mark-up	$1,806,213
Pounds sold	587,448
Mark-up per pound	$3.07 per pound sold

10.5.39 What is the mark-up per cent for B&B using the current cost structure. The following example illustrates this.

$$\text{Mark-up \%} = \frac{[\text{Total non-material costs} + \text{Return-on-investment}]}{\text{Total material costs}}$$

Implementation issues

10.5.40 Using the above mark-up percentage formula where the 'numerator costs' represent all the costs not included in the denominator costs.

10.5.41 The calculation of the mark-up percentage is as follows.

$$\text{Mark-up \%} = \frac{[\$1{,}456{,}213 + (\$35{,}000 + \$315{,}000)]}{\$2{,}205{,}775} = 81.89\%$$

10.5.42 An example of applying the mark-up percentage can be illustrated using a 5 lb bag of Columbia French Roast. Cost per pound to mark-up is as follows.

Bean cost ($2.84×5 lb)	$14.20
Shipping ($0.58×5 lb)	2.90
Packaging cost (5 lb bag)	0.45
Total cost per pound	$17.55

10.5.43 B&B is concerned about marking up shipping costs. They believe that excessive shipping costs may make the customer feel 'taken advantage of'.

Cost per pound to mark-up	$17.55
×mark-up %	81.89%
Amount of mark-up	$14.37
Cost per pound to mark-up	$17.55
+mark-up	$14.37
Wholesale price	$31.92
Current wholesale price ($6.15×5 lb)	$30.75

10.5.44 The $1.17 difference per pound may not seem significant but considering that B&B sold 18,321 5 lb bags of Columbia French roast in 1995, that difference represents $25,080 in operating income.

Computation of shipping costs per pound

Direct material costs	$2,205,775
Less: cost of beans sold	1,761,400
Less: cost of packaging ($50,100 + 45,184 + 11,404)	106,688
Cost of shipping	337,687
Number of pounds shipped (523,236 + 64,212)	587,448
Shipping cost per pound	$0.58

Target cost management

10.5.45 In this context target costing focuses on; (1) identifying appropriate product sale prices by assessing the market, (2) determining required return on investment, and (3) identifying target costs for which they should produce their products. As a result, B&B can use a target cost analysis as a control mechanism to monitor their overall cost structure.

Sales by product information

10.5.46 The three products with the largest sales volumes are; (1) Costa Rican SHB, $761,723, (2) French Roast, $678,075, and (3) Sumatra Mandheling, $620,478. Total sales of these three products are $2,060,276 with the remaining products accounting for sales of $1,887,474. Based on the market research results, it is possible to re-price the products and their approximate sales from those products. See Figure 10.11 for competitor information. The process is as follows.

	Current	Re-priced
Costa Rican SHB	$761,723	$790,000
French Roast	$678,075	$685,000
Sumatra Mandheling	$620,478	$600,000
Total of analysed products	$2,060,276	$2,075,000
Other product sales		1,887,474
Re-priced sales		$3,962,474

Competitor	Market strategy
1. Starbucks	1. Retail locations – sales of specialty coffee and coffee drinks
2. Seattle's Best Coffee (SBC)/Torrefazione Italia	2. Wholesale and grocery store sales of coffee beans
3. Coffe Bean, Inc. (CBI)	3. Retail locations
4. Allegro	4. Retail locations
5. Peet's Coffee & Tea	5. Retail drink sales in a coffeehouse format
6. Barney's Coffee & Tea	6. Retail sales of coffee beans
7. Gloria Jean's Coffee Bean	7. Retail sales of coffee beans
8. First Colony Coffee & Tea	8. Retail sales of a wide variety of foods and premium coffees in a coffeehouse format
9. Folgers and Maxwell House	9. Grocery store sales of standard (low quality) coffee; plus introduction of limited specialty brands

Figure 10.11 Analysis of competitors

Determine income required

10.5.47 The income required by B&B given their capital structure has been computed as $315,000. With a pre-tax required rate of return of 21 per cent, one can see the cost reduction pressure placed on targeted costs.

Determine target cost

Re-priced sales	$3,962,474	
Excluded expenses:		
Beans	1,761,400	
Administrative	387,662	
Income required	315,000	
Target cost	$1,498,412	
Target costs:		
Packaging/shipping	$444,375	($2,205,775 − $1,761,400)
Direct labour	437,559	
Mfg overhead	281,874	
Selling expenses	349,118	
Current cost levels	$1,512,926	

10.5.48 Current costs exceed target costs by $14,514 (only 1 per cent of current costs). The results indicate that B&B appears to be operating very close to the target costs indicated by market forces. What is relevant to note is that functional areas throughout B&B can see how all costs interact. Key points for managers include; (1) cost reduction plans for the target costs, (2) impact on other functional areas if administrative costs are *not* included in target costs, and (3) impact of rapid sales growth on current cost structure.

- Most production costs are determined before production. Therefore, cost reduction activities at the production stage might be seen as misguided.

- Many product prices are market determined and not cost determined. Therefore, to focus on cost as a determinant of product price is to risk bringing a product to market that is not price competitive or that returns an unacceptably low profit.

- The absence of cost as a design specification may lead to inefficient product design (e.g., features that cannot be cost justified may be added to a product).

- The changing business environment has caused more and more costs to be determined in the product planning and product design stages.

Target cost management

- The focus of target costing is on cost reduction at the product planning and product design stages. Target costing can thereby link strategic and profit planning to product cost by determining target costs only after target prices and profits have been calculated.

A case study: redesigning the product

10.5.49 Target costing is widely regarded as a management technique to cost products based on customers' perceptions of the product's worth and as a tool for reducing costs over the entire life-cycle of a product. As suggested above it helps companies to set ceiling costs which enable target profits to be achieved. Most case studies suggest that organisations practising target costing do so in different ways. A variety of approaches underpin how products get redesigned within the parameters of maximum allowable costs to earn desired profits within different companies. Bhimani and Neike (1999) discuss target costing within one division of the global enterprise Siemens to illustrate how target costing deals with time, quality and cost issues in redesigning product features.

The need for market-led costing

10.5.50 Siemens is a global leader in electrical and electronic products industries. Its product range spreads over 260 product areas in a variety of market sectors including semi-conductors, power generators, defence components, medical engineering and transportation systems. The Fiber Optics business unit (HLFO) provides the site for investigating target costing. HLFO is one of 16 business units within the semi-conductors group. HLFO products principally comprise passive networking equipment and fibre optical transmitters and receivers (referred to as transceivers). These devices change electrical impulses within computers into light impulses which are then transmitted, via optical fibres, to other transceivers. Transceivers are composed of optical, electrical and mechanical parts.

10.5.51 HLFO was among the first players in the customised products market. However, the growing number of entrants into the industry since the mid-1990s and the increasing complexity of HLFO products has led the company to pursue an enhanced cost management focus. To retain its competitiveness, HLFO projected early on a cost reduction target for its transceivers of 70 per cent. Achieving reduced costs of this level of magnitude cannot but necessitate a reconsideration of existing production and technical configurations of the product lines for this type of enterprise.

10.5.52 HLFO managers decided that the necessary cost reductions had to come from alterations to the actual design of the transceiver and the accompanying changes that this would entail for the production processes. Design engineers were given responsibility to alter the product and production processes to align the total manufacturing costs for the transceivers with emergent market conditions.

10.5.53 HLFO launched what it termed the 'Phoenix' project as a consequence of the unprecedented competition within the fibre optics market. This was a re-engineering exercise to alter the product and the manufacturing process. The Phoenix project entailed restructuring the reconfiguration of manufacturing such that all basic products would run on one automated line prior to mass-customising the product. Products would thus make use of modularised production steps according to individualised product specifications. Design engineers at HLFO, faced with the prospect of enhanced production and technical complexity combined with increasing price competition, perceived a need for more extensive accounting information relating to manufacturing processes and market prices of fibre optics products. Although their primary role had traditionally been to develop leading edge technological innovations and to seek ways of further improving product specifications, performance and efficiency, the Phoenix project incited HLFO design engineers to seek more detailed cost information.

10.5.54 The traditional accounting system in place at HLFO had been designed to allocate, rather than trace, costs and used volume-based allocation methods. Under this approach, material and production elements were divided into cost blocks, and direct material and direct labour costs served as a basis for the application of different overhead costs using predefined overhead rates. This approach made it difficult for the design engineers to relate changes in components to changes in production, and generally to compare costs for different generations of re-engineered products. Thus, if a process change resulted in the production throughput time being reduced by 50 per cent, the overhead cost amount would then have to be allocated to a smaller base thereby doubling the allocation ratio. The resulting overhead allocation would not tally with the resources perceived to be consumed by the new process. To overcome this problem a different approach had to be sought in order to identify the origins and flows of costs.

10.5.55 Overhead cost allocation was not the sole problem. Although the Phoenix initiative focused on the production process, material cost inputs were also analysed because they represented a large proportion of the total cost of the final product. Meaningfully identifying cost changes of product components proved difficult, because, for different product generations, substantial variations existed as sub-component costs decreased with production volume and as suppliers learned to reduce their costs. Further, basic

Target cost management

product components were continuously re-engineered and consequent global cost interactions needed to be monitored and analysed.

10.5.56 The production process of transceivers was, in large part, reflective of product design requirements, which determined the basis of production workflow, timing and ultimately costs. It was difficult for the design engineers to address questions about the impact of component changes on the production process and its costs. What was desirable was a linkage between the decisions made at the design stage and the resultant effects on the production costs. If such information could be made available, it would enable design decisions to take account of production implications which themselves had to be seen in the context of customer requirements. The cornerstone of the project was to apply target-costing concepts to set market-defined parameters affecting production cost, timing and quality factors. To do this, the Phoenix team drew upon two engineering and accounting techniques: functional analysis and activity-based costing. The intent was to focus on processes rather than functions, which led to what essentially was process-based target costing (PBTC).

Process-based target costing

10.5.57 At HLFO many product design projects were concerned with incremental alterations of existing designs rather than with radical new designs. What was desired was for product improvements aimed either at increasing value to the customer or at reducing the cost to the organisation. The value-engineering technique used within HLFO focuses on functional values. Under this approach, engineers concentrate their design efforts on relevant function areas. The aim is to cost the different product functions and to assess the value of these functions to the customer. Once this is done, it becomes possible to determine whether the costs that are necessary to achieve product functions are in line with accorded customer value. In order to conduct such an analysis, the product has to be mapped into its different function areas and costs allocated to these function areas.

10.5.58 To understand customer requirements better, HLFO products were stripped down to product functions using value-engineering techniques. The aim was to analyse each production process step independently and to derive costing data on single processes as well as information on quality levels and process times. All transceivers produced within the HLFO components group had the same functional areas (notably mechanical, electrical and optical). Two types of functional analyses were undertaken – one engineering driven and another customer driven (see Figure 10.12). Ultimately, for each product, the process costs at different steps were linked to a customer defined production function. The product design could then

Implementation issues

be altered so as to avoid 'over-engineering' the product with features upon which customers placed little value but which increased the final product costs.

Product Function Areas (Engineering orientated)

Mechanics
- Provide optical connector socket
- Provide electrical contact to computer motherboard
- Physical mounting on the motherboard
- Physical positioning on the motherboard
- Mechanical protection of electronic parts
- Identification
- Cooling
- Packaging

Electronics
- Electromagnetic shielding (internal/external)
- Connection of electronic components
  Receiver, RX:
  - Signal amplification
  - Data-flow cycle/sequence correction   1-(for parallel transceiver only)
  - Parallelisation   1-(for parallel transceiver only)
  Transmitter, TX:
  - Serialization   1-(for parallel transceiver only)
  - LED/diode diver

Optics
  Receiver, RX:
  - Focusing
  - Optical → Electronic signal conversion
  Transmitter, TX:
  - Electronic → Optical signal conversion
  Focusing

Product Function Areas (Customer orientated)

Mechanics
- Provide optical connector socket
- Provide electrical contact to computer motherboard
- Physical mounting on the motherboard
- Physical positioning on the motherboard
- Mechanical protection of electrical parts
- Identification
- Cooling
- Packaging

Electronics
- Electromagnetic sheilding (internal/external)
- Connection of electronic components
- Receiver/Transmitter

Optics
- Focusing
- Optical → Electronic signal conversion

Figure 10.12 Engineering and customer-related product function areas

Target cost management

10.5.59 Activity-based costing within HLFO has been implemented on a pilot basis to generate information about the cost structure of HLFO products. The objective is for activities rather than volume levels to provide the basis for allocating overhead costs. To achieve this, single production processes were initially identified as activities. Since these production activities represented the cost drivers, it was possible to choose between different production activities at the design and development stage. Under this approach, overhead costs could be allocated to production steps rather than to the total production as had been done traditionally. This enabled production process related costs to be pinpointed directly to the source.

10.5.60 The value added to the product during production can be monitored through production activities and may be analysed more closely. As an example, using information relating to the production and testing of a standard component (called Maeva 2) and interviews with different production engineers and supervisors, production was divided into four main activities: chip on board (electronic assembly), coupling units (optical assembly), module assembly (mechanical assembly) and the production of transmitter receiver shells (TRS) (final assembly, testing and packaging). These four activities were further divided into a total of 15 sub-activities (see Figure 10.13). It was essential to ensure that each process could exist on its own and was not directly interrelated with other sub-processes.

10.5.61 In order to cost processes, design engineers sought information on quality, time and cost components. The production starting point is for work in procress (WIP) and material to enter the process. The process produces WIP for input into the subsequent production step. During processing, further material and labour inputs are required at each subsequent production steps which increase the value of the WIP. Some resources required for production are not volume dependent. These costs include depreciation, interest, some energy costs, rent, supervision, maintenance, IT systems and other indirect material. These costs are allocated as period costs at each production step. Some costs are variable, such that there may be a trade-off between automation (fixed cost) and manual labour (variable cost) in different production cells. Activities such as control and quality test procedures increase fixed costs and some defective product costs must be borne by good products. This is of prime importance at the planning and production stage as these can amount to 30 per cent of a good product.

10.5.62 Once value engineering and activity-based costing were applied to HLFO production processes, it was then possible to move towards market-derived production cost parameters. This was essential for the development of process-based target costing. This integration of market-led costing, func-

Implementation issues

1.0 COB (Chip on board)
1.1 Entrance testing and heat sink assembly (redundant)
1.2 Setting of active and passive components
1.3 Wire bonding
1.4 Lasermaking
1.5 Cutting and gluing of PCB
1.6 Final test
1.7 Pressing and bonding of coupling units (CU)
2.0 Coupling units
2.1 Assembly of duplex nose
2.2 Laser spot welding of CU
3.0 Module assembly
3.1 Casting
3.4 Assembly of distance ring (redundant)
3.5 Gross leak testing
4.0 TRS (Transceiver receiver shell)
4.1 Assembly
4.2 Electrical and aging testing
4.3 Packaging

Figure 10.13 Production processes for Maeva-2

---

tional analysis and activity-based costing within the context of tracking cost, time and quality elements, culminated in what the Phoenix team termed a Function-Process Relationship Map (FPRM). Within FPRM, the magnitude of the cost of quality is represented by a square (at the bottom left of each box) whereby size reflects the importance of the quality cost compared with the total cost of the process (see Figure 10.14). A consideration deemed important by product designers in tracking costs was the delayed discovery of defects. If, for example, a defect was caused by a process X, but was only identified much later in the production process, say at process $(X+4)$, the value of the work performed to date would have increased at each process step between X and $X+4$. The process X production cell could then be accorded full responsibility and bear all 'value added' costs which the defect caused up to the process point $X+4$. Broadly, activity-based costing concepts and value engineering are both combined and depicted within the FPRM to produce a modular function-process relationship whereby market factors are tied to design changes via cost, quality and timing issues.

10.5.63 The proportion of the time consumed by the process compared with the total time consumed in the course of production is represented by the size of the vertical bar in each process box, as shown in Figure 10.14. The

Target cost management

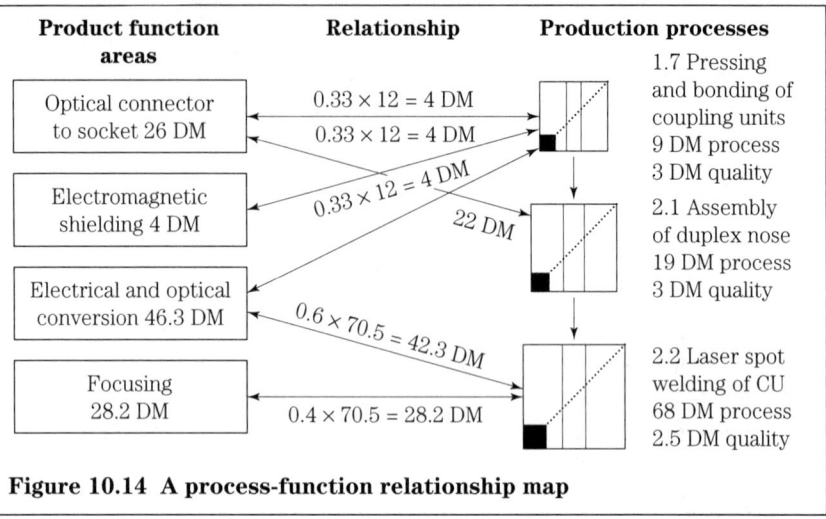

Figure 10.14 A process-function relationship map

FPRM shows the fixed and variable cost distribution for each process. It provides insights into the cost structure trade-offs and shows how cost changes are associated with single process alterations. It also continuously reports on quality levels and costs and it illustrates the time flow of the process and value creation at each production step.

10.5.64 The FPRM enables customer requirements to be identified alongside company costs; time and quality linked factors. Production process and product material costs can be linked to specific customer requirements in order to achieve enhanced product designs. The functional analysis identifies customer needs on a product level basis and the FPRM subsequently enables the production cost structure to be assessed. Both sets of information together enable optimal product design to be established within the backdrop of production process implications.

10.5.65 With PBTC, design and production engineers can relate product function areas to the production processes. Every production process can likewise be linked to the function areas. The allocation of costs proceeds from the processes to the functions because the costs of a process are allocated to functions. When process costs are allocated, a substantial part of the costs may be the material costs. Ultimately, costs can be assigned to customer functions served by the products in addition to providing total product cost information. Overall, PBTC enables the cost of a function to be compared to the perceived customer value for that function. It also permits a functional cost driver to be backtracked from the function to the production

Implementation issues

process and allows a depiction of the trade-offs between material and processes, or automation versus labour costs. Effectively, production flow can be visualised at the design stage, and production and cost factors can be rendered more directly controllable at the early product development stages. Design engineers who traditionally only dealt with product specifications now have a visual and quantitative understanding of the effects of different design decisions on specific production process decisions.

10.5.66 The basic theme of PBTC is embedded in the generic target cost philosophy underlying cost-based adjustments to meet market value expectations. But PBTC pursues this cost management objective in a highly differentiated and organisationally specific manner. As noted earlier, different companies adopt styles which are organisation specific rather than purely represented by the nature of the product. PBTC allows the cost allocation to product functions to be highlighted visually. All process costs are allocated to the function and depiction is communicated by means of diagrammatic as opposed to purely quantitative information. Within a FPRM, some processes can have many relationships and others have only one. Quality costs weightings in the process function relationship are reflected by the size of the lower left box within each process box. Each line also indicates the significance of the relationships. The importance of time and quality measurements can be examined by managers within the design, production and marketing departments via visual representation of the production flows and the incremental value accruing at each stage. PBTC was developed from a design engineer's perspective. Traditionally, design-engineering decisions at HLFO have tended to make heavy use of flow charts, graphs and technical illustrations. Since target costs for the Phoenix re-engineering project had to be met principally from design alterations, PBTC information structuring did not depart from the visual emphasis to which design engineers have traditionally been accustomed. PBTC has brought together, through its emphasis on the function process relationships, the requirements of the customer and the technical expertise of the company. The objective has been for design engineers to concentrate their design efforts on the functions valued by the customer and to understand the cost structure implications. PBTC has achieved a combination of both external and internal requirements to guiding design engineering within a technical, production and market conscious context. The target cost can be broken down to the product functions and, hence, the whole design process can be broken down into analysable sub-modules. Ultimately the design engineers are able to retain the traditional design imagery whilst managing value from the customer's perspective.

10.5.67 The manner in which PBTC can be used to monitor planned cost reductions also reveals the extent to which it is organisation specific. During

Target cost management

the design stage, process optimisation goals can be set. Subsequently, the costing system can monitor the cost reduction due to process optimisation, by comparing the actual cost of each process to the targeted cost goals and identifying the variances. In order to be able to gather the actual cost at a process level, the accounting system has to be adapted by way of sub-accounts. The FPRM information is linked to the accounting information system in order to provide actual time, quality and cost information on single production processes. Using the actual cost at the process level, the system feeds back information on the process costs for each product function. In Figure 10.15, for example, 26 DM were targeted as the cost for the optical connector to socket function. If the accounting information system triggers 28 DM back through the FPRM, the engineers will know that they should look for a saving of around 0.50 DM in the first and 1.50 DM in the second process round. Hence, the design engineers can focus their efforts on achieving cost reductions on customer relevant functions since they would be able to identify the cost drivers for any process level to see if they match the target cost goals. Ultimately, they would have a dynamic system which enables control of the value flow of the product.

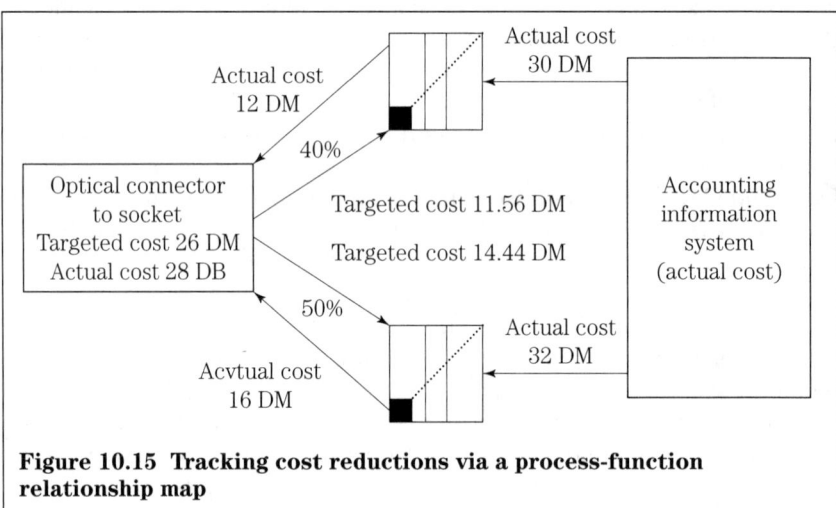

Figure 10.15 Tracking cost reductions via a process-function relationship map

10.5.68 At HLFO, the PBTC system enables the quality of the production output at each process stage to be monitored. If, for example, a quality defect is found at a particular process stage, and this defect is due to a much earlier process stage, then this earlier process stage is problematic in terms of the subsequent process costs incurred as the product moves through the value chain. For responsibility accounting purposes, the costs are allocated to the process where the problem arises. Thus, if a weld is destroyed by a laser cutting process, the welding process can be made to bear all the costs including those of value added post-welding. This is particularly useful for guiding designers through value engineering activities whereby process decisions have a cascading influence on total defect costs. The process planning engineers can trade-off quality tests at different places within the production process and calculate how far it is worthwhile to check quality at earlier stages and eliminate the possibility of significant amounts of value being added to a defective product.

10.5.69 One other significant feature of PBTC is that HLFO design and production engineers can use this as a tool to plan the production flow. The idea of breaking the production path down into easily manipulated processes makes planning of the process layout easier. Since the technique gives information about the value creation of each process, the engineers can analytically assess and influence the production layout. This may include altering the time requirements of processes and aspects of total quality management to optimise value creation.

10.5.70 PBTC has in part been implemented so as to assist HLFO to engage in organisational learning (see Chapter **11**). During the PBTC implementation phase a computer programme was developed to automate the steps required for PBTC information output. The primary aim was to support the decision-making process at the design stage. However, although the programme was intended as a decision support tool it was also designed as an experimental tool in that it points the design engineers in directions which they would perhaps not naturally have considered. In providing this capability, PBTC supports an intuitive approach by giving an analytical basis for the design process. Design engineers now have to consider customer aspects (targeted prices, production function, etc.) as well as internal constraints which exist in actual production plants. Moreover, the distance which lies between the R&D department and the rest of the company (marketing and production departments) is reduced through PBTC because the information needed to run the system stems from outside the traditional R&D databases. Different scenarios as to the impact of design changes on other functions can be explored and such information is useful in assessing the potential of design changes. HLFO sees PBTC as playing an employee empowerment role. Information about the target price and target functions is given through the application value engineering techniques, and knowledge relating to the internal cost structure is derived through ABC and the FPRM. PBTC offers design engineers a tool which gives individuals all the necessary information to design a product to a set target cost. This empowers the design engineer

Target cost management

since the costing technique relies on assessing the whole cost structure at the design stage of the product life-cycle. PBTC can then have wide implications for the company because it alters the information flows within the enterprise and, in so doing, may influence the organisational structure.

(Source: Bhimani and Neike, 1999. Reprinted with permission. For more information, visit www.wglcorpfinance@riag.com)

A case study: dealing with market pricing pressures

10.5.71 Whilst target cost management deals with associating internal costs with external value expectations, the issue of market pricing pressures is a real concern for most commercial organisations. The MosCo deals with ways in which cost management can assist with this issue.

10.5.72 The evening before the annual two-year budget review, Cosmos 'Chip' Offtiol, MosCo's director of operations, was confident. While he waited for the latest financial estimates, he thought of the plan he and his staff had methodically prepared, which successfully addressed all the crises this new business unit was facing: developing competitive transfer pricing on an aging product, developing and marketing new products to external customers against an established market leader, reducing manufacturing costs, improving manufacturing utilisation and improving its slim levels of profitability.

10.5.73 When Jonathan Janus, MosCo's controller, solemnly delivered the requested pro forma income statements, Offtiol's mood changed dramatically. Instead of sustained profit, Offtiol was shocked to see significant projected operating losses. He wondered why his extensive planning had not improved MosCo's 1995 and 1996 financial results. With less than 24 hours before he was to offer senior management a viable business plan, he felt abandoned and hopeless.

Background

10.5.74 MosCo, a semi-conductor design and manufacturing company, is a wholly owned subsidiary of Computer Systems Inc. (CSI), a leading manufacturer of client/server systems, workstations, and personal computers. During 1993 and 1994, MosCo manufactured and sold to CSI a single product, the $\times 100$, a 100MHz, 10 nanosecond microprocessor. The $\times 100$ is a 0.75 micron device packaged in a 339 pin-grid array (PGA) and is used in CSI's servers and workstations. MosCo has sold CSI 150,000 units of the $\times 100$ in each of the past two years.

10.5.75 Although MosCo sells entirely to its corporate parent, the company was required to establish competitive prices for its devices by Q3 '94. Previously, the $\times 100$ had been sold to CSI at full cost. Establishing competitive

Implementation issues

prices was but one of many changes CSI required MosCo to make. In 1995, CSI planned to change all its major business units into profit centres. CSI management felt each business unit needed flexibility and independence to react to rapidly changing market conditions. CSI believed that if its business units were profit centres, they would be more accountable for their own financial success. Their strategies and annual performance would be more visible and measurable as well. This change meant they could sell their devices to external customers using available manufacturing capacity. MosCo could also recover the large development costs for future products and control their destiny.

10.5.76 MosCo established the competitive market selling price of the ×100 at $850, based on industry price/performance comparisons. CSI approved of this market-based method of establishing transfer prices, which ensured that CSI could purchase internally at a competitive price while placing the burden of cost management appropriately on MosCo. Jonathan Janus, MosCo's controller, prepared revised financial statements applying the $850 transfer price to MosCo's 1993 and 1994 shipments (see Figure 10.16). Gordon Scott, MosCo's vice president and general manager, was pleased to see MosCo had generated profits of $4.9 million and $1.9 million for 1993 and 1994, respectively, on annual revenues of $127.5 million, after applying the newly-established transfer price. The profit decline in 1994 reflected the establishment and staffing of MosCo's new marketing department. This department was created to identify and open external market opportunities for new products currently under development.

	1993	1994
Revenue		
×100: 150,000 @ $850	$127,500,000	$127,500,000
Cost of sales		
Wafers: (16,595 @ $45)	$746,775	$746,775
Packages: (175,000 @ $50)	$8,750,000	$8,750,000
Mfg. spending	$91,112,000	$91,112,000
Total cost of sales	$100,608,775	$100,608,775
Gross margin ($)	$26,891,225	$26,891,225
Gross margin (%)	21%	21%
Process development	$14,000,000	$14,000,000
Product development	$5,000,000	$5,000,000
Marketing & administration	$3,000,000	$6,000,000
Operating profit	$4,891,225	$1,891,225

Figure 10.16 MosCo Inc. income statement

Target cost management

10.5.77 As fiscal year 1995 approaches, MosCo management is faced with a number of pressures and unknowns. CSI is under severe competitive pressures in their server and workstation product lines and is already demanding a price reduction on the ×100. They also insist MosCo remain profitable. Carlotta Price, head of MosCo's new marketing department, determined from industry studies that the price/performance for microprocessors halves every 18 months (Moore's law). To remain competitive, merchant semiconductor companies were consistently offering some combination of price reductions and/or performance improvements, so that their products' price/performance (price per unit of speed) halved every 1.5 years. Thus, for the ×100 and for every CPU MosCo developed and manufactured, Price believed the market would require similarly timed price/performance offerings. Price knew any price reductions would require offsetting cost reductions if MosCo was to remain profitable and wondered what the manufacturing organisation was thinking.

10.5.78 As product development was no longer working on any ×100 performance improvements, Price computed required price reductions on the ×100 following the industry model. The ×100 would continue at the $850 price through Q1 '95, then drop to $637.50 at the start of Q2 '95, drop to $425.00 at the start of Q1 '96, and to $318.75 at the start of Q4 '96. Price was troubled by these prices as she knew CSI was requesting 150,000 units in FY95 but only 75,000 in FY96. CSI indicated it expected a customer shift away from workstations and into CSI's new personal computer line.

10.5.79 Product cost for the ×100 had remained constant during FY93 and FY94 at approximately $665 (see Figure 10.17). Price computed that cost reductions of approximately $166.25 per year (to $498.75 in FY95 and

DESCRIPTION	COST/WAFER	COST/DIE	CUM COST/DIE
Yielded raw wafer	$50.00	$1.00	$1.00
Wafer production cost	$5,245.15	$104.90	$105.90
Probe production cost	$785,71	$15.71	$121.62
Probe yield		25%	$486.47
339 PGA package cost		$50.00	$536.47
Assembly production cost		$9.26	$545.73
Assembly yield		90%	$606.36
Test production cost		$32.14	$638.51
Test yield		96%	$665.11
TOTAL ×100 PRODUCT COST			$665.11

Figure 10.17 MosCo Inc. FY94 product cost worksheet

Implementation issues

$332.50 in 1996) would be necessary to maintain the ×100's current gross margin of ~22%. She wondered if manufacturing could achieve a cost reduction that steep.

10.5.80 Concurrent with the ×100 pricing activities, P. J. Watt, head of product development, sent an urgent request to Scott, Price, Janus, and Offtiol for $3 million in funding. This funding would accelerate the completion of an integer-only microprocessor, the ×50 and the follow-on CPU, the ×75. The ×50, a new product already under development, could be completed with $1 million of the additional funding and made available for volume shipment by the beginning of FY95. The remaining $2 million would be spent during FY95 and FY96 to complete development and ready the ×75 for volume shipment by the beginning of FY97.

10.5.81 The ×50 was a 50MHz, 20 nanosecond CPU, manufactured like the ×100, using the present .75 micron technology. But unlike the ×100, the ×50 did not have a floating-point processor. The elimination of the floating-point processor reduced the size and power requirements of the CPU. The ×50 and ×75 could be packaged in a 168 pin-grid array (PGA) that cost $15, that is, $35 less than the 339 PGA used by the ×100. However, the testing parameters of the ×50 and ×75 were significantly different than for the ×100 and required a Bonn tester, which MosCo did not currently own. This $2 million tester, if purchased, would add $1.2 million in annual depreciation and other direct operating costs and $800,000 in incremental annual support costs to the present level of manufacturing spending.

10.5.82 The ×50 and ×75 were targeted as entry devices for CSI's personal computer business. NoTel was the market leader in .75 micron integer-only microprocessors. Their N50 CPU (also 50MHz, 20 nanoseconds) sold for $500. The N50 had just been announced with volume shipments to coincide with the beginning of MosCo's FY95. MosCo's new marketing department estimated the demand for the ×50 from CSI and potential new external customers could easily exceed 1,000 units per year. To break into this market, Price recommended heavy market promotion and a price/performance two times the competition's. Estimates for unit sales potential from advertising were 100,000 for the first $1,000, up to 500,000 for the second $1,000, and over 1 million for a third million-dollar advertising expenditure.

10.5.83 With the increased pricing pressures from both CSI and the external market place, product cost reduction became critical. This fact, coupled with the request from product development for additional funding, had Gordon Scott very concerned. He knew it was important to bring out the ×50 and ×75 quickly, but the pricing pressures for their market entrance and the

Target cost management

pricing pressures from CSI on the ×100 seemed almost impossible to meet and still achieve a profit in FY95 and 96. He knew, however, that if he did not maintain a profitable operation, his tenure would be short.

10.5.84 Reduced product costs leading to competitive manufacturing appeared to be the critical factor necessary to sustain MosCo's slim profit levels. Scott asked Offtiol, the director of operations, to formulate a series of recommendations for developing and manufacturing an expanded CPU product line in FY95 and FY96. He asked that the recommendations be completed by the annual two-year budget review, scheduled to commence in a month. Scott knew that soon after MosCo's budget review he would have to present a credible business plan to CSI management. He worried how he could develop a viable plan in light of the obstacles.

Overview of the semi-conductor manufacturing process

10.5.85 Semi-conductor devices are made from silicon, which is material refined from quartz. Silicon is used because it can be altered easily to promote or deter electrical signals. Electronic switches, or transistors, that control electrical signals can be formed on the surface of a silicon crystal by the precisely controlled addition of certain elements designed in microscopically small patterns.

10.5.86 Silicon is first melted to remove impurities and grown into long crystals (ingots), which vary in size from 0.5 inches to 16 inches in diameter (typical sizes in use today are 6 and 8 inches). The purified silicon is sliced into wafers on which integrated circuits are patterned. As the size of an integrated circuit is extremely small, hundreds, even thousands, of circuits can be formed on a wafer at the same time.

10.5.87 Integrated circuits (typically referred to as 'chips' or 'dies') are an array of transistors made up of various connected layers, designed to perform specific operations. Each layer is a specific circuit pattern (approximately 20 are used in present processes). A glass plate (called a reticle) is used to pattern each layer on the wafer during the fabrication process.

Fabrication

10.5.88 In the fabrication process, blank wafers are first insulated with a film of oxide, then coated with a soft, light-sensitive plastic called photoresist. The wafers are masked by a reticle and flooded with ultra-violet light, exposing the reticle's specific circuit pattern on the unmasked portion of the wafer. Exposed photoresist hardens into the proper circuit layer outline. Acids and solvents are used to strip away unexposed photoresist and oxide,

Implementation issues

baring the circuit pattern to be etched by either chemicals or superhot gases. More photoresist is placed on the wafer, masked, and stripped, then implanted with chemical impurities, or dopants, that form negative and positive conducting zones. Repeating these steps builds the necessary layers required for the integrated circuit design to be completed on the wafer.

Probe
10.5.89 In the probe process, an electrical performance test of the functions of each of the completed integrated circuits is performed while each die is still on the wafer. The non-functioning dies are marked with ink; the functioning dies are left unmarked and moved to assembly.

Assembly
10.5.90 In the assembly process, each die is cut from the wafer with a diamond saw. The good dies are placed in the cavity of a ceramic package. The bonding pads from the dies are connected by very thin aluminium wires into the leads of the package, creating the necessary electrical connection from the chip to the package. The package is then sealed, with a metal lid placed over the exposed dies in the package.

Test
10.5.91 Once the device is completely packaged, it is tested to ensure all electrical specifications of the integrated circuit are met.

10.5.92 The completed, packaged semi-conductor device is now ready to be soldered to a printed circuit board, which in turn will be installed into a computer system.

Overview of the product costing process
10.5.93 Semi-conductor product costing is a multiple-step process in which manufacturing costs measure value added to raw material as it is processed. Value added typically is defined as production or capacity throughput divided by spending. The cost system collects, accumulates and yields material and manufacturing costs through each stage of production.

- First, the costs of raw materials used and the unit costs of each stage of manufacturing are established.

- Next, raw wafer and wafer production costs are converted to die costs. In wafer fabrication and probe, manufactured material is in wafer form.

- As such, the unit costs of the raw wafer and manufacturing in these stages are captured initially as cost/wafer. In assembly, where the wafer is cut into dies, the unit of measure also changes to dies. Thus,

Target cost management

to complete the costing of the final product, which is in die form, cost/wafer must be converted to cost/die.

- Finally, the unit die costs are accumulated in the sequence of the manufacturing process and yielded at each stage. Yield refers to the production units successfully manufactured in each stage. The semi-conductor manufacturing process typically loses much of its production due to misprocessing or non-functioning dies. Yielding the accumulated unit cost at each manufacturing stage applies the cost of lost production units to the cost of good production units.

10.5.94 At MosCo, the unit production cost of each major manufacturing stage (wafer, fabrication, probe, assembly, test) has been determined by applying that stage's annual spending to the annual volume of production (see Figures 10.17 and 10.18) or capacity (see Figures 10.19 and 10.20).

OPERATION	PER YEAR	MFG. SPENDING	COST/UNIT
Planned wafer capacity	16,595		
Engineering test wafers	1,040		
Planned wafer starts	15,555		
Wafer fabrication yield	90%		
Planned wafer production	13,999.50	$73,429,500	$5,245.16
Planned probed wafer starts	14,000	$11,000,000	$785.71
Gross die/wafer (×100 = 50)	50		
Total gross die through probe	700,000		
Probe yield for ×100	25%		
×100 probed die output	175,000		
Planned assembly starts	175,500	$1,620,000	$9.26
×100 assembly yield	90%		
Planned assembly completions	157,500		
Planned test starts	157,500	$5,062,500	$32.14
×100 test yield	96%		
Planned test output	151,200		
TOTAL MANUFACTURING SPENDING		$91,112,000	

Figure 10.18 FY94 used capacity and process costs worksheet

Implementation issues

	Manufacturing				Research & Develop		SG&A	
Organization	Fabrication	Probe	Assembly	Test	Prod devp.	Proc. devp.	MKT & ADM	TOTAL
Direct mfg.	$57,000,000	$11,000,000	$1,620,000	$5,062,500				$74,682,500
Res & Devp.					$2,000,000	$9,000,000		$11,000,000
Mkt. & Admin.							$5,000,000	$5,000,000
Support Org's								
Facilities	$5,500,000				$1,000,000	$3,000,000	$500,000	$10,000,000
Yield Eng.	$2,000,000							$2,000,000
Cimt	$4,000,000				$2,000,000	$2,000,000	$500,000	$8,500,000
Qual. & Rel.	$3,537,500							$3,537,500
Purchasing	$1,392,000							$1,392,000
Tot. support	$16,429,500				$3,000,000	$5,000,000	$1,000,000	$25,429,500
Tot. spending	$73,429,500	$11,000,000	$1,620,000	$5,062,500	$5,000,000	$14,000,000	$6,000,000	$116,112,000

Fabrication	$73,429,500
Probe	$11,000,000
Assembly	$1,620,000
Test	$5,062,500
Tot. mfg. spending	$91,112,000

Figure 10.19 FY94 spending summary by organisation

Target cost management

	Manufacturing				Research & Develop		SG&A	
Activity	Fabrication	Probe	Assembly	Test	Prod devp.	Proc. devp.	MKT & ADM	TOTAL
Direct mfg. (see Fig 10.21)	$57,000,000	$11,000,000	$1,620,000	$5,062,500				$74,682,500
Res. & devp.					$2,000,000	$9,000,000		$11,000,000
Mkt. & admin.								
Marketing							$3,000,000	$3,000,000
Administration							$1,000,000	$1,000,000
Finance/Hr							$1,000,000	$1,000,000
Total							$5,000,000	$5,000,000
Total support (see Fig 10.21)	$10,392,000	$2,000,000		$3,037,500	$3,000,000	$6,000,000	$1,000,000	$25,429,500
Total spending	$67,392,000	$13,000,000	$1,620,000	$8,100,000	$5,000,000	$15,000,000	$6,000,000	$116,112,000

Fabrication	$67,392,000
Probe	£13,000,000
Assembly	$1,620,000
Test	$8,100,000
Tot. mfg. spending	$90,112,000

Figure 10.20 MosCo Inc. – FY94 Activity-based spending summary by organisation

Implementation issues

10.5.95 Figures 10.18 and 10.24 highlight the computation of unit cost at each stage of manufacturing. In wafer fabrication and probe, the production unit is a wafer. Unit cost through these two stages is computed as wafer cost. In assembly and test, the wafer has been diced to remove the dies. The good dies continue through assembly; the non-functioning dies are discarded. Unit cost through these two manufacturing stages is computed as die cost.

10.5.96 At each stage of production, production loss (or yield) is experienced. Yield loss is typically greatest during probe, when each die on the wafer is first tested to determine if it is functioning as designed. At probe, the effectiveness and quality of the wafer fabrication process, through which the multiple circuit layers have been placed on the wafer, is revealed. In wafer fabrication, the wafers used solely for engineering testing (to ensure equipment is properly calibrated, and not used for production) are also eliminated (treated similar to production yield loss) in the calculation of wafer cost.

10.5.97 Figures 10.17 and 10.19 highlight the computation of product cost. The unit cost of each manufacturing stage is listed. For the raw wafer, wafer fabrication, and probe, the unit cost (wafer) is converted to die cost. The material cost is reflected at the manufacturing stage at which it is introduced. To determine a final or complete product cost, the cost per die is accumulated through each manufacturing stage and yielded for the production loss experienced in that stage. Yielding the accumulated die cost has the effect of placing the total cost of manufacturing on the good production units (or expected good production units if the total production capacity costing method is used).

10.5.98 Figure 10.17 highlights the accumulation of costs the $\times 100$ incurs during manufacturing. The cost and application of raw material can be seen at the start of wafer fabrication and assembly. Wafer to die conversion, based on the $\times 100$'s specification of 50 die on each wafer, is used to compute the equivalent die cost from the raw wafer, and at wafer fabrication and probe. Finally, the treatment of production loss (yield) can be seen throughout the costing process, as the accumulated cost at each stage of production is increased by the planned or expected yield at that stage, resulting in an accumulated cost that reflects the total cost of production applied to the good dies produced or expected after each stage.

The Offtiol plan
10.5.99 Offtiol started his preparation by reviewing the detailed $\times 100$ product cost (see Figures 10.17, 10.18 and 10.19). He immediately assembled a team comprising Janus from Finance, T. Q. Marcel from Quality, and Beeb Ruby from Training. The team, led by Marcellus deStepper, manager of wafer fabrication, conducted a cost review by activity. Offtiol, like Scott,

Target cost management

believed significant cost reductions would be necessary to maintain profitability. He had recently taken an executive development course in activity-based costing and knew it was a proven method for better understanding cost structures and cost drivers and highlighting non-value added work. Offtiol was excited, given the size of the assignment and his belief there were both cost reduction opportunities in manufacturing and necessary improvements in the current standard cost system. He felt the current standard cost system did not properly capture the complexity of MosCo's production process. He felt an ABC analysis could provide the insight necessary to reduce the ×100 product cost by the $166 which marketing had requested.

10.5.100 The team mapped the processes of the entire operation and then reassigned costs to the newly defined activities (see Figures 10.22, 10.23 and 10.24). The direct manufacturing operation was now better delineated by equipment use (see Figure 10.23). The manufacturing support organisations were also better understood. Their key activities were costed, then each was aligned to the manufacturing operation it supported (see Figure 10.24). MosCo's ABC team reset the ×100 product cost in line with the true practical capacity of the manufacturing process. The team saw capacity utilisation as a major driver of product cost. The old product costing methodology was based on the planned utilisation of each manufacturing process with underutilised manufacturing costs absorbed into product costs.

10.5.101 The revised ×100 product cost (see Figures 10.19 and 10.20) was pleasing but not totally surprising to Offtiol. It confirmed his belief in the inaccuracies of the old costing method. The new ×100 product cost of $437.50 was $227.61 lower than the $665.11 original cost shown by the old system. It did not make sense to charge the ×100 for the costs of resources it did not consume. Offtiol felt he could commit immediately to Price's 1995 product cost reduction request of $166.

10.5.102 To achieve the 1996 product cost goal of $332.50, Offtiol and his team looked further into the activity-based costing results. The study clearly showed that wafer fabrication was the largest area of manufacturing cost. Offtiol, with the help of Janus, computed that if the ×100 wafer cost was reduced from the 1995 level of $3,000/wafer to $1,866/wafer, the ×100 total product cost would be lowered by $105, achieving the desired $332.50. To obtain a wafer cost of $1,866, spending reductions of ~$25.5 million or 38 per cent in wafer fabrication would have to be achieved (see Chart I). Offtiol again asked deStepper to review the fabrication area for further cost reduction opportunities. He asked deStepper to formulate a plan that could reduce direct wafer fabrication spending by ~$25.5 million (from $67.4 million to $41.9 million).

Activity	Manufacturing				Research & Develop		SG&A	TOTAL
	Fabrication	Probe	Assembly	Test	Prod devp.	Proc. devp.	MKT & ADM	
Equipment capacity: driven by equipment installation								
Depreciation	$30,000,000	$3,500,000	$520,000	$1,400,000				$35,420,000
Utility costs	$5,000,000	$1,000,000	$50,000	$500,000				$6,550,000
Property/site	$5,000,000	$500,000	$50,000	$100,000				$5,650,000
Total	$40,000,000	$5,000,000	$620,000	$2,000,000				$47,620,000
Equipment capacity: driven by equipment uptime								
Equip. engn'rs	$8,000,000	$2,000,000		$1,762,500				$11,762,500
Monitor wafer	$1,000,000							$1,000,000
Op'n supplies	$1,000,000	$1,000,000	$100,000	$300,000				$2,400,000
Total	$10,000,000	$3,000,000	$100,000	$2,062,500				$15,162,500
Equipment capacity: driven by production								
Direct labor	$5,000,000	$2,000,000	$800,000	$700,000				$8,500,000
Monitor wafer	$1,000,000							$1,000,000
Op'n supplied	$1,000,000	$1,000,000	$100,000	$300,000				$2,400,000
Total	$7,000,000	$3,000,000	$900,000	$1,000,000				$11,900,000
Tot. dir. mfg	$57,000,000	$11,000,000	$1,620,000	$5,062,500				$74,682,500
Tot. dir. mfg: (new Bonn tester)				$1,215,000				

Figure 10.21 MosCo Inc. – FY94 Direct activity-based spending summary

Target cost management

Activity	Manufacturing				Research & Develop		SG&A	TOTAL
	Fabrication	Probe	Assembly	Test	Prod devp.	Proc. devp.	MKT & ADM	
Facilities:								
D/I water	$1,000,000						$500,000	$1,500,000
Site support	$500,000			$100,000	$500,000	$500,000		$2,100,000
Utilities	$3,000,000			$400,000	$500,000	$2,000,000		$5,900,000
Chemicals	$500,000							$500,000
Total	$5,000,000			$500,000	$1,000,000	$3,000,000	$500,000	$10,000,000
Yield eng: yield improvement:		$2,000,000						$2,000,000
Cimt:								
Shop floor system	$1,000,000				$1,000,000			$2,000,000
Networks	$500,000			$1,000,000		$500,000	$250,000	$2,750,000
Field svc	$500,000			$500,000	$500,000	$500,000	$250,000	$1,750,000
System devp				$500,000		$500,000		$1,000,000
Equip. connection						$1,000,000		$1,000,000
Total	$2,000,000			$2,000,000	$2,000,000	$2,000,000	$500,000	$8,500,000
Quality:								
Doc. control	$1,000,000							$1,000,000
Fail analysis	$500,000			$100,000		$250,000		$850,000
Equip. calibrate	$500,000			$437,500		$750,000		$1,687,500
Total	$2,000,000			$537,500		$1,000,000		$3,537,500
Purchasing	$1,392,200							$1,392,000
Total sup. spend	$10,392,000			$3,037,500	$3,000,000	$6,000,000	$1,000,000	$25,429,500
Total sup. spend: (new Bonn tester)	$2,000,000			$810,000				

Figure 10.22 MosCo Inc. – FY94 Support group activity-based spending summary

Implementation issues

DESCRIPTION	COST/WAFER	COST/DIE	CUM COST/DIE
Yielded raw wafer	$50.00	$1.00	$1.00
Wafer production cost	$3,000.00	$60.00	$61.00
Probe production cost	$500.00	$10.00	$71.00
Probe yield		25%	$284.00
339 PGA package cost		$50.00	$334.00
Assembly production cost		$8.00	$342.00
Assembly yield		90%	$380.00
Test production cost		$40.00	$420.00
Test yield		96%	$437.50
TOTAL ×100 PRODUCT COST			$437.50

Figure 10.23 FY94 revised product cost worksheet

OPERATION	PER YEAR	MFG. SPENDING	COST/UNIT
Planned wafer capacity	26,000		
Engineering test wafers	1,040		
Planned wafer starts	24,960		
Wafer fabrication yield	90%		
Planned wafer production	22,464	$67,392,000	$3,000.00
Planned probed wafer starts	26,000	$13,000,000	$500.00
Gross die/wafer (×100 = 50)	50		
Total gross die through probe	1,300,000		
Probe yield for ×100	25%		
×100 probed die output	325,000		
Planned assembly starts	202,500	$1,620,000	$8.00
×100 assembly yield	90%		
Planned assembly completions	182,250		
Planned test starts	202,500	$8,100.000	$40.00
×100 test yield	96%		
Planned test output	194,400		
TOTAL MANUFACTURING SPENDING		$90,112,000	

Figure 10.24 FY94 used capacity and process costs worksheet

669

Target cost management

10.5.103 deStepper returned in two weeks with an alternative plan (see Chart II). His team found nominal spending opportunities by; (1) reducing monitor wafer usage, (2) redesigning wafer lot handling procedures, and (3) better placement of inspection stations. deStepper's most significant discovery was the 64 per cent increase in capacity attained by increasing equipment uptime (the time equipment is not undergoing repair or preventive maintenance). Higher uptime, however, required an annual investment of ~$1.8 million in additional equipment engineers. While this investment would increase wafer fabrication spending to ~$69.2 million, wafer fabrication capacity would increase from 26,000 to ~42,700 in annual wafer starts. The increased capacity actually decreased the cost/wafer to $1,845, which was $21 lower than Offtiol had requested.

10.5.104 Offtiol dismissed deStepper's alternative plan outright. 'Spending needed to decrease, not *increase*!' Offtiol exclaimed and reiterated his request to reduce fabrication spending by 38 per cent. Offtiol then focused his team's cost reduction efforts on packaging costs, another major cost component of the ×100. (MosCo had spent close to $8.8 million annually on chip packages). He asked MosCo's purchasing manager, Nomial, to pressure MosCo's 339 PGA supplier to lower their $50 price. Nomial told Offtiol she had already made this request and was reminded by the vendor that the 339 PGA was a unique design, used by only MosCo for the ×100. With order volumes declining by 50 per cent in a year, Nomial said it would be difficult to keep the $50 package price from increasing.

Chart I

×100 1996 target product cost analysis (×100 gross die/wafer = 50)			
Manufacturing area	**Cost / Wafer**	**Cost / Die**	**Cum. Cost / Die**
Desired wafer cost	$1,866.00	$37.32	$37.32
Yielded raw wafer cost	$50.00	$1.00	$38.32
Probe cost/wafer	$500.00	$10.00	$48.32
Probe yield		25.0%	$193.28
339 PGA package cost		$50.00	$243.28
Assembly cost		$8.00	$251.28
Assembly yield		90.0%	$279.20
Test cost		$40.00	$319.20
Test yield		96.0%	$332.50
Current fabrication spending:			$67,392,000
Desired level of spending: (22,464 annual wafer production @ $1,866)			$41,917,824
Required spending reduction:			$25,474,176 38%

Implementation issues

Chart II deStepper alternate capacity and spending plan

	Current level	Proposed level
Total wafer start capacity	26,000	42,707
Engineering wafer starts	1,040	1,040
Production wafer starts	24,960	41,667
Fabrication line yield	90%	90%
Annual wafer completions	22,464	37,500
Annual spending level	$67,392,000	$67,392,000
deStepper's added spending		$1,797,120
Proposed spending level		$69,189,120
Cost/wafer	$3,000	$1,845

10.5.105 The final area of review was the ×50 proposal. Offtiol and the team reviewed its product cost, necessary manufacturing process, and spending requirements (see Figures 10.25 and 10.26). Offtiol compared the ×50 product cost (computed assuming all production capacity was used to manufacture the ×50) with the product cost of the ×100 and noted a few significant cost differences. The reduced size of the ×50 (no floating point processor) increased the number of dies able to be placed on each wafer, thus reducing the fabrication cost/die 67 per cent from the ×100 ($61.00 for the ×100; $20.33 for the ×50). The increase in the number of dies on each wafer increased the probe time, however, and increased the probe cost per wafer by 25 per cent ($500 for the ×100; $625 for the ×50). He was pleased with the doubling of assembly capacity resulting from the smaller package required by the ×50 (202,500 annual assembly starts for the ×100; 405,000 for the ×50). The increase in assembly throughput reduced the ×50 assembly costs by 50 per cent. Offtiol was pleasantly surprised at the ×50's lower test costs. Even though the ×50 required a new tester, the lower annual operating costs versus the ×100, along with the reduced testing time (from

DESCRIPTION	COST/WAFER	COST/DIE	CUM COST/DIE
Yielded raw wafer	$50.00	$0.33	$0.33
Wafer production cost	$3,000.00	$20.00	$20.33
Probe production cost	$625.00	$4.17	$24.50
Probe yield		70%	$35.00
168 PGA package cost		$15.00	$50.00
Assembly production cost		$4.00	$54.00
Assembly yield		96%	$56.25
Test production cost		$5.00	$61.25
Test yield		98%	$62.50
TOTAL x50 PRODUCT COST			$62.50

Figure 10.25 MosCo Inc. – FY95

Target cost management

OPERATION	PER YEAR	MFG. SPENDING	COST/UNIT
Planned wafer capacity	26,000		
Engineering test wafers	1,040		
Planned wafer starts	24,960		
Wafer fabrication yield	90%		
Planned wafer production	22,464	$67,392,000	$3,000.00
Planned probed wafer starts	20,800	$13,000,000	$625.00
Gross die/wafer (×50 = 150)	150		
Total gross die through probe	3,120,000		
Probe yield for ×50	70%		
×50 probed die output	2,184,000		
Planned assembly starts	405,500	$1,620,000	$4.00
×50 assembly yield	90%		
Planned assembly completions	364,500		
Planned test starts	405,000	$2,025,000	$5.00
×50 test yield	96%		
Planned test output	388,800		
TOTAL MANUFACTURING SPENDING		$84,037,000	

Figure 10.26 MosCo Inc. – FY95

the elimination of the floating point unit), resulted in a per unit test cost of only $5 versus $40 for the ×100.

10.5.106 With the ×50's cost structure now soundly understood, Offtiol could better appreciate the high but achievable profit margins of the ×50. The margins ranged from 75 per cent during Q1-Q3 '95 to ~67 per cent in Q4 '95 when the marketing-required price reduction took effect (see Chart III). If deStepper could achieve the $1,866 wafer cost by the start of 1996 (see Figures 10.27 and 10.28), the ×50 could obtain a very respectable margin of ~59 per cent in the second half of 1996 at the required price of $125. Using the capacity available in 1995 and 1996 to produce 50,000 and 215,000 units, respectively, easily convinced Offtiol to fund the ×50 development effort and purchase the new tester. While the product specifications for the ×75 were not yet available, he also agreed to fund its development effort. He felt the ×75 would achieve the same product margins the ×50 demonstrated.

Implementation issues

DESCRIPTION	COST/WAFER	COST/DIE	CUM COST/DIE
Yielded raw wafer	$50.00	$0.33	$0.33
Wafer production cost	$1,866.00	$12.44	$12.77
Probe production cost	$625.00	$4.17	$16.94
Probe yield		70%	$24.20
168 PGA package cost		$15.00	$39.20
Assembly production cost		$4.00	$43.20
Assembly yield		96%	$45.00
Test production cost		$5.00	$50.00
Test yield		98%	$51.02
TOTAL x50 PRODUCT COST			$51.02

Figure 10.27 MosCo Inc. – FY96

OPERATION	PER YEAR	MFG. SPENDING	COST/UNIT
Planned wafer capacity	26,000		
Engineering test wafers	1,040		
Planned wafer starts	24,960		
Wafer fabrication yield	90%		
Planned wafer production	22,464	$41,917,824	$1,866.00
Planned probed wafer starts	20,800	$13,000,000	$625.00
Gross die/wafer (x50 = 150)	150		
Total gross die through probe	3,120,000		
Probe yield for x50	70%		
x50 probed die output	2,184,000		
Planned assembly starts	405,500	$1,620,000	$4.00
x50 assembly yield	90%		
Planned assembly completions	364,500		
Planned test starts	405,000	$2,025,000	$5.00
x50 test yield	96%		
Planned test output	388,800		
TOTAL MANUFACTURING SPENDING		$58,562,824	

Figure 10.28 MosCo Inc. – FY96

673

Target cost management

10.5.107 Just as Offtiol was completing his ×50 product development meeting, Nomial called and suggested outsourcing and then disinvesting MosCo's assembly operations. She had found an assembly house that could assemble the ×50 in its required 168 PGA for $5 per device (in volume levels of 500,000) with equivalent yields to those MosCo projected. Offtiol thought this idea had merit until he compared the $5 external assembly cost/device to the internal cost estimate of $4. He quickly concluded outsourcing would only increase the overall product cost and therefore was not a viable option.

Chart III

	Q1 '95–Q3 '95	Q4 '95–Q2 '96	Q3 '96 & Q4 '96
Price	$250.00	$187.50	$125.00
Cost	$62.50	$62.50	$51.02
Margin $	$187.50	$125.00	$73.98
Margin %	75.0%	66.7%	59.2%

10.5.108 A week before the budget review, Offtiol asked Janus to prepare new pro forma income statements for FY94, FY95, and FY96. He wanted to reflect all his cost reduction targets and product-funding levels. He was curious to see the levels of profit he would generate in 1995 and 96 from; (1) the revised ×100 product cost, (2) the 1996 cost reduction targets in wafer fabrication and their effect on the ×100 and ×50, (3) the funding of the ×50 and ×75, (4) the purchase of the Bonn tester the ×50 required, (5) the utilisation of 1995 and 1996 capacity for manufacturing the ×50, (6) the additional advertising expense necessary to promote the ×50 fully in the market place, and (7) the selling of the ×100 and ×50 using the marketing department pricing model. Offtiol was confident his decisions would prove sound and keep MosCo profitable in 1995 and 1996.

10.5.109 Now, after a second review of Janus' pro forma income statements (see Figures 10.29, 10.30 and 10.31), Offtiol had become very anxious. He had to present a viable set of recommendations to MosCo's senior management the following day. He thought he and his team had explored and included all viable options in Janus' statements. Finally, Offtiol concluded the cause of the projected FY95 and FY96 losses was the overly aggressive pricing model. He decided he would present Janus' projections, highlight the losses in spite of the cost reductions reflected, and suggest keeping the ×100 price at $850 for all of 1995 and at $637.50 for all of 1996. The $23.9 million increase in FY95 revenue would turn the ~$(15.2 million) loss into an $8.7 million profit. But the $17.9 million increase in FY96 revenue would only improve the loss of ~$(40.5 million) to ~$(22.6 million). Offtiol was convinced Scott would also agree that Price's pricing model was too aggressive. He was certain Scott

Implementation issues

	1994 REVISED	1995 RECOM'D	1996 RECOM'D
REVENUE:	$127,500,000	$115,312,500	$63,476,562
COST OF SALES:			
raw material cost	$9,496,775	$10,348,010	$8,282,255
production costs	$90,112,000	$59,063,500	$27,788,853
total product cost	$99,608,775	$69,411,510	$36,071,108
product gross margin	$27,891,225	$45,900,990	$27,405,454
%	21.9%	39.8%	43.2%
underutilized costs	$0	$33,071,500	$38,873,971
total cost of sales	$99,608,775	$102,485,010	$74,945,079
GROSS MARGIN:	$27,891,225	$12,827,490	($11,468,516)
%	21.9%	11.1%	−18.1%
PROCESS DEVELOPMENT:	$15,000,000	$15,000,000	$15,000,000
PRODUCT DEVELOPMENT:	$6,000,000	$6,000,000	$6,000,000
MARKETING & ADMINISTRATION:	$6,000,000	$7,000,000	$8,000,000
OPERATING PROFIT/(LOSS):	$891,225	($15,172,510)	($40,468,516)

Figure 10.29 'Offitol' pro forma income statement

would approve a revised ×100 price and be receptive to a higher price for the ×50, which could offset the remaining projected 1996 loss. Offtiol felt it would take a combination of his cost reduction efforts and higher prices to maintain MosCo's profitability and thus demonstrate to CSI MosCo's ability to transform itself into a competitive business unit.

Major internal and external factors affecting MosCo
10.5.110   Internal factors.

- MosCo has been changed from a captive cost centre to a business unit and profit centre; its goal has been changed from managing cost to making a profit.

- Products are now transferred to parent at price, not cost. Competitive pricing determination is critical.

- New products can be sold to the external market; MosCo must develop marketing skills and establish a market presence against an established market leader.

- Sustaining a gross margin of at least 24 per cent is needed to break even. To achieve respectable profit levels, gross margins in the 40–50 per cent range are required. Understanding and managing manufacturing under-utilisation and related cost drivers are critical.

Target cost management

	×100	×50	FY95
REVENUE:			
Q1: (37,500 @ $850)	$31,875,500		
Q2–Q4: (112,500 @ $637,50)	$71,718,750		
Q1–Q3: (37,500 @ $250)		$9,375,000	
Q4: (12,500 @ $187.50)		$2,343,750	
	$103,593,750	$11,718,750	$115,312,500
RAW MATERIAL COSTS:			
Wafers: (16,595 @ $45)	$746,775		
(583 @ $45)		$26,235	
Packages: (175,000 @ $50)	$8,750,000		
(55,000 @ $15)		$851,000	
	$9,496,775	$851,235	$10,348,010
PRODUCTION COSTS:			
Fabrication: (14,000 @ $3000)	$42,000,000		
(524 @ $3000)		$1,572,000	
Probe: (14,000 @ $500)	$7,000,000		
(524 @ $625)		$327,500	
Assembly: (175,000 @ $8)	$1,400,000		
(55,000 @ $30)		$220,000	
Test: (157,000 @ $40)	$6,280,000		
(52,800 @ $5)		$264,000	
	$56,680,000	$2,383,500	$59,063,500
UNDERUTILIZED COSTS:			
Fabrication: ($67,392,000 – ($42,000,000 + $1,572,000))			$23,820,000
Probe: ($13,000,000 – ($7,000,000 + $327,000))			$5,672,500
Assembly: ($1,620,000 – ($1,400,000 + $220,000))			$0
Test: ($8,100,000 – $6,280,000) + ($2,025,000 – $264,000)			$3,581,000
			$33,073,500

Figure 10.30 FY95 'Offitol' pro forma income statement worksheet

10.5.111 External factors.

- Product price/performance halves every 18 months. Shorter life-cycles and product performance or price reduction are constant and major market forces.

- Demand for the older, proprietary product is declining, while MosCo is being asked to establish a competitive market price that tracks with the external market.

Implementation issues

	×100	×50	FY95
REVENUE:			
Q1–Q3: (56,250 @ $425)	$23,906,250		
Q4: (18,750 @ $318.75)	$5,976,562		
Q1–Q2: (107,500 @ $187.50)		$20,156,250	
Q3–Q4: (107,500 @ $125)		$13,437,500	
	$29,882,812	$33,593,750	$63,476,562
RAW MATERIAL COSTS:			
Wafers: (7,991 @ $45)	$359,592		
(2,448 @ $45)		$110,160	
Packages: (86,875 @ $50)	$4,343,750		
(231,250 @ $15)		$3,468,750	
	$4,703,345	$3,578,910	$8,282,255
PRODUCTION COSTS:			
Fabrication: (6,950 @ $1866)	$12,968,700		
(2,203 @ $1866)		$4,110,798	
Probe: (6,950 @ $500)	$3,475,000		
(2,203 @ $625)		$1,376,875	
Assembly: (86,875 @ $8)	$695,000		
(231,250 @ $4)		$925,000	
Test: (78,187 @ $40)	$3,127,480		
(222,000 @ $5)		$1,110,000	
	$20,266,180	$7,522,673	$27,788,853
UNDERUTILIZED COSTS:			
Fabrication: ($41,917,824 – ($12,968,700 + $4,110,798))			$24,838,326
Probe: ($13,000,000 – ($3,475,000 + $1,376,875))			$8,148,125
Assembly: ($1,620,000 – ($695,000 + $925,000))			$0
Test: ($8,100,000 – $3,127,480) + ($2,025,000 – $1,110,000)			$5,887,520
			$38,873,971

Figure 10.31 MosCo Inc. – FY96 'Offitol' pro forma income statement worksheet

- New products that have a cost and price disadvantage are being readied for external sale against an established market leader. Determining the appropriate price and the potential actions of competition are critical.

10.5.112 This listing helps put the volatile and competitive semi-conductor market in perspective and focus on the need to keep the very capital-intensive manufacturing base fully utilised. The fact that the process life-cycle often exceeds a single product life-cycle is relevant to note.

Target cost management

What caused the 1995 ×100 product cost to drop by $227 after reflecting the results of the activity-based costing approach?

10.5.113 The redistribution of support costs and the increase in capacity utilisation allow the savings. A comparison of the product cost (see Figures 10.17 and 10.19) and the process cost (see Figures 10.18 and 10.20) given the ABC study show the following.

Wafer fabrication: cost/wafer decreased from $5,245.15 to $3,000.00

- Support costs for fabrication are reduced ($16,429,500 to $10,392,000) because of redistribution to the manufacturing areas they support as defined in the activity-based costing assessment.
- Wafer start capacity used in product costing has been redefined from the capacity planned to be used (15,555) to the total capacity available for manufacturing (24,960).

Probe: cost/wafer decreased from $785.71 to $500.00

- Probe manufacturing spending increased from $11,000,000 to $13,000,000 because $2,000,000 of the redistribution of fabrication support costs is now assigned to probe as defined in the activity-based costing assessment.
- Probe wafer start capacity has been redefined from capacity planned to be used (14,000) to the total capacity available for manufacturing (26,000).

Assembly: cost/assembly start decreased from $9.26 to $8.00

- Assembly capacity has been redefined from capacity planned to be used (175,000) to the total capacity available for manufacturing (202,000).

Test: cost/test start increased from $32.14 to $40.00

- Test manufacturing spending increased from $5,062,500 to $8,100,000 because $3,037,500 of the redistributed fabrication support costs is now assigned to test as defined in the activity-based costing assessment.
- Test capacity has been redefined from capacity planned to be used (157,500) to the total capacity available for manufacturing (202,500).

10.5.114 Process development: $1 million of fabrication support costs has been redistributed from manufacturing and assigned to process development.

Implementation issues

What are the cost drivers of process manufacturing and what are the other cost drivers contributing to total product cost?

10.5.115 Equipment cost and utilisation are the major cost drivers of process manufacturing. The semi-conductor manufacturing process is very capital intensive, and the cost of each piece of process manufacturing equipment drives depreciation, a significant process manufacturing cost element. More important, the size of the equipment base, its integration across the manufacturing process, and the amount of time the equipment is up and running will determine manufacturing capacity, the single largest process manufacturing cost driver. In addition, the size of the equipment base will drive equipment maintenance, monitor wafer (and other expendables) usage, and the size and cost of other related support functions. Line and probe yield, the per cent of usable wafer and die production versus the total manufactured are key factors in determining the amount of capacity necessary; thus also are significant cost drivers of process manufacturing.

10.5.116 Die size is probably the largest single product cost driver. As the size of the die increases, the amount of total dies on a wafer decreases and the amount of dies lost through probe yield increases; thus during product design, it is critical to balance functionality (which more usually means larger dies) and the resulting cost. Die functionality also may drive package type and cost. The concept of total product cost can be expanded to include other non-manufacturing costs related to products, such as marketing and sales. As is noted in the case, the new sales and marketing department is chartered to open new markets for the ×50 and ×75. In determining the total cost of these products, it would also be fair to include specific sales, marketing, and advertising costs in these analyses.

Was it practical or plausible to reduce wafer fabrication spending by 38 per cent or ~$25.5 million as Offtiol asked deStepper to do?

Wafer fabrication cost make-up		
Fixed/semifixed costs	$m	%
Depreciation	30.0	44.5
Utilities	5.0	7.4
Property/site costs	5.0	7.4
Equipment engineers	8.0	11.9
Direct labour	5.0	7.4
Facilities	5.0	7.4
CIMT	2.0	3.0
Quality	2.0	3.0
Purchasing	1.4	2.0
Total fixed/semifixed	63.4	94.0

Variable costs		
Monitor wafers	2.0	3.0
Operational supplies	2.0	3.0
Total variable	4.0	6.0
Total wafer fabrication costs	67.4	100.0

10.5.117 It was not practical to reduce wafer fabrication spending by 38 per cent or ~$25.5 million as Offtiol had demanded. The chart above highlights the large per cent of fixed and semifixed wafer fabrication costs. Depreciation alone is almost 45 per cent of the total wafer fabrication cost structure, which underscores the large capital infrastructure necessary in this industry. The remaining $33.4 million of fixed/semifixed costs is driven directly or indirectly by this extensive capital equipment base. Thus, while cost improvements or reductions are always possible, it is not likely that $25.5 million could be removed from the cost structure without severely affecting the capacity or efficiency of the wafer fabrication area. The reciprocal to this conclusion is also important to highlight. With a large fixed cost production base, increasing the utilisation has a dramatic unit cost reduction effect, usually better than can be achieved with cost reduction alone.

Should Offtiol have explored cost reduction opportunities in other manufacturing or non-manufacturing areas? If so, where?

10.5.118 Yes, other cost reduction opportunities in manufacturing and non-manufacturing areas should have been pursued. In the manufacturing area, improving probe yield for the ×100 should have been explored. Improving probe yield increases the amount of good dies available from a fabricated wafer, thus fewer wafers need to be started to produce a static demand and available wafer fabrication capacity is increased. This higher capacity could be utilised for the ×50. Also in the manufacturing area, the remaining production activities (probe, assembly and test) should be examined for all possible cost reduction and/or production efficiency opportunities. The assembly area, in particular, is a capacity bottleneck – unit production costs may be low, but its limited capacity limits the entire production capacity. Outsourcing should not have been dismissed so readily. This assembly capacity issue is further discussed below. Finally, cost/benefit analyses and benchmarking should have been pursued in the area of R&D and SG&A. These efforts might provide other cost saving opportunities.

Was Offtiol's ABC team staffed appropriately?

10.5.119 An ABC team should be cross-functional in nature with members having a skilled understanding of the operational and financial make-up of each area to be analysed. Offtiol's team had only wafer fabrica-

Implementation issues

tion represented. The remaining members were representatives from staff functions (finance, quality and training). No other manufacturing or non-manufacturing area was represented. A well-constructed and effective ABC team should ensure membership from, and coverage of, each phase of the entire product life-cycle. An ABC consultant, either an internally trained or external expert, should be used to facilitate the project from exploration and documentation to data analysis. Offtiol's ABC team was not staffed appropriately.

Is there still under-utilised manufacturing capacity when the ×50 is manufactured?

10.5.120 Yes, there is still available manufacturing capacity in fabrication, probe and test after the ×50 is produced. Figure 10.32 highlights the specific available production levels. Assembly, at full capacity, is also the process bottleneck preventing further ×50 production. Management should quickly assess the cost of this unused capacity versus the cost and benefit of additional internal or outsourced assembly capacity to balance the line and make available additional production of the ×50.

Is Price's pricing model too aggressive?

10.5.121 Falling prices, which is the nature of the industry, and short product life-cycles place great pressure on capacity utilisation. The physical and technological nature of a semi-conductor device requires extensive capital production equipment. The equipment life is typically much longer than the product life. This phenomenon places a great deal of risk on the potential return from the equipment investment.

10.5.122 *×100:* Changing to a market-based price centred on industry price/performance curves appears to be a management catch 22. The product was developed and production established to meet the demand of CSI, the sole customer and parent to MosCo. Their demand is falling, and the design of the product makes it unsuitable for external sales. Yet, because CSI now measures MosCo on profit, it is demanding a market price for this custom product. Given these circumstances, Price's pricing model is too aggressive for the ×100. This model is better suited for developing base prices for external business. MosCo and Offtiol should develop a negotiated ×100 price for this custom, legacy and declining demand product.

10.5.123 *×50 & ×75:* MosCo is not the market leader for these products and has a cost disadvantage due to the larger die size of the ×50 versus NoTel's N50. They must price at, or slightly below, the market to gain entry. Pricing at half NoTel's price would attract attention not only from potential customers but also from NoTel, which could easily match the lower price

681

Target cost management

(w) wafers (d) die	Total capacity available	×100 capacity used		Available capacity for ×50		Maximum used by ×50		Available capacity	
		FY 95 (150,000)	FY 96 (75,000)	FY 95	FY 96	FY 95	FY 96	FY 95	FY 96
Fab. starts	26,000 (w)	16,595	7,991						
Engineering starts	1,040 (w)	1,040	1,040						
Production starts	24,960 (w)	15,555	7,723	9,405	17,237	582	2,447	8,823	14,790
Production completes	22,464 (w)	14,000	6,950	8,464	15,514	524	2,202	7,940	13,312
×100 probe starts	26,000 (w)	14,000	6,950	12,000	19,050				
×50 probe starts	20,800 (w)			9,600	15,240	524	2,202	9,076	13,038
339 PGA assembly starts	202,500 (d)	175,000	86,875	27,500	115,625				
339 PGA assembly completes	188,250 (d)	157,500	78,187						
168 PGA assembly starts	405,000 (d)			55,000	231,250	55,000	231,250	0	0
168 PGA assembly completes	388,800 (d)			52,800	222,000	52,800	222,000	0	0
×100 test starts	202,500 (d)	157,500	78,187					45,000	124,313
×100 test completes	194,400 (d)	151,200	75,060					43,200	119,340
×50 test starts	405,000 (d)			405,000	405,000	52,800	222,000	352,200	183,000
×50 test completes	396,900 (d)			396,900	396,900	51,744	217,560	345,156	179,340

Figure 10.32 MosCo Inc. – FY95&FY96 capacity available

Implementation issues

and still earn a comfortable margin. MosCo could not afford to get into a pricing war at this time. Price's pricing model is too aggressive for these products as well. In addition, MosCo must be competitive in service and delivery. To compete successfully, the market will continue to place great pressure on cost management. Thus, a serious assessment needs to be made to determine if the firm can be competitive in the long run. This assessment should consider market share, marketing know-how, current and future product life-cycles, manufacturing process efficiencies, and an affordable cost structure.

What pricing advantages does MosCo's competitor, NoTel, have due to their N50 having 33 per cent more die on each wafer than the ×50?

10.5.124 Assuming a similar manufacturing process and cost structure (which is not likely given NoTel's market leadership), NoTel will still be able to produce the N50 for less than MosCo can. Using MosCo's $3,000 wafer cost applied to the N50 @ 75 per cent probe yield, the N50 would cost $51.34; $11.16 or 18 per cent less than the ×50. If NoTel's wafer cost was more competitive, say at the MosCo desired level of $1,866, then the N50 would cost $43.30; $19.20 or 31 per cent lower than the current ×50 product cost and $7.72 or 15 per cent lower than the ×50 after reflecting Offtiol's improbable wafer fabrication cost reductions.

10.5.125 Given these conservatively estimated cost advantages, the pricing advantages available to NoTel are obvious.

What other manufacturing, development, and/or pricing actions could be taken to improve MosCo's financial performance in 1995 and 1996 and can Offtiol's recommendations be improved?

10.5.126 In addition to the factors and issues highlighted above the following can also be considered.

- Build and sell more ×50. Product demand is estimated at more than 1 million units/year.
- Increase assembly capacity by reconsidering Polly Nomial's proposal and outsource the amount necessary to balance the production process and meet the ×50 demand. Attempt to renegotiate the outsourcing price; MosCo's internal cost is $4/unit, while the vendor is charging $5/unit.
- Implement deStepper's capacity proposal, which increases fabrication capacity and lowers unit costs below Offtiol's target. There is sufficient ×50 demand to utilise this additional capacity, although test capacity becomes the bottleneck.

Target cost management

- If deStepper's proposal is recommended, then increase test capacity by purchasing additional testers. While a tester is an expensive piece of equipment, the higher profit levels achieved by the additional sales easily justify the investment.

- Quickly redesign the ×50 to achieve a similar die/wafer level as the N50 and/or ensure that the design of the ×75 equals or exceeds the technology and cost of NoTel's comparable product.

- Improve yields on the ×50 as well as the ×100, not only in probe but also in assembly and test.

MosCo – Process map

Production process:				
Material	**Fabrication**	**Probe**	**Assembly**	**Test**
Silicon Wafers	Repeat process for layers Insulate (oxide) Coated Masked, UV light Strip	Test die Market rejects	Cut die Good die to package Seal	TEST
Cost map				
Wafer Cost Cost/wafer	+Fact OH +Direct L & M Cost/wafer	+Fact OH +Direct L & M Cost/wafer	+Fact OH +Direct L & M Cost/die	Cost/die
Final manageable unit cost is cost/die, the YIELD KEY				

(Source: adapted with permission from Nanni, 1998.)

Chapter 11
Performance measurement and cost management

11.1 The goals of performance measures

11.1.1 Performance evaluation is considered an important aspect of management accounting systems. Unfortunately, effective performance evaluation is complex and difficult to achieve. Ideally, performance measures should be quantifiable and should encompass all aspects of performance that are potentially relevant to outcomes. But these requirements often conflict because many relevant aspects of performance are intangible and difficult to quantify.

11.1.2 According to Bledsoe and Ingram (1997), performance measures should:

- encourage goal congruence (i.e., the alignment of employees' goals with those of the company as a whole);
- focus on future operating results;
- include both financial and non-financial criteria;
- provide a means of communication between operations and accounting.

Problems with traditional evaluation systems

11.1.3 Criticism of traditional performance evaluation systems have focused on their primary reliance on financial accounting information. Criteria based on sales, earnings, return on investment and budget variances have dominated performance standards. While these measures help managers evaluate financial performance, they do not lend themselves to the measurement of management effectiveness, manufacturing productivity, product quality and asset utilisation. They also tend to report historical performance (i.e., what has happened) rather than predict future performance (i.e., what will happen).

11.1.4 Like traditional financial accounting performance measures, traditional management accounting performance measures (e.g., those that concentrate on budget and production variances) do not necessarily indicate

Performance measurement and cost management

whether an operation is performing effectively relative to the goals of the organisation. Moreover, as Bledsoe and Ingram (1997) note, the incorporation of these traditional measures into evaluation programmes can cause employees to behave in ways directly opposed to the overall goals of the company. This can occur when management uses a performance measurement and reward system that fails to emphasise the articulated goals and objectives of the organisation as a whole.

11.1.5 For example, if a single performance measure (e.g., a standard cost variance) is over-emphasised in an employee's performance evaluation, the employee is encouraged to make decisions that maximise his personal performance in terms of that single measure. These actions may conflict with the achievement of the organisation's overall goals.

11.1.6 Efforts to improve traditional evaluation systems have emphasised the need to evaluate the ability of employees to increase the long-run effectiveness of their divisions consistent with organisational goals. Therefore, organisational goals, strategies for achieving the goals and performance measures are all relevant to a performance evaluation system.

Improvements to traditional evaluation systems

11.1.7 Bledsoe and Ingram (1997) believe that performance goals should be clearly defined and stated in terms of specific outcomes that are measurable. Performance measures can then be linked to these outcomes. The participation of employees in developing goals and performance measures plays an important role in whether the goals are achieved. The attainment of goals is affected by:

- the extent to which employees view the goals as necessary and attainable;
- the degree to which employees have control over the outcomes that affect performance evaluation.

11.1.8 Figure 11.1 provides a summary model of a performance evaluation system based on these principles. The system begins with the determination of goals. Strategies must be developed to achieve the goals, and expected outcomes must be specified. Next, quantifiable performance measures are identified consistent with the desired outcomes. After procedures are developed to collect and evaluate performance measures, the performance measures can be assessed in terms of whether the goals, strategies and the entire evaluation system are met. The ultimate success of the system depends on whether the organisation's goals are achieved.

Figure 11.1 Performance evaluation system model

| Performance goals | Strategies to achieve goals | Expected outcomes |
| Examine achievement and reassess goals | Performance evaluation procedures | Measure outcomes |

(Source: Bledsoe and Ingram, 1997.)

11.2 Which performance measures?

11.2.1 Traditional accounting measures are dominant in practice. Nevertheless there is evidence that new measures of performance, especially value-based metrics, are gaining increasing popularity. One study of divisional performance measures used in UK organisations (Francis and Minchington, 2000) suggests that 28 per cent make use of value drivers, 15 per cent use shareholder value analysis and 10 per cent use economic value added (EVA®) (see Table 11.1). Moreover, the study reports that 24 per cent use the balanced scorecard approach (see below). Whilst the balanced scorecard addresses financial and non-financial aspects of performance, value-based metrics are more focused on financial performance and shareholders. Value-based metrics seek to combine three essential characteristics of enterprises. These are cash flow generated, capital invested to generate the cash flows and the cost of capital of the investment. Amongst performance measures introduced by the organisations included in the study over the previous three years, the balanced scorecard seemed most popular (see Figure 11.2).

Table 11.1 Use of financial performance measure in the division

	Used	Being considered	Not being considered	Not aware of
Ability to stay within budget	99%	1%	0%	0%
Target profit	94%	3%	2%	1%
Return on capital employed	71%	6%	18%	5%
Target cash flow	70%	7%	17%	6%
Value drivers	28%	18%	35%	19%
Balanced scorecard approach	24%	21%	29%	26%
Shareholder Value Analysis (SVA)	15%	13%	53%	19%
Economic Value Added (EVA®)	10%	18%	46%	26%
Residual income (RI)	6%	2%	56%	36%

(Source: Francis and Minchington, 2000.)

Performance measurement and cost management

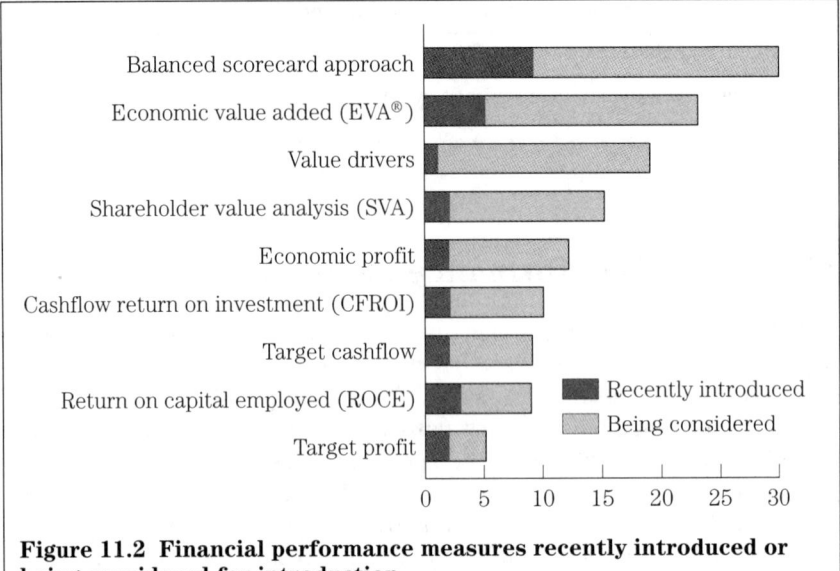

Figure 11.2 Financial performance measures recently introduced or being considered for introduction

11.3 Performance measures for stakeholders

11.3.1 In the development and implementation of improved business processes, it is vital to identify and monitor appropriate performance measures to evaluate progress in achieving plans and to prompt control actions when necessary. According to MacArthur (1996), a performance measure can be defined as, 'a quantification of how well the activities within a process or the outputs of a process achieve a specified goal'. Thus, performance measures should:

- be expressed quantitatively rather than qualitatively so that they are measurable;
- be geared to the purposes of the organisation;
- evaluate both the processes themselves (e.g., the way deliveries of products are scheduled) and the outputs of processes (e.g., the timeliness of product deliveries to customers).

11.3.2 The performance measures must seek to facilitate decision and actions that support strategies based on the needs of stakeholders (see Figure 11.3). These stakeholders include stockholders, internal and external customers, regulatory bodies, managers and employees.

Performance measures for stakeholders

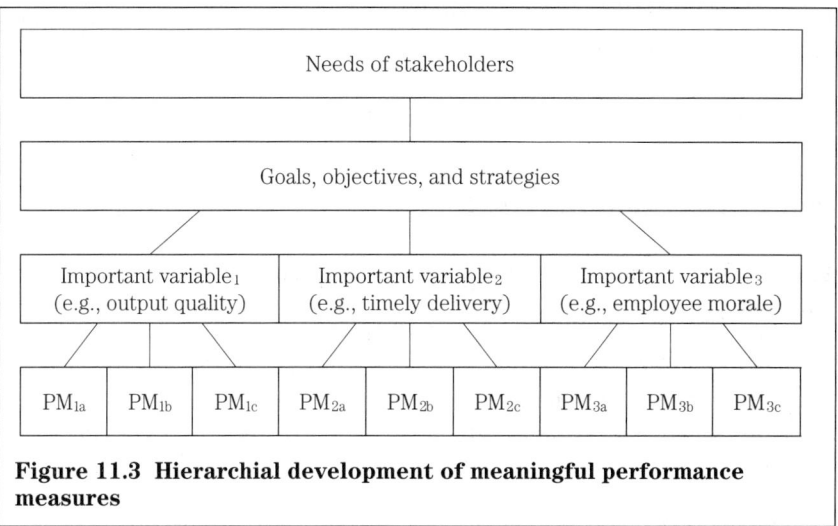

Figure 11.3 Hierarchial development of meaningful performance measures

The vital link

11.3.3 MacArthur (1996) provides a practical example of how to link performance monitoring to strategy. The goal according to him is to encourage the wider adoption of this link and the development of better quantitative performance measures as well as supplementary qualitative performance indicators.

11.3.4 Performance measures can monitor quantitative variables (e.g., a direct measure of lead time) or serve as proxies for qualitative variables (e.g., employees' turnover rates to help monitor trends in employee morale). Performance indicators can also monitor qualitative variables (e.g., a consultant's assessment of the level of employee morale as high, moderate or low) or represent quantitative variables (e.g., a manager's evaluation of lead time as satisfactory or unsatisfactory). Table 11.2 shows these relationships.

Table 11.2 Examples of variables monitored by performance measures and indicators

	Quantitative performance measures	Qualitative performance measures
Quantitative Variables	Direct measures of lead time	Manager's evaluation of lead time as satisfactory or unsatisfactory
Qualitative Variables	Employee turnover rates to help monitor trends in employee morale	Consultant's assessment of the level of employee morale as high, moderate or low

(Source: MacArthur 1996.)

Performance measurement and cost management

11.3.5 Qualitative performance indicators can sometimes be transformed into quantitative performance measures. For example, a qualitative value like employee morale might be evaluated by tracking the number of times employee morale is rated as high, moderate or low over specified periods of time.

Monitoring employee safety

11.3.6 To illustrate the development of performance measures and indicators comprehensively, MacArthur (1996) presents a case study on employee safety in the meat-packing industry. The case complements studies on monitoring the performance of more tangible aspects of production processes (e.g., physical product dimensions and cycle time). Since the case emphasises four significant features that generally apply to other types of organisations as well, the case study can be used as a model for similar systems.

11.3.7 Meat-packing is a labour-intensive industry. Front-line employees work with dangerous tools. To compensate for low profit margins (less than 1 per cent), employees must operate at fast speeds to maintain high volumes. In fact, MacArthur (1996) notes that the high-speed, mass 'disassembly' of hogs and cattle in meat-packing plants in the latter part of the nineteenth century provided Henry Ford with a model for the development of the assembly lines he used to mass- produce automobiles. In the meat-packing industry, the combination of sharp instruments and employees working at high speeds has led to exceptionally high rates of injury and illness caused by repetitive body movements, awkward body positions and other hazards of the workplace. Consequently, injuries and illnesses are a major concern to various stakeholders of meat-packing plants, including employees, management and the government. Reductions of workplace injuries and illnesses (e.g., through reductions in worker fatigue and stress) can improve worker productivity and efficiency. Therefore, employee safety is an area of strategic importance to top management in the meat-packing industry – an area that needs to be closely and continuously monitored.

Key variables

11.3.8 Given the need to minimise job-related injuries and illnesses, meat-packing companies pursue continuous improvement in employee safety by implementing new technologies and work techniques designed to reduce injuries and illnesses. Performance measures and indicators can be designed to monitor how these worker-safety strategies are implemented. Generally, safety standards require employers to provide a working environment that is clear of known serious dangers to worker safety.

Performance measures for stakeholders

11.3.9 Examples of worker safety quantitative performance measures and qualitative performance indicators are classified in Figure 11.4.

Figure 11.4 Examples of worker-safety process performance measures and indicators

Quantitative performance measures
• Job rotation frequency.
• Number of standby or relief workers.
• Number and percentage of deviations from the preventative maintenance programme.
• Number and percentage of deviations from knife-sharpening programme.
• Number and percentage of deviations from housekeeping programme.
• Number and percentage of deviations from medical management programme.
• Number of ergonomic improvements in terms of facilities, processes, materials and equipment.
• Number and percentage of mechanical or powered assists to eliminate extreme force.
• Number and percentage of heavy tools suspended to reduce extreme force.
• Number of full-time equivalent appropriately trained healthcare providers available per shift.
• Tool vibration measures (to check if within acceptable limits).
• Cost-benefit measures of workstation and equipment changes proposed to prevent and control ergonomic hazards.
• Trends in quantitative process safety measures.
Qualitative performance measures
• Periodic employee surveys regarding process safety features.
• Before and after surveys of job or worksite changes.
• Review of results of plant evaluations.
• Up-to-date records of logs of job improvements tried or implemented.
• Worksite analysis using ergonomic checklist.
• Preventative maintenance programme evaluation by experts.
• Knife-sharpening programme evaluation by experts.
• Housekeeping programme evaluation by experts.
• Medical management programme evaluation by experts.
• Training and education programme evaluation by experts.
• Employee interviews, testing and observation of work practices to evaluate training and education programme.
• Trends in qualitative process safety indicators.

(Source: MacArthur, 1996.)

11.3.10 Meat-packing companies can still use other performance measures and indicators to monitor strategic variables other than worker safety. For example, one meat-packing company measures the results of its continuous improvement process by using the following measures.

- Water usage and landfill charges (to monitor progress in environmental matters).

- Yield.
- Labour and material costs.
- Inventory levels.
- Customer returns.
- Rework.
- Absenteeism rates.
- Eliminating obsolete measures.

11.3.11 In addition to developing performance measures that support a company's mission and strategy, companies may also discontinue measures that are seen as inappropriate. Outdated performance measures compete with new, more appropriate performance measures and dilute their intended effect. The retention of obsolete performance measures tends to promote organisational 'paralysis'.

11.3.12 Discarding obsolete performance measures is unlikely to take place as a matter of course in most organisations. It requires directed management action. Sometimes the development of an improved performance measurement system may be easier than persuading organisations to eradicate obsolete measures with which they are familiar and feel comfortable.

11.3.13 Selecting an appropriate set of performance measures and indicators has, according to MacArthur (1996), been facilitated by advances in information technology, which have made data collection and data analysis in organisations far more efficient and cost-beneficial in recent times.

11.3.14 Despite advances in computer technology, however, practical considerations must prevail in the selection of performance measures and indicators. For example, the cognitive limitations of managers is a constraint on the number of measures and indicators that should be prepared for each important variable. Other practical questions that must also be considered include the following.

- Can the required information be obtained in a sufficiently timely manner to facilitate proper control actions?
- Are the collection costs greater than the benefits obtained from the performance measures and indicators?
- How frequently should performance measures and indicators be calculated and reported?

Performance measures for stakeholders

A case study: measuring workers' performance

11.3.15 Whilst worker performance measurement is an issue of considerable importance for many organisations, it is typically interrelated with other operational concerns. The Velky Potraviny case captures many operational concerns including flows and layout of a warehouse, capacity expansion issues, delivery priorities and broader corporate goals.

11.3.16 Juraj (pronounced 'Yurai') Zdenek, the warehouse manager for the Velky Potraviny ('Big Grocery' in Czech) grocery chain, was examining the operating results from the latest month when Jan, his senior warehouse picker, came bursting into his office. 'This is ridiculous,' Jan exclaimed. 'Last month was an incredibly busy month, especially with the addition of another store to service. Now I pick up my monthly pay cheque and find that this month's bonus is half what it should be. I wasn't happy with my last pay cheque either, but I didn't say anything. If this happens again, I'm quitting. There are plenty of other jobs in the Czech Republic.'

11.3.17 This was not the first time an employee had complained about the bonus system, and Juraj knew their grievances had merit. In fact, employee compensation was only part of the entire problem that he faced in running the Velky Potraviny (Velky) warehouse. Juraj decided to call a meeting, that would include a representative of each of the job functions in the warehouse, to discuss compensation issues, along with any other issues that might arise. Juraj knew he had to do a better job of controlling all his costs, particularly compensation.

Background
11.3.18 For much of the seventeenth, eighteenth and nineteenth centuries the Czech Republic was part of the Austro-Hungarian Empire. Czechoslovakia gained its independence in 1918 after World War I. Between the world wars, Czechoslovakia's economy was one of the most prosperous in Central Europe, as capitalism flourished. However, World War II and its aftermath proved devastating, as Czechoslovakia lost its independence in all but name. Throughout World War II, Czechoslovakia was occupied by Nazi Germany. After liberation by the Red Army, it became part of the Soviet sphere, behind the Iron Curtain. Communism completely changed or eliminated much of the economic infrastructure developed in the 1920s and 1930s.

11.3.19 Czechoslovakia first attempted to change the nature of communism in 1968 when the Prague Spring with the movement 'to put a human face on communism' was born. The Soviet invasion of Czechoslovakia in late

Performance measurement and cost management

1968 crushed this movement, which sought to bring more individual freedom. Although dissidents continued to fight, it was not until November 1989 that communism was overthrown by the 'Velvet Revolution'. In mid-1990, a freely elected government led by Vaclav Havel was formed, and capitalistic structures began to be created. Western companies found Czechoslovakia, with its political stability, its centralised location in Europe and its well-educated and relatively low-wage workforce, an attractive location for investment. Since the subsequent peaceful split of the Czech Republic and Slovakia in 1993, the Czech Republic has done well economically.

The company

11.3.20   Velky Potraviny was positioned as a one-stop, low-cost grocery store. It was established in the Czech Republic in 1991 and opened its first store in Prague in 1992. As of August 2000, the company had 37 stores operating in Prague and in the north-west region of the Czech Republic. Each Velky store was a full-service supermarket, offering an extensive variety of products, although Velky limited the number of brands available in an effort to keep its costs down (in 1996 it carried 1,300 stock-keeping units (SKUs) with a goal of 1,000 SKUs).

11.3.21   Velky had to face numerous challenges not typical of those faced by companies in the West. Some were caused by the complete transformation of an economy from communism to capitalism, for example, extremely high inflation due to price liberalisation; a non-convertible currency (the Czech crown); a poor to non-existent distribution system characterised by a lack of roads – let alone highways; an overburdened rail system; a lack of warehouse space; and an evolving business, regulatory, legal and taxation system. There was also the cultural hurdle of convincing potential customers to do one-stop shopping. The Czechs have not been in the habit of buying groceries in large quantities, instead preferring to shop daily at neighbourhood specialty stores such as bakeries, butchers and fruit merchants. Such specialisation lent itself to a perception of quality and knowledge about the product; thus, Velky's lack of specialisation was perceived by many as a detriment.

11.3.22   All of Velky Potraviny's retail stores were approximately 6,400–7,500 sq ft, with similar layouts. At the retail stores, storage facilities were kept as small as possible; nearly all goods flowed directly from the loading dock to the retail shelves. Customers could select individual units out of cartons (e.g., a single pencil from a large carton of pencils). Each store employed six cashiers whose responsibilities included memorising prices, checking out customers, collecting money and counting inventory with a small, hand-held device. The retail stores were not computerised, although

Performance measures for stakeholders

Velky's long-term plans included implementation of bar code scanning technology. Depending on the retail store, some sent their orders via modem to the warehouse every day; others ordered two to three times a week. Each store usually received shipments every other day from the warehouse.

The warehouse

11.3.23 Soon after establishing its first retail operations, and to support the growth anticipated by the company, Velky acquired a defunct, communist-era, military-tank-building facility in a Prague suburb north of the city. The current layout of the warehouse is shown in Figure 11.5.

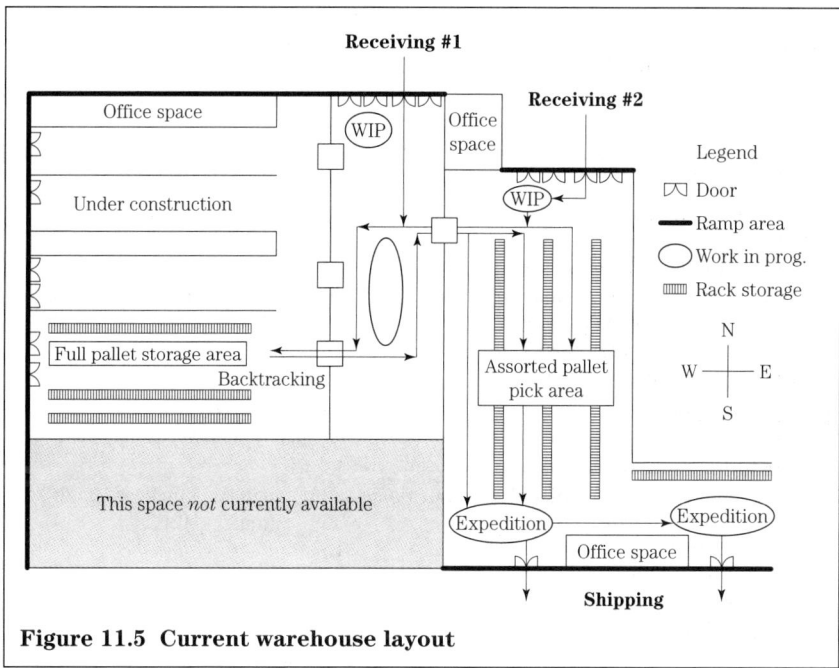

Figure 11.5 Current warehouse layout

11.3.24 The warehouse was responsible for holding non-perishable goods, approximately 70 per cent of Velky's product mix. Suppliers sent perishable goods such as fruits, vegetables, bread and cheese directly to the retail stores. The warehouse originally was arranged so as to facilitate the unloading of goods from suppliers and the loading of goods for stores. However, with the increase in the number of stores to service, and given the planned expansion to 67 stores within the next two years, Juraj was concerned about whether the warehouse could handle the additional demand that would be placed on it. See Figure 11.6 for a description of the capacity and activity level of the warehouse.

Performance measurement and cost management

Figure 11.6 Velky Potraviny Warehouse Data

Store expansion plans		Aug 96	37
		Dec 96	40
		Dec 97	52
		Dec 98	67
Warehouse area		97,000 square feet	
Area for containers, cases		2,700 square feet	
Capacity		7,500 pallets (shelving + floor space)	
Shelf dimensions	Depth	55 inches	
	Height	60–80 inches	
	Total Ht.	20 feet	
Number of items	Average	750	
	Max.	1,000	
Average value of stock		75 mil. CZK	
Highest turnover items		1. Beverages (milk, water, juice, beer)	
		2. Flour, Sugar	
		3. Stiff fat	
		4. Oil	
Warehouse inventory turnover		18–24 days	
Delivery to Warehouse Data (collected from 1/15/96–3/22/96 = 50 days)			
Total # of pallets delivered		30,012	
Total number of deliveries (vans)		2,728	
Total number of pallets delivered per day		600	{(max., min) = (876,412)}
Total number of vans per day		54.5	{(max., min) = (55,19)}
Total number of pallets per van		11	
Average unloading time / van		45 minutes	
Delivery to Store Data (collected from 1/15/96–3/22/96 = 50 days)			
Total of pallets delivered		26,204	
Total number of deliveries (vans)		1,746	
Total number of pallets dispatched per day		524	{(max., min) = 612, 393)}
Total number of vans per day		35	{max. = 42}
Total number of pallets per van		15	
# of shipments (van)		2.5 deliveries/truck/van	
Frequency of shipments to stores		Every other day	
Working hours		10 hours / day	
Paid breaks		1 hour / day	
Loading time at warehouse		1 hour / truck	
Average weight of pallet		1,270 lbs.	
Single vs. assorted pallets		40% / 60%	
# items sent as single-item pallets		70 SKUs	
Average delivery to store		475 SKUs, valued at 475,000 CZK	

11.3.25 Juraj was proud to be the manager of Velky's lone warehouse facility. It was only ten years before that an operation such as Velky's would have been illegal. The change from communism to capitalism in some ways seemed incredibly fast, and in other ways painstakingly slow. Fast in the sense that Juraj and many of his contemporaries had to learn capitalism quickly to survive. For Juraj, issues such as cost control, performance eval-

Performance measures for stakeholders

uation, bonuses, inventory turnover, productivity and efficiency, all vital to a company run in western style, had to be learned on the job and quickly. In addition, being a low-cost grocer in a country with per capita GDP only a fraction of that of other advanced economies and a lack of roads and telecommunications that caused costs and inefficiencies to skyrocket, made his job more difficult. Before meeting with his employees, Juraj thought it would be wise to go back to the basics and rethink what the purpose of the warehouse was.

11.3.26 He realised that corporate head office viewed his warehouse operation as a cost centre. The warehouse's goal was to provide inventory to the retail stores in a timely manner and to deliver exactly the goods the retail store ordered, in the correct quantity. Furthermore, this goal had to be accomplished with a conscious eye to the costs incurred to deliver this service to the retail stores. On the surface, this goal appeared simple enough, even more so since the warehouse dealt only with non-perishable goods. Spoilage was not a significant issue, yet even non-perishable goods had spoilage dates, so it was important to follow a first-in, first-out (FIFO) inventory flow. Another cost issue was breakage. The inventory had to be stored and moved with care. Any inventory loss due to breakage went directly to Juraj's total cost line. The total error rate for the warehouse was around 3 per cent.

11.3.27 Velky's buyers were located near the warehouse, and they were responsible for purchasing inventories from the suppliers. The buyers' bonus was determined solely by the lack of inventory stock-outs in the warehouse so the buyers clearly were motivated always to buy more than they thought was needed. After all, they saw no cost associated with having too much inventory. As far as what the buyers thought they needed, this quantity was based on very incomplete information. From the retail store perspective, because the stores lacked bar code scanning technology, the buyers did not have up-to-date information on what items were selling well or poorly. From the warehouse perspective, because the buyers were not located in the warehouse and the warehouse did not operate on a perpetual inventory system, the buyers did not know how much inventory was on hand at any given time. Juraj also found frustrating the fact that the buyers never consulted him about their buying decisions. As a result, excessive inventory was often being held at the warehouse.

11.3.28 When the buyers placed an order, the suppliers delivered goods to the warehouse. The warehouse staff knew what the buyers had ordered, but it was nearly impossible for them to plan ahead for the receipt of the inventory. First, the suppliers did not always deliver the quantities ordered. Although shortages were primarily a thing of the past, the supply chain in

Performance measurement and cost management

the Czech Republic was still far from efficient and reliable. As a result, buyers often ordered more than was really necessary, in case the supplier could not deliver the correct amount. Second, even if the correct amount was delivered, there was no telling when the goods would arrive. The rail system was overburdened and inefficient, and the roads, although far superior to what they had been in communist days, were still significantly below the distribution needs of the country. As a result, the receiving function occurred whenever a supplier's truck happened to pull up to the receiving dock.

11.3.29 As seen in Figure 11.5, the warehouse had a number of functional problems. The long ramp on the north side and a good portion of the ramp on the west side were not being used, as the height of the ramps did not match the height of the vans that Velky owned. Even though the south-side ramp accommodated up to six vans for loading at any given time, there were only two doors. Receiving docks no.1 and no.2 accommodated two vans each. The work-in-procress and expedition (goods ready to ship to the retail stores) often blocked the existing doors in the receiving and shipping areas. Velky also had a problem with empty water, juice and beer bottles returned by customers to the retail outlets. At least 1,000 pallets of these empty bottles had completely filled the unused ramps and had started flowing into the receiving and shipping ramps as well. (Pallets are approximately 4 ft × 4 ft at the base and can range from 3–5 ft high, depending on the weight of the merchandise on the pallet.) Velky had a tough time negotiating with the suppliers to take these bottles back because the bottles were all mixed up in terms of shapes, sizes and colours. The suppliers would take back only their own standardised glass bottles.

11.3.30 The offices were strewn all over the warehouse. The manager and the assisting staff were located in offices near the shipping area. The assistant manager's office was between the receiving areas. The office space in the north-west corner of the building was empty, and Juraj was thinking of ways to use this space productively. Construction was being done to increase storage space between the empty office space and the full-pallet storage area.

11.3.31 The warehouse had the following job functions: receiver, picker, stepper, output checker and driver. Their job descriptions and responsibilities are noted in Figure 11.7. Figure 11.8 schematically shows the order in which activity occured within the warehouse. Juraj realised that although everyone worked in the same warehouse, each job function seemed to work independently of every other. The performance evaluation system exacerbated that way of thinking among the employees. See Figures 11.9 and 11.10 for a description of the employees' compensation package.

Performance measures for stakeholders

Figure 11.7 Task Flow and Responsibilities by Job Title

Receiver (*warehouse delivery; 14 employees*)

1. Average of 55 truckloads per day are unloaded by the suppliers' drivers (80%) and/or the receivers (20%).
2. Receivers check orders as they are unloaded from trucks.
3. Full pallets get moved to full pallet area by the receivers.
4. Full pallets get moved to and stored in assorted pallet area by the steppers.

Picker (*order picking; 38–44 employees*)

1. Picker gets pick order from the assistant/deputy warehouse manager.
2. Pickers decide between themselves who picks which assorted items (e.g. beverage vs. dry goods, etc.).
3. Picker gets on his forklift.
4. Picker begins to pick order in assorted pallet area, shrink-wrapping pallet as he goes.
5. Picker picks orders which contain full pallets and delivers to expediting area.
6. Picker compares goods vs. items listed on pick for accuracy.
7. Picker checks item off list once it's picked.
8. If no goods in lower racks, picker tells stepper that item needs to be replenished.
9. Picker puts a circle around item on pick list which lets the buyer know that item needs to be reordered.
10. Picker completes pick order and finishes shrink-wrapping pallet.
11. Picker delivers pallet to the expediting area. Assorted pallets are arranged as closely together as possible, by store, in expediting area.
12. Picker puts 4 stickers on each side of assorted pallet order. Stickers identify store and order number. Identical sticker is placed on completed pick order paperwork; last sticker is left on the sticker sheet.
13. Completed pick order paperwork and sticker sheet are returned to warehouse manager.
14. Completed pick order is checked by the output/quality checker. Approximately 15% of a whole store order is checked. Errors (over/under) are brought to the attention of the warehouse manager who writes up the mistake and puts in the picker's file. The picker then corrects the error.

Driver (*store forwarding; 14 employees*)

1. Driver receives paperwork which tells him which stores he will deliver to and what orders/pallets he needs to load on his truck. Drivers' routes vary each day.
2. Driver gets his forklift.
3. Driver starts loading order from expediting area.
4. Once truck is fully loaded, driver leaves, drives to first store and unloads that store's order.
5. Driver picks up empty bottles which have been returned by customers to the store and loads onto truck.
6. The driver returns to the warehouse to pick up his next load, 90% of the time, and starts the process (steps 1–5) again.
7. Driver proceeds to a second store to deliver another order, 10% of the time.
8. Driver moves or off-loads bottles in order to get to pallet order to be unloaded.

9. Driver picks up 2nd store's empty bottles and loads onto truck (and so on, if delivering to more than one store).
10. Driver returns to Velky distribution centre throughout the day and repeats process either until 2 or 3 deliveries are made per day.
11. Driver washes/cleans inside of truck upon return to distribution centre.
12. Driver may fill truck with store orders and leave the fully loaded truck at the distribution centre overnight; returning at 6:00 in the morning to make delivery to the first store.

Stepper (*replenishment of picking area; 2 employees*)
1. Steppers receives verbal indication from pickers that an item needs to be replenished in a particular aisle.
2. Stepper continuously visually evaluates the inventory in each aisle and replenishes products as required.

Output Checker (*error checking; 2–3 employees*)
1. Output checkers review 15% of store orders throughout the day to check for accuracy.
2. When errors are discovered, output checker advises the warehouse manager who writes the error up and places in the picker's file.

Deputy Warehouse Manager (*assistant management; 5 employees*)
1. Deputy warehouse manager acts as an assistant to the warehouse manager
2. Reviews orders that come in from each store.
3. Compiles picking order sheets based on his experience and knowledge of how many items can fit on an assorted pallet.

Warehouse Manager (*management; 1 employee*)
1. Oversees all warehouse operations and manages staff of deputy warehouse managers.

The meeting

11.3.32 Juraj thought that a meeting of representatives from the various employee groups was needed to discuss the compensation issue. He wanted to include the employees in the compensation discussion so as to give them some ownership in the results. He wanted the compensation to be fair and yet reasonable, so as to control costs, but he knew this would be a difficult balancing act. One thing was certain – if nothing was done, employee turnover would only become worse. With unemployment levels in Prague at 0.3 per cent, there were simply too many other opportunities for workers at any skill level. Juraj thought that if he could control employee turnover, it would have a beneficial result on his costs.

11.3.33 The following people attended the meeting.

- Juraj, the warehouse manager.
- Jan, the senior warehouse picker.

Performance measures for stakeholders

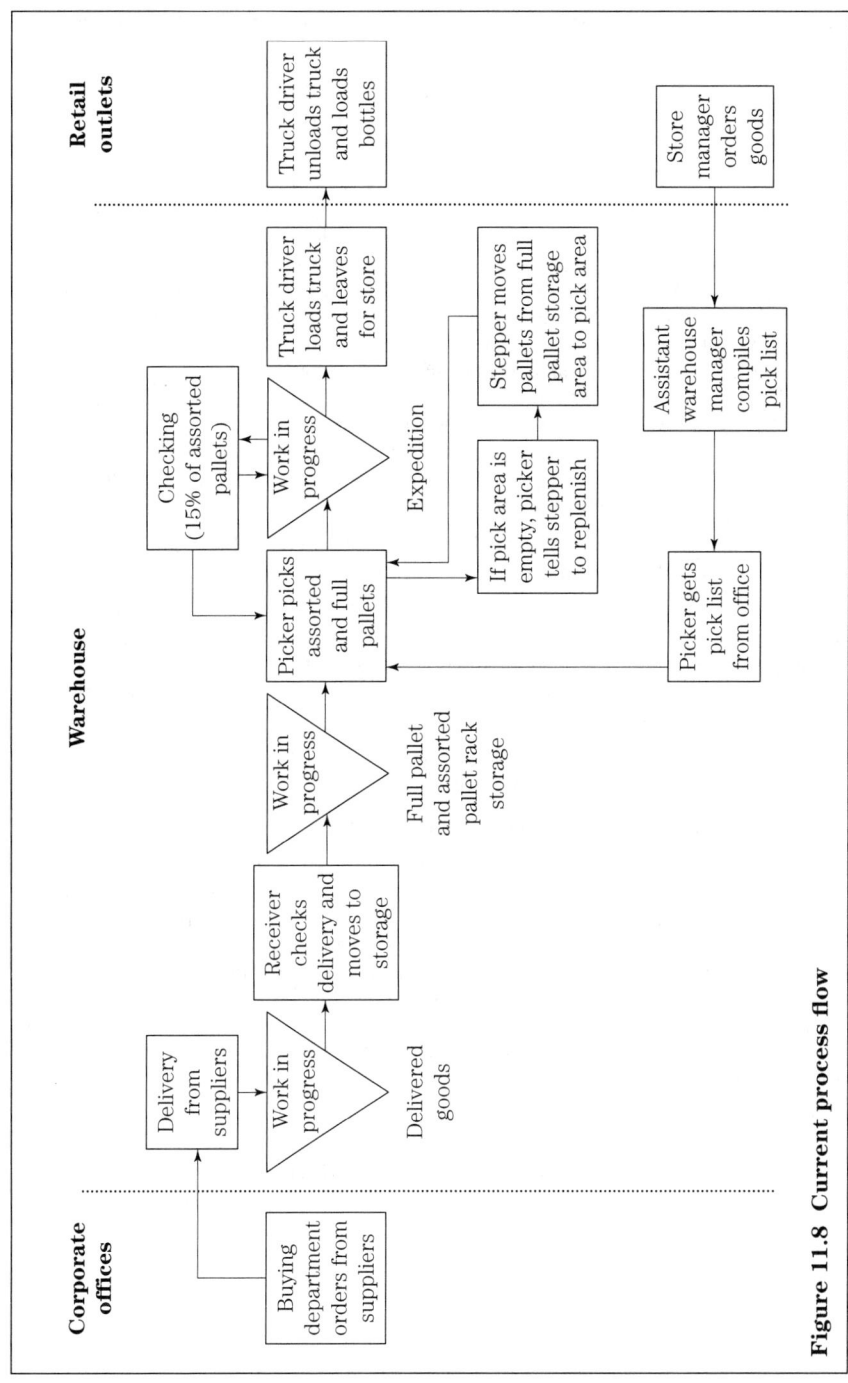

Figure 11.8 Current process flow

Performance measurement and cost management

Figure 11.9 Velky-Potraviny's Current Bonus Program for Warehouse Employees

An employee who has a permanent contract with the company and whose trial period has expired, may be given a bonus in addition to his base pay.

The amount of bonus depends on the quality of the work he delivers. It serves to compensate the employee for aspects of work which are difficult to express in quantitative measures. Among the evaluation criteria are aspects like willingness, pro-activity, commitment, speed but keeping with quality standards, proper handling of merchandise and technology, obeying safety rules and regulations and highway code regulations. The employee should have no absence without permission for the month in question and has not breached work discipline in any other way. Otherwise he is not entitled to any bonus. For any breach of work discipline he must be reproached in writing. The employee must have worked at least 75% of the monthly working hours in the position during the month in question. If he has worked less working hours than specified, the employee will receive a bonus amounting to the proportionate bonus of the last month. The bonus is due as of the regular payday together with the normal pay for the period and is subjected to tax and other deductions.

Based on poor quality, an employee's bonus is reduced in the following way: For each penalty point/error point CZK 50 is deducted from his bonus up to the point where he has no bonus.

In addition to mistakes found by inspection in the warehouse, also mistakes found during offloading goods at a retail store are taken into account. In such instance, however, only item 2) i.e., extra merchandise applies. The formula for computation of the final penalty points score is:

(Number of penalty points from the warehouse * 3 / number of inspections) + (number of errors found in a retail store)

The result is rounded to an integer (from 0.5 up).

Each employee is checked at least 3 times per month and the result of the inspection is recorded in a record signed by the warehouse manager or his deputy. Documents stating the amount of bonus are submitted to the payroll office together with other payroll paperwork. The manager of the warehouse is responsible for the contents and timely delivery of the paperwork. The bonus is paid together with the regular pay and is subjected to normal taxing and deductions (tax, social and health insurance). Should an attempt to influence the results of an inspection be determined, the employee will not be paid any bonus for that month.

Errors are evaluated according the following key:

Error description	Penalty points	Picker Error %	Receiver Error %	Stepper Error %	Drivers Error %
Missing merchandise item	3	12	33	—	—
Extra merchandise item	3	7	—	—	—
Interchange (confusion) of items	2	5	60	96	—
Missing pallet	5	5	—	—	41
Delivered an extra pallet	7	5	—	—	41

Performance measures for stakeholders

Incorrect record in the consignment sheet	2	9	—	—	—
Pallet not labelled	3	3	—	—	—
Pallet label with a different label	5	15	—	—	—
Improper storage of goods on a pallet	1	18	—	—	—
Issuance of "younger" goods	3	13	—	—	—
Breakage, damage, mishandling	2	8	7	4	18
Total percentage of errors by job		100%	100%	100%	100%
% of all errors attributed to each job		63%	17%	10%	10%

Error percentages are given for data collected in 1999 (for the whole year). The last line means that pickers were responsible for 63% of the errors made in 1999. Example: Suppose a picker is charged with 4 errors (1 extra pallet delivered, 1 pallet with different label and 2 damages) in a given month then the total penalty points = 16, i.e., 800 Kcs. will be deducted from his second bonus (see exhibit 11.7). The maximum second bonus he can get is 200 Kcs.

- Jiri, the senior warehouse receiver.
- Radek, the senior delivery driver.
- Pavla, one of the warehouse steppers.
- Karel, one of the output checkers.

11.3.34 After the preliminary greetings, the meeting quickly became a complaint forum. Juraj decided to let everyone vent frustrations and complaints.

11.3.35 Jan started by saying, 'I'm working too hard and getting killed over errors that aren't my fault. Yet I see Jiri in receiving reading the newspaper half the time, and it's partly his fault that I received a smaller bonus this month. For instance, a retail store orders a full pallet of tomato sauce, so naturally I go to the full pallet area where the tomato sauce is supposed to be. So what do I find – canned whole tomatoes instead. I know that's close, but close isn't good enough because not only will I get penalised by your mistake, it slows me down so I can't move as many pallets as I want to. And as you know, the more pallets I move, the greater the bonus I receive. With all the time on his hands, you would think Jiri could get it right. Or at least Pavla, you should have noticed it when you stacked it up or brought it down.'

Warehouse position	Responsibilities	# of employees	Measures of performance (Quantitative)	Measures of performance (Subjective)	Base pay component (Paid monthly)	First bonus (Subjective measures)	Second bonus (Quantifiable measures)
Receivers	Unload on average 65 pallets per day, check deliveries with invoice, check for damage, stack in correct SKU place and expiration order	14	Number of pallets unloaded per day	Cooperative, positive attitude, takes responsibility	9,000–12,000 CZK	Max. 2,000 CZK	Max. 3,000 CZK
Steppers	Replenish products, move correct pallets from higher stacks to lower, in correct expiration order	2	Number of pallets moved each day	Cooperative, positive attitude, takes responsibility	8,000 CZK	Max. 2,000 CZK	Max. 1,000 CZK
Pickers	Pick orders, visually check for correct product, hand-wrap pallet, put store i.d. on pallet, deliver pallet to expedite area, advise steppers that products need to be replenished, clean aisles, do technical maintenance of forklifts	38–44	Number of pallets picked each day	Cooperative, positive attitude, takes responsibility	7,000 CZK	Max. 2,000 CZK	Max. 1,000 CZK
Output/quality checkers	Check 15% of all outgoing orders; advise warehouse manager when order is wrong, incomplete	2	Number of pallets checked per month and number of errors found	Cooperative, positive attitude, takes responsibility	9,000 CZK	N/A	N/A
Drivers	Pick up orders from expediting area, load order on truck, deliver to stores, unload at stores	14	Speed of loading pallet orders onto truck, speed of unloading at stores, care of truck and truck contents	Willingness to travel to two stores located far from Prague	11,000 CZK	3,000	N/A
Warehouse manager	Manages overall warehouse operations, construction for expansion, employees' performance, quality	1			N/A	N/A	N/A
Deputy/assistant warehouse managers	Support warehouse manager, operations, quality, process flow	5			N/A	N/A	N/A
Total		77–82					

Figure 11.10 Current measures of performance by job/function

Performance measures for stakeholders

11.3.36 Jiri angrily replied, 'I'm a receiver. I have no idea when those suppliers are going to be pulling up to the receiving dock. And just like you, Jan, my bonus is based on the number of pallets I move. So when two or three supplier trucks are waiting, I'm going crazy. I have to make sure that the suppliers deliver the correct inventory in the correct quantities. Those suppliers are always trying to short us, yet I get blamed for it if I don't count it correctly. Moreover, the SKU number tags pasted on the stacks are so small they are barely readable. Well, as you said, Pavla could have warned me or helped me when he stacked them up.'

11.3.37 'Well, I also get paid based on the number of pallets I move,' replied Pavla. 'But when I get called by one of you to stack a pallet or bring it down, I don't notice the SKU numbers on the pallets. It's not my job. I'm not paid for that. Between moving Jiri's newly received inventory in and bringing Jan's requested down, I think I'm doing a great job maintaining the FIFO flow I am required to do and I get paid for. Yet I seem to get penalised for little mistakes that I don't think hurt anybody. Why can't a customer use a product that is one day old? We are not dealing with any meat here. And by the way, Jan, there is no proof that the pickers travel more distances within the warehouse than either the receivers or myself.'

11.3.38 'I don't see those types of errors,' Karel said. 'In expedition, most of the errors I see are the result of the pickers picking the wrong inventory. I don't see what's so difficult about their job. You have a list from the store, just pick the inventory that's on the list. And how difficult can the driver's job be, and yet they keep shipping the wrong pallets to the retail stores.'

11.3.39 'Before you get to the drivers, I have to respond,' Jan said. 'A picker's job is not that easy. Receivers and steppers are dealing only with full pallets. I am the one who creates the partial pallets and it takes more concentration and care than any other job here. However, I often see that full pallets are missing from the ground-level shelves, and I have to go hunting for the steppers. The receivers are always monopolising the steppers. It's such a waste of time for me, and I can't finish the number of pallets I want to in the day. Since you mentioned drivers, guess who gets blamed if a driver delivers the wrong inventory to the wrong store. Is it fair to blame me for a driver's mistake?'

11.3.40 'So you think all I do is drive around all day listening to the radio,' Radek said. 'The expedition area is such a mess, it's a wonder I get as much correct as I do. I should be able to pull up, have my store's shipment separately stacked, forklift the inventory onto the truck, and get out of here. I get paid based on the deliveries I make, and yet most of the time I'm waiting in

Performance measurement and cost management

the parking lot because Jan and Karel are so slow and disorganised. It takes forever to get a truck loaded around here, and I have to make at least two deliveries every day and a third delivery every other day.'

11.3.41 'Well, it would help if we knew when you were planning to pick up the inventory,' Jan said. 'You just expect to show up unannounced and we should be ready to serve you? How can we arrange the expedition area when the order in which you and the other drivers show up is a mystery? The only time loading inventory worked well was that special set of Sunday deliveries we made last fall for the Bohemian Festival.'

11.3.42 'I remember,' said Karel. 'There was so little activity that day, we were not only able to separate the different stores' deliveries clearly but also we were able to load the trucks in an order that facilitated direct stocking from truck to shelves at the retail store. The stores said they were able to unload the truck and stock the floor in about one-third of the time.'

11.3.43 'The only problem,' Radek said, 'is that we did all the work, but the retail store received all the credit and all the benefit. Another thing I think we can all agree on is that ridiculous attitudinal component to the bonus.'

11.3.44 'Do you all feel as Radek does?' asked Juraj, 'That the subjective component of the compensation package needs to be changed?'

11.3.45 'The problem with these subjective measures is that from period to period there is no consistency,' Jiri said. 'For instance, one month I'll make a suggestion to change a procedure and it will be viewed favourably, and the next month I'll be accused of being dissatisfied with how we do things around here.'

11.3.46 'How does management know what my attitude is, let alone all my fellow pickers and everyone else on the warehouse floor? Don't misunderstand me, Juraj. I appreciate the opportunity to discuss these issues with you today, but we live with these problems every day. You and the rest of management determine what our attitudinal performance is, but just having this meeting is an indication that you don't understand what we do. On the other hand, I think I speak for everyone when I say that I see you in your office every day, and I know you work hard, but I have no idea what you do. I have no idea what determines whether you've done a good job or not.'

Business setting and customer habits
11.3.47 The Czech Republic is new to capitalism and is undergoing rapid cultural and economic change. Traditionally, the Czechs have shopped for

their groceries on a daily basis and in small quantities. They are used to walking to the nearby small, mom-and-pop, speciality grocery store and buying fresh produce and meat. The reasons for this situation are many: everybody in the neighbourhood knows the grocer, they have a personal relationship with the stores and it is a good meeting place for neighbours. Czech apartments are small, and refrigeration and storage space is limited. Perhaps the chief reason is that the Czechs have had limited disposable income, and even if they have disposable income, they cannot buy groceries in large quantities. Few people have cars to carry the groceries home. Most people buy groceries on their way home from work, and public transportation is very popular. This fact again limits people to buying in small quantities. For instance, although the Czech Republic has the largest per capita consumption of beer, very few people buy a multi-pack of beer. People buy two or three half-litre bottles every night.

Business strategy

11.3.48 Velky wants to be the leading discount grocery store chain in the Czech Republic. This goal can be achieved in two ways: by increasing market share through rapid expansion, which it intends to do at the rate of 10–15 stores per year, and by providing the lowest-priced groceries with a product assortment that covers the basic needs of the Czech people.

11.3.49 Velky is facing a number of problems in trying to achieve this goal. There is the enormous task of dealing with traditional Czech habits, as mentioned above. Velky wants to change customers' habits to shopping two or three times a week and eventually once a week. The Czechs have always bought their produce fresh. How can Velky consistently and reliably offer fresh produce to so many outlets, given the lack of infrastructure for reliable delivery of fresh produce? There is also the issue of availability. The suppliers are unreliable. For Velky to change customers' habits, it first has to build customer loyalty through low prices; pleasant, convenient, service-oriented stores; and product variety. It is trying to keep costs low by not using fancy packaging, by shelving pallets directly from the warehouse into the retail store, and by letting customers buy in small units directly from the pallets (unlike in large discount warehouses in the United States such as Sam's Club, where you are required to buy in large quantities). Further, to maintain low costs for the customer, Velky has to keep its warehousing and distribution costs as low as possible.

11.3.50 A warehouse can reduce and control costs in several ways.
- Carry as little inventory as possible, achieve high inventory turnover.
- Minimise inventory waste and damage when handling.

Performance measurement and cost management

- Use the FIFO system efficiently.
- Lay out the warehouse to facilitate the optimal flow of goods.
- Use space within the warehouse efficiently.
- Maintain forklifts and material-handling equipment well.
- Build in flexibility to allow additions, deletions, and seasonal variations in inventory.
- Keep productive, stable and motivated employees.

11.3.51 In advanced economies, warehouses use sophisticated information systems and management techniques to achieve low costs, for example, bar coding, EDI (electronic data interchange), cross-docking, FCR (fast consumer response), and supplier partnerships for accurate and JIT deliveries. The warehouse should be seen as an integral and essential part of the supply chain, which is streamlined by co-ordinating activities of the purchasing department, suppliers, warehouse employees, retail store employees and managers.

Problems at the warehouse
11.3.52 Broadly the problems at the warehouse can be classified as problems related to capacity expansion, problems related to flows within the warehouse and problems related to employees.

Problems related to capacity expansion
11.3.53 Since Velky is in the rapid growth phase, a lot of construction is going on within the existing facility. It hampers the receiving, movement and shipping of inventory on a day-to-day basis. At the rate Velky is expanding, they will need to use more ramps for shipping and receiving.

11.3.54 Time to load 1 truck = 1 hour. Working hours = 10 hours/day with 1 hour of paid break

	August 2000	December 2000	December 2001	December 2002
Number of stores	37	40	52	67
Total shipments per day	37	40	52	67
Trucks loaded per hour	4.1	4.4	5.8	7.4
Number of vans / ramp	4	4	6	8

11.3.55 Currently there are some problems (see Figure 11.5). WIP is blocking some of the receiving doors. There are insufficient doors in the shipping area. However, within one year the warehouse will require more ramp space to accommodate more vans. There are 16 doors and enough ramp space all around to meet the expected need for loading and unloading by the end of 2002. However, either most of the ramps need to be adjusted for the van height or the vans need to be changed. This is assuming that there is no improvement in the time taken to load the vans (i.e., presently 1 hour/van). In addition to adding resources, existing operations could be improved by reducing the time taken to load one van to 45 minutes. For instance, greater co-ordination between pickers and drivers might allow Velky to make do with existing ramp space until the end of 2001. However, we know that Velky is having a number of internal co-ordination problems as well.

Problems related to flows within the warehouse
11.3.56 There are constant flow changes due to construction and high traffic and confusion in the expediting areas. At present there is suboptimal use of existing ramps and aisles. Suppliers arrive throughout the day, and there is no co-ordination between suppliers' deliveries. The warehouse employees do not know when the drivers will return from their deliveries, and this causes congestion in the expediting area. Also, there is an inventory build-up of 3,808 pallets in the warehouse over a 50-day period (30,012–26,204 pallets from Figure 11.6), primarily because the buyers are working independently without consulting with the warehouse manager. The buyers are given a bonus if there is no stock-out of any item, and so they order in large quantities. They order larger quantities for other reasons: unreliable suppliers, inconsistent availability of certain items, late deliveries and breakage. The gridlock with the suppliers of beverages in regard to recycling empty bottles is cluttering up the ramps.

Problems related to employees
11.3.57 There is a feeling of us versus them among the management and employees. Morale is very low and turnover is high. Each employee works independently, and there is little exchange of information or assistance among workers. If a worker spills a beverage on the floor, the other employees do not come to assist in the clean-up. This attitude is driven primarily by the performance and bonus measurement system: it is responsibility accounting. The receiver's compensation is based on the number of pallets moved. However, the receiver is at the mercy of the supplier and has little control over his own bonus. A closer examination of Figure 11.10 reveals a number of problematic issues regarding the bonus system: the subjective weight is often greater than the objective weight. Hence, it is possible that an employee might not receive the full bonus even if there were no errors in a given month. The subjective measures are not defined clearly.

Performance measurement and cost management

11.3.58 Consider the picker's monthly pay (see Figure 11.10).

Picker's monthly pay = base pay + bonus 1 + bonus 2

$$= 7,000 + \text{max. of } 2,000 + \text{max. of } 1,000 \text{ Kcs}$$

i.e., a max. of 20 penalty points for bonus 2

(because it costs 50 Kcs / penalty)

50 working days, 26,204 pallets delivered, i.e., 524 pallets/day

$$= 524 \times 20 = 10,481 \text{ pallets/month}$$
$$= 10,481/41 \text{ pickers} = 255 \text{ pallets / picker / month}$$
$$= 13 \text{ pallets / picker / day}$$

No. of errors = 3 per cent of pallets shipped/month

$$= 10,481 \times 0.03 = 314 \text{ errors/month} = 314 / 20 \text{ days/month}$$
$$= 15.7 \text{ errors/day} = 15.7 \times 0.63 \text{ (Exhibit 6 – picker error rate)} = 9.89$$
errors/day for the pickers (41 of them)
$$= 0.24 \text{ errors/day/picker}$$
$$= 4.8 \text{ errors/month/picker, that is, 240 Kcs per month average penalty}$$

11.3.59 Issues to be considered.

- Inordinate blame and responsibility placed on the pickers.
- Whether pay scale is proportional to seniority.
- Probably higher turnover among pickers.
- Dependence of errors or propagation of errors caused by previous handler but attributed to later handlers.

Short-term recommendations

11.3.60 The lack of communication between the drivers and the warehouse is causing an inventory build-up in the expediting area. It could be avoided if the warehouse knew when a particular van was returning for pickup. Cellular or van phones would help. Knowing the estimated time of arrival of a particular van at the warehouse would give the pickers time to start work on a particular outlet's order just-in-time (JIT) (see Chapter **5**).

11.3.61 The inventory build-up is caused partially by the lack of communication between the buyers and the warehouse manager.

11.3.62 A short-term plan to reduce employee dissatisfaction or boost employee morale is important. Formation of a team representing all employee groups to address the restructuring of the bonus system as well as formation of teams in the warehouse should begin immediately.

11.3.63 Make the SKU tags larger for easier identification.

11.3.64 The empty bottle problem should not overflow into the ramps presently being used. Take steps to store the bottles in places away from the receiving and shipping ramp areas and reduce the amount held.

11.3.65 Change the buyers' incentives. Are stock-outs really that detrimental? (Keep in mind that stock-outs were a normal occurrence under communism. What makes Velky different is that customers always feel the goods are there when they want them.) How costly is the current system of over-ordering? Better communication with the buyer by both the retail stores and the warehouse is needed.

Long-term recommendations

11.3.66 With such low unemployment in Prague, and given the cost to find and train a new worker and new workers' lower productivity as they learn the system, employee turnover is very costly. It may be worthwhile to pay more to maintain a stable workforce.

11.3.67 The need for teamwork is obvious. Velky is unlikely to have a labour union, so restrictive work rules are not stopping Juraj from breaking down the job description barriers. Tied to this fact, the compensation should not be based on the local optimums that the current system is focused on. The employee goals should be consistent with the overall warehouse goals. If everyone has one mission, to provide timely and accurate (in terms of both quantity and product) inventory deliveries, then teamwork is much easier to institute. If you believe in TQM, why are there output checkers?

11.3.68 Given the manager versus worker mentality of the workers, the development of the new compensation scheme should actively include representatives of the workforce. In this way, the workers have a sense of ownership. Also needed is continuous communication to all the workers about why a change is being made, and the process by which the change in compensation is being made. The concern is that without worker involvement, the natural inclination of the workers is to think that management is trying to reduce their pay by changing the pay structure.

Performance measurement and cost management

11.3.69 Successful variable pay-for-performance plans have several common characteristics. They should:

- be based on a clear vision of the organisation's strategy by tying rewards for individuals, teams or the entire organisation to the priorities of the business;
- be linked to specific goals and accomplishments and be measured against those goals;
- be clearly communicated to participants before the start of the performance period (participants should be properly trained);
- provide time for implementation;
- be evaluated continually to ensure that the team, department and organisation stays on course;
- have a 'sunset' period so that the variable reward isn't viewed as an entitlement, and employees can celebrate when the organisation reaches its goals.

11.3.70 Velky's employees should be evaluated on the basis of speed, accuracy, care and efficiency. Considerations for desirable traits such as being proactive, dependable and safety conscious should be factored into the performance review. Leeway for human error is imperative, but workers must be expected to meet established levels of satisfactory performance. The predetermined levels can come from one or a combination of the following sources.

- Engineering studies/time studies (published records of standardised times for certain warehouse activities).
- Historical performance data at the warehouse.
- Previously established management time standards.
- Work sampling or observation of warehouse employees.

11.3.71 The ultimate goal is zero errors, but a realistic expectation must be set to account for honest human mistakes. While employees should be rewarded for performances that meet or exceed management expectations, those who do not perform should be warned, and eventually fired, if poor level of work persists. Promotion schedules must be made clear. The following is a sample evaluation system based on four attributes: accuracy, speed, care and attitude. Velky should establish the standards for each criteria.

Performance measures for stakeholders

Accuracy	+	Speed	+ Care +	Attitude		
Velky standard	99%	95%	99%	100%		
Employee performance	99%	95%	99%	90%		
Weight of criteria	30%	30%	30%	10%		
Total	0.297	+ 0.285	+ 0.297 +	0.09	=	0.969

11.3.72 The bonus system could then follow a pattern similar to the one below.

Score	Result
1.0	bonus level 3
0.95 to 0.999	bonus level 2
0.90 to 0.949	bonus level 1
0.875 to 0.899	no bonus
0.8 to 0.874	warning (maximum of 3 before being fired)
Less than 0.8	one warning, fired if repeated

11.3.73 These measures of standards and weights are one possible solution. The standards and weights actually used should be decided by employees and management and adjusted accordingly.

11.3.74 Formation of teams and dedication of teams to stores and receiving/shipping ramps might be a better way of giving responsibility. By assigning a team of employees to a particular store's orders, workers feel a sense of ownership. The distribution centre can develop the team-building skills that will further lower costs in the warehouse and ensure that the end users will receive quality products. This process can sow the seeds for initiating direct communication between teams and store managers, eliminating layers of middle managers. Job rotation and training within store teams will break down barriers between different groups that exist now. Team rewards are essential as well.

11.3.75 Bar code scanning technology should be introduced at point-of-sale in the retail stores as well as in the warehouse. Furthermore, the two systems should be linked to order, distribute and monitor inventory flows more efficiently.

11.3.76 Given conditions in the Czech Republic, incentives such as stock options will not work. People need money now, and they may not understand capital markets yet. Training trips to the West might be a nice incentive.

(Source: adapted with permission from Juras and Dierks, 1998.)

Performance measurement and cost management

The need for measures that perform

11.3.77 An organisation's ability to operate successfully depends to a large extent on the availability of information upon which its managers can act. The role of information about performance, whether for use within the enterprise or for external parties, is crucial in determining economic or commercial viability. The pace of change of business activities and the need to remain responsive to market pressures means that a performance measurement system cannot remain static. Changes in production methods and in the organisation of work have led academics, consultants and commentators on industrial practices to encourage rethinking of performance evaluation approaches. In the case of manufacturing companies, critics of traditional performance measure systems have pointed to the existence of a drift between fundamental changes in the way in which manufacturing processes now take place and the traditional performance measures being used in many companies. Novel work organisation methods such as just-in-time purchasing and production (see Chapter **5**) have transformed production methods even in relatively small companies. Consequently, it is claimed that similarly radical alterations need to be made to the ways in which other enterprise activities are monitored.

11.3.78 The issue of appropriate performance measures is highly significant because it can affect commercial success, and because in the present economic climate many companies will be looking for appropriate information about their internal processes to establish ways of cost cutting, of enhancing performance and generally of building a better product in a shrinking market. Companies at this stage are finding more than ever before that the need for accurate and comprehensive information about their activities is intense.

11.3.79 A major study of manufacturing enterprises commissioned by the Department of Trade and Industry and carried out by the Chartered Institute of Management Accountants (CIMA) recently recently reported that:

> 'There appears not to be an optimal mix of specific financial and non-financial indicators applicable to all enterprises. Rather, each company must find a balance of measures which it views as sufficient for the management of its operational activities.
>
> There is no 'quick-fix-off-the-shelf' solution to performance measurement problems, but guidelines as to what may be appropriate can be developed. Thus, for financial measures, a company may develop its own measures in relation to the following: working capital, capital market, financial return and lender security. Likewise, for non-financial measures, the company could adopt the following

Performance measures for stakeholders

broad categories: quality, delivery, process time and flexibility. To an extent, the choice of measures should reflect specific company strategy relating to a variety of performance criteria. Companies have a preference for custom-developing their own such measures based on internal factors viewed as significant.' (CIMA, 1993)

11.3.80 Complex performance measures are not necessarily the answer to operating in a complex commercial environment:

'Performance measures need to take account of operational complexity. Yet, unless they are kept simple enough to be understood, they will not be used. Companies which ensure managers' understanding of novel performance indicators reap the most benefits from them.' (CIMA, 1993)

11.3.81 What cannot be denied is that companies can benefit from using an array of both financial and non-financial performance measures. Typically, financial and non-financial performance measures can be combined in complementary ways. A proper approach can be developed for combining non-financial and financial measures of performance to create a thriving firm. Dixon *et al.* (1990) suggest that measures of performance (especially non-financial ones) should directly support corporate strategic goals. McNair *et al.* (1988) point out that in a just-in-time environment financial and non-financial measures of performance may conflict with each other, but both may be useful. A pyramid performance measurement system is proposed to measure the achievement of strategic goals more meaningfully. Top-level management objectives are implemented by designing performance measures for individuals at process, activity or department level. At the lowest levels, specific enterprise cost accounting methods are applied to provide strategic cost information for management. It is not suggested that financial information is replaced, but rather that specific financial performance measures be used by management in conjunction with non-financial performance measures. Ultimately, such integrated information should contribute to 'continuous improvement' and the attainment of the firm's strategic goals.

11.3.82 Kaplan and Norton (1992) also stress the value of non-financial measures and link all relevant performance measures to 'strategy and vision'. They combine financial measures of performance with operational-level measures of performance (e.g., innovativeness and customer satisfaction). They advocate that employees at all levels should be given the flexibility to achieve their respective objectives and suggest that clearly defined goals should be established before being implemented through a 'scorecard' (see below). Non-financial performance measures (e.g., concerning product and/or service quality and timing) are part of a larger, firm-wide strategic

Performance measurement and cost management

plan. Thus, both firm-specific financial and non-financial performance goals should be defined, measured and integrated to some degree. However, financial performance measures are to be used primarily to the extent that they aid the firm in attaining its strategic goals.

11.3.83 The need to support the organisation's strategic mission through performance measures is felt clearly by many companies. The use of traditional performance measures in enterprises which are dynamic, outward-looking and technologically intensive is considered to be a priority. Table 11.3 identifies commonly used financial and non-financial measures which can be altered to address more directly the processes and/or functional structure specific to an enterprise.

Table 11.3 Financial and non-financial measures commonly used in assessing performance

Financial	Non-financial	
Production	Marketing/quality	
WORKING CAPITAL	GENERAL PRODUCTION	DEMAND
Cashflow	Capital utilisation	Market share
Creditor days	Inventory	Orders on hand
Debtor days		
CAPITAL MARKET	PROCESS	PRODUCT
Asset value per share	Manufacturing lead time	Price
Dividend cover	per cent rework and reject	Product quality
Dividend per share	per cent yield on production	
Earnings per share	Schedule adherence	
Price/earnings ratio	Set-up time	
(FINANCIAL) RETURN	LABOUR	CUSTOMER
Capital turnover	Direct labour productivity	Complaints
Working capital turnover	Indirect labour productivity	Warranty claims
Profit to turnover	Employee turnover	Repeat orders
Return on capital employed		On-time delivery
Profit		
Total shareholder returns		
Profit per employee		
Economic value added		
Sales per employee		
LENDER SECURITY	SUPPLIERS	INNOVATIVENESS
Gearing	Number of suppliers	New product frequency
Interest cover	Supplier lead time	New product time to market
Asset cover	Supplier product quality	

11.3.84 One company which has been reported to have a balanced system for providing financial and non-financial performance measures which couple operational with strategic factors is the A company (see CIMA, 1993

Performance measures for stakeholders

and Bhimani, 1994 for a fuller discussion). Company A was started in 1979 and is now, in terms of turnover, among the world leaders in the manufacture and sales of industrial inkjet printers. The group's structure consists of a UK-based holding company and operating subsidiaries in the US, Netherlands, France, Germany and Spain. Two of the four manufacturing plants are in the UK and two in the US. Around 350 people are employed in the UK. Initially, there was little demand for A's product as there was no apparent need for such relatively expensive equipment. At the start of the 1980s, however, EC legislation required product traceability on items such as drugs and foodstuffs, and stipulated that shops display product sell-by dates. The on-line capability of A's equipment made it the only product then in the market that could meet the exacting specification.

11.3.85 A's stated objective is clear: worldwide leadership in industrial markets for variable printing technology. Whilst offering a state-of-the-art product in which the company is constantly investing, it pays particular attention to product quality, in-house and externally. Management makes efforts to involve the whole workforce in the achievement of A's goal and a set of measures is in place to aid these efforts rather than inhibit them. The company recognises, and its results show, that a firm financial underpinning is also required. Therefore the principal monetary measures are growth, profitability and earnings per share. The second priority is cash management, measured by the major elements of working capital, debtors, creditors and inventory. The company's approach to performance measurement rests on the following.

- Having a standard set of figures which is reported regularly both to the board and to the banks.
- Reporting financial figures, apart from sales volumes, at the highest level in line with financial objectives. Thus sales, profitability and working capital all feature prominently in the reports.
- Using a few well understood and common non-financial measures at operational level, to motivate the workforce. These must be congruent with the top level financial measures.

11.3.86 The financial goals of the enterprise are filtered down to subsidiaries through interlocking measures. Non-financial measures are especially relied upon further down the organisation.

11.3.87 Financial measures include:
- total sales revenue broken down by product group; in this case machines, inks and spares; machines are further subdivided by type;

- sales revenue by geographical area, along with a breakdown of what percentage distributors account for;
- machine unit sales by geographical area;
- worldwide market share.

11.3.88 In terms of non-financial measures, quality is monitored, at the top level, by the physical performance of the machines already sold. 'Fault rates' and 'warranty calls per year' are two of the specific measures used. Particular emphasis is placed on customer satisfaction using repeat orders, on-time delivery and returns as the major monitors. Ex-post performance measures are also used. For instance, the company monitors whether a machine is capable of running for a year in a customer's premises without attention.

11.3.89 In addition to the standard measures, transitory performance measures are also used. For instance, A has benefited worldwide, and particularly within the EU, from the progressive introduction of legislation covering the coding of food and drink. It has therefore introduced a measure of how much of the market is determined by 'legislative pull' and how much by 'sales push'. Recognising that new legislation will not always be a major sales driver, the company has set itself targets in terms of the percentage of total sales they must achieve through sales push. When that target has been achieved, the measure will cease to be directly monitored at board level.

11.3.90 At the operational level, the key measures are as follows.
- Quality.
- Customer feedback: the percentage of quality feedback reports from the customer indicating an error on shipment.
- Monthly average number of faults: percentage of faults found at final test.
- Supplier quality performance: numbers of rejected incoming parts.
- Service.
- On-time delivery: percentage of deliveries on time.
- Cash.
- Stock turn days: numbers of days' stock.
- Debt turn days: numbers of debtor days.
- Productivity.

- Throughput per £ cost: resource usage to total production and materials group costs.
- Throughput £ per hour: the time is the manufacturing time at the facility.

11.3.91 While there is only an indirect link between these non-financial measures and the fixed elements of the profit and loss account, they do reinforce the company's overall goals. In general, A has given the same careful thought to the development of performance measures as it has to the rest of its business. The measures used are viewed as congruent with company goals. Where this has been found not to be the case, the company has made the necessary changes and has introduced transitory measures from time to time, to monitor problems which have transcended the scope of local management and which potentially impact on the achievement of company goals.

Strategic business information and performance measurement

11.3.92 Management information should form the vital link between strategic objectives and business performance. It can only do this if real management responsibility is closely linked to the information provided. Strategic business information (SBI) is a technique used to stress the need to develop information that reflects and supports organisations' strategies. Management information should have three characteristics: it should be balanced, relevant and consistent.

A balanced view
11.3.93 Information should provide top management with a balanced view of the overall performance of the business. It should include information from a number of different perspectives. Typically, a balanced view will include the following perspectives.

(1) *Customers:* many organisations recognise that understanding what their customers think of their performance is the only important way of ensuring that performance in key areas is up to the required standard. The alternative is to find out what customers think only when the sales figures change. It is generally recognised that protecting and developing an existing customer base is much more cost effective than constantly finding new customers. However, measures that indicate whether the company is being successful in this respect seldom form part of a company's regular reporting.

(2) *External environment:* the need to monitor and understand the dynamics of the business and competitive environment is more

important than ever. Many companies take an *ad hoc* approach to monitoring changes, rather than deciding what should be monitored, how, how often and assigning unambiguous responsibility for both collection and interpretation. This provides a sharp contrast to the systematic production of routine financial information.

(3) *Process and activities:* by understanding processes and their constituent activities, organisations can highlight areas of concern and focus attention and action accordingly. One of the advantages of activity-based approaches to accounting and cost management has been the insight into the key processes by which a company's strategy is realised. All too often, reporting remains functionally-based, telling managers little about key processes that cut across functional boundaries.

(4) *Continuous improvement:* how well an organisation and its people are learning and developing is crucial to the firm's long-term competitiveness. Some companies have in place formal procedures for measuring and tracking the skills and effectiveness of their people. However, these are the exceptions.

(5) *Financial:* this will continue to be a crucial measure of overall success, although tighter focus should reduce the volume of information produced. The appropriate balance of the different perspectives is different for each organisation so a rigorous process is needed to identify individual requirements. It is tempting for accountants to dismiss as unimportant those things that cannot be expressed in financial terms.

11.3.94 Management information needs to reflect the processes and activities of the business at least as much as it reflects the organisational structure. The consequences for roles and responsibilities within the organisation may be evaluated critically.

Consistency throughout the business hierarchy
11.3.95 The phrase 'what gets measured gets done' is well recognised and is often used to justify the measurement of activities that are vital to an organisation's success. Conversely, measures within a business can often drive managers to act against what the organisation is trying to achieve. Recognising this brings one to the starting point for consistent performance measures: what is the organisation trying to achieve? For example, an organisation keen to protect and develop its customer base will need to measure customer attrition rates and satisfaction as well as numbers of new enquiries and volume of new business. The organisation's objectives can be translated into critical success factors and then down the hierarchy into functions and processes and activities as suggested above.

11.3.96 One reason, often overlooked, for reluctance to change is the fact that management information, even if inadequate, often underpins existing organisation structures. Challenging and changing performance measures and making individual managers' responsibilities and accountabilities very visible can be very unsettling to the managers concerned. Outdated or irrelevant measures remain very attractive to an individual if they show that s/he is performing well.

11.3.97 Another difficulty is that many managers are cynical about the improvements that can be made to their management information. They will have tried to make changes in the past which have resulted in little more than the addition of graphics and commentary to existing information.

Sources of information
11.3.98 Information must come from a variety of sources if it is to be balanced, relevant and consistent. Much of the necessary information is likely to be already available somewhere within the organisations: its collection or production, and ensuring its integrity and reliability, are vital.

11.3.99 As organisations fundamentally re-examine their critical success factors and therefore their information requirements, they find that to extract some of the information will require additional effort. Finding out what customers' perceptions are will usually entail formal, regular and consistent surveys in order to track changes in perceptions and performance over time. In some industries – IT for example – such formal surveys have long been considered important indicators.

11.3.100 Tracking changes in the external environment in terms of the overall economy, technological changes and how competitors are behaving, can be very time consuming. The need for focused effort in this area is clear. Information on competitors can be gleaned from customers, the press, trade shows, public records, etc. Deciding what information is needed, where it is going to come from, who is responsible for its collection, who should see it and how it is to be presented and used are all details that should not be left to chance.

11.3.101 What strategic business information (SBI) attempts to do is to break a company's strategic objectives into *critical success factors* (CSFs), i.e., the things which must go right if the strategy is to succeed. Ways of measuring these are developed.

11.3.102 Once what must go well is recognised, it is important to know what things people must do to make them happen. The business activities necessary to achieve the critical success factors are identified. Measures are developed to track these activities.

11.3.103 Having identified what people must do, it is important to motivate them as well. To do this, it is essential to see if the reward systems help or hinder motivating managers and the workforce, and securing their emotional commitment. The reward system will only work if it is perceived as acceptable by the people. This means onr must understand their individual and collective motivations – in short, their culture.

11.3.104 The identification of CSFs is one of the major tasks of the strategy implementation approach. If they cannot be isolated at the planning stage, then it is unlikely that the follow-up processes involved in strategy implementation will be fully successful. There are two types of CSF. One is a set of general, all-encompassing industry-based factors. The other is specific to the organisation and is generated by differences in environmental situation, temporal factors, geographical location or strategic situation.

Key performance indicators (KPIs)
11.3.105 These can be developed for each CSF. A KPI is a measure of whether the CSF is being achieved. This gives a performance measurement indicator to track the achievement towards strategic objectives. A set of CSFs and KPIs can then be developed for the organisation as a whole and for each sub-unit of the organisation. It is worth noting that KPIs will contain financial and non-financial indicators. In many organisations, non-financial indicators, many of which monitor the outside world, will easily outnumber financial measures in board reporting. CSFs are underpinned by a set of activities necessary to make them successful. These are core processes and activities. Ultimately, what is sought is a clear link between the strategy agreed at board level and the lowest level of activities in the business.

11.3.106 There is usually a need to identify underlying human factors which may assist or impede the implementation of the proposed strategy. There are three key factors to consider.
- Organisation culture.
- Performance measurement systems.
- Reward systems.

11.3.107 Organisation culture can be thought of as beliefs and expectations shared by members of an organisation. These beliefs and expectations produce rules for behaviour – norms – that powerfully shape the behaviour of individuals and groups in the organisation. Both performance measurement systems and reward systems are significant subsets of organisation culture. The manner in which performance is measured – the elements which are emphasised and those discounted – has a direct bearing on the expectations placed on the workforce.

11.3.108   The following example illustrates the potential of SBI.

Example

11.3.109   A large multinational company had recognised for some time the need to improve its supply chain management. This need has been brought to a head because of the company's deteriorating financial performance. Reduction of inventory (which in most divisions represents between six and twelve months' sales) was seen as a major financial opportunity.

11.3.110   The company had made one previous attempt to develop new performance measures for the international supply chain. This attempt sought to develop a rational set of rules to support key supply chain decisions such as: when to hold inventory, the timing of production and when to invest in capacity rather than inventory. This project was regarded as a failure for two reasons.

- The international supply chain was too complex to be 'optimised' by a single set of decision rules.
- The rules were logically sound but could not be assigned to individuals or departments because the management framework did not exist in which they could be applied.

11.3.111   Hence the rules were not capable of implementation.

11.3.112   The company carried out a search of management literature and academia and could find no 'theory of optimisation' which could be applied to its business. It came to the conclusion that performance measures were perhaps the only way to drive improvement.

11.3.113   The objective for the company was to develop an integrated set of financial and non-financial performance measures to support the improvement of performance across the international supply chain. This was done by:

- determining and agreeing strategic objectives of supply chain management;
- identifying critical success factors (CSFs);
- decomposing CSFs into critical activities and identifying performance measures.

Performance measurement and cost management

Supply chain management

1 Effective use of resources	2 Effective material and information flow	3 Effective customer service
OBJECTIVE	OBJECTIVE	OBJECTIVE
1 Purchase at best value	2.1 Minimise forecast error	3.1 Integrate market needs into the business
CSF	CSF	CSF
2 Maximise cost-effective use of existing capacity	2.2 Conform to schedule	3.2 Meet agreed customer requirments
CSF	CSF	CSF
3 Minimise cost-to-serve	2.3 Reduce supply chain lead time	3.3 Build customer partnerships
CSF	CSF	CSF
4 Integrate operational targets/business objective	2.4 Respect social factors	3.4 Co-ordinate new process/product introductions
CSF	CSF	CSF
5 Highlight projected free capacity	2.5 Create and maintain a company-wide MRPII attitude	
CSF	CSF	

Figure 11.11 Application of the SBI process: supply chain management

Effective use of resources

1 Purchase at best value	1.2 Maximise the cost-effective use of existing capacity	1.3 Minimise the cost to serve	1.4 Integrate operational targets with business objectives	1.5 Highlight projected free capacity
		1.3 Supplier analysis		
1.1.1 Cost to supply	1.2 Supplier performance to	1.3.1 Cost to serve	1.4.1 Supply chain costs to sales ratio	1.5.1 Projected supply chain load versus capacity
2.3 Production conversion efficiency ratios	1.2.1 Manufacturing capacity analysis specifications	1.3.2 Stock level analysis	1.4 Activity analysis of purchasing department	1.5.2 Actual supply chain load/capacity versus projection
3.5 Activity analysis of logistics department	1.2.2 Changeover time	1.3.3 Ability to meet customer orders for ex-stock items	1.4.2 Business performance Indicators	
	1.2.4 Cost to manufacture	1.3.4 Flow time		

Performance measures for stakeholders

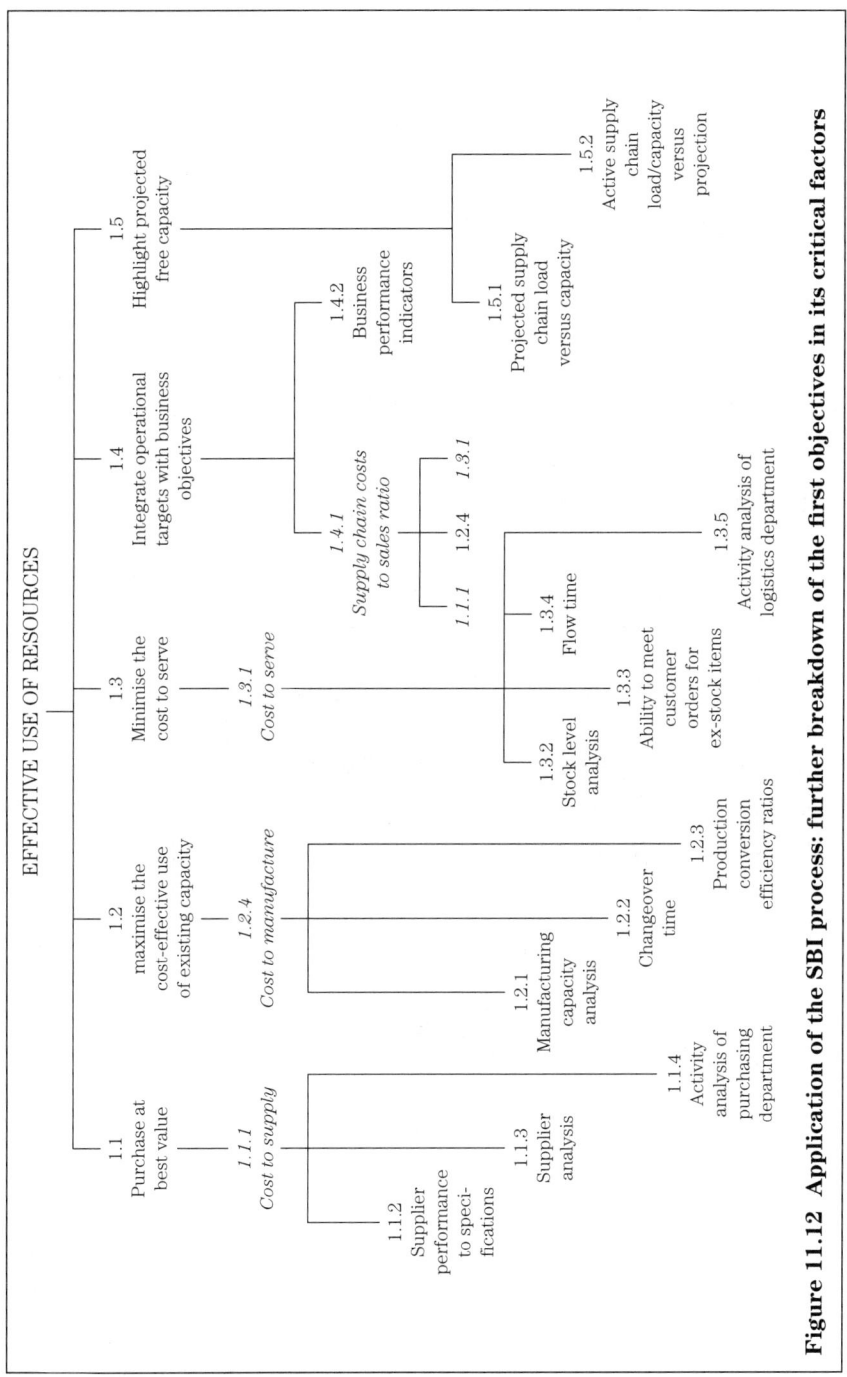

Figure 11.12 Application of the SBI process: further breakdown of the first objectives in its critical factors

Performance measurement and cost management

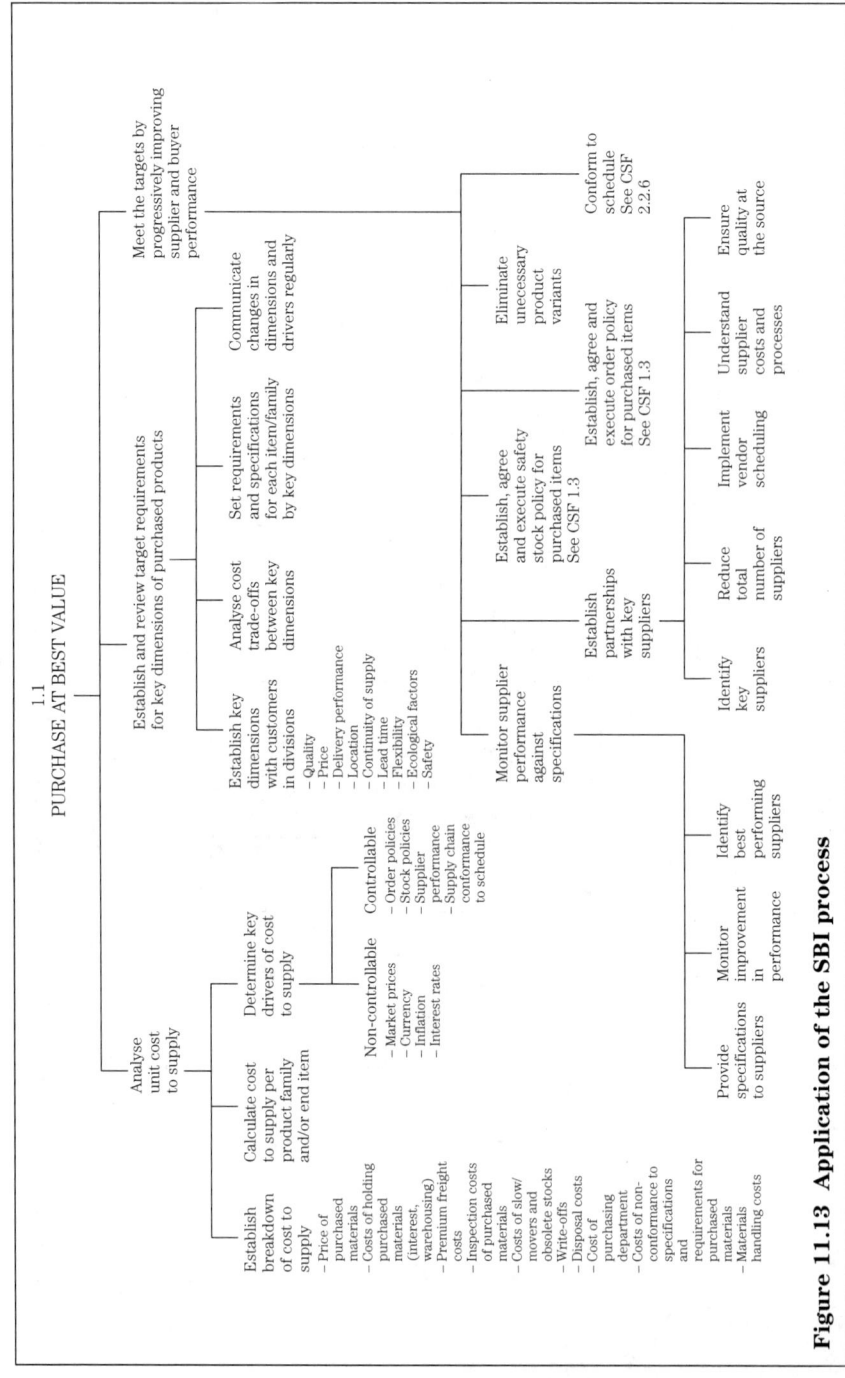

Figure 11.13 Application of the SBI process

Performance measures for stakeholders

Figures 11.11–11.13 indicate the application of the SBI process. The benefits to the company were as follows.

- Visibility of performance in all areas critical to effective supply chain management.
- Improved communication across functions.
- Support for a process of culture change towards a 'continuous improvement' culture necessary to compete in the business climate of the nineties.

Developing non-financial metrics

11.3.114 The study on performance measures in UK manufacturing companies discussed above (CIMA, 1993) concluded that no optimal set of measures has emerged in practice or theory to monitor comprehensively enterprise performance. Performance measures are, ideally, to be contextually determined. Certainly, a general roadmap approach may suggest a focus on some aspect of quality, delivery, process times and flexibility alongside the traditional working capital, accounting return and capital market financial monitors. However, a changing business climate and altered production and operational technologies and methodologies mean that 'performance measures useful at one time may become redundant at another' (CIMA, 1993). Thus a fine balance must be reached not just between reliance on financial and non-financial performance measures but also between the characteristics and activities which underpin an enterprise's success and the choice of representative performance monitors.

11.3.115 Introducing a broader set of performance measures by assessing core processes in terms of quality, speed and flexibility can move a company into a higher gear, bring balance to the way it is run and provide a radically different picture of the business from the one painted by financial figures. Luck (1994a) suggests that processes are core to a business if they focus on customer needs, are critical to success, are cross-functional in scope, focus on results and deliver competitive advantage (see Figure 11.14). While, on the surface, performance measures appear simple, many managers nonetheless grapple with what types of measure to use to find the right balance. This is because there is no standard formula to create the measures and they differ so dramatically between companies. One approach is to watch and learn from other companies and then apply relevant ideas to one's own organisation. Leading UK companies such as British Airways, ICI, Bass Brewers and Philips Electronics provide a useful insight into performance measures and how they can be applied. All of these companies use markedly

Figure 11.14 From design to sales

DESIGN	PURCHASING	PRODUCTION	FINANCE	SALES
Order fulfilment				
Compliance with regulatory constraints				
New product development				
Time Quality Flexibility Cost				

different measures but common traits emerge, such as the need for measures to be balanced and to show the performance of core processes that drive long-term business results, not the performance of functions.

11.3.116 In some cases, such as Northumbrian Water, finding the right balance with measures is complex. Northumbrian Water is one of ten UK water and sewerage companies providing water to 1.2 million customers and sewer services to 2.5 million. Since privatisation, its focus has been to show customers value for money while, at the same time, satisfying strict regulations governing water quality and environmental standards. Customers are required by law to fund expensive developments such as sewage treatment plants which must be built to meet EU requirements.

11.3.117 To satisfy the needs of both customers and regulators, Northumbrian Water has identified strategies which are each monitored by a set of measures. For instance, total lifetime cost of projects where price is balanced against risk. Rather than a 'belt and braces' zero-risk approach when setting out on projects, the company accepts a limited risk of failure to contain costs and satisfy customers and authorities.

11.3.118 With an annual capital programme of between £150 and £200 million, even small savings quickly become significant. British Airways has measures which form a hierarchy of strategic, tactical and operational indicators. This ensures that the number of measures that any one person has to deal with is manageable. The manager of operational performance at the airline suggests that 'the measures grew as the firm pursued its vision to be the world's favourite airline: we had to balance the needs of all of our stakeholders and so picked external and qualitative measures which focused on our customers and staff'.

11.3.119 When setting its measures, BA started by focusing on its customers, for without them it knew that no culture would be needed and no cash would exist: 'You gain bigger benefits by keeping customers loyal than by having to constantly gain new ones'. The airline analysed its key processes, including reservations, checkings, catering and baggage handling.

From its analysis, BA set goals, such as reducing customer complaints over baggage handling by two-thirds in one year, and used measures to see if they were achieved.

11.3.120 To cascade its vision through the organisation, BA's management developed a performance management system (PMS) which monitors department and team targets but also remains flexible enough for new customer satisfaction objectives.

11.3.121 At Bass Brewers it was the customer orientation that led the company to review its measuring system and look at its core processes. The director of new product development at Bass said the firm realised it had to move from measuring functions to measuring core processes: 'A core process approach allows customers' needs to drive the way our company operates and clarifies areas for improvements'. The firm lists customer service, logistics, brand portfolio management, product development, funds flow and information as its core processes and uses three methods to measure them: time, quality and productivity/cost. The benefits of the measures are twofold: 'Our business has a focus for continuous improvement and measures provide a baseline for re-engineering decisions'.

11.3.122 Bass' achievements in its product development unit provide a glimpse of how measuring core processes can dramatically improve efficiency. Developing new products at Bass was once the domain of a three-strong team buried within the company's marketing department. Projects were run by individuals within the unit, others were handled by different functions, and there was no senior director responsibility. With its new outlook, the company analysed the core processes of new product development, starting with the generation and development of ideas through to market testing and brand establishment. Managers then set objectives, introduced rigid feedback tools and measures and began balancing research against judgement. The results were dramatic, with the maximum time from product conception to launch reducing from 172 weeks to 85 weeks and the minimum time dropping from 84 to 36 weeks. To be customer-driven, managers must rely on a motivated workforce who look out to customers not up to managers, and with this reliance comes the difficult territory of culture.

11.3.123 Culture describes the complex and often vague set of values, beliefs and assumptions that guide staff behaviour in an organisation. Conflicts between functions and with a company's culture are a major stumbling block to implementing a consistent cascade of measures. No given culture is good or bad in itself, but it becomes appropriate or inappropriate by the degree to which it fits evolving strategies.

Performance measurement and cost management

11.3.124 By knowing the beliefs that drive it and by making those beliefs explicit, a corporation can see what contributes to its success and determine how and when changing circumstances require changes in culture. Managers must be aware of their company's culture, be flexible in their approach and know when and how best to change it, which involves communication, education, involvement, negotiation and agreement.

11.3.125 Philips provides a good example of what can be done when culture sensitivities are understood by management. At the start of the 1990s, Philips used a balanced set of measures to help it tackle dramatic change. The firm was in a financial crisis, productivity was 20 per cent below competitors' and 70 per cent of its business supported the other 30 per cent. The chairman and managing director of Philips Electronics UK said the firm had to change the attitudes of 300,000 people worldwide. 'We embarked on a change project called Centurion to improve profitability and bring commercial reality into the hearts and minds of our managers'.

11.3.126 At the same time, the firm introduced Philips Quality, incorporating the best TQM practices available. Managers were trained to be leaders, and all employees were trained to be customer-focused. To ensure that objectives cascaded through the firm, policy deployment was introduced. This involved senior managers setting improvement goals and ways to measure them. The measures were then used to agree on goals and measures for the organisation's next layer, and so on down through the company. For example, if customer service was the top goal and lead time its measure at the next level, the goal became reducing lead time. The result was a more open environment where staff were willing to face difficult problems. Philips was rewarded for its careful cultural and change management. In four years, its debt reduced by 30 per cent and sales volumes increased by 10 per cent: 'We are now convinced of the need to define the right set of performance measures, to set stretch targets and to have a rigorous follow-up process.'

11.3.127 While culture and customers are important, cash also matters – it is critical to any measuring system. The director of treasury and tax at ICL notes that, 'There are other things in business life but nothing is quite so important as cash'. In 1993, ICL had revenues of £2,623 million and was one of Europe's few profitable large IT companies. The firm uses strict cash measures to improve its asset management performance but is careful also to manage for long-term value. ICL management knows investors are attracted by a business' future ability to put cash in the till and not by its reported earnings. It therefore makes investment decisions that create shareholder value.

11.3.128 The company's finances were once centrally controlled, with each of its 26 business units conforming to one set of measures. However, this system was devolved and now each unit looks after its own finances. Financial controllers in units became financial directors and once cash targets are agreed with the central organisation, they are left to run their units as individual businesses. As a result, cash targets are consistently met and manufacturing asset returns have risen while working capital has fallen. ICL provides yet another context for the use of performance measures and, like the other firms mentioned, is developing performance measures as it goes.

11.4 Corporate board information and budgetary control

11.4.1 Members of the corporate board are the only persons whose interests tend to span both the external and the internal perspectives. As trustees for shareholders' interests, directors must work to ensure the integrity of externally reported figures. As the highest policy-level group of management, however, directors also have a vital interest in the internal financial and operating information system. Participation in the planning process is essential for directors. The process should consist of assessing the strengths and weaknesses of management strategies and examining the major assumptions used in developing the strategic or business plan. Directors should also evaluate the risk contained in the plan, and if necessary propose alternative strategies for review by management. Additionally, directors need to focus on their institution's financial risk at regular board meetings since the level of this risk significantly affects both the short- and long-term profitability and financial viability of the organisation.

11.4.2 Financial risk of an enterprise can be divided into eight elements.

- Capital adequacy risk.
- Asset quality risk.
- Liquidity risk.
- Interest rate risk.
- Off-balance sheet risk.
- Operating risk.
- Internal control risk.
- Litigation risk.

Performance measurement and cost management

11.4.3 Elements of financial risk are present in each business. Since every decision and completed transaction affects these risk factors, their relative balance must be controlled through policy guidelines designed to avoid excessive exposure in any single risk area. This balance is crucial since overexposure in any one area may lead to financial difficulties causing an institution to fail. Once one of these risk parameters is severely out of balance, the lack of necessary time and financial resources can make effective corrective action difficult to achieve.

11.4.4 Managers and directors of financial institutions need a comprehensive programme for monitoring and controlling each of the eight elements of financial risk. In order to accomplish this critical task, management must provide directors with accurate, timely information presented in a manner which will facilitate their understanding of the current financial condition of the institution and will provide a basis for an informed discussion of current and projected financial performance. 'Information for Corporate Directors' by the National Association of Accountants, provides an excellent case study of an enterprise which is concerned about financial risk evaluation and which has adhered to a 'value creation' perspective for its budgetary control activities. The organisation in question is the Sherwin-Williams Company.

11.4.5 The Sherwin-Williams Company was founded in 1866, and is today a major producer in the paint and coatings industry. The company ran into serious financial difficulties in the mid-1970s: a substantial loss of market share and a decline in earnings beginning in 1975 led to a deficit for the company's 1977 fiscal year. In January 1979 a new management team took over, implementing a new philosophy and revising management practices. The company's performance improved dramatically. The new CEO restructured the compositions and operations of the board by: firstly making a major commitment to improving internal controls and professionalising the finance and accounting functions. The implementation of new reporting systems and strengthening the internal audit function minimised the number of financial surprises each year and improved directors' perceptions of the integrity of the financial reporting systems.

11.4.6 Also, eing the architect of the design and implementation of a new management system effectively linking all facets of planning, control and performance evaluation. This system not only improved the operating performance of internal management but also provided a frame of reference for defining the board's role.

11.4.7 One of the most significant changes made by Sherwin-Williams was to develop an integrated and decentralised planning and control system.

Corporate board information and budgetary control

This system linked all facets of planning and control, beginning with strategic planning and goal formulation and ending with monthly control reports and planning for executive appraisal and compensation.

11.4.8 This new process stressed divisional planning and performance as the key to maintaining long- and short-term profitability. Introducing this formalised planning and control process also improved the relationship between the board and management; directors became more deeply involved in the workings of various parts of the planning and control system. As a result, the board/management relationship became more highly structured. Likewise, the board's involvement in the process encouraged management to review the amount of different types of information flowing to directors for adequacy.

11.4.9 For a full understanding of the board's role in the planning and control process and of the nature of the board information system, one needs an overview of Sherwin-Williams' managerial process, as shown in Figure 11.15. The process can be roughly divided into three phases: strategic planning, operational planning and control and executive appraisal and compensation planning.

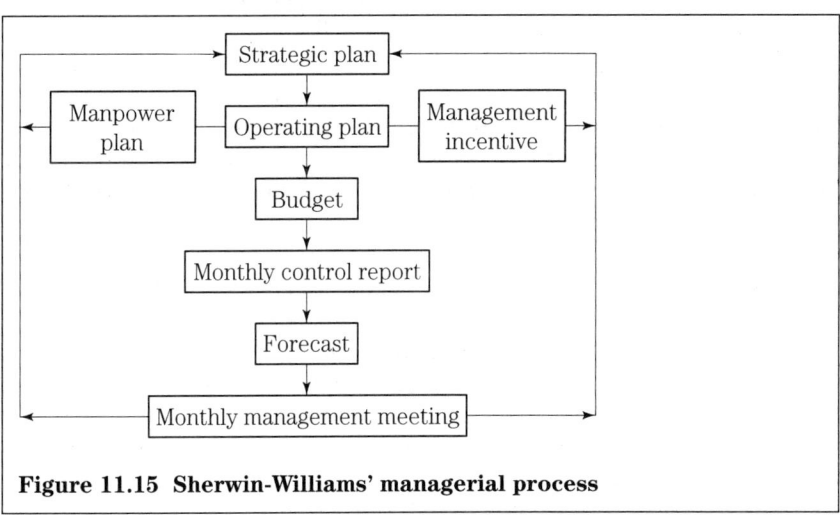

Figure 11.15 Sherwin-Williams' managerial process

11.4.10 Sherwin-Williams' planning process involves both short-term (operational) and long-term (strategic) planning. The process usually begins in June with the development of strategic plans and ends in January with the approval of operating budgets. The planning process seeks to integrate the short term and long term, and it involves corporate management, divisional management and the board.

733

11.4.11 Divisional strategies represent the operating unit managers' statements of the direction they believe their units should take in the next five years and beyond. Managers also explain how their units are going to achieve these objectives and why the strategies are the best ones available among possible alternatives. Strategies describe the opportunities, identify the resources needed and establish the major priorities for future growth. The management of each operating unit forms its own objectives and its own strategies without guide from corporate management.

11.4.12 Corporate management reviews objectives and strategies submitted by each sub-unit and then determines the compatibility of these strategies with overall strategies and plans. The outcome is the strategy or plan that has the commitment of the managers who prepare it and that reflects Sherwin-Williams' overall philosophy. Key operating managers present their strategic plans to directors at the October board meeting. The CEO firmly believes that the board should neither set nor approve the company's strategic plans but that it does have the right to provide advice and counsel and to hold the management responsible for results.

11.4.13 The second element of Sherwin-Williams' planning process, which usually begins in mid-September, is the development of the operating plan. This plan details the major actions that division managers should take to meet their objectives and strategies, and outlines how resources at the managers' disposal will be used to execute the strategy. In conjunction with the development of operating plans, the company prepares contingency plans that describe what the operating manager would do if an unexpected event should occur.

11.4.14 After the operating plan has been formulated, the next step is to develop the management manpower plan, the qualitative goals for Sherwin-Williams' management incentive programme and the consolidated budget for the coming year. One primary result of the operations planning process is the preparation of detailed budget schedules indicating each unit's expected financial performance for the next two years. A summary of the required budget documents appears in Figure 11.16, and illustrations of the three key summary budgets appear in Figures 11.17–11.19.

11.4.15 The financial measures in Figures 11.17-11.19 are crucial to planning and control for continued corporate profitability. Operating managers and directors regularly receive information on or comparisons of actual performance against the targeted performance for each of these measures. The board receives a summary of the corporate and divisional operating plans every year. These plans keep directors informed about the company's short-

Corporate board information and budgetary control

Figure 11.16 Sherwin-Williams: Summary of required budget documents

1. Summary budgets: annual income and expense, detail of interdivision transfers, cost of sales, two-year quarterly budgeted income and expense, five-year sales, profit, net assets employed and cash flow and analysis of profit before tax change
2. Market
   A. Profit and loss by new and existing product lines
   B. Profit and loss by major market segments
   C. International markets and developments, income from licences and royalties
   D. Key and major account objectives
   E. Sales promotion and advertising budget
   F. Market research
   G. Marketing department budget
3. Technical development: Technical development – new and current products/processes, technical development department budget, current product extension, new and current product and process development
4. Manufacturing
   A. Profit and loss by manufacturing plant or divisional profit centre
   B. Logistics
   C. Manufacturing engineering
   D. Energy
   E. Capital expenditures
   F. Manufacturing department budget
5. Materials management
   A. Major purchasing items
   B. Inventory management
   C. Physical distribution: distribution and warehousing
6. Cost reduction objectives
7. Administrative: Working capital, administration department budget
8. Human resources: Manpower summary
9. Acquisitions and divestitures
10. Contingency plan

term directions and serve as a benchmark for evaluating the corporation's monthly, quarterly and yearly performance, its major businesses and its key managers. Most important, the qualitative and quantitative objectives established for units and key operating managers during the planning process become an integral part of the system of executive appraisal and compensation.

11.4.16 After the operating plan and the budget are set, the operating division's actual results are compared each month with planned goals. These performance data are reviewed at corporate, divisional and board levels. Decisions made at these review sessions are fed back into the system to

Figure 11.17 Sherwin-Williams: annual income and expense summary

$	1978 actual $ per cent	1979 actual per cent $	1980 budget $ per cent	1980 estimate per cent $	1981 budget $ per cent	1982 plan $ per cent
1. NET SALES – EXTERNAL						
2. Inter: DIVN. transfers						
3. Total sales and transfers (1+2)	100.0	100.0	100.0	100.0	100.0	100.0
Cost of goods sold						
Standard cost of goods sold						
4. Material						
5. Mfg. direct labour						
6. Mfg. overhead – variable						
7. Mfg. overhead – fixed						
8. Distribution						
9. Administration						
10. Technical						
11. Total standard cost						
Other cost of goods sold						
12. Factory operations						
13. Other cost of goods sold items						
14. Total other cost of sales						
15. Total cost of goods sold (11+14)						
Gross Profit (3 – 15)						
16. Marketing, General and Administration						
17. Marketing						
18. Administration						
19. Total MG & A						
20. Corporate charge – working capital						
21. Corporate charge – fixed assets						
Corporate charge – Total (20+21)						
22. Other expense						
23. Other income						
24. Balance sheet conversion Gain or loss						
Profit before tax (16 – 19 – 22 – 23 + 24 \pm 25)						

Corporate board information and budgetary control

Figure 11.18 Sherwin-Williams: five-year sales, profit, net assets employed and cash flow summary

	1979 actual	1980 budget	1980 estimate	1981 budget	1982 plan
1. Net sales					
2. Gross profit					
3. PBT					
4. Accounts receivable (excl. interco.) Year-end					
5. Average					
6. Inventory year-end					
7. Average					
8. Accounts payable (excl. interco.) Year-end					
9. Average					
10. Working capital year-end (lines $4+6-8$)					
11. Average (lines $5+7-9$)					
12. Allocated working capital Year-end					
13. Net fixed assets (excl. alloc. assets) Year-end					
14. Alloc. net fixed assets Year-end					
15. Net assets employed $(10+12+13+14)$					
16. Pre-tax RONAE (lines $3+15$)					
17. PBT $+50$					
18. Depreciation					
19. Increase (decrease) in accounts receivable					
20. Increase (decrease) in inventory					
21. Decrease (increase) in accounts payable					
22. Subtotal – increase (decrease in working capital before adj. $(19+20+21)$					
23. Increase (decrease in alloc. working capital					
24. Subtotal – increase (decrease) in working capital $(22+23)$					
25. Inc. (dec.) in net fixed assets (excl. alloc. assets)					

26. Inc. (dec.) in alloc. net fixed assets
27. Net book value of assets disposed
28. CORE reported net cash flow (17 + 18 − 24 − 25 + 26 + 27)
29. Effect of foreign currency gain (loss)
30. Net cash flow

Figure 11.19 Sherwin-Williams: profit before tax change analysis

Total	Product line
1. 1979 profit before tax	
2. Selling price changes	

Sales volume changes
 3. Existing products
 4. New products
 5. Discontinued products

Product mix changes
 6. Existing products
 7. New products
 8. Discontinued products
 9. Total revenue changes (2 to 8)
10. Material cost changes
11. Direct labour changes
12. Other standard cost changes
13. Other cost of sales changes
14. Administrative changes
15. Marketing changes
16. Corporate charge changes
17. Other cost changes
18. Total cost changes (10 − 17)
19. 1980 profit before tax (1 + 9 + 18)

target year-end results. Management uses this information to modify and improve strategies and operating plans the next time they are submitted for review. The CEO holds monthly meetings with key corporate and group executives to review each division's performance and, if necessary, to recommend operating changes for the remainder of the fiscal year. Each quarter, the top corporate management meets group and divisional personnel to review each operating unit's progress to date.

11.4.17 Management provides directors with two types of information: a monthly 'core' report and other reports as needed. The core report summarises the financial performance of the corporation and its segments, and its format and content are similar to those given to line management. The most important data in these reports involve several key ratios. These measures are consistent with ones found in operating budgets and are used continually by line managers to run their businesses. Directors are particularly interested in each unit's return on net assets, net cash flow, profit before taxes as a percentage of net sales and utilisation of assets. Directors receive monthly and year-to-date information concerning actual versus planned and prior-year performance. In addition to the core report, which represents management's attempt to keep the board informed regularly, directors receive other reports on an as-needed basis to support a particular decision.

11.5 Metrics and customer satisfaction

11.5.1 Often the single most important improvement a company can make to increase customer satisfaction is to fix its order fulfilment process. Customers' expectations about delivery performance have changed dramatically over the last decade. A few years ago, a good supplier delivered on time about 70 per cent of the time. Now standards are nearing 99 per cent for many companies. One major step in the continuous improvement process is the identification of key measures of the process, or metrics. Schneiderman (1996a) discusses the development and use of metrics for the order fulfilment process at Analog Devices Inc. (ADI), a midsize semi-conductor manufacturer. He notes that improving the order fulfilment process is a good way to bring to light other areas in a company that need improvement. Starting with the order fulfilment process is similar to cutting inventory in a just-in-time management system. (Taiichi Ohno – the inventor of the Kanban system at Toyota – has pointed out that reducing inventory is like lowering the level of a river: when the water level falls, the rocks and boulders become visible.)

11.5.2 *Helping to overcome limitations in other processes.* As delivery performance improves, Schneiderman (1996a) notes that the limitations imposed by other processes become more visible. These processes include:

- yield enhancement;
- credit approval;
- quarterly revenue management;
- Dfx (Design for x, where x stands for manufacturability, testability, usability, serviceability, recyclability, etc.);
- management review.

Steps to improve customer satisfaction

11.5.3 To improve customer satisfaction, ADI established the following corporate-wide customer service commitment.

(1) To deliver all orders to all customers complete and when promised and to minimise lateness where we fail.

(2) To meet customers' delivery requirements – always.

(3) To offer even shorter lead times if doing so would give a competitive advantage by reducing total systems costs for the company and its customers combined.

11.5.4 ADI recognised that these objectives were likely to be met only one at a time and in the order given. The last commitment assumes that customers always value shorter lead times because it helps them build to order rather than forecast, thus minimising the excess inventory required to cover forecasting errors.

11.5.5 ADI also produced a detailed policy manual that considered market-driven trends in each area and expanded on each of the customer service commitments. Sample topics included the following.

- Taking *all* customers into consideration rather than focusing only on the largest.
- Partial shipments.
- Padded lead times with early shipments.
- Informing customers in advance of expected late shipments.
- Customers' needs versus wants.
- Transit-time responsibility.

11.5.6 The commitments, policy changes and other improvements helped transform ADI from a company that many of its customers considered difficult to work with to a company that one of its largest and most demanding customers ranked as number one.

Metrics versus measures

11.5.7 Confusion often arises over the distinction between *metrics* and *measures*.

Metrics and customer satisfaction

11.5.8 Metrics are a subset of those processes whose improvement is critical to the success of the organisation. Metrics are surrogates for stakeholder satisfaction and delight according to Schneiderman (1996a). (The term *stakeholders* refers to customers, stockholders, employees, communities, suppliers and even future generations.) As a good metric improves, stakeholder satisfaction will increase, either directly or indirectly. This relationship between improvement of a metric and improvement in stakeholder satisfaction must be significant.

11.5.9 Customers generally want high quality (as defined by conformance to specification and fitness for use (see Chapter **8**)), low cost, and timely availability. Measures of these characteristics are *results* metrics. To achieve these results, suppliers often focus on the following.

- Short cycle times.
- Inventory management.
- Scrap reduction.
- Training.
- Design for manufacturability.
- Statistical process control (SPC).
- Market research.

11.5.10 Measures of the items listed above are *process* metrics. Metrics associated with *activity*, such as the percentage of a company's associates who are on improvement teams or the hours of training per year per employee, are a subset of process metrics.

11.5.11 Results metrics represent the real objective of any process. They are the basis for the customer's decision about suppliers. They are where money can be made or lost. Ultimately, results and process metrics are not independent: they characterise a measurement system for delivering increasing value to customers.

11.5.12 The first requirement for a good metric according to Schneiderman (1996a) is that it should be a *reliable proxy* for stakeholder satisfaction. There is often a potential danger of over-complicating metrics to make them a 'better' proxy for customer satisfaction. At ADI, for example, a quadratic equation (using what is known as Taguchi's loss function) was proposed for measuring the impact of late shipments to customers. The equation (which used the number of days the order was late and worked on the assumption that being two weeks late was more than twice as bad as being one week late) used the square of the number of weeks late to measure the impact of the late shipment. Unfortunately, not all managers have the training to work easily with such sophisticated mathematical formulas. No one of ADI could produce either a real or hypothetical situation where the resulting action would be different based on the more complicated metric, so simplicity prevailed.

11.5.13 Among the characteristics of good metrics are the following.

- Well-documented, unambiguous operational definitions.
- Continuous values: metrics should be able to take on continuous values so that incremental improvement can be observed.
- Metrological standards: metrics should also meet such metrology tests as accuracy, precision, reliability and bias.

Making metrics useful

11.5.14 For metrics to be useful as part of an improvement effort, they should be all of the following.

- *Oriented toward weaknesses or defects* (i.e., metrics should measure weaknesses or defects in the process).
- *Timely*.
- *Accessible* to those responsible for improving the process.
- *Linked* to an underlying data system that facilitates the identification of root causes. In other words, if the value of the metric prompts managerial attention, then data should be available so that the responsible person can explain the cause of the variation.

11.5.15 As Schneiderman (1996a) notes, metrics evolve over time to reflect both the changing needs of constituents and process learning (i.e., the systematic mastery of a process). While financial measures have been in use for more than 100 years and are relatively stable, non-financial measures need to change to improve an organisation's alignment with rapidly changing customer requirements. Two vehicles were developed at ADI to improve the metrics continuously.

- The balanced scorecard.
- The metrics board of appeals.

The balanced scorecard at ADI

11.5.16 In 1987 ADI pioneered in the development of a balanced scorecard. The scorecard contains quarterly goals for both financial and non-financial metrics and is updated annually as part of the business planning process. At the start of the process, the quality steering council (QSC) chaired by the senior executive in change of quality performance reviewed the areas addressed on the scorecard to ensure that the right things were being targeted for improved corporate performance. To offset the historic bias in favour of financial measures, an organisation is likely to need an unbalanced scorecard at first which favours non-financial performance. The QSC included the following members.

- The CEO.
- The president.
- The vice-presidents of manufacturing, sales, technology and human resources.
- Two representative general managers of divisions.

11.5.17 This leadership group had the broad and balanced perspective to assure that ADI focused its improvement efforts on the right things. Schneiderman (1996a) states that even after detailed metrics are developed for a balanced scorecard, they and their associated supplemental metrics must evolve. Non-scorecard (or supplemental) metrics provide checks and can become candidates for future elevation to scorecard status. To this end, 'metrics boards of appeal' were established on an *ad hoc* basis.

11.5.18 For the order fulfilment metrics, a board of appeals was established. This board included the credit and warehouse managers and also operations managers from any affected divisions. Representatives from sales – and anyone else interested – were also invited to participate. The basis for an appeal was that a metric in use inappropriately penalised a sub-process for something either desired by customers or of no importance to them.

11.5.19 Based on ADI's experience, Schneiderman (1996b) states that a complete set of results metrics for the order fulfilment process should measure the following.

(1) How well commitments are met (lateness).

(2) How closely commitments match customer needs (excess lead time).

(3) The degree to which lateness hurts customers (severity).

(4) Timeliness of order quoting (responsiveness).

11.5.20 A set of results metrics must illuminate all significant undesirable trade-offs (i.e., where one metric may improve but overall customer satisfaction declines).

11.5.21 Process metrics assign responsibility for corrective action to individuals. The metrics must link up with internal data systems to facilitate root-cause analysis.

11.5.22 How metrics are displayed and distributed has a significant influence on how useful they will be.

11.5.23 Seamless integration into management planning and review systems assures the vitality of non-financial metrics.

11.5.24 Focusing on rates of *improvement* rather than on performance levels contributes directly to organisational learning.

11.6 The balanced scorecard

11.6.1 The balanced scorecard is an approach to performance monitoring which must be considered in the light of an organisation's broader performance system structure. Simons (2000) notes that the balanced scorecard is a complement, not a replacement, for an organisation's other performance measurement and control systems. He sees performance measurement and control systems as essential tools used by all effective managers in achieving their desired profit goals and strategies. These systems comprise profit planning and a variety of performance-management techniques. These systems also allow managers to balance the tensions between: profit, growth, and control; short-term versus long-term performance; expectations of different constituencies; opportunities and attention; and the differing motives of human behaviour. Simons (2000) believes that, properly applied, performance measurement and control systems can be used to overcome the organisational blocks that impede the true potential of individuals working in modern organisations. The balanced scorecard may be considered to cast a wide net over organisational performance issues in that it is concerned with a wide group of stakeholders rather than purely shareholders.

11.7 Four dimensions that matter

11.7.1 Kaplan and Norton (1996) argue that managers focusing on a single financial measure often tend to manage for the short term, which may lead to a failure to invest in assets essential to long-term growth. Investments to obtain motivated and skilled employees and to ensure customer satisfaction often pay off only over the long term. Therefore, managers need a performance measurement system that is balanced between outcome measures (the results of past efforts) and the measures that are to drive future performance. The balanced scorecard provides such a set of measures. As Ruhl (1997) notes in his comments on the conception of the balanced scorecard advanced by Kaplan and Norton (1996), the balanced scorecard is based on the premise that organisational performance needs to be viewed from four perspectives.

(1) The financial perspective.

(2) The customer perspective.

(3) The internal-business-process perspective.

(4) The learning-and-growth perspective.

The financial perspective

11.7.2 Kaplan and Norton (1996) argue that the goals of any profit seeking company are ultimately financial. Financial objectives establish the objectives and measures in the other three perspectives. It is unlikely that one financial metric (such as ROCE (see Chapter **4**)) can be appropriate across a wide range of business units. Financial objectives can differ at each stage of a business's life-cycle (see Chapter **7**). For instance, businesses in the growth stage may operate with negative cash flows and low returns on invested capital. For harvest-stage businesses, however, the overall financial objectives would probably be operating cash flow (before depreciation) and reductions in working capital.

11.7.3 Several financial themes drive business strategy across all stages of a business's life-cycle. One of these is revenue growth and mix. Companies can assess their progress in this area by tracking the following.

(1) The percentage revenues from new products, services and customers.

(2) Profitability of particular customers and product lines.

(3) Percentage of unprofitable customers.

The customer perspective

11.7.4 In the customer perspective, companies identify the customer and market segments in which they compete. As part of the customer perspective, companies identify and measure ways in which they deliver value to targeted customers and market segments. Once a business has identified and targeted its market segments, it can address the objectives and measures for these. Measures can include market share and customer satisfaction. The importance of customer satisfaction cannot be exaggerated. Research indicates that only when customers are completely satisfied can a company achieve their buying loyalty. Some Internet companies have recently found that even ensuring customer satisfaction does not translate into continued loyalty.

The internal-business-process perspective

11.7.5 For the internal-business-process perspective, managers identify the processes that are most critical for achieving customer and shareholder objectives. Managers define a complete internal-process value chain. This value chain starts with the innovation process (i.e., identifying current and future customers' needs, then developing new solutions for these needs), proceeds through the operations process (i.e., delivering existing products and services to existing customers), and ends with post-sales service (i.e., offering services after sale that add to the value customers receive from a company's products).

11.7.6 Kaplan and Norton (1996) provide measures for the three phases of the value chain. For example, measures for the innovation process could include the following;

(1) percentage of sales from new products; or

(2) new product introduction versus competitors'.

The learning-and-growth perspective

11.7.7 The learning-and-growth perspective develops objectives and measures to drive organisational learning and growth. Objectives in the learning-and-growth perspective provide the basis for performing on the other three perspectives.

11.7.8 There are three principal categories for this perspective.

(1) Employees' capabilities.

(2) Information-system capabilities.

(3) Motivation, empowerment and alignment ('alignment' refers to whether departments or employees have their goals aligned with the company's goals as articulated in the balanced scorecard).

The balanced scorecard and strategy

11.7.9 Employee capabilities are especially important, because organisations must hire individuals capable of creative problem solving and continual improvement. Employee capabilities can be assessed through measures of employee satisfaction, retention and productivity.

11.8 The balanced scorecard and strategy

11.8.1 A management accounting guideline published by CMA Canada (1999) on applying the balanced scorecard notes that managers can use the balanced scorecard as a means to articulate strategy, communicate its details, motivate people to execute plans and enable executives to monitor results. The prime advantage is that a broad array of indicators can improve the decision-making that contributes to strategic success, whether in big organisations or small, profit-focused or non-profit, whether at the executive level or the team level. Non-financial measures enable managers to consider more factors critical to long-term performance. These factors, flowing directly from the organisation's strategy, vary from how well the organisation concerns itself with customers to how fast it innovates.

11.8.2 The guideline by the CMA Canada (1999) notes that another reason managers strive for more non-financial measures is that traditional financial measures give a historical view of performance – 'through the rearview mirror'. The 'lagging' financial figures, like sales volume, help the firm keep track of the past. They often do not provide as much insight as forecasted data on quality and shipping performance for instance. In other words, financial measures tend not to offer the predictive information contained in many non-financial metrics.

11.8.3 By incorporating new measures in a balanced scorecard, an organisation's managers can be prepared for future competition imposed by the market it operates in, such as:

- to improve performance continuously;
- to implement more complex strategies;
- to run lean, decentralised organisations better;
- to feed systems for organisational learning;
- to drive organisational change.

11.8.4 The guideline from the CMA Canada (1999) notes that while managers have found they need a broader set of measures to manage within the organisation, they are also perceiving the need for a broader set of measures

Performance measurement and cost management

to identify external issues and manage external relationships. The organisation's success may depend on managing the partners, suppliers, customers, shareholders and other stakeholders via which the organisation creates value. To this end, a balanced scorecard can help in a variety of ways.

- To sense the demands of markets, competition and society.
- To broaden and deepen supply-chain relationships.
- To broaden and deepen relationships with stakeholders.
- To demonstrate accountability for performance.

11.8.5 The guideline notes that as organisations develop balanced scorecards, they can apply them in at least three ways: as part of a performance improvement system, as part of a strategic management system and as part of an internal and external accountability system. Using the balanced scorecard as a performance improvement system enables managers to deliver better results with current plans and processes. Top executives who are largely satisfied with strategic execution can use a balanced set of measures to drive continuous improvement such as with a total quality management initiative (see Chapter **8**). They can rely on the powerful linking of measures, in a cascading fashion, to the drivers of performance at every level. This cascading enables firm-wide, not just factory-wide, improvement of performance.

11.8.6 As Kaplan and Norton (1996) maintain, executives can translate the corporate vision, communicate strategy down through the organisation, integrate business and financial plans to deliver the strategy, and stimulate feedback that indicates how to change the strategy to increase its effectiveness (see Figure 11.20). Each of these processes is useful by itself; together they can play a decisive role in organisational success, especially when a firm launches a new strategy or undergoes considerable change.

Figure 11.20 Balancing four dimensions of strategic concern

What is the vision?
What is the communicating objective?
How is learning to take place?
What business targets need to be set?

11.8.7 The guideline notes that the third way to apply the balanced scorecard is as part of a corporate accountability system. When managers use measures as a performance-improvement system, or as a strategic management system, they are largely restricting themselves to an internal focus. They consequently develop strong internal accountability – systems for defining goals, meeting them, and gathering intelligence on improving.

The balanced scorecard and strategy

A case study: organisational processes and the balanced scorecard

11.8.8 Organisations are managed not simply by technical means. Political and social dimensions are essential to consider. Ultimately, a multi-dimensional outlook must be adopted. The Tempest case considers how a balanced approached might be achieved.

11.8.9 Bill Jennings had a tough choice to make. Bill was Activity-Based Project Manager of Tempest Inc., a large European manufacturer of industrial and consumer detergents and paints. Joe Smith, his boss and Chief Financial Officer of Tempest, had offered him the position of Manager, Capital Spending. This new position would give Bill responsibility for managing the financial planning and monitoring of Tempest's $415 million capital budget, a position of major importance. However, it would also mean leaving his current role in leading highly visible performance improvement projects involving activity-based management and organisational re-engineering. Furthermore, it was June and Tempest's lengthy, tedious, capital budgeting process, disliked by many in the company, would begin in about a month.

11.8.10 The entire capital budgeting process took about six months. First, each subsidiary would propose investment in several projects. These proposals would reach the European head office in July and August. They typically represented a significant increase in expenditure over the previous year. Over the next few months, Joe Smith's staff would gather various pieces of information about project costs and specific benefits to prepare for year-end meetings. Held in December, these were a series of annual planning meetings during which the subsidiary CEOs and CFOs presented projected year-end results and negotiated performance targets for sales, net income, headcount and capital, for the new year. Tempest's overall capital target was then established as a percentage of total expected revenues.

11.8.11 January was a very busy month. Each subsidiary would lobby and negotiate for changes in the resources and results targets established in December, even while year-end performance numbers were being finalised. Finally, by mid-February, final targets were established. It seemed that no sooner did one cycle end than it was time for the next one to begin.

11.8.12 Joe Smith believed that Tempest needed a repeatable and reliable capital budgeting process and that Bill Jennings was the right person for the job. After much discussion, Bill accepted the position. He was excited. He now saw this as a highly visible opportunity to apply his process improvement skills to a far-reaching process which had major business impact.

Performance measurement and cost management

Additionally, since his boss was also very interested in improving the process, he would have all the support he needed to get the job done. The sea of life appeared calm and untroubled.

The business climate

11.8.13 Tempest Inc. had been in business for 30 years at that point. Each of its five subsidiaries (two located in Europe, two in Asia and one in the US), were organised around product groups (industrial and consumer detergents and paints), and each had its own plants. Each subsidiary's board reported in to the Executive Board in Europe, with CFOs reporting to Joe Smith. Bill now had responsibility for co-ordinating worldwide capital budget development activity with the CFOs of the subsidiaries.

11.8.14 For decades, the company had been the market leader in most of the categories in which it competed. With sales of $4 billion, an unshakeable reputation with the trade, and a large base of customers for its premium priced, high quality, innovative products, it had operating power that could not be matched by the competition, which, for the most part, had no critical mass to pose a serious threat. In recent years Tempest had fuelled its growth with heavy investment in the latest manufacturing technology, and believed this would be an insurmountable barrier to any new competitor. Tempest's highly automated state-of-the-art plants were the benchmark for the industry and a considerable source of pride for the Executive Board. Several 'high tech' projects which returned less than cost of capital were approved by the board, because of the 'strategic value' of an investment in new technology.

11.8.15 The problem had been that the company had no problem. Tempest was incredibly successful. The only group apparently concerned about capital spending was the finance division which felt that more attention needed to be addressed to cash flow issues. The company's board had ample experience, very good judgement, and an excellent reputation in the industry for aggressive business strategy. There simply was no apparent need to 'over-analyse' things. Nonetheless, in recent years a disturbing trend had emerged.

11.8.16 Small regional manufacturers, whose products matched Tempest's quality at much lower prices, were operating in several key markets. Consumers in these markets had unique needs which Tempest's large scale production capability could not economically accommodate. The new competition's flexible manufacturing facility produced small runs of product for the local trade, and provided a highly customised service to small localised industrial clients. Furthermore, with 'value pricing' becoming an issue in the consumer markets, many of Tempest's retail outlets were begin-

The balanced scorecard and strategy

ning to stock their shelves with 'house brands'. The small local producers were the major source of such products.

11.8.17 Individually these regional manufacturers were no threat to the giant. Collectively, however, they were an increasingly troubling force. Two of the largest of these regional producers had recently merged and the company's strategic planners were now concerned that further consolidation would pose a serious threat to Tempest's position in the market place. For the first time in 20 years sales were flat and expected to show a growth in the next three years – despite anticipated continuing market growth. A major business publication noticing this trend, included it in a major report on the impact of generic manufacturers on major brands. The event crystallised many board concerns and became a catalyst for change within Tempest.

Planned changes to capital spending

11.8.18 In mid July, Tempest's board, which prided itself on its ability to make quick decisions, responded. It was decided that, given market conditions, price must remain flat. The heavy capital investment programmes had resulted in explosive growth of depreciation expenses. In order to sustain income growth targets (which had to be maintained as a separate issue from sales growth), costs of production would have to be reduced. Simultaneously return on investment targets were raised to strengthen overall financial performance. Given this 'get better' versus 'get bigger' philosophy, it was agreed that capital investment should be focused on improvement rather than expansion. Capital investment had to decrease as a percentage of sales. Allowing continued growth of capital spending at current rates would lead to depreciation charges which would significantly erode the bottom line. The board hoped that this new focus would yield results in two ways: first, projects which did not yield solid benefits would not be implemented, and second, projects which held the promise of very good returns would be implemented without excessive spending. This new focus would allow 'more to get done with less' (capital).

11.8.19 Many people asked Bill what all this meant. Would capital projects already begun be stopped? Were there particular types of projects that would not be funded in the future? What was the target for the new capital budget? Bill was concerned. A storm seemed to be brewing.

11.8.20 Cost-cutting teams were deployed throughout the company. A few examples of the new focus were widely discussed in the company. In one instance, the number of engineers scheduled to visit the US to evaluate new equipment was reduced from 14 to 4. Some managers complained that instead of cutting 'fat', 'muscle' was being sliced away (translation: *their* budget had the biceps and should not be cut). However, this was an expected reaction to the new lean focus.

11.8.21 Many agreed that this new cost consciousness was appropriate. It stood in conflict, however, with a major motivator for many managers. Many of Tempest's directors liked the power of having a substantial capital budget. Indeed, at times, it seemed that the size of your capital budget, along with the number of staff in your department, signalled your importance to the rest of the organisation. Thus, much attention became focused on the capital budget.

11.8.22 By the end of August, two camps had emerged. The first group consisted of a stream of anxious visitors to Bill Jennings' office. They (and their representatives) had questions about how much would be 'cut' out of the total budget. They emphasised how important their projects were to the success of the company, especially in the face of the emerging competitive threats. They also wanted to know how their obviously superior projects could be guaranteed inclusion in the capital budget. Perhaps there could be two tiers of projects: an 'A' list (which would presumably include many of their own projects), and a 'B' list of inferior projects (of which many seemed to be in a variety of departments other than their own). The second camp seemed to have decided that the power of their influence with the board and the obvious superiority of their projects would guarantee them inclusion in the budget. Bill was unhappy. The waters were decidedly choppy.

11.8.23 This wasn't an easy time for Bill. The directors were a formidable group of people with power to impact his career, and they all expected that he could recognise the unique value of their projects. He grew thin and pale. He wore a hunted look and took to ducking into the nearest empty office when he saw a director approach, to avoid painful discussions of why a particular project just *had* to be funded. He wished for the old days when he facilitated teams in their pursuit of performance improvement. Joe Smith noticed Bill's pain. 'Surely,' said Joe, 'some of those performance improvement principles could be applied to the capital budgeting process.' Bill felt sick. The waves were higher than he had ever seen them.

Strategy and capital planning

11.8.24 In late August the board hired a consultant for advice on issues of strategic importance. The consultant had the board attend a senior management course on 'Competitive Strategy'. This was a change from previous strategy meetings where the board would retire for a week to the sumptuous surroundings of a luxury resort. Directors noted this and commented on

The balanced scorecard and strategy

it. When they returned, they assembled the company's 6,000 employees in five cities for a satellite broadcast of a meeting at which the chairman discussed the competitive challenges facing Tempest. 'Strategic intent', 'Competitive advantage', and 'Critical capabilities' were addressed, as were 'Cycle time', 'Delighting the customer', and 'Empowerment'. When the issues came around to 're-focusing' capital spending, the chairman referred to 'Your Chief Financial Officer, Joe Smith and his team, who are working on a solution'. The chairman was 'confident that this revised capital strategy would re-energise the company by allowing it to concentrate on only those opportunities that could deliver the best results'. In no way would the new capital plan impair Tempest's ability to compete. Cycle time would improve and manufacturing processes would become more nimble as a result of this new focus. The chairman said he would have Joe Smith report to the board in November on how the process redesign was progressing and how he intended cutting $65 million from the capital budget. Joe Smith smiled as the camera zoomed in on him. Bill was glad the camera crew did not know who 'Joe's team' was. Bill felt the waves batter at him as he sank under the surface.

11.8.25 That evening Joe and Bill had a long discussion. How would they manage the expectations of the directors with ideas for capital investments? They had to overcome the 'squeakiest wheel gets his/her project funded' syndrome. How would they deliver results to the board? How could they be sure that they could select the 'best' capital investment ideas and reject the rest? Should the value of a capital project be measured only by a discounted cash flow? Should an attempt be made to reflect what value the project could deliver to customers, the trade and the employees? How did these issues relate to each other? Were some more important than others? Were there other issues they were missing? Would this new process take too long to implement? What if it didn't succeed? Should they work with a group of directors to validate their thoughts?

11.8.26 Validation, they decided, was a must on two fronts – first, to test how sound their ideas were, but second, and as important, to test the 'political' ramifications of a new approach. Bill recalled an approach he had read about which may have some application here; the balanced scorecard model. They called in Joyce Shu, the director of strategic planning. Joyce had perhaps the best cross-functional overview of how things should work in the company. The three worked late into the night and when the meeting ended they had a plan.

11.8.27 Over the next few weeks Bill led Joe, Joyce and a small cross-functional team of managers in two meetings where they identified a series of performance factors that capital investments should impact. This brainstorming process ended with close to a hundred such factors. There were too many to use effectively and Bill referred to research papers for a method which would help narrow the list down to a few key performance factors. He found one that worked: the Performance Measurement Questionnaire. The method was a democratic, consensus-oriented way to distil a wide variety of potential measures of performance into a short list of the few most important to Tempest. It began with a list of all the performance measures. Each member of the cross-functional team 'voted' for each measure by circling a number on a scale from 1 to 7 where '7' was most important. The measures with the highest average scores became part of a final set of 25 measures.

11.8.28 Bill was amazed at how much he had contributed to the tool. He was back in a mode of improving the performance of a process – in this case, the capital budgeting process. He was happy. The waves were rough, but he was riding them well.

Implementing the process

11.8.29 A series of video conferences with key subsidiary VPs and directors followed, explaining the new capital evaluation process. The new process included a decision tool which evaluated each project on the basis of the value it was expected to deliver. 'Value' was defined from the perspectives of several 'stakeholders' including 'Customers', 'Shareholders', 'Internal business processes', and 'Innovation and learning'. Each of these stakeholders was represented by specific performance factors. Projects would be valued on the basis of how much they could contribute to these factors, and therefore, to 'value' (see Bill Jennings memo). Initially, many directors were sceptical – only they really *knew* their project. Only they were therefore qualified to decide whether it should be funded or not. How could anyone else know this better? Besides, it was argued, nobody was genuinely unbiased in their recommendations. People would obviously rate their projects ahead of everyone else's.

11.8.30 Bill responded to the concerns with confidence. He believed that the new process was theoretically and practically sound and, because of the sound logic backing his conviction, opposition to the process gradually weakened. The subsidiaries proceeded to gather project proposals as they always had. Joe Smith asked for the subsidiary CFOs' support in rolling out the new process in mid-October.

11.8.31 Each subsidiary formed a Capital Evaluation Committee (CEC) consisting of key board members. Directors submitted lists of recommended

The balanced scorecard and strategy

capital investment projects, which the CEC rated (scored) according to the 'value' they promised to deliver. The maximum score a project could earn was 1,000 points. Projects were ranked by their scores and an estimate of the capital required for each was made. Each subsidiary was told to assume they had 20 per cent less capital than the previous year. When the capital available 'ran out', the expectation was that other projects could not be funded. Given the current capital budget of $415 million, this would result in planned investment of $332 million and allow some flexibility in meeting the $350 million target established by the board. These ranked lists of projects were sent by the subsidiaries to Tempest headquarters during November. Bill consolidated the information into a single ranking for the year-end meetings and found that when $332 million was assigned completely, 215 projects fell 'below the line' – they could not be funded.

11.8.32 One point of contention was that the final list of projects differed from a simple pooling of the separate subsidiary level lists. For instance, eight of the projects that were below the line for the Asian subsidiary had higher scores than accepted projects at the European subsidiary. Thus, in the final list, these eight Asian projects were ranked as fundable while several previously accepted European subsidiary projects fell below the line. In the past, choices about which projects to implement had not been a critical issue since most capital projects had been approved. Now the Board had to reach an understanding as to whether the European projects had priority, given that region's rapidly changing environment. The political ramifications of this discovery could not be addressed by the new capital evaluation process alone. Instead, they required management judgement. However, the list of projects for which discussion was now necessary was much smaller and could be examined in depth.

11.8.33 The CEC meetings proceeded smoothly when participants realised that the process was actually very sound – it did not allow individuals' biases to overvalue a project. For instance, a project that did nothing to help the 'Customer' could not get a high score from the 'Customer' perspective. Weak projects were exposed for what they really were now that there was a consistent basis of evaluation. People even withdrew projects that only weeks before 'just *had* to be funded'. Bill felt he was getting his 'sea legs' now.

11.8.34 Despite the progress made, there were those who grumbled about the process in the washrooms. It took too long. Judgement and creativity were being stifled. How could they be expected to do their jobs if they did not get the resources to function? They would talk with their board if they had to. The grapevine conveyed these things to Bill and he grew concerned – but not for long.

Performance measurement and cost management

11.8.35 Joe Smith and Bill met with the Chairman and introduced the new process to him. He was delighted. He led the Executive Board in an active discussion of the process, with the CEOs and CFOs of the subsidiaries participating via video conference. At the end of the meeting the Chairman announced that he was well satisfied with the new process and its results. He was especially pleased with the focus provided by the process. As a direct result, the time required for senior management to review capital projects had been reduced by 50 per cent to 75 per cent. He congratulated Joe Smith and Bill on their excellent work. He also recommended using a similar approach for other areas in the company where priority calls, once made, locked the company on a course of action which was expensive to change. With this, many of those who had recently expressed dissatisfaction with the new process re-examined their positions. Bill was pleased. He had found his core competence. He began thinking seriously about taking up sailing.

Memorandum

TO: Joe Smith, CFO

FROM: Bill Jennings

SUBJECT: Internal memo: THE BALANCED SCORECARD AT TEMPEST INC.

DATE: December 3

BACKGROUND

The new capital evaluation process (The Balanced Scorecard) is a flexible management tool which helps define and execute business strategy. Designed correctly, it provides a balance for the entire organisation, focusing it in a structured manner on key results, without stifling creativity and judgement. Best of all, once designed, its application is simple and consistent. It also has the capacity to evolve quickly, growing with management experience and absorbing the best emerging business practices and academic thinking. Companies like Apple Computer, Advanced Micro Devices, Analog Devices and FMC Corporation are pioneering its use with great results. Tempest Inc. is solidly in this category of advanced, successful users.

WHAT NEEDS IT SERVES

The tool provides a remarkably simple and comprehensive approach to address critical issues for which no coherent alternatives exist. First, it clarifies strategic focus by requiring definition of the relative importance of the company's key stakeholders. Second, it helps define and set targets for the results management expects to deliver as the direct result of the chosen strategy. Third, it provides a structure which channels investments and resource assignments into divisions and departments such that the strategy is executed well.

Not having this clarity results in mixed signals to managers and forces them to make trade-offs between different aspects of performance. Such trade-offs are made by different managers in different ways, resulting in a lack of operating consistency

The balanced scorecard and strategy

over time and between divisions. This dilution of the organisation's capability to focus on a few key areas and deliver superior results in them is undesirable and, although often recognised as such, is managed ineffectively.

WHAT IT IS

The tool establishes a limited number of critical performance indicators for the entire company which are directly derived from the organisation's strategic objectives and competitive demands. In Tempest, the scorecard requires 'business value' to be defined from four key 'stakeholders" perspectives: (1) The customer, (2) Internal business processes, (3) The shareholder, and (4) Innovation and learning. These perspectives of what 'good' performance means are crystallised into a few specific performance measures and are given weights reflecting the company's intent to satisfy its different stakeholders' needs.

A simple scoring process follows. Each project or investment scores points for its potential to succeed in each chosen performance measure. Projects are ranked on their scores and investments are prioritised on that basis. Management decisions can override this ranking allowing for the guidance of judgement and experience.

Since the scores provide a ranking, top projects and very weak projects are generally not debated. Instead, only projects at the 'cut-off' point (the limit at which resources to implement run out) are scrutinised. The method is remarkably robust and does not allow an individual's biases to override what 'value' means (e.g., a project that does nothing for the 'customer' cannot receive a high score in the 'customer' category).

INTERESTING POSSIBILITIES

(1) This tool begs the use of a top management quarterly review book that contains four sections – one for each 'stakeholder'. Each section would map Tempest's progress since the last review in a few critical performance areas. Divisions that are key contributors to these areas would be accountable for specific aspects of performance.

(2) It offers a specific and rational vehicle for the post audit of investments. As such, it can be used to encourage project champions to focus on specific project performance targets. This could avoid unfortunate instances where an individual's project responsibility ends with successful project justification.

(3) Performance targets could be set for stakeholder measures to focus streamlining and redesigning activity. This focus also provides a basis for concentrating on only a few key improvement efforts at one time.

CONCLUSION

This new approach has received refreshingly enthusiastic response because of its greatest strength – its ability to translate very clearly a 'strategy' into operating terms which are commonly understandable, communicable, actionable, and measurable. In this context, it is flexible enough to operate with any acronym (BPR, TQM, ABM, ABC, etc.), and, in fact, significantly strengthens them all. It focuses the enterprise.

Performance measurement and cost management

Balanced scorecard versus DCF

11.8.36 Traditional DCF methods (see Chapter **4**) favour investments that have documentable revenues or savings associated with them. Thus, the automation or expansion of existing production facilities is an area where traditional DCF is likely to work well. However, DCF is not very easily applied in a situation where the benefits are unknown, where they are inextricably intertwined with other initiatives, or where the cost of *not* investing is loss of long-term competitive advantage.

11.8.37 The balanced scorecard approach described in the case ranks investment initiatives based on their contributions to a variety of strategic ends. Furthermore, it sanctions the use of judgemental scoring on these dimensions. Thus, it emphasises strategic coherence in capital spending. There is no doubt that DCF *is* theoretically correct. The problem is that the practical world does not always co-operate by providing access to all of the relevant data.

11.8.38 Tempest's current woes seem to be related to price pressure from generic label manufacturers. However, there does not seem to be any desire in the organisation to switch from an innovator/prospector strategy to a price leader/defender strategy (see Chapter **9**). Tempest's management just want to make sure that the money they spend will provide the most competitive advantage. The balanced scorecard approach does not preclude the use of DCF analysis in providing, say, a score on the stockholder value dimension. However, it does expand the decision model to include explicitly all major strategic dimensions.

Determinants of the proposal's success
11.8.39 Some of the points that are likely to arise include the following.

- Tractability – Although the approach requires analysis of each proposed investment along each of the four stakeholder dimensions, the output of that analysis is a judgement in relative terms. Concrete data is desirable, but not required.

- Understandability – The method does not require mysterious calculations and manipulations. Everyone is capable of grasping the technique of rating on a 1 to 7 scale.

- Democracy – While DCF relies on its input parameters and an inviolable process to find an output value, the inputs can be manipulated. The balanced scorecard approach described in the case openly employs a subjective rating method. However, the ratings must be justified and the 'voting' approach can be used to average out individual biases. Finally, as a voting process, its results represent an inherent consensus and an unassailable 'judgement of the majority'.

- Improved focus and time requirement – The rating methodology created 'clear winners' and 'clear losers' at the top and bottom of the ranked list. Thus, discussions could be fruitfully focused on the proposed investments clustered around the spending cap. The time requirement for the final board decisions was thereby significantly reduced.

- Use of opinion leaders – The early roll-out of the new method involved 'key subsidiary VPs and directors'. Bill clearly oriented his approach toward convincing these critical opinion leaders of the rationality and fairness of the approach.

The balanced scorecard approach at Tempest

11.8.40 At Tempest, the scorecard is comprised of a weighted matrix of scores on four dimensions: stockholders (i.e., accounting-based financial results), customers, internal business processes and innovation and learning. Each of the scores within a cell of the matrix is weighted by a multiplier related to the relative importance of that dimension to Tempest's strategic development. Suppose the following weights were applied at Tempest:

Stockholders (30%)	Customers (30%)
Internal business processes (20%)	Innovation & learning (20%)

11.8.41 Within each cell in the matrix, a list of evaluation criteria can be placed, against which the project's expected results can be judged. These lists can be sub-categorised under the headings cost, time, quality and flexibility.

11.8.42 Stockholders

(1) Financial survival (cash flow, profit, ROI)

(2) Success (sales growth and market share)

(3) Time to market

11.8.43 Customers

(1) Price/cost of ownership

(2) Operating performance

(3) Availability

11.8.44 Internal business processes

(1) Procurement

(2) Customer acquisition

(3) Distribution

11.8.45 Innovation and learning

(1) Product technology

(2) Process technology

Information management

(Source: The Tempest case, Carr, 1997. Reprinted with permission. For more information visit www.wglcorpfinance@riag.com)

11.9 Balanced scorecards can fail!

11.9.1 Although the balanced scorecard can offer a variety of benefits as identified by Kaplan and Norton (1996), implementing the technique is not without shortfalls. Some commentators have noted that 70 per cent of balanced scorecard implementations fail (see McCunn, 1998). McCann (2000) suggests that there are a number of key elements to launching a successful balanced scorecard solution, the first of which is that it must be enterprise-deployable. The balanced scorecard methodology is only valuable when rolled out across all divisions and down all management levels. If only the management team knows what the strategy is, then employees could be pulling in different potentially non-strategic directions. Putting a balanced scorecard on the desktops of employees is a way to ensure that they have an understanding of performance issues and how their day-to day decisions affect them according to McCann (2000)

11.9.2 In order to support a wide user base, a balanced scorecard ought to be easy to use. Key requirements for usability include: a graphical user interface (GUI) to enable users simply to point and click to obtain information. Also, to make administration easy, a balanced scorecard should enable the administrator to create as many groups and users as required by the organisation, including adding and maintaining groups, users and applications.

11.9.3 McCann (2000) remarks that a balanced scorecard must also consist of a great deal more than just numbers and measures. It must have

Balanced scorecards can fail!

scope for qualitative commentary as part of the assessment process and also for actions resulting from the knowledge put into the system.

11.9.4 In building a scorecard, an organisation will go through the process of building a new way of managing. Areas which are likely to be assessed will include clarifying and agreeing strategy, educating (or re-educating) the organisation, aligning business processes throughout the company and introducing a feedback system.

11.9.5 The first step according to McCann (2000) should be to organise a team of people who will be instrumental in the implementation. This is not like implementing ABM (see Chapter **6**) or total quality management (see Chapter **8**). The team should spend time discussing and reaching a consensus on what the company's vision is, identifying strategic issues and how they can be understood and communicated to the rest of the company. It is imperative that scorecard development has the commitment and attention of senior executives. McCann (2000) believes that implementing a scorecard is not a middle-management task. There are three critical roles for the team:

- a designer who takes ownership of the project, educates the executive team and turns strategy into action;
- an executive sponsor should also be selected according to McCann (2000). If the scorecard is to be properly implemented, it should be endorsed by a senior member of the company. This person should have a direct relationship with the CEO, as the role requires looking at how managers will need to adapt their roles to reflect the new strategy;
- a key advocate should be responsible for ensuring the aims of the scorecard are understood throughout the rest of the organisation.

11.9.6 Strategic objectives are the foundation of any scorecard, so identifying them becomes the first key step in implementation. The designer should gather information on areas such as competitors, trends in market size and growth, customers and current and future technology innovations. These then need to be considered in the context of the four perspectives developed by Kaplan and Norton (1996).

11.9.7 McCann (2000) notes that once the new strategy is decided, it should be communicated to the middle managers in the organisation. This should involve the people who constitute the top three layers of management. Strategy should be taught and discussed with them to ensure that the way forward is clear. Projects, programmes or initiatives that do not reflect the new corporate strategy should be eliminated rapidly.

Performance measurement and cost management

11.9.8 The finalised corporate scorecard should be used as a basis for allowing each business unit to formulate its own objectives, targets and strategy according to McCann (2000). Strategic business units will all have their own products, customers and communication channels. Mission and strategy statements should be established for each department, taking into account their individual needs and aims, but always linking them back to the corporate scorecard. The balanced scorecard should become part of the management process and highlight possibilities to link individual objectives and financial reward back into the scorecard.

11.9.9 Rousseau and Rousseau (2000) note further pitfalls in the implementation of a balanced scorecard. They suggest that since the balanced scorecard concept is normally introduced from the top down, the organisation often starts with the development of its first scorecard at the top level of the organisation. The selected measures are therefore applicable to the executive committee and the senior management team. According to these authors, for strategy to be realised successfully, it must be translated into actions. Moreover, it should involve people at all levels of the organisation, not just at the top.

11.9.10 The performance measures of a balanced scorecard are sometimes not mapped to the value drivers of the financial institution or the subsection of it to which the scorecard relates. Moreover, the sensitivity of the value drivers should be used to select those performance measures that relate to the value drivers which create the most value for any given improvement.

11.9.11 A good balanced scorecard is sometimes developed and integrated into the reporting process, which continues to report as usual, but on different measures. Thus the balanced scorecard is turned into just another reporting engine. The link between the scorecard and improvement actions is not considered since this is not a standard function of typical reporting systems. Performance measures need more than just reporting. Each performance measure needs a target, defined actions to reach this target, and an owner to lead the implementation of these actions. The difference between performance reporting and performance management needs to be clearly identified according to Rousseau and Rousseau (2000).

11.10 Commandments of balanced scorecards

11.10.1 McCunn (1998) has identified ten 'commandments' of balanced scorecard implementation as follows.

Commandments of balanced scorecards

Do...	In other words...
– Use the scorecard as an implementation pad for strategic goals	– it can be an ideal vehicle for rolling the corporate strategy down through the organisation.
– Ensure strategic goals are in place before the scorecard is implemented	– do not invent the strategy as you go along, or the scorecard will drive the wrong behaviour.
– Ensure that a top-level (non-financial) sponsor backs the scorecard and that relevant line managers are committed to the project	– the scorecard project is too big to be anything other than top priority, and it should never be left to the accountants to do.
– Implement a pilot before introducing the new scorecard	– it provides valuable lessons and avoids 'big bang' risks.
– Carry out an 'entry review' for each business unit before implementing the scorecard	– this minimises the risk of going ahead in unfavourable circumstances and allows one to customise the project to suit the organisation's needs.
Do not...	
– Use the scorecard to obtain extra top-down control	– people will rebel.
– Attempt to standardise the project. The scorecard must be tailor-made	– the organisation's strategic imperatives are unique – a ready-made scorecard will not fit.
– Under-estimate the need for training and communication in using the scorecard	– do not be fooled by the simplicity of the idea – one has to deal with the huge change it brings.
– Seek complexity nor strive for perfection	– avoid 'paralysis by analysis'.
– Under-estimate the extra administrative workload and costs of periodic scorecard reporting	– gathering information for the scorecard is more time-consuming than one might expect.

A case study: strategy and budgetary control

11.10.2 This case involves budgeting over a five-year time horizon as part of the long-term strategic management of The Repertory Theatre of St Louis, a not-for-profit, professional theatre with an annual budget of about $4.5 million. This case involves two parts; (1) a projection of revenues and expenses over a five-year horizon and a resulting realisation that the theatre will run into severe financial problems if earned revenue (capacity) cannot be increased, and (2) an incident process part where managers must seek information to formulate solutions to the first problem and then revise their budgets accordingly.

11.10.3 Since this is in a not-for-profit setting, the solution to the capacity problem (building a second theatre space) does not involve discounted-cash

Performance measurement and cost management

flow analysis (see Chapter **4**). Since capital would be contributed for a new building there is no cost of capital. Managers have to wrestle with operating assumptions of a new space and then explore whether additional capacity is financially feasible over the long haul.

The Repertory Theatre of St Louis

11.10.4 In June 1993, Steve Woolf and Mark Bernstein, the Artistic and Managing Directors respectively, of The Repertory Theatre of St Louis (The Rep) were preparing for a long-range planning meeting to be held the following month with the board of directors. The long-range planning process at The Rep consists of four parts. First, a steering committee made up of Woolf, Bernstein, The Rep's President, and one or two other members of its Executive Committee, lay out a general agenda for the meeting. This group tries to identify possible problems and opportunities and to prepare information needed for a full analysis by the entire board. The second stage is a day-long meeting of the entire board of directors and key staff members along with a professional planning consultant. Woolf and Bernstein report on their respective areas, the issues proposed by the steering committee are discussed, and a full day's discussion ensues to deal with these issues as well as others that either board or staff bring up. Third, as a result of this meeting, the steering committee constitutes several task forces to deal with specific issues and to report back to the board. This stage takes about two months. Finally, the board meets again for a second full-day session in which the task force reports are discussed and actions recommended.

11.10.5 In the first stage, the steering committee posed the following four questions for the long-range planning session.

(1) Where are we today and how did we get here?

(2) Why do we need growth? What does growth mean to us?

(3) What do we want next and why do we want it?

(4) How do we go about achieving it?

11.10.6 They also asked for the following information to be provided at the planning session.

(1) Vision Statement (1990).

(2) Plays performed 1985–86 through 1992–93.

(3) Historical financial and attendance data (seven years actual plus 1993–94 budget).

(4) Financial projections (five years).

Figure 11.21

The Repertory Theatre of St. Louis
Vision Statement (1990)

The Repertory Theatre of St. Louis, a professional, not-for-profit corporation is dedicated to producing live theatre of uncompromising quality. In celebrating the joy of live performance, this theatre is committed to building and sustaining a vital connection among its stakeholders.

In this spirit, we will:

1. Be the pre-eminent theatre in the St. Louis region.
2. Be identified as an indispensible institution by the St. Louis community.
3. Enhance public awareness of the essential contribution theatre makes to the quality of human life.
4. Function in such a way that our stakeholders expect a consistent standard of quality in every facet of our operations.
5. Attract outstanding professionals in the field to join our work.
6. Achieve and maintain financial strength and stability in order to accomplish the above.

The Repertory Theatre of St. Louis
Guiding Principles (1990)

I. Stakeholders

The Rep exists to develop, maintain and celebrate the art of live theatre. Many constituencies have a stack in The Rep. These include:

- our subscribers
- our audiences
- to-be-developed audiences
- our artists
- our staff
- our donors;
- our volunteers;
- our Board
- our vendors;
- Webster University
- the City of Webster Groves;
- the Community at large

While we recognize the primary importance of our audiences, it is essential to them and to us that we also meet the desires and needs of the other stakeholders. Thus, this theatre works to lead without losing them.

II. Artistic Principles

The Rep's main purpose is to inform, entertain and enrich our audience through the art of live theatre. We seek to achieve in our programming an array of theatrical styles and periods. We believe we have a responsbility to our theatrical heritage, while simultaneously developing new works to add to this heritage.

By its nature live theatre involves risk and we recognise the need to take risks in programming which may occasionally offend. While the ultimate decision of what we produce and the artistic quality of the productions are the responsibilities of

Performance measurement and cost management

the Artistic Director, the Artistic Director must be sensitive to how these decisions affect the various stakeholders and stability of The Rep.

III. Quality of Operation
The Rep experience is more than that which happens between artists and audience during performance. It includes – and is dependent upon – every aspect of the operation which supports that performance for patrons, artists and staff. Our standards of operation for all facets of the theatre should result in a sense of integrity, quality and consistency for every person we serve.

Management of The Rep

11.10.7 Professional staff manages The Rep. Over its life, the titles of the top executive officer(s) have changed as has the organisational structure. Until 1983, the organisation was managed by a single individual who was called either Producing Director or Artistic Director. Starting in 1983, leadership was shared between the Artistic Director and a Managing Director.

11.10.8 As a not-for-profit corporation, The Rep is governed by a board of directors consisting of 48 members from the Greater St Louis area. There is a balance of power between the board and professional leadership. The board's main functions are to set general policies, map the long-range direction of the theatre, help fund the resources needed to mount the programme it has accepted from the Artistic Director, and oversee the finances of the theatre. Within the approved budget, the professional managers are given fairly free rein to choose a season and to expend funds in order to bring that season about. An organisation chart for the staff is contained in Figure 11.22.

Background of The Repertory Theatre of St Louis

11.10.9 The theatre was founded in 1966 to bring a professional repertory company to the St Louis area and as an enhancement of Webster College's (now Webster University) Theatre Conservatory programme. From the beginning, it was a professional theatre, as contrasted to a community theatre, or one that was an outreach of the university where students and instructors put on their performances. Thus, while the theatre was originally a division of the college, it was separate from its academic theatre programme.

11.10.10 The Rep has gone through two significant cycles over its life. At the beginning, after a few successful years, audience attendance dropped and finances suffered. In fact, because of the great losses the college endured, the theatre 'went dark' (closed down) for a year in 1970. At this point, since the theatre was such a financial burden to the college and the president thought the theatre could only prosper if it were independent from

Commandments of balanced scorecards

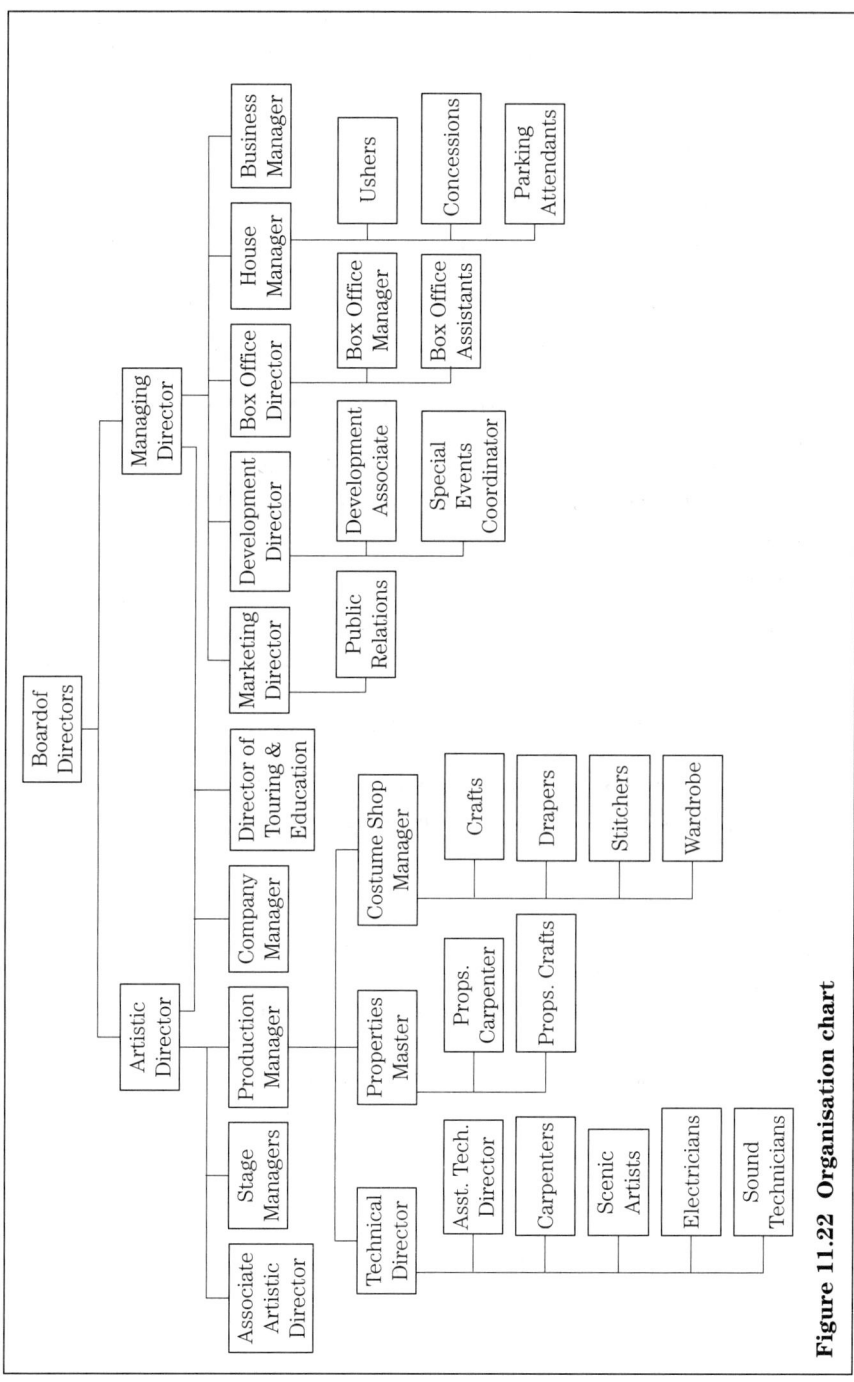

Figure 11.22 Organisation chart

the college, an independent, not-for-profit corporation was formed, the Loretto-Hilton Repertory Theatre Inc., and an independent board of directors was recruited from various community and business leaders interested in theatre and the arts. This organisation continues today and is now known as The Repertory Theatre of St Louis or The Rep.

11.10.11 During the 12 seasons after The Rep became a separate not-for-profit corporation (1971–83), attendances grew and then started to decline (see Figure 11.22). Differences in artistic vision led to the Artistic Director leaving in 1983 and, while a nationwide search was conducted for a new Artistic Director, for two years Steve Woolf, then the Managing Director, assumed the title of Acting Artistic Director as well as performing the duties of Managing Director. A new Artistic Director was hired and embarked on an aggressive but unsuccessful programme that left The Rep with a $400,000 deficit after the 1985–86 season. At this point, Woolf became Artistic Director and Mark Bernstein was hired as Managing Director in early 1987.

11.10.12 As a result of the 1985–86 season, the theatre was at a low in attendance. Attendance began to improve in the 1986–87 season, but costs associated with the transition in artistic leadership and an enhanced marketing effort drove the deficit up to $500,000 at the end of that season. From that point through to the present, the theatre has prospered under its professional and lay leadership. At the time of the preparation for the long-range planning meeting, the deficit was down to about $90,000. Figure 11.23 shows the history of subscriptions over this period including estimates for the upcoming year.

11.10.13 Figure 11.27 disaggregates Figure 11.24 expenses for 1992–93. This breakdown is typical of the other years included in Figure 11.24 and 11.26. Figure 11.28 further breaks down costs in Figure 11.27 showing detailed line items. Figure 11.29 deals only with artistic costs and shows costs traceable to each production as well as common overhead. This Figure also shows the mainstage and studio plays for 1992–93, a typical set of choices for these two performing spaces.

11.10.14 A long-term analysis of artistic versus administrative expenses shows a steady pattern with the bulk of expenses (over 60 per cent) going for artistic purposes. Expenses for productions seem within national ranges and appropriate for the level of excellence that The Rep seeks to maintain. The number of people on staff is appropriate for this size theatre; in fact, it's a bit lean in some areas. In addition, the theatre has continued to delay items such as retirement plans for its long-time employees.

Commandments of balanced scorecards

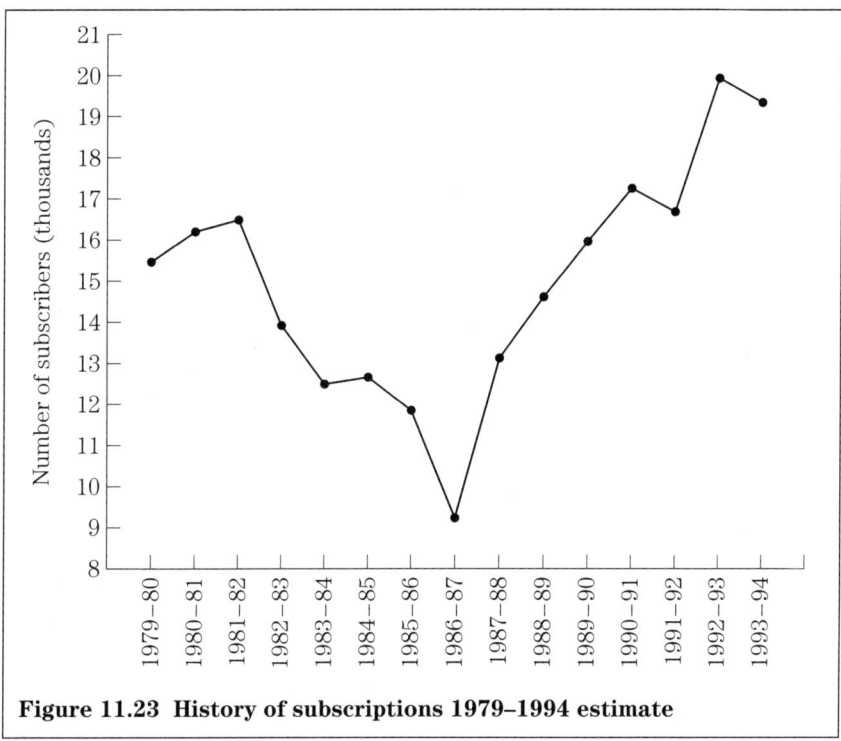

Figure 11.23 History of subscriptions 1979–1994 estimate

11.10.15 Expenses are a function of the season that Woolf chooses. His choices are limited by the amount of revenue that the theatre expects that year. With this in mind, the expenses of The Rep have been under control over a long period of time. While there might be some variances from budget in some items, overall expense targets are achieved with Woolf and Bernstein making adjustments as the season goes on to balance costs. For example, if the sets and costumes on one production are over-budget, management tries to make cuts in other productions or in administrative expenses so the entire expense budget is achieved for the season.

Programmes

11.10.16 The Rep produces six plays a year for its mainstage space, three for its studio space, and also has a travelling theatre educational outreach, the Imaginary Theatre Company (ITC), which performs at schools throughout Missouri. Mainstage and studio productions are performed from September through April and the ITC performs throughout the normal school year. Mainstage productions include, for example, plays by Shaw, Shakespeare, Williams, Miller, Moliere and Sondheim. Some are plays that

Performance measurement and cost management

	1986-87 Actual	1987-88 Actual	1987-88 % change	1988-89 Actual	1988-89 % change	1989-90 Actual	1989-90 % change	1990-91 Actual	1990-91 % change	1991-92 Actual	1991-92 % change	1992-93 Actual	1992-93 % change	1993-94 Actual	1993-94 % change
Earned revenue															
Mainstage subscriptions	$654	$928	41.9%	$1,072	15.5%	$1,218	13.6%	$1,365	12.1%	$1,452	6.4%	$1,883	26.2%	$2,000	9.1%
Mainstage single tickets	388	392	1.0%	388	-1.0%	417	7.5%	336	-19.4%	420	25.0%	462	-14.5%	395	-14.5%
Studio subscriptions	20	21	5.0%	23	9.5%	30	30.4%	31	3.3%	40	29.0%	49	22.5%	50	2.0%
Studio single tickets	15	17	13.3%	19	11.8%	35	84.2%	23	-34.3%	28	21.7%	23	-17.9%	20	-13.0%
Ticket sales revenue	$1,077	$1,385	26.1%	$1,502	10.6%	$1,700	13.2%	$1,755	3.2%	$1,940	10.5%	$2,367	22.0%	$2,465	4.1%
Imaginary Theatre Co.	65	27	-58.5%	51	88.0%	66	29.4%	74	12.1%	68	-8.1%	71	4.4%	70	-1.4%
Other earned revenue	121	121	0.0%	141	16.5%	187	32.6%	179	-4.3%	189	5.6%	189	0.0%	200	5.8%
Endowment earnings	44	46	4.5%	36	-21.7%	46	27.8%	45	-2.2%	30	-15.6%	40	5.3%	30	-25.0%
Total earned revenue	$1,307	$1,552	18.7%	1,730	11.5%	$1,999	15.5%	$2,053	2.7%	$2,235	8.9%	$2,667	19.3%	$2,765	3.7%
Contributed revenue															
Corporations	$77	$134	74.0%	$139	3.7%	$120	-13.7%	$162	35.0%	$174	7.4%	$162	-6.9%	$180	11.1%
Foundations	53	38	-28.3%	48	26.3%	49	2.1%	46	-6.1%	54	17.4%	14	-74.1%	55	292.9%
Individuals	232	243	4.7%	260	10.8%	293	12.7%	272	-7.2%	301	10.7%	346	15.0%	360	4.0%
Special events	143	98	-31.5%	138	40.8%	140	1.4%	127	-9.3%	161	26.8%	161	0.0%	150	-6.8%
Public funding	631	668	5.9%	747	11.8%	731	-2.1%	760	4.0%	751	-1.2%	720	-4.1%	680	-5.6%
Webster/in kind	221	226	2.3%	241	6.6%	237	-1.7%	211	-11.0%	209	-0.9%	219	4.8%	210	-4.1%
Restricted grants	20	53		24						29					
Total contributed revenue	$1,377	$1,460	6.0%	$1,597	9.4%	$1,570	-1.7%	$1,578	0.5%	$1,679	6.4%	$1,662	-3.4%	$1,635	0.8%
Total revenue	$2,684	$3,012	12.2%	$3,372	10.5%	$3,569	7.3%	$3,631	1.7%	$3,914	7.8%	$4,289	9.6%	$4,400	2.6%
Expenses															
Administrative expenses															
Administrative	$585	$583	-0.3%	$649	11.3%	$712	9.7%	$748	5.1%	$774	3.5%	$869	12.3%	$879	1.2%
Marketing	358	316	-11.7%	398	25.9%	457	14.8%	440	-3.7%	438	-0.5%	434	-0.9%	460	6.0%
Fundraising	92	109	18.5%	120	10.1%	130	8.3%	136	4.6%	150	10.3%	142	-5.3%	161	13.4%
	1,035	1,008	-2.6%	1,167	15.8%	1,299	11.3%	1,324	1.9%	1,362	2.9%	1,445	6.1%	1,500	3.8%
Production expenses															
Production	626	663	5.9%	718	8.3%	781	8.8%	854	9.3%	898	5.2%	1,041	15.9%	1,075	3.3%
Artistic	806	873	8.3%	971	11.2%	1,079	11.1%	1,095	1.5%	1,265	15.5%	1,382	5.0%	1,450	9.2%
	1,432	1,536	7.3%	1,689	10.0%	1,860	10.1%	1,949	4.8%	2,163	11.0%	2,369	9.5%	2,525	6.6%
Other expenses															
Imaginary Theatre Co.	77	79	2.6%	92	16.5%	117	27.2%	137	17.1%	142	3.6%	154	8.5%	165	7.1%
Webster/in kind	221	226	2.3%	241	6.6%	237	-1.7%	211	-11.0%	209	-0.9%	219	4.8%	210	-4.1%
Rent	20	53		24						29					
Restricted grants	318	358	12.6%	357	-0.3%	354	-0.8%	348	-1.7%	380	9.2%	373	-1.8%	375	0.5%
Total expenses	$2,785	$2,902	4.2%	$3,213	10.7%	$3,513	9.3%	$3,621	3.1%	$3,905	7.8%	$4,187	7.2%	$4,400	5.1%
Net income/loss	($101)	$110		$114		$56		$10		$9		$102		$0	
Accumulated surplus/deficit	($490)	($380)		($266)		($210)		($200)		($191)		($89)		($89)	
Year-end cash balance	$96	$283	194.8%	$546	92.9%	$846	54.9%	$929	9.8%	$1,242	33.7%	$1,553	25.0%		
Peak borrowing	$475	$425	-10.5%	$260	-38.8%	$200	-23.1%	$125	-37.5%	$125	0.0%	$0	-100.0%		
Average monthly borrowing	$312	$96	-54.7%	$65	-32.3%	$42	-35.4%	$21	-50.0%	$17	-19.0%	$0	-100.0%		

Figure 11.24 Financial data 1986–87 through 1993–94

Figure 11.25 Glossary

Revenues:

Mainstage Subscriptions	Revenue from sale of subscriptions from the six-play Mainstage season
Mainstage Single Tickets	Revenue from sale of tickets to individual shows in the six-play Mainstage season
Studio Subscriptions	Revenue from sale of subscriptions to the three-play Studio season
Studio Single Tickets	Revenue from sale of tickets to individual shows in the three-play Studio season
Imaginary Theatre Company	Booking fees for performances by the Imaginary Theatre Company, a touring company which performs theatre for children in schools and community centres throughout the region
Other Earned Revenue	Revenue from program advertising, concession sales, parking and interest on short-term investments
Endowment Earnings	Earnings from the theatre's endowment fund, transferred to the operating fund to support operations (a portion of endowment fund earnings is also reinvested)
Foundations	Grants from private foundations
Individuals	Contributions from individuals; includes annual giving (contributions expected to be renewed annually) and special gifts (usually one-time)
Special Events	Funds raised from two major special fundraising events held each season; reported on a net basis
Public Funding	Grants received from the Arts and Education Council of Greater St. Louis (a private funding agency) and three public funding agencies: National Endowment for the Arts, Missouri Arts Council, St. Louis Regional Arts Commission
Webster/In-Kind	For financial reporting purposes, a value is assigned to the in-kind contribution of facilities provided by Webster University
Restricted Grants	Grants received for special expenditures outside of the operating budget (usually for purchase of capital equipment)

Expenses:

Administrative	Expenses related to general administration and management, financial management, box office and patron services
Fundraising	Expenses related to generating contributions
Production	Expenses related to physical production elements: sets, props, costumes, lighting, sound, overhead for shops, vehicles and equipment
Artistic	Expenses related to artistic personnel: actors, directors, designers, musicians, stage managers, travel and housing for guest artists; royalties; overhead for rehearsal facilities

Imaginary Theatre Company	Production, artistic and administrative expenses for the Imaginary Theatre Company, a touring company which performs theatre for children in schools and community centres throughout the region
Webster/In-Kind	For financial reporting purposes, a value is assigned to the in-kind contribution of facilities provided by Webster University (cancels out the corresponding revenue item; no bottom line impact)
Rent	Anticipated rent payments to Webster University, beginning in 1995–96
Restricted Grants	Expenses incurred to satisfy conditions of special grants received outside of the operating budget (usually for purchase of capital equipment)

have just finished Broadway runs, but are not considered good commercial ventures to have road companies.

Relationship with Webster University

11.10.17 From its inception until the present, Webster University has been the host site for The Rep. The Loretto-Hilton Center on its campus provides performing and production space for the theatre and a separate building, the Carriage House, provides staff office space. The Rep shares the mainstage and studio space with the university's Theater Conservatory as well as a local orchestra. After The Rep's season, the Opera Theatre of St Louis uses the mainstage to produce four operas for a season that lasts from late May through June.

11.10.18 The university provided free rent for the use of its facilities from the inception of the theatre through the end of the 1994–95 season. At that time, although a lease had not been fully negotiated, it was the intent of the university and The Rep to enter into a lease whereby The Rep would pay $100,000 per year for its use of the facilities starting in 1995–96. These fees would cover maintenance, utilities and housekeeping. Included in the free rent, and to be dealt with in the lease, was the use of the performing and production space at the Loretto-Hilton Center and the office space at the Carriage House. Under separate lease agreements, The Rep rents rehearsal space in a nearby shopping centre and apartments (the Garden Apartments) used by visiting actors and directors. All these spaces are within easy walking distance of one another.

Commandments of balanced scorecards

	1986-87 Actual	1987-88 Actual	1988-89 Actual	1989-90 Actual	1990-91 Actual	1991-92 Actual	1992-93 Actual	1993-94 Budget
Mainstage								
Subscriptions	9,165	13,232	14,622	16,054	17,303	16,672	19,798	19,800
Ave. subscription price	$71.32	$70.10	$73.29	$75.89	$78.91	$87.09	$92.58	$101.00
Total main sub. revenue	$653,648	$927,563	$1,071,646	$1,218,338	$1,365,380	$1,451,964	$1,832,899	$1,999,895
Single tickets	48,098	37,896	33,251	35,674	24,178	32,099	29,765	23,330
Ave. single ticket price	$8.07	$10.34	$11.67	$11.69	$13.90	$13.08	$15.52	$16.93
Total main single revenue	$388,000	$392,000	$388,000	$417,000	$336,000	$420,000	$462,000	$395,071
Total mainstage revenue	$1,041,648	$1,319,563	$1,459,646	$1,635,338	$1,701,380	$1,871,964	$2,294,899	$2,394,966
Studio								
Subscriptions	662	760	1,038	1,190	1,168	1,245	1,385	1,300
Ave. subscription price	$30.21	$27.63	$22.16	$25.21	$26.54	$32.13	$35.38	$38.60
Total studio sub. revenue	$20,000	$21,000	$19,000	$30,000	$31,000	$40,000	$49,000	$50,178
Single tickets	3,037	2,922	1,537	3,504	2,155	2,564	1,906	1,525
Ave. single ticket price	$4.94	$5.82	$12.36	$9.99	$10.67	$10.92	$12.07	$13.17
Total studio single revenue	$15,000	$17,000	$19,000	$35,000	$23,000	$28,000	$23,000	$20,077
Total studio revenue	$35,000	$38,000	$42,000	$65,000	$54,000	$68,000	$72,000	$70,255
Total ticket revenue	$1,076,648	$1,357,563	$1,501,646	$1,700,338	$1,755,380	$1,939,964	$2,366,899	$2,465,221
Total attendance	103,088	117,288	120,983	131,998	127,996	132,131	148,553	142,130
Capacity (215 perf × 733 seats)	157,595	157,595	157,595	157,595	157,595	157,595	157,595	157,595
Attendance as a % of capacity	65.41%	74.42%	76.77%	83.76%	81.22%	83.84%	94.26%	90.19%

Figure 11.26 Attendance and revenue data 1986–87 through 1993–94

Figure 11.27 Expense Breakdown 1992–93

Administrative expenses		
Administration	$386,399	
Marketing	247,982	
Subscriptions	186,390	
Development	142,354	
Box office	198,476	
Front of house	113,263	
Publications	170,404	$1,445,268
Production expenses		
Artistic Production	$1,328,422	
Sets	137,131	
Props	452,652	
Electrics	87,828	
Sound	89,327	
Costumes	61,869	
	212,376	2,369,605
Other expenses		
Webster in kind	$219,000	
imaginary theatre	153,541	372,541
		$4,187,414

Seating capacity

11.10.19 There are two configurations for seating in the mainstage theatre space. The Loretto-Hilton Center mainstage theatre has two bays at the sides of the house that can be closed off. With the bays closed, the capacity is 733 people per performance. With the bays open, it is 953. Woolf and the board have decided for artistic reasons that while they will open the bays from time to time to satisfy demand, they will not operate the theatre with the bays as part of the regular ticket inventory (for either subscriptions or single ticket sales). This mainly has to do with artistic choices. With the norm of 733 seats, certain plays can be selected that play well to this size audience. In addition, natural acoustics can be used and actors do not have to be wired with body microphones. At 953 seats as the norm, this all changes. The board and staff are quite happy with the current arrangement. There is also a studio space where seating capacity is a function of how the room is set up. The Rep budgets on a basis of 125 seats for this space.

11.10.20 In addition, the number of performances are regulated by two main factors. First, the total time for a mainstage (and for a studio) production is a function of the total number of weeks The Rep can occupy the

Commandments of balanced scorecards

Figure 11.28 Expense Detail 1992–93

Administrative Expenses			
Administrative		Marketing	
Salaries	$177,523	Salaries	$79,330
Payroll tax	15,065	Payroll tax	7,534
Medical insurance	7,720	Medical insurance	4,632
Pension		Pension	
Postage	8,958	Single ticket advertising	117,258
Telephone	24,723	Institutional advertising	6,669
Data processing	10,020	Photography	13,671
Equipment maintenance	13,922	Press releases	12,758
Office supplies	13,927	Houseboards	973
Mileage	521	Mileage	1,769
Audit	9,244	Dues/Subscriptions	1,580
Insurance	68,868	Miscellaneous	1,808
Interest			247,982
Dues / Subscriptions	15,568		
Managing director	5,449	Development	
Utilities	8,470	Salaries	$89,170
Facilities maintenance	4,610	Payroll tax	8,167
Depreciation		Medical insurance	1,544
Miscellaneous	1,811	Pension	
	$386,399	Backers board	25
		Corporate cultivation	932
Front of the house		Individual cultivation	5,325
Salaries	$38,993	Annual giving	25,447
Payroll tax	4,853	Special fund drive	
Medical insurance	1,033	Special events	6,613
Pension		Board expense	1,581
Lobby	18,135	Dev. director expense	2,518
Houseboards	2,015	Mileage	122
Parking	4,639	Miscellaneous	910
Concessions/bar	30,345		142,354
Rep shop	8,936		
Licenses	1,527	Subscriptions	
Miscellaneous	2,787	Renewals	$27,519
	113,263	Direct mail	62,197
		Telemarketing	47,234
Publications		Advertising	49,440
Salaries	$14,918		186,390
Payroll tax	1,233		
Medical insurance	1,033	Box office	
Program	133,999	Salaries	$127,676
Newsletter	13,791	Payroll tax	13,411
Study guide	5,430	Medical insurance	5,923
Annual report		Pension	
	170,404	Tickets	4,809
		Printing	10,033
		Postage	9,513
		Supplies	1,882
		Credit card expense	25,229
			198,47
		Total administrative expenses	$1,445,268

Production Expenses

Sound		Sets	
Salaries	$33,902	Carpenters salaries	$101,446
Overtime	6,884	Scenic artists salaries	54,487
Payroll tax	4,012	Overtime	87,354
IATSE benefits	11,696	Student labour	22,571
Sound materials	1,285	Payroll tax	28,018
Sound equipment	4,090	IATSE benefits	47,347
Depreciation		USA benefits	7,971
	61,869	Set materials	91,495
		Shop supplies / equipment	11,519
Props		Mileage	444
Salaries	$50,117		452,652
Other labour	9,622		
Payroll tax	6,282	Electrics	
Medical insurance	3,486	Salaries	$33,210
Pension		Overtime	12,299
Prop materials	16,683	Student labour	17,133
Shop supplies / equipment	933	Payroll tax	6,396
Mileage	705	IATSE benefits	12,047
	87,828	Electrical materials	2,463
		Electrical equipment	5,779
Artistic		Depreciation	
Artistic salaries	$133,546		89,327
Payroll tax	8,827		
Medical insurance	6,632	Costumes	
Pension		Shop salaries	$88,034
Stage manager salaries	95,082	Wardrobe salaries	17,281
Payroll tax	9,351	Other labour	23,981
Pension/welfare	18,298	Payroll tax	13,817
Actors' salaries	380,920	Medical insurance	7,619
Payroll tax	47,898	Pension	
Pension/welfare	72,188	Costume materials	49,717
Directors' fees	49,325	Shop supplies/equipment	7,624
Pension/welfare	6,345	Wardrobe expense	3,977
Designers' fees	75,500	Mileage	326
Pension/welfare	3,992		212,376
Musicians' salaries	33,445		
Payroll tax	3,229	Production overhead	
Artistic director expense	19,837	Salaries	$61,725
Rehearsal expense	3,825	Payroll tax	6,024
Company meals	3,340	Medical insurance	1,162
Actor travel/housing	76,485	Pension	
Director travel/housing	4,070	IATSE benefits	11,555
Desinger travel/housing	12,268	Vehicles	9,488
Music rental/equipment	4,493	Rent/Utilities	40,048
Royalties	163,888	Depreciation	3,297
Scripts	2,006	Miscellaneous	3,382
Casting fees/expense	26,756		137,131
Playwrights' expense	660		
Lab project	7,126	Total production expenses	$2,369,605
Education programs	6,090		
Rent	55,000		
	1,328,422		

Imaginary Theatre Company		**Other Expenses**	
Administrative expense	$39,839	Webster in kind services	219,000
Advertising / promotion	7,506	Total other expenses	$372,541
Artistic expense	87,535	Total expenses	$4,187,414
Production expense	10,592		
Misc. tour expense	8,072		
	153,541		

Loretto-Hilton Center and other uses within that time period. Webster University has a Theater Conservatory programme and puts on student productions in both performing spaces. A local community orchestra has an ongoing contract with the university for performances four times a year. This not only eliminates four performances, but also means that The Rep cannot sell a subscription series on that night of the run. Thus, The Rep is fairly limited in its ability to extend a run – it is impossible on the mainstage and only possible for one week each for two productions in the studio space. Second, The Rep is a professional, union operation. This is the norm for professional theatres. National contracts with unions such as Actors' Equity limit the number of performances per week at regional theatres. The Rep operates at the peak number allowed under the contract. Thus, there is not much room to increase the number of potential seats sold for any production or for the season overall.

Long-term financial expectations
11.10.21   While the theatre realises that it is possible to have an operating deficit in some years, on balance the organisation must break even over the long haul. The board is also committed to erasing the accumulated deficit. Thus, for several years there was the implication that operations should provide a surplus. In fact, for several years The Rep operated at a surplus and consistently reduced the accumulated deficit. The important fact is not that every year breaks even but that the organisation breaks even over the long term.

Cashflow
11.10.22   While the theatre has a fiscal year ending May 31, its cash flow runs on a cycle that ends in March. Annual subscriptions are renewed (and paid for) during the last of the six mainstage productions. Many grants come in at the beginning of the fiscal year. Cash needs are minimal during the summer and pick up in the Autumn. Cash outflow for administration is fairly evenly spaced over the fiscal year. Cash needs for artistic expenses either lead (sets, costumes, design) or track with (actors, director) productions. Thus, there is a timing difference between cash inflows and outflows. This

Performance measurement and cost management

	Mainstage plays					Studio plays			Unallocated costs			Total costs
	Madam Butterfly	Dracula	Forum	Six Degrees	Women in Mind	Pygmalion	Show & Tell	Irma Vep	Sight Unseen	Personnel	Overhead	Lab	
Prod. overhead										$82,183	$54,948		$137,131
Sets	$13,306	$59,993	$16,920	$14,272	$28,903	$45,861	472	1,373	1,749	246,345	12,316		452,652
Props	3,889	2,282	728	1,173	2,267	12,892				59,379	1,624		87,828
Electrics	4,559	9,575	3,099	2,701	3,073	5,361	1,252	1,051	732	50,785	7,183		89,327
Sound	1,730	2,856	498	443	756	1,295	295	26	270	49,610	4,090		61,869
Costumes	13,857	9,843	12,313	6,786	5,393	20,678	855	3,305	1,414	126,037	9,895		212,376
Artistic	134,594	144,165	252,323	137,741	108,796	111,627	44,070	24,947	29,854	278,281	41,333	20,692	1,328,422
Total production	$171,935	$228,714	$285,881	$163,116	$149,188	$197,669	$50,912	$36,783	$38,706	$894,620	$131,389	$20,692	$2,369,605

Figure 11.29 Production expense report

means even though the theatre ran its accumulated deficit to $500,000, the timing of cash flow allowed the theatre to use a short-term line of credit to cover shortfalls in cash which occurred. At its highest need for cash, the theatre only borrowed from December through early March. As the theatre began to cut down the accumulated deficit, it also reduced the time that there were outstanding balances on the line of credit and the amount of such loans. Borrowing became unnecessary after the 1991–92 season and the theatre began to accumulate a cash balance to invest. However, the theatre still maintains a line of credit from a local bank in order to provide a cushion in case of an emergency.

Long-term vision
11.10.23 The Rep developed both a vision statement and a statement more fully delineating its guiding principles. The most current statements (1990) are in Figure 11.29. Part of the upcoming planning process will be the review and revision of these two statements. While there might be some changes in wording, the basic tenets of the existing vision statement and guiding principles will remain.

Financial background
11.10.24 Figure 11.23 reflects actual results from the 1986–87 season through the 1992–93 season and the budget for the 1993–94 season. Figure 11.25 is a glossary of terms used in Figure 11.24.

Revenues
11.10.25 The theatre gets its funds from earned income (revenue from sales of subscriptions and single tickets, as well as some other items such as parking, refreshments, programme advertising, etc.), from funding agencies and from contributors. Funding agencies include regional, state and federal money as well as private and community foundations interested in the arts such as the Arts and Education Council of St Louis.

Subscription and single ticket revenue
11.10.26 Figure 11.26 provides a history of ticket prices and revenue (subscriptions and single tickets). The totals in Figure 11.26 tie to the ticket sales revenue line in Figure 11.24. Each year the Finance Committee of the board reviews competing ticket prices in the area. These include The St Louis Symphony, The Muny (a large, outdoor theatre providing summer performances), series prices for national companies of Broadway shows (usually performed at The Fox Theatre), and the Opera Theatre of St Louis (which also uses the Loretto-Hilton Center during May and June). Marketing studies show that there is a high correlation between Rep subscribers and subscribers to the symphony and opera.

11.10.27 The Rep divides the mainstage audience space into four sections and prices the sections differently. In addition, prices are differentiated by day/time of performance (previews, matinees and week nights, and Friday/Saturday evenings). Over the years, the theatre has tried to keep the prices for Section IV, the least expensive seats, fairly constant. The total number of seats in Section IV is small and this provides a service to the community by keeping attendance affordable. Otherwise, the theatre has been fairly aggressive in raising prices over the past several years. The Finance Committee and staff are concerned about how high prices can go before there is some resistance. However, with the high number of subscribers in Sections I and II, so far no resistance has been evident. In addition, The Rep does not want to be in a position where it has to lower prices to increase attendance. Both the board and staff believe that prices should not rise to a level where they are seen by the general public as too high. (Recent road shows (e.g., Phantom of the Opera) have met resistance with high prices ($60) and some rock concerts with $75 tickets have had a hard time selling out.)

Contributed income

11.10.28 Contributed income comes from individual and corporate donors, federal/state/local funding agencies, and community charitable institutions. Over the years, The Rep has done a good job attracting major corporations as sponsors and donors (e.g., Southwestern Bell, Monsanto, United Missouri Banks and General American Insurance). These corporations (or their charitable foundations) provide a steady stream of funds to help underwrite plays. There is not a great potential to increase this base by large amounts over the years; but it should increase principally as a function of time as long as the economy holds strong. Individual donors provide annual gifts as well as special gifts. These should also grow as a function of time and the economy, as well as relevant tax laws. Funding from agencies such as the National Endowment for the Arts and the Missouri Arts Council has been steadily declining. The theatre does not look to these sources for increased funding. Funds also come from a tourism tax levied on hotel and motel guests. These funds are a function of economic, convention and sports activity in the area. At the time of this case, St Louis was looking for a professional football team for its new stadium then under construction and this was before the strikes in professional baseball and hockey. However, without a professional football team, projections for the tourism tax were flat. Finally, St Louis has a community fund-raising organisation for the arts: the Arts and Education Council of St Louis. This organisation operates under the same principles as other community-wide charitable organisations by organising individual giving within companies and other organisations. The Rep gets the highest allocation of

Commandments of balanced scorecards

funds from this council, but the theatre does not expect funding to increase much beyond the cost of living over time.

11.10.29 Annual and special contributions are used as part of sources for the operating budget as are earnings of the endowment fund. (The Finance Committee of the board sets limits of how much of endowment earnings can be used for annual operations.) Public funding has varied over the years principally as a function of the economy and politics.

Expenses
11.10.30 Expenses include the general overhead of running the theatre (management personnel, marketing, fund raising, accounting, utilities, etc.) and the production and artistic expense of putting on the theatre's programmes.

Assumptions about the budget
11.10.31 It is also important to understand the difference between the fiscal year budget and cash flow. At present, the theatre has cash of $1,500,000 at the beginning of its fiscal year. Funds are needed for salaries and other expenses over the fiscal year. Currently, for about eight months or more, there is a balance of at least $1,000,000 that can be invested and interest used for current operations. This is quite different from the manner in which revenues and expenses are recognised as the season progresses. Thus, even in lean years, the theatre did not have a long-term loan. As the case points out, even with the original accumulated deficit of $500,000, a short-term line of credit was sufficient and it could be paid down to zero for several months given the huge inflow of cash during the subscription renewal period. At its height, the outstanding line of credit was about $500,000 for a period of December through to early March. This amount kept reducing so that in the final year the line was used, the maximum outstanding balance was $125,000 and there was an outstanding balance for only two months.

11.10.32 Figure 11.30 shows the budget that The Rep's staff created. This shows that the 1994–95 season should show a deficit and that this condition will be ongoing and growing. There is not much room to reduce expenses or to increase revenues to take up the slack over the long term. Even if the projections are too pessimistic for 1994–95, it seems apparent that The Rep will have rising annual deficits unless something is done beyond the current production model.

The five-year budget
11.10.33 Managers may want to deal with the existing budget and fine tune it. Below are some typical questions which could be addressed.

Performance measurement and cost management

	1992-93 Actual	1992-93 % change	1993-94 Budget	1993-94 % change	1994-95 Projected	1994-95 % change	1995-96 Projected	1995-96 % change	1996-97 Projected	1996-97 % change	1997-98 Projected	1997-98 % change	1998-99 Projected	1998-99 % change
Earned revenue														
Mainstage subscriptions	$1,833	26.2%	$2,000	9.1%	$2,080	4.0%	$2,163	4.0%	$2,250	4.0%	$2,340	4.0%	$2,433	4.0%
Mainstage single tickets	462	10.0%	395	-14.5%	411	4.0%	472	4.0%	444	4.0%	462	4.0%	481	4.0%
Studio subscriptions	49	22.5%	50	2.0%	52	4.0%	54	4.0%	56	4.0%	58	4.0%	61	4.0%
Studio single tickets	23	-17.9%	20	-13.0%	21	4.0%	22	4.0%	22	4.0%	23	4.0%	24	4.0%
Ticket sales revenue	$2,367	22.0%	$2,465	4.1%	$2,564	4.0%	$2,666	4.0%	$2,773	4.0%	$2,884	4.0%	$2,999	4.0%
Imaginary Theatre Co.	71	4.4%	70	-1.4%	73	4.0%	76	4.0%	79	4.0%	82	4.0%	85	4.0%
Other earned revenue	189	0.0%	200	5.8%	208	4.0%	216	4.0%	225	4.0%	234	4.0%	243	4.0%
Endowment earnings	40	5.3%	30	-25.0%	35	16.7%	40	15.0%	46	15.0%	53	15.0%	61	15.0%
Total earned revenue	$2,667	19.3%	$2,765	3.7%	$2,879	4.1%	$2,998	4.1%	$3,123	4.1%	$3,253	4.2%	$3,389	4.2%
Contributed revenue														
Corporations	$162	-6.9%	180	11.1%	187	4.0%	195	4.0%	202	4.0%	211	4.0%	219	4.0%
Foundations	14	-74.1%	55	292.9%	57	4.0%	59	4.0%	62	4.0%	64	4.0%	67	4.0%
Individuals	346	15.0%	360	4.0%	374	4.0%	389	4.0%	405	4.0%	421	4.0%	438	4.0%
Special events	161	0.0%	150	-6.8%	156	4.0%	162	4.0%	169	4.0%	175	4.0%	182	4.0%
Public funding	720	-4.1%	680	-5.6%	653	-4.0%	627	-4.0%	602	-4.0%	578	-4.0%	554	-4.0%
Webster/in kind	219	4.8%	210	-4.1%	210	0.0%	110	-47.6%	110	0.0%	110	0.0%	110	0.0%
Restricted grants														
Total contributed revenue	$1,622	-3.9%	$1,635	0.8%	$1,638	0.2%	$1,543	-5.8%	$1,550	0.5%	$1,559	0.6%	$1,571	0.8%
Total revenue	$4,289	9.4%	$4,400	2.6%	$4,517	2.7%	$4,541	0.5%	$4,672	2.9%	$4,812	3.0%	$4,960	3.1%
Expenses														
Administrative expenses														
Administrative	$869	9.8%	879	1.2%	905	3.0%	993	3.0%	961	3.0%	989	3.0%	1,019	3.0%
Marketing	434	2.3%	460	6.0%	474	3.0%	488	3.0%	503	3.0%	518	3.0%	533	3.0%
Fundraising	142	-5.3%	161	13.4%	166	3.0%	171	3.0%	176	3.0%	181	3.0%	187	3.0%
	1,445	6.1%	1,500	3.8%	1,545	3.0%	1,591	3.0%	1,639	3.0%	1,688	3.0%	1,739	3.0%
Production expenses														
Production	1,041	20.6%	1,075	3.3%	1,118	4.0%	1,163	4.0%	1,209	4.0%	1,258	4.0%	1,308	4.0%
Artistic	1,328	2.1%	1,450	9.2%	1,505	4.0%	1,568	4.0%	1,631	4.0%	1,696	4.0%	1,764	4.0%
	2,369		2,525	6.6%	2,262	4.0%	2,731	4.0%	2,840	4.0%	2,954	4.0%	3,072	4.0%
Other expenses														
Imaginary Theatre Co.	154	7.7%	165	7.1%	172	4.0%	178	4.0%	186	4.0%	193	4.0%	201	4.0%
Webster/in kind	219	0.5%	210	-4.1%	210	0.0%	110	-47.6%	110	0.0%	110	0.0%	110	0.0%
Rent							100		100		100		100	
Restricted grants														
	373	7.0%	375	0.5%	382	1.8%	389	1.8%	396	1.8%	403	1.9%	411	1.9%
Total expenses	$4,187	7.0%	$4,400	5.1%	$4,553	3.5%	$4,711	3.5%	$4,875	3.5%	$5,045	3.5%	$5,222	3.5%
Net income/loss	$102		$0		($36)		($170)		($203)		($233)		($262)	
Accumulated surplus/deficit	($89)		($89)		($125)		($295)		($497)		($730)		($992)	

Figure 11.30 Five-year projections 1994-95 through 1998-99

Can ticket prices be increased?
11.10.34 While there have been some substantial increases over time, the board and staff do not want to raise prices too much. Thus, one can be aggressive, but there is a limit. The Rep does not want to raise prices so high that they might alienate subscribers or funding agencies given the educational mission of the theatre. They never want to be in the position where demand drops due to external or internal reasons and they have to retreat on ticket prices. They also do not want to be perceived as a premium priced form of entertainment. As the case discusses, there is some resentment in the area about rising prices for road shows and rock concerts. While increasing ticket prices might yield a short-term answer, the long-term answer lies in capacity rather than in price per ticket.

How about having all performances in the 953 seat configuration?
11.10.35 There are artistic considerations in opening the house to 953 seats for all performances. Given the number of performances per week and per production, a larger house would put additional voice strain on the actors. In addition, actors might have to wear body microphones. This takes away from the intimacy of the performance, something that is important to the audience. Finally, different plays work best in different sized performing spaces. Thus, consistently working in a 953 seat environment would mean some changes in the plays Woolf selects. Woolf believes this would change the nature of the theatre. A consistently larger house would eliminate certain plays that Woolf believes important to produce; they might fill 733 seats over the run, but not 953. The Board has discussed this issue at length and is satisfied that planning should involve the 733 seats with overflow handled by opening up to 953 seats.

Is there any room to get more time from Webster University to have a longer season?
11.10.36 Not for the mainstage. There is some room for change in the studio space.

Is there any other theatre space available to rent or own?
11.10.37 Besides the Loretto-Hilton Center, the next biggest theatre is 4,500 seats (The Fox). There are no other spaces available or projected to be available.

What about producing some large shows in a bigger theatre?
11.10.38 This would put The Rep in direct competition with commercial theatre for the only other viable space in St Louis, The Fox. In addition, it would greatly affect staff time and costs as well as changing the focus of programming and, therefore, the mission.

Performance measurement and cost management

What about cutting out the ITC?
11.10.39   The ITC is the core of the educational programming of The Rep. Private and public funding are based not only on supporting the mainstage and studio, but also the educational programme. Funding agencies, the board, and both Woolf and Bernstein believe that the ITC is an important programme that must be supported.

What about cutting artistic and/or administrative expenses?
11.10.40   As the case points out, the level of spending by The Rep is in line with national averages and there is a good ratio of production to administrative expenses. While one can always point to areas that could be trimmed a bit here and there, you would not be able to find savings substantial enough to solve the problem over the long run.

Is there an angel out there to provide an annual donation to make up the difference?
11.10.41   No. While contributions can and should increase over time, the theatre does not see such an angel existing. In addition, the board and staff want to make sure that the theatre does not rely too much on contributed revenue as compared to earned revenue.

Options for additional capacity

11.10.42   The theatre has looked at several options for different or expanded capacity over the years. Some of these options are as follows.

1. Move the theatre to another site and build all new facilities.

    (i) Build in another part of west St Louis County in an area where current patrons live.

    (ii) Build in a proposed theatre/entertainment district near The Fox and the St Louis Symphony (Grand Centre).

2. Create a second theatre space.

    (i) Build a second theatre at another location as above.

    (ii) Build a second theatre at Webster University.

11.10.43   Moving the entire operation to another site would be very costly. In addition, the Grand Centre project has been languishing for years and does not seem to be developing. While moving would allow complete freedom in space use, The Rep has some ongoing relations with Webster University that it needs and wants. Rep staff act as adjunct faculty. Theatre Conservatory students play some small roles in Rep productions and students are willing and easily available for ushering and backstage crew assignments.

11.10.44 If a second space were built, it would be logistically difficult to have this space separated from Webster University. Trying to rehearse and produce shows at two locations separated by several miles would significantly add to costs of operations. Thus, the best space solution seems to be to build a second theatre on the Webster University campus.

11.10.45 The university has recently acquired some land at its periphery which will help solve its parking problems on the main campus. The space near the Loretto-Hilton Center is currently used for parking and the university's planners and administration are amenable to the idea of an additional theatre in that area.

Building a second theatre on the Webster University campus
Funding
11.10.46 If a second space were to be built, The Rep would engage in a capital fundraising drive. The goal of such an effort would be to fund the new building completely. It is a matter of conjecture as to whether the initial effort would produce 100 per cent funding, but ONE should NOTE that there really is no cost of capital or opportunity cost of funds, per se. Thus, rather than looking at a new building from a discounted-cash flow perspective, it is more a matter of incorporating the new revenue opportunities and projected ongoing costs in the long-range budget to see if the deficit problem can be solved by additional capacity. One can decide whether to include interest on unpaid pledges for a new building. If the new facility costs about $15 million, pledges will come in over a five-year horizon. This means some significant interest costs for several years during and after the facility is built.

How The Rep might operate with two theatre spaces
11.10.47 Instead of having all six productions on the mainstage in one facility, The Rep would rotate between the two buildings. This would allow longer technical rehearsal time (currently only two days before previews), longer regular runs of each of the mainstage (and studio) productions, the ability to extend a play if it is doing well, and the energy and enthusiasm that might be generated with two plays overlapping in time in the two facilities. In addition, new space would have to include increased scene and costume shops, but this might result in some savings on space rented in other areas for painting sets, for example.

11.10.48 The current schedule is 30 weeks for the mainstage and 9 weeks for the studio. Current plans call for only one studio space (in the new building). Thus, if all spaces are operating at the same time, there would be three stages occupied.

Performance measurement and cost management

Other use of new theatre

11.10.49 The staff and board were interested to see if the Opera Theatre of St Louis (OTSL) would be interested in sharing the space as a tenant. The current OTSL season consists of four operas sung in English that are performed in rolling repertory over a five-week season in late May through June. Since each production is extremely expensive to stage, the theatre wonders if OTSL would benefit from a larger house. A new building could be constructed to accommodate not only a smaller house for The Rep (about 750 seats), but also additional space that could be opened up for a 1,200 seat house for opera. While this would increase the cost of a building, it would provide needed rent over the summer. The cost of the theatre ($15 million) and operating assumptions do not include OTSL at this point.

Budgetary impact (mainstage and studio)

11.10.50 Staff salaries (including benefits and based on current costs) are as follows.

For additional work weeks in extended season:	
Actors, musicians, stage managers	$220,000
Backstage running crew	75,000
Seasonal production staff	40,000
Box office and front-of-house staff	10,000
Additional production staff (to accommodate increased production activity)	70,000
Total staff budget impact	$415,000

11.10.51 Webster University would own and maintain the new facility. At present, The Rep pays a user fee to reimburse the university for out-of-pocket costs of maintenance, utilities, and housekeeping.

11.10.52 There would be proportional increases in these fees. This might amount to about $75,000 to $100,000 per year.

Potential revenue – mainstage

11.10.53 Potential ticket sales revenue from additional performances (at current prices):

> 8,800 new subscription seats @ $110 average revenue per seat = $968,000

11.10.54 Potential contributions from additional subscribers:

> 4,000 subscriber households × 25 per cent donor conversion @ $200 = $200,000

11.10.55 Note that these estimates do not include additional single ticket sales for the mainstage nor any additional revenue from the studio.

Building schedule

11.10.56 If The Rep were to decide to pursue building a second theatre, it would take about a year to negotiate terms with Webster University and to conduct feasibility studies on costs and fundraising. Construction would take about another year or so.

(Source: adapted with permission from Carr, 1997.)

Bibliography

Adams, 'Quality Dairy Case', *Issues in Accounting Education*, Fall 1997, pp.385–398.

Anthony, RN, *Planning and Control Systems: A Framework for Analysis*, Harvard University Press, 1965, p.16.

Argyris, C and Kaplan, RS, 'Implementing new knowledge: the case of ABC', *Accounting Horizons* 8 (3), 1994, pp.83–105.

Armstrong, G, 'Information technology', *The Financial Management Manual*, ABG, 2000.

Atkinson, J, Hohner, G, Mundt, B, Toxel, R and Winchel, W, *Current Trends in Cost Quality*, NAA, 1991.

Balderstone, S and Keef, S, 'Throughout accounting: exploding an urban myth', *Management Accounting*, October 1999, pp.26–28.

Barfield, R, 'Think like an investor', *Professional Manager*, March 1994a, pp.17–19.

Barfield, R, 'Business accounting: shareholder value analysis', *Television Education Network*, March 1994b, pp.41–46.

Barfield, R, 'How much should the piper be paid?', *Accountancy*, May 1994c, pp.35-36.

Barton, B, 'Application of the balanced scorecard in a manufacturing company', paper presented at the ACCA/IAFA Seminar on the Balanced Scorecard, 25 October 1997, Dublin.

Barton, TL, Shenkir, WG and Marinas, BC, 'Main Line vs Basinger: a case in relevant costs and incremental analysis', *Issues in Accounting Education*, Spring 1996, pp.167–174.

Batson, J and Brown, A, *Spreadsheet Modelling Best Practices*, Coopers & Lybrand, 1991.

Bendell, T, Kelly, J, Merry, T and Sims, F, *Quality: Measuring and Monitoring*, Century Business, 1993.

Bennett, R, Hendricks, JA, Keyes, D and Rudnicki, E, *Cost Accounting for Factory Automation*, NAA, 1987.

Bibliography

Berliner, C and Brimson, J, *Cost Management in Today's Advanced Manufacturing: The CAM-I Conceptual Design*, Harvard Business School Press, 1988.

Bierman, H and Smidt, S, *The Capital Budgeting Decision*, Cornell University Press, 1981.

Bjornenak, T and Mitchell, F, 'A study of the development of the ABC journal literature 1987–1998', paper presented at the LSE Seminar on Management Accounting Change, April 2000.

Bhimani, A, 'Monitoring performance measures in UK manufacturing companies', *Management Accounting* vol. 72, January 1994, pp.34–37.

Bhimani, A, 'Control à la Française: the tableau de bord', University of Warwick Working Paper, 1995.

Bhimani, A (ed.), *Management Accounting: European Perspectives*, OUP, 1996.

Bhimani, A and Bromwich, M, 'Accounting for just-in-time manufacturing systems', CMA: *The Management Accounting Magazine*, February 1991.

Bhimani, A and Bromwich, M, 'Activity based costing', *International Encyclopedia of Business and Management*, Routledge, 2001.

Bhimani, A and Keshtvarz, MH, 'British management accountants: strategically oriented?', *Journal of Cost Management*, March/April 1999, pp.25–31. Reprinted with permission. For more information, visit www.wglcorpfinance@riag.com.

Bhimani, A and Neike, C, 'How Siemens designed its target costing system to redesign its products', *Journal of Cost Management*, July/August 1999, pp.29–34. Reprinted with permission. For more information, visit www.wglcorpfinance@riag.com.

Bhimani, A and Okano, H, 'Targeting excellence: target cost management at Toyota', *Management Accounting*, March 1995.

Bhimani, A and Pigott, D, 'Implementing ABC: a case study of organisational and behavioural consequences', *Management Accounting Research* 3 (2), 1992, pp.119–132.

Bledsoe, NL and Ingram, RW, 'Customer satisfaction through performance evaluation', *Journal of Cost Management*, Winter 1997, pp.43–50. Reprinted with permission. For more information, visit www.wglcorpfinance@riag.com.

Booth, R, 'Avoiding pitfalls in investment appraisal', *Management Accounting*, November 1999, pp.22–23.

Borthick, AF and Roth, HP, 'Faster access to more information for better decisions', *Journal of Cost Management*, Winter 1997, pp.25–30.

Brausch, J, 'Beyond ABC: target costing for profit enhancement', *Management Accounting* (US), November 1994.

Bremser, WG and Dierks, P, *Cases from Management Accounting Practice* vol. 14, Institute of Management Accountants (US), 1998.

Brimson, JA, *Activity Accounting: An Activity Based Costing Approach*, Wiley, 1991.

Bromwich, M, 'Accounting for strategic excellence', *Management Accounting and Strategies: New Ideas, New Experiences*, SYSTIME (Denmark), 1991.

Bromwich, M and Bhimani, A, 'Strategic investment appraisal', *Management Accounting* (US), March 1991.

Bromwich, M and Bhimani, A, *Management Accounting: Pathways to Progress*, CIMA, 1998.

Bromwich, M and Wang, Q, *Accounting for Overheads: Critiques and Reforms*, CIMA research report, CIMA, 1993.

Burnstein, M, 'Life-cycle costing', *Cost Accounting for the 1990s*, NAA, 1988.

Busby, JS and Pitts, CG, *Assigning Flexibility in Capital Investment*, CIMA, 1998.

Buzzell, R and Gale, B, *The PIMS Principles: Linking Strategy to Performance*, The Free Press (US), 1987.

Camp, R, *Benchmarking*, ASQC Quality Press, 1989.

Carr, LP, 'Cost of quality – making it work', *Journal of Cost Management*, Spring 1995, pp.61–65.

Carr, LP, *Cases from Management Accounting Practice* vol. 11, Institute of Management Accountants (US), 1997. Reprinted with permission. For more information, visit www.wglcorpfinance@riag.com.

Chapman, C, *Instructional Notes on Electronic Spreadsheets*, LSE, 1994.

CIMA (Chartered Institute of Management Accountants), *Draft Standards of Competence in Management Accounting*, CIMA, 1992.

CIMA, *Performance Measurement in the Manufacturing Sector*, CIMA, 1993.

Bibliography

CIMA, *Management Accounting Official Terminology*, CIMA, 2000.

CIMA/IPE, *Justifing Investment in Advanced Manufacturing Technology*, CIMA/IPE, 1987.

Cheatham, CB and Cheatham, LR, 'Redesigning cost systems: is standard costing obsolete?', *Accounting Horizons*, December 1996, pp.23–31.

Chiapello, E and Lebas, M, 'The tableau de bord, a French approach to management information', paper presented at the 19th Annual Congress of the European Accounting Association, Bergen, Norway, 2–4 May 1996.

Chow, CW, Hwang, Y and Toga, DF, 'ACE company: a case for incorporating competitive considerations into the teaching of capital budgeting', *Issues in Accounting Education*, Fall 1995, pp.389–401.

Coate, CJ and Frey, K, 'Integrating ABC, TOC, and financial reporting', *Journal of Cost Management*, July/August 1999. Reprinted with permission. For more information, visit www.wglcorpfinance@riag.com.

Cobb, I, *JIT and the Management Accountant*, CIMA, 1993.

Cokins, G, Stratton, A and Helbling, J, *An ABC Manager's Primer: Straight Talk on Activity-Based Costing*, Institute of Management Accountants (US), 1992.

Cooper, G, 'Strategic business information', paper presented at the Management Accounting Research Conference at LSE, 2 April 1992.

Cooper, R, 'The two-stage procedure in cost accounting – II', *Journal of Cost Management for the Manufacturing Industry*, Summer 1987.

Cooper, R, 'You need a new cost system when . . .', *Harvard Business Review*, February 1989.

Cooper, R, 'Activity based costing and the lean enterprise', *Journal of Cost Management*, Winter 1996, pp.6–14. Reprinted with permission. For more information, visit www.wglcorpfinance@riag.com.

Cooper, R and Kaplan, RS, *The Design of Cost Management Systems: Text, Cases and Readings*, Prentice Hall, 1991.

Cooper, R and Kaplan, RS, *The Design of Cost Management Systems*, Prentice Hall (US), 1999.

Corboy, M and O'Corrbui, D, 'The seven deadly sins of strategy', *Management Accounting* (UK), November 1999, pp.29–30.

Darlington, J, Innes, J, Mitchell, F and Woodward, J, 'Throughput accounting: the Garrett Automotive experience', *Management Accounting* (UK), April 1992.

Dedera, CR, 'Harris Semiconductor ABC: world-wide implementation and total integration', *Journal of Cost Management*, Spring 1996, pp.44–58. Reprinted with permission. For more information, visit www.wglcorpfinance@riag.com.

Develin, N and Bellis-Jones, R, *No Customer – No Business: The True Value of Activity Based Cost Management*, ABG, 1999.

Dixon, J, Nanni, A and Vollman, T, *The New Performance Challenge*, Irwin, 1990.

Donelan, JG and Kaplan, EA, 'Value chain analysis: a strategic approach to cost management', *Journal of Cost Management*, March/April 1998, pp.7–15.

Drtina, RE and Monetti, GA, 'Controlling flexible business strategies', *Journal of Cost Management*, Fall 1995, pp.42–49. Reprinted with permission. For more information, visit www.wglcorpfinance@riag.com.

Drucker, P, *Management*, Heinemann, 1974.

Drury, C, 'Standard costing: a technique at variance with modern management', *Management Accounting*, 1999, pp.56–58.

Dutton, JJ and Ferguson, M, 'Target costing at Texas Instrument', *Journal of Cost Management*, Fall 1996, pp.33–38. Reprinted with permission. For more information, visit www.wglcorpfinance@riag.com.

Epstein, M, 'Customer profitability analysis', *Management Accounting Guideline*, SMAC (Canada), 2000.

Epstein, M and Manzoni, J, 'The balanced scorecard and tableau de bord: translating strategy to action', *Management Accounting* (US), August 1997, pp.28–36.

Estrin, T and Kantor, J, 'Accounting for throughput time', *Advances in Management Accounting* vol. 6, 1998, pp.55–74.

Faletti, PF and Harty, HE, *The Illustrated Guide to Preparing Director Information Reports*, US League of Savings Institutions, 1990.

Fargher, N and Morse, D, 'Quality costs: planning the trade-off between prevention and appraisal activities', *Journal of Cost Management*, January/February 1998, pp.14–22.

Fariah, M, 'COOMS and ERP: any hope behind the hype?', *Engineering Computers*, May 1993, pp.12–15.

Fess, PE and Warren, CS, *Managerial Accounting*, South-Western Publishing Co., 1985.

Bibliography

Fisher, J, 'Implementing target costing', *Journal of Cost Management*, Summer 1995, pp.50–59. Reprinted with permission. For more information, visit www.wglcorpfinance@riag.com.

Fitzgerald, L, Johnston, R, Brignall, S, Silvestro, R and Voss, C, *Performance Measurement in Service Businesses*, CIMA, 1993.

Flegm, EH, 'The future of management and financial accounting', *Journal of Cost Management*, Winter 1996, pp.44–49. Reprinted with permission. For more information, visit www.wglcorpfinance@riag.com.

Foster, G, 'Management accounting in 2000', *Journal of Cost Management*, Winter 1996, pp.36–39. Reprinted with permission. For more information, visit www.wglcorpfinance@riag.com.

Foster, G, Gupta, M and Sjoblom, L, 'Customer profitability analysis: challenges and new directions', *Journal of Cost Management*, Spring 1996, pp.5–17.

Francis, G and Minchington, C, 'Value based management in practice', *Management Accounting*, February 2000, pp.46–47.

Galloway, D and Waldron, D, 'Throughput accounting: the need for a new language for manufacturing', *Management Accounting*, November 1988.

Gardiner, M, 'Financial ratios: can you trust them?', *Management Accounting*, September 1997, p.30.

Goldratt, EM, *The Haystack Syndrome: Sifting Information Out of the Data Ocean*, North River Press (US), 1990.

Goldratt, EM and Cox, J, *The Goal*, Gower, 1984.

Greenberg, H, 'Alphabet dupe: why EBITDA falls short', *Fortune*, 10 July 2000, pp.90–91.

Hamel, G, 'Strategy as revolution', *Harvard Business Review*, July/August 1996, pp.69–82.

Hamel, G and Prahalad, CK, 'Competing for the future', *Harvard Business Review*, July/August 1994, pp.122–128.

Handy, C, *The Age of Unreason*, Arrow, 1998.

Hartley, VH, *Cost and Managerial Accounting*, Allyn and Bacon, 1986.

Hayes, RH and Abernathy, WJ, 'Managing our way to economic decline', *Harvard Business Review*, Winter 1980.

Holmen, JS, 'ABC vs TOC: it's a matter of time', *Management Accounting* (US), January 1995, pp.37–40.

Horngren, CT, 'Contribution margin analysis: no longer relevant/Strategic accounting: the new paradigm', *Journal of Management Accounting Research*, Fall 1990, pp.3–24. Reprinted with permission. For more information, visit www.wglcorpfinance@riag.com.

Horngren, CT, Bhimani, A, Foster, G and Datar, S, *Management and Cost Accounting*, Prentice Hall (UK), 2001.

Horngren, CT and Foster, G, *Cost Accounting*, Prentice Hall, 1991.

Horovitz, J and Jurgens-Panak, M, *Total Customer Satisfaction*, Pitman, 1992.

Hubbell, WW, 'Combining economic value added and activity based management', *Journal of Cost Management*, Spring 1996, pp.18–24. Reprinted with permission. For more information, visit www.wglcorpfinance@riag.com.

Innes, J, Mitchell, F and Sinclair, D, 'A tale of two surveys', *CIMA Research Update*, CIMA, Spring/Summer 2000, p.4.

Johnson, HT and Kaplan, RS, *Relevance Lost: the Rise and Fall of Management Accounting*, Harvard University Press, 1987.

Jones, L, 'Competitor cost analyses at Caterpillar', *Management Accounting*, October 1988, pp.32–38.

Juras, PE and Dierks, P, 'Blue Ridge', *Management Accounting*, December 1993, pp.57–59.

Juras, PE and Dierks, P, *Cases from Management Accountancy Practice* vol. 13, Institute of Management Accountants (US), 1998.

Kahn, J and Garine, F, 'Presto chango! Sales are huge!', *Fortune*, 27 March 2000, pp.66–70.

Kaplan, RS, 'New roles for management accountants', *Journal of Cost Management*, Fall 1995, pp.6–14. Reprinted with permission. For more information, visit www.wglcorpfinance@riag.com.

Kaplan, RS and Norton, DP, 'The balanced scorecard: measures that drive performance', *Harvard Business Review*, September/October 1993.

Kaplan, RS and Norton, DP, *The Balanced Scorecard*, HBS Press (US), 1996.

Kaplan, RS and Norton, DP, 'Using the balanced scorecard as a strategic management system', *Harvard Business Review*, January/February 1996.

Kato, Y, Böer, G and Chow, CW, 'Target costing: an integrative management process', *Journal of Cost Management*, Spring 1995, pp.39–51. Reprinted with permission. For more information, visit www.wglcorpfinance@riag.com.

Bibliography

Kim, I, 'ABM and corporate downsizing', *Journal of Cost Management*, May/June 1998, pp.12–19.

King, AM, 'Three significant digits', *Journal of Cost Management*, Winter 1997, pp.31–37. Reprinted with permission. For more information, visit www.wglcorpfinance@riag.com.

Lebas, M, 'Management accounting practice in France', in Bhimani, A (ed.), *Management Accounting: European Perspectives*, Oxford University Press, 1996, pp.74–99.

Lefley, F and Sarkis, J, 'The decline of the accounting rate of return (ARR)', *Management Accounting*, June 1997, pp.50–52.

Lewis, C and Cooper, G, 'Threat or opportunity? The new management information', *Financial Focus*, November 1992.

Lewis, C and McFadyen, K, 'World class finance', *Management Accounting*, September 1993a.

Lewis, C and McFadyen, K, 'World class finance – 2', *Management Accounting*, October 1993b.

Lewis, C and McFadyen, K, 'World class finance: moving toward the goal', *Management Accounting*, November 1993c.

Loomis, CJ, 'Amazon so far has produced nothing but loses . . .', *Fortune*, 1 May 2000, pp.61–63.

Luck, V, 'Made to measure', *Accountancy Age*, 1994a.

Luck, V, 'Performance measurement: translating strategy into performance', presentation made at The Economist Conference, 25 March 1994b.

Luther, R and O'Donovan, B, 'Cost–volume–profit analysis and the theory of constraints', *Journal of Cost Management*, September/October 1998.

Lynch, D, 'Focus on quality', *Management Accounting*, September 1999, pp.30–31.

MacArthur, JB, 'Performance measures that count: monitoring variables of strategic importance', *Journal of Cost Management*, Fall 1996, pp.39–45. Reprinted with permission. For more information, visit www.wglcorpfinance@riag.com.

McCann, M, 'Turning vision into reality', *Management Accounting*, January 2000, pp.36–37.

McCunn, P, 'The balanced scorecard . . . the eleventh commandment', *Management Accounting*, December 1998, pp.34–36.

Bibliography

McHilhattan, 'How cost management systems can support the JIT philosophy', *Management Accounting*, September 1987.

McNair, CJ, 'To serve the customer within', *Journal of Cost Management*, Winter 1996, pp.40–43. Reprinted with permission. For more information, visit www.wglcorpfinance@riag.com.

McNair, CJ, 'The new finance: shaping functional relevance for the new millennium', *CMA Magazine*, February 1997, pp.11–14.

McNair, CJ, Musconi, W and Norris, T, *Meeting the Technology Challenge: Cost Aaccounting in a JIT Environment*, NAA, 1988.

Maskell, B, 'Management accounting and just-in-time', *Management Accounting*, September 1986.

Maskell, B, 'Performance measurement for world class manufacturing – I', *Management Accounting*, July/August 1989a.

Maskell, B, 'Performance measurement for world class manufacturing – II', *Management Accounting*, September 1989b.

Massot, 'Residual income captures sustainable growth creation', *Equity Research Report*, Morgan-Stanley Dean Witter, 8 May 2000.

Monden, Y and Hamada, K, 'Target costing and *kaizen* costing in Japanese automobile companies', *Journal of Management Accounting Research*, Fall 1991.

Morrow, M, *Activity Based Management*, Woodhead-Faulkner, 1992.

Morse, W, *Cost Accounting: Processing, Evaluation and Using Cost Data*, Addison-Wesley, 1981.

Morse, W, 'Rantoul Tool Inc.', *Issues in Accounting Education*, Spring 1990, pp.78–89.

Moyes, J, 'The dangers of JIT', *Management Accounting*, February 1988.

Musgrove, CL and Fox, MJ, *Quality Costs: Their Impact on Company Strategy and Profitability*, Technical Communications Ltd, 1991.

NAA, *Information for Corporate Directors*, NAA, 1993.

Nanni, AJ, *Cases from Management Accounting Practice* vol. 12, Institute of Management Accountants (US), 1998.

Naylor, J, *Management*, Pitman, 1999.

Newing, R, 'Out with the old, in with the new', *Accountancy Age*, July 1994.

Newing R, 'Wake up to the balanced scorecard', *Management Accounting (UK)*, March 1995.

Bibliography

Noreen, S, Smith, D and Machey, JT, *The Theory of Constraints and its Implementation for Management Accounting*, Institute of Management Accountants (US), 1995.

Nugus, S and Remenyi, D, *Forecasting, Planning and Budgeting Using Lotus 1-2-3*, Glentop, 1988.

O'Hara, M, 'Financial planning and the micro-computer', in Ashton, D, Hooper, T and Scapens, R (eds.), *Issues in Management Accounting*, Prentice Hall, 1991, pp.219–232.

O'Neill, B, 'Application of the balanced scorecard in an insurance company', paper presented at the ACCA/IAFA Seminar on the Balanced Scorecard, 25 October 1997, Dublin.

Pasework, WR, 'The evolution of quality control costs in American manufacturing', *Journal of Cost Management for the Manufacturing Industry*, Spring 1991.

Peskett, R, 'Beyond DCF', *Management Accounting*, November 1999, pp.60–61.

Piercy, NF, 'Strategic management: strategizing your way to the future', *Business Digest*, June 1999, pp.1–42.

Player, RS and Keys, DE, 'Lessons from the ABM battlefield: getting off to the right start', *Journal of Cost Management*, Spring 1995a, pp.26–37. Reprinted with permission. For more information, visit www.wglcorpfinance@riag.com.

Player, RS and Keys, DE, 'Lessons from the ABM battlefield: developing the pilot', *Journal of Cost Management*, Summer 1995b, pp.20–34. Reprinted with permission. For more information, visit www.wglcorpfinance@riag.com.

Player, RS and Keys, DE, 'Lessons from the ABM battlefield: moving from pilot to mainstream', *Journal of Cost Management*, Fall 1995c, pp.31–41. Reprinted with permission. For more information, visit www.wglcorpfinance@riag.com.

Plunkett, J, Dale, B and Tyrrell, R, *Quality Costs*, DTI, 1985.

Porter, M, *Competitive Advantage*, Free Press, 1985.

Porter, ME, *Competitive Strategy*, Simon and Schuster, 1998.

Porter, ME, quoted in Surowiecki, J, 'The return of Michael Porter', *Fortune*, 1 February 1999, pp.135–138.

Prahalad, CK and Hamel, G, 'The core competence of the corporation', *Harvard Business Review* vol. 68 No. 3, 1990, pp.79–91.

Pryor, T, 'Making new things familiar and familiar things new', *Journal of Cost Management*, Winter 1997, pp.38–42. Reprinted with permission. For more information, visit www.wglcorpfinance@riag.com.

Pryor, T and Sahm, J, *Using Activity Based Management for Continuous Improvement: A Step by Step Approach*, ICMS (US), 1995.

Radharkrishnan, S and Srinidhi, B, 'Avoiding the death spiral: a case for activity based costing', *Journal of Cost Management*, 1997, pp.19–24. Reprinted with permission. For more information, visit www.wglcorpfinance@riag.com.

Raffish, N and Turney, P, 'Glossary of ABM', *Journal of Cost Management*, Fall 1991.

Ray, M, 'Cost management for product development', *Journal of Cost Management*, Spring 1995, pp.52–60. Reprinted with permission. For more information, visit www.wglcorpfinance@riag.com.

Reeve, JM, 'Projects, models, and systems – where is ABM headed?', *Journal of Cost Management*, Summer 1996, pp.5–16. Reprinted with permission. For more information, visit www.wglcorpfinance@riag.com.

Rigelsford, K and Sharp, I, 'Accounting for the new economy, *Accountancy*, May 2000, pp.124–125.

Roberts, A and Pitt, S, 'Strategy implementation: a dynamic process guide', LBS Working Paper, March 1990.

Roberts, MW and Silvester, KJ, 'Why ABC failed and how it may yet succeed', *Journal of Cost Management*, Winter 1996, pp.23–35. Reprinted with permission. For more information, visit www.wglcorpfinance@riag.com.

Roslender, R, Hart, S and Ghosh, J, 'Strategic management accounting: refocusing the agenda', *Management Accounting* (UK), December 1998, pp.44–46.

Rousseau, Y and Rousseau, P, 'Common pitfalls of the balanced scorecard', *CMA Management*, December/January 2000, pp.26–29.

Ruhl, JM, 'ABC for continuous improvement, the theory of constraints, and open book management', *Journal of Cost Management*, Fall 1995, pp.80–89.

Ruhl, JM, 'Activity based management. Lessons from the ABM battlefield and world class manufacturing; the next decade', *Journal of Cost Management*, Spring 1996, pp.26–37. Reprinted with permission. For more information, visit www.wglcorpfinance@riag.com.

Ruhl, JM, 'An introduction to the theory of constraints', *Journal of Cost Management*, 1996, pp.43–48. Reprinted with permission. For more information, visit www.wglcorpfinance@riag.com.

Bibliography

Ruhl, JM and Kreuze, JG, 'Startup Inc.: linking financial accounting, managerial accounting and strategic management', *Issues in Accounting Education,* Fall 1997, pp.435–456.

Scapens, R, Jazayeri, M and Scapens, J, 'SAP: integrated information systems and the implications for management accountants', *Management Accounting*, September 1998, pp.46–48.

Schneiderman, AM, 'Metrics for the order fulfilment process (I)', *Journal of Cost Management*, Summer 1996, pp.30–41. Reprinted with permission. For more information, visit www.wglcorpfinance@riag.com.

Schneiderman, AM, 'Metrics for the order fulfilment process (II)', *Journal of Cost Management*, Fall 1996, pp.6–17. Reprinted with permission. For more information, visit www.wglcorpfinance@riag.com.

Schonberger, R, 'The transfer of Japanese manufacturing approaches to US industry', *Academy of Management Review*, 1982.

Shanahan, YP, 'Implementing an ABC system – lessons from the Australian Post', *Journal of Cost Management*, Summer 1995, pp.60–64. Reprinted with permission. For more information, visit www.wglcorpfinance@riag.com.

Shank, JK, 'New wines in old battles: Reichard Maschinen GmbH', *Journal of Cost Management*, Summer 1996, pp.49–59. Reprinted with permission. For more information, visit www.wglcorpfinance@riag.com.

Sheridan, T, 'The changing shape of the finance function', *Management Accounting*, 1998, pp.18–20.

Shields, MD and McEvens, MA, 'Implementing ABC systems successfully', *Journal of Cost Management*, Winter 1996, pp.15–23. Reprinted with permission. For more information, visit www.wglcorpfinance@riag.com.

Shields, M and Young, M, 'Managing product life cycle costs: an organisational model', *Journal of Cost Management*, Fall 1991.

Simmonds, K, 'Strategic management accounting', in Cowe, R (ed.), *Handbook of Management Accounting*, Gower, 1988, pp.26–29.

Simmonds, K, 'Strategic management accounting: the emerging paradigm', paper presented at the European Accounting Association Conference, Stuttgart, 5–7 April 1989.

Simons, R, *Performance Measurement and Control Systems for Implementing Strategy*, HBS Press (US), 2000.

Smith, K and Leksan, M, 'A manufacturing case study on activity based costing', *Journal of Cost Management*, Summer 1991.

Smith, M, 'Realising the benefits from investment in ERP', *Management Accounting*, November 1999, p.34.

Stalk, G and Hout, T, *Competing Against Time*, Free Press, 1990.

Stern, JM, Stewart, GB and Chew, DH, 'The EVA® financial management system', *Journal of Applied Corporate Finance*, Summer 1995, pp.32–46.

Stewart, GB, *The Quest for Value*, Harper Business (US), 1991.

Titard, PL, *Managerial Accounting: An Introduction*, Dryden, 1983.

Tomkins, P, 'SAP and the Hibernia experience', *CMA Magazine*, November 1997, p.34.

Tully, S, 'America's best wealth creators', *Fortune*, 28 November 1993, p.143.

Umble, MM and Umble, E, 'How to apply the theory of constraints' five-step process of continuous improvement', *Journal of Cost Management*, September/October 1998.

Wallace, JS, 'EVA® financial systems: management perspectives', *Advances in Management Accountancy* vol. 6, 1998, pp.1–15.

Walsh, TJ, 'Electronic batch recording: a vendor's perspective', *Pharmaceutical Engineering*, July/August 1992.

Williamson, OE, *Markets and Hierarchies: Analysis and Antitrust Implications*, The Free Press (US), 1975.

Yoshikawa, T, Innes, J, Mitchell, F and Tanaka, M, *Contemporary Cost Management*, Chapman and Hall, 1993.

Young, D, 'Economic value added: a primer for European managers', *European Management Journal*, August 1997, pp.335–343.

Index

accountants,
  increasing numbers of, 1.2.17
accounting ratios, 3.7.
  internet companies, 3.7.1
achieving balance, a case study,
    6.15.22–6.15.67
  background information, 6.15.25–6.15.30
  complexity of, 6.15.15–6.15.21
  control, loss of, 6.15.23–6.15.25
  developing intensity factors,
    6.15.61–6.15.67
  heading up, 6.15.7–6.15.12
  information system, 6.15.45–6.15.60
  new customers and new problems,
    6.15.31–6.15.35
  pilot system, usefulness of,
    6.15.13–6.15.14
  politics of change, 6.15.43–6.15.44
  replacing gut fact with information,
    6.15.39–6.15.42
  stepping into the future, 6.15.36–6.15.38
activity accounting, 6.0
  activity, determining a, 6.6.1–6.6.3
activity-based budgetary control,
    6.20.1–6.20.27
  benefits of, 6.20.5–6.20.8
  implementation of, 6.20.8–6.20.10
  order receiving department,
    6.20.13–6.20.16
  performance evaluation, standards for,
    6.20.23–6.20.27
  preparation of budget, 6.20.17–6.20.18
  product costing first, 6.20.11–6.20.12
  resource requirements, questioning,
    6.20.19–6.20.22
activity based control and theory of
    constraint, integrating, 7.11
  bottleneck follows, 7.11.19–7.11.21
  bottleneck parallels, 7.11.22–7.211.24
  bottleneck precedes, 7.11.17–7.11.18
  constrained activities, 7.11.12–7.11.15
  financial reporting, effects on,
    7.11.25–7.11.29
  interdependencies among activities,
    7.11.16
  non-constrained activities, 7.11.12–7.11.15
activity based management,

achieving balance, a case study,
    6.15.22–6.15.67
  actuals only, 6.17.24–6.17.31
  background to, 6.1.1
  business objectives, clarifying, 6.15.6
  change strategies, 6.13.1–6.13.2
  complexity of, 6.15.15–6.15.21
  cost analysis versus business analysis,
    6.18.5–6.18.72
    barrel depreciation issue,
      6.18.60–6.18.72
    Chalice Wine Group, 6.18.13–6.18.17
    distributor, the, 6.18.31–6.18.33
    Lyford Winery, 6.18.46–6.18.50
    overall value chain, 6.18.35–6.18.39
    project, description of, 6.18.9–6.18.13
    retailer, the, 6.18.34
    The Vineyard, 6.18.25–6.18.30
    value chain analysis, 6.18.51–6.18.59
    Winery, 6.18.18–6.18.24
    Winery costs revisited, 6.18.40–6.18.45
  cost based decisions, 6.8.8–6.8.21
    investment justification, 6.8.28–6.8.38
    performance management,
      6.8.39–6.8.45
    product pricing, 6..22–6.8.27
  cost behaviour, 6.5.1–6.5.3
  cost centre control, 6.17.8–6.17.13
  costing system, replacing a, 6.7.1–6.7.4
  costs drivers, 6.2.1–6.2.4
    determining, 6.8.1–6.8.7
  design issues, 6.9.1–6.9.3
  design trade-offs, 6.17.21–6.17.23
  economics versus organisational reality,
    6.12.1–6.12.6
  effective design of an ABM system,
    6.16.10–6.16.29
    acting on ABC information,
      6.16.21–6.16.25
    cost incursion, understanding,
      6.16.12
    evaluation, packaging, 6.16.20
    implementation, packaging,
      6.16.15–6.16.19
    manufacturing plant overhead,
      6.16.26
    objectives, packaging, 6.16.14

803

Index

outcome, 6.16.27–6.1.629
value chain, understanding, 6.16.13
heading up, 6.15.7–6.15.12
lean enterprises and, 6.9.4–6.9.10
  clarity of objectives, 6.9.25
  consultants and, 6.9.23–6.9.25
  death spiral and, 6.14.1–6.14.16
  failure of, reasons for, 6.11.1–6.11.5
  increasing revenue, 6.11.6–6.11.7
  long term use of, 6.14.18–6.14.21
  product discontinuance, 6.14.17
  product redesign, 6.11.11–6.11.13
  reducing cost, 6.11.8–6.11.10
  right fit, achieving the, 6.10.1–6.10.2
  service context, in the, 6.13.18–6.13.26
  success of, 6.13.3–6.13.17
  theory and practice, 6.15.1–6.15.67
  top management support for, 6.9.11–6.9.16
  training, 6.9.17–6.9.22
literature on, 6.1.2–6.1.3
logic of, 6.3.1–6.3.5
lot-level control, 6.17.17–6.17.18
lot-level tracking, 6.17.19–6.17.20
outdated habits, 6.18.1–6.18.4
pilot system, usefulness of, 6.15.13–6.15.14
resistance to change, 6.16.1–6.16.9
scope versus scale, 6.4.1–6.4.2
software, choice of, 6.19.1–6.19.2
strategy versus finance, 6.15.5
tangible costs versus intangible benefits, 6.17.1–6.17.7
activity level control, 6.17.14–6.17.16
activity mapping, 7.12
  bottlenecks and, 7.12.10–7.12.11, 7.13.11–7.13.29, 7.13.60–7.13.79
  case study, 7.12.12–7.12.17
  computer simulation models, 7.13.30–7.13.38
    results, analysis of, 7.13.39–7.13.45
    summary, 7.13.46
    XCELL+, use of, 7.13.56–7.13.59
  dependency grids, 7.12.7–7.12.9
  Gantt chart, 7.12.6
  line balancing, 7.13.80–7.13.81
  non-financial performance measures, 7.14.1–7.14.16
  simulations, 7.13.82–7.13.87
  theory of constraints and, 7.13.1–7.13.10
backflush cost accounting system,
  cost reductions, 5.2.11
  point of sale and, 5.2.10
  use of, 5.2.9
break-even analysis, 2.4.1
  break-even point, 2.4.2–2.4.4
  calculations of, 2.4.5–2.4.17

budget, preparation of, 6.20.17–6.20.18
business environment,
  change in, 1.1.1

capital budgeting in action, 4.4.28–4.4.46
cash flow return on investment, 3.7.71
change, management of, 1.3.1
changing technologies, 5.0
company information, 3.7.33–3.7.38
  additional accounting information, 3.7.39
  additional financial information, 3.7.40
computer aided design and computer aided manufacturing, 5.5
  coverage of, 5.5.1
  decision to use, 5.5.2
  problems and potential solutions, 5.5.3
contribution margin analysis, 2.5.1–2.5.6
  case studies,
    Kim Basinger, replacement cost of, 2.5.32–2.5.59
    Quality Dairy, 2.5.7–2.5.31
control, approaches to, 1.2.25
corporate treasury, development of, 1.2.22
cost analysis versus business analysis, 6.18.5–6.18.72
  barrel depreciation issue, 6.18.60–6.18.72
  Chalice Wine Group, 6.18.13–6.18.17
  distributor, the, 6.18.31–6.18.33
  Lyford Winery, 6.18.46–6.18.50
  overall value chain, 6.18.35–6.18.39
  project, description of, 6.18.9–6.18.13
  retailer, the, 6.18.34
  The Vineyard, 6.18.25–6.18.30
  value chain analysis, 6.18.51–6.18.59
  Winery, 6.18.18–6.18.24
  Winery costs revisited, 6.18.40–6.18.45
cost based decisions, 6.8.8–6.8.21
  investment justification, 6.8.28–6.8.38
  performance management, 6.8.39–6.8.45
  product pricing, 6..22–6.8.27
cost behaviour, 6.5.1–6.5.3
cost centre control, 6.17.8–6.17.13
costing system, replacing a, 6.7.1–6.7.4
cost management,
  activity based costing, 2.1.6–2.1.8
  background to, 2.1.1–2.1.3
  behaviour, 2.2.1–2.2.3
  estimation, 2.3.1–2.3.16
    account classification, 2.3.2
    engineering method, 2.3.3–2.3.5
    regression analysis, 2.3.8–2.3.16
    scattergraphs, 2.3.6–2.3.7
  job costing, 2.1.4
  standard costing, 2.1.5
costs drivers, 6.2.1–6.2.4
  determining, 6.8.1–6.8.7
customer profitability analysis, 9.9.1–9.9.3

Index

implementing, 9.10.6
information, developing, 9.9.4–9.9.11
new directions in, 9.10.15–9.10.30
key features, 9.10.1–9.10.5
strategy and, 9.10.7–9.10.14

earnings per share, 3.7.56
economic value added, 3.5
  advantages and disadvantages of, 3.7.73–3.7.79
  calculating, 3.5.2, 3.5.6, 3.7.65
    financing approach and, 3.7.69
    operating approach and, 3.7.66
  capital asset pricing model, 3.5.4
  cost of equity, 3.5.3
  definitions of, 3.5.1, 3.5.5
  financial improvement and, 3.7.21–3.7.32
  impact on managers, 3.5.11
  implementation of, managing the, 3.7.87–3.7.90
  incentive plans, features and benefits of, 3.7.92–3.7.97
  managing the firm by, 3.7.80–3.7.86
  reconciling results, 3.7.70
  residual income,
    measure, 3.5.9, 3.5.10
    versus, 3.6.1–3.6.7
  small service firms, in, 3.7.91
  stock prices, changes in, 3.5.7, 3.5.8
Emerging Issues Task Force, 3.7.1
employment,
  trends in, 1.2.18
enterprise resource planning, 5.3
  applications for, 5.3.10–5.3.11
  business change, importance of, 5.3.16
  decentralisation of certain functions, 5.3.20
  integrated information systems, adoption of, 5.3.15
  integration through, a case study, 5.3.21–5.3.29
  materials requirement planning, 5.3.1–5.3.3
  move to, 5.3.8–5.3.14
  object orientated approach, 5.3.4–5.3.7
    business objects, 5.3.5
  systems, applications and products package, 5.3.17
    customising, 5.3.18
    role of, 5.3.19
  total quality management, 5.3.1
equity equivalents, 3.7.61–3.7.64

finance and accounting,
  change management through, 1.3
  function of, 1.1.2, 1.2.1
  orientation of, 1.2.3–1.2.8
  processes, 1.2.9–1.2.10
finance teams, role of, 1.2.3, 1.2.4
financial analysis, 3.1 *et seq.*
  acid test ratio, 3.3.4
  asset turnover ratio, 3.2.3–3.2.7
  comparative balance sheet, 3.2.2
  current ratio, 3.3.3
  debtor's turnover, 3.3.6
  departmental analysis, 3.3.10
  inventory turnover, 3.3.9
  number of days' sales in stock, 3.3.11, 3.3.12
  profitability ratios, 3.2
  quick ratio, 3.3.4
  ratio analysis, 3.3.16–3.3.18
  shareholder's equity, rate earned on, 3.2.8–3.2.16
  solvency ratios, 3.3.1–3.3.18
  total plant assets, ratio of, to long-term liabilities, 3.3.13–3.3.15
  working capital ratio, 3.3.2
Financial and Management Accounting Committee,
  work of, 1.1.7
financial management,
  world-class, achieving, 1.2
financial risk management, 1.2.23
flexible manufacturing systems, 5.6
  accounting problems and solutions, 5.6.3
  CAD/CAM and, 5.6.2
  investing in AMT: a case study, 5.6.39–5.6.181
    activity-based costing,
      design objectives, 5.6.126–5.6.128
      indirect costs, 5.6.129–5.6.132
      objectives of, 5.6.149–5.6.155
      perceived need for, 5.6.141–5.6.148
      project team, 5.6.123
      resistance to, 5.6.180–5.6.181
      use of, 5.6.138–5.6.410
    actual contract cost, 5.6.92–5.6.103
    as-sold costs estimates, 5.6.92–5.6.103
    computer integrated manufacturing process, 5.6.110–5.6.122, 5.6.162–5.6.179
    computer simulation of major activities, 5.6.132–5.6.137
    cost drivers, determining the, 5.6.156–5.6.161
    cost estimation, 5.6.107–5.6.109
    cost system, existing, 5.6.61–5.6.67
    engineering and production process, 5.6.52–5.6.60
    environment, understanding the, 5.6.68–5.6.83
    labour-focused costing system, concerns with, 5.6.104–5.6.106

Index

major products, 5.6.50–5.6.51
manufacturing capacity, 5.6.41
market and competitive environment, 5.6.42–5.6.50
principal business, 5.6.40
product engineering, 5.6.107–5.6.109
Tube Shop, modernisation of, 5.6.84–5.6.91
workforce, impact on the, 5.6.84–5.6.91
material handling systems, 5.6.4, 5.6.5
meaning of, 5.6.1
plant layout, rethinking, 5.6.6–5.6.38
information requirements,
impact of, 1.4.4
non-financial, management of, 1.4.6
transparency in, 1.4.5
internal rate of return, 3.7.71
Internet-based transactions,
advent of, 1.2.16
impact of, 1.2.17
Internet companies, 3.7.1
aggregator,
agent, as, 3.7.8
status of, 3.7.7
barter transactions, 3.7.14–3.7.16
cash flow figures, 3.7.19
fulfilment costs, toying with, 3.7.17
gross sales figures, 3.7.9–3.7.13
marketing expenses and, 3.7.2
revenue,
recognition, 3.7.4–3.7.6
treatment of, 3.7.3
Investment appraisal,
accounting rate of return, 4.3.2–4.3.3
cost benefits of investment decisions, 4.3.6
counting to discounting, 4.3
discounting cash flows, case for, 4.2.1–4.2.2
income, expressing, 4.3.5
initial capital method, 4.3.4
internal rate of return, 4.3.23–4.3.36
calculating the, 4.3.24, 4.3.25
capital budget decisions, 4.3.27
case study, 4.3.29–4.3.33
discounting cash flows, 4.3.28
primary advantage of, 4.3.26
introduction to, 4.1
new technology investments, 4.3.7
return on investment, 4.3.1
alternative investment proposals, considering, 4.3.21
anticipated net cash flow, 4.3.20
average rate of return, 4.3.10–4.3.13
calculating the, 4.3.8
discounted cash flow, 4.3.22–4.3.36
net present value, 4.3.18–4.3.22
opportunity cost of capital, 4.3.19
payback, 4.3.14–4.3.17
real options-based capital budgeting, 4.3.37–4.3.42

just-in-time,
accounting needs and, 5.2.12
non-financial monitors, 5.2.15–5.2.16
performance under, 5.2.16
purchasing, 5.2.13
work re-organisation, *See* work reorganisation

management accountants,
corporate treasury, development of, 1.2.22
financial risk management, 1.2.23
future role of, 1.2.24, 1.4.8, 1.4.9
opportunity for, 1.2.21
role of, 1.2.12–1.2.14
strategic role of, 1.4.10
training of, 1.4.7
management accounting,
approaches to, 1.1.4
changing role of, 1.1.3
defining, 1.1.5
future of, 1.4.1–1.4.13
research into, 1.1.6
traditional objective of, 1.1.3
management information,
design of systems of, 1.4.11
market value added, 3.7.21–3.7.32
calculating EVA and MVA, 3.7.57–3.7.60
comparing EVA and MVA, 3.7.52–3.7.56
equity equivalents, use of, 3.7.61–3.7.64
understanding, 3.7.41–3.7.51
See also Economic value added

net operating profit after tax, (NOPAT), 3.7.57
net operating tax before tax, 3.7.59
net present value, 3.7.71
determining, 3.7.72
non-financial performance measures, 7.14.1–7.14.16
numerical control machines, 5.4.1–5.4.3

Outsource Inc., a case study,
additional accounting information, 3.7.39
additional financial information, 3.7.40
calculating EVA and MVA, 3.7.65
financing approach, using the, 3.7.69
operating approach, using the, 3.7.66–3.7.68
company information, 3.7.33–3.7.38
PayNet, development of, 3.7.38
understanding the EVA and MVA results, 3.7.98–3.7.101
outsourcing, transaction processing, 1.2.15

806

Index

people,
  decline in numbers employed in finance, 1.2.17
  organisation of, 1.2.11–1.2.24
performance evaluation,
  indicators, 5.2.14
  standards for, 6.20.23–6.20.27
performance measurement and cost management, 11.1
  balanced scorecard and, 11.5.16–11.5.24, 1.6.1
    commandments of, 11.10.1
    failure of, 11.9.1–11.9.11
    organisational processes and, 11.8.8–11.8.45
    strategy and, 11.8.1–11.8.7
  budgetary control, strategy and, 11.10.2–11.10.56
  corporate board information and budgetary control, 11.4.1–11.4.17
  customer satisfaction and, 11.5.1–11.5.2
    making metrics useful, 11.5.14–11.5.15
    metrics versus measures, 11.5.7–11.5.13
    steps to improve, 11.5.3–11.5.6
  dimensions that matter, 11.7.1
    customer perspective, 11.7.4
    financial perspective, 11.7.2–11.7.3
    internal-business-process perspective, 11.7.5–11.7.6
    learning and growth perspective, 11.7.7–11.7.9
  goals of performance measures, 11.1.2
  key variables, 11.3.8–11.3.14
  measures, selecting, 11.2.1
  monitoring employee safety, 11.3.6–11.3.7
  need for measures that perform, 11.3.77–11.3.91
  non-financial metrics, developing, 11.3.114–11.3.128
  stakeholders and, 11.3.1–11.3.5
  strategic business information and, 11.3.92–11.3.113
  traditional evaluation systems,
    improvements to, 11.1.7–11.1.8
    problems with, 11.1.3–11.1.6
  worker's performance, measuring, a case study, 11.3.15–11.3.76
price bid, determining a, 2.5.7–2.5.31
  basic mix strategy, assessing, 2.5.27
  competitors, position of, 2.5.12
  cost accounting system, 2.5.14
  cost centres in factory, 2.5.17
  current allocation procedures, consequences of, 2.4.29
  delivery schedules, 2.5.13
  marketing information, 2.5.11
  minimum price, calculating, 2.5.25
  mix department, 2.5.20
  non-manufacturing costs, 2.5.15
  offer of new business,
    assessing, 2.5.22–2.5.24
    strategic value of, 2.5.28
  selling and administration costs, 2.5.16
product costing first, 6.20.11–6.20.12

quality and cost management, 8.0
  achieving quality improvements, 8.4.46–8.4.165
    activity analysis, 8.4.56–8.4.67
    build-up group for 737 engine, 8.4.81–8.4.87
    build-up group for 767 engine, 8.4.79–8.4.80
    change process, 8.4.148–8.4.165
    cost drivers, choice of, 8.4.88–8.4.91
    engineering organisation, 8.4.113–8.4.118
    improvement alternatives, 8.4.137–8.4.147
    objective of the process, 8.4.46–8.4.51
    process analysis, 8.4.68–8.4.78, 8.4.124–8.4.136
    process identification, 8.4.119–8.4.123
    process improvement, 8.4.100–8.4.112
    propulsion systems division, 8.4.52–8.4.55
    quality improvement initiative, 8.4.96–8.4.99
    vertical versus lateral perspectives, 8.4.92–8.4.95
  assessing quality and product line performance, 8.4.24–8.4.45
  conformance, 8.2.8–8.2.23
  cost of quality information,
    breakthrough improvement efforts, 8.3.42
    customers, 8.3.16–8.3.17
    developing, 8.3.3–8.3.50
    external failure, 8.3.24–8.3.31
    incremental improvement efforts, 8.3.37–8.3.41
    internal failure, 8.3.19–8.3.23
    new order entry system, 8.3.45
    on-line configurator, 8.3.43–8.3.44
    order entry department, 8.3.11–8.3.14, 8.3.33–8.3.36
    quotes, tools for, 8.3.46–8.3.50
    study commissioned, 8.3.9–8.3.10
    suppliers, 8.3.15
  cost of quality,
    making it work, 8.4
    returns on quality, 8.4.10–8.4.23
    successful use of, 8.4.4–8.4.9
  defining quality, 8.2.1–8.2.7

807

Index

environmental management, 8.4.166–8.4.213
  activities in, 8.4.173–8.4.178
  corporate environmental directive, response to, 8.4.169–8.4.172
  cost of quality in, 8.4.179–8.4.183, 8.4.198–8.4.202
  customer requirements, 8.4.184–8.4.189
  future clean-up, cost of, 8.4.203–8.4.213
  large expenditure categories, 8.4.190–8.4.196
  related measures, 8.4.167
  review of issues, 8.4.166–8.4.168
  hidden costs and customers, 8.2.24–8.2.25
  how much is enough?, 8.1.1–8.1.3
  non-conformance, 8.2.8–8.2.23
  quality costs, 8.3.1–8.3.2
Quality Dairy,
  case study on, 2.5.7–2.5.31

residual income, 3.7.71
  calculating, 3.6.4, 3.6.5
  definition of, 3.6.3
  focus of, 3.6.1
  stock, fair value for, 3.6.7
  value creation, capturing, 3.6.2
resource requirements,
  questioning, 6.20.19–6.20.22
return on assets, 3.7.55

service centres,
  establishment of, 1.2.11
standard costing and variance analysis, 2.6.1–2.6.12
  fixed cost variances, 2.6.5
  flexible budget, preparing a, 2.6.4
standard costs, costing using, 2.7.1–2.7.6
  use of, 2.7.7–2.7.17
strategic investment appraisal, 4.4
  appraisal, 4.4.4, 4.4.16–4.23
  benefits tracking, 4.4.6, 4.4.26–4.4.27
  positioning, 4.4.3, 4.4.7–4.4.15
  selection, 4.4.5, 4.4.24–4.4.25
strategy and cost management,
  achieving strategic cost analysis, 9.8.16–9.8.76
  analysis, extending the, 9.8.62–9.8.67
  competitive environment, 9.8.17
  consensus solution, 9.8.68–9.8.75
  cost information, 9.8.30–9.8.31
  economics versus marketing, 9.8.33–9.8.39
  market shares, 9.8.18
  price changes, impact of, 9.8.49–9.8.57
  pricing, 9.8.25
  relevant costs and profits, 9.8.40–9.8.48
  replacement parts, 9.8.19–9.8.20
  steel vs plastic rings, 9.8.21–9.8.25
  strategic considerations, 9.8.58–9.8.62
  business planning, 9.1.1–9.1.3
  competitive differentiation, 9.2.8–9.2.15
  core competencies, 9.2.16–9.2.21
  customer value to product costs, linking, 9.8.1–9.8.15
  environmental analysis, 9.3.9–9.3.11
  failure of strategy, reasons for, 9.5.1–9.5.9
  linking pans to strategy, 9.2.1–9.2.7
  mission,
    building a sense of, 9.4.7–9.4.13
    development of, 9.4.1–9.4.6
    statements, 9.4.14–9.4.22
  strategic management accounting, 9.6.1
    criteria, 9.6.3–9.6.26
    implementing, 9.6.27–9.6.33
    need for, 9.7.1–9.7.14
  structured strategy generation, 9.3.12–9.3.14
  SWOT analysis, 9.3.1–9.3.8
strategy and financial reporting,
  a case study, 9.8.77–9.8.131

target cost management,
  basis for, 10.2.1–10.2.14
  consumer perspective, 10.4.25–10.4.27
  corporate planning, 10.2.2
  critical activities, 10.4.28–10.4.36
  implementation issues, 10.5.1–10.5.7
  implementing, a case study, 10.3.2–10.3.16
  integrative management process, as, 10.4.1–10.4.18
  kaizen costing versus, 10.1.1–10.1.2
  management planning systems, 10.4.19–10.4.21
  market pricing pressures, dealing with, 10.5.71–10.5.125
  market strategy and, 10.5.8–10.5.48
  new project, developing the, 10.2.3–10.2.9
  principles for, 10.3.1
  procedural aspects of, 10.4.22–10.4.24
  product design, 10.2.10
  production transfer plan, 10.2.11–10.2.14
  redesigning the product, 10.5.49–10.5.70
  reducing costs, 10.4.37–10.4.47
technology,
  just-in-time systems, 5.2.1–5.2.8
    case study, 5.2.9
  kanban system, 5.2.4
  processes and accounting, 5.1.1–5.1.5
theory of constraint and activity based control; integrating, 7.11
  bottleneck follows, 7.11.19–7.11.21
  bottleneck parallels, 7.11.22–7.211.24
  bottleneck precedes, 7.11.17–7.11.18
  constrained activities, 7.11.12–7.11.15

Index

financial reporting, effects on, 7.11.25–7.11.29
interdependencies among activities, 7.11.16
non-constrained activities, 7.11.12–7.11.15
time and cost management, 7.0
　constraints,
　　controversies about, 7.8.5–7.8.7
　　goal of the company, 7.8.8–7.8.9
　　managing, 7.8.3–7.8.4
　　theory of, 7.8.1–7.8.9
　continuous improvement, 7.7.1–7.7.19
　　steps to, 7.7.11–7.7.19
　cost and time drivers, 7.4.4–7.4.9
　life-cycle costs, 7.3.1–7.3.3
　new product development, 7.4.1–7.4.9
　product life-cycle costing, 7.1.1–7.1.7
　strategy, role of, 7.6.1–7.6.5
　throughput accounting, 7.9.1–7.9.28, 7.10.1–7.10.41
　　bottlenecks and constraints, 7.9.20–7.9.26
　　calculating throughput time, 7.10.29–7.10.41
　　inventory, 7.9.7–7.9.10
　　operating expense, 7.9.11–7.9.19
　　preventing wasting constraint time, 7.9.27–7.9.28
　　redirecting managerial attention, 7.10.7–7.10.28
　time and product life-cycles, 7.2.1–7.2.6
　total quality management, role of, 7.5.1–7.5.4
　trade-offs between cost and time, 7.2.4–7.2.6
transaction processing,
　outsourcing, 1.2.15

treasury,
　corporate, scope of, 1.2.20
　strategic role of, 1.2.19

Urgent Issues Task Force, 3.7.1
work reorganisation,
　case study, 5.2.17–5.2.22
　costing systems, implications for, 5.2.47–5.2.79
　inventory management, 5.2.23–5.2.25
　key performance indicators, 5.2.88–5.2.94
　key success factors, 5.2.30–5.2.35
　management response, 5.2.151–5.2.165
　new inventory management, 5.2.41–5.2.46
　new purchasing management, 5.2.36–5.2.40
　non-financial metrics, 5.2.143–5.2.150
　previous production environment, 5.2.26–5.2.29
　previous purchasing, 5.2.23
　product costing, 5.2.95–5.2.142
　profitability indicators, 5.2.88–5.2.94
　profits and cost control, focusing on, 5.2.80–5.2.87
working capital management, 3.4
　average payment periods, 3.4.15
　case study, 3.4.5–3.4.11
　checklist, 3.4.4
　comparative ratio analysis, problems with, 3.4.12
　difficulty in managing, 3.4.1
　e-business, investment in impact of, 3.4.17
　efficiency, evaluating, 3.4.15
　gearing levels, 3.4.16
　profitability ratios, 3.4.13
　reasons for, 3.4.2
　solvency ratios, 3.4.14